Handbook of Black Librarianship

Handbook of Black Librarianship

Compiled and edited by
E. J. Josey
and
Ann Allen Shockley

Libraries Unlimited, Inc.
Littleton, Colorado

1977

Copyright © 1977 E. J. Josey and Ann Allen Shockley
Printed in the United States of America
All Rights Reserved

LIBRARIES UNLIMITED, INC.
P.O. Box 263
Littleton, Colorado 80160

Library of Congress Cataloging in Publication Data

Main entry under title:

Handbook of black librarianship.

    Includes index.
    1. Afro-Americans and libraries. 2. Afro-American librarians. 3. Afro-Americans--Library resources.
4. Libraries--Special collections--Afro-Americans.
5. American literature--Afro-American authors.
I. Josey, E. J., 1924-   II. Shockley, Ann Allen.
Z711.9.H35   021   77-21817
ISBN 0-87287-179-7

TABLE OF CONTENTS

    INTRODUCTION 11

PIONEERS AND LANDMARK EPISODES

1. A Chronology of Events in Black Librarianship
   by Casper LeRoy Jordan and E. J. Josey 15

2. Afro-American Forerunners in Librarianship by Casper LeRoy Jordan. . 24

3. The Hampton Institute Library School by Lucy B. Campbell 35

EARLY LIBRARY ORGANIZATIONS

4. The Alabama Association of School Librarians
   by Carrie C. Robinson 47

5. The Librarians' Section of the Georgia Teachers and Education
   Association by Laura S. Lewis 51

6. The North Carolina Negro Library Association
   by Albert P. Marshall 54

7. The South Carolina State Library Group by Rossie B. Caldwell 57

8. The Division of Librarians of the Virginia State Teachers
   Association by Harriet M. Hill 62

CONTEMPORARY BLACK LIBRARIANSHIP

9. Black Caucus of the American Library Association by E. J. Josey ... 66

10. California Librarians Black Caucus by James E. Crayton
    and Lucy Wilson 77

11. Chicago Area Black Librarians by Alfred L. Woods 81

12. New York Black Librarians Caucus, Inc. by Cynthia Jenkins and Ernestine Washington 84

13. Statistical Facts Pertaining to Black Librarians and Libraries in 1976 88

14. Black Librarians with Doctorate Degrees 89

VITAL ISSUES IN BLACK LIBRARIANSHIP

15. Library Services to Black Americans by Wendell Wray 90

16. Children's Library Service and Black American Children by Jessie M. Birtha 93

17. School Libraries and Black American Children by Ann Stewart Watt 106

18. Multi-Media Resources, Libraries, and the Education of Black Ghetto Youth by Robert B. Ford, Jr. 118

19. The Future of the Black College Library by E. J. Josey 127

SIGNIFICANT BOOKS AND PERIODICALS FOR BLACK COLLECTIONS

20. A Selected Annotated List of Reference Books Reflecting the Black Experience by Sue P. Chandler 134

21. A Descriptive Bibliography of Selected African and Afro-American Periodicals by Ann Allen Shockley 143

22. The Best Seller List and Black Authors by Ann Allen Shockley 153

23. Best Selling Books by Black Authors by Dorothy Lake 154

24. Afro-American Authors Represented on the ALA Notable Book List by Geraldine Clark 156

25. Black Librarians as Creative Writers by Ann Allen Shockley and E. J. Josey 160

AFRICAN RESOURCES

26. Procurement of Materials from Africa: A Bibliographic Essay by Mohammed M. Aman 167

27. Major African Collections in the United States 179

AFRO-AMERICAN RESOURCES

28. Establishing Afro-American Collections by Ann Allen Shockley 182

29. The Role of the Curator of Afro-American Collections
    by Ann Allen Shockley 192

30. Archival and Fugitive Afro-American Literature: The Duties of
    the Archivist by Daniel T. Williams 202

31. Experiences of a Black Private Book Collector
    by Charles L. Blockson 209

32. Black Special Libraries by Vivian D. Dewitt 222

33. Library Holdings on Afro-Americans by Ernest Kaiser 228

34. Major Afro-American Collections 245

35. Major Black Oral History Programs 253

36. Afro-American Museums 258

37. Afro-American Historical Societies 263

UNDERGRADUATE LIBRARY SCHOOL DEPARTMENTS IN
  PREDOMINANTLY BLACK COLLEGES AND UNIVERSITIES 266

PREDOMINANTLY BLACK GRADUATE LIBRARY SCHOOLS 269

LIBRARIES OF PUBLIC LIBRARY SYSTEMS SERVING
  PREDOMINANTLY BLACK COMMUNITIES 271

BLACK ACADEMIC LIBRARIES 332

ADDITIONAL LIBRARIES NAMED FOR AFRO-AMERICANS 359

SELECTIVE LIST OF BLACK-OWNED BOOKSTORES 360

BLACK BOOK PUBLISHERS 363

INDEX 367

Dedicated to

Mrs. Clara Stanton Jones

First Person of African Descent
Elected President
of the
American Library Association

INTRODUCTION

The *Handbook of Black Librarianship* is designed to provide reference information on the relationship of Afro-Americans to various aspects of librarianship and libraries. It fills a void for a variety of people needing Afro-American and African materials and information on the location of those materials. Additionally, it preserves the heritage of blacks in librarianship and chronicles current thinking among Afro-American librarians. Not only blacks will be interested in this work. It seeks to serve all people by identifying those materials essential to an African/Afro-American collection (large or small), by providing information on black publishers and their specializations, by identifying selected bookstores specializing in African and Afro-American materials, by identifying those libraries (both public and academic, with descriptions of services) that serve predominantly black populations, and by instructing them as to how to establish and maintain archives and special collections. Also, two directories provide information as to the location of both undergraduate and graduate library training schools primarily attended by Afro-American students. Thus, since it provides a view of past and present, as well as a guide to the future for all Americans concerned with an accurate portrayal of their country, the *Handbook* can be of inestimable value to librarians, publishers, educators, writers, students, booksellers, scholars, and researchers in need of such resources.

Black Americans have a distinguished history in American librarianship, as evidenced by the careers of Richard T. Greener and Edward C. Williams, to name two of the pioneers. Greener was librarian of the University of South Carolina in 1875, one year before the American Library Association was founded, and Williams was librarian of Adelbert College (at Western Reserve University) in 1894. Now, one hundred years after the founding of the ALA, an Afro-American presides over the activities of the organization. Spanning over one hundred years of library history, Afro-American contributions to libraries, library education, and learning in general are feats of no small means when one considers the discrimination with which their work and indeed their persons were often met.

Naturally, then, the *Handbook of Black Librarianship* is concerned with the history of those achievements. "Pioneers and Landmark Episodes" covers that history with a chronological list of achievements, and the outline is followed by biographical sketches of pioneers and by a history of the Hampton Institute Library School, the first such school for blacks. "Early Library Organizations" presents more detailed histories of the early organizations of black librarians that were established because Afro-Americans were denied membership in white organizations.

Yet the *Handbook* is concerned with the present and the future as well as the past. "Contemporary Black Librarianship" presents histories of contemporary library organizations, including the ALA Black Caucus and three regional groups. Included here, as well, are statistics concerning the present status of Afro-Americans in the profession and a list of those black librarians holding doctorate degrees as of July 1977. Too, since the concerns of black librarians are not always articulated in mainstream library literature, "Vital Issues in Black Librarianship" includes discussions of serious issues in the Afro-American community, concerns relevant to all librarians. The essays presented pinpoint serious gaps in and express concern for strengthening children's services, public library services, school libraries, and the black college library.

For those in need of guidance to basic resources for a collection, whether just beginning or already in operation, "Significant Books and Periodicals for Black Collections" lists works essential for a core collection. For the first time, books by Afro-American authors who are represented on the ALA Notable Books List are listed and annotated. In addition to pointing out basic reference works and periodicals, this section also deals with "best selling" books by black authors. Finally, this section includes short biographical sketches of those black librarians who are creative writers.

This book concentrates, of course, on Afro-Americans. Reflecting American librarians' growing interest in Africa, however, "African Resources" provides an essay on the procurement of African materials and also lists the major African collections in the United States. The treatment here is not exhaustive, but it provides a sound introduction to the resources and problems currently at hand.

Of interest to most librarians will be the section "Afro-American Resources." The task of starting an Afro-American collection is discussed here, as are the role of the curator, the duties of an archivist in preserving contemporary and recent history, and, as a bonus, private collecting of materials on blacks, this essay by a preeminent collector of Afro-Americana. Two other essays describe the nature of black special libraries (and their locations and services) and the extent of major library holdings on Afro-Americans (including discussions of bibliographies and archival material as well as general collections). These essays are then followed by directories to major Afro-American collections, major black oral history programs, Afro-American museums, and Afro-American historical societies, each directory entry describing the extent of the collection and the services available as well as its location.

Prospective librarians will be interested in the directories of undergraduate library schools in predominantly black colleges and universities and of predominantly black graduate library schools. These schools are ALA-accredited, and a brief history of each is presented.

Never before has an attempt been made to collect in one source a list of the branch libraries of public library systems that serve predominantly black communities. Rather than cover every United States community, though, the compilers sent questionnaires to public libraries in cities with populations of 100,000 or more. Over 275 of these responded as serving black neighborhoods, and for these, the following data are provided in "Libraries of Public Library Systems Serving Predominantly Black Communities": name; address; telephone number; name of branch librarian; number of professional and non-professional staff; library materials and operating budgets; number of volumes and number of periodicals received; description of audiovisual materials; information on interlibrary loan, photocopying, and teletype services; hours of service; names of former librarians; and subject specialization of collections. "Black Academic Libraries" provides this same information for over 70 academic libraries that replied to questionnaires, along with a brief history of each library.

In these sections, libraries named in honor of prominent Afro-Americans are starred (*) and the significance of the name is explained in the history of the institution. Among the 39 public libraries so identified, the name of Dr. Martin Luther King, Jr. occurred most frequently. Forty-six black academic libraries honor

Afro-Americans in their names, as do the libraries in three predominantly white institutions of higher learning. Too, a directory lists special libraries named in honor of Afro-Americans.

The information on these libraries will be of great value to those who need access to information on blacks contained in these institutions, but it will also aid publishers and authors in identifying them for the purposes of apprising them of materials related to their collecting interest.

For those people lacking ready access to Afro-American materials, the compilers have included a selective directory of black-owned bookstores that they could identify as being active at the time of compilation. The final directory lists publishers of Afro-American materials, complete with address and specialization of each.

Our appreciation goes to the many people who aided in the compilation of this *Handbook*, the many librarians, museum staff members, historical society members, colleagues, book publishers, and book dealers, all of whom gave so generously of their time and efforts. We give special thanks to our contributors, whose essays provide invaluable insights for the users of the book. Also, we are very appreciative of the excellent typing assistance received from Mrs. Barbara E. Hendon and Mrs. Verdelle Barlowe. Finally, while the compilers acknowledge their feelings of professional interest and responsibility, it should also be said that this book was undertaken as a labor of love, involving personal time, without the aid of research funds.

E. J. Josey
Chief, Bureau of Specialist Library Services
New York State Education Department
Albany

Ann Allen Shockley
Associate Librarian for Public Services
and Associate Professor of Library Science
Fisk University Library
Nashville

PIONEERS AND LANDMARK EPISODES

1. A Chronology of Events in Black Librarianship
   by   Casper LeRoy Jordan, Associate Professor of Library Science and University Librarian, Atlanta University
   and
   E. J. Josey

1808   *An Inquiry Concerning the Intellectual and Moral Faculties and Literature of Negroes* was published by Henri Grégoire.

1816   A school and library were established for Afro-Americans in Wilmington, Delaware.

1832   The Library Company of Philadelphia was established by Afro-Americans as a literary society.

1871   Daniel Alexander Payne Murray joined the staff of the Library of Congress as personal assistant to Ainsworth Rand Spofford, Librarian of Congress.

1875   Richard T. Greener served as University Librarian at the University of South Carolina during 1875, where he reorganized the library and prepared a catalog. Professor Greener was also the first black person to receive a degree from Harvard University.

1880   Daniel A. P. Murray was appointed assistant librarian at the Library of Congress.

1894   Edward Christopher Williams was appointed librarian of Western Reserve University's Adelbert College.

1896   George Washington Forbes was appointed assistant librarian, West End Branch, of the Boston Public Library, where he served generations of Jews and Gentiles for over thirty years.

The United States Supreme Court Decision *Plessy v. Ferguson* established the "separate but equal" doctrine as a "reasonable" use of state police power and was responsible for segregated library facilities of Afro-Americans. The decision remained in effect until the 1954 *Brown v. Board of Education* ruling.

1897   Alexander Crummell founded the American Negro Academy to promote literature, science, and art and to foster higher education.

1900   A Carnegie Library was built at Tuskegee Institute, Alabama.

Daniel A. P. Murray edited his *Preliminary List of Books and Pamphlets by Negro Authors* for the Negro Exhibit prepared for the Paris Exposition of 1900.

Edward C. Williams graduated from the New York State Library School, the first professionally trained Afro-American librarian.

1901   S. W. Starks was appointed West Virginia State Librarian and held the position until 1906.

1903   Charlotte, North Carolina, Public Library created a separate library for Negroes with an independent governing board, the earliest example of an independent Negro library.

Cossitt Library, Memphis, Tennessee, entered into a contract with Lemoyne Institute to give library service to blacks.

The General Education Board was founded to promote education without discrimination, and became a great force for progress in Afro-American education and librarianship.

1904   Carnegie Library buildings were erected at Alabama A.& M. College, Atlanta University, Benedict College, Talladega College, and Wilberforce University.

Edward C. Williams joined the library school faculty at Western Reserve University.

Rosenberg Library of Galveston, Texas, established a Negro branch to serve as a public library agency for the entire black population of Galveston. This was the first structure erected to provide public library quarters for exclusive black use.

1905   Atlanta University Press published *A Select Bibliography of the Negro American*, compiled by W. E. B. DuBois.

Carnegie Libraries were erected at Cheyney State Teachers College, Johnson C. Smith University, Livingstone College, and Fisk University.

The Hampton Institute Library began special black collections with the gift of the George Foster Peabody Collection on the Negro.

The Louisville (Kentucky) Free Public Library established the first public library in America exclusively for Afro-Americans. It was operated and administered entirely by blacks, although supervised from the main library.

Thomas Fountain Blue joined the staff of the Louisville Free Public Library, becoming the first black to head a public library branch.

1906   A Carnegie Library was erected at Wiley College, Marshall, Texas.

1907   Carnegie Libraries were erected at Howard University and Knoxville College.

Savannah, Georgia, established independent governance for Negro branch service, the second instance of this type of action.

1908   The Department of Records and Research was founded by Monroe Work at Tuskegee Institute.

1910   James H. Gregory of Marblehead, Massachusetts, funded a traveling library extension service for Southern blacks; distribution was effected through the Atlanta University Library. The service was known as the Marblehead Libraries.

In the Louisville (Kentucky) Free Public Library, an apprentice class for blacks was established, the first example of any attempt in the South to provide library training for the prospective black librarian. The last classes were held in 1928-1929.

1911   The Negro Society for Historical Research was begun.

1912   The first edition of the *Negro Yearbook* appeared, edited by Monroe Work. Nine editions in all were published (1912-1938).

1913   William F. Yust attempted, perhaps for the first time, to establish the status of the Negro in the American public library scene with his "What of the Black and Yellow Races?" *ALA Bulletin* 7:159-167 (July 1913).

1914   The Moorland Foundation Collection was formed at Howard University as a gift of Jesse Moorland, a Howard trustee and bibliophile.

1916   *A Bibliographical Checklist of American Negro Poets* was published by Arthur A. Schomburg.

1917   *Negro Education, a Study of the Private and Higher Schools for Colored People in the U.S.*, by Thomas J. Jones, was published by the U.S. Bureau of Higher Education.

1921   The American Library Association established the Work with Negroes Round Table.

Daniel A. P. Murray retired from the Library of Congress after 52 years of service.

J. Arthur Jackson was appointed State Librarian for West Virginia.

Thomas Fountain Blue addressed a session of ALA in Detroit; he is believed to be the first black to have a place on an ALA program.

1923   Sadie Peterson Delaney started the library at Tuskegee Veterans Hospital and began her pioneering efforts in the field of bibliotherapy.

1925   The Division of Negro Literature, History and Prints was established at the New York Public Library.

Hampton Institute (Virginia) Library School was established with Florence Rising Curtis as director.

1926   Negro History Week was introduced by Carter G. Woodson and the Association for the Study of Negro Life and History.

The Schomburg Collection was purchased with funds provided by the Carnegie Corporation at the behest of the National Urban League for the New York Public Library.

1927 The Carnegie Corporation financed a conference of librarians at Hampton Institute.

Thomas Fountain Blue founded the Negro Library Conference at Hampton, Virginia.

1928 *Bibliography of the Negro in Africa and America* was compiled by Monroe N. Work.

Survey of Negro Colleges and Universities by Arthur J. Klein was published by the U.S. Office of Education.

1930 A Library Institute for Negro Librarians was held at the Morehouse-Spelman Summer School financed by the Rosenwald Fund.

Louis S. Shores published "Public Library Service to Negroes," *Library Journal* 55:150-154 (February 1930).

1931 A Negro Library Conference was held at Fisk University under the direction of Louis S. Shores, November 20-23.

1932 Arthur A. Schomburg was appointed curator of the black research collection, New York Public Library, which was later to be named for him.

1933 The Commission on Interracial Cooperation called a conference on "Education and Race Relations" to discuss the treatment of Negroes in textbooks.

1936 The American Library Association took a stand against holding segregated conferences.

1939 The Hampton Institute Library School closed.

1940 Eliza Atkins Gleason was awarded the first Ph.D. in librarianship to an Afro-American. Her University of Chicago dissertation was entitled "The Southern Negro and the Public Library."

1941 The Atlanta University School of Library Service opened with Eliza Atkins Gleason as dean.

The Carnegie Corporation and the General Education Board held a Library Conference at Atlanta University, heralding the opening of the School of Library Service.

The Carnegie Corporation made a number of grants to Negro colleges to assist in the upgrading of their library collections.

The School of Library Science, North Carolina College, Durham (now North Carolina Central University) opened.

1942 The Carnegie Corporation financed the establishment of a Field Service Program to improve Negro school libraries in the South; the program was under the direction of Hallie Beacham Brooks, Atlanta University.

Establishment of the James Weldon Johnson Collection was announced at Yale University Library as a gift from Carl Van Vechten.

1943 Arna Bontemps was appointed the first Afro-American University Librarian of Fisk University. Two illustrious white librarians, Louis S. Shores and Carl White, were Bontemps's predecessors.

The E. Azalia Hackley Memorial Collection on Negro music, dance, and drama opened at the Detroit Public Library.

The North Carolina Negro Library Association was given chapter status by the American Library Association.

1945   Virginia Lacy Jones received the second Ph.D. in librarianship awarded to an Afro-American; her dissertation was "The Problems of Negro High School Libraries in Selected Southern Cities" (University of Chicago).

North American Negro Poets: A Bibliographical Checklist of Their Writing was published by Dorothy Porter.

1946   The Arthur Spingarn Collection of Black Authors was purchased by Howard University to form the Moorland-Spingarn Collection.

The Henry Proctor Slaughter Collection was purchased by the Atlanta University Library as the nucleus of its Negro Collection.

1947   The Atlanta University School of Library Service held a six-day conference for 97 Afro-American public librarians.

1949   The Atlanta University School of Library Service initiated the graduate program leading to a master's degree.

1950   Gwendolyn Brooks received the Pulitzer Prize for poetry, becoming the first Afro-American to receive the coveted award.

1952   Clarence R. Graham, of the Louisville Free Public Library, became the first public library director in the South to open the main library to blacks.

1953   Augusta Baker was appointed Assistant Coordinator of Children's Services and Storytelling Specialist, making her the first black person to hold an administrative position in the New York Public Library.

1954   The American Library Association approved the idea of a single library association in a state, forecasting integrated associations in the South.

In *Brown v. Board of Education*, the United States Supreme Court ruled that school segregation was unconstitutional.

1956   The ALA Conference at Miami Beach, Flordia, was probably the first completely desegregated Association meeting held in the South.

Charlemae Rollins became the first black to receive the Grolier Foundation Award.

1957   Alma Jacobs became the first Afro-American elected president of the Pacific Northwest Library Association.

Charlemae Rollins became the first black elected president of the Children's Services Division of the American Library Association.

1958   Dorothy B. Porter edited and published *A Catalogue of the African Collection in the Moorland Foundation*.

Effie Lee Morris received the E. P. Dutton-John Macrae Award for advancement of library service to children and young people.

1960   Alma Jacobs was elected president of the Montana Library Association.

Rice Estes questioned ALA about its position on race and libraries.

1961   Albert P. Marshall served as first Afro-American president of the Missouri Library Association.

Annette Hoage Phinazee asked for an accounting from the American Library Association at the Cleveland, Ohio, conference as it pertained to race and American libraries.

John E. Scott served as the first Afro-American president of the West Virginia Library Association.

1963   *Access to Public Libraries*, a research study prepared for the American Library Association by International Research Associates, Inc., documented discrimination, both direct and indirect, in library service to Negroes in the United States.

Effie Lee Morris was appointed Coordinator of Children's Services, San Francisco Public Library.

1964   Alma Jacobs became the first black member of the Executive Board of the American Library Association.

E. J. Josey offered a resolution to the American Library Association conference (St. Louis, Missouri) that would prohibit ALA officers and staff members from attending in their official capacity or at ALA expense the meetings of state associations that continued to practice segregation. This resolution led to the integration of the remaining four state associations that would not extend membership to Afro-American librarians.

1965   A. P. Marshall became the first black member of the American Library Association appointed to chair a nominating committee.

The Atlanta University School of Library Service held a conference on "Materials by and about American Negroes." The school also sponsored a conference on the role of the library in improving education in the South.

Dudley Randall, a Detroit poet and librarian, founded Broadside Press.

E. J. Josey became the first black librarian given membership in the Georgia Library Association.

1966   ALA established an ad hoc Committee on Opportunities for Negro Students in the Library Profession, chaired by Virginia Lacy Jones.

In *Brown v. Louisiana*, 383 US 131, the United States Supreme Court held that "persons could not be punished for using the library peacefully to protest the illegal segregation of the library itself" (argued 1965).

The Negro Handbook was published by Johnson Publishing Company, Inc.

1967   The Atlanta University School of Library Services' Conference on the Georgia Child's Access to Materials Pertaining to American Negroes was held.

The first edition of *The Negro Almanac*, a comprehensive reference work, was published.

Hannah D. Atkins became the first Afro-American president of the Oklahoma Chapter of the Special Libraries Association, 1967-68.

Virginia Lacy Jones was the first black person elected president of the Association of American Library Schools.

1968 Milton Byam was appointed chairman of the Department of Library Science at St. John's University.

E. J. Josey was appointed chief of the Bureau of Academic and Research Libraries of the New York State Education Department.

1969 The Committee on Scientific and Technical Information (COSATI) established a Subcommittee on Negro Research Libraries.

A Conference on the Use of Microphotography and Black Studies was co-sponsored by the Atlanta University School of Library Service, the 3M Corporation, the United Negro College Fund, and the Maude Hill Family Foundation.

A Conference for the Evaluation of Materials about Black Americans (CEMBA) was held at Alabama A.&M. State University at Huntsville.

The Cooperative College Library Center, the first consortium of black academic libraries, opened in Atlanta, Georgia, with Hillis Davis as director.

Hannah D. Atkins became the first Afro-American elected president of the Southwestern chapter of the American Association of Law Librarians, 1969-70.

Howard University Library hosted a conference on black bibliography, chaired by Dorothy Porter.

1970 Alma Jacobs was appointed State Librarian of Montana.

The Black Caucus of the American Library Association was formally organized at ALA Midwinter meeting.

The first ALA Black Caucus Award to be given was received by Clara S. Jones for Distinguished Service to Librarianship.

The Black Librarian in America, edited by E. J. Josey, was published, the first book to deal exclusively with black librarians.

Burton E. Lamkin was appointed Associate Commissioner for Libraries and Educational Technology in the U.S. Office of Education of the Department of Health, Education and Welfare.

Charlemae Rollins became the first black woman to win the Constance Lindsay Skinner Award.

Clara S. Jones was appointed director of the Detroit Public Library, the first black and female in that position.

E. J. Josey became the first black to receive the *Journal of Library History* Award.

Fisk University sponsored the first summer Institute on Black Studies Librarianship, directed by Jessie Carney Smith.

The Library of Congress published *The Negro in the United States: A Selected Bibliography*, edited by Dorothy B. Porter.

1971   The Council of the American Library Association adopted a resolution alleging racial discrimination by the Library of Congress in its recruitment, training, and promotion practices.

Edward C. Mapp published *Books for Occupational Education Progress*.

Effie Lee Morris became the first black president of the Public Library Association Division of the American Library Association.

Joseph H. Reason became the first black president of the Association of College and Research Libraries (ACRL).

Rebecca T. Bingham became the first Afro-American president of the Kentucky Library Association.

The U.S. Office of Education funded the African-American Materials Project (AAMP), a six-state library project to identify holdings in Negroana in the Southeast.

1972   Charlemae Rollins became the first black to be given honorary membership in the American Library Association.

E. J. Josey published *What Black Librarians Are Saying*.

Edward C. Mapp published *Blacks in American Films*.

Fisk University Library sponsored the first conference to be held solely on Black Oral History, under the direction of Ann Allen Shockley.

Milton S. Byam was appointed the first black director of the District of Columbia Public Library.

Robert Wedgeworth became the first black to be appointed Executive Director of the American Library Association.

1973   Eugene Walton was appointed Coordinator of Affirmative Action Programs for the Library of Congress.

Lucille C. Thomas became the first black appointed to the New York State Regents Advisory Council on Libraries.

Sylvia Lyons Render was appointed Specialist in Afro-American History and Culture at the Library of Congress.

1974   Ann Allen Shockley and Sue P. Chandler published *Living Black American Authors: A Biographical Directory*.

Charles D. Churchwell was appointed director of Brown University Library.

E. J. Josey was elected chairman of the Association of Cooperative Library Organizations (ACLO).

Georgia McClaron became the first Afro-American president of the Tennessee Library Association.

Hardy Franklin became the second black named director of the District of Columbia Public Library, succeeding Milton S. Byam.

Milton S. Byam became the first black appointed director of the Queens Borough Public Library System.

Herman L. Totten was appointed Dean of the School of Librarianship of the University of Oregon, the first black to head a predominantly white, ALA-accredited library school.

Virginia Lacy Jones became the first black to receive the Melville Dewey Medal.

1975 Ann Allen Shockley received a special ALA Black Caucus award for editorship of the *Black Caucus Newsletter*.

Augusta Baker became the second black to be given honorary membership in the American Library Association.

Clara S. Jones was elected vice-president/president elect of the American Library Association.

The Clarence Day Award was received by Augusta Baker, the first black to do so.

Edward C. Mapp was elected the first black chairman of the Council of Chief Librarians of the City University of New York.

Louise Giles became both the first black woman and the first community college librarian to serve as president of the Association of College and Research Libraries (ACRL).

1976 Clara S. Jones became the first black inaugurated as president of the American Library Association.

Gwendolyn Brooks, Pulitzer Prize winner and Poet Laureate of Illinois, read her poem "Other Music," written for the inauguration of Clara S. Jones, at the ALA Centennial Inaugural Banquet, July 23, 1976.

Ella Gaines Yates became the first Afro-American to be named Director of the Atlanta Public Library.

Ina C. Brownridge was appointed Director of Libraries, State University of New York at Binghamton; Ms. Brownridge is the first black to direct a major library in the SUNY system.

Jack McDonald was appointed chief of the Loan Division, Library of Congress.

Jessie Carney Smith became the first Afro-American president of Beta Phi Mu, the international library science honor society.

The Library of Congress recognized the American Federation of State, County and Municipal Employees (AFSCME) as a bargaining agent for employees. Joslyn Williams, a black member of the ALA Black Caucus, is the Executive Director of the Federal Council to which the unit of the Library belongs.

Lucille C. Thomas became the first Afro-American president of the New York Library Club.

The North Carolina Central University School of Library Science sponsored a colloquium, "Southeastern Black Librarians," to celebrate its thirty-fifth anniversary.

Robert Hayden, professor of English, University of Michigan, was named Consultant in Poetry to the Library of Congress, to succeed Stanley Kunitz.

Virginia Lacy Jones became the third black granted honorary ALA membership.

Wallace Van Jackson was the only black person honored with an ALA Centennial Award.

1977   Lucille C. Thomas became the first Afro-American president of the New York Library Association.

Alex Haley won the National Book Award and the Pulitzer Prize for *Roots*.

Virginia Lacy Jones received the coveted Joseph Wharton Lippincott Award for distinguished service to librarianship, the first black so honored.

2. Afro-American Forerunners in Librarianship

    by   **Casper LeRoy Jordan, Associate Professor of Library Science and University Librarian, Atlanta University**

If we consider the year 1876 as the formal beginning of American librarianship, black involvement is fairly recent. The 1890s chronicled the career of Daniel A. P. Murray's achievements at the Library of Congress, and a little later, Edward Christopher Williams is considered to have been the first professionally trained black librarian at a time when most American librarians did not possess this training. Yet, in spite of these highly accomplished men's presence, in general, blacks in American librarianship were few.

Prior to the establishment of the Hampton Institute Library School in Virginia, professionally trained black librarians received their education at predominantly white institutions. The Hampton Library School was closed in 1939, and, in 1941, the Atlanta University School of Library Service assumed responsibility for educating the majority of black American librarians. From the ranks of the Hampton graduates, then, have come most of the pioneers in American librarianship who happened to be black. With about 75 years of involvement in the field by blacks, some parameters necessarily were placed on this study. Many "pioneering" librarians are alive, some still working, and others only recently retired, so this paper concerns only those librarians who were deceased as of 1960. Thus, consideration of the careers of Eliza A. Gleason, Virginia L. Jones, Hallie B. Brooks, Josephine Thompson, Wallace Van Jackson, Mollie Dunlop, Dorothy Porter, Carrie Robinson, E. J. Josey, Annette Phinazee, Augusta Baker, Clara S. Jones, Zenobia Coleman, Morteza Sprague, Mollie Huston Lee, Jean Blackwell Hutson, Albert P. Marshall, Lawrence Reddick, and Milton Byam, to name only a few, must be undertaken at another time.

However, three men who were not librarians were distinguished book men and have had a marked influence on black librarianship: Arthur Schomburg and Henry P. Slaughter were avid bibliophiles, and Monroe Nathan Work was an indefatigable bibliographer—three librarians without portfolios, we might say. The pioneers who are discussed after these three were, then, actual librarians.

Arthur Alphonso Schomburg (1874-1938)[1]

A. A. Schomburg ranks as the foremost bibliophile and collector of books by and about blacks. Schomburg was born in Puerto Rico, was educated there and in the Spanish West Indies, and from an early age, had an insatiable curiosity about the achievements of blacks in the world. Thus, he began his long career of collecting Negroana. He came to the United States in 1891, arriving in New York, where he read law for five years and served for five years as secretary of Las Dos Antillas, a Cuban/Puerto Rican revolutionary party. He also taught Spanish, worked as a journalist and editor in New York, and finally joined Bankers Trust. He was a member (and in 1922, president) of the Negro Academy of Washington, D.C., was founder and secretary-treasurer for the Negro Society for Historical Research, and was an ever-active collector.

Schomburg typified the private collector of this period who had a great interest in amassing sources on the history of the black man. (Libraries at Fisk University, Atlanta University, Howard University, Tuskegee Institute, and Hampton Institute also evidenced their growing assumption of stewardship in conserving the record of the black past.) Indicative of his interest in helping reclaim the black heritage, Schomburg served for a time as curator of the Negro Collection at Fisk University, starting after his retirement from banking in 1929. He had already received the Harmon Award for his work in Negro education in 1926.

Schomburg was a prolific writer and editor. "The Negro Digs Up His Past," one of his most important essays, was published in *The New Negro* (edited by Alain LeRoi Locke, 1925) and is considered a cornerstone of the Harlem Renaissance. His real passion, however, was collecting—books, pamphlets, manuscripts, documents, letters, photographs, paintings—anything to do with Negro history.

In 1926, the Schomburg Collection was purchased by the New York Public Library with a Carnegie Corporation grant for $10,000, obtained through the efforts of the National Urban League. Schomburg became curator of the collection in 1931, so he actively was able to further his desire that the collection be available for students of Negro life. His original collection was housed at the NYPL Harlem branch on West 135th Street, and is the nucleus of the matchless collection that bears his name. Schomburg died in 1938.

Henry Proctor Slaughter (1871-1958)[2]

Henry Proctor Slaughter was born in Louisville, Kentucky, in 1871. Fatherless at the age of six, he sold newspapers to support his mother and younger sister and brothers. He was educated in the Louisville public schools and graduated as salutatorian of his class. Young Slaughter served an apprenticeship as a printer with the *Louisville Champion* and later became an associate editor. He wrote articles for the local papers and was a contributor to the daily *Louisville Courier-Journal*.

---

[1] Earl E. Thorpe, *Black Historians, a critique* (New York: Morrow, 1971), pp. 145-46; Joel A. Rogers, *World's Great Men of Color*, Vol. 2 (New York: Macmillan, 1972), pp. 449-53; *Who's Who of the Colored Race* (Chicago: Mather, 1915), p. 237.

[2] "A Kentucky Leader," *Colored American* 10 (May 10, 1902): 1, 4; biographical files, Trevor Arnett Library, Atlanta University.

In 1892, Slaughter accepted the foremanship of the printing concerns of the *Lexington Standard* and served as the associate editor a year later. He was ambitious and worked to attend college; in 1894 he went to North Carolina as the manager-foreman of the African Methodist Episcopal Zion Church Publication House at Salisbury. He attended Livingstone College, retaining as well his editorial post at the publishing house.

Slaughter went to Washington, D.C., in 1896. He passed, with a high score, the Civil Service examination for compositor in the Government Printing Office, and thus began his long stint with the public printer. In 1899, he received a Bachelor of Law degree from Howard University and a master's degree in 1900. He was very active in the social, civic, and literary life of the Capitol and was editor of the *Odd Fellows Journal* from 1910 to 1937.

Henry Slaughter had a consuming passion for books and amassed a formidable private library of books, broadsides, documents, autographs, and other memorabilia about blacks. His passion for collecting once caused him to spend money his wife had given him to purchase a hat for some rare items he found in a bookstore enroute to the millinery shop. His home was literally crammed with materials, and along with Schomburg and Arthur B. Spingarn, Slaughter must be included among those outstanding bibliophiles in black studies.

In 1946, Slaughter sold his collection to Atlanta University, where it serves as the nucleus for their present Negro Collection, one of the foremost collections in the Southeast documenting the American black experience. Henry P. Slaughter died in 1958 at the age of 87.

Monroe Nathan Work (1866-1945)[3]

Monroe Nathan Work was the founder and Director of the Department of Records and Research at Tuskegee Institute in Alabama. In 1904, Work published the first of the famous Tuskegee reports on lynching in the United States. Then, in 1921, he began to compile an annual cyclopedia, the *Negro Yearbook*, which is still a treasury of facts on black life in America. The *Yearbook* went through nine editions (1912-1938) and was the most extensively used book of information on the Negro of its day. Work also compiled the monumental *Bibliography of the Negro in Africa and America*. This work, based on comprehensive study, listed the titles and authors of books, pamphlets, and serial articles about blacks in Africa and America, and it stands today without a peer in black bibliography.

Work was born of slave parentage in Iredell County, North Carolina, in 1866, to Alexander and Elizabeth Work. He grew up in Illinois and Kansas. He first tried his hand as a minister in the African Methodist Church (1892-1893); then in 1895, he studied for the ministry at the Chicago Theological Seminary. He realized that he had other aspirations, so he entered the University of Chicago in 1898 for graduate studies in sociology. He received his bachelor's degree in 1902, and in 1903, he was awarded a Master of Arts in Sociology, the first black man to receive the degree from Chicago.

---

[3] Juanita L. Horne, "The Sociological Contributions of Monroe Nathan Work" (Atlanta: unpublished master's thesis, Atlanta University, 1975); Jessie Guzman, "Monroe N. Work and His Contributions," *Journal of Negro History* (January 1949): 34; Earl E. Thorpe, *Black Historians*, pp. 137-39; *Who's Who in Colored America* (New York: Burchel, 1927), p. 229.

He then taught for a while in Georgia. In 1904, he married Florence E. Hendrickson, and his long and fruitful career at Tuskege began in 1908. In 1921, the Carnegie Corporation made a grant to the Tuskegee Department of Records and Research that enabled Work to begin the compilation of his *Bibliography of the Negro*. The compilation took a number of years, after which Work visited American and European libraries to verify the accuracy of his compilations. The finished tome, revised three times before publication, was finally published in 1928.

The Harmon Award was presented to Work in 1921 in recognition of "scholarly research and educational publicity through his periodic compilation and publication of *The Negro Yearbook*."

Work retired in 1938, at the age of 72, after thirty years of service. Howard University awarded him with an honorary Doctor of Letters degree. At that time, he had collected and organized more than 70,000 bibliographical citations for a new *Bibliography of European Colonization and the Resulting Contacts of People, Races and Culture*. He died at his beloved Tuskegee, May 2, 1945. His passion for truth continues as a blessing to scholars, who are in his debt forever.

S. W. Starks (1866-1908)[4]

Little is known about S. W. Starks, a black man who was West Virginia State Librarian, 1901-1906. Many holders of the position of state librarian did not have the traning for the position but were political appointees who worked up to the position from a state department. Governor A. B. White appointed Starks to the position of West Virginia State Librarian in 1901.

Starks was born in Charleston, West Virginia, March 11, 1866. He was educated in the schools of his hometown and, at the age of sixteen, he entered the service of the Kanawha and Ohio Railroad as a messenger boy and later became chief telegraph operator. He worked for a number of railroads and took courses in business at Chicago's Bryant and Stratton Business College. Starks was also active in a number of black business ventures in Ohio and West Virginia and was a leader in black fraternal circles. Politics took a great deal of his time, and in 1900, he was instrumental in beating back forces in West Virginia attempting to institute segregation in public conveyances.

The State Librarian's responsibilities included those of the register of copyrights and chief documents clerk. Starks appointed an assistant, J. Arthur Jackson, also a black man, as a messenger. In 1917, Jackson became Assistant State Librarian, and in 1921 he became State Librarian—the second black to hold the position in West Virginia. Starks died in 1908.

Daniel A. P. Murray (1852-1925)[5]

Daniel Alexander Payne Murray is a prime example of a librarian of great reputation who was not formally trained as a librarian. However, Murray made an

---

[4] Wallace Van Jackson, "Some Pioneer Negro Library Workers," *Library Journal* 64 (March 15, 1939): 215-17; *Colored American* 9, No. 2 (April 13, 1901): 1.

[5] *Who's Who of the Colored Race* (Chicago: Mather, 1915), p. 203; Wallace Van Jackson, "Some Pioneer Negro Library Workers," *Library Journal* 64 (March 15, 1939): 215-17; U.S. Library of Congress, *Report of the Librarian of Congress, 1923* (Washington, D.C.: Government Printing Office, 1923), p. 111; *Murray's Historical and Biographical Encyclopedia*. Prospectus. (Washington, D.C.: World's Cyclopedia Company, 1912).

unusual mark for himself at the Library of Congress during his long tenure. In the 1923 *Report of the Librarian of Congress*, the then Librarian, Herbert Putnam, opined that Murray's "extraordinary record, exceeded in the Library of Congress probably in but a single instance, was remarkable in the almost unbroken continuity and regularity of his attendance." However, regularity of attendance at L.C. was not the only claim to fame of D. A. P. Murray.

Murray was born in Baltimore, March 3, 1852, the son of George and Eliza Wilson Murray. He was apparently born of freemen and was educated in Baltimore public schools and the Unitarian Seminary in his hometown. In 1879, he married Anna Evans of Oberlin, Ohio, and seven children were the product of this union.

Murray joined the staff of the Library of Congress in 1871. From 1874 to 1897, he was personal assistant to Ainsworth R. Spofford, Librarian of Congress, and was also an assistant librarian beginning in 1880. Murray was "curator" of a collection of Negro books and pamphlets that was the outgrowth of an exhibit of Negroana prepared for the Paris Exposition of 1900; it later was called the "Murray Collection." Murray edited his *Preliminary List of Books and Pamphlets by Negro Authors* for the Exposition—a landmark bibliography of the American black experience.

In his position at the Library of Congress, Murray fostered an undying interest in black literature, which led to his editorship of *Murray's Historical and Biographical Encyclopedia of the Colored Race Throughout the World* (Washington, 1912). This work was planned to chronicle in six volumes the race's "progress and achievements from the earliest period down to the present time." The *Encyclopedia* promised "25,000 biographical sketches . . . a bibliography of over 6000 titles of books and pamphlets . . . a synoptical list of all books of fiction by Caucasian authors that deal with the race question and a list of nearly 5000 musical compositions by colored composers in every part of the world." This formidable task was to be undertaken with the aid of John E. Bruce, Arthur A. Schomburg, John W. Cromwell, L. M. Hershaw, Bishop J. Albert Johnson, William S. Scarborough, and R. R. Wright, Jr., and scholars from Africa and the Caribbean area. Twenty years of research was put in to the project, but it was never completed and published.

Murray was prominent in Washington's social and civic affairs, and was also a successful realtor. He was a member of the National Commission to escort Admiral George Dewey to Washington to receive the accolades of Congress after his Far East victories. He was either a member or officer of the Washington Civic Centre, Washington Board of Trade, and the Oldest Inhabitants Association. Mr. Murray contributed articles to the *Voice of the Negro* and collaborated in writing *Banneker, the Afro-American Astronomer* (1921).

On December 31, 1922, Murray retured from Library of Congress service at the close of fifty-two years. He died in Washington three years later, in 1925.

George Washington Forbes (1864-1927)[6]

Another great pioneer black librarian was George Washington Forbes of Boston, Massachusetts, who was appointed to serve a predominantly black

---

[6] M. Bendor, "A People's Tribute," *Opportunity* 5 (June 1927): 184; Wallace Van Jackson, "Some Pioneer Negro Library Workers," *Library Journal* 64 (March 15, 1939): 215-17; "George Forbes of Boston," *Crisis* 34 (July 1927): 151-57; Harold Wade, Jr., *Black Men of Amherst* (Amherst, Mass.: Amherst College Press, 1976), pp. 21-23.

neighborhood at the West End Branch of the Boston Public Library. However, the color and culture of the area changed, and Forbes soon found himself serving a largely Jewish clientele until his death in 1927.

Forbes was born in Shannon, Mississippi, in 1864, but he left the South at age fourteen to go west. In Ohio, he attended Wilberforce University; he then was graduated from Amherst College (Massachusetts) in 1892 and settled in Boston. In Boston, Forbes edited a small, black weekly newspaper, the *Courant*. Forbes was also a central figure in black Boston intellectual circles and was a close associate of W. E. B. DuBois and William Monroe Trotter.

Trotter and Forbes combined forces to establish a radical paper of the day, the *Boston Guardian*. The newspaper was an ardent foe of Booker T. Washington's advocacy of accommodation on the part of blacks, and Forbes wrote highly charged editorials critical of the "Washington Machine" at Tuskegee. The *Boston Guardian* served a very significant role during this period, as it provided a platform for progressive blacks to express various views. DuBois described the paepr as "bitter, satirical and personal; but it was well edited."

For a number of years, Forbes was assistant librarian of the West End Branch of the Boston Public Library, where he joined the staff in 1896 as the only black member. As librarian for the growing Jewish community, Forbes assisted in the education and encouragement of a generation of immigrant Jews. He was so popular at the branch that users referred to him as "Reference Librarian." Forbes was also greatly responsible for arranging the Theodore Parker Collection in the Boston Public Library.

In addition to his work as librarian, he was also a steady editorial assistant on the *African Methodist Episcopal Church Review* and wrote for the *Springfield Republican* and *Boston Transcript*. Forbes wrote continually on black history and biography for most of his adult life, and at the time of his death, he was just about to publish a book on the *History of the Black Men in the Life of the Republic*. Forbes succumbed to influenza, and his funeral was held on March 14, 1927. The West End Branch was closed for the services, and children who used the branch presented his widow with a floral offering and a gift box. The pallbearers were his white associates at the Boston Public Library.

The Jewish community felt the great loss of Forbes, as did the black community. *Opportunity* and *Crisis* both carried news of his demise, and *Crisis* reprinted a long eulogy which appeared in *The Jewish Daily Forward*. The final paragraph stated:

> Since his death everybody, especially the children of the West End, misses Mr. Forbes. They feel now like sheep without a shepherd. The joy and happiness that reigned every evening in the children's room is now gone. Though children still come to the Library with their problems they no longer have Mr. Forbes to assist them. The librarian, too, is in despair because the Library cannot easily find a person to fill his place. Though his death is being mourned by the Negro population which was justly proud of him, still now is he being mourned by the Jewish children of the West End of Boston.

Edward Christopher Williams (1871-1929)[7]

In the annals of American librarianship, Edward Christopher Williams is considered the first professionally trained black librarian. In 1894, E. C. Williams was appointed librarian of Western Reserve University's Adelbert College (the undergraduate men's division) in Cleveland, Ohio. In 1900, he was graduated from the New York State Library School, and, according to Eliza A. Gleason, Williams became the first trained black librarian as well as the first black man to earn his livelihood in the field of librarianship. After having received his certificate from New York (after one year's study rather than the normal two), Williams was appointed Instructor in Library Service in the library school of Western Reserve University and still retained his position at Adelbert College.

Williams was born of a mixed marriage—his black father came of a distinguished family, and his mother, Mary Kilkary, was Irish—on February 11, 1871. He was educated in the public schools of Cleveland, and in 1892, he was graduated from Western Reserve University. He had been elected to Phi Beta Kappa in his junior year. He was valedictorian of his graduating class. Upon his graduation, he was appointed first assistant librarian of Hatch Library at WRU, and in 1894, he was made librarian, a position he held until 1901. WRU was planning a library school, and prior to its establishment, Williams taught an elementary course in national bibliography to a few seniors. He later became instructor in bibliography and reference work. He then joined the new library school faculty in 1904, teaching courses in "public Documents" and "The Criticism and Selection of Books."

Williams married the eldest daughter of Charles Waddell Chesnutt, the distinguished black author; Ethel Chesnutt Williams was a graduate of Smith College. They had a son, Charles, who became a lawyer and wrote a biography of his father (which was never published due to the author's sudden death).

Williams devoted a great deal of his time to collection building at WRU and laid the foundation for the present eminence of the collection there. A charter member of the Ohio Library Association, he served as its secretary in 1904. He was second vice-president of the New York State Library School Association in 1904. He chaired the constitution committee of the Ohio Library Association and was chairman of OLA's college section. Williams was a member of the American Library Association, and addressed a session of ALA's College and Reference section on May 30, 1928, about "Library Needs of Negro Institutions."

After 15 years at WRU, E. C. Williams resigned his position in August 1909 to assume the principalship of M Street High School in the nation's capital. M Street School had a reputation of educating an inordinately large number of students who went on to greater heights after pursuing college work at the elite colleges of the East and New England. Williams brought to the school "the richest and most varied" scholarship of any principal in the school's history. He left M Street School in

---

[7]"Williams," *Crisis* 37 (April 1930): 138; Wallace Van Jackson, "Some Pioneer Negro Library Workers," *Library Journal* 64 (March 15, 1939): 215-17; E. J. Josey, "Edward Christopher Williams: A Librarian's Librarian," *Journal of Library History* 4 (April 1969): 106-122; "Some Schoolmen," *Crisis* 10 (July 1915): 118-20; Dorothy B. Porter, "Phylon Profile XIV: Edward Christopher Williams," *Phylon* 8 (4th quarter, 1947): 315-21; Eliza A. Gleason, "Negro Libraries and Librarianship," 1945, unpublished article.

June 1916 to become Professor of Bibliography, Director of the Library Training Class, and Librarian of Howard University. During the first year, he was also acting instructor in German.

Early in his career at Howard, Williams recognized the pressing need for improved quarters, personnel, and resources if Howard were to realize its goal as the "capstone of Negro education." He set up a library training class in 1917-1918; however, it was not until 1922 that instruction was resumed. In addition to his duties as librarian-instructor, he also served as director of student organization, member of the University-wide Library Committee, associate faculty editor of the *Howard University Record*, and a teacher in the Romance Languages Department.

Williams was an accomplished writer as well and wrote for the student drama group *The Exile*, an Italian classical two-act drama. He wrote two other dramas: *The Sheriff's Children*, an adaptation of his father-in-law's short story, and *The Chasm*, in collaboration with Willis Richardson. He penned a series of articles that were published in the *Messenger* from 1925 to 1926 based on the foibles of black society in Washington, D.C.

Advanced study at Columbia University was provided for Williams through a Rosenwald Fellowship in 1929-1930. He had hoped to receive the Ph.D. degree at the end of his studies, but this was not to be; after a brief illness, he died on December 24, 1929.

Crisis stated, in April 1930:

> But Edward Williams was more than a scientific librarian. . . .
> He died a comparatively young man in a career but half-finished,
> and left the memory of a scientist, a writer, and a loyal and
> genial friend.

Thomas Fountain Blue (1866-1935)[8]

When the Louisville Free Public Library began service in 1905, there was a plan for ten branch libraries, two of which were designated to give service to the blacks of that Kentucky city. The first branch was opened with a librarian and two assistants—all were black.

The system soon learned that it took more than mortar, bricks, and books to make a library; it also took trained library personnel to operate an effective library program. Thus, an annual library apprentice class was established for those interested in library work, the first example of any attempt in the South to provide library training for the prospective black librarian. Students from such cities as Houston and Memphis availed themselves of Louisville's project since no other means of training seems to have been available until the inauguration of the Library School at Hampton Institute in the 1920s.

The guiding light behind these library developments in Louisville was Thomas Fountain Blue. In 1905, Louisville authorities called Blue to head this first branch for blacks, and for 30 years, he worked in the branch. Western

---

[8] Eliza A. Gleason, *Southern Negro and the Public Library* (Chicago: University of Chicago Press, 1941), p. 23; R. D. Harris, "The Advantages of the Colored Branch Libraries," *Southern Workman* 64 (July 1915): 389-90; B. W. Bell, Colored Branches of the Louisville Free Public Library," *ALA Bulletin* 11 (May 1917): 170; Lillian T. Wright, "Thomas Fountain Blue, Pioneer Librarian 1866-1935," (Atlanta: unpublished master's theses [M.S. in L.S.] Atlanta University, 1955).

Colored Branch was joined by the Eastern Colored Branch in 1914, and Blue was given joint direction. Then in 1920, all work for blacks was consolidated under the direction of Thomas Blue. Louisville served as the prototype for service to blacks in the South, and Blue served with distinction in the vanguard of the development of branch library service.

Thomas Blue was the second child of Noah and Henri Ann Blue, born near Washington, D.C., March 6, 1866. His parents were former slaves. Blue attended Hampton Institute from 1885 to 1888 and received a Bachelor of Divinity degree from Richmond Theological Seminary in 1898. Although he was primarily educated as a minister, he never held a position as a church pastor. He served as YMCA secretary of the Sixth Virginia Regiment Volunteers in the Spanish-American War. He continued his association with the YMCA after the war, was called to Louisville to head the Colored Branch of the YMCA, and remained as its first regular secretary from 1899 to 1903.

In 1918, Blue was serving temporarily as an educational secretary in the First World War at a camp in Kentucky, where he helped teach thousands of new recruits to read and write. In 1919, he returned to library work. He developed a working arrangement with the schools through library stations and classroom collections, and heavy use of the buildings was evidenced by the numerous clubs and associations meeting regularly in the branches. From 1919 to 1935, Blue served as director of all the Negro work in Louisville.

Blue was also active in the American Library Association. During the Detroit meeting of 1922, he read a paper, "Training Class at the Western Colored Branch," before the "Work with Negroes Round Table" session. It is believed that Blue was the first black to have a place on the program of ALA. Too, Blue is listed as a delegate to the ALA 50th anniversary convention in Atlantic City in 1926.

Blue delivered the opening address to a conference of black librarians at Hampton Institute in 1927, speaking on "Arousing Community Interest in the Library." He instigated the Negro Library Conference of 1930, held at the dedication of the Fisk University Library, and he was a prominent speaker at the exercises. He became ill in 1935 and expired on November 10, 1935. In recent years, the surviving "Colored Branch" has been placed on the National Register as a landmark, a fitting tribute to the work of Thomas Fountain Blue, a pioneer librarian.

Susan Dart Butler (1888-1959)[9]

The provision of library services to blacks in the South was scanty at best up to the early twentieth century, and even the idea of free library service to all persons did not include the Southern black in all instances. As early as 1900, some provisions were made for separate facilities, but still the growth of the number of cities offering segregated library service could be described as sporadic and limited. Since 1920, however, growth has been more consistent. This change in growth and attitude has been due, in part, to individuals and groups having both an interest in library service and a cognizance of the presence of a racial dualism that demanded

---

[9] Ethel Bolden, "Susan Dart Butler: Pioneer Librarian" (Atlanta: unpublished master's thesis [M.S. in L.S.] Atlanta University, 1959); Virginia L. Jones, "Susan Dart Butler, *Dictionary of American Library Biography* (Littleton, Colo.: Libraries Unlimited, to be published 1977).

the leadership of achieving blacks in the field of library service. The reversal of the trend of not providing service to blacks can be considered as the result of a combination of efforts on the part of citizens, philanthropic organizations, and librarians. One such committed librarian was Susan Dart Butler of Charleston, South Carolina, who was obsessed with a desire from early childhood to provide library service to Charleston's black populace.

Susan Dart was born of free parents in Charleston in 1888. Her father, John L. Dart, an ordained Baptist minister, married Julia Pierre, and Susan was the first of five children born to the couple in the parsonage of the Morris Street Baptist Church in Charleston. She was educated in the schools of Charleston and Washington, D.C., and attended Atlanta University's Normal Department and the McDowell Millinery School in Boston. She also received some training in library science at Hampton Institute in Virginia in 1932. She married Nathaniel Lowe Butler in 1912, and the young couple moved to Charleston. They had one son, Nathaniel Lowe Butler, Jr.

After the death of her father and son, Mrs. Butler turned to civic activities. Her father had errected a building (Dart Hall) years before then to provide facilities for educating the young blacks of Charleston. Mrs. Butler assembled the family library in the building and made the collection available three times a week to the public. A regular story hour was held for youngsters, and the high school used the facility as well. Mrs. Butler also traveled widely and gained counsel from many library leaders on how to serve her patrons more effectively. The library was maintained at her own expense as she attempted to persuade the black citizens and the City of Charleston to provide financial support for it. Meanwhile, she motivated women's groups and churches to collect books and raise funds for the project.

The Rosenwald Fund became interested in promoting public library service to Southern blacks in the 1920s, and in 1925, Butler organized a bi-racial women's committee to investigate the feasibility of seeking Rosenwald support to start public library service. The Rosenwald interests were so impressed by Mrs. Butler's work that there was ferment for a five-year plan for the development of the library with Charleston County officials. Rosenwald and the Carnegie Corporation gave funds for the establishment of the Charleston County Free Public Library, and, for one dollar a year, Mrs. Butler gave the use of Dart Hall to the County Library as her contribution to the project.

In 1929, the County Library began service to all citizens. Dart Hall Branch was opened in July 1931, with Mrs. Butler serving as children's librarian. In 1932, she attended Hampton Institute Library School and returned to Charleston to become the librarian of Dart Hall Branch Library. However, Mrs. Butler's interests went beyond library service to blacks. Her organizational interests included the Librarians Section of the South Carolina State Teachers' Association, YMCA, Boy Scouts, Girl Scouts, American Red Cross, and she was founder/historian of the South Carolina Federation of Women's Clubs.

At the age of 69, in May 1957, Susan Dart Butler retired after serving as branch librarian for 26 years. She was acclaimed by both the library board and citizens for her exemplary pioneering spirit that inspired others in working toward similar goals. Mrs. Butler died in 1959.

Sadie Peterson Delaney (1889-1959)[10]

"What is bibliotherapy?" asked Eleanor Roosevelt in her column, *My Day*. She was writing about an unusual black librarian, Sadie Peterson Delaney. Bibliotherapy has been defined as "book treatment," the art or science of curing or improving the state of health of the ill and infirm (either physically or mentally) through the skillful selection and reading of appropriate books and use of other media.

Sadie Peterson Delaney was born in Rochester, New York, in 1889, the daughter of James and Julia Johnson. She received her early training at Poughkeepsie (New York) High School and at the College of the City of New York. Her first marriage ended in divorce, and she later was married again, to Rudicel A. Delaney (in 1928). Her library training was received in the training classes of the New York Public Library, and in 1919, she was assigned to the 135th Street Branch.

The 135th Street Branch, located in Harlem, was one of the focal points for the literary ferment that was later to burst into the Harlem Renaissance. Here, Delaney set a pattern of service that would hold for a lifetime—the consideration and use of books in relation to the practical interests and needs of people. Story hours were started, and special groups for parents and teachers, Boy Scouts, YMCA leaders, social workers, and others brought attention to the library resources and its programs. The first library art exhibits of black artists' works were held, and a book lovers club caught the interest of the young Countee Cullen, Claude McKay, and Langston Hughes. Delaney placed special emphasis upon building a Negroana Collection at the New York Public Library, and as a result of this interest, she came to know Arthur Schomburg, who later provided the nucleus for the world-famed collection on blacks now bearing his name.

While working with various groups and individuals, Delaney became interested in work with the blind; this interest became so great that she learned Braille and Moon Point. In 1923, she was called to organize the hospital library at the Veterans Administration Hospital at Tuskegee, Alabama. Thus, she began her work at the hospital as a pioneer in bibliotherapy, group therapy for the mentally ill, and organization of work for the blind, all of which would bring her international acclaim.

At Tuskegee, she found very little more than the need and desire for library service. She said in 1925, "We began work on the wards by carrying books and magazines to the bed patients in a wire paper carrier," and the first month's circulation was 275. She started the only VA library in the country with a literary society and reading classes, and from then on, she began to create a technique of dealing with hospital patients that has been discussed and imitated throughout the profession in this country and abroad. So marked were Delaney's achievements and

---

[10]Morteza D. Sprague, "Dr. Sadie Peterson Delaney 'Great Humanitarian'," *Service* 15 (June 1951): 17-18; Sadie P. Delaney, "Library Activities at Tuskegee," *Medical Bulletin of the Veterans Administration* 17 (October 1940): 163-69; *Who's Who in Colored America* (New York: Burchel, 1950), p. 48; Clyde H. Cantrell, "Sadie P. Delaney: Bibliotherapist and Librarian," *Southeastern Librarian* 6 (Fall 1956): 105-109; Sadie P. Delaney, "U.S. Hospital Library No. 91, Tuskegee, Alabama," *Crisis* 29 (January 1925): 116-17.

her theories that her library was for years a demonstration center for other VA hospitals, as well as the site of internships for library school students.

She was an extremely active member of the American Library Association and its Hospital Library section, and the library profession as a whole honored her at an ALA testimonial banquet at its convention in 1950. Also in 1950, Atlanta University, in recognition of her achievement, conferred upon her the Doctor of Humanities degree, and the citation stated in part that she was "a pioneer in utilizing reading materials in the rehabilitation of delinquent boys and girls, in the rehabilitation and cure of mental patients, and in the development of techniques for teaching the blind to read . . . a great humanitarian." In 1950, she received as well the National Urban League Award as Woman of the Year, and in September of the same year, she was applauded by *Look* magazine. In 1952, she was selected as one of America's outstanding women and given a national award of the National Council of Colored Women's Clubs. The Veterans Administration also cited Mrs. Delaney for distinguished contributions to library science and library science education in the United States and abroad. Mrs. Delaney died in 1959. A scholarship loan fund in her honor was begun at the School of Library Service of Atlanta University.

* * *

When one looks back over the more than one hundred years of the black presence in American librarianship, the record is not unimpressive. Blacks, both women and men, served in national, state, and local libraries, often pioneering in areas of service to all races. Too, they made available materials documenting the struggles of blacks in an often hostile society, materials that demonstrated how blacks surmounted the obstacles placed before them. In spite of overwhelming odds, these librarians and bookmen attained greatness, and their names are an indelible part of the annals of American librarianship.

3. The Hampton Institute Library School
by Lucy B. Campbell, Librarian, Hampton Institute

One cannot assess librarianship and the black librarian without a retrospective glance at the Hampton Institute Library School, for this library school has a unique place in the development of librarianship in the United States. Founded in September 1925 by a grant from the Carnegie Corporation, the library school was established mainly on the advice of officers of the General Education Board and the American Library Association, with the full endorsement of the Julius Rosenwald Fund. At the time the library school was established, there was only one other accredited library school in the South—the Emory University Library School at Atlanta, Georgia.[1]

---

[1] S. L. Smith, "The Passing of the Hampton Library School," *Journal of Negro Education* 9 (January 1940): 51.

Certainly a school was needed that could provide black librarians to the black community, but the problem was even more basic than that. As late as 1913, such large cities as Atlanta, Birmingham, Mobile, Montgomery, Nashville, New Orleans, and Richmond reported that there were no library facilities for Negro readers. However, in order to develop such service (as was done by Thomas F. Blue in Louisville, Kentucky, in 1905), librarians sensitive to the existence and needs of potential black patrons had to gain entry into the profession. Only after World War I would this happen on any large scale.

Thus it was that the development of librarianship as a field for professionally trained blacks occurred in the years following 1920. Too, this happened only through large endowments and grants, made principally by the General Education Board, the Carnegie Corporation, the Julius Rosenwald Fund, the Slater Fund, and other private philanthropic organizations, following conferences and studies on library needs in the South.[2] Summarizing this influx of monies into a new field, Louis Shores stated in his article, "Library Service to Negroes" (1931), that:

> The General Education Board has come forth with over a million dollars for Negro college library buildings. . . . Another half million dollars has been appropriated by the Julius Rosenwald Fund for county library development on condition that equal service is granted to both races. The Carnegie Corporation has helped a number of the colored public libraries and has given money for books to one or two Negro colleges. Finally, the Southeastern Library Association has written into its resolutions "that library service to Negroes should be part of every public library program."[3]

Money alone could not accomplish what was needed. Dedicated people, willing to work to the utmost to achieve their goals, had to emerge from the profession itself if the donated money was not to go for nothing. Such people did come forth, and the rapid growth of the profession during the period 1925-1939 can be attributed largely to the founder and director of the Hampton Institute Library School, Miss Florence R. Curtis. She was a graduate of the New York State Library School, taught for eleven years in the Library School of the University of Illinois, and for three years was Vice Director of the Drexel Institute Library School. She also visited each year a large number of public libraries, high schools, and colleges, both white and black, in the Southeast and Southwest; and through her visits, the New York Library School kept in close touch with its alumni. (The School served as an advisory bureau for libraries concerning building plans, library equipment, book purchases, and administrative problems.) Thus, Miss Curtis was in many ways an ideal choice to head the "experiment," the Hampton Institute's new Library School.

Hampton Institute (Virginia) was selected as the site for a library school since its library and resources would enable the school to be placed on a solid educational basis immediately. This first school for blacks to issue degrees in library

---

[2] *Ibid.*

[3] Louis Shores, "Library Service to Negroes," *Wilson Library Bulletin* 5 (January 1931): 311.

science was also accredited by the Board of Education for Librarianship of the Association of American Library Schools. The school began as a junior undergraduate school in 1925; the entrance requirement was then raised to three years of approved college work in 1929 and to graduate from a standard four-year college in the fall of 1934.[4]

Miss Curtis was also aware that the Hampton Library School had potential for great influence, both in the state and in the South. For the year 1927, the state of Virginia reported notable progress in all matters relative to the development of library service: several small public libraries were organized in towns and villages, there was marked improvement in the county situation, and at Hampton Institute Library School, an institute for colored librarians was held from March 15 to March 18. The general interest manifested by all who attended the conference, and the full discussion following the presentation of each topic, showed that such an annual conference of librarians might increase interest in libraries and help in their development. This meeting was called by Miss Curtis, and it was "probably the first of its kind in the South and was very largely attended."[5]

The conferees were educators and librarians of both races, representing different sections of the country and various types of libraries. Edward C. Williams, Librarian of Howard University, spoke on the problems of the college library at this meeting. When the Hampton Library School was established in 1925, he was the only Negro graduate of a library school in the entire country.[6] His soon-to-be-annual pilgrimage to the old Hampton Institute Library School, where he often presented lectures, was the occasion that he would use to urge Negro library school students to excel in their studies and join the ranks of the American Library Association. In his unique position as one of the best educated librarians of his day (he was elected to Phi Beta Kappa at Western Reserve University), he was frequently called upon to advise on library institutes and conferences.[7]

Thomas F. Blue, also one of six lecturers at the Hampton Librarians Conference (1927), discussed the topic "Community Interest in the Library." (He was graduated from Hampton Institute in 1888 and Richmond Theological Seminary [now Virginia Union University] in 1898.)[8] The success of library service for blacks in Louisville, Kentucky, can be attributed to Mr. Blue, when he became, in 1905, the nation's first black person to head a public library—i.e., the first branch for blacks in the South, "The Western Colored Branch." Mr. Blue also developed an excellent training program which produced a large number of library workers. With his assistant, Mrs. Rachel D. Harris, he organized many public library branches, among them the colored branches of Lynchburg and Roanoke, Virginia.

In 1928, the U.S. Bureau of Education issued a report that only underscored the concern of those working for library service, especially the concerns of black

---

[4] Smith, p. 51

[5] "Library Extension in Virginia in 1927," *Virginia Libraries* 1 (April 1928): 3.

[6] Parepa Watson, "The Development of the Negro College Library in North Carolina," *North Carolina Libraries* 3 (May 1944): 9.

[7] E. J. Josey, "Edward Christopher Williams: A Librarian's Librarian," *Negro History Bulletin* 33 (March 1970): 76.

[8] Wallace Van Jackson, "Some Pioneer Negro Library Workers," *Library Journal* 64 (March 15, 1939): 216.

educators about the availability of materials for their students. The Bureau's survey of colleges emphasized the library as a major department of every college, and it was further revealed that one of the prerequisites for developing adequate libraries was trained librarians. The black colleges had neither trained librarians nor modern library facilities. In 1931, there were approximately 64 universities, colleges, and normal training schools, 448 public and private high schools, and 53 public libraries in need of trained Negro librarians. Only one accredited library school existed for the sole purpose of training Negro librarians. (A few Negroes attended other accredited library schools.) As a result of this situation, several Negro institutions became interested in offering professional library training so that service in schools and public libraries as well as in college libraries might be provided.[9]

Under a three-year grant from the General Education Board, a program of instruction was initiated, in 1936, with representatives of Atlanta and Fisk Universities, Hampton Institute, and Prairie View State College, and state school library supervisors from Alabama, Louisiana, Kentucky, and Tennessee. From this cooperative effort, some 200 teacher-librarians received the instruction required by the Southern Association of Colleges and Secondary Schools for the high schools in which they were appointed.

Wallace Van Jackson's article "Negro Library Workers," written in 1940, contains statements that appear to be prophetic for these times:

> As the Negro enters the library field in large numbers, he will seek to participate in the professional activities of libraries. Already Negro colleges and universities are becoming members of the American Library Association, and the number of individual memberships is increasing. It is safe to say that in the future Negroes will join the Association and will attend the conference in larger numbers. . . . In the future complete participation in the professional affairs of the library field may be expected.[10]

Unfortunately, the Hampton Library School did not survive into the days of more complete participation. The school, dependent upon large grants, was forced to close in 1939, when those funds were no longer available. Rather than dilute the quality of instruction, those in charge of the school felt it better to close it at a time when its graduates were receiving the best available instruction.

Then, in 1944, Florence Curtis died. Wallace Van Jackson, a Hampton graduate, commented as follows:

> News has come to us of the passing of Florence Rising Curtis, director and founder of the Hampton Institute Library School, during the period of its existence, and friend of all who labored to improve library service in the United States. . . . She carried the program of Library Extension to every state in the South. Largely as the result of her foresight and hard work, scores of Negro schools and colleges have been accredited by regional agencies because, although she was primarily interested in libraries, she used her influence and

---

[9] Sarah C. N. Bogle, "Training for Negro Librarians," *A.L.A. Bulletin* 25 (April 1931): 133.

[10] Wallace Van Jackson, "Negro Library Workers," *Library Quarterly* 10 (January 1940): 108.

energy to improve the whole educational program of the school she visited. Miss Curtis was a familiar visitor at conferences and meetings of administrators of Negro schools during the period of service at Hampton.... Her many firends attest to her qualities of sincerity and unprejudiced acceptance of all persons as human beings of basic worth, regardless of race, religion, or status.

Speaking for myself and as a representative of many students of Miss Curtis, I wish to express our heartfelt thanks for her life among us and register the hope that many other librarians will follow her example of interracial goodwill to the end that America may practice as well as preach democracy.[11]

Yet, in spite of its closing and the death of its Director, the school continues to have influence in the persons of its graduates, some of them distinguished leaders in the profession as a whole. Too, Virginia, because it happened to be the residence of the Hampton Institute Library School, has the distinction of being the locale for the beginning of education in library service for blacks and for the library training of 183 of the nation's librarians from September 1925 through June 1939. The impact of the services of these Hampton graduates (coming from 22 states, the District of Columbia and the West Indies) has spread internationally, and graduates of this library school today are scattered throughout the nation. Although many of them have retired, they occupy positions of leadership throughout the nation, and some have achieved international fame.

SELECTED OUTSTANDING GRADUATES OF THE SCHOOL

Mrs. Virginia Young Lee (1928) spent the bulk of her career in Roanoke, Virginia. From its inception in 1920, the Roanoke Public Library Board sought to provide library service to all citizens. Thus, the main library was opened May 21, 1921, and the Gainsboro Branch, serving the black community, was opened December 13, 1921. An impressive article concerning Mrs. Lee, courtesy of the Roanoke Public Library and Florence B. Yoder (Virginia State Library) defines her contributions:

In 1928, a professional librarian, graduate of Hampton Institute, and a former library page at Gainsboro, Mrs. Virginia Young Lee, became head of the Gainsboro Branch. She retired in December, 1971 after forty-three years of extraordinary dedicated service to the library and her community.

Imbued with a steadfast devotion to education and a contagious enjoyment in sharing the rewards of reading, Mrs. Lee, with unswerving zeal, used her remarkable intellectual and artistic talents to create a community center where library users could confidently depend on unselfish, kindly service—rendered with competence, humor, and true Christian understanding.

---

[11] Wallace Van Jackson, "Florence Rising Curtis," *Library Journal* 69 (December 1, 1944): 1060.

Her development of Gainsboro Branch activities as a dominant influence in the community and her assiduous, untiring efforts in assembling an impressive collection on black history, comprising materials covering interests in the African background, culture, artistic endeavors, also the heritage of American blacks and their contributions, are an enduring legacy to the library system.

Her widely recognized capabilities as a librarian and the respect accorded her as a valued citizen have been the inspiration for others to emulate her achievements and continue in her standards of excellence.

In 1930, Mrs. Lee was a panelist at the Fisk University Negro Library Conference; her topic in the "Public Library Service" session was the "Value of Clubs in the Public Library." In 1970, she received a citation from Hampton Institute for her work in organizing a school for the rehabilitation of returning soldiers after World War II. She was chosen "Citizen of the Year" (1970) by the Gamma Alpha chapter of Omega Psi Phi and "Woman of the Year" (1972) by the Omega Zeta chapter of Zeta Phi Beta.

Mrs. Olive Durden Brown (1929) retired after 33 years as Head Librarian at Huston-Tillotson College, Houston, Texas.

Miss Alice A. Jackson (1930) retired as Education Librarian at Virginia State College in 1972. She has also served as Head Librarian at Fayetteville State University (1957-1960) and Delaware State University (1960-1962). She began her career in 1930 as an assistant librarian and cataloger at Virginia State College. From September 1945 until August 1947, Miss Jackson was Supervisor of Acquisitions at Howard University, and from 1947 to 1957, she was Cataloger at Manhattanville College of the Sacred Heart. The recipient of Rosenwald and General Education Board Scholarships, at Hampton Institute and Columbia University, respectively, Miss Jackson was designated by Florence Rising Curtis to assist Arthur Schomburg in coordinating his collection with the Negro collection of the New York Public Library.

Miss Jackson is the author of "Authors' Names in Negro Collections" (*College & Research Libraries*, October 1946), a digest of her master's essay at Columbia University's School of Library Service.

Miss Jackson has stated:

> At the beginning of my career in 1930 most libraries were makeshift ... housed in converted classrooms and staffed by nonprofessional personnel. Under the inspired leadership of Miss Florence R. Curtis ... the broadly trained professional appeared on the scene, dedicated to the principle of upgrading every type of library service to blacks. These professionals, by hard work and constant pressure on administrators, led the way to the fine facilities available in many libraries. May their spirit continue unabated!

Since retirement, she has been organizing archival material at Virginia State College.

Mrs. Gwendolyn Jordan Midgette (1932) retired in 1975 from Elizabeth City State University, Elizabeth City, North Carolina.

Mrs. Harriet Dorothy Miles Hill (1932) stated:

> Aside from the usual preparation and encouragement of children to read, librarians have to be counselors with the patience of Job, the knowledge of Methuseluh and possess an endless abundance of love! The majority of these librarians continue to do this willingly, quietly and without overtime pay or promotion.

A native of Virginia, Mrs. Hill, now retired, organized library science courses at Virginia State College (Summer 1937-1938) and taught library science courses at Hampton (Summer Session 1939-1942; 1948-1952). She was librarian for the Gainsboro Branch of the Roanoke City Public Library from October 1924 through June 1928.

Mrs. Hill also served as Librarian at Hampton Institute's Phenix Training School (1931-1962) and the Phenix Senior High School (1962-1967), which enabled her to work closely with the students of the Library School during their Practice Work Training period. She organized the library at the Roy Bright Private School, cataloged the collection of Hampton Institute's non-graded elementary school library and taught library usage (part-time), 1967-1969. She was lauded for her organization of the William Moses Library of the Department of Architecture at Hampton Institute, where she served as Librarian (1968-1974; 1975-1976).

For four years, Mrs. Hill was chairman of the Librarian's Division of the Virginia State Teachers Association, which had its first meeting at Virginia State College at the Forty-Seventh Annual Convention of the Virginia State Teachers Association (1934).

Mrs. Carrie Coleman Robinson (1932) was employed by the Alabama Department of Education (1946-1972) and was the first black librarian in America to serve as a state school library consultant (1946). She also organized the Department of Library Education at Alabama State College and served as its part-time chairman (1946-1962). With Mrs. Robinson at the helm, "the simultaneous undertaking of a Library Education Program at Alabama State College and consultative services to the public schools during the years 1946-1962, put the library programs in black schools out in front."[12] In 1969, she was successful in establishing the School of Library Media at Alabama A&M University (Normal, Alabama).

Mrs. Robinson, who received the M.L.S. from the University of Illinois, has also completed course work for the Ph.D. degree at the same university. She is a member of more than 30 organizations, committees, round tables, etc., including ALA, AASL, IASL, NEA, SELA, AEA, AIMA, ALA Council, Freedom to Read Foundation Board of Trustees, etc. She began her career in librarianship as a teacher-librarian in Georgia, at Dorchester Academy, and has served as Librarian at Southern University Laboratory High School, and as Head Librarian

---

[12] E. J. Josey, *The Black Librarian in America* (Metuchen, N.J.: Scarecrow Press, Inc., 1970), p. 280.

at three institutions—Grambling College, Louisiana State University (Baton Rouge Branch), and Alcorn College.

Mrs. Robinson filed suit in federal court against the Alabama State Department of Education in September 1970, alleging racial discrimination in the Department's employment practices. As a result, she was granted a significant increase in salary and a promotion in the Alabama State Department of Education in an out-of-court settlement announced in the November 27 issue of the *NEA Reporter*. (She was assisted by the NEA DuShane Emergency Fund in her legal action against the State of Alabama and the American Library Association also filed an *amicus curiae* brief with the court at the insistence of Eric Moon and E. J. Josey.)[13]

During the summer of 1970, Mrs. Robinson was a member of a Round the World Tour that attended the meeting of the WCOTP (World Confederation of the Teaching Profession) and the International Association of School Librarians in Australia. The recipient of numerous awards and honors, Mrs. Robinson also received the ALA Black Caucus award in 1974.

Mrs. Robinson's extensive experience and professional activities attest to her dedicated and distinguished leadership. During the summers of 1964 and 1967, she was a visiting professor at Purdue University, Lafayette, Indiana. As a consultant for many in-service education programs and as sponsor for numerous workshops and conferences, she has enabled many persons to extend their educational pursuits. Since 1971, Mrs. Robinson has been a member of the ALA Committee on Accreditation. The only woman and only black member of this committee, she has served as chairwoman and has been a member of COA Evaluation Teams for numerous schools of library science, including the University of Chicago, Kent State University, Syracuse University, State University of New York at Buffalo, North Carolina Central University, and Iowa State University.

In September 1975, she retired as Associate Professor of Educational Media at Auburn University, Auburn, Alabama, where she began her service in 1973. Although her career has spanned several states, her most notable contribution has been to the people of the State of Alabama, to which she came "for the building of a library training program, the training of school librarians and the building of libraries in the public schools."[14] Her mission was accomplished.

Mrs. Virginia Lacy Jones (1933), Dean of the Atlanta University School of Library Service since 1945, was the second black to receive the Ph.D. in library science (from the University of Chicago, 1945).

Following her graduate from Hampton Institute, she was designated by Miss Curtis to head the regional center at Prairie View A&M College in Prairie View, Texas. This center was designed, along with those at Hampton Institute, Atlanta University, and Fisk University, to offer courses for four consecutive summers to Negro school librarians to fulfill the need for their services. For Dr. Jones, this assignment was the beginning of the "challenges, problems, and gratification of library education."[15]

---

[13] "Justice Comes to Carrie Robinson," *American Libraries* 2 (April 1971): 333.

[14] Josey, *Black Librarian*, p. 283.

[15] *Ibid.*, p. 27.

In an introduction to a *Bio-Bibliography of Dr. Virginia Lacy Jones*, the late Joan Herring, a graduate of Hampton Institute (1972) and Atlanta University School of Library Service (1974), voiced the sentiments of other graduates of the Atlanta University School of Library Service when she said:

> Her writings express her feelings toward discrimination in the profession; and the material that has been written about her reflects the extent of her activities in the community and her untiring efforts in behalf of library education . . . this bibliography shows her deep concern for students and in particular the students at the School of Library Service in Atlanta University.[16]

It was a great tribute to Miss Florence Rising Curtis when Dr. Virginia Lacy Jones, her student, received the Melvil Dewey Award of the American Library Association at the ALA Conference in Las Vegas in June 1973. It reads:

> Librarian—Educator—Administrator—Diplomat
> Virginia Lacy Jones' time and talent have been dedicated un-unstintingly to her students, to library education, and to her chosen profession. At the forefront of creative library leadership in this country for more than a quarter of a century, Dr. Jones in accepting this distinguished medal, does honor to this Association and to those who have been so recognized in the past. As Dean of a library school which has provided opportunities for scores of distinguished black librarians, Dr. Jones has fought valiantly to maintain quality professional education even as the man for whom this medal is named struggled so tirelessly.[17]

During the 1976 Annual Conference of the American Library Association (the "Centennial" Conference), Dr. Jones received the ALA Black Caucus Centennial Award and was also one of eight librarians voted to receive an honorary membership in the ALA.

A distinguished scholar, notable administrator, and leader in librarianship, **Mr. Wallace Van Jackson** (1934) has also made many notable contributions to librarianship internationally. A graduate of Virginia Union University, Van Jackson received the B.L.S. degree from Hampton Institute and the A.M.L.S. from the University of Michigan. For two years, he was also a student at the University of Chicago Graduate Library School. His professional career began in 1923 as a teacher at Higgs Roanoke Institute in Parmelee, North Carolina.

He has served as Librarian at Virginia Union University (1927-1939); Professor, Atlanta University School of Library Service (1940-1941); University Librarian, Atlanta University (1941-1947); University Librarian and Head, Department of Library Service, Texas-Southern University (1949-1954); Library Director,

---

[16] Joan B. Herring, *A Bio-Bibliography of Dr. Virginia Lacy Jones* (Atlanta: Atlanta University School of Library Science, May 1974. Unpublished).

[17] *Ibid.*, p. 11.

Virginia State College (1954-1962, 1963-1968); Librarian (1968-1969), Mary Holmes College (West Point, Mississippi), and Assistant to Librarian (1969-1970); and teacher, summer faculty, Hampton Institute (1971-1974, 1976). Van Jackson has served also as a consultant and expert on acquisitions and buildings at Alabama State College and Alabama A&M College (1952-1954); Texas College (1952); Morristown College (1958); Claflin College (1957-1958); and Fayetteville State Teachers College (1961).

Because of discriminatory laws and the traditional position of the South with respect to mixed meetings, and since the American Library Association accepts members regardless of race, Van Jackson (a native of Richmond, Virginia) was among those librarians who expressed his opinion concerning the ALA convention policies in 1936, when Richmond was host city.[18] It was recommended by the Committee on Racial Discrimination and approved by the ALA Council at its opening meeting in Chicago, December 28, 1937, that:

> In all rooms and halls assigned to the American Library Association hereafter for use in connection with its conference or otherwise under its control, all members shall be admitted upon terms of full equality.[19]

Van Jackson (in 1963)[20] and the late Mrs. Alpha S. Rogers were later the first blacks to be accepted to membership in the Virginia Library Association. In 1972, he was made a life member of the Virginia Library Association.

A member of the ALA, Van Jackson served on the Council, the Committee of Intellectual Freedom, and the Economic Opportunity Programs Committee. He is also a member of the Texas Library Association and the Nigerian Library Association. As a member of the Virginia Teachers Association, he has served as Chairman of the Librarians' Division. In 1960, when the schools of Virginia had a special project, "Teaching Africa in Virginia Schools," Van Jackson worked closely with elementary and secondary pupils and teachers. He prepared an extensive preliminary bibliography on Africa as well. Too, he has served as a member of the editorial board of *Phylon* magazine and also as editor of the Richmond, Virginia, *Voice*. Since 1923, he has continuously contributed to scholarly journals.

The present library building at Virginia State College was designed, planned, and erected during his administration as library director. Since his retirement from that school in 1968, he has been, as noted, continuously involved in many library projects. In November 1974, Van Jackson journeyed to South Africa for a six-month assignment with the library faculty of the University of Botswana, Lesotho, and Swaziland to provide technical library assistance to that developing university. He went to this Southern African institution under an exchange program sponsored by the ALA Black Caucus Task Force on Librarians for Africa. (The African-American Scholars Council, Inc., of Washington, D.C., financed the

---

[18] Wallace Van Jackson, "A Letter to Negro Librarians, Readers Open Forum," *Library Journal* 61 (May 15, 1936): 387.

[19] "Report on the Committee on Racial Discrimination," *A.L.A. Bulletin* 31 (January 1937): 37.

[20] Letter from Florence B. Yoder, Virginia State Library, July 22, 1976.

assignment as part of its program to assist in the educational development of the African continent.) Mr. Van Jackson's appointment to the BLS University system and his willingness to assist this young Southern African institution were another milestone in his long and distinguished career. He had previously served as Public Affairs Officer in the American Embassy at Monrovia, Liberia (1947-1949), and somewhat later, he was Acquisitions Librarian and Deputy Director of the National Library of Nigeria in Lagos (1962-1963).[21] The ALA presented a Special Centennial Citation to Van Jackson during the Centennial Conference, July 19, 1976, in Chicago, Illinois. Excerpts from the Centennial Citation read:

> Wallace Van Jackson is a distinguished librarian whose leadership in the development of black academic libraries in the United States, in library education, and in the development of library service in Africa has made a lasting impact on librarianship. . . .
>
> Through his activities in the American Library Association and as a member of the ALA Council, he was a spokesman for black librarians in the 1930s and 1940s. . . .
>
> Throughout his career Wallace Van Jackson has inspired numerous black Americans and Africans to enter the library profession.
>
> The American Library Association is proud to honor Wallace Van Jackson for his significant contributions to librarianship.

The diversity of his services, contributions, and achievements reflects his great knowledge and wisdom. A brilliant man with an impressive record, and an exemplary leader, he is a symbol of the "history of librarianship" for blacks everywhere.

Miss Ollie L. Brown (1937), now deceased, served as Head Librarian at Alabama State College (Montgomery) for 40 years. She organized the black Alabama Association of School Librarians, a department within the Alabama State Teachers Association.

Miss Lois H. Daniel (1937) was Librarian, Tennessee A&I State University, Nashville, Tennessee.

Mrs. Hattie I. Durant (1938) served as cataloger and outstanding librarian at Norfolk State College, Norfolk, Virginia, from 1942 until her retirement in 1969.

Mrs. Minnie Slade Bishop (1939) has been Librarian at Sanford Bishop College, Mobile, Alabama, since 1943. This college was originally the Mobile Branch of Alabama State College.

Mrs. Alta M. Anderson (1939) began service at Norfolk State College in 1955, where she also served for many years as Librarian in the Acquisitions Department.

---

[21] "Personals," *Virginia Librarian* 20 (December 1974): 22.

Finally, several alumnae of the Hampton Library School had close associations with the North Carolina College for Negroes (now North Carolina Central University). **Mrs. Dorothy Shepard Manley** and **Mrs. Eva Glass Williams** (both now deceased) were faculty members of the college's Library School in September 1941, when the B.S. in L.S. degree program was begun. **Mrs. Parepa Watson Jackson** (1930) and **Mrs. Robbie Goodloe** (1932) served with distinction for many years on the college library staff, and **Miss Evelyn B. Pope** (1937) bridged the period of transition from North Carolina College for Negroes to North Carolina Central University and accreditation—serving also for a period of time as Director of the School of Library Science.

* * *

The librarians discussed above represent only a sample of Hampton's Library School graduates. An assessment of librarianship and the Hampton Institute Library School will include these graduates as well as others who have had impressive records of service, leadership, and achievement. Florence Rising Curtis and the Hampton Institute Library School will forever live through its 183 graduates—trailblazers and pioneers—who received their basic library education and training in Virginia. Their careers and contributions are an impressive record highlighting significant achievements of black librarians throughout the world.

SOURCES

Commencement Programs (1926-1939). Hampton Institute Archives.

Curriculum Vitae and Biographical Data Forms. (Received from Mrs. Hattie I. Durant, Mrs. Harriett M. Hill, Miss Alice A. Jackson, Mrs. Carrie C. Robinson, Mr. Wallace Van Jackson)

Hampton Institute Library School. *Distribution of Graduates, 1926-1936.*

News release: "American Library Association. Centennial Conference," Chicago, July 18-24, 1976. (Wallace Van Jackson, Virginia Lacy Jones.) (Courtesy Peggy Barber, Director, Public Information Service.)

"Potpourri—Mrs. Olive D. Brown, 1929, *Hampton Bulletin. Alumni Issue.* (January, February, 1976), p. 6.

Retirement Banquet Program. "Mrs. Gwendolyn Jordan Midgette," Elizabeth City State University, Elizabeth City, North Carolina, May 1975.

Roanoke Public Library, Roanoke, Virginia. "Mrs. Virginia Young Lee, Black Public Librarian." (Courtesy Florence B. Yoder, Head, Library Development Branch, Virginia State Library, Richmond, Virginia.)

Southern Workman, Hampton Institute, Hampton, Virginia, LII-LXVIII (1923-1939).

Virginia Libraries, Virginia State Library Extension Division, Richmond, Virginia, I-IV (1928-1931).

EARLY LIBRARY ORGANIZATIONS

4. The Alabama Association of School Librarians
   by   Carrie C. Robinson, formerly Associate Professor, Auburn University

Unfortunately, the Association's early records are no longer available, and only the scantiest of recorded information about the initial years of the Association exists. Oral history gathered from several individuals supports the recollections of Miss Ollie L. Brown (for many years Head Librarian of Alabama State College/University), who conceived the idea of having black librarians convene as a departmental unit of the Alabama State Teachers Association (ASTA). The earliest recorded meeting of those librarians was in March 1944, during the period when the President of Alabama State College, the late Dr. H. Councill Trenholm, was initiating a program for training school librarians for the black public schools of Alabama. It should also be noted that Alabama State College (now Alabama State University) was the headquarters for the ASTA from its inception in the latter decades of the 1800s until 1969, when there was a merger of AEA/ASTA.

In the summer of 1947, I met with the following people to organize formally a professional black librarians' organization in Alabama: Mrs. Jewett Langford Anderson (Librarian, Booker Washington High School), Miss Ollie L. Brown (Head Librarian, Alabama State College), Mrs. Lucille Green (Librarian, Carver High School), Mrs. C. Elizabeth Johnson (Assistant Professor, Department of Library Education, Alabama State College), Miss Mattie Lee Langford (Librarian, Elmore County Training School), Mrs. Bertha Pleasant Williams (Librarian, Union Street Public Library Branch, Montgomery), and Mrs. Elizabeth Jett Thompson (Librarian, Darden High School). However, to a great extent, my work with the organization for its first years was limited by my own graduate study. Too, since records of the Association's activities during its first four years of existence are almost non-existent, activities of the early years cannot be chronicled.

Recruitment of "desirable" persons for the profession of school librarianship, raising the standards of the profession (both generally and in the black schools of Alabama, specifically), and serving as a clearing-house for school library problems in Alabama were concerns to which the members of the group seriously addressed themselves. Benefiting recruitment efforts was the fact that as many as 95 percent of the black school librarians in Alabama enrolled over a period of years at Alabama State College for their initial training. But the program of library education was not the only means by which persons of high quality were encouraged to pursue the profession of librarianship. It was not the only means by which standards for school library services were to be raised. And it was not, indeed, the one source to which school administrators and school librarians could turn for solutions to their problems.

One of the major services of the Alabama Association of School Librarians (AASL) was to provide professional meetings to which outstanding leaders in the fields of education and librarianship were invited as keynote contributors. It was in March 1951 that Dr. Frances Henne (a leader in school librarianship) was the keynote speaker at the AASL annual meeting. Moreover, Dr. Henne appeared and spoke briefly at a general session of ASTA, the parent organization of AASL.

Guided by its rather simplistic constitution, the Association's Executive Committee was constantly involved in planning annual spring meetings and annual fall workshops, co-sponsored by the State Department of Education. In April 1952, responding to the convention theme "Appraising Ourselves as Teachers," the AASL engaged in efforts to appraise library services in both elementary and secondary black schools in Alabama.

In 1953, the Association began its formal acquaintance with a valued friend, and any account of the AASL must note the contributions made by Dr. Carol W. Hayes, former Director of Negro Schools of Birmingham. Few school administrators are identified with the development of school libraries as is Dr. Hayes, who spearheaded an effort to provide functional library services in every elementary school of Birmingham that served black children. Leaders in the upper echelons of education on both state and local levels were largely committed to effecting the accreditation of struggling high schools when Carol Hayes was stimulating inquiring minds in the teachers and children of Birmingham's black public schools. It was his conviction that libraries are essential in such a process and that "reading" is the key to successful teaching and learning. The following remarks by Dr. Hayes to the teachers with whom he worked gave impetus to the work of the AASL annual spring meeting of 1953 (Dr. Hayes's topic was "Have You Read Sufficiently?"):

> The teacher should do a wide variety of reading. The up-to-date teacher will be found reading not only books which deal with teaching as such but also books that will give her world points of view, good mental health, emotional balance and pleasure. Because of the stress and strain of living today, few teachers, if any, escape some form of neurosis. Neurotic or frustrated behavior patterns, which make good teaching and learning situations almost impossible, are often brought into many classrooms. The reading of books on mental health or emotional balance is especially needed during these times. In many cases, the teacher can be her own psychiatrist if she will read and apply what she reads from literature of this kind.

Under the strong leadership of Mrs. Ella McCain, the Association emphasized the importance of "Knowing Your Professional Organizations," and through our organization, the majority of black Alabama school librarians came to know the American Library Association, the American Association of School Librarians, the Southeastern Library Association and, indeed, the Alabama Library Association. It is also appropriate to state that the Alabama Library Association, the Alabama School Library Association, the Educational Media Association, and the Alabama Association of School Libraries, with the exception of EMA, existed entirely independently of each other, and solely because of race. The Educational Media Association, a bi-racial group, is to be commended for its lack of racial bias.

Within the first decade of the existence of the AASL, some effort was made to bring white and black librarians together. The exact dates of events elude me; however, the culminating event was the year of Gretchen Schenk's presidency of the Alabama Library Association. One who has had the pleasure of Ms. Schenk's acquaintance has no reason to doubt that she was completely unaware of the unreadiness of her Association to admit black members. She had appointed a bi-racial committee to iron out any difficulties that may have existed, and well in advance of the annual meeting of the Alabama Library Association, she called a meeting of the committee to which all concerned librarians, black and white, were invited. The purpose of the meeting was to outline procedures for acdeptance of black members into the heretofore all-white Association, this in anticipation of the newly recruited black members attending the forthcoming annual meeting. In attendance were the late Miss Ollie Brown, the late Mrs. Sadie Delaney (Librarian, Veterans Administration Hospital, Tuskegee Institute), Mrs. Sybil Baird (Librarian, Indian Springs School for Boys), Dr. W. S. Hoole (Librarian, University of Alabama), and many others, including myself.

The ease with which some members of the Alabama Library Association demeaned prospective black members was appalling. "Who," asked Dr. Hoole, "is stuffing these Negroes down our throats? I want you to know that I represent a conservative institution." "They would have to use the freight elevator," said someone else. "And they could not attend our dinner meeting," said still another. These comments left me with no doubt that I, or the school librarians for whom I was there to speak, had no desire to join an organization whose constituency had nothing to offer. Why were we black people subjecting ourselves to such insults? This was the question that overwhelmed me, a relative newcomer to Alabama. And why weren't we responding verbally to these people, I wondered. So incensed with their bigotry, insensitivity, and indeed their feelings that any black librarian stood to gain anything more than personal and professional degradation by joining such an organization, I was compelled to so inform them. I vividly recall the expeditious adjournment of that meeting.

The theme for the 1956 spring meeting of the AASL was "Meeting Our Crises through Education." It was a timely theme, and enthusiasm was evident among the membership. The organization voted to send its president, Ella McCain, as its official delegate to the 1956 Annual Convention of the American Library Association. As our constitution reveals, membership dues were minimal ($1.00 per year). Nevertheless, this organization of school librarians responded readily to the needs for professional growth, and sending a delegate to the ALA was considered a "must" in order to keep abreast of national professional activities.

Under the dynamic leadership of the late Miss Marie Peoples (Librarian, Prentice High School of Montevallo), the Association presented Mrs. Charlemae Rollins (Children's Librarian, Hall Branch of the Chicago Public Library) as the major contributor for the 1957 AASL Annual Meeting, speaking on the library as an idea source for children. During the business session, however, a discussion relative to the name of the Association was a top priority, as we had learned that the name of our organization had been taken by the organization of white school librarians of Alabama. At no time during the existence of the AASL were its members more appreciative of its 1948 constitution than at that 1957 Annual Spring Meeting. As a result of that conflict, the organization of white school librarians of Alabama became the Alabama School Library Association, after having to admit that they had failed to use the information resources with which they were entrusted.

In 1958, our Association conceived the idea of organizing student library assistants on a state-wide basis. Mrs. Emma Walton (Librarian, Carver High School of Dothan) was appointed state chairperson of this undertaking, and the state was divided into ten districts. Librarians were appointed as district chairpersons with the primary responsibility of working with librarians and their student assistants within the designated district. Then, in 1959, the annual meeting focused on the role of the student library assistant.

On Saturday, January 30, 1960, district chairpersons and their student representatives from seven districts met in the Conference Room of the Headquarters Building of the ASTA and organized the Student Library Assistants of Alabama (SLAA). Elected officers were: President, James Mixon (11th grade, Hudson High School of Selma), Vice President, Paulette Boykins (10th grade, D. A. Smith High School of Ozark), Secretary, Joan Owens (10th grade, Parker High School of Birmingham), and Treasurer, Howard Harris (11th grade, Druid High School of Tuscaloosa). During the years 1961-1964, then, the AASL concentrated its efforts on work with SLAA and the implementation of the 1960 national standards for school libraries.

The 1965 annual meeting of the Association had as its theme "Utilizing Professional Opportunities in Meeting the Changes in Education and Society." There was an awareness of pending changes in local organizations of school librarians, changes in library services (resulting from federal aid for library resources in elementary and secondary schools), changes in standards for school library programs, and changes in national (NEA) and local organizations (ASTA and AEA) that would affect the teaching-learning process of all schools and the library services within those schools.

Meetings of the Executive Committee and the annual spring meeting of 1966-67 centered on the implementation of the Elementary and Secondary Education Act of 1965 (ESEA). Significant points of interest were: lack of qualified librarians; the number of schools without library services; the average cost of library resources; the population explosion; human longevity; and the changing number of hours in a work day. It was also at this meeting that Mrs. Emma Walton presented a Resolution/Certificate making Dr. Carol Hayes an honorary member of the Alabama Association of School Librarians.

Of major concern during the 1968 annual meeting were the pending mergers of the Alabama State Teachers Association (parent association of the Alabama Association of School Librarians) with the Alabama Education Association and the three media associations. Recruitment of librarians from Alabama to attend a nine-month institute for the training of media specialists at Purdue University also created considerable discussion and much interest. It should be noted there that Carolyn L. Whitenack (Professor ahd Head, Media Sciences, Department of Education, Purdue University) made possible the organization's first and only Telelecture; her presentation on the implementation of *Standards for Media Programs* at a fall workshop held at Alabama State College and her contribution at a prior workshop held at A&M University are landmarks in the activities of the Association as well.

The 1968 and 1969 AASL meetings were concerned with the utilization of media in instruction, as well as the benefits which could accrue from the union of media specialists and librarians. Certainly the members were being kept up to date on developments in their field, even if all the resources discussed weren't yet available to them.

Mrs. Alpha A. Robertson (Assistant Librarian, Hayes High School of Birmingham) was president of the Association at the 1969 meeting, and she was also president of the AASL when its last meeting was held, March 12, 1970. The meeting convened at the A. G. Gaston Lounge in Birmingham, with the theme of "Au Revoir aux Choses commes Elles Etaient," (Farewell to Things as They Were). Our incoming president, Mrs. Geraldine W. Bell (Librarian, Hayes High School), challenged the group with remarks entitled "Focus on the Seventies," and it was my pleasure to give a progress report on the "Merger with the Alabama Education Association" and to say "adieu" to our association, which I had been privileged to serve for 22 years as Executive and Correspondence Secretary.

Dr. Carol Hayes was also listed on that program, both to speak briefly and to install the new officers. Well aware of going into a new organization (merging the Alabama Association of School Librarians, the Alabama School Library Association and the Alabama Educational Media Association), each Association sensed the importance of keeping its own group intact, so each was prepared with officers.

Unfortunately, illness prevented Dr. Hayes from attending this last meeting, and because of his support and encouragement over the years, he was indeed missed. The AASL thus came reluctantly to a pleasant end; pleasant because, in so doing, it was closing the first gap on racial segregation in our state professional organizations. Too, while Dr. Hayes was unable to join us, he sent a letter which admonished us that "as you integrate today ... be still and know that your training, experience, dedication and continuous study, qualify you to serve, with credit and distinction as a librarian for *anybody, anywhere*." Since then, school librarians and media specialists of Alabama have worked together in a new organization, the Alabama Instructional Media Association, with Geraldine Bell chosen as its first president.

5. **The Librarians' Section of the Georgia Teachers and Education Association**
   by   **Laura S. Lewis, Librarian, Union Street Library Branch, Lagrange Memorial Library**

The Librarians' Section of the Georgia Teacher and Education Association was established 25 years following the organization of its parent body, the Georgia State Teachers and Educational Association, in 1925. The parent group was the result of the merging of the "Old State Teachers Association," the Georgia

Business and Professional League, the Georgia Education Association North, the Georgia Education Association South and the Organization of Private Colleges and Schools.

A group of 13 librarians met with the State Library Consultant, Miss Clarice Jones, at the Lucy Laney School in Augusta on April 15, 1949, to share problems and seek solutions to them. The organizational meeting for the actual librarians' association took place a year later, on April 14, 1950, and the group had grown to 32 librarians when they met in Macon. The concern of the meeting was the organization of school librarians as a section of GTEA, and the parent body approved the organization, with Mrs. Theodosia Theus as chairman. As the parent association became better organized, with local and regional units, a definite line of communication was established for implementing the work of the Association. Thus, it was agreed that the librarians in the 11 GTEA regions would also organize into 11 regional organizations.

In 1951, as the group worked to formulate guidelines for the organization, they set forth the following purposes: the improvement and expansion of library service in schools as a means of strengthening the educational program; the promotion of professional growth and development of librarians; the cooperation with other educational organizations concerned with the welfare of children and youth. From its inception in 1950 until 1953, the management and direction of the Librarians' Section was guided by the State Library Consultant, Mrs. Clarice Jones Alston. As the organization of the Librarians' Section unfolded in 1953, the late Mr. William D. Beasley was elected as chairman and Leroy Childs as co-chairman. For its annual meeting in 1953, the librarians chose the theme "The Role of the Library in Dealing with Exceptional Children," and Mrs. Charlemae Rollins delivered the main address. In 1954, at the annual session at Atlanta University, Arna Bontemps shared his poetry in addition to delivering the main address. The meeting's theme was "A Functional School Library—A Foundation for Intellectual Growth and Democratic Participation." Under the leadership of William D. Beasley, then, the Librarians' Section began to emerge as a dynamic and guiding force in the development of library service in Negro education in Georgia.

In 1954, Miss Margaret L. Walker became State Library Consultant and gave untiring leadership to the organization until the time of the merger of Georgia's black and white education associations in 1969. During the formative years of the Librarians' Section of the GTEA, various groups, agencies, and individuals gave support, encouragement, inspiration and guidance, among them Mr. R. L. Cousins, Mr. T. A. Carmichael, and Dr. Virginia L. Jones, Dean of the Atlanta University School of Library Service, and her staff. The parent organization, the Georgia Teachers and Education Association, represented by Charles Lincoln Harper, Charles Butler, and Horace E. Tate, was also instrumental in providing the support so vital to the development of the Librarians' Section.

Work in the Section continued at each annual session thereafter, with topics such as new trends in scientific materials and the use and construction of bibliographies being covered. Consultants included Miss Augusta Baker (1956). Later, entertainment such as dance, jazz, and poetry was included in the conferences.

During the fifteenth anniversary session in 1966, under the chairmanship of Mrs. Nancy Beasley, black librarians pledged to work closely with all librarians in the State of Georgia and to continue to work for the growth of the Librarians'

Section. Too, a book called *Rising in the Sun: A History of the Georgia Teachers and Education Association* was published that year. Mrs. Laura Lewis as chairman in 1967 continued the work of the Association, using the theme "The Librarian; a Catalyst for Change in Learning." The librarians discussed the uses of instructional materials and their applications to the educational processes, and Dr. Virginia Jones, Dean of the School of Library Service, Atlanta University, served as consultant.

Membership in the organization was open to full-time school librarians, teacher-librarians, public and college librarians, and all other persons interested in the extension and improvement of library service. Many challenges and demands were made upon, and met by, the dynamic leadership of the organization during the almost two decades of service by the Librarians' Section. Two accomplishments stand out, however: the sponsorship of the statewide organization of Student Library Assistants of Georgia (SLAGS), and the annual Book Scholarship that was awarded to worthy SLAGS.

The contributions made by the Librarians' Section of Georgia Teachers and Education Association have been etched in the history of education in Georgia. Negro education in Georgia could not have progressed without the organization and the dedication of the members of the Librarians' Section. Then, with the merging of the black and white education associations in 1969, the organization became known as the Library Department of the Georgia Association of Educators.

OFFICERS OF THE ASSOCIATION

1951-1952	Mrs. Theodosia M. Theus, Chairman; Mrs. Corinne Long, Secretary-Treasurer
1953-1954	Mr. William D. Beasley, Chairman
1955-1956	Mr. Leroy C. Childs, Chairman
1957-1958	Mr. William H. Travis, Chairman
1959-1960	Mrs. Lenel L. Burnett, Chairman
1961-1962	Mrs. Rosebud Dixon, Chairman
1963-1964	Mrs. Doris P. Little, Chairman
1965-1966	Mrs. Nancy Beasley, Chairman
1967-1968	Mrs. Laura S. Lewis, Chairman
1969-1970	Miss Lillie Benjamin, Chairman

Mrs. Clarice J. Alston and Mr. E. J. Josey served as co-chairmen (to head the organization for the year following their election) for the years 1957-1958 and 1961-1962, respectively. Each moved out of the state prior to actually heading the organization.

WORKS CONSULTED

History Committee and Consultants of Georgia Teachers and Education Association. *Rising in the Sun: A History of the Georgia Teachers and Education Association.* Atlanta: GTEA, 1966.

Librarians' Section of Georgia Teachers and Education Association. *In Review.* Prep. by Margaret L. Walker. Atlanta: Librarians' Section, GTEA, 1962.

6. The North Carolina Negro Library Association

by   Albert P. Marshall, Dean of Academic Services, Eastern Michigan University

On April 20-31, 1934, 26 librarians gathered at Shaw University, Raleigh, North Carolina, to form what was to become the North Carolina Negro Library Association. This culminated a four-year dream of Mollie Huston Lee, librarian at Shaw University. Since moving to the state in 1930, this active, vivacious woman had felt, as she explained in the May 1944 *North Carolina Libraries*, that something needed to be done to "encourage and stimulate" black librarians working in school, college, and public libraries.

Several conditions obtained at that time that encouraged this action. First, there was an educational thrust among black people in North Carolina which probably surpassed any single statewide effort in the rest of the country. A dozen colleges existed in the Tar Heel State, each of which sought to provide the best possible undergraduate education for its students. The five state-supported institutions worked in harmony with seven privately controlled colleges and institutes to improve education for blacks in general. The Julius Rosenwald Fund, which supported Jeanes Teachers in all Southern states, provided the black youths of North Carolina with a stimulation to get as much education as possible (Anna T. Jeanes of Philadelphia funded the program for regional rural instruction that was named for her). The second condition resulted from a demand for trained librarians, a demand backed by foundation support for students wishing to attend Hampton Institute's Library School. Several were already working within the state, however, and a camaraderie developed, even without an organization, which created receptiveness for the idea. Third, the all-white North Carolina Library Association could not find it in its collective heart to invite or accept black membership, although the subject had been broached several times by some of its members, including Louis R. Wilson and Charles M. Adams. Fourth, since the start of the Hampton Institute Library School in 1925, several of its graduates had found positions in North Carolina, so that, by 1934, no less than 17 professional librarians, including graduates of Simmons, Columbia, and Michigan, were working in the state. (See the list at the end of this article.)

The fifth condition that helped to stimulate interest in an association was the presence of Mollie Huston Lee. A native of Columbus, Ohio, Mrs. Lee proceeded to become a "mover and a shaker," and she continued in this role most of her professional life. Rather than accept conditions as they were, she saw the many opportunities for practicing her profession and believed that if she could get librarians to work together for the promotion of libraries, then education in general would be enhanced.

There was a sixth condition which perhaps played as much part in the movement for a Negro Library Association as any. Two white librarians who worked for the state often went out of their way to provide guidance and encouragement to the struggling libraries that served black youth. Marjorie Beal was the Secretary and Director of the North Carolina Library Commission, and was often visiting librarians and school and college administrators, urging the provision and improvement of library materials and services for students. She was assisted in this effort by

Mary Peacock Douglas, a school library supervisor who worked out of the State Department of Education.

It was Mollie Huston Lee, though, who actually sent letters to all black librarians in the state early in 1934, inquiring about interest in such an organization. Responses varied, but almost unanimously they supported the idea. A few suggested that a national organization would be a better plan, and others felt that they should prod the existing state association to open its doors to them. However, a planning committee was formed, with Mrs. Lee as chairman, and including Pearl Snodgrass (St. Augustine's College, Raleigh), Jeannette Hicks (Washington High School Library, Durham), Marjorie Shepard (North Carolina College at Durham), and Marjorie Beal (North Carolina Library Commission).

The organizational meeting was held, then, in 1934, on the campus of Shaw University. In attendance were 11 college librarians, 13 school librarians, and two public librarians. Five of these people held library science bachelor's degrees, one held a library science master's degree, and 20 had little or no specialized training. The program included talks on various phases of library work by Dean Foster Payne (North Carolina College, Durham), Dean Robert B. House (University of North Carolina Library School), Miss Mary Peacock Douglas, and Mollie Huston Lee. Elected as the first officers were: Mollie Huston Lee, President; Mollie E. Dunlap, Vice-President; Josephine P. Sherrill, Secretary; and Pearl Snodgrass, Treasurer.

Throughout the existence of the Association, it played an important role in the improvement of library service to blacks within the Tar Heel State. It brought many professional leaders to the state as speakers, and before many years, most practicing black librarians, whether or not they held professional degrees, became members. An official journal was authorized in 1934, but this was a bit early for the fledgling organization. At the 1936 meeting, college, public, and school library divisions were established.

In 1939, Mary H. Hairston (Winston-Salem Teachers College Library) was given the assignment of compiling a library handbook. Completed in time for the 1940 meeting, this pamphlet provided statistical and other information about libraries serving blacks throughout the state.

In 1942, Albert P. Marshall, who had become librarian of the Winston-Salem Teachers College in 1941, sought financial help from the Association for publishing *A Guide to Negro Periodical Literature*. Although funds were scarce, the Association voted to provide limited financial support, but this publication was interrupted when Marshall entered the United States Coast Guard early in 1943.

A petition was presented to the American Library Association for chapter status and the North Carolina Negro Library Association became, on February 1, 1943, the first such group to be admitted, as recorded in the March 1943 *A.L.A. Bulletin*. Ordinarily only one professional affiliate was recognized in each state, but the ALA Council, acting for the Association while regular meetings were suspended for the duration of the war, decided to approve chapter status. Recognition meant representation, and Mollie Huston Lee became the first representative on the ALA Council for the chapter.

In the spring of 1944, the Association held two workshops, one for school librarians at North Carolina College, and one for public librarians at Shaw University. At the annual meeting, a request was sent to the State Department of Education for the appointment of a black person to work as School Library Supervisor, and this was eventually accomplished. Too, since the black association was hampered by a lack of funds to carry on its own publication program, the May 1944 issue of *North Carolina Libraries* (published quarterly by the North Carolina Library Association) was devoted to news of the "sister" organization.

The NCNLA encouraged the establishment of a library school at North Carolina College, which came into being in 1941, and it also played a role in the establishment of courses at other colleges which provided training for school librarians. At least three of the twelve North Carolina colleges offered such courses by 1947. Also in that same year the Association offered support for a *North Carolina Index*, a joint effort by the staff of Winston-Salem Teachers College.

Two librarians joined to promote the idea of an Association journal in 1947, resulting in the *Library Service Review*, with the first issue edited by Albert P. Marshall, Ben Smith (North Carolina College) serving as business manager. During the summer of 1948, both Smith and Marshall were granted leaves of absence to return to school, and a second, final issue, Volume I, Number 2, was published in November 1948.

Once the organization was begun, Joseph Ruzicka, Bookbinders, of Greensboro, provided printed programs for each conference. The November 1949 conference selected as its theme "Make Friends with Books." The President of Shaw University, Dr. Robert P. Daniel, provided the keynote address, entitled "The Illiteracy of the Literate." Other speakers included Thelma Nelson of Shaw, on "Student Library Assistants"; Joseph Reason of Howard University, on "Teacher-Librarian Cooperation"; Dr. S. E. Duncan, Supervisor of Negro High Schools, on "Administrative and Organizational Provisions for North Carolina Public School Libraries"; Hattie Coley, Bookmobile Librarian in Charlotte, on "Staff Public Relations"; and Louis S. Shores, Director of the School of Library Service, Florida State University, on "Trends in Reference Sources." The conference dinner meeting featured Dr. Hugh M. Gloster, Director of the Communications Center, Hampton Institute, who spoke on "Books and Our Struggle for Democracy."

At the 1946 meeting, Penny Perry of North Carolina College was named the Executive Secretary of the Association. She was followed by Ann M. Johnson, and then by Mrs. Ray N. Moore.

Constance Marteena, Librarian of Agricultural and Technical College, Greensboro, became President in 1953, with Elwyza Daniels as Treasurer, and Mrs. Moore as Executive Secretary. It was this group, along with other members of the Executive Board, that paved the way for the merger with the North Carolina Library Association. This action finally took place on November 4, 1955, when the black association was dissolved following a formal invitation to merge. Amid much nostalgia, the era of the North Carolina Negro Library Association came to an end.

PROFESSIONAL LIBRARIANS WORKING IN NORTH CAROLINA, 1934

Librarian	Institution or School	Library School
Marjorie Arlington	Palmer Memorial Institute	Simmons
Clarice H. Bizelle	Waters Training School	Hampton
John E. Bowen	New Bern CC Camp	Hampton
Lillie Daly	Palmer Memorial Institute	Hampton
Florence B. Davis	A&T College, Greensboro	Hampton

Librarian	Institution or School	Library School
Robbie L. Goodloe	Barber-Scotia College	Hampton
Fannie K. Gordon	Dudley High School, Greensboro	Hampton
Mollie Dunlap	Winston-Salem Teachers College	Michigan
Estella G. Grayson	St. Augustine's College	Hampton
Theodus L. Guss	Johnson C. Smith University	Hampton
Julia E. James	Rockingham Colored High School	Hampton
Mollie Huston Lee	Shaw University	Columbia
Charlotte Lytle	Charlotte Second Ward High School	Hampton
Josephine P. Sherrill	Livingstone College	Hampton
Rose D. Sully	Shaw University	Hampton
Parepa Watson	North Carolina College	Hampton
Selena W. Wheeler	Durham Dunbar Colored Library	Hampton

7. The South Carolina State Library Group

by **Rossie B. Caldwell, Associate Professor, Library Science Department, South Carolina State College**

The history of the organization of black librarians in the State of South Carolina is aligned with the history of the black state education association, whose official name was the Palmetto State Teachers' Association (PSTA). Later, the official name became "Palmetto Education Association" (PEA). One need only follow reports in journals, bulletins, and minutes of the association, which the executive secretary of the association was quite diligent in his efforts to preserve, in order to perceive historical trends. In 1967, when the Palmetto Education Association merged with the white state association known as the South Carolina Education Association, the black executive secretary became Associate Secretary and Special Service Director of the South Carolina Education Association. These journals, bulletins, and minutes accompanied Dr. Walker E. Solomon, who occupies this position and who has stored them in the SCEA Building.

"Black State Library Association" as it existed in South Carolina means "Black State Library Group" or "Department" as it existed and operated within the black state education association. The definition is necessary because the only state library association in South Carolina during the period 1936-67 was a segregated white association not visible in any black area. Too, in the beginning days of the group's activities, the term "librarian" included a few librarians who had received bachelor's degrees in library science from Hampton Institute and many teacher-librarians who were beginning to enroll or had already enrolled in library science courses at various colleges. In later years, the term "librarian" included many persons who had become certified according to state requirements and/or had received degrees from various library schools throughout the country. The term also includes school, public, and college librarians.

The first official record of black librarians organizing into a state group is a listing on the 1937 rolls of the journal of the Palmetto State Teachers' Association.[1] Three persons are listed as Librarians of Charleston: Sadie Burroughs, Susan D. Butler, and Mae H. Purcell. The actual organization of black librarians in South Carolina can be traced to an informal meeting of interested persons during March 1937. The minutes[2] indicate that interested persons met at the Waverly Branch of the Richland County Library on March 26, 1937, as a result of a questionnaire which had been distributed by Miss Agnes Crawford, a white assistant librarian in the Richland County Library.[3] The questionnaire sought to survey Negro librarians and teacher-librarians of the state and to encourage them to organize.

Following the above action, Mrs. Julia W. Talley, Librarian of Waverly Branch Library, called the groups together informally. Mrs. Susan Bart Butler, Librarian of Dart Hall Branch Library of Charleston, South Carolina, served as temporary chairman of the group, called in the minutes "The South Carolina State Library Group." Mrs. Charliese P. Sheffield, Assistant Librarian of South Carolina State College Library, served as temporary secretary. The stated purpose of the meeting was to organize a state library group, and the following actions were taken by the group: 1) they voted to appoint a State Library Committee which would apply to the Palmetto State Teachers' Association to become a functioning part of that organization, 2) they elected Mrs. Geraldine P. Zimmerman, a teacher-librarian from York County, as chairman and Susan D. Butler and Charliese P. Sheffield as secretaries, and 3) they scheduled their next meeting to be held during the Palmetto State Teachers' Association in March 1938.

The Waverly Public Library Branch was again the location for the meeting of the now state-association connected librarians' group in March 1938.[4] It was at this meeting that the pattern for the official structure of the group was set. New officers included representatives from the different types of libraries, and the chairmanship moved from a teacher-librarian, Mrs. G. P. Zimmerman, to a college librarian, Mrs. Charliese P. Sheffield. Mrs. Marian Miller, a school librarian, became secretary, and Mrs. S. D. Butler, a public librarian, was elected as vice-chairman. The "Library Group" met again at the Waverly Branch Library in March 1939, and it was decided that a fall meeting would be held at South Carolina State College (Orangeburg) in the new college library in November 1939. A Constitution Committee was appointed.

At its first fall meeting,[5] important actions were taken as follows: 1) a Basic Constitution for the "Palmetto State Library Association" was adopted, 2) for the first time, mention was made of the white state library association,[6]

---

[1] Palmetto State Teachers' Association, (Attendance Rolls) *The Teachers' Bulletin* XVII, No. 1 (March 1937).

[2] *Minutes*, First Meeting of the South Carolina State Library Group, March 26, 1937.

[3] Agnes Crawford, *Survey of Negro Librarians*, 1937. In a telephone interview, Nov. 15, 1976, Miss Crawford, now in retirement at Mt. Pleasant, S.C., stated that the survey was her independent project. She was found by tracing through Richland County Library and the State Library.

[4] *Minutes*, March 18, 1938.

[5] *Minutes*, November 24, 1938.

[6] *South Carolina Association Handbook*, 1969. (Date traced to source through conversation with Barbara Williams, Head, South Carolina State College Library, and Thomas Jones, Librarian at South Carolina Library.)

founded October 27, 1915, which was to meet in Greenville, South Carolina—members of the group expressed a willingness to attend if they were invited, but it would be 1962 before the invitation came;[7] 3) dues of $1.00 per year were levied.

The financial structure of the organization was not stabilized until a committee, led by Mrs. Muriel Potts, requested an allocation from dues of $5.00, which were regularly paid to the PEA.[8] In 1954, the group received an allocation of $150.00, and regularly thereafter this type of allocation was made.

The constituency of the first three meetings was representative of types of institutions from which members were to come throughout most of the existence of the Library Group, and these included colleges, junior colleges, academies, institutes, training schools, high schools, and branch libraries which were the segregated off-shoots of the white county library. When the term "school" was used to represent a librarian, "high school" was usually the meaning.

The minutes indicate that 28 persons were present for the first association-connected meeting; 26 persons were present for the second; 38 persons were recorded for the third. Some persons were with the "Library Group" until the black association merged with the white or until the white public library brought its branch librarians into the mainstream.

The names listed below are on the rolls of this constituency:

1938   Ethel Bailey, Sallie Bailey, Rosa Bush, S. D. Butler, A. M. Cloud, Evelyn Cuthbert, Elease Dawkins, D. M. Ellison, Lauretta Hammond, Hattie Harris, Ellen James, Marian Miller, Margaret Pendergrass, Betsy Perry, Birdie Peterson, Jessye Smith, F. M. Taggart, Julia Talley, R. G. Torrence, Etta Washington, Jane Watts, Katherine Wheeler, Wilma Wigham, G. P. Zimmerman, Bobbie Clark, Lucius Laster. (Charliese P. Sheffield was recorded as elected Chairman, but her signature did not appear; note presence of one man, Lucius Laster.)

1939   Ethel Bailey, Sallie Bailey, Louise Bogan, Rossie Brower, Susie Butler, Emily Copeland, Evelyn Cuthbert, Bertha Dorch, Claudia Dorrah, Dollie Ellison, Geneva Green, A. L. Lawrence, M. W. Miller, A. Nix, Nettie Petty, Josephine Sherard, Mattie Sherard, C. P. Sheffield, Julia Talley, R. G. Torrence, Etta Washington, Jane Watts, Minnie Webber, Katherine Wheeler, Lottie Williams, Wilma Wigam, Louise Worthy.

1940   E. M. Wade, Sallie Bailey, Geneva Green, Etta Washington, Bernice Latimer, S. D. Butler, Mamye Kendricks, Dollie Ellison, M. Richardson German, Jane Watts, Julia Talley, Katherine Wheller, Jayne Shelton, Marian Miller, Edgar Burke,* A. M. Winningham, Evelyn King, Margaret Pendergrass, H. K. Harris, A. L. Lawrence, Josephine Sherard, M. L. Pellman, Elizabeth Rogers, C. V. Garlington, A. R. Nix, C. P. Sheffield, Madge Perry, Eunice Fennell, Rossie Brower, C. H. Cloud, A. G. Hilderbrand, E. R. Cuthbert, Ethel Bailey, Sadie Johnson, Gracia Waterman, Brownlee Wade, J. H. McKissick, Helen Nance, S. D. Butler, A. L. Lawrence, and Marie Holland. (*Note one man present.)

---

[7] Program, Forty-first Annual Meeting, South Carolina Association, October 26-27, 1962.
[8] *Minutes*, March 27, 1953, and April 2, 1954.

The names for subsequent years were too numerous to include in an essay attempting to provide an historical perspective.

From the above constituency came a synthesis of goals, purposes, and programs which set a format that would be followed for the most part throughout the existence of the "Library Group." Program topics centered on goals or themes that reflected the concerns of the times, and the format emphasized single papers or papers in symposia. Open forums with time for questions and answers followed the papers.

The first program theme was "An Appreciation of the Possibilities of the Library and a Desire to Study and Know More of Books and Libraries." The first topics were "Teaching the Use of Books and Libraries" and "What Are Some Activities Included in Your Library Program?" The Palmetto State Teachers' Association *Bulletin and News* provided information concerning subsequent themes.

Other program thrusts were provided by the activation in 1946 of the position of state school library supervisor in the person of Miss Nancy Jane Day; by interest in a state student assistant program, reported in the meeting by Agnes Hildebrand Wilson;[9] and by interest in the provision of a profile of librarians, as exemplified in the production of a directory of Negro Librarians by the Public Relations Committee.[10] In this directory and its supplements may be found notes on many of the members of the Librarians' Group. A recent study by a former member of the group provides further information.[11]

Too, nationally known persons, state personnel, and persons from other states were presented at various meetings, and State Education Department personnel, principals, teachers, and students were provided with a forum in which to express their views to librarians. The list includes the following: Nancy Day and Margaret Ehrhardt (State School Library Supervisors); Marguerite Lovell (North Carolina State College, Durham); Virginia L. Jones (Atlanta University); Mollie H. Lee (North Carolina Library Association); Estellene Walker (South Carolina State Library Service); Joyce McClendon (North Carolina Librarian); Margaret Walker (Georgia State Department of Education); Sara Bond Davis (Georgia Librarian); Cora P. Bomar (North Carolina School Library Supervisor); Augusta Baker (New York Public Librarian and Columbia University Instructor); and Peggy Sullivan (Knapp School Library Project Director).

The Department of Library Service at South Carolina State College has been cited in the minutes as an encouraging force in several endeavors of the Librarians' Group,[12] and the promotion of workshops has been noted. In addition to this, the cause of recruitment was served when the student librarians' group was coordinated and provided with an annual meeting place on the college campus.

---

[9] *Minutes*, April 7, 1950. Also noted in telephone interview with Dr. Agnes H. Wilson, former teacher-librarian, November 13, 1976.

[10] Palmetto Education Association Department of School and College Librarians. Public Relations Committee, *Profile of Librarians*, ed. by Rossie B. Caldwell (Orangeburg: South Carolina State College, 1964). 1st Supplement, 1965; 2nd Supplement, 1966; 3rd Supplement, 1967.

[11] Lillie S. Walker, "Black Librarians in South Carolina," paper written for the Colloquium of the North Carolina Central University Library School, Durham, North Carolina, October 8, 1976.

[12] Nancy Burge, "Expression of Appreciation," in *Minutes*, April 2, 1954. (Miss Burge acting in place of Nancy Day, State School Library Association.)

Notable in extending support to these causes were departmental chairpersons Emily Copeland, Kathleen Moses, and Bernice B. Middleton.

The high quality of leadership and "follow-ship" of the Library Groups affiliated with the black state association is not debatable. The evidence is clear from the types of programs documented, from the survival techniques utilized, and from the continuity of professionalism exhibited. Limitations of space prevent the listing of many names and contributions which would further serve to document these assertions, and many names are recurrent on existing rolls.

The chairmanship of the organization was held by persons who remained active professionally over a long number of years. In addition to persons already named in this report, there were the following: Mrs. Athelma Nix, Mrs. Agnes Wilson, Miss Etta Washington, Miss Evelyn Cuthbert, Miss Emily Copeland, Mrs. Katherine Wheeler, Mrs. Claudine Ross, Mrs. Bernice B. Middleton, Mrs. Ollie Sherrard, Mrs. Mabel McKissick, Mrs. Ethel Bolden, Mrs. Harriet Jenkins, and Miss Mary Griffin. Numerous other people served in many capacities, of course.

Consistently present as officials from the public library field were Mrs. Julia Talley, Mrs. Susan Butler, Miss Etta Washington, Mrs. Katherine Wheeler, Miss Margaret Pendergrass, and Mrs. Annie Cloud.

Throughout its existence, the organization was predominantly female. However, it could be predicted from the constituency of the student librarians' groups as they entered the program arena that male librarians would be active in the future.

The organization—variously known as the "South Carolina State Library Group," "Library Science Group," "Palmetto Library Association"—had grown from its opening meeting strength in 1938 of 28 persons present to its closing strength in 1967 of 109 persons. It closed under the name of "Department of School and College Librarians."

Public librarians had generally withdrawn from attendance, since the South Carolina Library Association had opened its doors as noted. A feeling had also developed that the PEA-connected Library Groups should consist of school and college librarians. The Waverly Branch was gone, and its librarians were in desegregated branches. The place of meetings had been changed to the college library of either Benedict College or Allen University, but the final meeting was held at W. A. Perry Junior High School of the Columbia City School System.

The work of the segregated groups of librarians cannot be overrated, for they exhibited true professionalism in an organization founded and maintained with integrity. Thus, with hardly a break in their strides, these truly professional people moved with the tide of integration—many into the recognized South Carolina Library Association and/or continuing their professional activities with the integrated educational association of librarians.

8. The Division of Librarians of the Virginia State Teachers Association

by   Harriet M. Hill, Retired Librarian, Hampton, Virginia

Tommie Dora Barker, ALA Regional Field Agent for the South, 1930-1935, in her study on *Libraries of the South*, tells us of some of the problems that faced the Negro. In a section of the study entitled "Library Service to Negroes—School Libraries," she said that "the greatest stimulant to the provisions of libraries in Negro secondary and elementary schools has been the aid from the Julius Rosenwald Fund . . . for the purchase of unit collections of books." Commenting on the value of these collections, President Embree of the Julius Rosenwald Fund said, "The value of even a small collection of books to a rural school is almost beyond exaggeration. In many cases it represents the only supplementary reading in the school or the community. By furnishing well selected books of simple and interesting content, the educational influence of the school is multiplied and habits of reading are set up which may influence the school and the community to continue to develop their library facilities."[1]

These collections were used not only in the rural schools but in all the city schools. Where State Boards of Education had state supervisors of libraries, these books were distributed under their supervision and/or that of Jeanes Teachers (workers in a program to improve rural Southern instruction that was named for Anna T. Jeanes of Philadelphia, who funded it). Problems developed for the Virginia State Department of School Libraries and Textbooks, however, because of the lack of professional help available to supervise the use of these collections. Some schools also raised money to purchase needed materials; the state assisted with small sums to supplement what was raised. Aside from supplementing the Rosenwald books, a *New Tentative Course of Study for Virginia Secondary Schools* was being initiated throughout the state. This new course of study called for many more books, magazines, newspapers, audiovisual aids, etc.

C. W. Dickinson, supervisor, State Department of Libraries and Textbooks, with able assistants and the members of a special committee, compiled for the State Board of Education *Standards for High School Libraries*. To implement these standards, some courses in library science for teacher-librarians and librarians had to be introduced in three white colleges. Hampton Institute had opened a library school for Negro librarians in 1926, with the majority of students sent by their colleges, or else attending as recipients of grants from the Carnegie Corporation or scholarships from other sources. Graduates then returned to their former jobs or received better paying jobs than those offered in Virginia. However, activities followed, during the years 1934-1967, to improve the library situation within the state.

In 1933, Mrs. Alpha S. Rogers, librarian, Virginia State College, aware of the great need to help those untrained persons who were in charge of most of the book collections, organized a group which later became known as the Division of

---

[1] Tommie Dora Barker, *Libraries of the South: A Report on Developments, 1930-35* (Chicago: American Library Association, 1936), p. 55.

Librarians of the Virginia State Teachers Association. The following year, 1934, according to the editorial in the November 1934 issue of the Virginia State Teachers Association *Bulletin*, "The Conference of Librarians and Teacher-Librarians met for the first time at this Convention"[2] (47th Annual Convention).

Prior to this meeting, the Constitution of the Virginia State Teachers Association had been amended by an appointed committee to add Article XII—Departments; a seventh Department (Librarians) was added to the six of the previous year. The Convention was held at Virginia State College, November 28-30, 1934.

Miss T. Vivian Tucker, a Norfolk high school librarian, presented a paper at the 1935 Convention on "The School Library—A Field of Service." She said, in part, "This conference [in 1934] revealed the glaring need for trained librarians, not teacher-librarians, for trained workers can give their time and energies wholly to the course and not necessarily be buried with duties of the classroom.... It is necessary for scholastic and social purposes. It is the heart of the school...."[3]

Mr. Wallace Van Jackson, Librarian, Virginia Union University, in an address delivered at the Division of Librarians' Forty-Eighth Annual Convention, selected as his subject: "The Library: As an Essential Part of an Educational System." He stressed the importance of obtaining professional library training, getting a certificate or diploma for approved courses taken at the State Teachers College or Hampton Institute Library School. By being professionally qualified, he underscored, "We can make a beginning in our effort to equip our schools with libraries and to provide them with trained librarians so that we may successfully work under the new curriculum."[4]

The development of the Division of Librarians of the Virginia State Teachers Association can best be seen in the kinds of programs that the leadership of the Division fostered during some of the earlier years. A review of the *Virginia Teachers Bulletin* reveals that over the years not only school librarians but also college librarians, public librarians, and other educators attended the meetings. In all probability, the college and public librarians took an interest in the organization because, at the time, they were denied membership in the Virginia Library Association.

At the 49th Annual Conference of the Association, the Library Division held its Third Annual Meeting on Friday, November 27, 1936. More than 50 librarians, teacher-librarians, principals, supervisors, and teachers attended the session. Charles W. Dickinson, Jr., Director of School Libraries and Textbooks of the Virginia Department of Education addressed the group on the topic, "What Is Expected of a Good School Library."[5] The discussion period was dominated by the participants' concern with school library standards, book lists, and assistance to school libraries. In addition, Robert Sampson (of Virginia Union University, where the conference was held) conducted a demonstration of book repairing.

---

[2] "Editorial," *Virginia Teachers Bulletin* 11, No. 4 (March 1935): 2.

[3] Vivian T. Tucker, "The School Library—A Field of Service," *Virginia Teachers Bulletin* 12, No. 2 (March 1935): 11-12.

[4] Wallace Van Jackson, "The Library: As an Essential Part of an Educational System," *Virginia Teachers Bulletin* 13, No. 2 (March 1936): 4-5.

[5] Wallace Van Jackson, "Report of the Activities of the Library Division," *Virginia Teachers Bulletin* 14, No. 1 (February 1937): 40.

In 1937, at the Fourth Annual Meeting, 71 school officials, teachers, and librarians attended the Library Division meeting. Papers were read at this meeting by Laurette Gumbs ("What the School Principal Expects of the School Library and Librarian"), Mrs. Helen Cephas Reid, a Supervisor of the Chesterfield County Schools ("The School Supervisor's Suggestion for the Increased Use of Books"), Gwendolyn Jordan ("How to Make Work in the Elementary and High School Libraries Effective"), Carolyn L. Jones, of the Hampton Institute Library ("The Part the College Library Plays in Meeting the Demands of Our Schools"), and Florence R. Curtis, Director of the Hampton Institute Library School ("What the Library School Is Doing to Meet the Demands of Our Schools").

The following year the Library Division met in two plenary sessions. At that time Laurette Gumbs, Librarian of Addison High School, addressed the group at the first session on "Book Selection for School Librarians." James A. Hulbert, Librarian, Virginia State College, keynoted the second session, speaking on "The Library Science Curriculum for School Librarians at Virginia State College."

In 1940, the librarians centered their meeting on the theme "The Public Library," with the afternoon session divided into two parts: "Propaganda in the Public Library," and "Art in Schools, Colleges, and Public Libraries." Thomas Parker Ayer of the Richmond Public Library addressed the group on the "Handling of Propaganda in the Public Library," admonishing the librarians to acquire materials on both sides of the question and "not to clutter the library with propaganda material...."[6]

Although the librarian members of the Virginia State Teachers Association were isolated in a segregated, racist world, nevertheless, like their counterparts in other professions, they worked very closely and strengthened each other by developing programs that would not only educate newcomers to the profession, but also provide in-service education and training for those in the field. The "hands on" demonstration of book repairing has a parallel today, when the librarians of the seventies attend institutes and conferences and have "hands on" experiences in the utilization of the new technology applications for libraries. A recent conference in New York had a speaker who considered what the principal expects of the school library; this topic is as fresh in the 1970s in an integrated environment as it was to the early librarians in Virginia struggling in a segregated environment. While the librarians were interested in providing access to information, real interest existed in intellectual freedom as regards the provision of information on both sides of a question. While the program content was educational and meaningful to all the participants, exhibitions held during the meetings provided knowledge about new equipment and the latest techniques that proved invaluable to many of the librarians who were unable to attend national library or educational conferences.

The Library Division, through its programming, provided incentive for the members to engage in continuing education, and more importantly, it inculcated in principals and supervisors the importance of the library in the educational process, and at the same time, the Library Division inculcated the value of library service and the opportunity of providing genuine educational service to the school children as well as to the teachers.

---

[6]"Report of the Library Division of the Virginia Teachers Association," *Virginia Teachers Bulletin* 18 (January 1941): 34-35.

On January 1, 1967, the black Virginia Teachers Association, with more than 8,500 members, merged with the predominantly white group, the Virginia Education Association. The combined library group has thus increased in strength through the years. With the large group, it is rather difficult to find a place to meet, but because of districts there are also regional meetings. The Afro-Americans remain very active in the combined group, but white librarians dominate the leadership. Nevertheless, there seems to be a better spirit and a willingness to work together in the small and local district groups, and Afro-American librarians continue to play a vital role in the school library media centers in Virginia.

CONTEMPORARY BLACK LIBRARIANSHIP

9. Black Caucus of the American Library Association
by   E. J. Josey

INTRODUCTION

Those black professionals in every discipline who were members of national professional organizations realized at the close of the 1960s that white racism was embedded in their professional organizations. They further saw that, if black people were to have an impact on their professions and their professional development, it was necessary for them to band together, in a black caucus or an all-black organization, in order to ensure their contributions to the liberation of black people in general, and the liberation of themselves as professionals, in particular. As a matter of survival, black and other minority groups saw themselves forced to seek involvement and control of a greater part of their professional lives. In three instances, blacks severed ties completely with their former national professional organizations. The black political scientists organized themselves into the National Conference of Black Political Scientists, and the organization publishes an excellent bi-monthly newsletter. The black social workers established the National Association of Black Social Workers. The National Conference of Black Lawyers is another example of an excellent organization established to fight racism, in this case in the American Bar Association. A panel of 12 black law professors from this group defended Angela Davis.

Another approach to combatting racism was taken in Congress. The blatant insensitivity of the Nixon Administration created the need for the blacks in Congress to organize into a black caucus, and they boycotted President Nixon's State of the Union Message in January 1973, since Nixon had ignored their request to meet with him on the concerns of black people. In a letter to President Nixon, they declared, "We are the elected and legitimate representatives of the 25 million Negroes in the United States and in view of the fact that the opinions of black Americans have not been heard or considered by you, as they relate to the State of the Union for blacks, we only conclude that your views on the state of black affairs cannot possibly be accurate, relative or germane." These representatives had been trying to meet with Nixon for over a year, and he denied them an audience, but because of their boycott of the State of the Union Message and their solid unity, he finally met with them.

Because of white racism, there is a movement to establish a national federation of black caucuses. What is a caucus? It is a closed meeting of a group of persons belonging to the same political party or faction—usually for the purpose of deciding on policy. In terms of black caucuses in professional organizations caucus members constitute a highly visible faction of the membership, who happen to be black, and who, in spite of all of their accomplishments, are demeaned or ignored by many white professionals. In librarianship in general, and in the American Library Association in particular, blacks have not severed ties with their national professional organization. They organized themselves into a Caucus.

BLACK CAUCUS: GENESIS OF AN IDEA

Although the first conference of librarians convened in the United States in 1853, it was not until 1876, 23 years later, that the American Library Association was founded. In the American Library Association, the seeds for the establishment of the Black Caucus were sown during the 1930s and 1940s, when a few blacks began to attend the meetings of the American Library Association and met over lunch or dinner to share common concerns. During the 1950s, when I began to attend the annual ALA conference, the small number of blacks in attendance used to assemble in the hotel suites of colleagues. When the School of Library Service of Atlanta University began to sponsor alumni dinners, most black librarians, whether or not we were graduates of the school, would attend for the encouragement and knowledge we knew we could gain.

In 1968, Effie Lee Morris suggested that we meet to discuss mutual concerns. We met and shared our frustrations, but we did not organize around an issue or form an organization. In 1969, I was appointed to the 1969-70 ALA Nominating Committee, and, although anxious for a black presidential nominee, I knew that I could not accomplish the feat alone. In the fall of 1969, I sent letters to all black librarians who I knew would be in attendance at the January 1970 Midwinter meeting, and in addition, requested all of those who planned to attend the meeting to notify other blacks who did not receive a letter announcing the meeting. A large number of people responded. Many had not planned to attend Midwinter, for they were not active on ALA committees or boards, but they came, for there was a cause and an issue that they deemed important.

At the meeting I told them of my membership on the ALA Nominating Committee and asked their support in finding excellent black candidates and socially responsible white candidates to run for Council in the 1971 election. In addition, I indicated that it was time for a black ALA president. After serious deliberation, the group decided to back one candidate, Albert P. Marshall, for the presidency and agreed that they would submit names of potential Council candidates. It was then decided that we should have a formal organization.

I was elected chairman of the Black Caucus and appointed several committees, including a Planning Action Committee under the chairmanship of Thomas Alford. Binnie Tate indicated that the Black Caucus should express concern over the number of private schools established in the country to defeat integration of schools. I later summarized these concerns in *The Black Librarian in America* (pp. 318-19):

Black librarians are greatly concerned about the large number of private schools that are emerging in the country to thwart racial integration. Most of these institutions cannot afford libraries and are calling upon neighboring libraries to lend support. Black librarians at the ALA Midwinter meeting were determined to put ALA on record deploring this kind of action and in support of the Supreme Court's ruling on school desegregation.

For too long, blacks in ALA had been responding to the dictates of others. Our activism in the Social Responsibilities Round Table was a response to socially committed people, and several blacks circulated petitions to get SRRT started. We tried to work within the general framework of ALA but soon found out that the liberal whites' priorities were not our priorities. Blacks should never think that they can control and direct organizations when whites provide the lion's share of operational overhead for such organizations. Whoever provides financing will inevitably decide policy.

Too, a response to others can not be called self-determination. Thus, at our Midwinter meeting in Chicago, in 1970, we decided that ALA would not adequately respond to the needs of black professionals and that the Black Caucus would give professional black librarians a chance to take control of their professional destinies. Until this meeting, we had never confronted ALA as a group, but we decided that two things had to be accomplished: 1) a Statement of Concern from the Caucus had to be read as a matter of record, and 2) a resolution to Council had to be submitted to censure and bring sanctions against libraries and librarians that provide service to segregated schools established to circumvent the Supreme Court decision. The Council's agenda was closed, and to get these two items on the agenda, I made an appeal to President William Dix, who asked the Council to admit these items to the agenda. Effie Lee Morris then presented the resolution to the Council, and after a heated debate and much soul searching, the resolution passed and became an ALA policy statement. The resolution passed with only three negative votes, and it is my opinion that it passed because Hugh Atkinson, Ohio State University, requested a roll call vote, the first time historically that the Council had used the roll call vote. The resolution states:

> Racist institutions — opposition to support of
> WHEREAS, The United States Supreme Court of this land has called for the desegregation of public schools by February 1, 1970; and
> WHEREAS, Public, academic and school libraries in areas where desegregation has been ordered are in some cases lending and in other cases planning to lend materials to racist institutions conceived for the purpose of circumventing the law of the land; and
> WHEREAS, Such school administrators and many civic leaders in such areas have in fact asked for active support from libraries because funding for their schools and institutions is inadequate to provide libraries and textbooks; and
> WHEREAS, The American Library Association is cognizant of the social responsibilities of libraries serving the people of the United States and is on record as being opposed to racism in any and all of its forms;

THEREFORE, BE IT RESOLVED, That the libraries or librarians who do in fact through either services or materials support any such racist institution be censured by the American Library Association, and that the ALA staff give the widest possible publicity to this action.

The Caucus's statement is also short, and it gives an indication of our philosophical and professional viewpoint:

Black Librarians: A Statement of Concern,
ALA Midwinter Conference, 1970

On Wednesday night, January 21, 1970, 98 percent of the black librarians in attendance at the Midwinter Meeting of the American Library Association convened in a black caucus for the expressed purpose of addressing themselves to many of the pressing problems and issues facing this country, in general, and the American Library Association, in particular. Black librarians are especially concerned about the effects of institutional racism, poverty, the continued lack of educational, employment and promotional opportunities for blacks and other minorities. Although these socio-economic ills have been condemned by the Kerner Commission, the Commission on Violence, and many other studies, the library profession has been slow in responding to these problems.

As black librarians we are intensely interested in the development of our professional association and our profession; therefore, a committee of the Black Librarians' Caucus has been charged with the responsibility of preparing a program of action. The Black Caucus will continue to meet at American Library Association conferences for the purpose of evaluating progress being made by the Association in fulfilling its social and professional responsibilities to minority groups in this profession and in the nation.

ACCOMPLISHMENTS OF BLACK CAUCUS AT 1971 ALA MIDWINTER MEETING

1. The Black Caucus endorsed a "Program of Action" from Tom Alford's Planning and Action Committee.

2. Council endorsed the SRRT Task Force on Recruitment of Minorities Resolution, "Action Now to Achieve Racial and Sexual Parity in Library Staffing." The motion was moved by E. J. Josey, seconded by Arthur Curley, and passed unanimously, Wednesday, January 20, 1971.

3. A resolution to ensure black representation on library governing boards was offered by Mrs. Lola Johnson Singletary, Trustee, Washington, D.C., Public Library to the membership meeting. It was endorsed by the ALA Executive Board and approved by Council unanimously on Friday, January 22.

4. A resolution that would ensure that libraries play a more active and positive role in the application of fair employment practice laws was authored by Mrs. Clara Jones, Detroit Public Library. This resolution was historic legislation, for it asked libraries to seek fair employment practices from their suppliers of goods and services. William DeJohn introduced the motion, Arthur Curley seconded it; it passed unanimously.

5. David K. Berninghausen, Chairman of the Intellectual Freedom Committee, announced at the Friday, January 22, Session of Council that the IFC would investigate the five cases presented in the Report prepared by the Black Caucus. The Report stated that evidence indicated that five private segregated schools established to circumvent the U.S. Supreme Court decision were being provided library service by libraries and librarians. This concession was not granted until a special meeting held with Mr. Berninghausen and Mrs. Binnie Tate on Friday morning before the Council meeting, which will be described below.

BLACK CAUCUS REPORT ON LIBRARY SERVICE TO SEGREGATED SCHOOLS ESTABLISHED TO CIRCUMVENT THE U.S. SUPREME COURT DECISION

In Los Angeles, at the 1971 Midwinter meeting, I made a report, based upon an NAACP report, to the caucus which indicated that five segregated schools recently established to circumvent the Supreme Court decision were receiving library service and books. This report also pointed out indifference to black citizens, e.g., inadequate and/or no bookmobile stops in black communities, inadequate materials on black people in public and school libraries, fear of blacks to use library facilities in one Mississippi county, and very few blacks serving on public library boards of trustees, etc.

At the second session of Council on January 20, David Berninghausen made a report for the Intellectual Freedom Committee, and he indicated that at the Committee's meeting on December 1 and 2, Milton Byam (then Chairman of the Sub-Committee) indicated that he had no report to make. This was true, for I did not write the report until I had received the questionnaires from June Shagaloff, Director of Educational Programs, who queried NAACP branches with a questionnaire that she had asked me to prepare. Mr. Berninghausen then said that the Black Caucus had not provided information on this matter.

I attempted to set the record straight by indicating that a report had been mailed some time in the middle of December and that it could have been lost in the mail. At this point, Mr. Berninghausen conceded that a report had been sent to ALA Headquarters the previous week, but he had not had a chance to read it. Actually, I had prepared the report in December, but it had not been mailed until January 7.

On Thursday afternoon, I received a letter from Mr. Berninghausen asking that I see him before Friday's Council meeting and explain why I indicated that the report had been sent, when in my letter to Mr. Byam I had said that the report should be considered confidential until the following Midwinter Conference. Furthermore, he wanted me to make a retraction regarding the date the report was sent.

My immediate reaction was one of anger, for three reasons: 1) The confidentiality of the contents of a report cannot be confused with the existence of a report. It was hoped that the contents of the report would be kept private for obvious reasons. In short, I was protesting the withholding of knowledge of the existence of the report. 2) The actual date that the report was sent was rather unimportant; more importantly, a report was sent. 3) An ALA staff person indicated that he had knowledge of three schools established to circumvent the Supreme

Court decision and that he believed that there was no intention to bring sanctions and censure against the libraries and librarians involved.

Unable to convene a caucus strategy meeting on Thursday, I also began to hear rumors that, at the IFC meeting on Thursday morning, the report had been dismissed because of lack of documentary evidence. Those in attendance at the first BC meeting on this issue knew that I had named towns, counties and indicated public schools or public libraries, without being any more specific, as I said above for obvious reasons. I felt that the integrity of the Black Caucus was at stake and decided to meet with Mr. Berninghausen on Friday morning before Council.

Mrs. Binnie Tate and I represented the Caucus, and I invited Eric Moon, a member of the Council, as a neutral observer. David Berninghausen was accompanied by Alex P. Alain, a member of the IFC. Since it was stated that no documentary evidence existed, I shared the five questionnaires with Mr. Berninghausen, Mr. Alain, and Mr. Moon, without revealing the names of the persons who filled out the questionnaires. I informed them that I could not give them the questionnaires giving the specific documentation until I obtained approval from Miss Shagaloff in New York. After reviewing the evidence, then, a joint statement was prepared and read by Mr. Berninghausen, who indicated that the IFC would begin investigation. For the black caucus, however, this was a hollow victory. As Mrs. Tate asked them, "Why must black people always have to bear the burden of proof?" As we think of all our small steps toward freedom, including the historic 1954 U.S. Supreme Court decision, black people initiated the litigation. Yet even in 1971, the ALA Intellectual Freedom Committee insisted that the Black Caucus bear the burden of proof.

1971 DALLAS CONFERENCE

The Caucus continued its efforts through a sound committee structure, part of which was the important Planning and Action Committee. The report of this committee was approved at the January 1971 Midwinter meeting but was not released for publication until the Dallas Conference, and it adopted the following objectives:

1. Assess the utilization of the black community of library users in the development of relevant library services, necessary library outlets, involvement as active members on library boards of trustees, and the availability of materials which meet current issues and concerns.
2. Review, analyze, evaluate, and recommend to the American Library Association action on the needs of black librarians which will improve their status in the areas of:
    a. Employment welfare and general working conditions
    b. Library training programs
    c. State and local library programs
    d. The American Library Association
    e. Recruitment into the profession
    f. Contacts with national offices and agencies
    g. Activities Committee on New Directions for ALA
    h. Recruitment and development in a work setting of the black library employee at all levels.

3. Serve as a clearinghouse for black librarians:
   a. in promoting wider participation by black librarians at all levels
   b. in providing information on qualifications of black librarians.
4. Serve as a watchtower for black librarians in the profession and black library users:
   a. in terms of their needs in the profession
   b. in receiving complaints from individual black librarians and to channel these complaints to the proper body within ALA for action
   c. in disseminating information on current, successful library programs.
5. Review the personal records and analyze the platform statements of candidates for President of ALA to determine their potential impact upon black librarians and services to the black community.
6. Examine the inaugural address of the President of ALA for his statement of actions which will improve the status of black librarians and black communities served by libraries throughout the country. To examine critically the actions of the President of ALA during his term in office determining how well or where areas need to be improved as he fulfills social and professional responsibilities to minority groups throughout the nation.
7. To continue to be active and aggressive in the development of policy, planning and action in the field of librarianship and other related programs which affect black librarians.

In an action closely related to the substance of this report, Joslyn Williams, a black staff member of the Library of Congress, appealed to the Caucus for support of his resolution alleging the blatant practice of racial discrimination at the Library of Congress. The Caucus unanimously supported Mr. Williams because LC as the national library should serve as a model for other libraries.

William D. Cunningham was elected to succeed E. J. Josey as caucus chairman at the Dallas meeting, and at his first steering committee meeting as chairman, on November 12, 1971, the Library of Congress was a key item on the agenda. Joslyn Williams reported that LC was feigning a congressional barrier to the ALA investigation, and that ALA was wavering under the pressure. In response to this report, the Steering Committee sent a telegram to David Clift (ALA Executive Director) and Keith Doms urging ALA to carry out the investigation of the employment situation at the Library of Congress. Letters were also to be sent to each member of the congressional Black Caucus, asking their support, and to each member of the ALA Black Caucus, asking their support via letters to their congressmen. Letters to membership specifically asked that the Congressional Committee on the Library of Congress assume its responsibility for investigating the employment situation at LC.

For the next two and one-half years, the Caucus was actively engaged in helping the Library of Congress to eradicate racism and discrimination. ALA fielded two investigating committees, one chaired by David Kaser and the other by W. Carl Jackson, and the positive results of the investigations of LC are reflected in the increase in the employment of minorities at higher levels at this national institution.

BLACK CAUCUS AND NAACP

At the NAACP annual convention in 1971, the Association went on record commending the ALA Black Caucus in its efforts. In a resolution entitled "Public Library Services to White Academies" the NAACP resolution stated:

> BE IT RESOLVED that we commend the Black Caucus of the American Library Association for their efforts to end practices in public libraries and school libraries which are discriminatory, and call upon the American Library Association to act swiftly and vigorously on the findings of the ALA Black Caucus. . . .

The NAACP also adopted a variation of Lola Johnson Singletary's ALA resolution on equal representation on public library boards and urged its branches to use political participation to achieve this goal.

Fair and Equal Representation
on Public Library Boards of Trustees

> WHEREAS, a fair and inherent right to fair and equal representation at the policy making level is a basic right of all citizens served by public libraries, and
>
> WHEREAS, equal and fair representation is not practiced in the appointment of citizens to represent the total community on State and local library boards of trustees, and
>
> WHEREAS, since the public library is one of the important non-school agencies which contribute to the educational and informational needs of all citizens from pre-kindergarten to post-graduate, and since black and other minority Americans are in too many instances ignored, not included, and in too many instances are not appointed in sufficient number to represent a fair representation of the population, be it hereby
>
> RESOLVED that the National Association for the Advancement of Colored People vigorously supports fair and equal representation on boards of trustees of public libraries which will make for fair and equal representation of the total public served in the composition of all public library boards, and that this communication be sent to all branches of the Association as stated policy and further, that the National Education Director communicate this position to all known state and local officials who are responsible for appointments to public library governing boards.
>
> BE IT FURTHER RESOLVED that NAACP units urge use of political participation to achieve this goal.

INTERNATIONAL BOOK YEAR

At the 1972 January Midwinter meeting of ALA, I noted that ALA in its programming for International Book Year was thinking about every part of the world except Africa, and I urged the Caucus to take positive action to correct ALA's indifference to Africa. The Caucus unanimously adopted the following resolution:

Resolution in Support of International Book Year

WHEREAS, The year 1972 has been proclaimed as International Book Year by the General Conference of UNESCO at its sixteenth session in 1970, and

WHEREAS, The general theme for International Book Year is "Books for All," with the essential aim "to focus attention of the general public, governments, and international and domestic organizations on the role of books and related materials in the lives and affairs of the individual and society," and a correlative aim of "recognition of the worldwide need for full and unhindered access to good books by all people everywhere," and

WHEREAS, One of the goals of the members of the ALA Black Caucus is to strengthen library service to black communities through the provision of books, related materials, and the recruitment of black librarians; correspondingly, members of the ALA Black Caucus recognize that they have a duty and responsibility to foster and promote the international aims of IBY by contributing to our African black brothers and sisters in their struggle for nationhood and self-determination, therefore, be it

RESOLVED, That the Black Caucus (1) encourage members to spend a short period in Africa helping to provide library service by working in libraries during 1972, and (2) that the black college and university librarians send and support a staff member to work in an African library during the year and not only give professional service to Africa, but more importantly, become acquainted with the research resources of Africa that are essential to African Studies that have recently emerged in the Unite States, and further, that the ALA Black Caucus establish a Task Force on Africa to implement these goals by the Summer of 1972.

The resolution on International Book Year led to the formation of a Task Force on Africa, chaired by me. A large number of persons contributed their time and resources to the Task Force, and we were fortunate in having several librarians who had worked or traveled in Africa and were aware of African library needs.

Vivian Hewitt, Mohammed Aman, and I served as a sub-committee and wrote a proposal for funding of the project. After conferences with several potential funding organizations and foundations, we were successful in tapping financial resources from the African-American Scholars Council, Washington, D.C., to fund a pilot exchange program. Thomas Battle of the Howard University Library spent the 1972-73 academic year as an exchange librarian on the staff of the National Library Board in Freetown, Sierra Leone, and Harry Kamara of the National Library Board of Sierra Leone served on the Howard University Library staff. Mr. Kamara also gained invaluable experience at the District of Columbia Martin Luther King, Jr., Library. The funding from the African-American Scholars Council provided the Caucus the opportunity in 1974 to send Wallace Van Jackson, Librarian Emeritus of Virginia State College, to serve on the library faculty of the University of Botswana, Lesotho and Swaziland campus in the city of Manzini. Because of the critical shortage of professionally trained librarians in the country, no African librarian could be spared to journey to America. It is hoped that this successful pilot venture will encourage funding to support a larger exchange program between African and American librarians.

The African exchange program heightened the awareness of Afro-American librarians of the importance of participation in international librarianship. In 1974, under the aegis of the African Task Force, the Caucus sponsored a reception at the 40th Council meeting of IFLA (International Association of Library Federation) for Third World librarians. While the reception was designed to open communications with Third World librarians, a large number of non-minority American librarians participated.

CONTINUING CONCERNS

James Wright assumed the chairmanship of the Caucus at the Las Vegas ALA Conference in 1973, and during his tenure a Task Force on Telecommunications was organized. At the 1974 annual ALA conference, a special workshop on "Telecommunications: Information and Black Survival," was held. Too, it was at this conference that the Caucus opened its meetings to all who were in attendance at ALA to hear the guest speaker, Vernon Jordan, Executive Director of the National Urban League.

Harry Robinson and Avery Williams in 1974 and 1976, respectively, followed James Wright as chairman. During Robinson's tenure, the Caucus revised its constitution, and at the 1976 Centennial ALA Conference, it supported the Council on Interracial Books for Children's resolution on racism and sexism in children's books and featured black publishers and authors in the Chicago area. In addition, in cooperation with the Association of College and Research Libraries (Louise Giles, president), a reception in honor of Clara S. Jones, the first Afro-American President of ALA and the Honorable Julian Bond, State Senator of Georgia, was sponsored.

ACHIEVEMENTS OF THE BLACK CAUCUS

The Black Caucus has been active on many fronts, and as a result of those efforts, black librarians will not continuously remain dependent upon the resources of others. It is the notion of dependency that black librarians have changed through their support of the following programs:

1. An ALA Resolution which calls for the censure of libraries and/or librarians providing service or materials to racist schools established to circumvent racial integration.

2. Support of blacks at the University of Maryland's School of Library and Information Services who fought racism at the University of Maryland.

3. Supported the Black Employees Association at the Library of Congress in its struggle to eliminate discrimination in employment and promotion at the Library of Congress. The American Library Association is currently investigating the case.

4. Supported Barbara Ringer, a distinguished white lawyer and copyright expert, who was denied the position of Register of Copyright because she supported the black employees' allegation of discrimination at the Library of Congress as being valid. (After a court suit, Miss Ringer was given the position in September 1973.)

5. Supported the black and Chicano employees of the Los Angeles County Public Library System in their struggle for equal job opportunity and promotion. As a result of this case, one black librarian and a Chicano librarian were promoted to managerial positions.

6. Worked with the NAACP in gathering information on libraries serving in segregated academies in the South.

7. Made a survey on the number of blacks serving on the Board of Trustees of public libraries and state library boards/or commissions.

8. Supported the rights of other minorities in the American Library Association and in the library field.

9. Fostered a workshop on black publishing at the 1972 ALA Conference, under the leadership of Jeanne English and Donald Joyce, which resulted in a meaningful partnership between black librarians and black publishers.

10. Instituted an exchange of librarians between libraries in Africa and in America.

11. Publishes a quarterly newsletter, with Ann Allen Shockley as first editor and Casper L. Jordan as the present editor.

12. Plans are being developed for a black library periodical.

13. Developed regional black librarians' caucuses throughout the country as a result of the inspiration and encouragement from the ALA Black Caucus.

14. Conducted several conferences and workshops on librarianship as it relates to blacks, including the Institute for Training Librarians for Special Black Collections and Archives at Alabama State University.

15. Puts on an annual program at the ALA Conference each year.

16. Established a data bank on black librarians at Atlanta University.

The Black Caucus is not a separatist group. We have not left ALA and formed the Afro-American Library Association, and at this juncture in our history, we don't plan this kind of action. Blacks are a group that has an historical identity of being discriminated against, and although we represent the largest minority group in this country, we are but a small group in ALA. The Black Caucus is a group working toward a common goal of the elimination of racism in the American Library Association and in libraries. One of the salutary effects of the organization of the Black Caucus is the development of several new caucus groups: the Asian-American, the Italian-American, the Jewish, and the American Indian caucuses. Charles Townley, the first chairman of the American Indian Caucus, indicated that he was inspired to form a group for his Indian brothers and sisters, because of the Black Caucus. Such groups, working independently, will not be diverted from their most urgent, immediate tasks of professional, internal self-improvement and independent institution building. A strong coalition between all of these groups and other radical caucuses that have formed has pumped new blood into the American Library Association.

As long as there is racism in ALA and in America, there will be a need for the Black Caucus. We are, in 1976, a race of people still fighting daily indignities, patronizing attitudes, and pinpricks. Even those of us who think that we have made it in the system still suffer from or have to shrug off the smaller humiliations.

There have been some black groups who have denounced patronage of the black struggle by other groups seeking equality, and we do not quarrel with these groups. However, the ALA Black Caucus accepts support from all groups. Nevertheless, we must decide on the methods to be employed and set the pace of our struggle. We must seek an aggressive kind of political and professional freedom independent of the kinds of alliances that have made us slaves in the past. We must begin to seize power where we are. It is our hope that our efforts will forever do away with hearing only the rhetoric and never experiencing the reality of change.

10. California Librarians Black Caucus
by   James E. Crayton, Readers Advisor, Pasadena City College
and
Lucy Wilson, Public Services Librarian, Laney Community College

On April 22, 1972, the California Library Association (CLA) passed a resolution stipulating that there should be greater representation of minorities on its Council. In addition, the Council also passed a resolution in support of the Fair Employment Practice Commission suit against the Los Angeles County Public Library. These events provided the impetus for establishing the California Librarians Black Caucus. In addition to these facts, Council Members Kathryn P. Carr, Hermia Justice, and Elizabeth M. Smith felt a need to organize minority members within CLA in order to assure passage of future legislation and resolutions that would be beneficial to minorities in general.

Immediately, Council Members Carr and Justice began planning for the birth of a statewide Black Caucus, and the first planning session was held in San Francisco. Kathryn Carr, Barbara Coleman, Hermia Justice, Effie Lee Morris Jones, and James Crayton were present. From this session, initial plans were started to form an organization to deal with matters concerning and affecting both librarians and the minority community form a statewide perspective. It was also agreed that there would be two coordinators, one each for Northern and Southern California, for the purpose of organizing the membership and coordinating caucus activities.

On Sunday, May 21, 1972, the first series of meetings (North and South) were held. Librarians present were informed of the need for such an organized caucus with CLA, and a proposed organizational structure was developed. It was decided to form an informal Black Caucus and to call it officially the California Librarians Black Caucus (CLBC) in order not to exclude black librarians who were not members of CLA. Kathryn Carr (South) and Barbara Coleman (North) were elected coordinators.

*   *   *

IN 1972, most of the black librarians in Northern California were functioning in the San Francisco Bay area and its environs. Black librarians being graduated from library schools during the late 1960s and early 1970s found their professional area's boundaries to extend as far northeast as Sacramento, southeast to Merced in the San Joaquin Valley, and southwest to San Jose in Santa Clara County. Within these "extended" boundaries, public library services are provided by 11 county and approximately 30 municipal systems; 11 junior colleges, 5 universities, and many school library systems.

The 1976 *California Black Librarians' Northern Directory* lists 73 librarians employed and offering professional guidance and leadership in the Bay area. The caucus membership roster includes 44 percent of this group. Twenty-six are employed in municipal libraries, and 25 in school libraries; other areas of employment are: junior colleges (8), county systems (5), universities (4), federal (3), and unknown (2). This might imply progress in minority hiring in that the single token has been doubled, and persons are being hired for the job they can do regardless of racial origins.

Barbara Coleman, formerly of Hamilton Air Force Base in Northern California, worked diligently to locate and organize librarians in Northern California, and the first meetings convened at Laney Library, a community college library in Oakland. Our first efforts were given over to mainly structuring the group's goals and by-laws. However, as an organizing function and public relations project, we gave a book party in December 1972 for Bill Webster, then Assistant Superintendent of Schools in Oakland, California, and author of *One by One*. Later, some of our meetings were held at the Negro Historical and Cultural Society in East Bay and San Francisco. (Akilimali Funua, of San Francisco Public Library, is also volunteer librarian for the San Francisco Negro Historical and Cultural Society.)

We supported efforts to revive *Black World* by making a donation and encouraging other groups to do the same. Also, various areas of the community have asked us for assistance in areas relating to black materials and library leadership. Dean Buckland of the University of California School of Librarianship, Berkeley, has asked us to assist him in developing curriculum for library services to the disadvantaged. One of our proposals is that candidates for the MLS degree who plan to work with minority groups be thoroughly exposed to information about those groups and their historical and cultural heritages.

Few of us are free to visit other libraries during working hours. We are, therefore, nomadic with our monthly Sunday meeting dates, and we meet wherever we can arranged to have a different library open. Keeping shop is interesting, but many members express the need to have the opportunity to move around to see what other libraries are doing, which should be a concern of all black librarians who made decisions. When ALA met in California, few members were freed from their "storekeeping" duties to get beneficial experiences from the convention, and we propose that wherever ALA meets, libraries should allow regular staff adequate release time to attend.

* * *

The Southern area met for the first time on Sunday, May 21, 1972, to implement plans set in motion by black CLA Council members for a statewide organization. The Southern Area goals were to 1) encourage members to form a state organization, 2) to find and recommend black candidates for the CLA Council elections in December 1972, and 3) to provide support to those librarians involved in the Fair Employment Practice Commission suit against the Los Angeles County Public Library System.

Because of the efforts of Kathryn Carr, Hermia Justice, Ruby Ballard, Joyce Sumbi, Louise Moses, James Crayton, and others of the Southern Area, the first meeting was attended by approximately 25 librarians. Since 1972, the membership has grown to over 75 paid members, with members not only in Los Angeles, but also from the Riverside, San Diego, and Santa Barbara communities. The 1976 membership includes librarians in all areas of librarianship: administrators, children's, reference, catalogers, etc. Caucus members work in all types of libraries—public, college and university, community college, and special—and all are working to promote the goals and objectives set at the first annual conference in 1972.

Evidence of the dedication of Southern Area caucus members was never more apparent than the recent "Afro-American Materials and Library Services" workshop held at the Los Angeles Ambassador Hotel on May 14 and 15, 1976. Over 75 persons attended, and through the cooperation of the members, the caucus provided a successful workshop dealing with the selection, evaluation, and use of Afro-American materials and library services to the black community.

One of the most outstanding events of the year was the Southern Area's first autograph party. Over 400 persons attended, and the Caucus's first major affair was a financial success. Anne Ford, Ora Williams, Moss Humphrey, Nolan Davies, and A. S. "Doc" Young were the authors who appeared. Climaxing the affair was actress/author Beah Richards reading from her one-person play, "A Black Woman Speaks." On July 30, the Southern Area Caucus held its second autograph party, with actor William Marshall as the featured guest speaker.

* * *

On Thursday, November 30, 1972, the first annual Black Caucus of the California Librarians Association was held at the CLA Conference. Kathryn P. Carr, Southern Area Coordinator, presided. After formalities, members suggested that in order to further strengthen the Caucus, a set of by-laws should be developed by a committee. Further discussion concerned whether or not the Caucus should become a chapter of CLA, and after a lengthy discussion, members decided to remain autonomous. The by-laws committee then prepared a draft for membership approval. It became clear even before the conference was over that a strong need for our existence was evident. When the Caucus's ad hoc nominating committee attempted to fulfill its obligation to CLA regarding minority representation on the CLA Council, names submitted by the committee did not appear on the slate of nominations.

After the conference, Caucus members and committees, North and South, began working again on the by-laws and other related matters. The nominating committees began overseeing the activities of the CLA and the ALA nominating committees; the Library Training and Recruiting Committees began keeping data on job openings plus participating in "career day" programs; the Survey Committees started surveying libraries to see what kind of affirmative action programs, if any, were being developed by libraries in California; the Complaint and Grievance Committees began drafting guidelines for presenting grievances; the Public Relations and the Library Materials Committees started defining areas of responsibilities; and the Legislative Committees continued working on by-laws.

In 1973, members and committees continued their work. Accomplishments included the hosting of the ALA Black Caucus in Las Vegas in 1973, the monitoring of the Fair Employment Practice Commission suit, monitoring the activities of the California State Librarian, and campaigning for the election of four of our members to CLA Council. Eunice Parker, Assistant Chief of Branches, San Francisco Public Library, was CLBC Coordinator (Northern) during 1974 when the California Library Association held its 75th annual convention in San Francisco, and through her leadership, we were instrumental in having Clara Jones as the conference keynote speaker. A panel discussion was also held during this convention on "The Black Librarian and the Inner City Library," with black trustees from libraries in California as panelists.

Encouraged by our accomplishments, we saw in 1974 the refinement of the by-laws. Finally, in November, both North and South ratified the by-laws, which defined the Caucus's purpose and organizational structure. The members of the California Librarians Black Caucus defined its purpose as dedication to the welfare and concerns of black librarians with specific emphasis on the following aims:

1) Supporting all efforts to eradicate inequities that affect minorities within the profession;
2) Functioning as an ombudsman for black librarians in all communities;
3) Promoting library and information services to blacks;
4) Evaluating the quality of published materials concerning blacks.

Having thus fully decided on our purpose, we agreed that the Caucus would serve the needs of librarians, library school students, black directors of a library system, and black commissioners and trustees.

This conference saw minority members busy working on committees and various other activities. The CLBC, along with Reforma (National Association of Spanish Speaking Librarians in the United States), provided the children of San Diego with a storytelling session and the opportunity to view the exhibits. In addition to the community benefits, the Caucus sponsored an affirmative action panel, and Dr. Charles Thomas addressed the guests on "Media and Minorities." Ernest Gaines, author of *The Autobiography of Miss Jane Pittman*, was presented with an award, also.

In 1975, the new officers began planning activities, including continued monitoring of CLA activities, a push for the Los Angeles County Public Library to appoint a minority consultant to its staff, input to the National Commission on Libraries and Information Science, and participation in the Los Angeles Bicentennial plans.

In June 1975, the Northern Area hosted the second event for the ALA Black Caucus. Again, it proved a delightful and rewarding experience, with Richard Brown, Assistant City Librarian, Berkeley Public Library, serving as Coordinator during 1975. The tasks of providing program and cordial atmosphere for the American Library Association's meeting in San Francisco during the summer and the California Library Association's annual meeting (Fall 1975) were his challenge. Lucy Wilson, Public Services Librarian, Laney Community College, was Program Chairman and Coordinator-Elect. With Richard's patience, Lucy's persistence, and the membership's vote of confidence, Richard gave us the biggest year we have had. For ALA's delegates, the CLBC and Community Services of Laney College presented a concert at Laney Theatre featuring Dimensions Dance Theatre, Inc. (dance troupe) and Joyce Carol Thomas, poet, all of which followed a tour of the Oakland Museum and lunch at the Museum. We felt this program helped to give a more balanced view of the Bay Area to the delegates.

"Bicentennial '76, Should We Celebrate?" was the topic for the panel presented by the CLBC (Northern) during the 77th annual convention of the California

Library Association in San Francisco in November 1975. (*The California Librarian*, April 1976 issue, carries the full discussion of this event, billed as a Public Conversation with Community Leaders and Concerned Citizens.)

The Caucus ended the year with the Northern branch sponsoring the third annual program at CLA. The panelists included Dr. W. Hazaiah Williams (President-Director, Center for Urban Black Studies), Ms. Julia Hare (Director of Community Affairs, KSFO Radio), Dr. Raye Richardson (Lecturer in Humanities, California State University, San Francisco), and Ms. Naomi Madgett, a poet.

The California Librarians Black Caucus has now established itself as a part of the California library scene. The Caucus plays a vital role in ensuring that minorities both receive useful library services and have their legitimate place in the decision-making process and in the libraries and information centers in California.

11. Chicago Area Black Librarians
by Alfred L. Woods, Librarian, Blackstone Branch Library, Chicago Public Library

In the tradition of black librarians in Detroit and Dallas, Chicago area black librarians formed an ad hoc committee to plan a reception for librarians attending the 1972 annual conference of the American Library Association (ALA). Three years later, November 5, 1975, at the regular meeting of the Chicago Chapter of the National Black Caucus of the ALA, the report of the Goals and Objectives Committee was read and adopted by the general membership. This action formalized the group of librarians who, at their first meeting, were primarily concerned with planning a program and activities for librarians attending the annual ALA conference. However, the activities of all three groups of librarians, Detroit (1970), Dallas (1971), and Chicago (1972) were precipitated by a single act that is now a significant chapter in the history of American library service.

In January 1970, at the Chicago Midwinter meeting of the American Library Association, Afro-American librarians formed the Black Caucus of ALA. The Caucus was organized in response to a critical lag in the development of librarianship for blacks and for outlets for studies and reports dealing with social and economic issues relating to black American citizens in general, and black librarians in particular. Following this meeting in Chicago in 1970, and at subsequent annual conferences, local black librarians hosted an annual conference of the ALA Black Caucus under the leadership of the Chicago Planning Committee, co-chaired by Jeanne English and Donald Joyce in 1972. The Black Caucus for the 1972 ALA Annual Conference was formed to function in a similar capacity.

The Chicago Planning Committee was significant because it was the first time local librarians had rallied for a common cause. More importantly, it opened channels of communication that permitted other events to occur in the Chicago community of black librarians. The Chicago Planning Committee did not have a formal plan of action beyond its initial goal, but rather it attempted to respond to immediate needs.

After the 1972 ALA Annual Conference, the Chicago committee became inactive until its support from the community of black librarians was again needed. This support became necessary late in 1972 when Voree Gordon, a graduate library student, applied to the Illinois Manpower Advisory Committee for scholarship aid. When obstacles were placed before her, she appealed to the committee, which rallied to her support by sending a letter of protest to the Advisory Committee; subsequently, the scholarship was granted. It was necessary to follow a similar plan of action when a key administrative position in the Chicago Public Library was vacated, and filled, without what the committee felt to be adequate advertising. Telegrams by the committee protesting this oversight were sent to the Board of Directors of the Chicago Public Library, and the committee was joined in this protest by the Staff Association of CPL and representatives of the municipal employees' union. This action was also effective. However, in addition to responding as a crisis committee, local librarians were also interested in the educational and intellectual needs of the black community.

In September 1973, members of the Chicago Planning Committee were invited to participate in a panel discussion on library resources and black studies at the annual conference of the Association for the Study of Afro-American Life and History. During the 1974 ALA Midwinter meeting, members of the ALA National Black Caucus and Chicago librarians pooled their resources to present a symposium at the University of Illinois' Chicago Circle campus to consider the topic "Library Resources to support Black Studies." Participants from Chicago concentrated on library resources in the Chicago community (see *Illinois Libraries* LVII: 318-22, May 1975, for that information).

The Planning Committee of the Chicago Black Caucus was first conceived of as a program committee, but it also occasionally and successful met professional demands as both a crisis committee and as a contributor to the intellectual and educational needs of the local and national community of professional librarians, students, and scholars. Equally important is the fact that channels of communication were established among Chicago Afro-American librarians that served to facilitate the second stage of the CBC's development.

Jean E. Coleman, when appointed Director of the Office for Library Services to the Disadvantaged at ALA Headquarters, volunteered the facilities of that office to organize, solidify, and strengthen the local group.

The first meeting of what was to become the Chicago Chapter of the ALA Black Caucus was held in October 1973, with Jean E. Coleman as convener.

To the historian familiar with the development of organizations, the discussion at that first meeting should have been predictable. The convener asked the group at large what it wanted to do as an organization of black librarians, and the responses are somewhat indicative of the experience, needs, and orientation of those librarians present. For example, one librarian wanted an informal group to talk to about the profession, someone else wanted to reach out and touch the souls of all the black librarians in Chicago, and still another wanted neither talk nor touch but to locate a better professional position. Thus, many hours were spent discussing goals, objectives, and the reasons for having an association of local black librarians. The National Black Caucus of Librarians—Chicago Chapter was accepted as the official name of the organization which has met consistently since the first meeting in October 1973.

The group's emphasis during its first year was on building a strong organization, and under the leadership of Avery Williams, its first president, developing membership, organizational structure, purpose, goals, and programs were the primary topics of discussion. From these discussions evolved a cluster of working committees, which gave progress reports then to the regular meetings of the Chicago chapter. Among the committees established during the first year were a fund-raising and education committee; the latter keeps the chapter abreast of trends in the profession, as well as informing the community of the existence of the potential services of local black librarians. Ad hoc committees have investigated local affirmative action programs, the feasibility of registration with the state authorities for charitable organization status, author luncheons, book fairs, and Bicentennial/Centennial activities in commemoration of the American Revolution and the anniversary of the American Library Association. As the organization matures, it is conceivable that monthly business meetings will become less frequent and the organization will become more service oriented—i.e., rendering service to both the profession and the community.

The goals of the Chicago Black Caucus are the following:

1) To organize the black librarians in the Chicago area for the purpose of developing an educational, professional, political, and social organization which will assist the black community in achieving its potential goals.

2) To act as a catalyst in developing and executing relevant library services, programs, and activities relative to informing, creating, stimulating, and maintaining the black community's interest in libraries, and achieving self-development.

3) To expand the role of the black librarian in the profession and the total community by recruiting blacks into the field, provide and develop means of access to educational opportunities, and sustain and support library education.

Elected officers of the organization during its brief history were, for 1974-75, Avery Williams (President), Michael Baker (President Elect), Mary Biblo (Secretary/Treasurer), and Alfred L. Woods (Membership Chairman). For the year 1975-76, they were Alfred L. Woods (President), Emma J. Kemp (Secretary), Mary Biblo (Treasurer), and Alfred L. Woods (Membership Chairman).

As conceived, the National Black Caucus of Librarians—Chicago Chapter is committed to the needs of the local community; however, it also is supportive of the programs and principals of its parent organization, the ALA Black Caucus.

12. New York Black Librarians Caucus, Inc.

by Cynthia Jenkins, Librarian, Baisley Park/South Jamaica Branch Library, Queens Borough Public Library

and

Ernestine Washington, Librarian, Laurelton Branch Library, Queens Borough Public Library

Although desegregation in public libraries throughout the country began to take place before the 1954 U.S. Supreme Court decision which outlawed racial segregation, library services to black communities were still dependent upon two major factors. The first was the extent to which blacks fought for quality service, and the second was inherent in the various positions or attitudes taken by the boards of directors, city officials, and librarians themselves toward supporting these services.

In spite of the educational changes advanced by the Supreme Court decision, library resources in some black communities throughout the nation continued to be inferior as compared to those in non-black communities. This disparity was quite visible in the Queens Borough Public Library system; thus, whenever black librarians of Queens gathered on professional and social occasions, concerns were inevitably expressed about the inequities of library services to the black community of Queens. Additionally, there was the seeming insensitivity of the Queens Borough Public Library with respect to the elevation of black librarians in the organizational structure.

Ernestine Washington, the first black branch supervisor in Queens, became especially mindful of these problems affecting black library users and black librarians. With the leadership aid of Cynthia Jenkins, a children's librarian and community activist, the two women were instrumental in forming the Black Librarians Caucus of Queens, which was incorporated in the summer of 1970. The organization changed its name in 1974 to the New York Black Librarians Caucus to include librarians in the larger New York metropolitan areas. (The metropolitan area of New York includes the five boroughs of New York City, as well as Nassau, Suffolk, and Westchester Counties and Northern New Jersey.) In addition, the Caucus attracted not only public librarians but librarians from academic, school, special, and research libraries.

The focal points of the caucus were community needs in relationship to all libraries, both school and public, and upgrading the status of black librarians. Proposals were drafted delineating grievances, and were presented to both the late director of the Queens Borough Public Library, Harold W. Tucker, and a committee of four Board of Trustee members. The proposals dealt with existing policies and procedures bearing upon black librarians and the black target population. It was believed by the caucus that if the recommendations were accepted and implemented, positive changes would be the direct outgrowth.

Statement of Concerns

I. SPECIAL SERVICE DIVISION

The Special Services Division was questioned as to its personnel and programs. All programs that receive tax levied funds in the borough of Queens that have similar purposes, such as the Library Service and Construction Act, should be geared to up-grade blacks and other minorities. In communities where blacks make up the majority population to be served, the coordinator of the program should be black. Queens Borough Public Library is the only public library system in which this is the exception.

A. Coordinator: We as black professionals have the same academic training as the present coordinator. Furthermore, most of us live in a community served by the project, and many serve these communities in many other ways than making a livelihood. The most important input that we can bring to this program is that we have personal knowledge of the black community, and as black American citizens we are in the unique position of having inferior or no public library service. As a result of this, we can consciously and sub-consciously bring an innovative approach that only persons with the black experience can offer. We are deeply concerned that qualified black librarians were not given the opportunity to apply for the position of Coordinator of Special Services who would qualify by the simple virtue of their blackness and their years of devoted quality service to all the people served by Queens Borough Public Library. We feel this position should be held by a black librarian.

B. Assistant Coordinators: We are further concerned with the positions of the present assistants to the coordinator. Presently these are supervising positions. With the work entailed and the responsibilities accorded, we feel that these positions should be up-graded to principal librarians as is the case in the Extension Services Division and Program and Services Division.

C. Organization and Service: We request the opportunity to provide an input in materials purchased for circulation on all mobile units of Special Service projects and also library materials for the Operation Headstart Program in the Operation Headstart branches. The Black Librarians Caucus is also requesting to have an input in the Organizational structure of the Langston Hughes Cultural Center including its collection and its future development. Additionally, in any future projects being designed to serve the black population, we request an input from its infancy.

D. Para-professionals: It is imperative that in communities where the majority of the children who attend or should attend Operation Headstart programs are black, that the Operation Headstart para-professionals should be mostly black. And, furthermore, we question whether a para-professional can uplift library services without direct supervision and input of professional librarians.

II. BLACK CULTURE CENTER

We support the stand of the communities of Southeast Queens that the Saint Albans Branch Library house the Black Culture Center. As we observe the South Jamaica area with the development of York College and the type of housing to be built, the black population will be replaced by a predominantly white population and the area as we know it today will not be a black community.

III. EMPLOYMENT OF BLACK LIBRARIANS AND RECRUITMENT PROGRAMS

Twenty-two percent of the population of Queens is black and much less than 22% of the Queens Borough Public Library librarians are black. Recruitment of black librarians is at a crisis stage. Compute the average age of the few blacks we have and then project their retirement. Who will we have? We are requesting that at least one black librarian be part of the library's annual recruitment team.

IV. CITY SPONSORED CLASSES

Staff should be notified in general and black librarians specifically should be solicited for city sponsored classes pertaining to culturally deprived minorities.

V. BLACK LITERATURE

Pro-black literature or controversial literature as it is more popularly known, should be evaluated by black librarians.

VI. PROPORTIONATE REPRESENTATION IN POSITIONS

We request proportionate representation of black professionals on all levels of public service. There are no principal librarians in branches who are black and no supervising librarians as heads of divisions of the Central Library who are black.

VII. CAREER CONFERENCES

A black librarian should be sent to career conferences held by high schools and other organizations if the population to be served is black or majority black. The black child needs the black image in librarianship.

VIII. RELEVANCY OF PROGRAMS TO BLACK COMMUNITIES

Black programs, collections, and buildings should be made relevant to the black community they are supposed to serve.

IX. LIBRARIAN-FOR-A-DAY

For whatever reasons unknown to us, it seems that 99 percent of the students selected for Librarian-for-a-Day and other programs are usually white. We recommend that additional means be used along with the present selection practice in order that a larger percentage of black high school students may participate in the programs.

X. BLACK PERIODICALS

The Black Librarians Caucus would like to submit a list of black periodicals that we feel should be a must for all branches. We also request that a black librarian be a part of the periodical committee that formulates policies and the standards.

XI. WRITINGS OF YOUNG BLACKS

Publications of Broadside Press of young black poets should be heavily represented in the Queens Borough Public Library, because this is the only form available and the poetry is widely requested by both blacks and young whites.

XII. BLACK OBSERVANCES

We are hereby requesting that there be no stipulations in administrative policies and procedures which will permit or prevent persons from observing certain "Black Observances" based on staff consideration. In short, we wish to be considered with impunity to observe such days with the same consideration as the observances of Christmas, Yom Kippur and the like.

XIII. INADEQUATE COLLECTIONS

Libraries in Southeast Queens for years have been quite inadequate. Small physical plants, small budgets, small collections and inexperienced staff were the prevailing conditions. The new buildings going up in the communities are opening up with very inadequate collections. The black communities cannot use these branches as they should or as they desire because of the inadequate materials. Cambria Heights, Laurelton, Rochdale, Queens Village and the Central Library are easily accessible to the black communities and these branches are presently being used and will continue to be used by a large number of blacks until the libraries in the black communities have equal collections. Since this is a fact, we urge that the collections in these libraries be strengthened as quickly as possible. Children cannot travel for service, and children who are being denied adequate library materials now will have to compete with their white counterparts for high school placements and college placements. They will be taking the same tests and will not have been exposed to equal facilities and materials. Strengthening of the heavily used children's collection at St. Albans is urgent.

XIV. BLACK ARTICULATION

So that our concerns will not be unproductive, we state that there are differing degrees of readiness among blacks and therefore, in your consideration of these concerns, please note that all blacks do not automatically qualify for certain positions simply because of the color of their skin. In this period of rising expectations, it is imperative that blacks be placed in strategic positions based on their degree of readiness in articulating the black experience.

Some outstanding programs have been given by the Caucus. In July 1974, when the American Library Association held its annual meeting in New York City, the Queens Caucus hosted librarians from across the nation at Vincent's Place in Harlem, following a cultural tour of Harlem, a tour designed to emphasize the positive features of the community and noting its historic sites. Guest speakers were Dr. Anna Arnold Hedgeman (Consultant on Urban Affairs and African American Studies), Elton Fax (author, artist, and lecturer), and Lewis Micheaux (founder of the National Memorial African Book Store). A who's who of the black library world attended, including Clara Jones (Director, Detroit Public Library), Bertha Cheatham (Associate Editor of *School Library Journal*), Lucille Thomas (Supervisor of Libraries, District 16, Brooklyn, New York City Board of Education), Virginia Lacey Jones (Dean, School of Library Science, Atlanta University), Augusta Baker (author, lecturer and former Coordinator of Children's Service, New York Public Library), E. J. Josey (Chief, Bureau of Specialist Library Services, New York State Education Department), Major Owens (Librarian and New York State Senator from the 17th Senatorial District, Brooklyn), and Milton S. Byam (Director of Queens Borough Public Library, the first black director of a public library system in New York State).

The second outstanding program was designed to bring together authors, publishers, illustrators, librarians, and friends in an informal setting to discuss special needs related to black materials now being published. The program speaker was Dr. John Hendrick Clarke, author, historian, and professor at Hunter College. The third program was held during the New York Library Association's annual meeting in New York City in 1975. Dr. E. J. Josey was honored by a book party. The royalties from his book, *New Dimensions for Academic Library Service*, were donated to the Roy Wilkins Scholarship Fund of the National Association for the Advancement of Colored People.

Because of continued institutional racism, in spite of the many civil rights legislative actions and court decisions since 1954, black caucuses must continue their work and serve as the consciences and watchdogs of the institutions of which they are a part. Action issues by caucuses must take priority over programming, if the caucus is to serve as a catalyst for change. Caucus members must use their talents, strengths, and resources to influence equitable political decisions and see that the decisions are followed through to implementation. Only by this method will tax-supported institutions begin to become more responsive to all of the citizens.

In today's competitive climate and with continued budget cuts, black caucuses will have to be stronger, more forceful, more vocal, and more active than ever.

13. Statistical Facts Pertaining to Black Librarians and Libraries in 1976

Total number of black librarians in the U.S.	7,800
Total number of male black librarians in the U.S.	1,080
Total number of female black librarians in the U.S.	6,720
Total number of black librarians heading a state library agency	1
Total number of blacks heading a predominantly black ALA-accredited library school	3
Total number of black directors of major public library systems	4
Total number of blacks who direct a major research library serving a predominantly white research community	1
Total number of black libraries granted membership in the Association of Research Libraries	1
Total number of black female directors of predominantly white university libraries	1

Total number of black male directors of predominantly white university libraries	1
Total number of black academic libraries that were recipients of federal grants in FY 1975	75

14. Black Librarians with Doctorate Degrees

HOLDERS OF EARNED DOCTORATES

Elaine Parker Adams
Mohammed M. Aman
Robert Ballard
Lorene Byron Brown
Penelope L. Bullock
Charles D. Churchwell
Doris Clack
L. M. Collins
Dorothy Collings
James Cross
Gwendolyn Cruzat
Vivien Davenport
Elinor Ellis
Evelyn Fancher
Hardy Franklin
Carolyn Frost
Nicolas Gaymon
Eliza A. Gleason
Dorothy Haith
Epsy Hendricks
Miles M. Jackson
Ruth Moore Jackson
Virginia Lacy Jones
Patricia Jordan
Anne Kelsey

Sylvia Green Lomen
Eleanor Young Love
Inez Boddy McCord
Edward C. Mapp
Helen Matthews
Dorothy Obi
Annette Phinazee
Warren Palmer
Leo Pickett
Francie Pollard
Ann Knight Randall
Joseph H. Reason
Lelia Rhodes
Harry Robinson
Elinor Des Verney Sinnette
Benjamin Smith
Henrietta M. Smith
Jessie Carney Smith
Paul Smith
Benjamin F. Speller, Jr.
Herman L. Totten
Eric Winston
Johanna Smith Wood
James R. Wright
Tommie M. A. Young

HOLDERS OF HONORARY DOCTORATES

Alma Jacobs
Clara S. Jones
E. J. Josey

Dorothy B. Porter
Robert Wedgeworth

VITAL ISSUES IN BLACK LIBRARIANSHIP

15. Library Services to Black Americans
by   Wendell Wray, Professor and Assistant to the Dean, Graduate School of Library and Information Science, University of Pittsburgh

HOW LONG HAS THE TRAIN BEEN GONE

Viewing a recent documentary film about Watts, dealing with the 10-year period after the revolt which made it a symbol of black urban unrest, was a depressing experience. Analysis showed that there had been little or no apparent change in a community into which millions of dollars had been poured. The life of the people was much the same: unemployment was high and morale low. The cultural center was an empty shell full of echoes, and there was not even mention of a library. It was obvious that the solutions devised were a palliative and not a cure for social problems. If these are the final results of so much effort, what has happened in the development of library services for hundreds of other black communities across the nation?

It is now apparent that the soul train of social activism is gone, but unfortunately, many public library systems did not even get on board when it was passing through. If we put our ears to the track, we hear nothing to indicate that it is coming back, and any vibrations that we get from black communities are pretty deadening. Some people thought that the exposé of Daniel Moynihan's memo on "benign neglect" would counteract the virulent backlash policy which has been developed against the struggle to improve the lot of black people, but it continues to poison our country. This makes it difficult to talk about creative ideas and strategies to attract Afro-Americans to libraries. It is very easy for some battle-scarred librarian/soldiers of the War on Poverty to long for the good old days, dream about when money was plentiful and talk about what they could do, if only . . . There are, however, certain basic strengths in our communities and in our libraries which have not dried up and which should be tapped. These can be broadly categorized under three major headings: survival tactics, human and material resources, and cultural identity. This brief article does not try to deal with the total picture of the role of blacks within the framework of the American public library, but only with the critical problem when the library becomes derelict in its service to black people, flees to the suburbs and leaves a vacuum.

PUT DOWN YOUR BUCKETS WHERE YOU ARE

In another nadir, Booker T. Washington gave some good advice to black people that should be followed at this time. He was stressing that so often what is apparent and obvious for survival is overlooked. Many whites have fled to the suburbs of their own volition, with a concomitant increase in black urban populations. Libraries should, then, reflect this change in the make-up of communities. Many public libraries are now partially supported by other than city funds on a per capita basis, which means that blacks must make certain that directors of public libraries are held much more accountable in terms of minorities for how these monies are spent. Library personnel should also reflect this change in the community. Residency requirements will have to be enacted or enforced so that those who want to benefit from working for city organizations will also want to live within city limits.

The name of the game is politics. The only winners will be those who survive. Survival tactics must mean the discarding of the genteel, ivory tower manners that have pervaded libraries in the past. The library establishment (the "library mafia," if you will) has made little or no accommodation to broaden the participation of blacks, or any other minorities. They are still playing a game with blacks, and nothing but persistent exposure and challenge will bring about any significant change. Mr. Washington in his brilliant speech used the analogy of people cast adrift on the water yet dying of thirst. Blacks in this country are dying from a lack of information and knowledge. Instead of blindly squabbling among themselves for the one little bucket which "The Man" wants them to fight over, it is wiser that blacks lay claim to the political structure and library areas abandoned by the fleeing hordes. They can then make these organizations work for their own benefit.

RESOURCES AND LIBRARIES

Blacks have invariably inherited old, decaying sections of the cities. There are zero projections for starting new buildings, so the idle dreams of modern, functional libraries designed by young black architects must be shelved for a more promising day. There are, however, still solid library buildings (sometimes given to the community "forever" by Carnegie and his ilk) which can be made to meet the needs of black people. Nothing is more depressing than to find a library in a black community which does not reflect the life of the people. However, a little money and a lot of effort are enough to make these buildings literally shout blackness. Posters, art exhibits, and banners should say "uhuru—welcome" in a thousand ways; bright colors should be used to combat institutional drabness. Even more, the rhythms and vibrations of the surrounding community should be allowed to seep into the building, so that there is a liveliness and warmth which will make black people feel at home.

Since there has never been a significant number of black librarians, it makes it very difficult to provide personnel who will be interested in and identify with black patrons. Sometimes black librarians who are hired, due to affirmative action pressure, have turned out to have little interest in black concerns and are often hired because this fact is apparent. Black community leaders should thus be much more concerned about the type of librarians who are assigned to libraries in their neighborhoods. From what has been said previously, it is obvious that it should be black librarians who are dedicated to the aspirations and concerns of those communities. On the other hand, there are others, not black, who have developed a social awareness, and through continuous education and exemplary dedication are able to make a significant contribution.

The problem of material resources is a little harder to solve without money, but there has been significant progress made in the last decade to increase the amount of black materials which can be used effectively. The problems are in having these materials available for examination before purchase and, more basic, the very limited manufacture and distribution of these materials nationwide. With the cutback of federal funds, publishers are going to be much less susceptible to "demand." The well-trained librarian, however, is able to develop significant general collections of print and non-print materials which will appeal to black adults, young adults, and children. Wise use of available bibliographies developed by experts in the field can, of course, be very helpful. Unfortunately, neophytes in collection building often forget one of the basic rules of black survival—the necessity of sharing information, materials and ideas.

There is nothing really new under the sun, and those who believe that they can come up with truly revolutionary ideas of library services for black people are going to be very disappointed. We should retain all the elements of American public librarianship which will help us survive. It means instilling in our patrons what some might consider quaint, old-fashioned ideas such as the love of books and reading. We must remember that, in one generation, many black people have moved from one part of the country, where they rarely owned a book and never entered a public library, to another part, where reading a book or going to the library may be considered jive or totally irrelevant to survival.

A diametrically different approach which should be used is the application of the field of information science and the use of computers to solve the problems of our inner cities. Knowledge stored in great computer banks must be as accessible as the simple act of dialing a telephone. The underserved can and must have immediate availability to information about health care, employment opportunities, vocational training, legal advice, and accessibility to the inner workings of local government. Information centers designed for this purpose will have to compete with traditional library services for their share of the budget.

LIBRARY PROGRAMMING AND CULTURAL IDENTITY

Black library programming must have as its highest priority the development of the cultural identity of black people. Moving from large black cultural centers with a comparatively high level of cultural awareness to many more moderate size downs, nowadays one becomes aware that not only has the soul train not gone by but it has never arrived. With the appearance of Flip Wilson's Geraldine and the Jeffersons on television, *Jet* magazine on the newsstands, and Muhammad Ali in the boxing ring, there may be a misconception that there has been some significant penetration of black awareness in this country. Actually, it is almost as phantom as flickering figures on a TV screen. Great effort must go into developing a more positive national identity, but even more into the local one.

Blacks keep searching for sepia John Waynes and Charles Bronsons to emulate, when it is a local minister, physician, artist, school teacher, or civil rights leader who has really been the hero. A significant strategy must be designed to tie our black libraries more closely to the leadership resources of the black community. Whereas in the past, the more traditional library has tried to keep a clearly defined, separate image, survival will demand that these lines be blurred so that the library will be more closely related to the schools, community centers, churches and other agencies of city government. There will be less money for personnel, so the use of volunteers and expanded cooperative efforts will be the most important ways to offer significant cultural programs.

It is obvious that this combination of resources, personnel, and cultural identity will place a heavy responsibility on library program directors to make the library an integral part of the life of the community. The library should be the first stop in any search for information and education. The library in the black community should make it apparent, through its book collection, film festivals, lecture series, dance recitals, poetry readings, health programs, and consumer education, that black people are creating their own intellectual and cultural world. Black exploitation is too much with us, and with the limited resources and time at our command, there is little time for the frivolous or the irrelevant. There may be neglect, but there is no reason to be benign about it. There is a life or death struggle for survival in our black communities. The sturdy walls of our local libraries should be the bastions of our intellectual defenses.

16. Children's Library Service and Black American Children
by Jessie M. Birtha, Librarian, Nicetown-Tioga Branch Library, Free Library of Philadelphia

> As a responsibility of library service, books and other materials selected should be chosen for values of interest, information and enlightenment of all the people of the community.... The rights of an individual to the use of a library should not be denied or abridged because of his age, race, religion, national origins or social or political views.
> —Library Bill of Rights
> ALA Council, June 27, 1967

> Each child as an individual in the human community, has certain inalienable rights. He has the right to be accepted as the person he is, and to receive help in becoming the person he wishes to be. To this end, the San Francisco Public Library, through specially trained Children's Librarians, serves each child of this city and fosters the enjoyment of reading as the basis of our continuing relationship with him....
> —Children's Rights
> San Francisco Public Library

INTRODUCTION

The basic truths expressed in these two statements have not always been self-evident in library service to all children in America. Within the life span and recollection of many librarians still employed today are memories of a time when libraries were less liberal toward children and minorities. These were years when libraries greeted patrons with signs of "Silence"; a time when many libraries were officially designated and labelled for service to White or Colored. In comparison to the wide variety available today, children's books were few, and books about black children were even fewer. The value of *Little Black Sambo* as a delight to all children had not been challenged; children attended Shirley Temple movies and listened to Amos and Andy on radio instead of watching Bill Cosby and "Sesame Street" on television. The memory is of a period when America was younger, her people less critical and less disillusioned. Parents had not been liberated by Dr. Spock to the idea of rearing less inhibited, more free-thinking children, and over 30 was still a respectable and respected age for adults. School children studied reading, geography, and arithmetic instead of language arts, social studies, and the new math. The concept of school libraries was just beginning to emerge with no suggestion of the eventuality of Instructional Materials Centers. Children's librarianship was not a field widely publicized or promoted as a career for men and women. However, the three basic elements of library service to children were always present: librarians, children, and books.

The librarian, usually a woman, whether college-educated with a professional degree or trained through the school of experience, was one who had chosen this vocation and remained in it because of an inner satisfaction which may even have been subconscious. The librarian who served children was either a public librarian or a school librarian. The children came in all shapes, personalities, sizes and colors. And there were the books: the basic element, the silent factor, waiting to be awakened to life by the librarian placing the right book into the hands of the right child—or waiting to be discovered by those special children who possessed that insatiable curiosity to seek and find any books they had not previously read from the shelves.

There are still librarians, children, and books. But as the years have passed, many changes have occurred in libraries, changes as radical as the changes in America from the small corner grocery store to the supermarket syndrome, or from the Main Street department store to suburban shopping malls. Public libraries have developed with technological improvements demanding greater technical skill of librarians, more specialization of job classification, and fewer personal relationships with patrons. School libraries have become centers for the storage, use, and distribution of records, filmstrips, slides, films, and other audiovisual media and equipment, in addition to books. Book selection units have become materials selection units. To quote a National Library Week slogan of a few years past, "The library is not just books any more." Yet, books remain the basic ingredient.

As libraries have developed, children have also increased in their needs and demands. Exposed to matters involving social, economic, and emotional traumas at a younger age than were their parents, they reach a level of need for understanding, decision making, and problem solving earlier in life. Yet, the combined lessening of parental restrictions and constant exposure to life's problems while so young may help to decrease the sensitivity necessary in children for acute, perceptive evaluation. Acceleration of scientific progress has made as sudden a change in lives of children today as the Industrial Revolution made upon children at the close of the Renaissance. Nevertheless, children still have the same basic needs: security, love, knowledge, beauty, relaxation, self-identity and a philosophy of life. Librarians are still instruments for helping children to satisfy these needs through books and other library materials.

What about the books provided for children? How have they changed? Informational books for children are available in practically every field handled by adult books, and the content, depth and scope are frequently amazing to the adult who chances to pick one up. Beyond the picture books (which have also undergone changes), fiction deals more and more with the same issues covered by adult books: social problems, contemporary realism, scientific anticipation. Even fantasies, humor, and sport stories tend to employ plots interwoven with problems of the current world. Biographies no longer tend to paint people perfectly, but accurately and perceptively analyze the good and bad in human beings. History and historical fiction lean toward the accuracy of life as it really was rather than the glorified past that people often desire as a soothing memory. One change, however, has not taken place. Children still acquire from their reading an understanding of themselves, of life and the world, their attitudes toward others and their sense of values. The children's librarian remains the person whose responsibility and privilege it is to provide quality books to meet these needs.

CHILDREN'S LIBRARIANS

What is a children's librarian? One early poet laureate of the library world, at the 1906 American Library Association meeting, described the position as follows:

> See the Children's gay Librarian! Oh, what boisterous joys are hers
> As she sits upon her whirl-stool, throned amid her worshippers,
> Guiding youngsters seeking wisdom through Thought's misty morning light
> Separating Tom and Billy as they clinch in deadly fight;
> Giving lavatory treatment to the little hand that smears
> With the soil of crusted strata laid by immemorial years;
> Teaching critical acumen to the youngsters munching candy,
> To whom books are all two classes—they are either "bum" or "dandy"
> Dealing out to Ruths and Susies, or to Toms and Dicks and Harrys,
> Books on Indians or Elsie, great big bears, or little fairies;
> For the Children's gay Librarian passes out with equal pains
> Books on Indians or Elsie, satisfying hungering brains;
> Dealing Indians or Elsie, each according to his need,
> Satisfying long, long longings for an intellectual feed.
>
> —Sam Walter Foss
> Stanza III of *The Song of the Library Staff*

Adjectives have changed. The librarian is no longer termed "gay," and rarely does she (or he) hand out books to worshippers. The Indian books have become Native American books with new focus on accountability for action, and Elsie Dinsmore and her ladylike swoons have been banished to the historical collections in favor of non-sexist heroines. In many ways, however, public opinion of the children's librarian has not been altered. The children's librarian has been viewed as a glorified baby sitter and PLPF (private-leaning-post-forever) for harassed parents; an ever-present substitute mother to children of working mothers; a helping hand for adult room staff members to enable them to get the "serious, important" library work accomplished; and even a confidant for lonely retirees nostalgically reliving their childhood through the pages of children's books.

Although many laymen are unaware of the fact, the children's librarian is, first of all, a librarian with the same certification or accreditation demanded of other professional librarians. He or she is a specialist in children's work in the same way that another librarian may be a specialist in cataloging or science reference or business technology. A career in children's librarianship may also be directed toward school libraries or public libraries. A school librarian may serve either on an elementary or secondary level, and works closely with the teaching staff. Professional qualifications include teacher certification as well as library accreditation.

In most public libraries, the position involves service to persons from preschool through junior high or middle school, ages through 13 or 14 years, depending on specific library policy, as well as assistance to parents, teachers and other adults involved in working with children. Upon graduating from the Children's Department, children usually advance to a Young Adult Department for introduction to the adult collection, although many libraries are currently phasing out their young adult rooms as no longer useful or relevant. The responsibilities of the children's librarian include book and materials selection, talks to groups, displays, programming, story hours, film presentations, school visits, and participation in all that includes the children of the library in community outreach. The ideal children's librarian is endowed with a genuine interest in the welfare and development of children, an understanding that children are the most important resource of a nation, and a realization that children's librarianship is a career that affords a special position for guiding young minds into the creativity of widening horizons.

An important characteristic for any public librarian is enjoyment of people. One of the most essential characteristics for any children's librarian is a love for children; not only love for children in an idealistic way, but liking to be around children, a toleration for the good and bad which is as much a part of them as it is of adults, and an appreciation of the rewards of taking a vital role in the development of children through daily association. Children's librarians, of course, differ in personalities. Each person brings to the job his or her own personality and his or her own way of merging the two worlds of child and adult.

There are children's librarians who are great librarians in the total field of librarianship. The names of Augusta Baker, Charlemae Rollins, Spencer Shaw, and many others are known to library school students or readers of professional library literature throughout America. Librarians who have been so fortunate as to have an opportunity to develop under their guidance are as fortunate as those earlier librarians who enjoyed association with the great children's librarians of earlier years, Anne Carroll Moore or Mae Hill Arbuthnot. Important, also, to the children of America are the little-known, un-awarded librarians in the cities and towns and rural areas all over the country. They perform the often thankless, frequently little-paid tasks of children's librarians; thankless by many adult standards, it is true, but having instant as well as long-term rewards in the results achieved in the lives of individual children.

CHILDREN AND LIBRARIES

Who are the children served by these librarians? What kind of children are those who visit the library? Children are brought by parents, children come with friends, children first visit a library in a class visit, and some just wander in. Children come because of library programs and never reappear, and some come just to be with the crowd and talk with their friends; there are even those who come "just to bother the librarians." All are potential readers.

However, a distinction may be made between the two extremes of a child who visits the public library for his or her own purposes. The assignment-bent child is curriculum oriented, and comes because (s)he must. The assignment may be interesting but there is a difference from the self-motivated child in that the stimulus was teacher-initiated. The self-motivated child comes because (s)he wants to come. This is the special child, searching for something beyond the ingredients of his own daily routine, who challenges the children's librarian. Filling the ever-present need for an answer to the question "Isn't there more to life than this?" is the challenge frequently faced by the librarian in the inner-city community.

Up to this point, we have discussed children's library service in general with no particular consideration for color, race, or ethnic background. A children's librarian is a librarian to serve all children. It would be fortunate if there were no need to consider or evaluate the situation further. For long years, America ostensibly has worked toward an integrated nation, only to end with a country which is incredibly separate under the guise of pluralism or multi-ethnicity. We have reached a point of disillusion, a lack of belief in government, economics, and many of the organizations and institutions in which people had established faith and considered infallible. There is an absence of heroes for children growing up in a world so complicated that it is difficult for even grown-ups to find the necessary capabilities for coping. Libraries are thus experiencing crises which are changing patterns of library service in many areas. How are these changes affecting the children of America? Is library service today meeting the needs of black American children? Despite the straightforward approach toward equality of service for all ages and all races expressed in the American Library Association Bill of Rights, have the objectives been realized or has the great black American dream of equality become only another American dilemma?

LIBRARY SERVICE FOR BLACK AMERICA

A major concern in library service, as in many other fields, is to what extent service to the black American public becomes an integral part of total service to all. More and more black Americans are congregated in inner city and fringe areas, with the white population moving into white suburban ghettoes. Many white families returning to the city tend to choose selective white communities. Are libraries in predominantly black areas offering equal service to their readers, with adequate staffs and adequate budgets, or are they too frequently non-existent on a neighborhood basis because of activity not recorded by traditional library statistic-reporting techniques? Are materials concerning black people, their contribution, culture, and heritage as completely invisible in totally white areas as the black children themselves?

The children's librarian working in a suburban or upper middle class area may serve an all-white clientele or may have an integrated reading public. One of the major needs of black children in an all-white area is that their culture and contribution be recognized as a vital and positive part of American life, even though their community and life style may be different. It is the responsibility of the children's librarian, even if white, to be aware of materials about black Americans—not merely one week or month out of the year when black history celebrations are emphasized, but to provide a year-around total picture of all of the ethnic groups that make up our country. Any other course in selection or promotion of material can only result in all American children being deprived of accurate knowledge and understanding of their country's history and culture.

The patterns of library service to children (and to all other patrons as well) today tend to be set by the patterns of housing. In the integrated community, black children are not isolated from whites for library service, even though one or the other may be in a minority. A balance of programming must be maintained. A meaningful relationship must be established between all of the ethnic factors of the neighborhood, even though the library may prove to be the only place where the balance appears to work or the contact occurs. Where there is adequate financial, parental, and school support in achieving and maintaining an integrated life style, or some semblance of one, the librarian may follow the patterns of librarianship taught in library school, with recognition of each child as an individual in his own right and awareness of book selection and programming needs. In such neighborhoods, a librarian is not as frequently faced with the realization that the vast majority of the children are either reluctant readers or incapable of reading on the level of most of the books recommended for their grade on standard reading lists. Wtih the continued migration of white families from city to suburb, black minorities have become majorities of the library public in the inner city. Labelled with such adjectives as culturally disadvantaged, underprivileged, and economically deprived, and with municipal services diminishing as neighborhoods become more abandoned or neglected, families still remain with children who need educational facilities and require library service. The majority of these children are black American children.

LIBRARY SERVICE TO BLACK CHILDREN

The librarian in a black, inner city area has a demanding job. The basic elements of library service are theoretically the same as those in more affluent, politically favored areas: librarians, children, and books. Frequently, though, there are fewer librarians, more children to be reached, and fewer books. In most situations, the librarian must cope with lower reading levels, lack of home literacy or library support for the children, competition of outside influences (ranging from constant exposure to TV to gang membership for fear of gang violence, vandalism and mutilation of property), the problems of keeping balanced collections despite book losses, overdues, lower budgets, and general public apathy concerning the library and its program. The hours are long; the work is hard. Many times, service is not from a branch library but from a traveling bookmobile, a min-van, or a deposit collection in a location outside of the library. Why, then, would any librarian who has a choice have any inclination to be a children's librarian in an inner city black community? Many white librarians do not, feeling that the challenge is too demanding and the possibilities for success are too slim. Add to this the fact that they must prove their sincerity of purpose to the community (and sometimes to the black staff members) before achieving acceptance, and the combination of obstacles is one which few white librarians care to seek to overcome. However, may it be said for the record that there have been successful white librarians in inner city black areas, and there will be others for whom it does not prove "mission impossible."

Black librarians serving in black areas complete a cycle that began in 1905 in Louisville, Kentucky, with the first black staff of a "Colored Department"—a staff whose work began "with chief emphasis on service to children." After a period of conscious attempts at integration of branch library staffs in cities, the tendency has returned to assign black librarians to black areas, although there are rarely sufficient numbers of black persons on the staff of large city libraries to achieve this balance successfully. The reason for the earlier assignments was the law of segregation in the South. The reasons for recent assignments of black librarians to black areas may vary from reluctance of white librarians to accept employment in inner-city neighborhoods to a sincere interest on the part of the library administration to place librarians where they can be most effective through common interest with the reading public.

Whatever the reason, it is undoubtedly true that a black librarian feels a special responsibility and involvement in service to black children. Black librarians are usually able to establish an empathy with black children and their parents which a white librarian does not always achieve. This is particularly true with the intermediate and young teenage group, since the recent black awareness movement has provided an identity crisis for many young black people. The black experience is not identical for every black person; each has an individual background and form of reaction depending upon what is brought to a situation from the person's past, but a common sharing of racial history and culture creates a readiness for a more receptive relationships. This is not to imply that the total premise of children's library service and children's literature is to be subjugated to the dominance of black materials and culture to the exclusion of all other races, for if this happens, it is difficult to believe that balance will be achieved in developing black children into well-rounded adults prepared to take their places in the mainstream of American life.

The librarian who works with black American children in an inner city area is called upon to use all available inner resources of creativity, imagination and patience to motivate reading activity on the part of young patrons. The job has a two-part challenge: to get children to come to the library and to get them to remain and read. Often, it involves taking the resources of the library to wherever the children may be. Many of these are children of parents who are suspicious of anything related to the establishment, parents who are inherently skeptical of anything free, yet may have no desire or finances to pay for "unnecessary" services. The library is seen as part of the establishment. The children are not always shy, but are frequently deterred by parents fearful of overdue fines or disinterested in reading either for themselves or for their children. Many parents are working too hard providing a living, often without help, to have time for such non-essentials as library membership or parent-teacher meetings. Frequently, then, the children are turned off by the parent's attitude, although the parent's distrust may not be understood by the child.

The job is one of parent education as well as child motivation, and community outreach is important. This means taking the library message out into the community wherever possible, to churches, civic meetings, community fairs. The atmosphere of the library and attitude of every member of the staff toward the children are important as well. Children like to feel welcome. They dislike feeling stifled or disapproved, and often react to such treatment with resentment behavior. They need to have a feeling of belonging and a pride in the library as something of which they are a part. No child, no matter how lively, should ever be told that he is barred from the library forever.

Children need a sense of identity and self-esteem, a knowledge that someone knows and cares whether they visit the library. The feeling of helping things move along that comes through library helpers' clubs, child-created bulletin boards, or just through stamping the library's name on bookmarks is important to the child who lacks an opportunity to express himself at home. Children need the opportunity for creativity that comes from library activities like creative dramatics, puppet shows, creative poetry groups, and sometimes, just from the warm feeling that comes from showing an interested librarian an original story or picture, talking about it, and knowing that it is appreciated.

It is essential that children should have something to challenge them to strive toward improvement. They thrive on competition, for this is a way of life. Situations where little is required because little is expected are deadly for the development of inner city children; they serve only to limit achievement and result only in limited ambition in adult life. No ceiling should be placed on a child's ability, and reading clubs with unrealistically low requirements frustrate rather than help the child. Many children who withdraw in more structured classroom situations exert more effort toward reaching their potential in stimulating library activities.

STRATEGIES FOR STRENGTHENING LIBRARY SERVICE
TO INNER CITY CHILDREN

The child in the inner city needs exposure to the world outside. This exposure should come through books and other media, but also, wherever possible, library trips to plays and museums should be implemented to increase awareness. Trips provide a specific type of motivation to read, depending upon the nature of the trip and the library planned trip can be quite different from the school-oriented trip. The child needs both, but with limited staffs and finances, it is not always easy. Recruitment of parents and volunteers on a high school level is sometimes possible, however, and the librarian should explore all avenues of help from interested organizations. Communication with children of other libraries through correspondence, joint programs, and cooperative trips can also be a happy, meaningful association for all concerned.

Human resources within the city should be used to provide information, to inspire ambition, and to involve the surrounding neighborhood in children's programming. Programs featuring local authors can become multi-level, family programs. One need not wait for National Library Week or Book Week to have an Open House and invite the community, especially since many adults are unaware of the existence of juvenile material in the library. The children's room is one of the most important parts of the library, for today's picture "story hour" children are the reading public of tomorrow. It is indeed short-sighted that so many library staff members bestow upon the children's room the isolation treatment which is the subject of complaint by so many children's librarians.

Innovation is one of the key words for success, and should be limited only by the librarian's ingenuity, finance and staff available; ingenuity can help to compensate for lack of adequate finance and staff. Librarians have successfully sponsored such activities as fashion shows, chess tournaments, charm classes, and hair styling contests, all centered on books. Book contests, art contests, book fairs, and activities which culminate in ownership of books are incentives to reading. Paperbacks are both popular and inexpensive, and those available include many by black authors.

Close association between school and public library should certainly be encouraged, especially when the locations are in close proximity. Although one is curriculum oriented and the other planned for recreational reading, both have as their ultimate goal leading the child to greater adult literacy. School library and public library services, however, do not duplicate each other, nor could one satisfactorily replace the other. Each has a different function and fills a different need in the life and development of a child. A neighborhood book store, although business motivated, also will promote literacy as its business. It should thus be seen as an aid rather than a competitor to the library, and should be encouraged to stock children's titles.

DEVELOPING BOOK COLLECTIONS FOR CHILDREN

Book selection is one of the most important responsibilities of the children's librarian. It involves an astute coordination of knowledge of children and knowledge of books—one without the other is incomplete. The children's librarian must accept the responsibility of selection—not censorship, but the selection which parents depend upon the library to provide. Yet the child must not be deprived of freedom of selection. It is especially necessary that the librarian who serves black children should be knowledgeable about the availability of black materials and black authors, illustrators, and publishers. He or she must also exercise a sensitivity or awareness at all times for what is offensive, in poor taste, or poorly written. It is essential to provide books that are appropriate, appealing, and of excellent literary quality. A proper balance must be maintained, for there is no room in the job for personal censorship, prejudice or bias, faults possible whether the librarian is black or white.

There has long been a need for more and better black materials. The deluge of books that marked the late sixties and early seventies, following accusations of America as a racist nation, is receding, having climaxed as Virginia Hamilton won the National Book Award, Globe Horn Book Award and the Newbery Award simultaneously with the novel *M. C. Higgins, the Great*, thereby becoming the first black winner of either a Newbery or Caldecott Award. Children's librarians serving black American children should familiarize themselves with black authors and illustrators of award-winning or notable books, including those titles that have won the Interracial Books for Children contest for minority writers and the Coretta Scott King Award for books promoting world brotherhood, non-violent change, and peace.

The controversy over whether white authors can write successfully for black children has not been resolved. It is to be hoped that the current titles are being judged by the criteria of good, worthwhile books rather than by whether they are written by black or white authors. Nevertheless, a great need remains for more books on high interest/low reading levels on subjects of interest to urban children. Children's librarians like Lillie Patterson and Sharon Bell Mathis have sought to meet this need with excellent easy-to-read biographies. The poetry of Langston Hughes, Nikki Giovanni, Gwendolyn Brooks, and other black poets provides identity and inspiration for black American children. John Steptoe, Lucille Clifton, Eloise Greenfield, and others have provided realistic fiction of contemporary urban life on varied levels. Perhaps another challenge to children's librarians who live so close to the lives of their young readers will be to write books filling the need for more material for black urban children.

Where reading levels are low, book selection increases in importance, and multi-media materials should have the purpose of help and motivation toward reading as well as that of entertainment. Materials must be provided which give children a positive self-image, a sense of their identity, a knowledge of their racial contribution to civilization and to America, an appreciation of their cultural heritage and of their own potential for future achievement; but they also must have books that they are able to read. With the advent of television, multi-media materials and audiovisual equipment so readily available that many children (and adults) feel less need to acquire better reading skills. The substitution of filmstrips, records, and other media to compensate for a lack of literacy is not preparing children for a life in which they must compete with adults proficient in reading.

The addition of such media should be directed toward aid and motivation in reading as well as toward entertainment value. Libraries in inner city areas would benefit by having reading programs for children similar to the Adult Basic Education courses that many urban libraries have become involved in presenting. Tutoring programs and basic reading courses for children in a setting oriented toward leisure or pleasure could provide greater inspiration toward reading for enjoyment than the classroom situation. It might also alleviate the need for so many adult education programs in the future. It is encouraging to note that many libraries at present are advocating a return of libraries to reading as a basic element.

Story hours, both formal and informal, have always been one of the most important activities of children's libraries. One of the oldest arts and forms of communication despite the charm of audiovisuals, no pleasure for librarians or children surpasses the intimate relationship of a story told aloud. The first introduction for many children to the library is the picture-book story hour. Many children's librarians also plan read-aloud times and book discussion clubs, and few children's librarians neglect to have some type of summer reading program. Whatever their origin or content, though, programs must be varied and structured to meet the needs of the community served.

One important fact should be noted concerning the inner city librarian. The inner city library is not the place for the children's librarian who measures success by traditional library statistics. One working in such a community must realize the value of one-to-one service, must learn to cope with the unpredictability of program attendance, and must above all be dedicated. Furthermore, the inner city children's librarian is very much on his or her own resources; there are few affluent Friends of the Library groups upon which to rely. If the challenge seems too overwhelming, one should bear in mind that there are children's librarians in urban situations doing all of the things mentioned and more. The reward of the librarian in the inner city is that her one can truly feel that he or she fulfills the promise of librarianship as a service profession, the librarian's desire to be needed.

CHILDREN'S LIBRARY SERVICE AND THE FUTURE

What of the future of library service to children? With changing patterns of library service, discussions of eliminating children's service as a separate entity, and inter-shelving of children's and adult's collections, will special service to children in public libraries become a thing of a past era? With dwindling budgets in city library systems, closing of city branches and the absence of children's librarians in many of those remaining open, will service to the nation's children be found only in school instructional materials centers? With library school students discouraged by the idea of long hours and Saturday work in public libraries, elimination of non-teaching positions, and library schools placing less emphasis on children's service as a career, will children's librarianship survive as a viable career choice? Is there possibility of the replacement of the children's librarian by an AV or media specialist with more technical skill than empathy with children? How serious is the possibility that public librarians in the children's field will be forced to seek teacher certification to fit into school positions because of mergers of public library juvenile departments and school libraries?

Children's librarianship, since its beginning, has been an area in which opportunities for advancement while continuing to work with children have been limited. This has been both an asset and a liability. It has meant that those interested in economic advancement or prestigious fame have frequently moved out of children's service, while many who have remained have done so because of true dedication and a sincere belief in the importance of the reality of children's work as a field of librarianship. The question of whether there will ever be more promotional opportunities within children's library service can only be answered by the direction taken by children's services in the future.

What of the future of library service and black American children? It can not be denied that there is a need for more black professional librarians, including children's librarians. The library is broad-based in black non-professionals, with comparatively few black professionals at the top of the career ladder, and no imminent resolution of the problem of a bridge over the gap between the two classes. Since the close of the school of library science at Hampton Institute (Virginia) in 1939, Atlanta University, Alabama A&M, and North Carolina Central University remain the only ALA-accredited black schools supplying librarians to the field in large numbers. Correspondingly, Atlanta University has the most nearly complete data on black librarians employed or available for employment, although a few other schools are now compiling black librarian information. Encouragement of library schools and state libraries to provide more programs with financial aid to attract black people to the fifth year of graduate work required to become a professional children's librarian might be helpful. A study of the lines drawn between professional and non-professional workers and the establishment of some form of career development structure might also be helpful. In-service workshops and training courses for work with young people in urban black communities could also provide more workers trained in the philosophies and skills needed. The inner city library can not afford the professional hang-ups brought about by professional insecurity. Provisions should be made to train and use those persons available who are sincerely interested and capable of working with children in libraries.

Recognition of the types of programming most successful and most needed in black communities might increase the efficiency of libraries in inner city areas. An overall evaluation of the advantages and disadvantages of such experimental programs as Baltimore's High John the Conqueror program and Philadelphia's Action Library might also provide a key for further meeting the inner city library needs for children and young people.

Still more encouragement must be given to black writers and illustrators to provide more books that give all of America, not only black children, a greater understanding of black American life and culture. Much of the responsibility may fall upon independent or black publishers, but it is also a responsibility of white publishers. Concomitantly, there is greater need for black evaluation of materials in the area of selection, publishing, and editing. Editors and publishers, as well as librarians, should enforce a book selection policy that guards against discrimination and ensures proper recognition of minorities.

Furthermore, library administrators and others in charge of library funding must devise a more realistic method of allocating expenditures in inner city libraries, a method based on need rather than on circulation statistical figures (a method which invariably results in low budgets in areas where services are most sorely needed). Where library service is not easily available due to lack of neighborhood branches or understaffed facilities, black children are first to suffer. They miss receiving a library head-start and are deprived of their own cultural heritage, as well as denied the contact with the culture of mainstream America. In addition to neighborhood libraries, it would be of value to minorities if every large library system that serves minorities within its public area could plan one branch or library department with the idea of providing a collection strong in the materials important to that minority group, with relevant staffing.

The development of America has been as much an evolutionary process as a revolutionary one. It is comparable to the creation of a mosaic. In the process of the development of the art work, the colors of black America were almost always omitted. Concentration on this area in recent years has been necessary in order to provide American history, literature, and culture with the needed depth and color to complete a true picture of American life. Once this has been done, the task is one of merging it into the whole and maintaining it as a part of the American scene.

One looks forward to the day when black caucuses are no longer needed to protect the special concerns of black librarians or black library patrons, or to be assured that black American children are getting their share of library expenditures and service. The American Library Association took a major step in the right direction when a firm stand was taken against discrimination in libraries. We now ask if the present form of library services is adequately serving the black American children. Shall we split children up into white children and black children, Asian, and Native American while all are living together in the same country? As long as we adults continue to do this in our minds, will not the children continue to do likewise and view each other with suspicion and distrust? All children need the best available in libraries, in librarians, and in the quality of books. Best in libraries does not necessarily refer to the highest degreed librarians, but to those persons most sincerely dedicated to accomplishing the purpose of helping children to become well adjusted, literate, self-confident, adult human beings, prepared to share in making the world a better place for all.

Until we have solved the urban problems that are challenging all of America today, the problem of the deteriorating quality of life in our American cities, there will be need for children's librarians—both black and white—with the dedication and inspiration to lift children above the sordidness and inadequacies of their environment, to give them the knowledge and the power to help them reach beyond the present limits; to let them know that they, too, are a part of America, and that there is more to life than that which seems evident today.

BIBLIOGRAPHIES RELATED TO
BLACK AMERICAN CHILDREN'S LITERATURE

Titles that are no longer listed in *Books in Print* are listed as o.p. They are included here because they are still available in many libraries and may be consulted for perspective.

Africa, an annotated list of printed materials suitable for children, selected by a Joint Committee of the American Library Association Children's Services Division and the African-American Institute. Information Center on Children's Cultures, U.S. Committee for UNICEF, 1968. (o.p.)

"Black Culture Series for Young Readers," selected by the Chicago Public Library. In *The Ebony Handbook*. Chicago, Johnson Publishing Company, Inc., 1974. p. 190.

The Black Experience in Children's Audio-Visual Materials. Sponsored by North Manhattan Project, Countee Cullen Regional Branch. New York Public Library, Office of Children's Services, The Branch Libraries, 8 East 40th St., New York 10016, 1974.

The Black Experience in Children's Books. Selected by Barbara Rollock. New York, The New York Public Library, 1974. (Originally *Books about Negro Life for Children*, by Augusta Baker)

Dodd, Barbara. *Negro Literature for High School Students.* National Council of Teachers of English, 1111 Kenyon Road, Urbana, Illinois 61801, 1968.

Jackson, Miles M., Jr., ed. *A Bibliography of Negro History and Culture for Young Readers.* Published for Atlanta University by University of Pittsburgh Press, 1969.

Johnson, Harry A. *Multimedia Materials for Afro-American Studies.* New York, R. R. Bowker, 1971.

Katz, William Loren. *Teacher's Guide to American Negro History.* Chicago, Franklin Watts, 1968.

Koblitz, Minnie W., ed. *The Negro in Schoolroom Literature.* New York, The Center for Urban Education, o.p.

Latimer, Bettye I., ed. *Starting Out Right: Choosing Books about Black People for Young Children, Pre-School through Third Grade.* Washington, D.C., Day Care and Child Development Council of America. (Originally from Wisconsin Department of Public Instruction.)

Mills, Joyce W., ed. *The Black World in Literature for Children: Print and Non-Print Materials.* Atlanta, School of Library Service, Atlanta University, 1975

Red, White and Black: Minorities in America. Briarcliff Manor, N.Y., Combined Paperback Exhibit, 1969. This list was prepared for display at the American Library Association Conference, Atlantic City, in June 1969. (o.p.)

Rollins, Charlemae, ed. *We Build Together: A Reader's Guide to Negro Life and Literature for Elementary and Junior High School Use.* Urbana, Ill., National Council of Teachers of English, 1967.

Schmidt, Nancy J. *Children's Books on Africa and Their Authors: An Annotated Bibliography.* New York, Africana Publishing Company, 1975.

ADDITIONAL BOOK SELECTION AIDS

Broderick, Dorothy. *Image of the Black in Children's Fiction.* New York, Bowker, 1973.

Interracial Books for Children Bulletin. New York, Council on Interracial Books for Children. Eight issues per year, 1966– .

MacCann, Donnarae, and Gloria Woodard. *The Black American in Books for Children: Readings in Racism.* Metuchen, N.J., Scarecrow Press, 1972.

17. School Libraries and Black American Children

by   Ann Stewart Watt, Associate, Bureau of School Libraries, New York State Education Department

INTRODUCTION

In the context of government managed and government supported agencies, the literature of the profession, the courts, and public sentiment attests to a peerless role for education:

> Education is more than the impartation of information. At bottom, it is the molding of the character and personality of the young—the process through which children take on the motives, attitudes, and beliefs, the knowledge and skills, the ways of thinking, feeling and acting sanctioned by the society in which they live. . . . Education includes more than schooling. But in every society in which the school has existed, it has been established and supported primarily in order to ensure the "reproduction of the type." A society is not a collection of discrete individuals. It is a group of individuals bound together by a common pattern of behavior and belief, institutions and attitudes. But these individuals . . . do not transmit this pattern through the genes. They can maintain it from generation to generation only through education of the young. . . . In every land . . . the school undertakes to mold a specific kind of character and personality, able and willing

to participate effectively in the life of the society served by the
school. Hence education is ultimately a *moral* and *political*, as
well as an *intellectual* affair. [Emphasis supplied.]   Moreover, the
educator is the vicar of society; that is to say, he derives his authority
to educate in one way rather than in another from the society which,
as a teacher, he represents. But few civilized societies want to have
their culture reproduced exactly as it stands. It is, rather, an
idealized version of the culture that the school is expected to nurture
in its pupils.[1]

Here is an unparalleled, fundamental, institutional role, proclaiming both social and personal benefit. In American education, the ideals are the "Protestant work-ethic," honesty, fair play, the democratic way, respect for authority, "let each become all that he is capable of becoming," freedom, protection under the law, the land of opportunity, the highest living standard for the largest number of its population than any other country in the world. Realistically, this is juxtaposed against the rape of American Indians; a nation born through a bloody Revolutionary War; police brutality; a court and prison system weighted against the poor; draft evaders; Watergate; unjust wars; an institution of slavery which formed an ignominious cornerstone of this nation's flourishing free enterprise economy; a condescending attitude toward the education and role of women; large numbers of unemployed college graduates; an unconscionable use of three-fifths of the world's resources by one-fifth of its population; the assassinations of presidents, a presidential candidate, and a peaceful civil rights leader; calculated discrimination against the poor; a representative form of government that has 80 percent of its representatives drawn from the top third of the economic levels; and a nation where 80 percent of the wealth is held by 20 percent of the population.

If the public education system is to continue to have the support of the average taxpayer, the system must of course give "lip service" to the ideals of our culture rather than the realities. Yet, if it is to produce viable results, it must develop among its students, teachers, and administrators pedagogically sound approaches that give recognition to reality. Indeed, if it is to hold its clients beyond the limits of the compulsory age of attendance, it is obliged to become conversant with reality.

[A] major function of the American School seems to be an attempt
to insulate youth from the realities of life. This is especially true in
terms of a child's relationships to the adult world. The very real
generation gap in America is testimony to the success of schools in
separating the nation's youth from their elders. During the early teen
years when the transition from childhood to adulthood has just begun,
a youth desperately needs the stimulation of being with more mature
persons. Instead, the "adolescent island" realized by Ralph Tyler has
been created. Under the American system youths are systematically

---

[1] William O. Stanley et al., *Social Foundations of Education* (New York: Dryden, 1956), pp. 287-88.

excluded from fulfilling this need by being secluded in classrooms with their own age group. This isolation from the mainstream of society permits very little opportunity to learn about life from those who are grappling daily with the terrible, wonderful complexities of living in this modern age.[2]

Today's world of media will not permit the school the luxurious monopoly it once enjoyed in dispensing facts, attitudes, and values. It is in this media arena that the school library media center finds its validity as it accepts the challenge of education as a moral, political, and intellectual affair.

In placing emphasis on strategies and approaches to reach the needs and interests of young black students, one attempts to close a gap in the professional literature because concern for such approaches has been so long neglected and alien to the realm of "good education" and "real or relevant curriculum." This writer believes that any pedagogically sound program developed for or about culturally or ethnically different students would be of value for *all* students. An approach to multi-cultural studies that separates that content from the major ongoing curriculum emphases in our schools is an essentially useless afterthought. The proliferation of ethnic studies programs and the utilization of resources acquired in support of those programs rests on a very weak foundation without a comprehensive, interrelated approach.

Celia Burns Stendler and William E. Martin make this point, and others equally valid, in a more eloquent and definitive way in *Intergroup Education in Kindergarten-Primary Grades*:

> Principle 1. Intergroup education should be an integral part of democratic education; it should not be taught as a separate unit nor by singling out a minority group for special study.
>
> Principle 2. A school program which utilizes many different kinds of activities to build desirable intergroup attitudes will be more effective than one which relies upon a single approach.
>
> Principle 3. A program of intergroup education must help children to understand that members of minority groups are human beings who think and act like human beings.
>
> Principle 4. Intergroup education will be more effective if it is carried on with the total group rather than with individuals in a classroom.
>
> Principle 5. In so far as possible, the teacher should begin intergroup education with the close-at-hand, not the far-away.[3]

This posture has far-reaching implications for school library media centers serving black American children. Given the moral, political, and intellectual dimensions of education, these centers are challenged to give recognition to the depth and breadth of the black experience as it has been documented by the media and as it

---

[2] Lyndon Furst, "The Educational Fifth Column: An Expanded Role for Teachers," *Phi Delta Kappan* LVII, No. 1 (September 1975), p. 9.

[3] Celia Burns Stendler and William E. Martin, *Intergroup Education in Kindergarten-Primary Grades* (New York: Macmillan, 1953), pp. 57-61.

is known to black students. After eight years, the Kerner Report has not been proved inaccurate in its declaration: "Our nation is moving toward two societies, one black, one white—separate and unequal."[4]

INTERACTION OF BLACK CHILDREN WITH THE SCHOOL LIBRARY

Most black American children live in racially and economically segregated communities and attend schools that predominantly enroll students of their own racial background. The major organizations of the community—the churches, civic and social groups—follow this demarcation to a degree as well.

> [If] along with Ruth Benedict, A. L. Koreber, Franz Boas, and Melville Herskovits, one can assume that no particular way of life is superior, but rather than all culture is functional in nature (including lower-class or minority group culture), it is legitimate to expect, nay insist, that the public school of America meet the expectations of the youth of any given social class. These expectations can be "aspirationally" middle class in nature, or they can be those that will enable youth to cope better, in a highly relevant way, with their present life situation. If the life styles of minority groups and the lower class are granted functional validity, and if the school as a social institution creates programs based on the environmental and motivational correlates of this culture, then by this action the school would truly reflect the most cherished wishes of an operational democracy.[5]

The professional in school librarianship cannot ignore the clear moral challenge here. The library must be neutral turf. When the library is open to students to come in other than as class groups, many opportunities for pupil interaction present themselves. There is a constant need for techniques to lead pupils of different backgrounds to encounters with each other as educational experiences, to the end that they will learn skills of citizenship commensurate with the era of which they are a part. The librarian plans and conducts group activities such as role playing, dramatization, play reading, book discussions, media production, debates, choral reading, and peer teaching that mix pupils of varied backgrounds for meaningful interaction. The library club encourages participation from all types of students. Athletic, intellectual and artistic individuals can participate in book reviewing and book chats. The interaction is a vehicle for increased opportunities to develop leadership and initiative among young people, to establish wholesome intercultural peer relationships that may carry over into social, after-school pursuits. Such restructuring of groups and patterns of association is important for the black child, who frequently finds artificial age group barriers restrictive and fixed roles oppressive. The chance to enter another's role may lead to an understanding of another's point of view or rights.

---

[4] U.S. Riot Commission, *Report of the National Advisory Commission on Civil Disorders* (New York: Dutton, 1968), p. 1.

[5] Maurie Hillson, "The Reorganization of School: Bringing about a Remission in the Problems Faced by Minority Children," *Phylon: The Atlanta University Review of Race and Culture* XXVIII, No. 3 (1967), p. 231.

The rules established for the media center give lessons in morality. How often are students told they cannot take out another book because they have not returned an earlier one? Is care taken to see that students document sources used in preparing assignments? Are the assignments sufficiently differentiated, challenging, and meaningful to discourage students from copying each others' work? Does the library media specialist stand by while students Xerox mathematics homework with a few handwritten alterations to "confuse" the teacher? What kinds of selection and weeding practices are followed? What critical reviewing processes are used to validate the acquisition or retention of a title? Are enough resources available to present both sides of controversial issues fairly? Is the school's student handbook available in appropriate language and on cassette for students with reading difficulties? Are materials available on rights of students and young people? Have reasonable safeguards been established to prevent theft and vandalism? Are circulation procedures free from arbitrary restrictions? Is the child's privacy protected so that he feels free to ask: "My mother wants to know if she writes a letter to the landlord and she mad with him do she still have to start the letter with 'Dear'?" or other more revealing questions? A pupil requesting material for a parent should not be denied it. If pages must be reproduced or a limited loan period is set, this should be explained in a brief note to the parent. To deny the loan arbitrarily is to miss an opportunity to reinforce the importance of library resources and services to people in every level of life.

Is there a difference in the quality of assignments prepared under the supervision of the library media center staff and those done independently? Does something happen in the media center that contributes to the student's development, or is it a place to "fool around"? Whose responsibility is it to make the time productive when the students don't have assignments? How often do students and teachers get feedback from the library media center staff on the positive behavior that is observed? What prejudices do we transmit about black youths when we say they are irresponsible and deny a youngster, who regularly takes the family wash three blocks in a crime-ridden ghetto to the laundromat, the right to borrow a cassette or a filmstrip and viewer for home use? Do we reach out to students in a humane way or do they feel that to get our attention they must be disruptive? Have we anticipated their needs, interests, and enthusiasm?

Black students need the opportunity to develop pride in themselves, in their abilities, and in their schools and libraries. Along this line, many of the tasks performed in libraries can be performed by students under supervision. This is not to be construed as exploitation; it is to voice a need for paid student aides who review new materials, check in new materials, file, shelve, prepare displays and labels, write order cards, type notices and bibliographies, read stories, prepare cassette instructions on use of equipment, prepare mixed media presentations, suggest cross references and make copy slips for catalog cards.

Their involvement pays off in the development of a proprietary sense of responsibility for the library and its materials. The librarian cannot fail with this level of involvement to become more conversant with the needs, interests, and abilities of the young people (s)he serves. Students have library tasks, procedures, and standards of behavior translated into terms that are meaningful to them. Teachers have contact with pupils who can search for resources. Students get a chance to try on various types of career shoes. All of them won't, of course, become librarians, but careers in production, commercial art, teaching, and writing can be promoted through specialized library assignments. Consider James S. Coleman's projections in *Psychology Today* (February 1972), "The Children Have Outgrown the Schools":

> It is not clear just what the shape of future schools will be, but they must not have as their primary goal the teaching of children. Anomalous as this principle may seem, it is the key to successful educational institutions of the future. The failure to recognize this principle is a major source of malaise in present schools.
>
> Only if the new institutions resist the temptation to direct themselves principally to teaching the child can they fruitfully redirect their goals. One of these goals must be the development of strategies for coping with an information-rich and institutionally complex society; another must be the use of external activities where children are not students but contributors to a larger enterprise. Working with others under the discipline imposed by a common task and purpose is incompatible with the wholly individualistic goal of learning around which current schools are organized. And such involvement is necessary to provide both a direction to life and the motivation to learn how to implement it.

ASSEMBLING RELEVANT LIBRARY MATERIALS

It would be naive to ignore the fact that education is a political affair in America. Politics, defined as the science and art of government, is synonymous with power, and the degree of power one holds is determined by all those socioeconomic factors that balance against absolute tyranny. The prime factors in power are survival, followed by economics. First, then, the school must aid the black child to survive if he is to be a political entity. For the media center to be useful for young black students, then, it must acquire broad resources in the areas of mental health, physical fitness, the value of proper nutrition, and the dangers of drug abuse, including alcohol and tobacco. Resources that identify community agencies and legal rights are also needed. Beyond this, the will to seek to enjoy a wholesome quality of life is to be encouraged. As the effective library media specialist knows, it is not enough to simply purchase relevant resources. Some motivation must be given to encourage use of that information:

- Clusters of relevant resources (periodicals, books, pamphlets, filmstrips, filmloops, slides, transparencies, and tapes set up for viewing or listening) are gathered on a shelf, table or carrel captioned "Skillexchange" a figure control/physical development area with students giving demonstrations along with the media display. Names of students could be posted who are willing to give instruction in these areas in exchange for instruction or tutoring in another area.
- A "Budget Beauty Bar" with instructions and samples of health and beauty aids made from simple household substances such as lemons, baking soda, epsom salts, witch hazel, mineral oil, etc.
- "Economy Chef's Shelf" featuring cookbooks and other sources of menus and recipes emphasizing preparation of nutritious, inexpensive meals and party snacks.

- The library can provide assistance to community health and social agencies serving parents and children, e.g., Family Services, Family Court, Museums, Boys and Girls Clubs, Scouts, etc., by preparing bibliographies and kits of resources for loan highlighting the concerns of these agencies. This would include ecology projects, local history for the Bicentennial, problems of illness, divorce, personal adjustment, family disorganization.

- A "Baby-Sitter's Survival Kit" with first-aid information, types of emergency phone numbers needed, quiet games and activities, stories to read and tell, checklist for child's safety and the safety of the sitter.

Does this have anything to do with survival? When one reviews the infant mortality statistics among blacks, or the statistics on the institutionalized ill, the disabled and the life expectancy and imprisonment among blacks, the question is soon answered. More than one would like to admit, perhaps, there is a relationship between survival, quality of life and socioeconomic level. Social mobility and the comforts and luxuries of life are largely determined for children by the position or status of their parents. This position is largely, though not exclusively, attained through occupation. Black families are obviously the undergirding of survival for black children; they provide resiliency and insulation that buffer much of the racism youngsters meet away from home. Thus, resources on marriage, family life, and adjustment are valid acquisitions not only for the curriculum and insight into the youngsters' present situations but also for the many who are teenage parents.

Similarly, relationships among siblings in black families are found to be warm, with older siblings frequently having or assuming a responsibility for younger ones. So that these students may reinforce their own knowledge as well as assist the younger members of their families, in cooperation with the public library, older students should be encouraged to prepare models or projects using library resources to explain scientific and mathematical principles to younger children (e.g., Why does water boil?, Why does the moon come out at night?) with suggestions for observations the younger ones can make with their parents or sisters and brothers.

Using the home as an environment for early childhood and primary grade learning, both agencies could gather resources with suggestions for parents as to how concepts of shapes, colors, sizes, directions, order, contrasts and similarities, letter and number recognition, alphabetical and ordinal arrangement, following directions, and listening skills can be developed using everyday objects found in the home and children's ETV programs.

Take a cross-generation view of a local community, with vignettes of what the activities, setting, dress, and customs were during grandparents' childhood, parents' childhood and contemporary childhood and then make projections for the future. This could be banked in research into local history (newspapers, etc.) and illuminated by personal reminiscences.

The most consistent popular assessment of the quality of our schools is that the "good" schools are the ones attended by children from affluent or upper middle-class families. If this is an accurate assessment, then the chances of black students attending "good" schools, except by such synthetic means as busing, are diminished with each quarter's economic survey showing a widening gap between median income in black and white households and increasing unemployment among black males over 18. The need, then, for assistance in the development of coping strategies for economic exigencies is one to which the effective library media specialist serving black students responds:

- Clusters of relevant resources (periodicals, books, pamphlets, filmstrips, filmloops, slides, transparencies and tapes set up for viewing or listening, patterns for woodworking, needlework, or other crafts and art projects) could be gathered around a partly completed or a finished do-it-yourself project. Community craftsmen could spend time working on a project in the center so that students could interview them and/or watch demonstrations.
- "Resources to Recycle Rejects" emphasizing resources including periodical and newspaper clippings on how to make discarded household items and clothing useful once more. The display could show the discarded item in original form, directions taken from media resources, and materials, tools utilized, and the new item.
- A "Trading Post" where comic books, old magazines, paperbacks, records, toys, games, coupons, sewing patterns may be swapped.
- "Teen Task Force" could compile a listing of the service jobs they could offer; not only the traditional car washing, snow shovelling, window washing, babysitting, but also children's birthday party management or assistance, circular delivery service, pet and plant care or messenger and delivery services.
- A "Toyshop" display of homemade games and toys with directions for constructing them from the originator or from library resources.
- A "Micro-Mini-Course in Comparison Shopping," with a student made slide-tape kit showing costs of popular items—camera, mini-bike, tennis racquet, gym shoes, 8-track stereo, leather coat, purse, boots—purchased from different sources and using different payment plans.

Further, these students need to be convinced, despite a heritage of slavery that attests to the contrary, that work is honorable, can be remunerative at a level that provides more than mere subsistence, and employment can be found in a field that is satisfying. As many opportunities as the center can provide should be given to create an alliance between guidance counselors, representatives of varied career fields, and students, so that they may visit and interview people for firsthand views. Hence, a resource file of black and white community persons would be a well-advised undertaking. It will be especially important to provide the breadth and background found in biographies, biographical fiction, and drama behind some of the "glamourous" careers. Students who are aspiring to a legal career, for example, should share their reactions to the insights found in *To Kill a Mockingbird* with an empathetic, informed attorney.

The library media specialist who finds himself or herself serving black students, then, is not likely to be in one of the "best" schools according to the criterion above. Yet the responsibility to make education an intellectual affair—support and expand the curriculum, provide support for in-service to teachers, and challenge students to excellence—is both the charge and the reward of the position.

In providing inspiration as a springboard for creativity or providing opportunities for growth in appreciation of beauty, both the school and public library can support the humanities. Toward that end, collections of framed reproductions, recordings, as well as resources about composers or artists need to be circulated, and the appearance of a local or guest artist could be highlighted with relevant resources. Evidence of fine local architecture, landscape design, artistry, and craftsmanship may receive heightened appreciation by the community with similarities and contrasts being made with national or world-wide counterparts, this through research in appropriate library resources emphasizing both design and historical perspective.

The library media center serving black students should facilitate the integration of knowledge and disciplines. Not only then are parallels drawn that illuminate the black experience in this country, that help the student to be more competent in his present everyday pursuits and concerns, but stimulation is given to broaden and give depth to the concepts taught in classes. For example, teaching about the human body and the circulatory system could include information on Robert E. Gross, Adrian Kantrowitz, Daniel Hale Williams, or Charles Drew, which would add breadth to the unit by providing integrated corollary learning.

CLASSROOM TEACHERS AND SCHOOL LIBRARY SPECIALISTS

The library media specialist who expects to have an impact on the intellectual development of students is committed to working with classroom teachers to reach curriculum-related achievement goals. The faculty must be convinced that learning can take place in the media center and that something pedagogically sound happens to children there. In order to be of assistance to teachers, then, library media specialists know the curriculum, know the collection, and are supportive of sound educational objectives and practices. This is significant in keeping morale high among teachers, who frequently are frustrated and even bitter over assignments to predominantly black schools with their attendant inferior facilities and materials. Since many of these teachers are inexperienced in the profession and less than knowledgeable of black life styles, assistance to them is all the more crucial.

Jerome S. Bruner writes:

> The first object of any act of learning over and beyond the pleasure it may give, is that it should serve us in the future. Learning should not only take us somewhere; it should allow us later to go further more easily.

He then states that there are two ways in which learning serves the future:

> One is through its specific applicability to tasks that are highly similar to those we originally learned to perform. . . . A second way in which earlier learning renders later performance more efficient is through what is conveniently called nonspecific transfer of principles and attitudes.[6]

---

[6]Jerome S. Bruner, *The Process of Education* (New York: Vintage Books, 1963), p. 17.

It is with the issues of achieving interdisciplinary approaches in instruction, so that learning takes students somewhere and later allows them to go further more easily, and providing professional support for teachers that the remainder of this paper is concerned.

BIBLIOGRAPHIC AND REFERENCE SERVICES

In the midst of the daily whirl of activity an expectation exists on the part of many teachers that at some point the librarian will send out a list from the library. Students frequently have the same expectation. Library media specialists feel compelled to prepare lists if for no other reason than to advertise new wares.

Yet, there is a gap between expectation, delivery, and utilization in the matter of bibliographic services, just as there is in many other services of the center. Bibliographies may have many uses such as reading guidance, bibliotherapy, literature appreciation, puzzle solving, parent-community or inservice potential. Of interest here is the bibliography prepared by the library media specialist to support the curriculum unit and its inservice potential.

The most frequent response of the library media specialist in this matter is "There's never enough time to do bibliographies. Nobody pays any attention to them anyway. They just throw them in the wastebasket in the teachers' room." Visits with teachers and administrators have revealed "There just isn't enough material in the media center (to individualize instruction). It's hard to find what you want in the media center." Interestingly enough, this dichotomy is documented in the literature that addresses itself to what library media specialists do and what teachers want them to do.

The use of the term "bibliography" here has a multi-media connotation that includes a list of sources, classified by author, subject, or period with appropriate indication of point of retrieval and relevance. It is conceived of as a card file component of the resource unit, since the card file accommodates continual updating.

> A teaching unit is a collection of objectives, activities, materials, etc., on a specific topic, prepared by a teacher for a specified time, to be used with a particular group of learners. It often is carefully, logically sequenced. Many ideas in the teaching unit may have come, in turn, from a resource unit . . . A resource unit is a collection of suggested objectives, activities, and *sources* [emphasis supplied] on a broad topic, prepared by a group of people for a wide age or grade level range of learners, to be used by a teacher in planning a teaching unit. . . . If one visits schools and classrooms where exemplary teaching is taking place; if one reads suggestions for the improvement of teaching by subject matter experts or by curriculum leaders; if one reviews the few fragments of research that exist on the effects of this organization of teaching plans, such as that reported by the National Council for the Social Studies, unit teaching is close to the crux of recommended organization of content, process, and attitudes for use by learners.[7]

---

[7]Marcella Hannah Nerbovig, *Unit Planning: A Model for Curriculum Development* (Worthington, Ohio: Charles A. Jones Publishing Co., 1970), pp. 4-7.

The bibliographic services of the library media specialist are useful to assist in the development of the curriculum resources unit in the following ways:
1. Structure of the unit to insure depth and breadth topic
2. Interdisciplinary approaches to instruction
3. Multi-media approaches to instruction
4. Provisions for optional instructional tasks
5. Development of cooperative/team patterns of instruction
6. Individualization of tasks for learners.

In the areas of staff development of and development of library media services to support the curriculum, the bibliographies provide:
    a. An assessment of the adequacy of the collection
    b. An exploration into the resources available through inter-library loan provisions
    c. An identification of items to be considered for acquisition.

When teachers, curriculum specialists and library media specialists plan a unit cooperatively, utilizing the media center, certain basic tools are available. First, the professional collection is culled to gather materials on methodology, teachers' manuals for series texts, State Education Department and school district curriculum guides (annotated to show what resources are available in the school library media center), professional eclectic bibliographies and section guides, catalogs of new resources, and materials developed by other teachers. The reference collection provides encyclopedias (both general and special subject), indexes and other reference sources (such as film catalogs and union catalogs from other libraries), vertical files, and a community resources file. The card catalog and shelf list complete the search for circulating print and non-print resources. Special services include ETV programming via video, student production, and inter-library loan referrals.

In schools following the traditional subject matter program, where teaching is based for the most part on a textbook with perhaps one or two supplementary books, there is little occasion for the use of library materials. In the more creative and dynamic elementary school programs which are now becoming widely developed, extensive use of library materials becomes an absolute necessity. In school systems where there is close connection between the curriculum and the library, the library collection is developed and planned in the light of curriculum needs. . . .
Many courses of study are now organized so that they require the extensive use of library resources, and include in the course of study bibliographies related to each unit of work. Frequently these "unit bibliographies" include page references in specific books and give suggestions for the use of related library materials. The materials listed in the unit bibliographies include various levels of reading in order to take care of the individual reading capacities in any class. Including library references in courses of study is one of the most effective ways of assuring a close connection between the library and the curriculum. Where extensive use is made of library materials, it becomes important to include such references in courses of study as a means of saving time for both teachers

and children. While it might appear that this procedure would deprive children of needed opportunity to do reference work, it will be found in practice that this is not the case.[8]

The bibliography eliminates the need to remove large segments of the collection for lengthy periods from their normal location. By avoiding this type of "spoon feeding," the students' retrieval skills are reinforced, and they grow in the ability to function independently in their own local libraries as well as others. In this way, each time the media specialist assists, it is done in such a way as to make the student more independent in a similar setting. The bibliography is not designed to discourage students from finding additional resources. The entire bibliography is available; however, students would generally be given the references and general topic resources and be directed in their search for specific sources. The need for such direction would then decrease as students become more familiar with the patterns and logic of research methodology. Indeed, up through junior high school, the exceptional student should be assigned research in written form that culminates in more than a thoroughly researched, annotated bibliography. The results of these student explorations may be added to the resource unit's bibliography file after being assessed by teachers and the library media specialists for usefulness.

Using this approach, students have more time to examine and absorb data from the available resources and to decide on the materials that would be useful in the creative tasks that are assigned. Students thereby become increasingly aware of the interrelated nature of learning as they experience creativity banked in research. Utilizing this approach, then, students creating a time-line mural of U.S. history from the Age of Exploration up through the Emancipation Proclamation would not show a red Volkswagen in the 1855 scene of an antebellum plantation.

While teachers will most appropriately be involved in the resource selections for curriculum bibliographies, this writer believes that library media specialists should assume the leadership for their development. The most important reason for this is that the broadest single collection of organized materials, in the greatest variety of formats, ideally is located in the library media center, for both economy of acquisition and administration and for greatest utilization. Resources housed in other areas of the building are keyed there, selection tools and tools for the organization of resources are there, and professional time and resources are not wasted in replication of units by individual classroom teachers. A structure for drawing on the holdings in other, larger, or more specialized library collections, and a constant feedback for evaluation of the collection and for filling gaps in need of curriculum resources exists there as well.

This may appear to be a time-consuming approach, but it is time well spent. As the bibliographies are developed, they become part of the library media specialists' and teachers' professional repertoire. The procedure is telescoped as one becomes accustomed to working in this mode. While a single library media specialist may develop not more than three or four such bibliographies per year, it is incumbent upon each of us to reach out to colleagues in the profession and share those that have been developed, so that all children are enriched and all teachers

---

[8] Jewel Gardiner, *Administering Library Service in the Elementary School* (Chicago, American Library Association, 1954), p. 23.

grow. This practice of bibliographic support bears an honest relationship to teaching and learning that does not leave one apologizing for or rationalizing the worth of a media specialist in the school.

The process for organizing commercial materials to meet the curriculum needs of a reading program is especially well-delineated in Wayne Otto and Eunice Askov's *Wisconsin Design for Reading Skill Development: Rationale and Guidelines*. Davies has a useful outline for the study of world cultures in social studies in her book, *The School Library: A Force for Educational Excellence* (1969), that closely parallels the one suggested by Jarolimek in *Social Studies in Elementary Education*. The Davies source is strong in suggestions for other curriculum areas as well. Also useful in this regard is the New York State Education Department, Bureau of School Libraries' minipaper, "The Effective Elementary School Library."

NEW EFFORTS FOR STRENGTHENING PROGRAMS

Finally, this writer would make two other pleas to the library media specialist serving black students. First, do not allow standards of achievement to be diluted out of condescension; provide a level of service that reinforces the best teaching practice. A sixth grade teacher once asked her class for a synonym for the word "clean." One student volunteered "Not dirty." "Use just one word," the teacher responded. "Neat" was another reply. "Tidy" was another. Finally, the superintendent who was observing, said, "I want to hear a sixth grade level synonym." A seemingly disinterested youngster turned to him and said "Fastidious." Another volunteered "Impeccable." What you see (read, expect) is what you get.

Second, keep the center a place for students and teachers to work by providing an atmosphere conducive to learning, with displays that engage students and provisions for storage and easy retrieval of assignments or work in progress.

Library media specialists must keep the faith with their profession and with black students, not by doing the same thing over and over, or doing what everybody else is doing, but by breaking new ground, being movers and shakers, by being in the center of the action.

18. Multi-Media Resources, Libraries, and the Education of Black Ghetto Youth

by Robert B. Ford, Jr., Chief Librarian and Associate Professor, Medgar Evers College, City University of New York

Like all social institutions, American libraries in the twentieth century have been deeply affected by many external forces, especially by the ever-increasing expansion of knowledge and the resulting flood of available information. Perhaps the most significant of all these recent developments have been the rapid technological advances of computer science and the pervasive influence of mass media. In other words, the computer and the television set have radically changed the fabric of contemporary society. Since the library is a communication and information agency, it was inevitable that it, too, would change with the changing times. Melvil Dewey, writing in the first issue of the *American Library Journal,* was never more on target than when he observed: "the time *was* when a library was very like a museum and a librarian was a mouser in musty books . . . the time *is* when a library is a school, and the librarian is, in the highest sense, a teacher, and the visitor is a reader among the books as a workman among his tools."[1]

With the passage of time, the library has evolved from a mere book repository to a media and information center that must serve the diverse needs of one of the most pluralistic populations to be found on the face of this earth. Most perceptive observers would agree that this is a complex task, especially since information comes in many different forms, of which the book is only one. The focus of this essay is on the nonprint or multi-media resources that the modern library must possess in order to fully serve its patrons. Furthermore, the relationship between multi-media resources and the education of culturally different youth, who usually live in the black ghettos of this nation, will be explored.

Within the last decade, the library has been referred to as the information center, the instructional materials center, the educational media center, and finally, the learning resources center. The new labels suggest a perception of the library as a place where learning takes place rather than a place where materials are stored. This has been especially true of the school and the academic library because of its natural function of supporting instructional programs. By emphasizing a one-to-one student-teacher-librarian relationship that focuses on the individual student's academic achievement, the place of learning is no longer confined to the classroom but encompasses the entire learning complex, including the laboratory and the library. This concept has given rise to a new movement in education called the "library-college." It is, of course, best to remember that what takes place within the library is far more important than what it is called. However, as one author observed, the significance of the new appellations represent a "concerted effort to redefine the function of the library."[2]

As has been stated earlier, there has been a dramatic increase in the production of nonprint or multi-media materials. Marshall McLuhan, in his book *Understanding Media*, set the tone for a society dominated by sophisticated electronic communications technology. The knowledge explosion was already too great to be contained in books and came packaged as films, filmstrips, audio or video tapes, microform, phonorecords, etc. From all sides, the eyes and ears of modern man were frequently assailed by information emanating from the movie screen, the television set, or the high fidelity phonograph. In essence, a new information environment had been created whose main task was to "expand and train our consciousness—in order to exploit it."[3] In educational circles, Dr. Louis Shores, considered the father of the library-college concept, discussed the "generic book," that includes knowledge and information in all the various formats and media.

---

[1] Melvil Dewey, *The American Library Journal* 1:1, cited in *Library Journal* 101 (January 1, 1976): 1.

[2] Warren B. Hicks and A. M. Tillin, *Developing Multi-Media Libraries* (New York: Bowker, 1970), p. 4.

[3] Hans Mangus Enzensberger, "Industrialization of the Mind," *Partisan Review* 36 (Winter 1969): 105.

The modern library/resource center, in order to be truly effective, should be divided spatially into five areas to accommodate: (a) printed materials, (b) audio-visual materials, (c) materials (media) production, (d) television, and (e) computer/data processing. This is not to suggest that without sufficient space for these five activities a librarian cannot start to create a media center. In fact, the physical integration of print and nonprint resources is perhaps the most basic feature that distinguishes the progressive library from a more conventional one. To cite one author:

> In many instances, the integration of print and non-print resources is more beneficial for the user than is their separation . . . viewing and listening facilities can be incorporated within the area traditionally reserved for books.[4]

What must be continually stressed is that the modern library/resource center provides its patrons with sufficient access to information regardless of its format and creates an internal atmosphere conducive to achieving this goal.

At the risk of alienating many of my colleagues, this writer openly states that most librarians are too cautious and conservative to break away from the traditional pack. They are fearful of failure and refuse to try any new approach unless success can be guaranteed. Of course, the reality of the situation is that nothing is completely foolproof, but if one is courageous and resourceful, (s)he meets the challenge head-on. That is what is necessary to implement a successful program in a modern library/resource center; not sophisticated equipment or elaborate spatial arrangements or an unlimited budget, but a librarian who is enthusiastic, knowledgeable, and determined to make the concept work. As one writer has stated the case:

> The truly creative librarian is the one who realizes the vast potential of the multi-media library for increased services and who, even though all of the conditions are not ideal, initiates immediate action. . . . even though budget and space may be inadequate, he assures continuous library service by bringing knowledge to his patrons in all of its various and changing forms.[5]

A great deal of rhetoric exists in the profession about innovation. The time has come to move beyond the rhetoric and make the idea a reality. Before the idea can become reality, however, it is necessary to examine the attitudes toward media in the library profession. We have traditionally been a print-oriented profession and a certain aura of reverence has been created to preserve this fact. The problem is that technology has shattered that situation, and we can no longer afford the luxury of living in the past. In fact, the essence of this essay is that we, as a profession, must learn to cope with change. If not, there is a danger that some other group in the society will take over our function and that librarianship will cease to exist.

---

[4] Hicks and Tillin, p. 5.
[5] *Ibid.*, p. 9.

While generalizations are dangerous, this writer will presume that attitudes are a reflection of one's perspective; and the perspective of the library profession toward media has been too diverse and ambivalent. As one writer has observed:

> What seems needed is for the profession to arrive at an understanding of media as McLuhan saw them, as *codes of communication.* When media as a concept is limited to *audiovisual aids* or *nonprint*, when media mean filmstrips, transparencies, and simulation games, few are likely to deem such codes equal partners of the powerful and sophisticated language of words. But when media are viewed as those sources of information which dominate us, a total concept of a *new information environment* created only in the last hundred years becomes apparent.[6]

If one accepts the goals of librarianship, as expressed by the late Allie Beth Martin in her landmark study, *A Strategy for Public Library Change*, i.e., "to provide user-oriented service and information for all," then a new perspective, based on a new understanding of media as an integral part of a totally different information environment, is a basic necessity for all librarians.

One basic reason for many librarians' reluctance to accept media on the same level as the printed word may be traced to a basic fear of technology. This fear, as it is with so many fears, is based on a lack of knowledge and the "competent professional" feels that (s)he must never admit a lack of knowledge about something that (s)he *should know.* Professional reputation and, more important, ego, are placed in a perilous position. The fact of the matter is that simply no competent professional simply can know everything all of the time but must be adaptable enough to learn and relearn whatever is necessary to succeed in a given situation. Alvin Toffler, in one of the most significant books of recent vintage, *Future Shock*, warned us that: "new knowledge compels those for whom it is relevant ... to reorganize their store of images. It forces them to relearn today what they thought they knew yesterday."[7]

Another reason for the average librarian's relegation of media to second-class status lies in the way media courses are taught in library schools. There is too much theory and not enough practical experience in the use of audiovisual equipment. Although some would argue that the operation of equipment is a technician-level assignment, the mature librarian should know *how to do it* even if the need never arises.

Without giving serious consideration to the ramifications of the new information environment and the role that media must play therein, libraries will increasingly lose their vitality and credibility. Estelle Jussin, library school professor at Simmons, states it in the most succinct manner when she observes:

> The functions and services of all professions are determined by the technologies at their disposal. Librarianship is no exception. If the

---

[6] Deirdre Boyle, "Libraries and Media," *Library Journal* 101 (January 1, 1976): 126.
[7] Alvin Toffler, *Future Shock* (New York: Bantam Books, 1971), p. 157.

profession fails to understand and appropriately utilize the communications technologies which are available, it has failed in its social function.[8]

Let us briefly review and identify the spectrum of materials known as multimedia resources. Fundamentally, these materials can be divided into six categories: 1) *still-projection materials* such as filmstrips, microforms, etc., 2) *motion-projection materials* such as 8 and 16 millimeter films, video tapes, etc., 3) *audio materials* such as disc and tape recordings, 4) *flat graphic materials* such as art and study prints, charts, etc., 5) *three-dimensional materials* such as dioramas, games, globes, etc., and 6) *programmed materials* for individual study and use with teaching machines, etc. This constitutes, then, a broad range of materials that should be as carefully selected as are books and periodicals.

Two essential principles must be dealt with when selecting materials, regardless of format: a) a thorough knowledge of the user population and their needs, and b) a variety of information about the sources of all types of materials that fit the particular group of users that you serve. It is important to remember that criteria are only guidelines that must be flexible enough to be utilized in a variety of situations. Moreover, relevancy, which changes according to different conditions and clientele, must be constantly dealt with. There are seven criteria that are usually examined when evaluating materials under consideration for selection: authenticity, appropriateness, scope, interest, organization, special features and physical characteristics. When dealing with audiovisual materials, the technical quality of the product is especially important. The merits of multi-media resources should not be compared with their counterparts in printed form but must be judged in terms of the unique contribution that they can make toward satisfying the needs of that particular clientele.

After acquiring multi-media resources, decisions must be made about how they will be organized, processed, cataloged and circulated. These decisions will in turn generate certain rules and regulations that must avoid rigidity and permit sufficient flexibility in order to facilitate the patron's use of these resources. Certain questions must be faced, such as: does the format of these materials dictate the kind of circulation policy to be formulated? have the initial cost of or the subsequent expenses that will be needed for repair been taken under consideration when formulating the circulation policy? has the economic level of the community (in terms of availability of certain audiovisual equipment) been taken into account *before* formulating the policy? will the multi-media materials be classified and shelved together with the print materials or do restrictions of space dictate otherwise? if multi-media materials are *not* classified and shelved along with the monographic materials, will you use an accession number system?[9]

All of the answers to these questions will ultimately determine the level of service that your library/resource center will offer to its patrons. A great deal of libraries with which this writer is familiar make rules and regulations that favor the

---

[8] Estelle Jussim, comments cited by Deirdre Boyle "Libraries and Media," in *Library Journal* 101:128 (January 1, 1976).

[9] Hicks and Tillin, pp. 18-25.

library staff rather than the library patron. Avoidance of proliferating bureaucratic rules and regulations is greatly to be desired. However, rules and regulations are *not* holy writ; they *can* and *should* be changed when necessary. Often we get so institutionalized that we forget this basic premise.

With the above background material, then, it is appropriate to examine urban education in the ghetto and to explore the role of multi-media resources and educational (or instructional) technology might have in improving the situation. It is common knowledge in educational circles that urban education for minority youth has failed miserably. This failure can be attributed to several factors: an obsolete and irrelevant curriculum, inadequate teaching techniques, poorly trained teachers, a shrinking school budget that has no place for innovative programs, etc. In 1966, a report (entitled *Equality of Educational Opportunity*) was published by the U.S. Office of Education and was popularly referred to as the "Coleman Report." This 737-page report, based on data collected from more than 3,000 public schools representing 650,000 students in five grades, substantiates the failure in a statistical way that leaves no doubt that a crisis situation exists that is likely to explode into something very ugly. A distinguished educator, Dr. Kenneth B. Clark, has painted a picture that is stark and grim indeed:

> Urban public education is a national disaster ... a catastrophic, inefficient situation ... a social and political powder keg, awaiting just a capricious spark to set off a tremendous social explosion ... the public educational system has broken down in terms of fulfilling the responsibility of preparing these children [from low income families] for a meaningful role in our society ... drop-outs are excessive, and analysis of the drop-outs leaves at least this observer to believe that these children are probably more intelligent, in that they escape from a dehumanized and intolerable situation.[10]

Now, though Dr. Clark's comment may seem overly dramatic, there is no doubt in this writer's mind that his assessment describes the cold, hard facts of a real situation that could escalate into a overwhelming tragedy.

Somehow, this drift toward abject tragedy and despair must be reversed, but the redirection and revitalization must go beyond the cosmetic. A basic restructuring of the curriculum in urban education is in order. To design a curriculum that has relevance for the socially and economically deprived youth of this nation, mostly black, is a task that must be faced honestly if the school systems in our urban enclaves are to survive. To quote Harry Johnson, an outstanding black professor who is an educational media specialist:

> Our great concern is that of providing minority children and youth with an educational environment in which they can identify, and a secure and comfortable atmosphere in which they can continue to identify and learn; an atmosphere in which they value themselves as persons and take pride in their own ethnic heritage.[11]

---

[10] Kenneth B. Clark, "Unstructuring Education," *New Relationships in ITV* (Washington, D.C.: Educational Media Council, Inc., 1967), p. 8.

[11] Harry A. Johnson, *Multimedia Materials for Afro-American Studies* (New York: Bowker, 1971), p. ix.

This educational environment can be created through increasing individualized instruction, using multi-media resources, and building in instructional technology as an integral component of the educational process.

Before discussing the role of instructional technology as relates to the education of the urban poor, however, the background and characteristics of black ghetto youth must first be examined. Even though he lags behind his suburban counterpart academically, he has mastered the art of self-survival in a situation that is tenuous at best. Dr. Johnson has observed that "when he comes to school, [the ghetto youngster] comes with more of a complexity of burdens than any children anywhere in the world." Furthermore, when he gets to school, as if to add insult to injury, he is subjected to "the abuses of a battery of middle-class rules and regulations from middle-class school personnel with middle-class values and an obsolete middle-class curriculum planned around a scheduled set of time blocks that won't move an inch."[12] This presents an impossible situation, in which the ghetto youngster is programmed for failure and under-achievement from the outset.

Other characteristics also help define economically disadvantaged and culturally different young people. Their level of verbal articulation and expression is low, making it extremely difficult for them to understand the "textbook English" that they hear in the traditional classroom. Their perception discrimination is weak; they find it difficult to concentrate; their attention span is limited—all of these factors make it difficult for them to cope with abstract theories. Unfortunately, the grim realities of poverty and discrimination have also left them with low self-esteem and lower educational aspirations, since the hopelessness of ever escaping from the dismal ghetto has greatly influenced their behavior and their attitudes. Much has been written about the irrelevance of intelligence and standardized tests as they relate to culturally different youngsters. Since the test designers come from traditional middle-class backgrounds, the tests that they produce, likewise, measure middle-class experiences. It is only logical, therefore, that ghetto youngsters cannot be expected to do well on such tests. Finally, mention must be made about the relationship between student achievement and teacher expectations. Research has proven that when teachers expect low achievement, that is what they will most likely get from their pupils.

One of the most positive characteristics of ghetto youth relates to their unique learning style, and perhaps this characteristic lends itself most to the multi-media approach to learning. When planning strategies for working with ghetto youth, the wise educator would do well to remember that those patterns do, indeed, exist and should be taken into account.

If ghetto youth are, then, to be catapulated into the mainstream of our society, change must come to the urban educational system. There is no longer any question of whether change *will* come but, indeed, whether it will come fast enough to avoid the tragedy that I referred to earlier. The Commission on Instructional Technology has stated the problem in a most objective manner:

> Formal education is not responsive enough: the organization of schools and colleges takes too little account of even what is now known about the process of human learning, particularly of the range of individual

---

[12] *Ibid.*, p. 34.

differences among students ... moreover, formal education is, in an important sense, outmoded—students learn outside schools in ways which differ radically from the ways they learn inside school ... researchers in human learning agree that individuals differ markedly in the ways they learn, in the speed at which they learn, in their motivation to learn, and in what they desire to learn ... most schools and colleges are still locked into conventional patterns of grade structure, time span, and subject-matter division that fail to exploit each student's individual capacities, interests and personalities.[13]

Now, exploitation of the individual differences among students will prove to be the cutting edge that will radically change the educational environment in the ghetto.

In the last decade, we have heard a great deal of talk about systems analysis or the systems approach to various educational issues. In taking a system approach to the education of ghetto youth, many pieces of the puzzle fall into place: the redesign of the curriculum, the retraining of teachers and other school personnel, and last, but hardly least, the proper utilization of instructional media resources—each component acting and interacting with each other will produce a new educational process and environment that will result in quality education for ghetto youngsters. The systems approach will set up specific and explicit educational goals and behavioral objectives as an initial step in the process.

Individualized instruction is an important component in achieving quality education in the ghetto. The foundation of individualized instruction is programmed learning, i.e., materials organized in a logical manner, with frequent testing of the concepts presented, which permit the individual student to learn and advance at his own rate of speed. Through immediate feedback, a sense of confidence and mastery is achieved. Dr. Johnson notes that "study carrels and independent learning facilities equipped with single concept 8 millimeter film, record players, filmstrips, and color slides with earphones, lend a person-to-person excitement to learning."[14]

Two other recent developments in instructional technology and their potentialities for upgrading ghetto education will be considered briefly, computer-assisted instruction (C.A.I.) and educational television. Some educators believe that computer-assisted instruction is one of the greatest breakthroughs for individual instruction since the computer can serve large groups of students simultaneously. If one perceives the computer as a tool for problem solving, then, it can be more resourceful in a much shorter time span than an individual teacher can be. Dr. Johnson has observed:

> A ghetto school with limited resources, poorly prepared teachers, and a low level of achievement can turn to computers to make quick decisions based on assessments of student performance, and then match available resources to individual student needs.[15]

---

[13] Commission on Instructional Technology. *To Improve Learning: A Report to the President and the Congress of the United States* (Washington, D.C.: U.S. Gov't. Printing Office, March, 1970), p. 6.

[14] Johnson, p. 13.

[15] *Ibid.*, p. 16.

Many educators perceive educational television as one medium that has great potentialities for improving instruction in urban education. Many of us have watched the productions of the Children's Television Workshop, notably "Sesame Street" and "The Electric Company," and observed its positive influence on pre-schoolers and young people. Through careful and sensitive programming, many new horizons and vast reservoirs of knowledge could easily unfold for ghetto youth. Through this medium, a ghetto child's sense of ethnic heritage can be developed through programs that deal with the accomplishments of outstanding black people in all walks of life, and the forgotten people in American history books can be made truly visible, in the best sense of the term.

The ultimate success of instructional technology, the use of multi-media resources and any other innovative practices, will rest upon the skill of the individual classroom teacher. Unfortunately, ghetto teachers seem to be among the most ill-prepared. Therefore, if the quality of ghetto education is expected to change substantatively, the ghetto teacher must be retrained to function more as a manager of the learning environment rather than a mere presenter of information. School systems must change their internal reward systems so that teaching in the ghetto will become as attractive as teaching in the suburbs. As we have implied, the intelligent use of instructional technology in the ghetto school will make the difference in the level of success that is achieved. However, the attitude of the individual classroom teacher towards minority and poor children must change as well as that teacher's attitude toward the use of instructional technology. Skepticism and indifference must change to compassion, optimism, and concern. In other words, they must become true believers and, if that is not possible, they should seek employment elsewhere. If they can't help our children, they should stop crippling them.

Like all modern children, ghetto youngsters are heavily influenced by mass media, especially movies and television. Regardless of their socio-economic level, everyone owns or has access to transistor radios, portable tape recorders, phonographs and stereo systems that blast their electronic message with blaring intensity. These messages help to shape young people's attitudes about everything from love to war to death, and they receive their heroes, their idols and their villains in the same manner. Somehow, libraries and schools must build upon and exploit this natural interest engendered by electronic media and then lead subtly back to the printed page. Some experiences may well *not* lead to the printed page, and librarians, as a profession, must learn to cope with that reality as well.

19. The Future of the Black College Library*
by   E. J. Josey

The plight of the black man in America has been described by two black psychiatrists as follows:

> For the black man in this country, it is not so much a matter of acquiring manhood as it is a struggle to feel it is his own. Whereas the white man regards his manhood as an ordained right, the black man is engaged in a never ending battle for its possession. For the black man, attaining any portion of manhood is an active process. He must penetrate barriers and overcome opposition in order to assume a masculine posture. For the inner psychological obstacles to manhood are never so formidable as the impediments woven into American society.[1]

In another section of their book, *Black Rage*, William H. Grier and Price M. Cobbs assert that

> the culture of slavery was never undone for either master or slave. The civilization that tolerated slavery dropped its slaveholding cloak but the inner feelings remained. The 'peculiar institution' continues to exert its evil influence over the nation. The practice of slavery stopped over a hundred years ago, but the minds of our citizens have never been freed.[2]

There can be no doubt that the black college library, an inextricable part of the black college, must dedicate its program to militate against this kind of hopelessness, bewilderment, and futility in order to free the minds of young American black men and women.

Before we can assess the future of the black college library, let us take a look at the black college. Every institution must serve society or it will not last very long. However, the question remains as to what special, unique service a black college can render. Since May 17, 1954, when the United States Supreme Court declared segregation in the public schools unconstitutional, we have been talking about integration. When we attempt to define integration, most white people and most blacks define it in terms of sending a few blacks to white schools and colleges. Very few people have considered sending whites to predominantly black schools and colleges. The only meaningful integration would be sending both blacks to former all-white institutions and whites to former all-black institutions. Yet, because of the lack of a real program of integration in the colleges in this country, the majority of black recipients of higher education will be trained in black colleges. In 1977, more than half of the young black men and women enrolled in the nation's colleges and universities are in predominantly black institutions.

---

*Reprinted from *Library Journal*, September 15, 1969. Published by R. R. Bowker Co. (a Xerox company). Copyright © 1969 by Xerox Corporation. The essay has been updated and slightly revised.

[1] William H. Grier and Price M. Cobbs, *Black Roger* (New York: Basic Books, 1968), p. 59.

[2] *Ibid.*, p. 26.

Since no meaningful plans have been formulated for a restructuring of American society (in spite of the Kerner report and, more recently, the special study by Urban America, Inc. and the Urban Coalition on events since the National Advisory Commission on Civil Disorders' report 9 years ago) black young people have become disillusioned. They agree with the findings of the special study that America is "closer to being two societies, black and white, increasingly separate and scarcely less unequal." The realities of American society indicate that black colleges are here to stay, and these 120 institutions have a unique service to perform for the nation.

To return to the question of the special, unique service a black college can render the nation an answer that I gave nine years ago (Winter 1968, *Library-College Journal*) still seems germane. "Negroes will attend these institutions primarily because they are relatively inexpensive, they offer remedial work (which is a necessity for many young people who are enrolled in poor Southern high schools), and because of proximity of these institutions and/or their geographical accessibility."

Several reasons have been advanced by educators and civil rights leaders to support the view that large numbers of young black people will continue to depend largely upon black colleges for their undergraduate education. This is simply because most young black people come from economically poor circumstances and cannot afford the high tuition costs of most predominantly white institutions. Certainly in the late 1960s and the early 1970s, youngsters were recruited from economically depressed urban areas into the most prestigious colleges and universities in the nation. However, recent attacks on affirmative action in the form of reverse discrimination suits have discouraged many blacks. The *Allan Bakke v. the Regents of the University of California* suit is primary evidence that supports this fact, and *The Chronicle of Higher Education* (April 4, 1977) reports that "whatever the eventual resolution of the Bakke case many members of minority groups have become discouraged from applying." These unwarranted attacks upon admissions programs to attract blacks and other disadvantaged minorities to higher education affirm Allen B. Ballard's thesis, in his *The Education of Black Folk* (Harper and Row, 1973), that "there has never been a national commitment to educational opportunity for black folk."

Furthermore, since American society seems to be "moving toward two societies, one black, one white—separate and unequal," young blacks are seeking their true identity at black colleges or in Afro-American societies in predominantly white colleges and universities. Few people would have thought, even a few years ago, that black students would have given up on integration and now be demanding black institutions and organizations.

Some years ago there were those who felt that black colleges would close their doors. A reassessment has led a large number of people to envision a great future for black institutions of higher learning. John U. Monro, the former dean of Harvard College and now head of the freshman program at Miles College, is a distinguished educator who sees a unique role for the black college. In a *New York Times* report on March 2, 1969, Monro stated

> It is idiotic or worse to talk about depending on Harvard or the University of Alabama to educate black children.... The black community is here to stay, and I am persuaded that the black colleges are too.... the whole metaphor for what you're supposed to be thinking

and doing has changed remarkably. . . . The faculty at Miles has spent years trying to prepare their students to enter the mainstream of white American life. Suddenly the students don't want that. They don't think of white society as something especially worth integrating into. . . . As far ahead as anybody can see, the black colleges will not become obsolete. . . . Here are 120 places really run by and for the black community, and there are damn few places where you have this kind of chance to build leadership and institutions.

Historically, libraries in black colleges have not been supported with good budgets, excellent facilities and strong staffs, primarily because legislatures, foundations, and society have all failed to support the black colleges per se. Consequently, administrators of predominantly black colleges have had to spread funds so thinly throughout their institutions that libraries never received more than a pittance. Inadequate budgets only allowed librarians a chance to amass meager book collections which hardly supported the instructional program. Resources for research and recreational reading could not even be considered. With only a small but dedicated staff, librarians were enmeshed in clerical routines and pedestrian activities which rarely gave them the opportunity to perform real professional service or to work with students and faculty in exploiting the few library resources that were assembled for study and research.

In too many instances, library service was offered in small, unsightly, and uncomfortable quarters that hardly provided enough shelf space for books and periodicals, much less provision for nonbook materials. The cramped quarters rarely provided 25 square feet per reader for one-third of the student body, as recommended by the standards. The three main components of a library—resources, facilities, and staff—were woefully inadequate and remain inadequate in many black colleges today. The results of my study of "Negro College Libraries and ACRL Standards," published 14 years ago (September 1, 1963, *Library Journal*) are still pertinent today, i.e., very few black college libraries meet standards. Even in 1977, if we apply the revised 1975 ACRL Standards for College Libraries, we find that the black college libraries in the country are in a more critical situation than ever before.

In "A Comparison of Quality Characteristics in Negro and White Public Colleges and Universities in the South" (Spring 1969, *Journal of Negro Education*), Alan L. Sorkin of the Brookings Institution states that "the data indicate that Negro colleges have 11 fewer library books per student" than the white colleges in the region. In 1977, no library of a predominantly black college or university can claim to have one million volumes. Even the great Howard University Library, which supports several Ph.D. instructional programs, had a collection of only 837,055 volumes as of June 30, 1975. What has really helped this institution in supporting its excellent curriculum and the research of a first-rate faculty has been its membership in the Consortium of Universities of Washington, D.C. and its proximity to the Library of Congress.

Although the past has been bleak, conditions are changing slightly. New library buildings are now being erected and larger budgets for state-supported institutions in addition to federal funds have increased collections, although much remains to be done to provide adequate resources in both private and public institutions. Library staffs are also updating their education via institutes, etc., and one of the most ambitious of such efforts is at the Atlanta University Library School, where a program for technical services personnel of predominantly black colleges has been funded by the Ford Foundation.

The last two administrations in Washington did not have a commitment to the support of higher education, and most black academic librarians were alarmed at the squandering of millions of dollars for aiding foreign governments and the spending of billions of dollars on defense. They very seriously ask why the same kind of mobilization of resources cannot be utilized to provide for the nation's educational program the adequate resources necessary in college libraries, generally, and in black colleges, specifically. The Carter administration seems to be concerned about human services, and black librarians view the new administration's concern for human rights and education as a very encouraging sign for the future.

* * *

Obviously, the library in a black college is irretrievably tied to the purpose and goals of its parent institution. The ordinary test of action and the test of its purposes and goals will be meaningless if it does not address itself to the special problems that black colleges face. The most crucial test that the library must meet is responding to the needs of its disadvantaged students who, because of their poor high school education, need extra help and assistance. One vital aspect of special assistance to young black students is the inauguration of special library counseling programs which could include unique orientation programs utilizing programmed instruction. The use of teaching machines should not preclude the personal aid that the librarians, serving as special counselors, can give in selecting suitable materials for students who have reading difficulties and who, in too many instances, have not had the opportunity to use good libraries. By providing advisory assistance to students, librarians can contribute immeasurably to a developmental curricular program, which takes the student from his low academic freshman status and molds him into a full-fledged promising college student.

Such suggestions of activity by librarians presuppose that members of the professional staff, of necessity, must be uncommonly sensitive to the needs of culturally deprived students who enter college saddled with many handicaps. At this point, the reader may ask whether this breed of librarians must be only black librarians, and the answer is a resounding, No! Whites have served on the faculty of black colleges for many years; and they are welcomed to black colleges if they are committed to the goals of black students and can demonstrate that severe social, economic, and other sanctions cannot deter them from risking voluntarily what blacks have had to suffer involuntarily because of their color. Nevertheless, all librarians—black and white—who serve on the staffs of black college libraries in the future must have an affinity and empathy with these young black college people as well as belief in their dreams and hopes for the future. These young black students, in black and nonblack colleges, are very sensitive to social currents today and more than ever desire to throw off the bondage of discrimination, inequality, and inferiority. They would reject librarians who are not attuned to their aspirations.

In addition to a sensitivity and responsiveness to the needs of college students at black institutions, there must also be a reexamination of the neanderthal structure of college and universities in general that has led to the unrest on campuses.

Supporting this view, Dr. Kenneth B. Clark, the eminent psychologist and only black member on the New York State Board of Regents, has declared that

> there is abundant evidence that the causes of unrest and generalized restlessness among a highly sensitive and intelligent minority of white and Negro students are quite real, serious and pervasive throughout our society. Our major educational institutions have not delivered the services to humanity which could be reasonably expected of them.

While black college libraries must be cognizant of the special needs of black students as a top priority item, equally important should be the effort to assemble a first-rate collection of resources. To ensure that these resources are available, state legislatures, the federal government, and foundations have a moral obligation to pour millions of dollars into the black institutions that are educating more than one-half of all black college students today. It is virtually impossible to engage in substantive instruction and research without adequate library resources, and in addition to book resources, new information media materials and processes (audiovisual, reprographic, miniaturized, and automated) should be included.

Even if all of the black college libraries could meet minimum standards in 1977, the day of envisioning the single, self-sufficient library has passed. Therefore, it is imperative that these institutions join regional cooperatives as called for in the National Advisory Commission on Libraries' report, which suggests that

> for long-range college library development, plans should be developed for centralized services to college libraries in acquisitions, processing, and storage of little-used materials; in effecting cooperative arrangements that will give college students and faculty members efficient bibliographic and physical access to the resources of research libraries; in arranging for advisory services to college librarians, especially with respect to the utilization of technological aids to library work....

In short, it is essential for black college libraries to work cooperatively with all libraries in their regions to ensure the transmission of the entire intellectual resources of libraries and information centers, locally and nationally, to their students and faculty to support instruction, learning, and research.

Closely related to building basic collections in black college libraries is the need to provide new buildings. It is true that during the 1960s, several libraries were built at black institutions. The writer was attracted to Savannah State (Georgia) in 1959 because of the opportunity to plan service in a spacious, air-conditioned, modern building. Several new college library buildings have been dedicated at a few of the predominantly black institutions of higher education in recent years, and this has been the occasion for rejoicing, for so many of the institutions have had to make past library quarters in buildings that were not built solely for library purposes.

Although a few new library buildings have been constructed at predominantly black colleges, not nearly enough desperately needed facilities have been provided. Jerrold Orne's surveys of new academic library buildings for 1967 and 1968 (in the December 1 issue of *Library Journal*) indicate that eight new libraries were constructed at predominantly black colleges. Several of these libraries received federal aid. However, in the listing of institutions that received federal aid under Title II of the Higher Education Facilities Act (compiled by Katharine M. Stokes and published in the February 1969 ACRL *News Issue of College and Research Libraries*), it was revealed that not a single predominantly black institution received a grant under this title. Facilities must be built to house and support a viable library program in black colleges. Excellence in buildings cannot be equated with excellence in library service, but adequate buildings do provide a great potential for excellence.

In the first chapter of *Black Rage*, Grier and Cobbs contend that:

> The growing anger of Negroes is frightening to white America. There is a feeling of betrayal and undeserved attack. White people have responded with a rage of their own. As the lines become more firmly drawn, exchange of information is the first casualty.
>
> If racist hostility is to subside, and if we are to avoid open conflict on a nationwide scale, information is the most desperately needed commodity of our time.
>
> And of the things that need knowing, none is more important than that all blacks are angry. White Americans seem not to recognize it. They seem to think that all the trouble is caused by only a few "extremists." They ought to know better.[3]

Because most black Americans, including this writer, do not go around burning the town or joining the Black Panthers, it does not necessarily mean that they are not seething with anger because of the racial discrimination, the injustices, and the inequities which still exist in American society.

Grier and Cobbs sound a clarion call for an exchange of information, and this exchange or transfer of information is a primary function of libraries. The black college library has a yeoman service to perform in the information transfer process, for in most instances, these libraries over the years have been amassing books and materials on the black experience in America. Indeed, many of these institutions will be the only source for information on Afro-Americans in their communities.

It is quite clear that many whites have no knowledge of black life in America. Very few have visited a black community, a home, or a church, and they have no conception of the quality of life in black communities, in spite of the fact that large numbers of black Americans barely subsist above the poverty level. Thus it is that black students in high schools and colleges are demanding Afro-American studies, for they are not only anxious to know about their heritage, but they also are aware of the fact that white Americans are not cognizant of the contributions that Afro-Americans have made to this country. Furthermore, these young people are convinced that the exchange of pulpits by black and white ministers during brotherhood week, the trotting out of black civic leaders to speak once a year during Negro History Week, and the pre-empting of television time to honor the late Dr. Martin Luther King hardly touch the surface in terms of really educating white America.

Newspapers across the country rarely carry news about activities in the black community. Thus, this community has had to rely upon the black press to cover its churches, clubs, weddings, and other activities. Since white Americans very seldom

---

[3] Grier and Cobbs, p. 4.

see a black paper, Doctors Grier and Cobbs are justified in calling for an exchange of information. In fact, most white Americans do not know that, over the years, black college libraries often developed as repositories in an effort to preserve for posterity massive information files on the local community. One excellent example of such massive gathering of materials about the black community is the work of Louella Hawkins, former reference librarian of Savannah State College, who has collected virtually everything that has appeared in print on the black community in Savannah.

The question of whether the library in a black college has a special role to play would be only partially answered, unless we realize that, more than any other department or organization on campus, the library has the special competency to help the college overcome the students' charges of irrelevance, inconsistency, and dehumanization—charges heard on all campuses these days. The library can humanize the learning situation with its more leisurely atmosphere and individualized study stations or carrels. With a staff dedicated to liberating the minds of young people, it has the special competency to help the student overcome his educational deficiencies. And via a good program of publicizing and making available the resources and services of the library, young deprived youngsters will be ushered into a new world of hope with their spirits renewed.

As we move into the twenty-first century, the libraries of black colleges must play an increasingly important role on their campuses. In order to be a viable library, there must be an appropriation of sufficient funds from federal, state, local, and private agencies. With adequate resources and excellently trained staffs, these libraries will then be able to develop programs that will include remedial reinforcement, with compensatory as well as enrichment components. In addition to having a staff that will have the proper rapport with young people who need special counseling, the black college library also possesses the special ability to reach the unreached in the community—those who desperately need information on the contributions of blacks to American civilization.

The 1968 annual report of the Ford Foundation states that "the survival and improvement of the predominantly Negro college are vital, however, if black students as a group are to achieve equality of educational opportunity." An excellent library is central to the intellectual life of a black college, and the future of the black college may very well depend upon the quality of its library.

SIGNIFICANT BOOKS AND PERIODICALS FOR BLACK COLLECTIONS

20. A Selected Annotated List of Reference Books Reflecting the Black Experience

by Sue P. Chandler, Assistant Librarian for Public Services, Fisk University

INTRODUCTION

A reference book is a book referred to for factual information and not one to be read in its entirety. Many reference librarians will agree that reference book reviewing is indeed a very difficult task, for very often the true value of a reference book may not be tested until an informational crisis arises.

The following list of briefly annotated reference books reflecting the black experience is by no means intended to be comprehensive. The books selected for this list are in the Special Collections of the Fisk University Library. They have been heavily used, and it is felt that all of them contain information valuable to researchers.

* * *

Adams, Russell L. **Great Negroes Past and Present.** Chicago: Afro-Am Pub. Co., 1963.
Readable and for use in elementary or secondary schools, this collective biography has been divided into twelve sections covering such subjects as our African heritage, education, religion and literature. Antar, Peter Salem, Robert Smalls, Theodore K. Lawless, Frank L. Gillespie, and Mary Church Terrell are some of the people included.

Afro-American Encyclopedia. Chief compiler and editor, Martin Rywell; consulting editors, Charles H. Wesley and others. North Miami, Fla.: Educational Book Publishers, 1974. 10v.

This ten volume set, not designed for scholars, is a readable source of information on black people from earliest times to the present. Biographical material is provided as well as information on historical events, countries, ideas, and movements.

Bailey, Leaonead Pack. **Broadside Authors and Artists.** Detroit, Mich.: Broadside Press, 1974.

This illustrated directory contains one hundred ninety-two sketches of Broadside Press authors. These artists and writers were sent questionnaires, and when replies were not returned or persons were deceased, information was secured elsewhere. Writers in the Heritage Series (edited by Paul Breman) are also included, since Broadside distributed this series.

Brawley, Benjamin G. **Negro Builders and Heroes.** Chapel Hill: University of North Carolina Press, 1937.

This work was intended as an introduction to Negro biography. Some parts are concerned with literature and history, while earlier chapters deal with individuals. The latter chapters each are concerned with several persons. Some of those included are Daniel A. Payne, John Jasper, Paul Cuffe, and John Chavis.

Brown, Hallie Q. **Homespun Heroines and Other Women of Distinction.** Xenia, Ohio: The Aldine Pub. Co., 1926.

This work was intended "as an evidence of appreciation and a token of regard to the history making women of our race." It is illustrated and contains approximately fifty-three biographical sketches (Martha Payne, Phillis Wheatley, Sojourner Truth, Harriet Tubman, Mary A. S. Cary, C. J. Walker and Fannie J. Coppin, among others).

Bruce, John Edward. **Eminent Negro Men and Women.** Yonkers, N.Y.: Gazette Press, 1910.

This work contains biographical sketches of twenty-one persons, including Hannibal, Benjamin Banneker, Toussaint L'Overture, Aleksandr Pushkin, Henry Ossawa Tanner, Phillis Wheatley, and Ida B. Wells.

California. San Fernando Valley State College, Los Angeles, Library. **The Black Experience in the United States: A Bibliography Based on Collections of the San Fernando Valley State College Library.** Dennis C. Bakewell, Compiler. Northridge, Calif.: San Fernando Valley State College Foundation, 1970.

This bibliography is a selected list of the holdings of San Fernando Valley State College felt to be of value to the black experience in the United States. The arrangement is by the Library of Congress classification system. Included are an author index and a list of newspapers and periodicals.

Chapman, Dorothy. **Index to Black Poetry.** Boston: G. K. Hall and Co., 1974.

The *Index to Black Poetry* was built upon the earlier works of Dorothy Porter and includes old and newer works of poetry. The index includes black poets as well as poets who have in some way written in the black experience. The non-black poets are indicated by the use of an asterisk following their name in the author index. Some of the names easily recognizable in this category are Stephen Vincent Benet, Hodding Carter, Hart Crane, Henry Wadsworth Longfellow, Carl Sandburg, and Walt Whitman.

The preface states that ninety books and pamphlets by individual poets and thirty-three anthologies have been indexed. The major portion of the books used were selected from *The Negro in the United States: A Selected Bibliography* and *North American Poets: A Biographical Checklist of Their Writings, 1760-1944*, both by Mrs. Porter. Information given in the title and first line index includes author, source(s) and page number(s). The author index gives a list of poems by each author.

Directory of Black Literary Magazines. Washington, D.C.: The Negro Bibliographic and Research Center, Inc., 1970.

According to the preface, the term literary magazine has been used loosely to include those magazines containing fiction, poetry, book reviews, and articles. Not intended to be by any means complete, this publication has listed approximately forty-eight titles. Magazines have been annotated where review copies have been made available.

Duignan, Peter. **Handbook of American Resources for African Studies.** Stanford, Calif.: Hoover Institution on War, Revolution, and Peace, Stanford University, 1967.

A guide intended to point out the resources for African studies found in American libraries. Information was gathered by use of questionnaires and by consulting other bibliographic aids. The handbook has been divided into library and manuscript collections, church and missionary libraries and archives, art and ethnographic collections, private U.S. collections, and business archives.

The Ebony Handbook. Editor: Doris E. Saunders. Chicago: Johnson Publishing Co., 1974.

A revised edition of the 1966 publication, this compilation of various types of information on American blacks is a ready reference tool. It has been divided into twenty sections, including such topics as population, vital statistics, employment and government, sports and obituaries. The nature of the publication makes it necessary to include numerous statistical tables, and an index to these tables has been provided. Included also is a career guide; a list of black oriented institutions of higher learning; a list of available scholarships, fellowships, and loans; a list of significant books; and an index.

The Ebony Success Library. By the editors of *Ebony*. Chicago: Johnson Pub. Co., 1973. 3v.

Volume 1, *1,000 Successful Blacks*, contains biographical sketches of approximately 1,100 blacks from Hank Aaron to Andrew Young. Arrangement is alphabetical.

Volume 2, *Famous Blacks Give Secrets of Success*, contains seventy-two articles about persons who have achieved success in such fields as entertainment, politics, business, etc. Includes such persons as Barbara Jordan, Leontyne Price, and Cicely Tyson.

Volume 3, *Career Guide: Opportunities and Resources*, is divided into two sections, "Careers and People" and "Careers and Resources." The first section is an alphabetical listing of approximately ninety persons in various careers, giving job descriptions and job responsibilities. The second section gives tips on how and where to apply for information on scholarships and financial aid.

Haley, James T. **Afro-American Encyclopedia or, The Thoughts, Doings, and Sayings of the Race.** Nashville, Tenn.: Haley and Florida, 1895.

A retrospective source containing valuable material on the Negro. Contains an alphabetical table of contents and is illustrated.

Henderson, Edwin B. **The Black Athlete.** New York: Publishers Co., 1968.

This volume deals with black men and women in sports from the time they made inroads.

Hornsby, Alton. **The Black Almanac.** Woodbury, N.Y.: Barron's Educational Series, Inc., 1975.

The *Black Almanac* is designed as a chronology of important dates and facts concerning the role of blacks in United States history. Covering the period after 1870 in great detail, the work has been divided into ten sections. A brief history and explanation of each of the sections is given in the introduction. Also included is a selected bibliography of general and specific sources.

Index to Periodical Articles By and About Negroes. March 1950– .

Replaces the *Guide to Negro Periodical Literature* compiled by A. P. Marshall. Title varies: Mar. 1950-Summer 1954, *Index to Selected Negro Periodicals*; Fall 1954-1965, *Index to Selected Periodical Articles*; 1966– , *Index to Periodical Articles By and About Negroes*.

Presently this publication is prepared by the staffs of the Central State University Library and the Schomburg Collection. Authors, subjects, and references are listed in dictionary form. Included are obituaries, poems, music, drama, etc. A list of the periodicals indexed is also included.

Miller, Elizabeth W. **The Negro in America: A Bibliography.** Cambridge: Harvard University Press, 1966.

The Negro in America: A Bibliography, with a foreword by Thomas F. Pettigrew, concentrates on works appearing during the time span between the Supreme Court Decision of May 17, 1954, and the enactment of the Voting Rights Bill in August 1965. However, when necessary for purposes of clarity, older sources have been included. Selective, it is divided into fourteen sections; the last is "Tools for Further Research." Also included is an index of authors.

Miller, Elizabeth W. **The Negro in America: A Bibliography.** 2nd ed., rev. and enl. Cambridge: Harvard University Press, 1970.

The second edition was revised by Mary L. Fisher. The scope has been enlarged and contains 6,500 entries, almost twice as many as the first edition. Greater coverage has been given to black history and social institutions. Introducing new sections on music, literature, and the arts, the compiler has also expanded the last chapter "A Guide to Further Research."

Morais, Herbert M. **The History of the Negro in Medicine.** New York: Publishers Company, 1968.

The History of the Negro in Medicine includes biographical material and recollections of those persons engaged in the struggle against Jim Crow in medicine. It tells of the discrimination against blacks as patients and blacks as physicians. The topics discussed are black doctors, nurses and patients; however the editor states that he realizes that contributions have been made by Negro dentists and pharmacists to their professions as well.

The National Cyclopedia of the Colored Race. Montgomery, Ala.: National Pub. Co. Inc., 1919.

This cyclopedia is illustrated and contains long sketches of famous persons and institutions. Some of the subjects covered are education, churches, and national and fraternal organizations. The arrangement is not alphabetical. The first part of the index is arranged by states.

The Negro Handbook. Ed., Florence Murray. N.Y.: W. Malliet and Co., 1942-49.

Issued four times, the *Negro Handbook* was compiled to present factual information concerning Negroes in the United States.

Negro Year Book and Annual Encyclopedia of the Negro. Tuskegee, Ala.: Tuskegee Institute Department of Records and Research, 1912-52.

The *Negro Year Book* was begun in 1912 and there were eleven volumes published at irregular intervals until 1952. Monroe N. Work edited the first nine editions, designed to present concise and accurate information concerning the black race. Contains statistical tables and a detailed index.

Patterson, Lindsay. **Anthology of the American Negro in the Theatre.** New York: Publishers Co., 1968.

Dedicated to Langston Hughes, this compilation attempts to record the Negro's achievement in the theatre.

Patterson, Lindsay. **An Introduction to Black Literature in America: From 1746 to the Present.** New York: Publishers Co. Inc., 1968, 1969.

Covers prose as well as poetry, from Lucy Terry's "Bars Fight" to Julia Fields's "No Time for Poetry." Arrangement is chronological, and a bibliography is included. The index is by author.

Patterson, Lindsay. **The Negro in Music and Art.** New York: Publishers Co., 1967.

The first eleven sections of this work deal with the Negro and his music, treating such topics as spirituals, minstrels, post-minstrel, ragtime, blues, gospel, jazz, rock and roll, composers, singers, and classical music. The next five sections are devoted to the Negro in art, starting with the African heritage and finishing with contemporary artists.

Ploski, Harry A. **The Negro Almanac: A Reference Work on the Afro-American.** 3rd ed. New York: The Bellwether Pub. Co., 1976.

The bicentennial edition of *The Negro Almanac* was compiled by Harry A. Ploski and Warren Marr, II. (The work was first published in 1967 and revised in 1971.)

This third edition has paid particular attention to the black role in colonial and revolutionary America and to the contribution of blacks to the growth and development of the American nation since its inception. It has been divided into twenty-three sections, covering such topics as "Significant Documents in Afro-American History," "Historic Landmarks of Black America," "Legal Status of Black Americans," "Black Voter and Elected Officeholder," and "Black Capitalism." Containing numerous photographs, this volume provides biographical data and statistical material, including tables, charts, and graphs on the history and culture of the black man in the United States, and other parts of the world as well.

Porter, Dorothy B. **Early Negro Writing: 1760-1837.** Boston: Beacon Press, 1971.

This book makes available a selected number of writings by Afro-Americans which have appeared in print (as books, pamphlets, broadsides, or as parts of books) between the years 1760 and 1837. The work has been divided into seven parts: Mutual Aid and Fraternal Organizations, 1792-1832; Societies for Educational Improvement, 1808-1836; Significant Annual Conferences, 1831-1837; To Emigrate or Remain at Home? 1773-1833; Spokesmen in Behalf of Their Colored Fellow Citizens," 1787-1815; Saints and Sinners, 1786-1836; Narratives, Poems and Essays, 1760-1835.

Porter, Dorothy B. **The Negro in the United States: A Selected Bibliography.** Washington, D.C.: Library of Congress, 1970.

This bibliography emphasizes holdings in the collections of the Library of Congress. Entries have been given brief annotations when deemed necessary for clarification, and they are arranged alphabetically by author under broad subject headings such as art, biography and autobiography, economic conditions, social conditions, etc. An index of names and subjects is included.

Porter, Dorothy B. **A Working Bibliography on the Negro in the United States.** Ann Arbor, Mich.: Xerox, University Microfilms, 1969.

Designed as a selection aid to guide persons interested in acquiring materials for public, private, and university collections of Afro-Americana, this bibliography lists primarily books with a few periodical references included. Some of the category headings used are biography, cultural milieu, economic conditions, education, history, law, and sports and recreation.

Race Relations Information Center. **Directory of Afro-American Resources.** Edited by Walter Schatz. New York: R. R. Bowker Co., 1970.

The directory was started in 1967, as a project of the Southern Education Reporting Service, to identify organizations and institutions in the United States which have materials relating to black Americans. The arrangement is geographical, by states, then by city, and then by institutions within the cities. There is an index to directory entries and an index to personnel in these organizations and institutions listed. The bibliography which has been included is one of the items the project staff felt useful to their research.

Robinson, Wilhelmena S. **Historical Negro Biographies.** New York: Publishers Co., 1968.

Over five hundred biographical sketches of persons living and deceased are divided into three parts: "The Fourteenth through Eighteenth Centuries," "The Nineteenth Century," and "The Twentieth Century." Bibliography and two indexes are provided, as well as a name index and a major activity index.

Rollock, Barbara. **The Black Experience in Children's Books.** New York: New York Public Library, 1974.

Entries are arranged geographically in the following sections: the United States, South and Central America, the Caribbean, Africa, and England. The section on the United States is the longest, and England is the shortest. Previous editions of this work were compiled by Augusta Baker, and Ms. Rollock attempts to follow Mrs. Baker's philosophy. Information given includes author, title, publisher, price, and a brief annotation. There is also an author and title index.

Romero, Patricia E. **I Too Am America: Documents from 1619 to the Present.** New York: Publishers Co., 1968.

Documents were chosen on the basis of revealing dramatic aspects of the struggles for equality. Some familiar documents included are Martin Luther King's "Letter from a Birmingham Jail," and Mary McLeod Bethune's "Last Will and Testament to Her People." The arrangement is chronological, and some of the material has been edited. Index has been included as well as illustrations.

Rush, Theressa Gunnels. **Black American Writers Past and Present: A Biographical and Bibliographical Dictionary.** Metuchen, N.J.: Scarecrow Press, Inc., 1975.

This two volume dictionary was compiled by Theressa Gunnels Rush, Carol Fairbanks Myers and Ester Spring Arata. Containing over 2,000 entries, it is intended to cover writers from the 18th century to the present. Photographs have been supplied in some cases, and the information given varies from two lines to several pages. The bibliography includes all known books published by a person. Biography and criticism are listed under those headings, but in some instances, it may be difficult to distinguish one from the other.

Salk, Erwin A. **A Layman's Guide to Negro History.** New York: McGraw-Hill, 1967.

This guide lists books, pamphlets, periodicals, recordings, song books, film strips, and visual materials pertaining to the history and contributions of the Negro in the United States. The book was prepared for the use of the layman and is not aimed at the scholar.

Shockley, Ann Allen, and Sue P. Chandler. **Living Black American Authors: A Biographical Directory.** New York: R. R. Bowker Co., 1974.

This work was compiled to identify the many black writers who were published in the late sixties and early seventies, as well as those writers of long standing. The word author as used in the book includes persons who have written books or have been published in anthologies, newspapers, journals, or periodicals. The arrangement is alphabetical by name of author. The list of abbreviations used and a list of black publications are included. A title index is provided.

Simmons, William J. **Men of Mark.** Cleveland, Ohio: George M. Rewell and Co., 1887.

Contains over one hundred seventy biographies of eminent black men, including clergymen, educators, editors, martyrs, legislators, artists, singers, musicians, scientists, etc. There are over one hundred illustrations. Articles cover several pages each. The arrangement is not alphabetical, but there is an index to the sketches.

Smythe, Mabel M. **The Black American Reference Book.** Englewood Cliffs, N.J.: Prentice-Hall Inc., 1976.

The Black American Reference Book is based upon the *American Negro Reference Book*, originally published in 1965. It brings together information on black Americans' history, social and economic status, political activities, and contributions to the arts. It contains scholarly articles written by well-known persons, and an index is provided. Some of the contributors include John Hope Franklin, Constance Baker Motley, Vernon E. Jordan, Jr., and Ernest Kaiser.

Wesley, Charles H. **In Freedom's Footsteps.** New York: Publishers Co., 1968.

This volume (first of a series of three) traces the history of the black man from the African background to the Civil War. Illustrated, it contains a bibliography and an index.

Wesley, Charles H. **Negro Americans in the Civil War.** New York: Publishers Co. Inc., 1968.

This volume deals with slavery as the underlying cause of the Civil War, as well as emancipation, the armed forces, the battles, the aftermath, and the period of transition.

Wesley, Charles H. **The Quest for Equality.** New York: Publishers Co. Inc., 1968.

This book concerns the history of the black man starting after the end of the Civil War and up to the civil rights struggle. Illustrated, it contains a bibliography and an index.

Who's Who among Black Americans. Northbrook, Ill.: Who's Who among Black Americans, Inc., Pub. Co., 1976.

Includes biographical sketches of approximately 10,000 living black Americans. Primary consideration was given to those blacks who were felt to be of reference interest. After that, the interest was focused on two factors: 1) "the position of responsibility held," and 2) "the level of significant achievement attained in a career of meritorius activity." Contains a glossary of abbreviations, a geographic index, and an occupational index.

Who's Who in Colored America: An Illustrated Biographical Directory of Notable Living Persons of African Descent in the United States. Yonkers, N.Y.: Christian E. Burchel and Associates, 1927-50. 7v.

Issued at irregular intervals between 1927 and 1950, *Who's Who in Colored America* is arranged alphabetically and identifies black Americans in all fields. Selection was based upon two factors, position and personal achievements. Many of the brief sketches are accompanied by photographs.

Williams, Ethel L. **Biographical Directory of Negro Ministers.** 3rd ed. Boston: G. K. Hall and Co., 1975.

Designed to make available information about black ministers and their achievements, this third edition contains the six hundred and forty-three biographies that were in the second edition. These have been revised, however, and seven hundred and ninety-nine new biographies have been included.

Williams, Ora. **American Black Women in the Arts and Social Sciences.** Metuchen, N.J.: The Scarecrow Press Inc., 1973.

Designed to acquaint Americans with the names and achievements of black women, this bibliography contains over 1,000 entries and lists approximately 2,000 works. The book is divided into five categories "A Comprehensive Listing," which includes such entries as bibliographies, guides to collections, autobiographies, and biographies; "Selected Individual Bibliography," including Nikki Giovanni, Ann Petry, Dorothy Porter; and "Other Arts," concerning painters, illustrators, sculptors, arrangers, composers, lyricists. There are also sections devoted to audio-visual materials, and black periodicals and publishing houses.

Work, Monroe N. **Bibliography of the Negro in Africa and America.** New York: Octagon Books, 1970.

This volume is a comprehensive listing of over 17,000 selected books, pamphlets, and periodical articles, covering publications in different languages issued prior to 1928. The material has been grouped under two main divisions: "The Negro in Africa" and "The Negro in America," and each has been subdivided into classified chapters. An author index has been included.

21. A Descriptive Bibliography of Selected African and Afro-American Periodicals
by Ann Allen Shockley

INTRODUCTION

This descriptive bibliography of thirty-six selected African and Afro-American periodicals was designed to assist librarians and educators in selecting basic titles for Afro-American collections and to supplement Black Studies curricula. In addition, it should be of interest and value to readers seeking personal reading guidance for academic as well as recreational needs. The criteria for selection were the following: 1) longevity of the publication, 2) relevance to scholarship and the individual disciplines, 3) general reader interest, and 4) overall value to librarians, educators, and library patrons of public, academic, school and black research-oriented centers.

The evaluative descriptions attempt to delineate contents, worth, and usefulness. Stress was placed on Afro-American titles more than African because the list is geared primarily for Afro-American collections. The bibliographic form is modeled on Bill Katz's *Magazines for Libraries*. Entries are in alphabetical order by title giving: 1) date founded, 2) frequency, 3) address, 4) editor, and 5) price.

AFRICAN

Africa; an international business, economic and political monthly. 1971. Monthly.
Africa Journal Ltd., 28 Great Queen Street, London WC.2, England.
Editor, Ralph Uwechue. $12.50.
Captivating newsmagazine with timely articles, reports, features, and surveys focusing on Africa, Africans, and African relationships with the world. Regular interviews are published with leading world-wide figures such as Guyanese author, E. Braithwaite; former West German Minister for Development Aid, Erhard Eppler; and Mayor Maynard Jackson of Atlanta. The book reviews are of books by and about Africans and Afro-Americans. There are special reports, along with sections on African sports news, art, culture, and business. Liberal use of photographs and illustrations combine for a good format. Recommended for academic, public, and high school libraries.

Africa; journal of the International African Institute. 1928. Quarterly 210 High Holborn, London WCIV 7B W. Editor, John Middleton. Individual membership, $22.00; corporate membership, $32.00.
A highly scholarly journal which contains articles in French and English on various subjects relating to all sections of Africa. The articles are written by African scholars in Africa, Europe, and America. The book reviews are extremely noteworthy and the list of books received should be useful to librarians developing African collections. The annual fee covers a combined subscription to the separate quarterly publications, *Africa, International African Bibliography*, and *IAI Notes and News*.

Africa Quarterly; a journal of African affairs. 1961. Quarterly. Indian Centre for Africa, ICCR Azad Bhawan, New Delhi-110001. Editor, Dr. Vijaya Gupta. $7.00.

This journal is unique in its attempt to provide a forum for Indian/African coexistence, mutual concerns, and interests. Scholars and specialists whose objective "should be promotion of knowledge about Africa and better understanding between the peoples of India and Africa" are invited to contribute. The articles are on "various political, economic, social, cultural and literary subjects of interest to the people of Africa." Of special note is the "India and Africa" quarterly chronicle of world news and the "Africa through Indian Eyes" which is a "documentation based on coverage of Africa in Indian newspapers and periodicals." The latter arrangement is in classified order with broad subject headings, and in a few cases, brief annotations. Essential for both African and Asian Studies.

Africa Report; magazine for the new Africa. 1956. Bimonthly. African American Institute, 833 United Nations Plaza, New York, New York 10017. Editor, Anthony J. Hughes. $11.00.

"A nonpartisan magazine of African Affairs," this newsmagazine is geared toward an American audience's enlightenment about Africa and Africans. The articles are non-scholarly and range from five to six pages in length. The most valuable feature of this publication is the "African Update" section, which gives news capsules "monitoring economic and political developments around the continent" for the bimonthly period. In addition, there are interviews, photographs, and occasional book reviews. Recommended for academic and public libraries.

African Affairs; journal of the Royal African Society. 1901. Quarterly. 18 Northnumberland Avenue, London, WC2N 5BJ, England. Editor, Anthony Atmore. $21.00.

Contains articles of scholarly interest to academicians, researchers, scholars, and students of African Studies. Especially commendable are the well-written and perceptive book reviews, the bibliography of publications listed under sectional headings such as "Africa General," "North Africa," "West Africa," and the list of articles on Africa in non-Africanist periodicals. Recommended for academic libraries and research centers with African collections.

African Arts. 1967. Quarterly. African Studies Center, University of California at Los Angeles, Los Angeles, California 90024. Editor, John Povey. $14.00.

Glossy and handsome with striking color illustrations, the magazine has interestingly written articles, without heavy overtones, that span a broad range of the African arts. This scope includes sculpture, dance, theatre, music, film, literature, and contemporary and traditional art. Book and record reviews, along with news of exhibitions are informative. The periodical should be of value to teachers, collectors, and African art buffs.

African Studies Review; journal of the African Studies Association. 1957. 3/yr. 218 Shiffman Center, Brandeis University, Waltham, Mass. 02154. Editor, Alan K. Smith. $18.00.

The journal carries scholarly articles, bibliographic essays, and book reviews of note. Recommended for academic libraries and African Studies Centers.

Africana Journal; a bibliographic and review quarterly. 1970. Quarterly. Africana Publishing Company, 101 Fifth Avenue, New York, New York 10003. Editor, Abe Goldman. Individuals, $20.00; libraries and institutions, $35.00.

Formerly the *African Library Journal*, this serves as an excellent bibliographic tool for Africana and can be used by scholars, academicians, researchers, and librarians. It offers bibliographic essays and timely book reviews on African literature in both foreign and English publications by authoritative scholars. Bibliographies are by subject and geographical sections. An invaluable guide for bibliographic and review resources for African Studies.

Journal of African History. 1960. Quarterly. Cambridge University Press. 32 East 57th Street, New York, New York 10022. Editor, A. G. Hopkins. $23.00.

In French and English, eight or nine scholarly articles treat all periods of African history. Brief summaries of the articles appear at the end. The Table of Contents is on the verso. Book review essays range from eight to sixteen per issue with four to six shorter reviews as well. Valuable for African collections and academic libraries.

Journal of Modern African Studies. 1963. Quarterly. Cambridge University Press. 32 East 57th Street, New York, New York 10022. Editor, David Kimble. $12.50.

English/American African oriented with occasionally an overabundance of non-African contributors, although "contributors are invited from all over the world." Designed to be "a quarterly survey of politics, economics and related topics in contemporary Africa," its six to eight articles historically analyze topics pertinent to present day African issues. The "Africana" addition has short critical articles on current developments. An extensive number of book reviews with related topics are highlights. A good selection for academic African collections.

Présence Africaine; revue culturelle du monde noir. 1947. Quarterly. Revue Présence Africaine. 25 bis rue des Ecoles, 75005 Paris, France. Editor, Alioune Diop. $5.60.

A singular bilingual French and English "Cultural Review of the Negro World" founded by Africans in Paris. Essays and articles are on historical, social, political, cultural, educational and linguistic topics affecting Africans as well as blacks in all parts of the world. Special issues have been on "Black Civilization and Religion," and "Black Civilization and Education." African identity, originality, and awareness are promoted amidst overtones of African liberation and freedom. Some poetry is included, as well as four or five book reviews, and a "Books Received" list. An excellent review that should be in all Afro-American and African collections.

AFRO-AMERICAN

Black Books Bulletin. 1971. Quarterly. Institute of Positive Education. 7850 S. Ellis Avenue, Chicago, Illinois 60619. Editor, Haki R. Madhubuti (Don Lee). $8.00.

This quasi-literary magazine provides important information that is not easily located about the publications of black publishers, as well as books by and about blacks. There are bibliographic essays, interviews, and critical reviews of books, plays, records and films. Although the editor states that the "pages are open to the expression of a diversity of ideas and beliefs about the black experience," the socio-political commentaries and reviews have reflected heavily the black nationalistic concepts of the Institute. Current focus is on issues devoted to special topics with accompanying subject bibliographies. The bibliographies under the heading "Biblio One" are not consistent in style or form; however weak, they are useful. The "Books for the Young" comprise a regular section which is needed for information of this type. Occasional poetry and short stories are included. An acquisition for all Afro-American collections.

Black Collegian. 1970. 5/yr. Black Collegiate Services, Inc., 3217 Melpomene Ave., New Orleans, La. 70125. Editor, Kalamu ya Salaam. $7.50 (2 yrs.).

For black college students, the colorfully illustrated national magazine has articles by such well known scholars as John Henrik Clarke, Robert Staples, Nathan Hare, and Benjamin Quarles. The annual Careers, Jobs, and special Summer Work-Study issues are especially important to students. Usual features are the black art section, book and record reviews. "Campus News" pipelines national reports about the activities of black students on both predominantly black and white campuses. A highly informative and entertaining publication from which all black college students should benefit.

Black Enterprise. 1970. Monthly. Earl G. Graves Publishing Co., Inc., 295 Madison Ave., New York, New York 10017. Editor, Earl G. Graves. $10.00.

An award winning, leading magazine with a good format, the publication supplies otherwise scarce information on black-owned businesses, businesspeople and their achievements. Well researched articles center on the problems of the black economy, employment and corporate minority involvement. Useful and factual news is presented about careers, job opportunities, money management, and investments. Recommended for not only the business minded, but for students and consumers.

Black Law Journal. 1971. 3/yr. University of California, Los Angeles, 2 Dodd Hall, Los Angeles, Calif. 90024. Editor, David S. Chaney. Student, $5.00; General, $10.00; Institutions, $25.00.

In 1970, five black law students and two black law professors at the UCLA Law School planned a journal with "a format of articles discussing the impact of law on black people, feature stories on outstanding black people in the law, past and present, and analyses of proposed legislation, laws, and cases." Black law students, law school faculty, practicing attorneys, judges, educators, and scholars share the pages of this publication. The journal's readable articles, special symposia, and proceedings of conferences place this publication not only in the realm of interest for black law students, but for all persons involved in social justice. Book reviews are of political and legal works.

Black Perspective in Music. 1973. Semiannually (Spring and Fall). The Foundation for Research in the Afro-American Arts, Inc., P.O. Box 149, Cambria Heights, New York 11411. Editor, Eileen Southern. $5.00.

Articles are on current and past history of traditional and non-traditional Afro-American and African music, as well as musicians of all kinds. Interviews with famous personalities in the performing arts are discerning. Contributing to its importance to composers, performing artists, music educators, students, and librarians are the bibliographic listings and reviews. Under "New Music" are various categories such as "Orchestral Music," "Band," "Chamber," "Music for Ballet," and "Music for Films." Titles of dissertations and those in progress, with black author identification, are given. The book, record, and music reviews are outstanding. Announcements of special events, conferences, symposia, and festivals can be found in the "Commentary" section. Without a doubt, for all academic music collections.

Black Scholar; journal of black studies and research. 1969. Monthly. (Bimonthly in January-February and July-August.) P.O. Box 908, Sausalito, Calif. 94965. Editor, Robert L. Allen. $12.00.

This is one of the few publications born out of the black liberation thrust of the late 60s and early 70s that has survived the rigors of time and economic woes. Originating as a publication to combine "the writing of the black academy and the street," and "to take a stand against the bias of white scholarship," its early articles were heavily laden with black nationalistic ideology and activism. The second phase of 1975 witnessed a change in publisher and editor because of a purported swing to Marxism. Articles are written by noted black scholars, educators, and writers. There are in-depth book reviews, a descriptive list of "Books Received," interviews, poetry, and prose. Recently added is the "Black Books Round-Up" of all publishers' listings of black books, previews, and news of black publishers. A journal, despite wavering political directions, for black and ethnic collections.

Black Sports. 1970. Monthly. Black Sports, Inc., 31 East 28th Street, New York, New York 10016. Editor, Allan P. Baron. $9.00.

A good, all-around illustrated popular sports magazine, featuring articles of interest to anyone sportsminded. There are spotlights on college and high school athletes of the month. The "Rap" interviews are entertaining, and the "Historically Speaking" department dishes out tasty portions of black sports history. At least two or three sports related books are reviewed. An inclusion for school, public and academic libraries.

CLA Journal. 1957. Quarterly. College Language Association. Morgan State University, Baltimore, Md. 21239. Editor, Therman B. O'Daniel. $8.50.

As an organ of the CLA, the journal publishes critical and scholarly articles pertaining to the literature, language, and linguistics of Afro-Americans, and other nationalities. Book reviews range from two to four per issue. Organizational and professional news, announcements, reports, and transactions complete the format. The only black journal of this type, it is a necessity for collections.

Crisis. 1910. Monthly. National Association for the Advancement of Colored People. 1790 Broadway, New York, New York 10019. Editor, Warren Marr, II. $6.00.

Occupying a venerable position among the traditional black publications, the NAACP magazine offers not too scholarly articles on various subjects relating to blacks, news of the organization, "Crisis Editorials," and a "Book Corner" of one or two reviews. Important because of its source, for high school, public and academic libraries.

Ebony. 1945. Monthly. John H. Johnson Publishing Co., 820 S. Michigan Ave., Chicago, Ill. 60605. Editor, John H. Johnson. $12.00.

Now incorporating Johnson Publishing Company's literary *Black World*, this slick publication is the best known and most highly circulated of the black general magazines. As specified in its initial November issue, the focus is to "try to mirror the positive, everyday achievements" of black life. Utilizing photographs in the manner of the defunct *Life*, the 122 to 154 pages have topics for all interests. Popularly written articles focus on black history, personalities, sports, race, education, business, and health. The regular fashion and "Date with a Dish" features are colorful and have appeal. The "Sounds" column is valuable for record news, and the "Book Shelf" briefly notes various titles. There are occasional special issues devoted to themes similar to the "Black Male" and "Africa." An inclusion for all general reading collections, Afro-American or otherwise.

Encore; American and worldwide news. 1972. Biweekly. Ida Lewis Publisher, Tanner Publications Co., Inc., 515 Madison Ave., New York, New York 10022. Editor, Ida Lewis. $15.00.

An illustrated biweekly of American and worldwide news that began as a monthly, this thin imitation of *Newsweek*, with a twist, has a mixture of current news capsules, profiles, a smattering of black history, travel tips, and career guides along with record, film, and book reviews. The magazine claims to offer "information and service" geared to a black audience with emphasis on analyzing and interpreting the news. Signed articles are by both black and white writers, and the reviews are not exclusively of black oriented books and films. This is apparently in keeping with the magazine's "Panracialism" as coined by the editor. The articles do not have too much depth, but the overall magazine idea is good and refreshing.

Equal Opportunity; the minority student magazine. 1970. 3/yr. Equal Opportunity Publications, Inc., P.O. Box 202, Centerport, New York 11721. Editor, Alfred Duckett. $25.00.

An interracial publishing venture created by white publisher John R. Miller, III, with the editorial assistance of black writer Alfred Duckett, the magazine attempts to serve as a "communications channel between the world of business and work and college people seeking career, job and 'own your own business' opportunities." The stimulating articles on the personal experiences of those who have succeeded are honest and well-written. Additional articles on minority subjects by such people as Vernon Jordan, Maynard Jackson, and Senator Edward Brooke serve to hold interest and give balance. Even though the purpose is to inform minority students of economic opportunities, the magazine does not underplay racial hurdles. Of significance are the "Special Regional Section," which lists companies that recruit in specific geographic areas; the "Free Career Resume Service" offered by the publication to students; and the national "Corporate Profile Directory." For students with literary talents, fiction and poetry contributions are invited. The magazine is directed to all minority groups, women, blacks, Chicanos, Puerto Ricans, Cubans and Africans. The publishers also issue the *Collegiate Women's Career Magazine*. Of special value to college and graduate students of all minority groups needing information about job training and opportunities.

Essence. 1970. Monthly. Essence Communications, Inc., 1500 Broadway, New York, New York 10036. Editor, Marcia Gillespie. $8.00.

At one time the only continuing black magazine for black women, the slick format of fashion, cooking, home decoration, child rearing, and beauty tips mirrors white women's magazines. The publication has improved in quality throughout the years by changing its concentration, finally veering away from the all-consuming emphasis on black female/black male relationships. There are regular forums that comprise the "Congressional Black Caucus" where black congresspersons impart "information, analyses and positions on legislation," and "Education by Degrees," which discusses educational trends and problems. The "Your Sexual Health" column sometimes borders on a sex manual. Record and book reviews are slight, but the film reviews are occasionally quite perceptive. For buyers, "Consumer Concerns" is informative and serviceable. The black woman who has the time, inclination, and money for travel can get advice in a travel feature. The "Sign Time" appears to occupy considerable space, which must indicate that the editors perceive black women as horoscope-minded or dependent. Articles dealing with social, economic, and race issues confronting black women, as expected, are not too thought-provoking or weighty. The magazine attracts well known black writers, but the fiction is light and contributed by the lesser known as well as those of the stature of Bessie Head, Orde Coombs, and Toni Cade Bambara. The poetry section also has established writers to fill the page in the persons of Dudley Randall, Audre Lorde, and Mari Evans. Some black female intellectuals may view the magazine as one-sided or an affront to the black woman's image and intellect. The publication has survived, and if the big name advertisers occupying space are any indication, surviving well. It is widely read by all ages of women, and surprisingly, by some black males. It may be that the publication is filling a gap for the black bourgeois reading audience to which it is targeted, or that black women are so hungry for their own publication that anything will do until the real thing comes along. Entertaining reading for high school, public and academic libraries.

First World; an international journal of black thought. 1977. Bimonthly. First World Foundation, 1580 Avon Ave., S.W., Atlanta, Ga. 30311. Editor, Hoyt W. Fuller. $15.00; Foreign $18.00.

The discontinuation of *Black World* caused the founding of this new literary magazine by the First World Foundation, with Hoyt W. Fuller and Carole A. Parks together again as an editorial team. The premier January/February issue states one of the major objectives is to: "confront the world—and the issues and events of importance in the world—from a Black perspective." Contributions are sought from "thinkers and activists of the black world who have something of consequence to say." The origin of the title and background founding information is given in this soon-to-be collector's item. The publication, of newsmagazine size, will publish articles dealing with black history and culture and black social and economic concerns on a national and international scale. Short stories, poems, book reviews, and a descriptive list of "Recent Books Received" are included. A thankful continuation is the "In Perspective" column (similar to *BW's* "Perspectives"), which gives news of forthcoming and new publications, conferences, literary contests, authors, writers, artists, and art. This is most certainly for all library collections.

Freedomways; a quarterly review of the freedom movement. 1961. Quarterly.
Freedomway Associates, Inc., 799 Broadway, New York, New York 10003. Associate Editors, John Henrik Clarke, Ernest Kaiser, and J. H. O'Dell. $4.50.

Highly distinctive, this journal is in the rare position of being a black review not affiliated with an academic institution or professional organization that has withstood the test of time. The magazine covers the broad issues of racism within the context of the social, economic, and political systems affecting Afro-American, Africans, and other Third World peoples. The articles are not overly scholarly, but quite informative. Poetry inclusions and the too infrequent appearance of a short story serve to give a creative literary flavor. There does not appear to be a set format, but recurrent features making this publication especially valuable are the book reviews and current titles bibliographies that are of outstanding quality. Lengthy and critical reviews by knowledgeable persons average from six to nine per issue. "Recent Books" lists from forty to eighty-one titles with excellent annotations that refer to and compare similar works. In addition, authors are identified and other of their works noted. The books in this bibliography are by and about blacks in the United States and a few may include Africa and the Caribbean. One drawback is that copyright dates are not given. This is a basic title for all Afro-American collections.

Integrated Education. 1963. Bimonthly. Northwestern University, 2003 Sheridan Road, Evanston, Ill. 60201. Editor, Meyer Weinberg. $10.00.

Originating as a magazine for "clarifying the need for integration in education," the publication has changed its format from pocketbook to newsmagazine size. Illustrious educators, such as Robert Coles, Kenneth B. Clark, Charles V. Willie, and Thomas F. Pettigrew are among those on the editorial advisory list. The articles are of value and documented. Topics cover analyses, reports, and trends of the impact of school integration on urban development and attitudes, as well as social and economic implications which concern all minority groups. The "Chronicle of Race, Sex and Schools" gives reports of activities and news across the country. A "Race and Schools and Related Topics: Bibliography" lists books, dissertations, articles, and microfilm under subjects. One to two book reviews are in each issue. Informative for teachers, educators and administrators.

Jet. 1952. Weekly. John H. Johnson Publishing Co., Inc., 820 S. Michigan Ave., Chicago, Illinois 60605. Editor, John H. Johnson. $24.00.

The only black weekly newsmagazine and one of the most popular of the Johnson Publications line, the pocket-sized periodical provides an excellent, succinct round-up of black national and international news, along with non-black news of interest to black readers. Some of the articles give an inside coverage of stories that white newspapers fail to do. All facets of the news are presented, and the special feature stories are commendable. Routine entertainment guides of "Soul Brothers Top 20" and blacks on television appear weekly. This should be in all library collections.

Journal of Black Studies. 1970. Quarterly. Sage Publications, Inc., 275 South
  Beverly Drive, Beverly Hills, Calif. 90212. Editor, Molejik Assante.
  Institutions, $20.00; Individual, $12.00.

This is an interdisciplinary scholarly journal published with the assistance of a consortium of Black Studies Departments which include SUNY at Buffalo, Cornell University, Fisk University, Northwestern University and UCLA. Approximately eight to ten articles per issue cross-cut economic, political, historical, literary, and sociological subjects "related to persons of African descent." Topics ranging from "African Cultural Dimensions in Cuba," "The Dozens: An African Heritage Theory," to "Broadcaster Misperceptions of Black Community Needs" are covered. The original scholarly articles are well-documented, objective, and not grossly opinionated or political. Unfortunately, there is a conspicuous absence of the book reviews normally expected in a publication of this kind, although one might appear sporadically.

Journal of Negro Education; a Howard University quarterly review of issues
  incident to the education of black people. 1932. Quarterly. Editor-in-chief,
  Charles A. Martin. $7.50.

The oldest of the education subject journals is published under the auspices of Howard University's Bureau of Educational Research, with the assistance of an editorial/advisory board of scholars and educators from various schools and academic institutions. Scholarly articles cover educational research, history, trends, and developments involving all facets and levels of the field of education. The special summer issues have comprised "The Yearbook," which is a more inclusive edition devoted to one theme of importance arising during the year. Book reviews are under the "Current Literature on Black Education" and are of good quality. A publication basic for all academic collections.

Journal of Negro History. 1916. Quarterly. Association for the Study of Afro-
  American Life and History, Inc., 1401 14th Street, N.W., Washington, D.C.
  20005.

The prestigious ASALH's journal is the most distinguished in the discipline of Afro-American history. Each issue contains from five to six scientific articles that are heavily documented, in addition to a biographical treatment of a black's role in history. A large number of the articles view Afro-American history retrospectively. The "Document" series presents reproductions of primary source documents, letters, addresses, announcements, deeds, and minutes, with short introductions placing them in historical perspective. The January 1976 issue contained documents relating to "The Quest for Freedom" which had "Selected Documents Illustrative of Some Aspects of the Life of Blacks Between 1774 and 1841." The book review essays are excellent, as well as the book reviews. Clearly a good scholarly publication for academic libraries.

Negro Educational Review. 1950. Quarterly. P.O. Box 2895, General Mail Center,
  Jacksonville, Fla. 32203. Editor, J. Irving E. Scott. $10.00.

Originated by the National Teachers' Research Association, the publication presents articles, research reports, and critical analyses of issues confronting educators on the primary, secondary, and college or university levels. Primarily geared to teachers, the review can supplement the stronger *Journal of Negro Education*.

152 / Significant Books and Periodicals for Black Collections

Negro History Bulletin. 1937. Monthly. (October-May). Association for the Study of Afro-American Life and History, Inc., 1401 14th Street, N.W., Washington, D.C. 20005. Editor, J. Rupert Picot. $8.00.

Purposely designed not to be as scholarly as its companion publication, the *Journal of Negro History*, the magazine is mainly for lay historians, students, and schools; nevertheless, academic and some public librarians will certainly find it useful. The approximately twenty-two page format is attractive and nicely illustrated. Articles, averaging two to five pages in length, are interesting to read, informative, and have source notes. Biographies are about both famous and lesser known blacks, and some poetry is included. In addition, an "Editorial Comment" gives news of the Association's activities, and a "Preview" column that defines the subject concentration for the following month. Book reviews range from two to three per issue.

Phylon; the Atlanta University review of race and culture. 1940. Quarterly. Atlanta University, Atlanta, Ga. 30314. Editor, John D. Reid. $7.00.

The maiden issue stated as its *raison d'être*: "This quarterly review proposes to study and survey the field of race and culture, and of racial and cultural relations." Founded and edited by the eminent scholar W. E. B. Dubois, the publication was given the name "Phylon," which was transliterated from the Greek word "race." The eight to nine scholarly articles cover a broad gamut of topics, varying from "The Black Beauty Parlor Complex in a Southern City" to "Trends in Racial Differences in Political Efficacy: 1952-1972." The section entitled "Literature of Race and Culture" contains five to eight interpretive book reviews of high caliber. The publication is one that would enhance all academic collections.

Review of Black Political Economy. 1970. Quarterly. Black Economic Research Center, 112 W. 120th Street, New York, New York 10027. Editor, Lloyd L. Hogan. Individuals, $12.50; Institutions, $15.00; Full-time students, $8.00.

With the concept of providing a "hospitable arena in which black people could explore ideas as to how they might bring about effective and substantial improvement in their collective economic position," the journal offers a forum for articles on black economic development. Articles focus on all phases of the black economy, usually within the framework of the affects of racism and politics. Five to eight articles appear per issue, along with four lengthy book reviews. Some past issues have had a list of books received. A highly specialized journal for black economists.

Sepia. 1954. Monthly. Sepia Publishing Co., P.O. Box 2257, 1220 Harding Street, Fort Worth, Texas 76101. Editor, Ben Burns. $10.00.

An *Ebony* imitation, this pictorial general magazine's articles and photographs are of a substandard quality in comparison, besides having a minus for being printed on poor quality paper. Recurrent features are the "Sepia Scrapbook," which has news items; "Quote," similar to *Jet*'s "Words of the Week" of sayings by famous personalities; black history brevities in "This Month in Black History"; and "Black Humor." The largest, "Just Ask Me," answers gossipy questions about celebrities. Abounding with wig and corset advertisements, only for inclusive collections.

22. The Best Seller List and Black Authors
by Ann Allen Shockley

Books on the Best Seller Lists are not necessarily the "best books" in terms of their literary value. Such listings indicate only those books that are being sold the most. The people who usually buy these books for recreational reading or personal enlightenment are those who both can afford to buy them and have the leisure time to either read, or at least thumb through, the pages.

This reading class can be assumed to be typically white, middle-class, and affluent. Because of this, best seller lists are top-heavy with books reflecting the interests of the white reading populace; they indicate the taste, mood, and absorption of mind of this group against the backdrop of the country's literary, social and political currents. To have books by black authors represented on the Best Seller List is indeed remarkable, then, for few black authors have "made it."

In scrutinizing Alice Payne Hackett's pioneer compilation *Fifty Years of Best Sellers, 1895-1945*, it is pathetic to note that not until 1945 did a black author appear on the list, although books about blacks by white authors DuBose Heyward (*Mamba's Daughters*, 1929), Julia Peterkin (*Scarlet Sister Mary*, 1929), and Lillian Smith (*Strange Fruit*, 1944) were entries on the list. During this span of time, black writers such as James Weldon Johnson, Jessie R. Fauset, Zora Neale Hurston and Nela Larsen were writing, Langston Hughes was being widely read, and a rich period of black literature was flourishing in the Harlem Renaissance.

With the advent of Richard Wright's autobiographical *Black Boy* in 1945 on the Best Seller List, a "first" was made in the chronology of black literature. The book sold 195,000 copies and had book club sales of 546,000. The time was ripe for a black author to be nationally read and recognized, and the story of a Mississippi black boy growing up as an underdog in America arrived at a stage when a small egg of liberality was being hatched on the American scene. The nation was going through a metamorphosis of conscience. World War II was being fought to preserve democracy, black soldiers were losing their lives to save a country in which they were only half-free, and the propagation of white supremacy by the Nazi, coupled with their deliberate extermination of eight million Jews, precipitated a re-examination of America's own racial attitudes.

This re-evaluation of moral obligation was indicated in the literary trend. The best selling novel *Gentleman's Agreement* (1947), by Laura Z. Hobson, had a theme of anti-Semitic prejudice, and on the same list that year was Sinclair Lewis's *Kingsblood Royal*, a fictionalized account of a white man's dilemma at discovering "a nigger in the woodpile" somewhere down the ancestral line. These books mirrored a new boldness in American letters and the public's reading concern. Social themes were being read, if not adequately chewed or digested.

In 1946, Frank Yerby made his triumphant debut on the list with his swashbuckling historical costume novel *The Foxes of Harrow*. Since that time, Yerby, with entertaining historical novels devoid of rabid racial themes or heavy overtones, has captured a place on the list nine times—a record within itself for any writer.

Maya Angelou, in 1970, became the first black female author to make an appearance on the Best Seller List with her autobiographical *I Know Why the Caged Bird Sings*. In comparison to the number of white female writers who have written best sellers, as well as black males, this one small drop in the bucket is not even a tear in a needle's eye.

The list of black authors on the Best Sellers List compiled by Dorothy Lake should not be looked upon merely for statistical or reference information, but viewed critically for all of its ramifications. The fact that only nine black authors have appeared on the Best Seller List, one nine times, and another, James Baldwin, twice, is indeed a pathetic picture. It shows another side of racism in the publishing world, inherent within the publishers' promotion of books by black authors, booksellers' attempts to sell black books, book club selections and the book reviewing media.

Black writers can be "made" into best selling authors in the same ways as whites. All this necessitates is that publishers put forth more effort, time, and money into promoting their books. This is clearly apparent in the all-out promotion activity connected with Alex Haley's *Roots*. The results were far-reaching and satisfying.

With more support and cooperation between those segments which band together to make a best seller (for they *are* made through strenuous advertising promotions, personal interests of publishers, and word-of-mouth) black authors can too get a fairer and bigger slice of the Best Sellers Pie.

23. Best Selling Books by Black Authors

by   Dorothy Lake, Acquisitions Librarian, Fisk University

1945   Wright, Richard. *Black Boy*. New York: Harper, 1945.

1946   Yerby, Frank. *Foxes of Harrow*. New York: Dial Press, 1946.

1947   Yerby, Frank. *The Vixens*. New York: Dial Press, 1947.

1948   Yerby, Frank. *Golden Hawk*. New York: Dial Press, 1948.

1949   Yerby, Frank. *Pride's Castle*. New York: Dial Press, 1949.

1950   Yerby, Frank. *Floodtide*. New York: Dial Press, 1950.

1951   Yerby, Frank. *Woman Called Fancy*. New York: Dial Press, 1951.

1952	Yerby, Frank. *Saracen Blade.* New York: Dial Press, 1952.
1953	Yerby, Frank. *The Devil's Laughter.* New York: Dial Press, 1953.
1954	Yerby, Frank. *Benton's Row.* New York: Dial Press, 1954.
1963	Baldwin, James. *The Fire Next Time.* New York: Dial Press, 1963.
1965	Brown, Claude. *Manchild in the Promised Land.* New York: Macmillan, 1965.
1968	Baldwin, James. *Tell Me How Long the Train's Been Gone.* New York: Dial Press, 1968.
	Cleaver, Eldridge. *Soul on Ice.* New York: McGraw-Hill, 1968.
	Grier, William, and Price M. Cobbs. *Black Rage.* New York: Basic Books, 1968.
1970	Angelou, Maya. *I Know Why the Caged Bird Sings.* New York: Random House, 1970.
1976	Haley, Alex. *Roots.* New York: Doubleday, 1976.

Sources: *New York Times Book Reviews*; *Seventy Years of Best Sellers, 1895-1965*; *World Almanac and Book of Facts.*

24. Afro-American Authors Represented on the ALA Notable Book List

by Geraldine Clark, Assistant Director, Center for Library Media and Telecommunications, Board of Education, City of New York

The annual list of Notable Books is selected and published by the Reference and Adult Services Division of the American Library Association to call attention to books published during the year which are significant additions to the world of books (Notable Books Manual XIV-N 2-6). The list is intended for use by both the general reader and librarians who work with adult readers. As is true with any award prize or special listing officially sanctioned by ALA, the authority and prestige of the organization stand behind the selections and insures their wide representation in public library collections.

Although the general aim of the program has remained the identification of books which make significant contributions to knowledge or are of unusual aesthetic value, the method of selection and criteria have changed over the years. The lists began in 1944, when the chairman of the ALA Lending Section, with the cooperation of the editors of *Booklist*, drew up a list of "One Hundred Noteworthy Books of 1944." These titles were presented to the ALA membership, and on the basis of the membership vote, fifty were chosen as outstanding books for the year. Those chosen were ratified by ALA Council. This process continued through 1946. In 1947, the task was taken over by the Public Library Division and the name of the list changed to Notable Books. ALA staff members continued to assist a committee of 8 (later 12) in the selection, and Council continued to give its approval. In 1955, the Notable Books Council was established, with twelve members and a number of cooperating libraries. Since 1958, the Adult Services Division and its successor, Reference and Adult Services Division, have been responsible for the lists.

The original criteria stated that the list would include "books of permanent value or immediate significance, which have wide appeal." Today the criteria have been enlarged to read:

1. A book may be selected as significant for many reasons. It may possess literary merit; it may offer inspiration or pleasure; it may expand the horizons of man's knowledge or aspirations; it may make specialized knowledge comprehensible to the non-specialist; it may give promise of making a contribution toward the solution of a contemporary problem.

2. Each book will be considered in relation to the general adult reader. Books of limited interest, and books requiring highly specialized knowledge for their use will not be eligible. Books will not be excluded on the basis of their unsuitability for younger readers.

3. a) Each book shall have been published between December 1 of the preceding year and November 30 of the current year. In case of doubt, the actual date of publication shall be verified by a letter from the publisher indicating the exact date of publication or some other reliable bibliographic source. Forecast dates for publication will not be accepted.

b) The books selected will be limited to titles published in the United States of America, but may include translations from other languages.

c) Materials previously published in periodical form, revised or extended editions, or anthologies which have drawn together portions of previous publications may be included.

Over the years, thirty-three titles by Africans or Afro-Americans have appeared on the list. They include:

Abrahams, Peter. *Tell Freedom* (1954)
The pain and pathos of growing up in Johannesburg when one is of mixed racial ancestry is told without bitterness in a moving autobiography.

Anderson, Marian. *My Lord, What a Morning* (1956)
With great sincerity and without embellishment, a great American artist recounts her life from her Philadelphia childhood to her triumphs on great concert and opera stages of the world.

Angelou, Maya. *I Know Why the Caged Bird Sings* (1970)
In a powerful testament to the resilience of the human spirit, a sensitive poet overcomes the corrosive effects of the degrading racist milieu of her childhood. It is the story not only of personal triumph, but a tribute to the staying power of an impoverished Afro-American southern community as well.

Baldwin, James. *Nobody Knows My Name* (1961)
Penetrating, perceptive essays, flawlessly crafted, probe the relationship of Africans and Afro-Americans to the larger society in Europe and the United States.

Baldwin, James. *The Fire Next Time* (1963)
Two essays explore our common humanity by examining race relations in the United States. A critique of the Black Muslim movement provides a very personal look at a unique phenomenon by a master of the essay form.

Brooks, Gwendolyn. *In a Mecca: Poems* (1968)
A Pulitzer Prize poet looks at the universality of human experience through the joys and sorrows, triumphs and failures of the Afro-American inhabitants of a decaying apartment building.

Brown, Claude. *Manchild in the Promised Land* (1965)
Harlem in the thirties and forties is brought to life in the autobiography of a young man with an intense will to survive and the determination to overcome the devastating social pressures related to drugs, poverty, and broken families. It is a searing portrait of a community, of those who made it, and of those who did not.

Clark, Kenneth. *Dark Ghetto; Dilemmas of Social Power* (1965)
This searching, erudite examination of Harlem's social pathology refutes the allegation that the poor and deprived are responsible for their conditions. Dr. Clark underscores the irrelevancy and ineffectiveness of too many of the social agencies in American ghettos.

Cleaver, Eldridge. *Soul on Ice* (1968)
   Essays and letters of a former revolutionary describe his growing awareness of his blackness, of his place in American society.

Cole, Ernest, and Thomas Flaherty. *House of Bondage* (1967)
   The remarkable photo-journalism of a South African photographer make vivid the horrors of apartheid.

DuBois, W. E. B. *Color and Democracy* (1945)
   An incisive indictment of world-wide colonialism and racism by a scholar whose knowledge and influence was legendary.

Ellison, Ralph. *Invisible Man* (1952)
   Perhaps the greatest American novel of the twentieth century charts an Afro-American's efforts to give meaning to his existence. Told with humor, wisdom and consummate art.

Frazier, Edward Franklin. *The Negro in the United States* (1949)
   A distinguished sociologist presents his controversial theories of Afro-American history and status buttressed by exhaustive, scholarly research.

Gaines, Ernest. *The Autobiography of Miss Jane Pittman* (1971)
   A novel of an Afro-American Everyman in the guise of a one hundred-and-ten-year-old woman who reminisces about her long life from the end of the Civil War through the civil rights protests of the sixties. A celebration of the indestructibility of the human spirit, of the grace, humor, pride, courage, fear, and weakness of a remarkable people.

Grier, William H., and Price M. Cobbs. *Black Rage* (1968)
   Using case histories from their practices, two Afro-American psychiatrists explore the need for Afro-Americans to develop defensive mechanisms for survival.

Haley, Alex. *Roots* (1976)
   An extraordinary investigation into the past of an Afro-American family. This provocative history of a family is a panoramic view of the history of Afro-Americans, beginning in 1732 in West Africa with the author's ancestor, Kunta Kinte, being captured and brought to America as a slave.

Jackson, George. *Soledad Brother: Prison Letters* (1970)
   Letters from an Afro-American inmate of Soledad prison reveal an original intelligence and unmitigated rage at the repression of his people.

King, Martin Luther, Jr. *Stride Toward Freedom: The Montgomery Story* (1958)
   A compelling argument for non-violence as an instrument of social change coupled with a provocative commentary on southern race relations.

King, Martin Luther, Jr. *Strength to Love* (1963)
   Seventeen sermons containing Dr. King's conceptions of Christian love and a personal God.

Lamming, George. *In the Castle of My Skin* (1953)
   An autobiographical novel of the coming of age of a sensitive, talented youth reveal the complexes and values of the Bajan culture. The lyricism and curious empathy of the poet pervade the work.

Logan, Spencer. *Negro's Faith in America* (1946)
: A successful businessman's personal and largely uncritical assessment of the status of Afro-Americans at the close of World War II.

Luthuli, Albert. *Let My People Go* (1962)
: The courage and tenacity of this truly great man as he works to build a non-racist society in South Africa permeates this autobiography.

Meriwether, Louise. *Daddy Was a Number Runner* (1970)
: A Harlem family's disintegration during the Great Depression as seen through the eyes of the twelve-year-old daughter.

Parks, Gordon. *A Choice of Weapons* (1966)
: A brilliant photographer turns to hard work, dignity, and love as weapons in the fight against racism.

Redding, Joy Saunders. *Lonesome Road; The Story of the Negro's Part in America* (1958)
: The resilence of a people skillfully portrayed through the lives of twelve who left their distinctive mark on American society.

Robeson, Eslanda Cardoza. *African Journey* (1945)
: Returning from a trip to Africa, a careful observer and skillful anthropologist examines the African's predicament in the southern part of his continent.

Rowan, Carl T. *South of Freedom* (1952)
: With sharp insight and telling accuracy, an experienced journalist compares the climate in the South for Afro-Americans in 1951 with that of 1943.

Rowan, Carl T. *The Pitiful and the Proud* (1956)
: A cogent and thorough analysis of Southeast Asia during the fifties and also a candid picture of a reporter at work.

Tolson, M. B. *Harlem Gallery. Book I, The Curator* (1965)
: The quintessence of Harlem life in the powerful symbolism and soaring imagery of a major poet.

Waters, Ethel. *His Eye Is on the Sparrow* (1951)
: Despite the discrimination, poverty, and sordidness that were a part of her life, Ethel Waters's autobiography conveys a sense of her impressive achievement both as an artist and as a woman.

White, Walter F. *Man Called White* (1948)
: In his autobiography, a former secretary of the NAACP, whose whole adult life was spent in fighting bigotry, providing an exciting and incisive look at the fight for social justice and human dignity.

White, Walter F. *How Far the Promised Land* (1955)
: An optimistic look at Afro-American progress during the forties and fifties in education, politics, trade unionism, use of public accommodations and employment.

Wright, Richard. *Black Boy* (1945)
The cruelty and suffering of one life give insight into social conditions of many. The autobiography of a superbly talented artist is an almost unbearably moving account of childhood and youth in the Mississippi of the first quarter of this century.

These titles represent a remarkable collection which documents the Afro-American and African experience as only those who have lived it can. Almost half the entries are autobiographies or autobiographical fiction. Although Wright and Robeson appeared on the 1945 list, in most of the early years there was little representation of the black experience. This was perhaps a reflection of the tendency to include well established authors and stay away from controversial positions or the exploration of unpopular intellectual and philosophical theories. There are some noticeable omissions, for which it is impossible to account, Ann Petry, Langston Hughes, Franz Fanon, and John Killens among others. Nevertheless, the Notable Book List is an effective means of bringing the work of outstanding African and Afro-American writers to the attention of a large public.

25. Black Librarians as Creative Writers

by   Ann Allen Shockley

and

E. J. Josey

ANNE SPENCER (1881-1975)

Anne Spencer was a poet writing prior to the Negro Literary Renaissance who later contributed to it. She was born Anne Bethel Scales in Henry County, Virginia, on a plantation, February 6, 1881. Her father, Joel Cephus, was a descendant of mixed black, white, and Indian ancestry, and her mother, Sarah Louise, was a former slave and the daughter of a wealthy Virginia aristocrat. She learned to read and write at the age of eleven by starting with the *Bible*, *Police Gazette*, and the *Child's Picture Story of the Bible*. In 1893, she enrolled in the Virginia Seminary and Normal School in Lynchburg, Virginia, and was graduated with honors in 1899.

Two years later, she married her schooltime admirer, Edward Alexander Spencer, who built a home for his bride at 1313 Pierce Street in Lynchburg. Wanting his wife to have a place where she could write in solitude, Edward Spencer added a small one-room cottage next to her garden. Anne Spencer taught school for a while before becoming the first librarian at Dunbar High School, a position she held for over 20 years. Most of the books in the library were her personal copies. She also studied for a short time at the Hampton Library School.

Besides being a poet and librarian with a national reputation, she was a close friend of many famous people, including James Weldon Johnson, W. E. B. DuBois, Langston Hughes, and Georgia Douglas Johnson, who were frequent visitors to her home. Anne Spencer is described as being "a truly gifted and creative writer whose subject matter was not limited to race and protest" and as "a woman—and a black woman at that—succeeding in an art-form almost solely dominated by men." Her poetry has been included in such major anthologies as *The Poetry of the Negro*, *The Negro Caravan*, *Cavalcade*, and *Carolina Dusk*.

The mother of three children, she died on July 25, 1975. Her home and the little study-cottage, "Edankraal," have been restored and selected to be in the Virginia Landmarks Register by the Virginia Historic Landmarks Commission. The residence has been nominated also to the National Register of Historic Places.

[Mr. L. Garnell Stamps, president of the Friends of Anne Spencer Memorial Foundation, and Dr. J. Lee Greene, professor of English, University of North Carolina, Chapel Hill, are credited for this biographical information on the poet. Dr. Greene has authored a recent biography of Anne Spencer.]

[AAS]

ARNA BONTEMPS (1902-1973)

The name of Arna Bontemps is well known and remembered in both literary and library circles. He was a poet, librarian, editor, children's author and critic. One of the most prolific writers of his time, Bontemps was born in Alexandria, Louisiana, on October 13, 1902, and moved with his family at an early age to California. There he graduated with a Bachelor of Arts degree from Pacific Union College in 1923, and in 1943, received the Master of Arts degree from the University of Chicago.

Bontemps was a member of one of the most noted group of black writers and artists of the Harlem Renaissance. A man who once said that writing came natural to him, he won his first literary prize at the age of 24, when he was awarded the *Crisis* magazine's Alexander Pushkin poetry prize in 1926, and again in 1927. A short story award was presented to him by *Opportunity* magazine in 1932 for "A Summer Tragedy." For his *The Story of the Negro*, he was honored with the Jane Addams Book Award in 1956. He was a Julius Rosenwald Fellow, 1938-39; John Simon Guggenheim Fellow, 1949; and a National Endowment for the Humanities grantee, 1973.

His library career began as librarian at Fisk University in 1943. He remained at Fisk until 1965 when he left to become a professor at the University of Illinois in Chicago. In 1969, he went to Yale University to take a position as curator of the James Weldon Johnson Collection and visiting professor of English literature.

Bontemps returned to Fisk in 1971 to be writer-in-residence. He was named Honorary Consultant in American Cultural History at the Library of Congress in January, 1973. Honorary degrees were bestowed upon him by Berea College (L.L.D.) in 1973, and Morgan State University (L.H.D.), 1969. He was a member of the Omega Psi Phi fraternity, Dramatic Guild, and Author's League.

Among his creative works were *God Sends Sunday* (New York: Harcourt, Brace & Co., 1931), which was later dramatized as "St. Louis Woman"; *Black Thunder* (New York: The Macmillan Co., 1936); *Drums at Dusk* (New York: The Macmillan Co., 1939); *Chariot in the Sky: A Story of the Jubilee Singers* (New

York: Holt, Rinehart and Winston, 1951); and *The Old South* (New York: Dodd, Mead, 1973).

The author's literary career came to an end in Nashville, Tennessee, on June 4, 1973, when he died of a heart attack. But in his poem entitled "Miracles," he wrote: "A man may crumble into dust/And straightway live again."

[AAS]

OLIVER AUSTIN KIRKPATRICK (1911-   )

Oliver Austin Kirkpatrick was born in Jamaica, West Indies, on June 12, 1911. Prior to earning a B.S. degree in journalism from New York University in 1950, he was a sports editor and columnist for the *Jamaica Standard* from 1937 to 1941. During the period 1940-42, he was also a newscaster for the Jamaica radio station ZQI. After completing his studies at the Columbia University School of Library Service in 1953, Mr. Kirkpatrick began work as a librarian with the New York Public Library. In 1964, he joined the staff of the Brooklyn Public Library as Supervising Librarian.

His talents gained recognition when New York University awarded him the Joyce Kilmer Award for short stories. He has contributed poems to various magazines, and his juvenile book, *Naja the Snake and Mangus the Mongoose: A Jamaica Folktale* was published by Doubleday in 1970.

Kirkpatrick and his wife, Carol, have two sons, Ian and Brian. He is currently a librarian at the Bushwick Branch, Brooklyn Public Library, 340 Bushwick Avenue, Brooklyn, New York 11206.

[AAS]

DUDLEY RANDALL (1914-   )

Dudley Randall holds the unique distinction of being both a celebrated poet and publisher. As a librarian, his enthusiasm about black books, authors and writing spurred him in 1965 to found a revolutionary small, black publishing company, Broadside Press, in Detroit with only $12.00. This company is now one of the leading black publishers in the United States.

The path to success was not an easy one for Dudley Randall. Born in Washington, D.C., on January 14, 1914, he was graduated from Detroit's Eastern High School in 1930, and worked as a laborer for the Ford Motor Company from 1931 to 1937. Next, he joined the ranks of blacks who found the postal service one of the few respectable occupations open to them during that time. He entered Wayne State University in 1946, majoring in English, and was graduated in 1949 with a Bachelor of Arts degree. His education was continued at the University of Michigan where he earned an M.L.S. in 1951.

The fresh library school graduate gave up his job as a letter carrier to join the library staff at Lincoln University (Missouri) as a reference librarian, cataloger, and instructor in reference books. Here he remained until 1954, when he went to Morgan State University to become the Associate Librarian for Technical Services, 1954-55, and subsequently, Associate Librarian for Public Services the following year. He returned to Michigan in 1956 to work with the Wayne County Federated Library System. After thirteen years of service, he left this post to be poet-in-residence and librarian with the University of Detroit, until his retirement in 1975.

Although Dudley Randall was writing poetry during the blooming 1940s period of Gwendolyn Brooks, Margaret Walker and Robert Hayden, his first book of poetry was not published until 1966, when his own Broadside Press issued *Poem*

Counterpoem, written with Margaret Danner. For his poetry, he has been awarded the Wayne State University's Tompkins Award in both 1962 and 1966. In 1973, he was honored with the Kuumba Liberation Award.

As an editor and publisher of collected works, he has helped to call attention to the works of young black poets who perhaps would not have been known. According to *Black Books Bulletin* (Winter 1972): "Just about every major black poet to emerge out of the Sixties sprouted with Broadside Press."

He is married to Vivian Barnett Spencer and has one daughter, Mrs. Phyllis Ada (Randall) Sherron, III, by a previous marriage. The Randalls reside at 12651 Old Mill Place in Detroit. Always active, he belongs to Kappa Alpha Psi fraternity, the Arts Extended Gallery for the Advancement of Culture and Education, the Committee on Small Magazine Editors and Publishers, and the Michigan Council for the Arts Advisory Panel on Literature.

His books comprise *Poem Counterpoem*, with Margaret Danner (Broadside Press, 1966); *Cities Burning* (Broadside Press, 1968); *Love You* (Paul Breman, 1970); and *More to Remember* (Third World, 1971). He has edited *The Black Poets* (Bantam, 1971); *After the Killing* (Third World, 1973); and the Broadside series of Broadside Press.

[AAS]

LESLIE MORGAN COLLINS (1914-   )

Leslie Morgan Collins ("L. M. Collins") is a Louisianian by birth, born in Alexandria on October 4, 1914. He was graduated from Dillard University in 1936, and went on to do graduate work at Fisk University, where he received the A.M. degree. He held teaching positions in southern schools before undertaking additional graduate work at Case Western Reserve University, which awarded him the M.S.L.S. and Ph.D. degrees.

Dr. Collins joined the English faculty of Fisk University in 1945, where he remains as professor of English. He has been the recipient of a Rosenwald Fund Fellowship, Ford Foundation Fellowship, and an Institute of International Education Fellowship. Post-doctoral study has been at the Universities of Havana, Oslo, Florence, and Madrid.

Possessing a profound love and appreciation for books and authors, Dr. Collins serves as a senior book reviewer for the *Nashville Tennessean*. A poet of note, his works have appeared in the *Poetry of the Negro*, *American Negro Poetry*, *Beyond the Blues*, and *Ik Zag Hoe Zwart Ik*. His poetry received international acclaim when read on "Anyone for Tennyson" (Public Broadcasting Service TV), at the Edinburgh International Festival, and the telecast on the British Broadcasting Corporation at London, September, 1976. He resides on the campus of Fisk University, 926 A 17th Avenue, North, Nashville, Tennessee 37208.

[AAS]

ANN ALLEN SHOCKLEY (1927-   )

Ann Allen Shockley is both an academic librarian and a writer of fiction. Born in Louisville, Kentucky, on June 21, 1927, she was educated as well in the Blue Grass State. After being graduated from Fisk University with a B.A. degree in 1948, majoring in history and minoring in English, she went to Case Western Reserve, where she received her M.S.L.S. in 1959. Her career in academic librarianship has taken her to Delaware State College (1959), the University of Maryland, Eastern

Shore Branch (1960-69), and then back to Fisk, where she is currently Associate Librarian for Public Services with the faculty rank of Associate Professor of Library Science.

Her initial experience as a writer was as a newspaper writer and contributor. This paved the way for her unique contribution to the Black Caucus of the American Library Association, for she served most capably as the first editor of the *Black Caucus Newsletter*. In 1975, the ALA Black Caucus bestowed upon her its Special Service Award not only for her yeoman performance as the first editor of the *Newsletter*, but also for her creative contributions. Ms. Shockley published an essay in *College and Research Libraries* (January 1974) on "Black Book Reviewing: A Case for Library Action" that has been selected for *Library Lit. 5—The Best of 1974*. She also wrote "A Soul Cry for Reading" for *The Black Librarian in America*.

Ann Allen Shockley's short stories and essays appear often in magazines, journals and anthologies, and the American Association of University Women honored her with its National Short Story Award in 1961. She also published a reference book compiled with the assistance of Sue P. Chandler, *Living Black American Authors: A Biographical Directory* (R. R. Bowker, 1973). Her novel, *Loving Her* (Bobbs-Merrill, 1974) is an attempt by her "to create an understanding and compassion for people who choose another type of life-style."

A divorcee, she has a son, William Leslie Shockley, Jr., and daughter, Tamara Ann Shockley. She resides on the campus of Fisk University.

[EJJ]

MARGARET PERRY (1933-   )

Margaret Perry was born in Cincinnati, Ohio, on November 15, 1933. In 1959, she graduated from the School of Library Science at Catholic University, five years after receiving her Bachelor of Arts degree from Western Michigan University. Her first library post was with the New York Public Library in 1954, where she served for two years as a young adult and reference librarian. She spent the summer of 1956 studying at the Université de Paris in France, and from 1959 to 1967, she was a U.S. Army librarian in Europe. While in this post, she also pursued her creative writing. As a result, she was awarded honorable mention in the Armed Forces Writers League Short Story Contest in 1965, and first prize in the following year.

Upon returning to the states in 1967, she became chief of circulation at the U.S. Military Academy Library, West Point, N.Y., where she remained until 1970. Leaving this position, she was named Head of the Education Library at the University of Rochester. A joint appointment was offered in 1973 as assistant professor of English, and two years later, she advanced to associate professor. She is currently Acting Director of Libraries at the University of Rochester.

Margaret Perry is known in library circles for *A Bio-bibliography of Countee P. Cullen, 1903-1946* (Greenwood Press, 1971). She has also been an associate editor of the *University of Rochester Library Bulletin*. Her articles appeared in *Phylon*, *Panache*, and the *Ball State University Forum*.

As a short story writer, Margaret Perry was influenced by what she terms as "the traditional practitioner—the short story writer who writes the well-made story, the poet who adheres to form." In addition to her army literary awards, she has won the Certificate of Merit of the Writers Digest Short Story Competition in 1968, and second place for the Francis Steloff Prize the same year.

[AAS]

AUDRE LORDE (1934-   )

Poet Audre Lorde is rapidly rising in the orbit of contemporary successful black poets. Her poetry has appeared in anthologies and national magazines, and in 1974, she was nominated for a National Book Award for her collection of poetry, *From a Land Where Other People Live.*

The Hunter College graduate (English major, 1959) is a native New Yorker, born in that city on February 18, 1934. Before receiving her M.L.S. from Columbia University in 1961, she held a myriad number of jobs: nurse's aide in Bellevue Hospital, factory worker for Crystal Ribbon, library clerk for the New York Public Library, arts and crafts supervisor for the Police Athletic League, and social investigator for the Bureau of Child Welfare. From 1960 to 1962, she was Young Adult Librarian at the Mt. Vernon Public Library. For three years, 1962-65, she was self-employed. After this period, she became Head Librarian at the Town School and remained there until 1968. Presently, she is an associate professor of English at the John Jay College of Criminal Justice, lectures at various universities, and gives poetry readings.

Audre Lorde received the Creative Artists Public Service Award from the New York State Council of the Arts in both 1972 and 1976. The National Endowment to the Arts gave her a grant in 1968, and she spent the summer of that year as poet-in-residence at Tugaloo College. Her two children, Elizabeth and Jonno, are a treasured part of her family and writing life on Staten Island.

Her books of poetry include: *The First Cities* (Poets Press, 1968); *Cables to Rage* (Breman Ltd., 1970); *From a Land Where Other People Live* (Broadside Press, 1973); *New York Head Shop and Museum* (Broadside Press, 1975); *Coal* (W. W. Norton & Company, Inc., 1976); and *Between Ourselves* (Eidolon Editions, 1976).

[AAS]

SHARON BELL MATHIS (1937-   )

Sharon Bell Mathis, a former school teacher and renowned author of children's books, is a recent and welcome addition to the field of librarianship. Born February 26, 1937, she was a magna cum laude graduate of Morgan State University (1958), where she excelled as a sociology major. The 1957 Benjamin F. Jackson Prize, the Emmanuel Chambers Memorial Award, and the Eliza Jane Cunnings Medal (all in sociology) were awarded to her in 1958. Upon graduating, the young sociologist worked as a caseworker for the District of Columbia's Children's Hospital for a year.

As a Washington school teacher, Sharon Bell Mathis taught at the Holy Redeemer Catholic School, 1960-65, and the Charles Hart Junior High School, 1965-75. On May 9, 1975, she received her M.S.L.A. from Catholic University and she began work as a librarian at the Benning Elementary School, remaining there for a year. Now she is at the Friendship Educational Center, Elementary and Junior High School.

Her writing talent was perceived in 1970 when Coward-McCann Publishers nominated her for the 1970 Weekly Reader Children's Book Club Fellowship given to a writer of children's literature who has displayed unusual promise. She won the award, which was presented to her at the Bread Loaf Writers' Conference in Vermont.

Since the publication of her first book in 1970, she has become an award-winning author. For *Sidewalk Story*, she received the Council on International Books for Children Award (1970), The 1974 Coretta Scott King Award was hers for *Ray Charles*, and *The Hundred Penny Box* was designated a 1976 Newberry Honor Book. She has been a writer-in-residence at Howard University since 1972.

Sharon Bell Mathis divides her writing and library work time between her husband, Leroy Franklin, and their three children, Sherie, Stacy, and Stephanie at the family home, 131 Elmira Street, S.W., Washington, D.C. 20032. Her books are entitled: *Brooklyn Story* (Hill & Wang, 1970); *Sidewalk Story* (Viking, 1971); *Teacup Full of Roses* (Viking, 1972); *Ray Charles* (Crowell, 1973); *Listen for the Fig Tree* (Viking, 1974); and *The Hundred Penny Box* (Viking, 1975).

[AAS]

AFRICAN RESOURCES

26. Procurement of Materials from Africa:
    A Bibliographic Essay
    by   Mohammed M. Aman, Dean, Palmer Graduate School of
         Library and Information Science, Long Island University

Problems of selection and acquisition of African library material have increased because of the publishing "explosion" in African studies in Europe, the United States, and Africa itself in recent years. The widespread increase in the demand for all kinds of Africana materials, the creation of many new African collections, and the expansion of established collections to support African and Afro-American studies in American and European institutions have all contributed to the demand for more Africana to support intensified research interests.

Acquiring library materials from Africa is not an easy task. It is difficult and sometimes frustrating for several reasons. Paramount among these are: 1) an underdeveloped book industry, 2) a lack of organized bibliographic control to identify new publications, and, 3) the reluctance of African publishers to accept mail order business.

THE AFRICAN BOOK INDUSTRY

The development of book industries in Africa and the problems these industries face have been the theme of various conferences and projects. "Publishing in Africa" was the theme of a conference held from December 16-20, 1973 at the University of Ife in Nigeria.[1] The conference was directed by Hans Zell and included papers by publishers, printers, librarians, booksellers and writers. Primarily, the conference brought to surface the widening gap between indigenous and expatriate publishers, and advocates of Africanized publishing attacked "expatriate" publishing houses on the grounds of their insensitivity to the needs of African readers. During the

---

[1] The full report of the Conference was published by the University of Ife in 1974. A summary was published by Eva-Maria McLean under the title "Publishing in Africa, Conference Examines the Problems of an Indigenous Industry," *Publishers Weekly* 18 (1974):58-59.

conference, one of Nigeria's indigenous and most successful publishers, Gabriel Onibonoje, managing director of Onibonoje Press, Ltd. in Ibadan, stated that publishing should be entirely Africanized as soon as possible. Similar views were expressed by Walter Harders, who declared that African nations ought to be far less dependent on foreign printing and publishing than they are at the present time. In his report, Harders made very specific proposals and recommendations on equipment, manufacturers, costs, space requirements and staffing.[2]

In a piece on "Publishing in Africa in the Seventies," Hans Zell pointed out that "one of the major advantages the expatriate publisher enjoys in Africa aside from his reputation is his access to capital." He added that "the chronic problem of insufficient capital continues to be a major problem for the indigenous African publisher."[3] Lack of sufficient capital, however, is by no means the only reason that indigenous African publishers have failed to expand significantly. There is also the lack of an adequate readership.[4]

In 1968, a meeting of experts on book development in Africa was held for the first time at the initiative of UNESCO in Accra, Ghana. At this meeting, 23 nations discussed important problems of the modern African trade. The meeting was held pursuant to a decision taken by the General Conference at its fourteenth session (Resolution 4.222) which considered that efforts to develop book publishing should be "fully integrated into overall economic and social planning" and should contribute to the promotion of mutual understanding. . . ."[5] Participants made it clear that they also recognized the lack of the fundamental informatory media necessary for developing and promoting the present standing of the African book trade and for rendering book trade contacts between Africa and other countries. The report on the meeting was published by UNESCO under the title *Book Development in Africa: Present Problems and Perspectives* (Paris, UNESCO, 1969), and it is comprised of two parts. The first reviews the problems of book development in Africa as they emerged from the discussion and working papers. The second summarizes the main suggestions of the meeting for a program of action.

Also in 1968, a final report entitled *Book Development Project in Nigeria* was published by Franklin Book Programs, Inc. The report was based on a study conducted between 1964 and 1968 in Nigeria by the Franklin Book Programs, Inc., under a grant from the Ford Foundation and with financial cooperation from the Government of Nigeria and the U.S. Agency for International Development. The report covered all aspects of book publishing in Nigeria. Similar studies were

---

[2] Walter Harders, *Report from Africa: A Modern Approach to Improved Publishing* (Tripoli, Libya: Author, 1970).

[3] Hans M. Zell, "Publishing in Africa in the Seventies: Problems and Prospects," in D. A. Clarke, *Acquisitions from the Third World* (London: Mansell, 1975).

[4] *Ibid.*, p. 107.

[5] UNESCO, *Book Development in Africa: Problems and Perspectives* (Paris, 1969), p. 7.

conducted by the Franklin Book Programs to determine the future needs of book development programs for Tanzania,[6] Kenya,[7] and West Africa.[8]

Recent developments clearly show that African publishing industry has undergone a rapid change during the past few years, progress that may be attributed to the spread of education at all levels in African countries. The number of universities established in Africa has been increased, and consequently, a great deal of research and publication is being conducted in these institutions. Postgraduate studies are also being developed in Africa and consequently, more research and publications are coming out of these institutions. Modern publishing houses are thus now producing quality books for African students and scholars.

In his account of "Publishing in Africa in the Seventies," Hans Zell gives a brief account of the major publishing houses in Nigeria.[9] According to him, growing awareness exists among African universities of the need for their own university presses, especially in West Africa. In Nigeria, there are two very active university presses, and a third one has recently come into operation. The Ibadan University Press is the largest university press in Africa, and has a list of well over one hundred titles, all produced at its own plant.[10] Ibadan University books are distributed in the United States through Africana Publishing Corporation in New York.

The University of Ife Press is expanding its list of books, which currently emphasizes books on African law, history, and public administration. Ife has also been associated with the important reference tool *African Books in Print*. Other Nigerian universities which have a press of one kind or another are Ahmadu Bello University (Zaria), The University of Nigeria (Nsukka), and Lagos University (Lagos).

In Ghana, a consortium of universities known as the Ghana Universities Press was formed. In Ethiopia, the Haile Selassie University Press (Addis Ababa) publishes a small number of titles in cooperation with Oxford University Press. The Universities of Nairobi, Dar es Salaam and Makerere largely rely on the East African publishing house for the publication of books by their academic staff.

Non-academic presses include the Tanzania Publishing House, set up in 1966 as the result of a partnership with the Macmillan Company and the National Development Corporation of Tanzania. The company first concentrated on publishing primary school books, but the program is now being considerably expanded to include other areas of publishing, particularly books for adult education in Swahili. In Nigeria, the Northern Nigerian Publishing Company was set up in 1966 by a consortium of the Gaskiya Corporation (Zaria) and Macmillan. A newly

---

[6] Franklin Book Programs, Inc., *A Book Development Program for Tanzania: Prepared for the United States Agency for International Development under Contract No. AID/CSD-465-Task Order 10* (New York, 1966).

[7] Franklin Book Programs, Inc., *A Book Development Program for Kenya: Report and Recommendation. Prepared for the United States Agency for International Development under Contract No. AID/CSD-464-Task Order 10* (New York, 1966).

[8] Franklin Book Programs, Inc., *Nigerian Book Program: Proposal by Franklin Publications, Inc.* (New York, 1962), p. 22.

[9] Zell, pp. 111-119.

[10] *Ibid.*

established state-sponsored publisher in Nigeria is the Ethiope Publishing Corporation, which has the backing of the Midwest State Government. The Ghana Publishing Corporation was established in 1965. It has highly sophisticated printing equipment which produces quality school, academic and children's books. The National Education Company of Zambia (NECZAM) was established in 1967, as a subsidiary of the Kenneth Kaunda Foundation, to act as the Foundation's publishing arm in its commitment to "Zambianize" the production and distribution of educational books.

The commercial East African Publishing House (Nairobi) is East Africa's largest independent general publishing house and was founded in 1965. Its publications range from professional academic studies to primary school readers. In addition to a wide range of books, EAPH also published such periodicals as: *East African Journal of Rural Development, Busara, Transafrican Journal of History, African Adult Education, African Scientist, African Review*, to mention only a few. These and other publications are also valuable sources for identification of new and local publications in various subject areas.

Another major East African publisher is the East African Literature Bureau, which, since its inception in 1948, has been the publishing outlet of the East African community, with offices in Nairobi, Dar es Salaam and Kampala. Also in Nigeria, the Nwamife Publishers (Enugu) produces primarily books on literature and some scholarly books. However, the Onibonoje Press and Book Industries (Ibadan) is the pioneering indigenous African publisher. In Lagos, there is the John West Publications, and in Ibadan, the Daystar Press is now getting away from religious publications to scholarly book publishing. The Di Nigro Press (Lagos) is owned and run by Nigeria's controversial and flamboyant writer, Naiwo Osahon. In Ghana, Anowuo Educational Publications is run by the novelist, Asare Konadu.

The expansion of educational resources has created an expanded market for books of every type. According to Jerry James,[11] pride, economy, language, and unique educational programs provided the stimuli for indigenous publishing. As a result, the number of indigenous publishers is growing rapidly. It is estimated that outside of South Africa, eleven indigenous African publishers now have over 100 titles in print.[12] Nigeria and Nairobi, Kenya, can be considered the publishing centers for sub-Sahara Black Africa, but cities in other countries are rapidly emerging as centers for book industries.

While the development of publishing industries in Africa paves the way for more quality books from that continent, bibliographic control is a necessity for the identification of these publications. The present lack of bibliographic control is considered one of the main difficulties in acquiring current materials from Africa, especially since the continent seems to lack adequate bibliographic control over its general publications as well as non-commercial titles, such as institutional and governmental publications, in particular.

---

[11] Jerry James, "The Establishment of an Overseas Acquisitions Center: A Personal Reminiscence," *The Quarterly Journal of the Library of Congress* 27 (July, 1970):206-212.

[12] Hans M. Zell, ed., *African Books in Print: An Index by Author, Title and Subject* (London: Mansell, Part 1, 1975).

BIBLIOGRAPHIC CONTROL

The problems surrounding bibliographical developments in Africa were the subjects discussed at the various sessions of the International Conference on African Bibliography, held in Nairobi from December 4-8, 1967. The proceedings and papers of the Conference were published in a volume entitled *The Bibliography of Africa*, edited by J. D. Pearson and Ruth Jones (London: Frank Cass, 1970). Angela Molnos also reviewed some of the issues discussed in the Conference.[13]

The papers prepared for the Nairobi Conference covered a wide variety of subjects, ranging from the acquisition and recording of Africana to problems in Africana library classification and surveys of bibliographic developments in various African countries.

It is only recently that some African countries began to compile and publish their national bibliographies, and these are primarily based on effective deposit laws, which require the cooperation of book publishers and libraries. As a result, the bibliographies vary in their coverage and comprehensiveness from one country to another. Most notable are the bibliographies of Nigeria, South Africa, Ghana, Tanzania and Egypt. Less advanced ones are available from Algeria, Botswana, Ethiopia, Ghana, Ivory Coast, Malagasy Republic, Malawi, Mauritius, Morocco, Rhodesia, Senegal, Sierra Leone, and Uganda. With the possible exception of Senegal and the Ivory Coast, no current national bibliography exists for any of the French West African countries and very few book deposit laws are enforced.

About twenty-three African countries are covered by two current regional bibliographies, the *Accessions List Eastern Africa*, published by the Library of Congress Office in Nairobi, and the *Bibliographie nationale courante des pays d'Afrique d'expression française*, published by the Library School of Dakar. According to Ernst Kohl, the countries covered are Cameroon, the Central African Republic, Chad, the Comoro Islands, the Congo, Dahomey, the French Territory of the Afars and Issas, Gabon, Guinea, Kenya, Mali, Mauritania, Niger, Réunion, the Seychelles, the Somali Republic, the Sudan, Tanzania, Togo, Uganda, Upper Volta, Zaire, and Zambia.[14]

Publications of the former Portuguese territories of Angola, the Cape Verde Islands, Mozambique, Guinea and Sáo Thomó are included in the *Boletin de bibliografia Portuguese* and also listed in the *Bibliografia Cientifica de Junta de Investigacoes do Ultramar*. Publications of Angola are also recorded in the *Boletin bibliografico* of the Centro de Documantação Cientifica do Instituto de Investigação Cientifica de Moçambique.

The recent publication of *African Books in Print* in two parts, with English/ African language and French volumes to be issued in alternating years is a useful tool for identifying trade books published in Africa. This trade bibliography,

---

[13] Angela Molnos, "Whither African Bibliographies? An Observer's Afterthoughts to a Recent Conference," *East Africa Journal* (February, 1968):17-25.

[14] Ernst Kohl, "Acquisition Problems of Africa South of the Sahara," in D. A. Clarke, *Acquisitions from the Third World* (London: Mansell, 1975), p. 86.

compiled by Hans Zell, has the potential for becoming a reliable, functional reference tool and buying guide to African published materials currently in print. Zell also hopes that ABIP will help stimulate further interest in African books among librarians and scholars in all parts of the world (ABIP, Pref., xii). Previous attempts were made to publish the equivalents of the American *Books in Print.* In 1969, the Nigerian Publishers Association with the support of Franklin Book Programs, Inc., issued *Nigerian Books in Print.* In Ghana, a *Ghanaian Books in Print*, was published in 1971 but with no subsequent supplements or editions.

The lists of publications announced in the *African Book Publishing Record*[15] are useful for both the acquisition and Africana librarians. The bibliographies are compiled in collaboration with over 200 African publishers, research institutions, learned societies, professional associations, and other organizations with publishing programs. ABPR includes books in English and in French as well as selected significant new titles in the indigenous African languages. It covers books, pamphlets, reports, series (including regular series), but does not include periodical publications or magazines other than yearbooks or annuals. For the time being, at least, government and official publications are also excluded. Bibliographic listings in ABPR provide a supplementary and updating service to *African Books in Print.*

In addition to ABPR and ABIP,[16] *Africana Journal*[17] (formerly *Africana Library Journal*), *A Current Bibliography on African Affairs*[18] and the *International African Bibliography*[19] provide valuable information such as bibliographic listing of books and periodicals. Also useful is the *African Research and Documentation*[20] published under the auspices of SCOLMA.

UNESCO's *Bibliography, Documentation, Terminology* is another useful source for the identification of current and retrospective bibliographies. The reports on bibliographic activities of various nations, including those in Africa, are compiled by national libraries or bibliographic centers and can be considered semi-official reports. The acquisition librarian will find the published surveys to be very valuable for ascertaining guides to Africana literature.

Bibliographic and research information centers are emerging inside and outside Africa, and they constitute yet another source for the identification and the discovery of African publications. The East African Research Information Center, sponsored by the East African Academy, is a new institution aiming to collect, collate, and disseminate information on past and current research in the social sciences with special reference to East Africa.

---

[15]*African Book Publishing Record* (Oxford, 1975–).

[16]Zell, *African Books in Print.*

[17]*Africana Journal* 1:1– . New York: African Publishing Corporation, 1970– . (Formerly *Africana Library Journal.*)

[18]*Current Bibliography on African Affairs*, edited by Daniel Matthews (Washington, D.C.: African Bibliographic Center, 1:No. 1– , January, 1968–).

[19]*International African Bibliography*, edited by John Pearson (London: Mansell, 1971–).

[20]*African Research and Documentation, the Journal of the African Studies Association of the UK and the Standing Commission on Library Materials on Africa* (Birmingham: Centre of West African Studies, University of Birmingham, No. 1, 1973–).

The Standing Conference on Library Materials on Africa (SCOLMA) has initiated, among other things, a number of projects to improve the coverage of publications needed for African studies. SCOLMA's first efforts were mainly bibliographical, and the standing conference has produced an annual bibliography of United Kingdom publications on Africa and a list of theses in Africa. Its newsletter, *Library Materials on Africa*, was first published in 1962. Like SCOLMA, CARDAN (Centre d'Analyse et de Recherche Documentaire pour l'Afrique Noire) is responsible for the setting up of regional special collections. CARDAN also publishes an information and liaison bulletin which aims mainly at listing in-progress African research in French.

Periodicals, especially those emphasizing bibliography (such as *Africana Journal*) are also a good source for information on Africana. AJ includes a regular column entitled "The Acquisition of Africana," which is a good source for information on news, research in progress, new reference sources, etc. The column also provides a directory of government printers throughout English speaking Africa.

Accession lists of African and non-African libraries with extensive African collections are a good source for identification of publications. Northwestern University began in 1962 to publish a bi-monthly *Joint Acquisitions List of Africana*. Twenty libraries cooperate in this project by reporting their acquisitions of African material to the publisher (African Department, Northwestern University Library, Evanston, Illinois). Another joint acquisition list is *Africana i nordiska Vetenskapliga bibliotek* which records recent acquisitions of the Scandinavian libraries that specialize in Africa. New additions to the International African Institute appear in the Institute's quarterly journal, *Africa*.

The *Library Accessions List*, published by the University College Library in Nairobi, attempts to identify not only as many Kenya publications as have been acquired, but also "all material" about East African countries. In Uganda, the Makerere University, which is the nation's depository center, publishes a *Quarterly Bulletin and Accessions List* including a section entitled "Ugandan Bibliography." The bibliography consists mainly of government documents. The University College at Dar es Salaam also publishes its *Quarterly Bulletin and Accession List* (since 1961).

ACQUISITION AND IDENTIFICATION OF SERIALS

In addition to monographs, periodicals constitute one of the largest and most complex problems confronting Africana librarians. Because of the relatively poor state of bibliographic control, many serials published in Africa are unknown to their potential users. The African section of the U.S. Library of Congress is an important bibliographic center for African studies. The section publishes retrospective and current bibliographies of African periodicals, tools valuable to the Africana librarian for the identification and acquisition of African serial publications.

Among the bibliographies of African periodicals published by the section are the following: *Sub-Saharan Africa, a Guide to Serials*, 1970, 409p.; *Nigerian Publications*, 1963 (Nigerian Periodicals and Newspapers, 1962, pp. 44-48). To ascertain what African newspapers are in American libraries, see also *African Newspapers in Selected American Libraries: A Union List* (3rd ed., comp. by Rozanne M. Barry, 1965).

SOLMA also issued a list of periodicals published in Africa. Four sections have appeared so far: Parts 1 and 2 cover French speaking Africa; Part 3 includes Ethiopia, Libya, Somali Republic, and the Sudan; Part 4 includes Liberia, Mauritius, St. Helena, and Seychelles.

OFFICIAL PUBLICATIONS

A good Africana collection must constantly be enriched by African government publications. African governments are active publishing houses, and they cover topics in various fields of knowledge, with particular emphasis on the social and political sciences, business, industry, economics, science and technology, history, and statistics.

The acquisition of African official publications is not an easy task. Dealers are helpless and librarians are faced with the dual problem of identification first and acquisition second. Most African governments do not maintain government printing offices and, government printers, when they exist, are not equipped to publicize their publications as commercial publishers do. Government publications are not frequently deposited in the national libraries of the countries and their identification for current bibliographic listings is hopelessly lacking.

To help identify African government publications, libraries in the U.S. and Europe have compiled and published retrospective bibliographies. The African section of the Library of Congress is active in this field, and among its publications are:

Madagascar and adjacent islands; a guide to official publications. Comp. by Julian W. Witherell, 1965.

Nigeria; a guide to official publications. (Rev. ed.). Comp. by Sharon Burdge Lockwood, 1965.

The Rhodesias and Nyasaland; a guide to official publications. Comp. by Audrey A. Walker, 1965.

Ghana; a guide to official publications, 1872-1968. Comp. by Julian W. Witherell and Sharon B. Lockwood, 1969.

French Speaking West Africa; a guide to official publications. (Rev. ed.). Comp. by Julian W. Witherell, 1967.

Official Publications of Sierra Leone and Gambia (Guide). Comp. by Audrey A. Walker, 1963.

Official Publications of British East Africa. Comp. by Helen Conover and Audrey A. Walker, 1960-63. 4v.

Official Publications of French Equatorial Africa, French Cameroons, and Togo, 1946-1958. Comp. by Julian W. Witherell, 1964.

Portuguese Africa; a guide to official publications. Comp. by Mary Jane Gibson, 1967.

The problems of acquiring African government publications are detailed in an article written by Thompson Omoerha, Sub-Librarian, University of Benin, Nigeria and published in *Libri* (1973).[21] Omoerha enumerates methods used by libraries in

---

[21] Thompson Omoerha, "African Government Publications: Problems of Acquisition and Organization," *Libri* 23, No. 4 (1973):298-306.

acquiring government publications: (a) by purchasing directly from the government agency, (b) by exchange or by receiving complimentary copies, which is considered by many Africana librarians to be the best method for acquiring this type of material. The acquisition and bibliographic control of official publications in East Africa was also the subject of a paper delivered by J. Ndegwa at the Nairobi Conference.[22] The paper also dealt with other problems facing libraries and other institutions dealing with such documents.

Because of the bibliographic problems mentioned above, Africana specialists are relying for their acquisitions on standing, blanket orders with dealers in Europe and the United States, the dealers acting as jobbers. Blanket order arrangements, in spite of their limitations, work effectively for Africa where a systematized, well organized publishing industry and current bibliographic coverage are in the developing stages. One of the limitations is that blanket orders place the burden of selection on the dealer, who cannot realistically be expected to know what is and what is not considered to be of research value. Also, there is no guarantee that the library is receiving all current publications.

However, most dealers handle only "trade" books, leaving the library with the difficult task of trying to identify and obtain government documents and publications of quasi-official publications. Even when a blanket order arrangement is followed, the library may have to rely also on direct order from publishers in Africa. This can be frustrating as well, since many of these publishers do not respond to librarians' correspondence from overseas.

Names and addresses of various book dealers in and outside Africa are published in *Africana Journal*, and Beverly Gray's two-part article, "Selected List of Sources Specializing in Current Africana,"[23] contains a good list of sources which supply publications from African countries.

Major book shops in the individual African countries, along with the government printers, are listed in a booklet entitled *Directory of Government Printers and Prominent Bookshops in the African Region* (Addis Ababa, United Nations Economic Commission for Africa, 1970, p. 48; E1CN.14/LIB/Ser.D/1).

Official and semi-official publications can successfully be obtained through exchange, especially in countries with an organized library profession. In some African countries, such as in French-speaking Africa, where the library profession is not organized, exchange plans are difficult to implement.

R. A. Christopher's remarks in 1969 are to a large extent still valid today:

> The basic assumptions of exchanges of material has not, however, proved entirely workable for Africa. With many countries there is no suitable organization at the other end with which to exchange. The Arabic speaking countries of the North are not bibliographically organized and there are constant political difficulties. The French speaking countries

---

[22] J. Ndegwa, "Official Publications in East Africa," in International Conference on African Bibliography, Nairobi 4-8 December, 1967, *The Bibliography of Africa*, edited by J. D. Pearson and Ruth Jones (London: Frank Cass, 1970), pp. 57-74.

[23] Beverly Gray, "Select List of Sources Specializing in Current Africana," in *A Current Bibliography on African Affairs* 3, No. 6 (June, 1970):5-20 and 3, No. 7 (July, 1970:5-21.

have new national or university libraries to receive, and many are loath to send materials, even a subscription. Here only limited headway has been made in acquiring official gazettes, an occasional statistical bulletin and little more.[24]

The success of any exchange depends as Bowyer points out "upon the sustained, energetic co-operation of both partners and failure on one or both sides can generate as much correspondence and frustration as unrequested orders to book dealers."

PUBLICATION SURVEY TRIPS

Publication survey trips, albeit expensive and time consuming, are always interesting and very useful for the Africana librarian of a major research library. The person assigned to this duty normally visits publishing centers, libraries and archives of various countries in Africa, bookdealers, booksellers, and university presses. The idea is to strengthen ties, develop personal contacts, and explore new material and various channels of bringing more material to the sponsoring library or cooperating libraries. Acquisition tours are also valuable for establishing exchange arrangements, especially on one-to-one basis. Franklyn Bright states "a buying trip by a qualified member of your own staff is, potentially, the most effective thing you can do if the planning for it is well done."[25]

Interesting and informative accounts of such acquisition trips to Africa have been published. Moore Crossey, Curator of African Collections at Yale University Library, describes the trip she made in February and March, 1971, to East, Central, and North Africa and parts of Western Europe. She went partly to buy publications in countries where Yale experienced difficulty in doing any kind of business by mail, and to arrange for future source supply, and to survey research resources in libraries along the route.[26] A report on similar trips to Khartoum, Addis Ababa, Nairobi and Dar es Salaam was published in AJ by Susan Knoke, African Bibliographer, Michigan State University Library.[27] Ms. Knoke points out

> the value of a library acquisitions trip to Africa such as this lies as much, if not more, in the personal contacts made and acquisition information obtained as in the actual book purchases. . . . Another valuable service that such a trip may render is the spread of good will between American and African universities through personal contacts made with staff members and through such things as arrangements for exchanges of publications,

---

[24] R. A. Christopher's "Resources for African Studies in the British Museum, In SCOLMA, *Conference on the Acquisition of Material from Africa*, University of Birmingham, 1969. *Reports and Papers* (Zug, Switzerland: Inter Documentation Co., 1969), p. 8.

[25] Franklyn F. Bright, "The Acquisition of Book Materials from Africa, Asia and Latin America: The Technical Services Viewpoint," In *Institute on the Acquisition of Foreign Materials for U.S. Libraries*, compiled and edited by Theodore Samore (Metuchen, N.J.: Scarecrow Press, 1973), p. 260.

[26] Moore Crossey, "Account of an Acquisition Contact Trip to East, Central and North Africa, and to Parts of Western Europe," *Africana Journal* 2 (Summer, 1971):4-9.

[27] Susan Knoke, "Report on a Library Acquisition Trip to Africa," *Africana Journal* 4 (Winter, 1970):14-23.

of duplicate library materials and even staff members. One of our greatest needs in connection with these acquisition trips is to find good, dependable, local nationals in every country to work as agents for American university libraries in informing the latter about new publications available, constantly buying materials on the spot, before they go out of print, and arranging for them to be dispatched. Until such agents are found in every area where library materials are sought, it would be beneficial for universities to continue periodically sending African librarians, or similarly qualified persons, on trips to Africa to survey and purchase research materials, but also to maintain and renew contacts with book dealers, university and research institute personnel and the like.[28]

Julian Witherell of the LC African Section reported on her 1972 publication survey trip to Nigeria, Southern Africa, and Europe in *Africana Acquisitions* (Washington: Library of Congress, 1973). Among her objectives were the following: to survey the many publishing centers, libraries, and archives of Nigeria and South Africa; to strengthen LC's contacts with educational institutions; and to improve the flow of publications of state governments to LC.

NATIONAL PROGRAMS FOR ACQUISITIONS

The National Program for Acquisitions and Cataloging (NPAC) is an LC operation, developed in close cooperation with the Association of Research Libraries and authorized by an Act of Congress (Title II-C of Higher Education Act of 1965).

To accomplish this aim in Africa, LC established an overseas office in Nairobi, Kenya. The office works very closely with dealers and national bibliographies, thereby providing books and catalog copy promptly to the Library of Congress. This office, coupled with the Public Law 480 office in Cairo, Egypt, gives LC and participating American libraries wide coverage of Africa's publications.

The Nairobi office was established in 1966 and is responsible for several countries or areas, in addition to Kenya: Ethiopia, Djibouti (Territoire Francais des Afars et Issas), Somali Republic, Kenya, Uganda, Tanzania, Zambia, Malawi, the Malagasy Republic, la Réunion, Mauritius and the Seychelles. A review of the program was published by Alvin Moore, Jr., Field Director, Library of Congress, Nairobi.[29] A more detailed description of the origin and progress of the Library of Congress Program in Eastern Africa is found in Jerry R. James' paper published in the Nairobi Conference proceedings.[30]

---

[28]*Ibid.*, p. 23.
[29]Alvin Moore, Jr., "A Review of the Library of Congress Program in Eastern Africa," in SCOLMA, *Conference of the Acquisition of Material from Africa*, University of Birmingham, 1969. *Reports and Papers* (Zug, Switzerland: Inter Documentation Co., 1969), pp. 1-6.
[30]Jerry R. James, "The Library of Congress Program in Eastern Africa," in International Conference on African Bibliography, Nairobi, 4-8 December, 1967, *The Bibliography of Africa* (London: Frank Cass, 1970), pp. 75-82.

The Nairobi Office has compiled and published since 1968 a quarterly list *Accessions List: Eastern Africa*, complemented by an *Annual Serial Supplement*. In its first year, the Accession List recorded 843 monographic entries and the *Annual Serial Supplement*, 585 entries, including the annual reports of government offices and institutions and societies.

Another national acquisitions program for Africana is the Cooperative Africana Microfilm Project, an agency in which many institutions can work together to provide support to African studies programs. This means that materials needed for research, from either archives or libraries, can be microfilmed for preservation or for wider dissemination and made available to scholars related to member institutions. CAMP began in 1963 on the theory that the most efficient use of funds for such a project is to purchase, whenever possible, a negative microfilm from which members can have positive copies made at cost. A recent catalog was published by CAMP and the Research Liaison Committee of the African Studies Association to identify published monographs and periodicals.[31]

BIBLIOGRAPHY

African Book Trade Directory, 1971— . Munchen Pullach, Verlag Dokumentation, New York: Bowker, 1971— .

Aman, Mohammed M. "Bibliographical Activities of the Arab Countries of North Africa," *International Library Review* 2 (July, 1970):263-73.

Bloomfield, Valerie, ed. *The Acquisition of Africana.* Zug, Switzerland: Inter Documentation, 1972.

Brasseur, Paule. "The Bibliography of the Countries of French Speaking Black Africa," *Africana Journal* 2 (Winter, 1971):13-16.

Brigges, Michael. "Acquisition of Materials from Africa," In: *Institute on the Acquisition of Foreign Materials for U.S. Libraries.* Compiled and edited by Tehodore Samore. Metuchen, N.J.: The Scarecrow Press, 1973, pp. 211-220.

Clarke, D. A. *Acquisitions from the Third World: Papers of the Ligue des Bibliothèques Européennes de Recherche Seminar 17-19 Sept. 1973.* London: Mansell, 1975, pp. 85-103 and pp. 105-123.

Conover, Helen F. *Africa South of the Sahara: An Introductory List of Bibliographies.* Washington, D.C.: Library of Congress, 1961.

Duignan, Peter, ed. *Guide to Research and Reference Works on Sub-Saharan Africa.* Compiled by Helen F. Conover and Peter Duignan. Stanford, Calif.: Hoover Institution Press, 1971.

International African Bibliography of Current Publications in Africa. 1971— , Quarterly.

---

[31] The Cooperative Africana Microfilm Project. *CAMP Catalog*, published by the Cooperative Africana Microfilm Project and the Research Liaison Committee. Waltham, Mass.: African Studies Assn., Brandeis University, 1972.

International Conference on African Bibliography, Nairobi, 4-8 December 1967. *The Bibliography of Africa*, edited by J. D. Pearson and Ruth Jones. London: Frank Cass, 1970.

Kotei, S. I. A. *Persistent Issues in African Bibliography*. Legon: Department of Library Studies, University of Ghana, 1972.

Kotei, S. I. A. "Some Notes on the Present State of National Bibliography in English-Speaking Africa," *Africana Journal* 2 (Winter, 1971):13-18.

Leunox, G. W. "Bookselling in Nigeria," *Nigerian Libraries* 2 (Sept., 1966):83-89.

Musiker, R. *South African Bibliography. A Survey of Bibliographies and Bibliographical Work*. Hamden, Conn.: Archon Books, 1970.

Omoerha, Thompson. "African Government Publications: Problems of Acquisition and Organization," *Libri* 23, No. 4 (1973):298-306.

Panofsky, Hans E. *A Bibliography of Africana*. Westport, Conn.: Greenwood Press, 1975.

Standing Conference on Library Materials on Africa. *Periodicals Published in Africa*. London: Institute of Commonwealth Studies, 1965– .

Stanley, Janet L. *Nigerian Government Publications, 1966-73: A Bibliography*. Ife, Nigeria: University of Ife Press, 1975.

UNESCO. *Book Development in Africa, Problems and Perspectives*. Paris: UNESCO, 1969.

27. Major African Collections in the United States

Center for Research Libraries
5721 Cottage Grove Avenue
Chicago, Illinois 60637   (312) 955-4545
Ray Boylan, assistant director; 12 prof, 50 non-prof staff; ILL; copying; restrictions.

The Center for Research Libraries, established in 1963, houses the Cooperative Africana Microform Project (CAMP) which has an overall subject scope of African Studies. Microfilm reels total 3,342, and microfiche sheets, 3,734, which have 1,950 titles. The center subscribes to two newspapers.

Manuscript and Archival Collections: The Cooperative Africana Microform Project holds negative microfilm of archival materials from various parts of Africa, primarily south of the Sahara. These materials are listed in the CAMP catalog and supplements.

Publications: *CAMP Catalog* (with supplements).

Indiana University Library
Bloomington, Indiana 47401 (512) 337-1481
Jean E. Meeh Gosebrink, librarian for African Studies; 1 prof staff; ILL; copying;
  no restrictions.

Africa-related resources are located throughout the library with additional materials in the Fine Arts Library, Library of the School of Public and Environmental Affairs, science branches and the Lilly Library of Rare Books. The African Studies Program houses relevant materials as well as the Audio-Visual Center. The University's Archives of Traditional Music/Folklore Institute is one of the world's largest repositories of oral documentation, maintains the Center for African Oral Data, including recordings of music, verbal folklore and oral histories. In conjunction with the Cooperative Africana Microform Project, transcripts of the Transcription Centre, London, were acquired. Although the African Collection covers all of sub-Saharan Africa, special emphasis has been given to anthropology, linguistics and folklore, as well as geography and political science. Periodicals currently received average 397 and 5 newspapers. There are ca. 250 vertical files. Microforms comprise 1,000 reels of microfilm, 60 microcards, and 1,500 sheets of microfiche. Audiovisual materials include 132 items in the Audio-Visual Collection, 21 in the African Studies Program, and 26,000 slides in the Fine Arts Slide Library, 6,000 in the African Studies Department.

Six small manuscript collections are located in the Lilly Library of Rare Books. These include the Atliya of Arabic, Coptic and Turkish manuscripts on papyrus and paper, ca. 700 to 1700 A.D.; papers of diplomat Burton Yost Berry; papers of William Arnold Stevens and his wife, Caroline (Clarke) Stevens; and the collection of Charles Boxer, historian of Portuguese and Dutch expansion.

Publications: *Films on Africa: A Descriptive List of Motion-Pictures in the Indiana University Audio-Visual Center and the African Studies Research Collection*, 1975; *African Music and Oral Data: A Catalog of Recordings, 1902-1972*, 1975; and *Handbook of American Resources for African Studies* (being revised).

Northwestern University Library
Melville J. Herskovits Library of African
  Studies
Evanston, Illinois 60201 (312) 492-7684
Hans E. Panofsky, curator; 6 prof, 4 non-prof staff; ILL; lit searches; copying;
  restrictions.

The Melville J. Herskovits Library of African Studies was founded in 1929 and named after the director (1929-1963) of the first program of African Studies in the United States, who actively supported the growth of the collection. The collection's focus is in the humanities and social sciences concerning the African continent and surrounding islands, emanating from Africa or elsewhere, with some concentration for the collecting of natural sciences in relation to Africa. Housed in the collection are 76,963 volumes, along with approximately 2,000 periodicals currently received and 58 newspapers. Pertinent materials are stored in 180 drawers of vertical files. Microfilm reels number 1,728 with 359 titles, and 81 titles are on 1,620 microfiche. The audiovisual segment contains 6 films and 150 slides.

Northwestern University Library (cont'd)

There are three manuscript and archival collections. These comprise the 57 file drawers of the correspondence and papers of Melville J. Herskovits (closed until 1988); 40 drawers of the Carter/Karis Collection of the African National Congress of South Africa (restricted); 10 drawers of the papers of Northwestern University's *Economic Survey of Liberia*, 1962, and the correspondence of Lavinnia Scott, missionary to South Africa, 1932-1959.

Publications: *Catalog of the Melville J. Herskovits Library of African Studies and Africana in Selected Libraries*, 1972; and *Joint Acquisition List of Africana*, bi-monthly.

Stanford University
Hoover Institution on War, Revolution, and Peace
Stanford, California 94305 (415) 497-2072
Peter Duignan, curator; 3 prof, 1.5 non-prof staff; limited ILL; lit searches; no
  bibliog compilation; copying; some restrictions.

The collecting of African material began in 1919 with the organization of the Africa Collection in 1922. The broad structure of subjects range from history, politics, government and economics from 1870 to the present in Africa south of the Sahara. The collection has 47,000 volumes, 4,800 pamphlets, and receives 355 current periodical and 59 newspaper titles. Microfiche number 20. Approximately 1,000 photographs and 350 slides serve to supplement the holdings.

The Hoover Institution serves as a repository for 27 manuscript and archival collections. These include the African Revolutionary Movements; William H. Friedland Collection (Tanganyika trade unions); Rene Lemarchand Collection (political development in Zaire, Rwanda, Burandi, 1920-1964); Southern African Collection; Lewis H. Gann Collection (Rhodesia); Allen S. Drury Collection (South Africa); and the David B. Abernethy Collection (Nigeria, 1949-1964).

Publications: *Catalog of the Western Language Collections*, 63 vols., 1969, supplement, 1st vols. 1-5, 1972; *Catalogs of the Western Language Serials and Newspaper Collections*, 3 vols., 1969; *Index Africanus*, 1975. A complete listing can be secured from the Hoover Institution.

AFRO-AMERICAN RESOURCES

28. Establishing Afro-American Collections
by Ann Allen Shockley

The 1960s can be characterized as the movement years—the years of change, years of confusion, and years of identity searching—all sparked by a new black assertiveness. In his stirring book, *Why We Can't Wait*, the leading spokesman for the black revolution, Dr. Martin Luther King, Jr., wrote: "The revolution of the Negro not only attacked the external cause of his misery, but revealed him to himself. He was *somebody*. He had a sense of *somebodiness*. He was *impatient* to be free."[1]

This impatience to be free, to be somebody, spilled like a tidal wave from the streets and jails into the sacrosanct walls of white academia. Within these ivory-towered structures, more black students were enrolled than ever before, aided and abetted by federal monies and pseudo-liberal white administrators. Black faces abounded in institutions that in the past had adhered to blatant tokenism.

These young black collegians, entrapped mentally and physically amidst an academic sea of white racism, heard the hue and cry of the streets, and listened to the thunderous revolutionary rhetoric of Stokeley Carmichael and Eldridge Cleaver condemning the subjugation inherent in racism. Black students in *all* academic institutions began to look at themselves, not only through the physical reflection of a mirror, but deep into their souls to ponder, who am I? what are my roots? what is my history?

The quest was on, and the key for unlocking many of these answers was to be found in the written records of the past, the books and other relevant documents unearthing the history of an obfuscated black past. Such items were found to be in the libraries of major black academic colleges and universities—Hampton Institute, Atlanta University, Tuskegee Institute, Howard University, and Fisk University—which had a long and noble tradition of collecting and preserving the black experience. There were also treasured resources in public library branches serving

---

[1] Martin Luther King, Jr., *Why We Can't Wait* (New York: New American Library, Inc., 1964), p. 30.

predominantly black communities. These included the Schomburg Center for Research in Black Culture, a branch of the New York Public Library, and the Vivian Harsh Collection, originally a part of the George Cleveland Hall branch, but now housed in the new Carter G. Woodson Regional Library of the Chicago Public Library system.

These black collections were revered products of the years, assembled without benefit of special monies or staffs. They were acquired largely through: 1) gifts from collectors, friends, faculty, 2) purchase out of library budgets or other monies, 3) endowments by benefactors, and 4) development from a small in-house collection. The collections were fostered by painstaking care, guided by knowledgeable curators and librarians, and supported by private collectors who were seasoned bibliophiles. (One in-depth history of major collections can be found in Arna Bontemps' "Special Collections of Negroana," published in *Library Quarterly*, July, 1944.)

Black libraries had the books needed for study and research that were not in other libraries—books that authenticated and documented black antiquity. Thus, the frantic search began for similar materials to be placed in other libraries having a need for them. Immediately, "instant" collections were hastily assembled to mollify black students and support Black Studies programs, but many of these collections were staffed by librarians with little or no knowledge of the subject matter.

To hastily establish the collections, some librarians began indiscriminate buying sprees, purchasing books mainly because they had black authors or the contents concerned blacks. Taking advantage of this burgeoning demand for black books, some publishers flooded the market, and more books than ever before were published by and about blacks. White writers became "overnight" experts on Afro-Americans and Africans. Young black writers, who would have probably never been given a raised eyebrow previously, were courted and made instantaneous successes. Sloppy anthologies with repetitive themes and misleading titles glutted the bookstores, and, to deepen the well of despair, reprint publishers appeared like a scramble of ants to make fortunes with the least amount of work or investment. By photo-offset, out-of-print books and those in the public domain were ferreted out of libraries, private collections, and antiquarian bookstores to be sold in cheap reprints at astronomical prices to libraries.

Books and more books were being published, and librarians were in the exalted position to buy, for this was the golden epoch of federal library patronage. It was a period that can be described more adequately in the classic words of Charles Dickens: "It was the best of times, it was the worst of times, it was the age of wisdom, it was the age of foolishness. . . ."

All of this caused headaches and heartaches for librarians assigned the task of organizing Afro-American Collections. To have books was the aim, with little thought to the fact that, in effect, special collections were being established and special collections are indeed entities unto themselves.

Randall and Goodrich in their book, *Principles of College Library Administration*, define a special collection as:

> an assemblage of materials in some field of knowledge which includes unusual items and greater proportion of other titles, bearing upon the special subject that would be included ordinarily in a library . . . the

simple gathering of a considerable number of books on a special subject does not constitute a special collection.[2]

In focusing on Afro-American Collections within the framework of special collections, a working definition can be ascribed to them as books and related materials by and about blacks.

The first consideration to be given in attempting to establish an Afro-American Collection should be the type or scope of the collection. The collection can be formed to be: 1) an exhaustive or definitive one, international in coverage, designed to acquire secondary and primary sources of blacks in America, Africa, Europe, Asia and the Caribbean; 2) a collection having only Afro-American materials of secondary and primary sources; 3) an assemblage of Afro-American and African primary and secondary sources; or 4) one with materials only for supplementing Afro-American Studies programs and to promote personal reading enrichment.

Collection interpretations will vary with libraries. Variations will be contingent upon: 1) the primary purpose (objective) of the collection; 2) budget or the amount of money to subsidize the collection, which in turn, places limitations and restraints on purchasing and organization; 3) staff to carry out functions, services, and operations; and 4) quarters for housing, supervising, and maintaining the collection.

For acquiring materials, librarians normally resort to announcements, brochures, flyers, antiquarian booklists, private collectors, and reviews from various sources. There is another side of the coin when trying to go the professional route for securing black materials. Librarians, in many cases, may find themselves somewhat stymied for lack of information, not knowing where to look, or how to start.

The best initial approach would be to select basic retrospective and current titles by utilizing the special catalogs, checklists and bibliographies on blacks as guides in determining the matrix for the collection. Xerox University Microfilms has a *Catalog of Out-of-Print Titles* from Dorothy Porter's *The Negro in the United States*, which includes relevant titles published during the 19th and 20th centuries. The Chatham Bookseller catalog (Chatham, New Jersey) lists out-of-print as well as new books and pamphlets on blacks using bibliographic checklists. McBlain Books (Des Moines, Iowa) has catalogs of scarce, rare, out-of-print and used books relating to Black America and Africa, and Universal Books (Hollywood, California) offers scarce items.

Bibliographies are, of course, invaluable aids for assisting with selection. Regrettably, with due respect to bibliographies, the nagging problem of fecundity has arisen. Because of this, bibliographies should be critically evaluated before using, taking into consideration the compiler, purpose, scope, methodology, and organization. The need now is for more annotated and critical bibliographies in black-related subject areas by specialists, which would be quite helpful to librarians and academicians.

Some standard bibliographies and guides recommended for checklists are:

1. Abajian, James De T. *Blacks and Their Contributions to the American West: A Bibliography and Union List of Library Holdings through 1970.* Boston: G. K. Hall, 1974.

2. Chicago Public Library. George Cleveland Hall Branch. *The Chicago Afro-American Union Analytic Catalog.* 5 vols. Boston: G. K. Hall, 1952.

3. Comitas, Lambros. *Caribbeana 1900-1965, A Topical Bibliography.* Seattle: University of Washington Press, 1968.

4. Deodene, Frank, and William P. French. *Black American Fiction since 1952: A Preliminary Checklist.* Chatham, N.J.: The Chatham Bookseller, 1970.

5. Deodene, Frank, and William P. French. *Black American Poetry since 1944: A Preliminary Checklist.* Chatham, N.J.: The Chatham Bookseller, 1971.

6. Dodds, Barbara. *Negro Literature for High School Students.* Champaign, Ill.: National Council of Teachers of English, 1968.

7. East, N. B. *African Theatre: A Checklist of Critical Materials.* New York: Africana Publishers' Corporation, 1970.

8. Fisk University. Library. *Dictionary Catalog of the Negro Collection of the Fisk University Library.* 6 vols. Boston: G. K. Hall, 1974.

9. Hampton Institute, Hampton, Virginia. Collis P. Huntington Library. *Dictionary Catalog of the George Foster Peabody Collection of Negro Literature and History.* 2 vols. Westport, Conn.: Greenwood Publishing Company, 1972.

10. Howard University, Washington, D.C. Library. Moorland Foundation. *A Catalog of the African Collection in the Moorland Foundation, Howard University Library.* Washington, D.C.: Howard University Press, 1958.

11. Howard University, Washington, D.C. Founders Library. Moorland Foundation. *Dictionary Catalog of the Arthur B. Springarn Collection of Negro Authors.* 2 vols. Boston: G. K. Hall & Company, 1970.

12. Howard University, Washington, D.C. Founders Library. Moorland Foundation. *Dictionary Catalog of the Jesse E. Moorland Collection of Negro Life and History.* 9 vols. Boston: G. K. Hall & Company, 1970.

13. International African Institute. Library. *Cumulative Bibliography of African Studies: A Classified Catalog.* 3 vols. Boston: G. K. Hall & Company, 1973.

14. Jackson, Miles M., Jr., Mary W. Cleaver, and Alma L. Gray. *A Bibliography of Negro History and Culture for Young Readers.* Pittsburgh: University of Pittsburgh Press, 1968.

15. Jahn Janheinz. *A Bibliography of New African Literature from Africa, America and the Caribbean.* New York: Praeger, 1965.

16. Mathews, Geraldine O. *Black American Writers, 1773-1949: A Bibliography and Union List.* Boston: G. K. Hall, 1975.

17. Miller, Elizabeth, and Mary L. Fisher. *The Negro in America: A Bibliography*, 2nd ed. Cambridge: Harvard University Press, 1970.

18. New York Public Library. Schomburg Collection. *Dictionary Catalog of the Schomburg Collections of Negro Literature and History.* 9 vols. Boston: G. K. Hall, 1962. (Supplements, 1967, 2 vols.; 1972, 4 vols.)

19. Northwestern University Library. *Catalog of the Melville J. Herskovits Library of African Studies.* 8 vols. Boston: G. K. Hall, 1972.

20. Porter, Dorothy B. *Early Negro Writing, 1760-1837.* Boston: Beacon Press, 1971.

21. Porter, Dorothy B. *The Negro in the United States: A Selected Bibliography.* Washington, D.C.: Library of Congress, 1970.

22. Porter, Dorothy B. *North American Poets: A Bibliographical Checklist of Their Writings, 1760-1944.* Hattiesburg, Mississippi: The Book Farm, 1945.

23. Porter, Dorothy B. *A Working Bibliography on the Negro in the United States.* Ann Arbor: Xerox, University Microfilms, 1969.

24. Schomburg, Arthur Alfonso. *A Bibliographical Checklist of American Negro Poetry.* New York: C. F. Heartman, 1916.

25. Vail Memorial Library. Lincoln University, Lincoln, Pennsylvania. *Catalog of the Special Negro and African Collection.* 2 vols. Lincoln, Pa.: Lincoln University, 1970.

26. Whiteman, Maxwell. *A Century of Fiction by American Negroes 1853-1952: A Descriptive Bibliography.* Philadelphia: Albert Saifer, 1955.

27. Work, Monroe. *A Bibliography of the Negro in Africa and America.* New York: Octagon Books, 1970.

In utilizing these resource tools, librarians should naturally adhere as much as possible to the tenets of their library's acquisition policy and to the basic philosophy for the existence of the collection.

Most academic institutions offer at least some courses on Africa. The once misnomered "Dark Continent," whose postwar zeal for independence spread from North Africa in 1960 through West Africa and now South Africa, has made this continent and its peoples a requirement for study and recognition. Dr. Adelaide E. Hill, African specialist, states flatly that "no university library would be complete without acquiring some materials in this field."[3] For securing basic works for African collections, Dr. Hill recommends:

> Perhaps the easiest to secure but the costliest to own are the so-called traditional or classical books on Africa. These books, historical in treatment, form the background or core of any good African collection: *Stanley's Travels, De Chaillu's Tales, Bruce's Travels, Baker's Explorations* and so forth, to mention only a few.[4]

There are catalogs as well that are useful in procuring books on Africa. Among these are the *International African Bibliography*, published quarterly by Mansell, London, which lists current books, articles and papers in African studies; *Books on Africa Catalogue*, one of the various catalogs of the University Place Bookshop in New York; academic African Collection catalogs; the *Africana Journal* for timely reviews; and the *African Book Publishing Record.*

---

[3] Adelaide C. Hill, "Developing a Collection of Africa, South of the Sahara," *College and Research Libraries* 22 (November 1961):443.

[4] *Ibid.*

Most certainly the foundation for all African and Afro-American Collections will be basic retrospective titles. To secure these, librarians, in most cases, have to rely on reprints if the works are out-of-print or not available from antiquarian bookdealers. In the past, librarians have had problems with reprinters who had questionable reputations, an illustration of which is a publisher's announcement of forthcoming titles which were never produced, because not enough libraries had placed orders to sustain or justify the reprinting costs. Another illustration is in the inaccuracy of bibliographic information about titles.

When considering reprints, it is advisable to check carefully and thoroughly *all* bibliographic information to avoid duplication. A book may well already be in a series purchased, but brought out by another reprinter fanfaring a new introduction by a well-known scholar who is "putting the book in its proper perspective." A good reprint series is *The American Negro: His History and Literature* (published by Arno Press and the New York Times).

Recently, the quick-buck, fly-by-night reprint entrepreneurs have either cashed in since library budgets are tight, or have been crowded out by the entrance of commercial publishers into the market. Some commercial firms that have bought out reputable reprinters are: Harcourt Brace and World, who now has the Johnson Reprint Company; Lord Thompson, whose British Press owns Kraus Reprint; and Atheneum, which garnered Russell and Ressell. This turn of events can comfort librarians, who know that legitimate leaders of publishing are now at the helm.

Highly selective reprints whose formats meet the standards set forth by the Council on Library Resources are a necessity, for they make difficult-to-find titles available. Reputable reprinters usually have an advisory board of scholars and librarians to assist in making quality selections, whereas the more dubious ones simply rely on whether the book is in the public domain or out-of-print.

Astronomical costs prohibit extensive reprint buying; therefore, only those that are needed for buttressing the disciplines should be considered for purchasing. To offset this limitation, academic institutions in close proximity could share reprint titles through inter-library loan and inter-library use.

Current titles, like reprints, can also present problems. Thankfully, the sixties' boom of commercial publishers exploiting the black gold of print has diminished. On the other hand, there appears to be too much of a slowing down with the publishing of worthy black books, and the old, subtle publishers' quota for black titles and black authors appears to be in vogue again. The feeling is that blacks are not "fashionable" anymore, and consequently, neither are black books.

Perhaps the business heads of the publishing domain should be made aware of the study conducted by Professor Roger Whitlow, a teacher of American Literature and Black American Literature at Eastern Illinois University. Professor Whitlow, while making a survey of individual English departments throughout the United States on black literature courses, discovered that 59.7 percent of the 648 public, private and two-year academic institutions responding offered courses in black literature. Professor Whitlow's study further showed that even though there has been a fifty percent decline in English majors, who are the largest group of students traditionally enrolled in literature courses, the fact that, "at almost 80 percent of the senior institutions enrollments in black literature courses are either holding stable or actually continuing to increase indicates clearly that black literature is very much "alive and well."[5] With black literature seemingly in good health, then, publishers should be made to feel obligated to continue the supply of noteworthy titles. Quality books are the nourishing injections needed to keep black literature an integral part of American literature.

In assessing titles being published, librarians must learn to be objectively critical. Book reviews, even by librarians, are not always dependable or "the last word." Reviewers have prejudices, and oftentimes, many are simply not qualified or well-versed enough on the subject to adequately review the book. If a review raises hidden questions, seek other critiques. In the event additional ones cannot be found, write the publisher for a review copy, and *read* the book.

The publication in which the review appeared should also be closely observed. The book could be excellent as far as scholarship is concerned, but not in line with the publication's editorial direction. When reading reviews, the difference between such biased reviews and descriptions of other books or short announcements should be readily recognized.

Criteria for judging books for inclusion in special Afro-American Collections are essentially the same as for any quality collection, except for a few modifications. Some standard principles for selection could include the following:

1. What is the purpose or scope of the work? Is it definitive? Was it written to fulfill a quick publishing need for a title on a subject of timely interest, or does it show significant substance and coverage? Is the scope too broad, thereby causing digression from the main premise?

2. Is the work authentic as to reliable facts and sources, verification of data, and accurate documentation, all of which should exhibit scholarly research?

3. Has the book a good format with index, bibliography, and commendable physical features?

4. What are the author's credentials as to experience, past research, or background knowledge on the subject? Is the author's critical judgment sound?

5. If fiction, does the work have literary merit? For non-fiction, is the subject matter presented in a good writing style for readability?

6. Will the work add to scholarship and be a good supplement to support the curricula, or provide stimulating personal reading enrichment?

7. Is the work black distorted with emphasis on black dogmatism, making it totally "black distorted" with too much accentuation on the positive, therefore not offering a balanced view?

8. Conversely, is it "white distorted"?

9. How effective is the work in offering fresh information of historical or cultural value to past or present scholarship?

---

[5] Roger Whitlow, "Alive and Well: A Nationwise Study of Black Literature Courses and Teachers in American Colleges and Universities," *College English* 36 (February 1975):648.

10. Will the work give non-blacks more of an appreciation and understanding of black people's role in world history?

Book selection should be an enjoyable and rewarding task, for this is the fundamental enterprise in building a collection. (For other selection insights, read "Developing Collections of Black Literature" by Jessie Carney Smith, *Black World*, June 1971.) Personal biases causing censorship must be avoided, and the assistance of faculty, staff, and other knowledgeable individuals should be sought to aid in collection building. For public libraries, the cooperation of staff, community specialists, patrons, writers, and academicians in surrounding institutions should be enlisted to assist in getting the "right books on the shelves."

Students must not be overlooked or ignored in attmpting to have an outstanding collection. From students can be ascertained the reading needs and tastes of the younger generation, since they, too, expose the intellectual trend of the times so important in capturing for library posterity. All young people should be made to feel that a creditable collection houses the history of the struggles, hopes, dreams and contributions of black people, and that to help keep it distinctive is their thing too.

Along with books, selectivity must be exercised with other materials. Periodicals should be chosen with diligence, concentrating on the basic titles that have withstood the long test of time. A number of black periodicals have notoriously uneven life spans, appearing once, twice, and then fading away for a long length of time, frequently forever. This is lamentable, for some, such as *Black Creation*, *Black Spirit*, *Black Images*, *Black Theatre*, and *Journal of Black Poetry* had good potentials. In most cases, though, because of financial, staff, or other problems, they have not been able to keep afloat.

A few prestigious scholarly journals that have shown stability and are of immense supplementary value to Black Studies are the *Journal of Negro History*, *Journal of Negro Education*, College Language Association's *CLA Journal*, *Phylon*, and *Black Perspectives in Music*. Before subscribing to a new periodical, and possibly taking a chance of money being thrown down the drain because of a quick demise, librarians should try to work out a prior arrangement in which the publisher will agree to refund the money. Library budgets are tight, too.

Newspapers are an important adjunct to periodicals for keeping abreast with current developments. Indeed, at one time, only black newspapers kept the black public informed of events pertinent to it. This, in large measure has changed; however black newspapers are still surviving because of their wider and more inclusive black news coverage. Local black newspapers should therefore be a part of all collections, for within these pages are news stories that will someday serve to document local black history. Also, newspapers in close geographic proximity should be purchased for surrounding black regional news and should be microfilmed for preservation, if possible.

The old-line, established newspapers, the *Afro-American*, *Pittsburgh Courier*, *New York Amsterdam News*, *Chicago Defender*, and *Atlanta Daily World* are standards which give excellent local and national news. Oddly enough, *Black Times*, a tabloid monthly emanating from Palo Alto, California, frequently has good stories on events or persons not normally considered for front page features, for instance, the one on librarian Emily Copeland. This publication also has a regular book section entitled "Read All About It" which lists quite a number of current and new black titles with short descriptions.

Newspapers that are organs of political or religious organizations should be considered for penetration into ideas, opinions, and activities of these diverse groups. Movement newspapers, regardless of leanings, promote research and aid in balancing the collection. Examples of these are the *Black Panther*, a weekly published in Oakland, California, and heavily mixed with Black Panther activities and racial exposés, and the *Bilalian News*, the Black Muslim weekly with good international news articles; in spite of their biases, they have merit and supplementary value in presenting other views.

In addition to books, periodicals and newspapers, non-print materials are essential for new instructional approaches and documentation. Dr. Harry A. Johnson, media specialist and activist for promoting more media inclusion in Afro-American collections maintains:

> Libraries of all kinds and others charged with the storage and retrieval of information must take the responsibility of looking beyond the printed word as the model for transmitting Black history.[6]

Non-print materials can include slides, cassettes, phono disks, films, filmstrips, phonographs, tapes and video tapes. The selection of these media materials, as for others, should be evaluative and within the structure of a sound acquisition policy. The *Standards for School Media Programs* could be used for a guide, since the recent deluge of non-print materials makes careful selection more important than ever. There are, however, some excellent media resources on the market. One is a filmstrip entitled "Profiles of Black Achievement" (Guidance Associates, Pleasantville, New Jersey), in which eight noted blacks (among them Arna Bontemps, Aaron Douglas, Eubie Blake, and Alma Thomas) give poignant autobiographical narrations. Harry A. Johnson's book, *Multimedia Materials for Afro-American Studies* is a useful source for assembling a collection, providing as it does annotated bibliographies of resources.

The amount of non-print materials that should be included in Afro-American Collections depends upon: 1) need, 2) the predetermined amount of concentration to be given to non-print resources, 3) type of collection, 4) supplementary value to the collection, 5) relevance to library patrons' interests and needs, 6) budget, 7) staff, 8) quarters for housing and use, and 9) maintenance.

The inclusion of oral history interviews is most certainly beneficial for supplementing and complementing archival and manuscript collections. Such narrations are primary sources and add to the value of the overall research content of a collection. When budgets are limited, interviews can be confined to conducting them on a local basis, even if only on campus. At least, the institution's history is being preserved, and students, faculty, and community volunteers alike can be resources for interviewers. First-hand personal accounts can do much to document and fill in the gaps of black history.

---

[6] Harry Alleyn Johnson, "Developing a Current Awareness of Non-Print Media: Duplications for Afro-American Collections," (background paper for the Conference on Bibliographical Control of Afro-American Literature; University of Oregon School of Librarianship Conference, Chicago, Illinois, July 16-17, 1976), p. 33.

For those concentrating on a research-oriented library, the soliciting of personal papers and collecting non-current official papers of the institution are mandatory for organizing manuscript and archival collections. To do this work, an archivist should be assigned who has the knowledge for collecting, processing, and preserving those rare and irreplaceable primary sources in the repository. University Archivist Nicholas C. Burkel, University of Wisconsin—Parkside, advocates that "the archivist's first obligation, of course, is to preserve all significant non-current records of the university. That includes every type of record: budget, financial, student, faculty and administrative."[7]

Although some libraries might hesitate about establishing archival and manuscript collections because of budget, staff, and space, college and university records should be preserved. Priorities must be given to collecting official board minutes, annual reports, catalogs, programs, publications, yearbooks, photographs, brochures, and the official papers of the faculty. If limitations prevent the active soliciting of manuscript collections, the personal papers of faculty members who are eminent scholars or writers could be sought. These papers are those not officially connected with the institution. The personal papers of distinguished alumni are other sources to tap for manuscript collections. Regardless of the actual type of material gathered in forming archival and manuscript collections, always bear in mind that these collections require *special* handling, servicing, maintenance, and trained staff. The appointing of an Archival Committee of faculty, staff and administrators can do much toward supporting such an important endeavor.

For those needing guidance on archival practices and theory, the Committee on College and University Archives has compiled a valuable bibliography entitled "College and University Archives: A Select Bibliography" (*American Archivist*, January 1974). Also, Frank B. Evans' recent *Modern Archives and Manuscripts: A Select Bibliography* is an important aid.

The establishing of special Afro-American Collections can be a most gratifying experience, but the organization and development should be shared by students, faculty, staff, and all interested persons. The purpose and scope of the collection should be clearly defined, accompanied by a discerning but flexible acquisition policy styled with an eye to future resources and problems.

Collections are not created to stand alone. They are to be used and this calls for servicing. Adequate services must meet the needs of the clientele and should be effectively designed to promote the use of the collection. As succinctly stated by Amy S. Doherty, "Library services for a black studies program should be developed aggressively by librarians working in direct contact with both faculty and students to provide the kinds of services that will be most fruitful."[8]

To have services beneficial to users means that the collection must be a growing one, keeping abreast of new trends, spheres of research, and instructional technology developments. Coinciding with collection growth and services, the collection must be sold to the community by publicizing it. Special exhibits, news releases, booklists, bibliographies, book talks, programs and discussions help to make the collection known, which it must be.

---

[7] Nicholas C. Burckel, "Establishing a College Archives: Possibilities and Priorities," *College and Research Libraries* 36 (September 1975):387.

[8] Amy S. Doherty, "Black Studies: A Report for Libraries," *College and Research Libraries* 31 (November 1970):386.

Special Afro-American Collections, regardless of scope or size, house resources that document and interpret the thoughts, feelings, experiences, motivations, and efforts of black people. These collections are book monuments to black people all over the world, and as such, they should stand out as keepers of the dream.

29. The Role of the Curator of Afro-American Collections
by Ann Allen Shockley

There has been a paucity of literature on the role of the curator or librarian (the two terms will be used synonymously) who administers Afro-American Collections, for essentially two reasons. The first was the flagrant lack of interest predominantly white institutions had in attempting to collect and preserve black history and culture. Only with a few rare exceptions did white librarians actively seek to acquire materials on Afro-Americans.

One of these librarians was Bernhard Knollenberg, Yale University Librarian, who in 1942 perceived the need for having black books in the library of that prestigious institution. In soliciting Carl Van Vechten's rich private collection of books, manuscripts, phonograph records, letters, and photographs pertaining to blacks, Knollenberg forthrightly informed Van Vechten that they did not have any Negro books at all. Unfortunately, other librarians of predominantly white institutions, instilled with racist attitudes, did not see the need or simply did not care to acquire black collections. When depositing his collection at Yale, Van Vechten credited the institution with being "the first white college in the North . . . to make any determined effort to secure such material."[1]

The second reason for this scarcity was the negative stance taken by academic institutions in establishing a Black Studies curriculum. Naturally, a new curricular program demands the support of a complementary collection of library books and related materials for undergirding not only classroom instruction but scholarly research in the discipline. During the soul-searching sixties, black students gave the snowballing impetus to instituting Black Studies by their evangelistic quest for self-identity. Afro-American Collections were hastily assembled, and oftentimes, curators were appointed without subject or even reading background in the field. In most instances, the qualifying credential was a black face. It is common knowledge that black skin does not automatically denote erudition in black books, history, culture, or black people. But that did not matter, so long as tempers were cooled and minds assuaged.

---

[1] Carl Van Vechten, "The J. W. Johnson Collection at Yale," *Crisis* 49 (July 1942):222.

To some concerned black librarians, it did matter. Rallying to block a waste of money, time, and effort, while upholding the status of black librarianship, special institutes, workshops and seminars were given, focusing on Special Afro-American Collections. In doing this, black librarianship came to be a recognized entity within itself, having its own uniqueness and specificity. There was no longer a search for simply a "custodian" for an Afro-American Collection, but someone with a curator's acumen for collecting, preserving, and organizing.

A special role was realized for those who administered collections of books and related materials on blacks. The long established collections, as well as the performances of their curators, at predominantly black institutions (Howard University, Atlanta University, Hampton Institute, Tuskegee Institute, and Fisk University all had a strong tradition of collecting black history) were studied for models. It was discovered that these collections, similar to any other special collections, housed rare and unique items constituting both secondary and primary sources. These included books, journals, newspapers, ephemeral materials, artifacts, photographs, archival and manuscript collections, along with oral history narratives. Such collections require special supervision, for many of the items are irreplaceable if lost, stolen, or multilated.

The main function of the curator is to collect and preserve these materials for scholarly use. This task may seem simple, but as with the spider who spins a meticulously fine web with ease to human sight, "there is more to this than meets the eye." Not only is effective administrative organization involved, but the personal characteristics of the curator are at issue as well. The latter can be witnessed in the formation and growth of the pioneering historic black collections, for these collections did not grow alone. They were nurtured and loved by dedicated individuals who perceived the urgency to acquire and safeguard the history of black people. These early curators were visionaries who foresaw the impending relevancy of collecting all that was possible for the unborn black and white generations to come. The curators sought to authenticate the fact that blacks did have a history and had made valuable contributions to the broad spectra of world cultures. By acquiring books, records, documents, and other materials to substantiate this fact, these curators were paving the way for blacks to be properly identified as world leaders, builders, archievers, and persons of valor, wisdom and strength.

Forty-six years ago, Carl W. White, a caucasian librarian at Fisk University, presented in his annual report a highly meaningful interpretation and case for a "Negro Collection" at Fisk:

> The term "Negro Collection" is closely associated ... to works dealing strictly with the Negro and in particular to works of Negro authorship. As used here, the term has a broader significance; it refers to materials which in any way bear significantly upon the career and fortunes of the Negro. Works dealing with minority groups the world over, with the origin and distribution of races, with racial types and characteristics, with race contact, conflict and adjustment—these are considered quite as necessary for research purposes as Negro materials in the narrow sense of the term.[2]

---

[2] Fisk University Library, *Report of the Librarian of Fisk University, 1936-37*, p. 6.

Librarian White, even at that time in American history which was wrought with unprincipled racist and segregationist patterns, knew the significance of Afro-American collections to the curriculum and to research. Simultaneously, he was cognizant of bibliographic control when he further stressed the necessity for "a place in America for a limited number of research centers where scholars may concentrate upon problems dealing with the Negro."[3] With this in view, he presented logical reasons for Fisk to be this center in the south. To implement his program for bibliographic control, White encouraged the Committee on Delimitation of Fields of Interest (DFI), which was created by the Nashville Library Club in 1935 and composed of representatives from all major libraries in the city, to withdraw from the Negro field in deference to Fisk.

Another foresighted librarian, who followed White in the south, was Wallace Van Jackson. In 1943, he sought to form a separate collection of black books at Atlanta University. A comprehensive black savant, Van Jackson was "convinced that the University should have a considerable collection on the Negro if it was to be a great center of information on the Negro."[4]

Academic librarians were not alone in envisaging the imminent importance of Afro-American Collections. Ernestine Rose, Librarian at the One Hundred and Thirty-fifth Street Branch of the New York Public Library, was quick to discern the future of the branch as a black research center. In endeavoring to collect and save, Miss Rose called together to discuss preserving the books in the city, then known as the Black Mecca, "a group of influential scholars and leaders from the community including Schomburg, James Weldon Johnson, Hubert H. Harrison and John Nail."[5] Out of this conference emerged a reference room set aside for patrons interested in black resources. On May 8, 1925, the Division of Negro Literature, History and Prints formally greeted the public. From this meager beginning, spearheaded by a longsighted Jewish immigrant librarian, the now renowned Schomburg Center for Research in Black Culture evolved.

These curators of diverse ethnic origins had a sense of purpose inbred in their innate characteristics. In naming others with identical traits, Arthur A. Schomburg, Lawrence Reddick, Jean Blackwell Hutson, Arna Bontemps and Dorothy B. Porter stand out in their dedication to the work of preserving black history. Intrinsic in this determination are the virtues of ability, intellectual curiosity, knowledge, and an overwhelming regard for the power of books. As to this belief in books, Arthur A. Schomburg stated: "I am here with a sincere desire to awaken the dormant fibres in the soul, and to fire the racial patriotism by the study of the Negro books."[6]

---

[3] *Ibid.*, p. 7.

[4] Katherine Estelle Leonard, "A Study of the Negro Collection in the Trevor Arnett Library at Atlanta University," (unpublished M.S. thesis prepared for the School of Library Service, Atlanta University, 1951), p. 16.

[5] Jean Blackwell Hutson, "The Schomburg Collection," *Freedomways* 3 (Summer 1963):432.

[6] Arthur A. Schomburg, "Racial Integrity—A Plan for the Establishment of a Chair of Negro History in Our Schools and Colleges, etc." (Society for Historical Research Occasional Paper, No. 3). Yonkers, New York, p. 5.

Without a doubt the curator must be a bibliophile. Having a knowledge of books is fundamental for acquiring what is pertinent and of value. The quality of the collection is strengthened, thereby giving it distinction. Despite computerization, allowing information to be found more easily and quickly, the curator is still obligated to know his collection and be familiar with its contents. Through this familiarity, personal assistance can be given to users and rapport is established.

The curator must have the attributes of a professional bibliophile as delineated by Frederick B. Adams, Jr.: "a person trained in the use of books and manuscripts who has an abiding faith in their importance and a veneration for them as physical objects."[7] Curators as bibliophiles must also have a fervor for collecting. Dorothy B. Porter, curator emeritus of the Moorland-Spingarn Research Center, amassed materials "from various historical societies and numerous libraries situated in the United States, in European countries or in other countries of the world, reproductions or copies of documents and publications."[8]

A continuous acquisition program is required, for collections cannot afford to become stagnant. They have to be developed to keep abreast with research needs. There is now being published a growing mass of new information on blacks in both printed and audiovisual forms, and this creates a demand for collection expansion in order to offer adequate research materials. Such expansion represents a commitment to the professor/scholar diligently seeking fresh information. For these users, James D. Hart noted: "a scholar must have an enormous accumulation of books, journals and all the ancillary materials of a great library. This is the stuff of his research."[9]

The curator is also accountable to the student using the collection to supplement classroom work and personal investigation. Analyzing his choice of Yale for his collection donation, Carl Van Vechten rationalized as to its worth to students: "[it] might become an active and growing source of propaganda, for no student, hitherto uninformed on the subject, could read these letters, the inscriptions in the books, or even the books themselves, without asking himself, and others, many questions."[10]

Intellectual curiosity motivates research, especially by interested students, and special subject collections help to stimulate such exploratory study. However, students must not look upon the special collections area housing black materials as merely a showplace exclusively, nor in the manner satirically drawn by Lucius W. Elder as a place where students go "to study in quiet and leave the books therein to rot at leisure."[11] Indeed, these materials should not be allowed to rot at all. An Afro-American research collection can open new vistas of research methodology for

---

[7] Frederick B. Adams, "Long Live the Bibliophile," *College and Research Libraries* 16 (October 1955):344.

[8] Maurice A. Lubin, "An Important Figure in Black Studies: Dr. Dorothy B. Porter," *College Language Association* 16 (June 1973):515.

[9] James D. Hart, "Search and Research: The Librarian and the Scholar," *College and Research Libraries* 19 (September 1958):366.

[10] Van Vechten, p. 222.

[11] Felix Hirsh, "Why Special Collections in College Libraries?" *College and Research Libraries* 3 (June 1942):243.

students. Herein can be the introduction to using primary sources, by handling letters, documents and manuscripts under proper direction. Students can learn to become research oriented, and as a result of this ongoing educational process, could become well-seasoned scholars early. Students who are aware of the richness of a collection can also be instrumental in its development. They can offer recommendations for acquisitions and siphon information to prospective donors. Students can also provide leads to persons for conducting oral history interviews, and, if they are sufficiently interested, make excellent interviewers.

All recommendations for collection building should be considered in order to fulfill the research appetites of faculty, students, and scholars. To do this, the curator has to combine what Hart has called "the main ingredients necessary in forming a collection that will be of scholarly value [which] are imagination and perseverance."[12]

Armed with these principal components, the tangible, which is embedded in the overall scope of the collection, must take priority. A collection could be exhaustive in its Afro-American holdings with an international coverage of blacks, or limited to blacks in America. Of course, the decision as to scope should be determined by the initial purpose of the collection in relation to the supporting institution. For example, it might be organized as a center for black research in collecting primary and secondary sources, or as a small departmental library set up to supplement the curriculum. In any case, the curator must know where and how to acquire materials. Aside from the usual library methods of publishers' lists, reviews, bibliographies, and antiquarian catalogs, the curator must know private book collectors. Hart wisely points out: "Today's private collectors provide materials for tomorrow's libraries."[13]

A number of prominent black collections have been given support by the purchasing and depositing of collections belonging to private collectors. The purchase of Schomburg's private collection formed the nucleus for the Schomburg Center for Research in Black Culture. The Collection at Atlanta University was firmly established as a separate entity in 1946 with the purchase of Henry P. Slaughter's private library of books and manuscript materials. The valuable private collection of Harold Jackman, who was described as "an omnivorous reader, his interests being as wide as the whole field of literature and human knowledge,"[14] formed the Countee Cullen-Harold Jackman Collection at Atlanta University.

When acquiring private collections, a number of manuscripts are usually included. It is, however, the curator's duty to seek others, since primary sources are the materials from which books, theses and dissertations are born. Above all, they are the foundation for structuring distinctive research libraries. Many predominantly white institutions are now actively engaged in purchasing the personal papers of leading black figures. To pinpoint a few, the University of Massachusetts purchased the highly sought W. E. B. DuBois Collection. Boston University is a deposit for the papers of Nikki Giovanni; and Syracuse University has the personal papers of Arna Bontemps.

---

[12] Hart, p. 346.

[13] *Ibid.*

[14] Harold Jackman Memorial Committee, "Harold Jackman," 1973 (mimeograph).

Unfortunately, black universities, plagued with financial woes, do not have the funds to compete in the outright purchasing of valuable personal collections. Because of this, curators of these beleaguered black institutions must work doubly hard to impress upon donors the importance of having black institutions house the papers of blacks. Here the papers would be more accessible to a larger number of black students and serve as a source of pride as well. Curators must, then, approach donors and present a strong and valid case for papers to be either placed on deposit or given to their respective institutions, bearing in mind that the future of black-controlled research centers is at stake.

Coinciding with this, administrators of predominantly black institutions must be made to realize the significance of having manuscript collections. To be the repository for the personal papers of W. E. B. DuBois, Jean Toomer, Charles Chesnutt, and more recently, William L. Dawson, Marcus Garvey and Aaron Douglas (as at Fisk University) establishes a university as a renowned research center. An academic institution's esteem can be enhanced through its special collections, since the acquiring of invaluable collections can attract not only scholars and researchers, but prominent faculty and serious students who want to work and study at an institution known for its rich repositories.

Analogous with the acquiring of personal papers, university officials must be apprised of the importance of archival collections. Preserving the official papers of presidents, deans, librarians, faculty and other administrative offices is vital to the history of the institution, black education, and for information about the originators themselves. Sadly, there have been and perhaps are still administrators who do not realize the value of archival materials. This is because they have no idea about what constitutes them or how they can be utilized. They cannot understand that a letter or memo from a president to a faculty member or alumnus can provide a key to a historian's research premise.

Black academic officials must work with curators in forming archives of papers already in their institutions. As affirmed by Dorothy B. Porter:

> Indeed, the task of collecting, preserving, putting into systematic order and administering the manuscript and printed materials relating to a university should be enthusiastically welcomed and supported by every department and all the officials of that university, for it is their duty to assure future generations the abundance of information that will be needed to follow the complex development of the institution and to interpret the relation of various influential movements and personages to its success.[15]

The archives of organizations should be solicited, too, whether created by professional, ecclesiastical, or business organizations. The Julius Rosenwald Archives at Fisk contain 500 boxes of correspondence, manuscripts, minutes, reports, expanse books, bank statements, and information on rural black education. The Library of Congress houses some two million items of the National Association for the Advancement of Colored People.

---

[15] Dorothy B. Porter, "Current Literature on Negro Education," *Journal of Negro Education* 11 (October 1942):527.

To procure these enriching resources of both archival and manuscript collections, along with books and related materials, requires financial and administrative support. Afro-American collections are usually sustained through: 1) a separate budget apart from the library, 2) allotment from the library's budget, 3) endowment, or 4) grants from federal and private agencies. The curator who operates on a small independent budget or allotment from the regular library's budget is decidedly limited as to what can be done. Limited budgets place constraints on acquisitions, staff, equipment, supplies, travel, and services. If the curator desires to expand operations, outside funding must be sought. In essence, budgets control the quality and quantity of collections.

Fortunately, private foundations have been known to aid collection building. The Carnegie Corporation purchased Schomburg's private library for the One Hundred and Thirty-Fifth Street Branch in 1926, and in 1932, awarded a gift to retain Schomburg as curator. Schomburg held this post until his death in 1938.

For securing federal monies, the curator must be a proposal writer. According to R. E. Mahoney: "The library that has determined how corporate contributions can be effectively used, and approximately how much money will be needed to each project has taken the first step in securing a contribution."[16] In writing proposals, guidelines should be carefully studied, and the assistance of the staff and financial officers should be sought. This is an important undertaking and should be a cooperative venture.

To assist in matching gifts and raising other outside funding, a Friends of the Library group or special committee could be formed. These associates could be comprised of historians, authors, publishers, teachers, collectors, editors, and anyone else interested in preserving black history and culture. A most recent illustration of a committee activity at work is the Committee for the Schomburg Center which is seeking funds to match a National Endowment for the Humanities grant for conserving and preserving the collection. It is co-chaired by Mrs. Ralph J. Bunche, John Hope Franklin, and Robert C. Weaver, people who are participants themselves in black history.

Besides pursuing funding, the curator must actively solicit gifts. An outright gift of a rare collection can attract similar ones when a depository has the reputation for maintaining and safeguarding its collection. The curator must be prepared to show the benefactor that there are rules and regulations for protective utilization of the materials, and any reasonable stipulations placed on gifts should be rigidly adhered to by the curator.

Policies will have to be reexamined periodically. In working with researchers, experience has proven that new and unusual problems confront curators from time to time. This is particularly true of photocopying. There can be overly excessive demands for duplicating items, and a firm policy must be made for handling unreasonable requests. In formulating policies for use of the collections, accessibility should be kept in mind, buttressed by the need for securing and controlling the collection. All of these precautions are due to the benefactor who has entrusted valuable and rare materials to the institution's care.

---

[16] R. E. Mahoney, "It Pays to Give," *Library Journal* 78 (March 1, 1953):400.

Faculty members can be both donors and solicitors of seeking gifts. The curator should serve on faculty committees and circulate on campus to keep an open ear attuned for clues to collection locations and possible gifts. A faculty member may own a valuable private library or know of others with significant collections. Visiting scholars are sources for leads to collections and should be viewed as potential donors, too. The papers of the poet and publisher Naomi Long Madgett Andrews were secured in this manner when she visited Fisk to do research. Scholars are usually pleased to be asked for their papers, especially if they are researching in a depository that already houses prestigious collections.

A strong staff is a prerequisite for supervising, maintaining and making the collections available, but to secure a well-trained staff requires an adequate budget. The curator, in requesting funds, must make it known that a qualified and ample staff is of prime importance in assisting with the administration of the collections. The curator does not and cannot operate alone. Previously, because of limited and sometimes no budget at all for black collections, persons without library training or experience were hired to supervise the "little collection of Negro books" in the traditional black institutions housing them. Frequently, a part-time or in-between time circulation or reference librarian would divide time from these areas to work in the collections. Obviously, services were curtailed. Now, with the growth of Afro-American collections, even greater need exists for a competent staff, the size of which will depend completely on the budget, need, and services offered. A professional staff can consist of librarians, catalogers, archivists, researchers, and the non-professional staff of clerical workers, paraprofessionals, and student assistants.

For an Afro-American Collection, it would be ideal to hire professionals with some subject background in Afro-American history and culture. These persons could assist more knowledgeably with acquisitions and in working directly with the faculty and researchers. A staff member with a background in black literature could meet with faculty members in this area, inform them of new materials, prepare subject bibliographies, and participate in campus seminars. In addition, staff members with special backgrounds would find the work more challenging because of their own interests.

The curator should look for persons who are research minded. These staff members would know how to provide information and would be personally geared in tracking down elusive information. If the collection does not contain what the researcher is seeking, then a staff person should be able to direct the researcher to other depositories that might have it. Staff members should be able to: 1) converse intelligently with users, 2) know the basic reference sources, both current and retrospective, 3) be able to answer telephone inquiries, 4) respond with clarity to mail inquiries, and 5) be capable of performing the job assigned.

Staff members with a history specialization should make satisfactory archivists. They should be able to relate to their work and be capable of compiling effective finding aids for the archival and manuscript collections. Good listeners with inquiring minds have the potential to be capable interviewers for oral history projects. This is tantamount to structuring probing questions and connecting events, topics, places, and persons in eliciting information.

Too, staff members should be stimulated to develop professionally by attending meetings, workshops, and engaging in scholarly research for publication. They should participate actively in professional organizations such as the American

Library Association, Society of American Archivists, Oral History Association, and the Association for the Study of Afro-American Life and History. Memberships should be held also in state and local historical societies, since this provides a personal and professional liaison with other organizations having an identical focus and interest.

The relationship between the curator and staff should be cooperative, with all striving together to meet common goals and objectives. As the leader in the organizational framework, the curator must not assume the role of an autocrat, but should allow others to make decisions. In assessing the democratic leadership style, Paul Wasserman, former dean of the University of Maryland School of Library Science, states: "Democratic style strives for maximum participation by group members with the end that decisions tend more to be the result of interactive process. Individual responsibility in decision-making usually engenders more creative response . . . ."[17]

There must be a sharing of decisions and ideas between the curator and staff. Staff members need to feel free to offer suggestions and recommendations, and be assured that they will be taken into consideration. When attempting to design new policies, the curator must be mindful that the staff works closely with users. They are "out there," and because of this, are more aware of problems that need attention and improvements to be made. The curator's mind should, then, always be hospitable to staff viewpoints and innovations. Blatant authoritativeness on the part of the curator can produce low staff morale. If morale is low for any reason, no matter how efficient a staff, work will bog down, input will be stifled, and goals left unrealized.

The curator should also have a high regard for special talents of staff members. Creative persons could assist with exhibits, programs, and publicity strategies. No curator should want to be the "whole show" or become a prima donna. Authority and responsibilities should be delegated to those persons with ability and leadership characteristics, and staff members should be permitted to develop independently, so long as it is for the promotion and good of the whole organizational structure.

Hiring is an undeniably important factor in having a good staff. In this procedure, the curator should try to be as competent as possible in attempting to judge applicants. Glittering academic credentials do not always produce practical, sound, or good employees. Some persons, by temperament and interest, but with fewer academic credits, could be better suited for the position. For instance, a person may teach archives more effectively than work as an archivist. Librarians and archivists should face the fact that oftentimes, some routines can become decidedly boring, particularly to the more active, outgoing and imaginative person. When interviewing future employees, curators must condition themselves to look beyond the facade and more into the individual's personality, likes, dislikes and what has gone before. This will in time save a lot of headaches. Academic credentials may be excellent for college catalogs and accreditation committees, but an employee's ability to fit harmoniously into the organization's program should be the principal reviewing measure.

---

[17]Paul Wasserman, *The New Librarianship: A Challenge for Change* (New York: R. R. Bowker, 1972), p. 71.

If there is discord between staff persons, the curator must be a fair negotiator in settling disputes. Aside from equity in handling staff conflicts, the curator must exercise impartiality and honesty in making decisions about promotions, salaries and tenure. The curator is a leader, and workers respond more positively to a leader who is respected.

Certainly, non-professionals must not be forgotten in promoting healthy staff relationships, for they are important for assisting with maintenance, routines, and services. The staff normally has more direct contact with these workers, but this does not preclude the fact that the curator should not be acquainted with job assignments and work performance. This is markedly true of student assistants in academic environs employed in the special collections of a library. They should be informed of the magnitude of their responsibilities in maintaining and safeguarding the collections. This sense of duty can be strengthened by educating them as to their fortune in working in a section of the library that is attempting to preserve the black heritage. They may well come face to face with some of the world's foremost scholars and authors of books which they have read or used for classroom work. Student assistants, then, should see that their fellow students utilize the materials wisely and do not abuse privileges. A manual for student assistants should be distributed in the same manner as for other staff workers, and it should contain specific instructions about duties, routines, services, and what exactly is expected of them.

Student assistants can be valuable promoters of the special collections. By being proud of the historic significance of the collections, they can be inspired to help attract donors and funds. At Fisk, the Ladies of Jubilee Hall solicited five hundred dollars to purchase books by and about black women for the Special Negro Collection. These young women, who resided in the now landmark dormitory of Jubilee Hall, were cognizant of their institution's tradition of preserving black materials, and this, in turn, helped to make them conscious of themselves as black women in America.

Any special programs or events sponsored by special collections should include student assistants as ushers, receptionists, or program participants. Students are to be made to feel that they are not just workers but an integral part of the entire operation, since the ideas they offer are often just as important in accomplishing aims as their work.

A well-organized and dedicated staff is not the means to an end, for the collections exist to be utilized, and their availability must be made known through promotion and publicity. Publicizing requires imagination and creativity. A printed brochure, giving an account of the history, purpose and holdings of the collections, not only is a promotion aid, but saves considerable time in answering inquiries. Printed catalogs, special bibliographies, and finding aids for primary sources are extremely valuable, too. Special programs based on collection presentations are inspirational in enticing future donors, and newspaper, radio, and television coverage should be secured as well for formal presentations. Articles and notices to professional journals communicate the additions to the scholarly world. This is accomplished also by reports to the *National Union Catalogue of Manuscript Collections*, the *Directory of Special Libraries and Information Centers*, and Ash's *Subject Collections.*

Specially arranged tours for local and visiting groups make the collections visible to the public. In cooperation with other libraries, museums, and centers, materials can be sent on loan for exhibits. Finally, lectures by the staff members on resources engender an awareness of them.

Concomitantly, of utmost importance is the curator whose personal image upholds the image of the resource center. The curator must be a known figure to the academic community and public, and as a public relations link, the curator must convey the prominence of the special collections within the total library's organization. This focuses attention on the entire library to students, faculty, alumni, and public. In mirroring the collection's image, the curator as scholar is a potent force. By writing scholarly articles and books, the curator augments the library's stature through individual scholarship and demonstrates that productive research can be accomplished by utilizing the resources at hand. Maurice A. Lubin noted of Dorothy B. Porter: "Living among the company of books was not enough for Dorothy Porter. She immersed herslef in the documentation which she handled each day. She exploited the knowledge that she amassed and wrote a great deal."[18]

Together with a devotion to scholarship, the curator must exhibit a warmth toward the users. The curator's love for books and scholarship should shine out like a beacon to those seeking advice and direction. The user of today may become the world's recognized authority on black history in the future.

Books provoke thought, ideas and aspirations. Great black leaders have emerged from using libraries, and creativity has been instilled by reading the works of black novelists and poets. Indeed, the black race is ennobled in its history, which is a history of mankind. The curator of Afro-American collections who reads, thinks, and reflects upon this rich heritage recognizes the challenge of the job and its unique implications. In the role of curator, the fundamental tasks are to: 1) collect and preserve black materials, 2) make the materials available for use, 3) promote scholarship and research, and 4) be an efficient and capable administrator.

There are still black books unwritten, black deeds to record, and black lives to document. Black history flows on, no longer hidden or warped, but alive, and conspicuous to all. The work of the curator of an Afro-American Collection is never done. In fact, it is just beginning.

---

[18] Lubin, p. 515.

30. Archival and Fugitive Afro-American Literature: The Duties of the Archivist

by Daniel T. Williams, Archivist, Tuskegee Institute

Manuscripts and archives are the scholar's most important sources for the study of Afro-American history. These, of course, are supplemented by contemporary newspapers, broadsides, caricatures, and pamphlets where can be found both the facts and flavor of the period under study. Years ago, when manuscripts were mentioned, the student thought only of slave narratives, diaries, and legal papers. Now the field has broadened and become far more exciting, and the librarian or archivist is faced with the problem of collecting, processing, and administering the business papers of individuals and corporations, archives of national governments, states, and cities, manuscripts of authors, sketchbooks of artists, and the scores of musicians. The archivist has the chief responsibility and rare pleasure of bringing together these records and making them available to the scholar.

The mission of archival systems, in general, is to provide access to documentary evidence of the past, a function shared by other social institutions, including libraries and museums. But the scope of this mission for the archival system—unlike that of libraries and museums—is narrowed and defined by the kinds of input deemed appropriate to such a system. The mission of any particular archival system is further limited by the character of its parent organization, whose purposes and activities determine the quantity and the quality of the records available for incorporation into the system.

Obviously, interest in the study and writing of black history is widespread. As a research field, it now appears to be eclipsing all others; books, scholarly journals, magazines, and newspapers present the results, some of lasting value and much more that is ephemeral. However, a precondition for the proper writing of such history is the accumulation of primary sources. Although these may be varied in kind, it is generally recognized that manuscript and archival sources are preeminent. Many libraries have been accumulating such manuscript and fugitive materials on blacks for decades, and especially within the last five years. The result is a gathering of collections possibly unparalleled in their richness, diversity, and volume for the study of Afro-American history.

Black history is now fashionable and has taken on a new and vital role in American life, while only a short decade ago it was generally treated as a fringe subject. Unfortunately, the rapid rise in the popularity of and necessity for the history of the country's largest ethnic minority has produced certain anomalies. There has been an outpouring of research and publications and the utilization of these materials with too little of it grounded in thorough knowledge of the black community's history.

The events of the 1960s produced a new pride among blacks and a new search for historic roots. Negro Collections—uncataloged, yet often effectively used—are an essential tool for the study of the Negro's economic, social, and demographic history. They must continue to be coordinated with libraries possessing strong and workable collections in this area to fully utilize both collections, whether in the area of books, manuscripts, or other archival materials.

Archival literature in many black colleges is relatively new as far as organization and administration is concerned. This fugitive literature or material can be defined in many ways, as previously stated, depending on the structure of the archival institution. A rare book, photograph, or even a manuscript from a collection could fit within the definition of "fugitive."

New techniques of documenting Afro-American history by archival literature will mean, then, a broadening of collection policies, more active solicitation, and imaginative methods of acquiring and using the information. Obviously most college archives that focus on Afro-American history and function within the black experience document only one segment of the academic community, that is, the school's history. Rather than simply receive fugitive documents here and there, the archivist should actively solicit the papers of regents, trustees, or directors of the college. Papers of these people, especially in a predominantly black institution, could be important in determining the values, philosophies, and lifestyles of those who have guided and shaped the university's policy, along with their contributions to Afro-American history.

Similarly, the archivist should be in frequent and cordial contact with the alumni and their director on campus. Through regular newsletter features, the archivist can solicit papers, diaries, memorabilia, or specific types of items from publication files that may be missing. He can also play an active role in preparing displays for reunions, as well as occasional articles on the history of the college in the alumni newsletter or magazine. Because the archivist collects all items concerning the history of the institution, he may have duplicate files which can be put to use by alumni staff who might need, for example, an old yearbook or past issue of the campus newspaper.

One of the most important responsibilities of an archivist is establishing and maintaining a file of university publications, including not merely periodicals, newspapers and newsletters, but many other items such as memoranda, announcements, and programs. These can easily be traced to the office of origin and then classified accordingly. The problem, however, is to assure that the archives receives all of these publications. Trying to be on all mailing lists is not always adequate. A partial remedy is to contact the campus printing or duplicating shop. This shop usually files one copy of its work with each work order submitted, and it would increase their costs only marginally to keep an additional copy of each order run for the archives to collect on a periodic basis. This is a typical procedure at Tuskegee Institute. Another important source would be the city and county records dealing with the history and establishment of the institution. These are very helpful in tracing property rights, deed transfers, and other items.

Papers of prominent persons associated with the university or files of publications by the college do not comprise the complete records of any university. The *raison d'être* for most institutions of higher education is teaching, and the viability of most institutions of higher education rests on enrollment; yet archivists have done little to gather biographical data on students who pass through their institutions. Because administrators and faculty comprise a fairly stable constituency and are the salaried personnel who hold positions of responsibility, they are often mistaken for the institution itself. Because students are an unstable or rapidly changing element in the university, they are not always accountable to the board of trustees or the state legislature; therefore, they become mere statistics in administrative files. These records are worthwhile, but they are incomplete, just as oral history interviews would be alone.

To complete the picture, there are several ways of more fully documenting students' experiences. One possibility would be to choose randomly or selectively incoming students and introduce them to an experimental program. In addition to periodic oral history interviews, these students could be asked to save their term papers, exams, and notes on all courses, or courses taken in their major. Over a number of years, such records could be important in evaluating the quality of education, consistency of the grading system, and innovation or lack of it in instruction, all of this capturing outstanding experiences within the black milieu.

A more specific approach, with which this writer has had successful experience, has been to cooperate with members of the English department who teach the introductory composition and rhetoric courses required of all students. In this instance, professors assign at least one autobiographical essay or personal reminiscence per semester. Either assignment requires students to do some research on their own family, pattern of settlement, socio-economic status, education, customs and values. These essays are of value not only for judging the writing skills, style and ability of college freshmen of the 1970s, but also for determining the kinds of families from which the student population is drawn. Over a number of years, these essays provide a profile of the types of students attending the school, or in the cases where the school draws mainly from a given geographical location, the information contributes to a history of the area, especially its ethnic pattern. The archivist could speak at one session of each class concerning how diaries, journals, and autobiographies have been used by historians to uncover valuable history.

The main objective of any archival institution remains the collection, preservation, and administration of the official records of that respective agency. Persons engaged in the collection of Afro-American literature have a unique mission in assembling the recorded history of a people and movements.

Those archival records in Negro history are included in the following:

I. Personal Papers of Individuals
   Correspondence or letters, diaries, reminiscences, notebooks, manuscript books, and articles.

II. Official Records of the College or University
   Records creating the institution, government board minutes (trustees or regents), and official correspondence of the president and other executive administrators.

III. Papers of Organizations
   Minutes of meetings, memoranda, field reports, affidavits, speeches, agendas for meetings, information sheets, general correspondence, donation correspondence, local correspondence, student correspondence.

IV. Photographs, tapes, etc.

Another aspect of a university's history must be the intellectual and cultural atmosphere which it engenders, but this can hardly be determined from transcripts or college catalogs. With the increasing use and decreasing costs of video tape, plays, concerts, and important meetings can be recorded for future use. Such recordings can be used for archival preservation as well as for classroom and recreational use. Student music recitals, productions of the artist-in-residence, and choral groups would not only show the quality of education, but could be used in the classroom for comparison and criticism. Although many prominent speakers who appear on campuses reflect the popularity of certain evanescent causes—political, environmental, racial, or educational—their ideas and the presentation thereof should be preserved. Such recordings can be of immediate use both in the classroom and for students unable to attend lectures. They also emphasize popular trends on campus, reaction of the audience, and depth of the presentation.

This is not to say that problems of copyright or of expense in recording do not exist and might prove beyond the archivist's budget. Yet these are practical problems of implementation, not determinants of the program's value. An obvious extension of this type of collection policy would be a comprehensive attempt to acquire ephemera most often associated with student clubs and organizations, which often have a relatively short institutional life.

The technique of using oral history interviews as an important method of documenting black or institutional history is only now beginning to gain wide acceptance. All too often, however, this approach focuses narrowly on the biography of the person interviewed, or else the narrative presents the mellow recollections of a person who has retired amid recognition dinners and adulatory resolutions. These people are often unwilling or unable to critically appraise the university or their role in it. To balance these accounts, the archivist should strive to obtain interviews with known faculty dissidents or administrators who have announced a move to another university. With the guarantee of some restrictions or the promise of limited confidentiality, these people may be willing to discuss their view of the movements or the university and their own role within it. A person who has been at a university for a relatively brief time may have better insights about the institution than a senior faculty member who has not been employed at any other school. We have far too long concentrated on the people successful in the system. Perhaps we could learn as much from those who have rejected it, or been rejected by it.

Oral history is also a valuable tool for gauging student life and activity. The archivist could develop a random sampling of students and meet with them individually or in groups to record their college experiences. Over a sustained period, this could be a valuable research tool for anyone studying the effects of school and society on each other, the changing mores of college students, and student interaction with faculty and administration.

Another source for documenting student life is the record of demonstrations and causes espoused by students. Perhaps an archivist circulating among demonstrators with a tape recorder in hand might justifiably arouse suspicion among students. To allay this suspicion, the archivist might have student assistants, with some minimal training in oral history, interview their fellow students.

Oral history as part of a general collecting policy is useful, but limited in what it can provide. It is good for providing flavor, giving opinion, citing examples, but sometimes limited in disclosing specific factual material, the evolution of a policy, or the intricacies of negotiation. For these things, the archivist might turn to the formal history of the institution.

Programs devoted to the solicitation of papers, recording oral history interviews, developing a publications file, recording and preserving campus events, and collecting papers of students, can help to document more fully the role of Afro-American and institutional history in society. They are concerned with the collection, and in some sense the creation, of records which will be used by future researchers. Present collecting for future use is a necessary but not sufficient condition for a university archives. Present use of past records is the reverse side of the coin, and this in turn suggests new services an archivist can provide to assure use and recognition of the collection by faculty, students, and administrators.

The archivist and the faculty can and should enjoy a close working relationship. By surveying the faculty, the archivist could determine the type of research being done and the courses taught. In only a few instances can faculty members be expected to solicit help in the most obvious areas, such as a history course on methodology or original research. Students' records, alumni files, instructional reports, all provide enough material for students both to learn the technique of statistical work and to experience what their professors often do with primary records in researching articles and monographs.

The possibilities of research papers using the university's records are infinite, but the archivist must suggest them, have them ready, and be willing to work directly with faculty and students in exploiting those possibilities. Most faculty members are as interested in research as in teaching, and the archivist can also be of service here; however, this requires more than providing faculty members with a guide to the collection, a card catalog, or a container list. The problem is to supply the faculty with the archivist's knowledge of the collection as a whole and how it might further benefit research.

In the position as custodian of the university's records, the archivist is in a unique situation to determine the gaps that exist in the documentation of the school's history. Gaps that occur as a result of theft, accident, or destruction are probably left forever, but archivists might be of service to the university in suggesting certain kinds of data which would be of historical importance. The archives can also be of service through efforts to develop and maintain vertical files of newspaper clippings organized by subject or person. These are often useful for quick reference and people who want only a cursory answer to certain questions. There is no need to dismiss such people as a nuisance or to inundate them with inventories and container lists. A file of answers to frequently asked questions avoids having to rely on memory or on searches for the material each time the question is asked. These questions are most often about school colors, date of founding, tenure of the presidents, dates and cost of buildings, sports records, or the origin of the motto, logo, or traditions.

Particularly helpful in this regard and for researching the school's history is a comprehensive subject index of important campus publications. Although a tedious project at the outset, this catalog, once current, would not be difficult to maintain. It should include the campus newspapers, alumni magazine, departmental publications, minutes of the board of trustees and faculty—a mammoth project for an institution over a century old, but realistic for any institution less than 25 years old.

All of these service and research ideas point to a broader and more active role for the archivist on campus. The archivist's duties comprise: 1) surveying faculty to determine their research interests, 2) exploring ways of using archival material for instructional use, 3) offering courses, 4) searching and writing articles based on collections in the archives, 5) developing vertical files for frequently used materials, 6) creating certain types of records, and 7) serving on various committees. These leave little time for anything else.

Complementary to these services are collecting policies and techniques that more fully document the development of the college and Afro-American history generally. In conclusion, after deciding on a collecting focus based on the location or type of institution, the functions of the archivist should be: 1) soliciting the papers of trustees, alumni, students, and general donors in the areas of Afro-American history and civil rights, 2) establishing files for ephemera, media and publications, 3) inaugurating a systematic oral history project aimed at securing community, student, faculty, and administration input, and 4) experimenting with a possible inter-institutional loan program. All of these still do not exhaust the possibilities for collecting.

The following is a list of records common to colleges and universities:

1. Alumni association records and minutes
2. Alumni personal files
3. Audit reports
4. Budget records and ledgers
5. Contracts and grants
6. Correspondence and other papers. Includes correspondence reports received and sent, speeches, etc., of the president, deans and heads of non-academic offices, and department heads.
7. Gift and contribution records
8. Grade sheets or cards
9. Infirmary case records
10. Infirmary x-rays
11. Investment records
12. Judicial board cases
13. Ledgers (general, appropriation, and allotment ledgers)
14. Minutes of committees, faculty, school and/or department, councils, and other bodies.
15. Maintenance and operations building files
16. Monthly report on the budget
17. Payroll records
18. Personnel records (employees)
19. Printed materials (catalogs, programs, pamphlets, promotional material, etc.)
20. Purchase orders, requisitions, invoices
21. Placement records, relating to students and graduates and including resume, recommendations, record of interviews, etc.
22. Student folders (individual folder for students). Includes correspondence, personal data, activity records, academic reports, application for admission, disciplinary matters, transcript of secondary grades, etc.
23. Student ledger cards, for student accounts
24. Student organization files (including student governmental association)
25. Student organization reports. (Annual or periodic reports of student organizations to college or university administration, if such are made.)
26. Transcripts (permanent record). Shows courses taken, grades received, test results, degrees granted, etc.

31. Experiences of a Black Private Book Collector
by   Charles L. Blockson,* Private Book Collector,
       Philadelphia, Pennsylvania

When I was in the fifth grade, curiosity caused me to inquire of my teacher, "Do Negroes have a history?" Her reply was, "Negroes were meant to serve white people." This response did not answer my question and furthermore, I could not accept that statement as fact. Those words were much too painful for me. After all, I was a Negro, and even at that tender age, I knew I wanted to do something else with my life besides serve white people. Thus began the quest for my heritage—the quest for myself.

I was subconsciously guided to the Salvation Army and the Good Will Stores, which sold books for ten cents apiece and occasionally had half-price sales. I was the oldest of nine children and extra money for splurging on books was hard to acquire. Many times in those stores that I frequented I hid a desirable book behind others, hoping that it would still be there on half-price day. I bought anything which contained the words Negro, black, colored, or African. We lived in Norristown, Pennsylvania, and my father, who was a plasterer, would allow me to accompany him on his assignments to the homes along the Philadelphia Mainline— a wealthy area. While there, I would search through the trash cans and in any other accessible part of the homes where I thought an old book could be hiding.

My hunt continued through church bazaars and rummage sales. Through this process of rummaging, I found a battered and torn copy of Alain Locke's *The New Negro*, which today is worth over thirty-five dollars. At that time, I didn't realize the pecuniary value. My consuming preoccupation was to prove my teacher wrong. I discovered that blacks did have a history—as ancient and glorious as any other people if not more so. I was so ecstatic with my discovery that thereafter, book collecting and sports competed for my attention.

As time went on and I rested securely in my newly found knowledge, I became engulfed in sports activities. Because of my prowess in football and track, I received a scholarship to Penn State, and while there, I learned that my idol, Paul Robeson, the great athlete and singer, was also a book collector. I read Shirley Graham DuBois' *Paul Robeson: Citizen of the World*, and the very next month, I read an article in the *New York Times* about Arthur Schomburg, the eminent black American book collector. (His collection is the largest in the field of black literature, and is now housed in the New York Public Library, Harlem Branch.) "The Negro must remake his past in order to make his future," Schomburg theorized, and his unfailing energies in unearthing lost bits of information won him the tag "Sherlock Holmes of African History." My interest in book collecting was reawakened— Blockson's Renaissance, I called it.

---

*Author of *Pennsylvania: Black History*. Philadelphia, Pa.: Portfolio Associates, Inc., 1975.

During my years at Penn State I was able to visit many bookstores in various states while travelling with the football team. None of these stores impressed me more than did Harlem's National Memorial Bookstore. Mr. Lewis Michaux, the proprietor, had been in direct communication with most of the recognized and unrecognized literary people of the black world in this century, and he recommended that I read W. E. B. DuBois' *Souls of Black Folk*. I did, and to say that the book had a profound impact on me would be to understate its influence, for it prompted me to delve more deeply into black literature. I had come far from the days of the rummage sales. No longer was I seeking to find a heritage, but to amass a collection to explain that heritage.

Like the medals and trophies I acquired as an athlete, each book signified another conquest along the research route. It was with this conviction that I set out to investigate the Schomburg branch of the New York Public Library. As I entered the unpretentious building, I found an astounding statue of Ira Aldridge in the foyer. The Shakespearean actor was posed as Othello, his black hand clutching the stark white handkerchief of Desdemona, one counterpoised against the other in symbolic contrast. I was arrested by the sight of that dramatic figure and felt myself throbbing with wholeness, as if just for once I could imbibe the untampered essence of human integrity, colorless. Then I was lured in deeper, past this overwhelming countenance, to the cramped little reading room where stood six wooden tables surrounded by forty or so old chairs. The statue of Aldridge as Othello set the mood for an amazing experience, one so influential in my life that I have since added a reproduction of it to the library in my home.

Behind the reading room, I searched the compressed stacks, with row upon row of documented centuries of black culture. Just to wander along the length of shelves, browsing through ancient titles was a personal awakening, a meeting with my ancestors, bound as they were in cloth and vellum. I glanced over book titles and felt overwhelmed at the abundance of literature by and about blacks. "Everything in this room pertains to the black man," I whispered to myself. It made me feel complete.

From the central floor with its little reading room, I climbed the iron stairs to the Rare Books stacks. There was something about rare, leatherbound books that imparted that attraction that I have for book collecting in general. Here were volumes I had heard about previously but had never actually seen, such as *The Life and Travels of Gustavus Vassa*, tales of Ignatius Sancho, and Phillis Wheatley's poetry. Until now my contact had been limited to current literature. For the first time, I saw books from an earlier time, some with foreign names, others relating to the West Indies or slavery.

In another part of the library, I found a huge collection of blacks who belonged to the Masonic Lodge. There were even the Stetson Kennedy papers on the Ku Klux Klan. I recognized the contributions of Leigh Whipper, Alexander Crummell, William Pickens, Paul Laurence Dunbar, and others. Some of these I had already read about in Joel A. Rogers' *Great Men of Color*, which I had borrowed from the Pennsylvania State College Library. Here, however, I was surrounded by the histories of black scholars and artists, feeling engulfed in a unifying sea of blackness, and for a moment I could imagine the sense of inclusion that must have characterized the academics at the ancient University of Sankore.

Schomburg wrote many highly respected books before becoming curator of the Negro collection at Fisk University, books that forecast the upsurge of interest in black literature that would come a half century later. In 1916, he compiled his notable *Bibliographic Checklist of the American Negro*, and I credit this source with many of my own discoveries, since it guided me especially to those authors whose racial identity has generally been submerged.

The first visit to the Schomburg library refined my life's purpose dramatically. Viewing books as an index to a complete history raised my respect for collecting black memorabilia, a pursuit which I had considered as just a diversion up to that point. Feeling more and more like a historian myself, I returned to the Penn State library to borrow Rogers' *From Man to Superman*, covering three thousand years of black excellence and literacy that was for the most part otherwise unacknowledged. To read about the University of Alexandria in Egypt, the magnificent Songhay cities of Jenne and Gao, the cultural advances of Timbuktu, and the scholastics at Zimbabwe in the fifteenth century, was to credit a high level of black intelligence that existed even before there was a European civilization.

In the weeks that followed, I experienced a joy in my identity fed by the awareness of our cultural strengths, since my research was proving that blacks had an important tole in the formation of American civilization, too. A true American history, it seemed to me, would necessarily include the many contributions of American blacks, and to defeat the hopelessness in most Afro-Americans required that they discover what these hidden literary gems offered to reveal. And so I daydreamed, saying to myself: "My books are food for my soul; they are the inspiration of my being." With eloquence, Henry David Thoreau had said it in *Walden*: "Books are the treasured wealth of the world, the fit inheritance of generations and nations." Amy Lowell had observed also, in *The Boston Athenaeum*:

> For books are more than books, they are the life
> The very heart and core of ages past,
> The reason why men lived and worked and died,
> The essence and quintessence of their lives.

Ralph Waldo Emerson wrote in his *Journal*, 22 December 1839: "Some books leave us free and some books make us free." On February 11, 1964, President Lyndon Johnson would provide federal aid for library services with the words: "Books and ideas are the most effective weapons against intolerance and ignorance."

To this quiet battle I dedicated my energies. I was ready to begin collecting black literature seriously. Today I have over six thousand books, broadsides, prints, and pamphlets in my collection, all of which speak to the breadth of the black experience. They are written in many languages, including Hebrew, French, Yiddish, German, Dutch, Arabic, and Amharic, and other various African languages. Some of the authors are celebrated and others virtually unknown. I have works of Leo Africanus, the African historian who lived in the Middle Ages, and books written by early European travelers in Africa. There are descriptions of blacks visiting Africa, such as Martin Delany, Robert Campbell, and Wilmont Blyden. The experience of blacks in the West Indies from the time of the slave trade is represented as well. I have slave documents from the West Indies and a copy of the rare Haytian Papers by Prince Saunders, which includes a letter written by King Christophe. I have books concerning the anti-slavery as well as the pro-slavery movement. These include, among others, the original works of William Wells Brown, the

1847 narrative of Frederick Douglass and some of his letters, the works of George Washington Williams, William Still, and books by known black abolitionists. Also, I have included the work of white abolitionists Garrison, Whittier, and Charles Sumner, to name a few. I might also add that I collect the works of Thomas Dixon, Joel Chandler Harris, and Charles Carroll. The latter's *The Negro a Beast*, published in 1900, is a classic of hate, but I collect the writings of those who hate the black man because they too are important parts of black literature.

I am lucky to have one of the few known copies of the Nat Turner Confession, a signed copy of a book of poems by Phillis Wheatley, the works of Gustavas Vassa, and the untranslated pamphlet of Jacobus Elijah Capitein, the first black to graduate from the University of Leyden in Amsterdam, Holland. I have the first two copies of Benjamin Banneker's Almanac, sermons by Lemuel Haynes, the rare biography of the black cowboy Nate Love, and a pamphlet on how to play chess, written by a black man in 1872. I have most of the works from the Harlem Renaissance, and I keep up to date on the contemporary works of black authors from around the world. Black art, folklore, poetry, and sheet music are on my shelves, and there are good collections on the black church and blacks in sports. Perhaps the high points in my collection are the works on the Underground Railroad and the material on the life and times of Paul Robeson.

A collector may endeavor, as I have done, to gather the whole of black literature; on the other hand, he may wish to specialize in one or another phase, for instance, pre-Civil War, the writings of Langston Hughes, or even Frank Yerby, whose popularity makes his works more available. A person may wish to specialize in black humor, history, or even blacks in sports; or they may concentrate, as I do, in anti-black literature, or conversely, in anti-white literature written by blacks. Included in a collection of black literature may be books about Africa written by Africans or non-Africans, or works about the West Indies. Early black sheet music is also a possibility for the collector whose interests lean towards the musical. The ever-expanding literature of jazz is another interesting possibility. Black militant writing and Black Muslim and Black Panther newspapers are other fields of interest in black literature. The various aspects of the black or pseudo-black theater, such as the minstrel show, are still other possibilities. Poets ranging from Phillis Wheatley and Jupiter Hammon to the young poets found in recently published Broadside Series publications would be only one more of a long list of categories which would be available to the collector of black literature.

Some collectors assemble collections in a hit-or-miss fashion, much in the way I gathered what I could locate during my grammar school years. If such a collector enjoys this pastime, so be it. In short, the hobby, the avocation, the disease, the addiction, whatever, has no rules except those the collector makes. I, for instance, accept into my collection books with library markings; some collectors do not. I will purchase a book lacking a dust jacket; some will not. While I prefer first editions, I will purchase a reprint, if the first edition is not readily avaialble. I have purchased paperbacks, but prefer paperbacks which have not been first printed as hardbacks.

Many people question me about the rarities in my collection, and how I go about finding them. Certainly a collector does not begin a quest in a bookstore where, unarmed, the individual is already a victim. Bibliographies are among the more obvious sources of what is available in whatever the chosen field of collection happens to be. I have found Grégoire's *An Enquiry Concerning the Intellectual and*

Moral Faculties, and Literature of Negroes, 1810, quite helpful in finding what I seek, but I happen to have a copy of Gregoire's work. Finding a copy of it may be the greatest problem a young collector may encounter. More easily found are *Early American Negro Writers* by Dorothy Porter; *Bibliography of the Negro in Africa and America* by Monroe Work; *The Negro Author in America* by Vernon Loggins; *A Century of Fiction by American Negroes 1853-1952* by Maxwell Whiteman; *The Negro Caravan*, edited by Sterling Brown; *A Bibliography of Antislavery in America* by Dwight Lowell Dumond; and *The Catalogue of the Caribbeana Section of the Nicholas M. Williams Memorial Ethnological Collection: Negro History 1553-1903* by the Library Company of Philadelphia. For modern works, I find the *New York Times Literature Supplement*, *Freedomways* magazine, and works listed in the *Association for the Study of Negro Life and History* all valuable.

Also, I rely heavily on book dealers' catalogs. I live in a Pennsylvania area which is a rich resource for collecting my material because this was a focal point for the anti-slavery movement. Consequently, an abundance of material on that subject was published in Pennsylvania. Also, I am situated close to Lancaster County, the Pennsylvania Dutch area, where quite a few blacks kept collections. Flea markets are a popular sight near my home in Montgomery County, and rare items can sometimes be found in these places. Philadelphia was the mecca for book collecting in colonial times, with an abundance of bookstores, and it was also the capital of the black bourgeoisie. It had one of the largest free black communities dating from shortly before the American Revolution to the early 1840s. Among other firsts, the free blacks established literary societies, and the Library Company of Colored People had an outstanding collection of books by blacks. Some of the private black book collections were preserved by family members, such as the collection of Dr. Nathan Mosell, who established the Frederick Douglass Hospital, which was preserved by his wife, an aunt of Paul Robeson. Unfortunately at times, whole collections would disappear after the death of the book lover, as in the case of Robert Purvis, a wealthy black abolitionist. Of course, I am willing to drive to Washington or New York if I hear of something interesting, and I have even been known to make a transatlantic call in hopes of locating a rare item.

I was dumbfounded twelve years ago at the attitude of an ignorant bookseller in Baltimore, Maryland. I was in town for the Baltimore Colts-Los Angeles Rams game, wherein my two former college roommates, Lenny Moore and Roosevelt Grier, were set to oppose each other. Before the game I sought out the local bookstore as usual and approached the proprietor for some guidance.

"I'm looking for something used," I told him casually. "Do you have any books written by black authors that I could look through?"

"You mean 'coon' books? Ain't got none!" he snapped.

He turned his back and pretended to ignore me after that, but I wandered around for a few minutes and came up with some very collectible first editions. When I checked back at the register I was carrying James Baldwin's *Giovanni's Room*, Ann Petry's *The Street*, a few of Frank Yerby's novels that I am sure the bookseller never dreamed were the works of a black man, and two translations of works by the Russian black Alexander Pushkin. As I paid him a pittance for these new additions, he mumbled half at me and half into the register, "You really want this junk? That's just 'coon' books, anyway." I grabbed my change and took off, knowing that he was all the poorer for his lack of appreciation. I was learning not to take such foolishness personally, and safely tucked under my arm were treasures of yesterday that would be gems of tomorrow.

Another time, I stumbled on a stack of valuable books used merely for display in a Greenwich Village shop window. I liked to roam the streets of that artists' colony, savoring the Bohemian atmosphere much as I responded instinctively to the liveliness of Harlem. One particular afternoon, I passed a boutique window draped in exotic beads. My attention was caught by a grouping in a corner, a hill of leather books piled high beneath cascades of garish yellow chains and pendants. I stopped to examine the titles of the books lying sidewise and saw with pleasure *Prince Le Boos*, printed on the second uppermost book.

"*Prince Le Boos*, the biographic sketch of the wealthy New Bedford whaler," I gasped.

I knew that it was the story of the black Quaker merchant, Paul Cuffe, who had early advocated the "Back to Africa" movement, along with James Russwurm. Together they felt that life in the African Sierra Leone colony would restore the ethnic manhood that had been robbed from blacks in North America. They were in the vanguard of a movement that would again be echoed by Marcus Garvey. I had considered Cuffe an astute thinker, and it was impossible to walk away from that window without the book. I entered the store prepared to offer the manager five dollars for the *Prince Le Boos* volume.

"Impossible," she said when she heard my request. "It's part of the display—sets off the pendants just the way I want them. I'm awfully sorry."

"Look," I persisted. "Couldn't you find some other way to raise them up for view? You know, on a box or something? Here, I'll show you," I added, grabbing a small shipping carton from the floor near the counter. "Take this box and fold this scarf over it this way," I said demonstrating. "There. Can't you let me have the book now?"

"Well," she considered as she viewed my innovation, "it does look okay, I must admit. All right, you can have the book."

I paid her the five dollars and walked away with a gem far more precious than all her golden jewelry lumped together.

On another occasion I was visiting a Pennsylvania Dutch curiosity shop. I had gone there with no particular quest in mind and was haphazardly browsing through a box of documents that had been purchased from the estate of a former professor from Lafayette College. With no thought of finding anything relating to my own collection, I was simply enjoying the historical details revealed in the old maps, broadsides, and letters contained in that grouping. Towards the bottom of the box, I spotted a faded blue-gray book that looked irresistable to a collector's eye and immediately dug deeply into the box to extract the book, curious to see its title. To my surprise it was the elusive *Haytian Papers*, advertised for several hundred dollars. I was able to purchase the collector's item for only five dollars, because again the shop owner failed to recognize the value of pieces relating to black history.

Most of the books searched for are considered rare because of a special quality about them, but when they disappear from circulation and become equally scarce, researchers horn in on the literary treasure hunt, concentrating their attention and increasing the demand for the book. Time and again they pick like scavengers through catalogs, communications, book sales, flea markets and auctions, ever hoping to uncover one of the fragments of history that has been obliterated when a book of consequence evaporates from sight. By the time the long-sought book turns up, dealers usually have accumulated waiting lists of people who have already asked for the item. Luck, timing, and personality—the success ingredients in this kind of buying—combined with just the right amount of pressure and interest, can determine who will secure the book that is so dearly wanted. *Medga*, a novel by black writer Emma Kelley (1891), is such a book.

Early in 1973, I read a news article which disclosed that Harvard University had purchased a copy of *Megda* from David O'Neill, an antiquarian dealer in New Hampshire. The news of this curiosity, advertised in O'Neill's catalog for thirty dollars, required prompt action in the interest of keeping my library as comprehensive as possible. I immediately called O'Neill to see if another copy might be available. His wife answered my call and explained that he had received over fifteen requests already, but agreed to add my name to the waiting list if I wished. One month later, a letter arrived from O'Neill which I tore open impatiently in the hopes of a new offer. The letter explained that since I was the last to call, he had decided to offer it to me for a slightly higher price. I asked about the one advertised in his catalog, and he replied that it had been sold to the library at Harvard—the only other known edition. However, because I was a collector with such a vast knowledge of black history, he preferred to sell it directly to me than to an institution or another dealer.

I was anxious not to miss out on this "find" a second time, and also very much flattered to think that I had been singled out to receive this offer. I called O'Neill that afternoon to confirm the price and order the book. O'Neill was very enthusiastic when he heard my voice and promptly advised me that the copy he was now holding was in "mint" condition, far better than the one that he had sold to Harvard. Again, I was impressed by the arbitrary luck that governs the appropriation of collector's items, and we finished the conversation with assurances from him that the volume would be securely wrapped and mailed to me that day.

For several days I literally paced, waiting for the mail to arrive. Finally, the little yellow card appeared, notifying me of a special delivery package by registered mail. I received the book safely intact in its New Hampshire newspaper wrapping, and like a child given a birthday package, I flew to the car, where I broke open the box and glanced through the story. After a brief appraisal of the book's contents, I drove directly home to settle in my favorite chair and read the entire story. Afterwards, I locked the book safely away, satisfied that I now possessed two books written by an early black female novelist in this country.

It is interesting that once a new book comes to light, more and more copies of it are successively uncovered. In the same year that both of these copies of *Megda* were discovered, still a third one was unearthed. Mr. O'Neill sold the third copy to the library at Boston University. What this means to me is that I can continue to hope optimistically that some books now thought to be extinct actually do exist somewhere on an unrecognized shelf, waiting to be found by someone who has learned what to look for. The dollar value of the books, as collector's items, has far less importance in my own mind, comparatively speaking, than the hope that enough interested people can be educated to help retrieve this literature for the benefit of all mankind.

Megda, in its scarcity as only one of three known copies, and its rarity as one of the first publications of its kind, is one of many such items that I have continued to unearth as I have collected over the years. One of the oldest rare books I own, a 1632 edition of the *Travels of Leo Africanus*, is another special treasure. I bought it from Walter Goldwater, a noted white bookseller who specialized in black literature, and found that not only is the 3½" by 3½" book exceedingly well preserved and unique simply because of its age (albeit a fourth edition), but it is also written in Latin and apparently published by Abraham Elzvier, head of one of the world's greatest publishing houses at that time.

The text contains the observations of an African slave who was abducted and educated in Italy during the sixteenth century. On his return to Africa as a scholar, Leo Africanus studied the living conditions of the time and was the first to describe the culturally rich city of Timbuktu. At the request of Pope Leo X, Africanus elucidated the conditions he found in Africa, describing the magnificently crafted embroideries, carving, jewelry, and leatherwork that typified the society. He extolled the University of Sankore, of the Songhay empire, as a versatile center of learning and thereby documented its existence for the future of mankind. With the help of Leo Africanus' book, we can begin to make a substantial case for the existence of a significant and respectable African heritage—one that has been erroneously overlooked and devalued.

The collector of the rarities of black literature must be blessed with an abundance of patience, since so many of the most prized works by black writers are among the rarest of the rare. Offhand I could list one hundred of these works, and with a little thought, one hundred more. Were I to research the subject, I am sure I could unearth at least a thousand.

One such rarity would be Juan Latino's *Austriad*, published in 1573 in Granada, Spain. While Latino did not gain the worldwide reknown of Cervantes, Latino is of more interest to me. Ironically, however, a similarity exists between the well-known Cervantes and the lesser known Latino, as both had known slavery, Cervantes in North Africa, Latino in Spain. Interestingly, Cervantes was Spanish and Latino was African.

Latino was born in Guinea and brought to Spain as a slave. From his position as a slave, Latino earned his Doctor of Arts degree at the University of Granada, where he eventually was awarded the Chair of Poetry. His poems have placed him safely in the annals of Spanish literature.

A number of other Africans earned fame under adverse conditions. One would be Jacobus Elisha Joannes Capitein, who earned his fame far from the land of his birth. Brought to Holland as a slave, much in the same manner Latino was to Spain, Capitein, after years of incredible advancement, earned his doctorate degree at the University of Leyden in 1740. Two years later, his dissertation, *Politico-Theologica de Servitute, Libertati Christianae Non Contraria*, was published in Amsterdam. Twentieth century blacks will be surprised to learn that Capitein was pro-slavery, as his *Devocatione Ethnicorum* (1742) reveals. First editions of either his dissertation or his pro-slavery work are extremely rare, and I have seen them only in my wildest fantasies. However, I am fortunate to possess one Capitein item, a paperback entitled *De Negerpredikant Jacobus Elisha Joannes Capitein*, a collection of Capitein's letters published centuries after his death; but is a first edition. I find this paperback of special interest because its frontispiece is a copy of a portrait executed by Van Dyke, and to my knowledge, it is the only extant portrait of Capitein.

There are many books that eager collectors now possess only in their dreams. One such book is Ludolph's *History of Aethiopia*, written in Latin and Coptic, and published in four huge tomes, 1691-1694. Gustavus Vassa's autobiography would be another, and a third would be the *Collected Poems* of Lucy Terry, a black slave of the pre-Revolutionary War era. The latter work is one I have imagined—such a work most likely was never published. That Lucy Terry existed is well-documented; that she wrote poetry is equally well-documented. It is also true, however, that not a single one of her poems is extant. Somewhere, perhaps in an attic or in a barn or buried with treasure, there may be a sheaf of poems by Lucy Terry. I would like to find it.

Still another rarity is Walker's *Appeal*, published in 1829. It is one of many anti-slavery tracts, unique only in that it is the rarest of them. Following the publication of the pamphlet, a concentrated effort on the part of the pro-slavery forces was so successful in destroying almost all copies that, despite the fact that the *Appeal* went through three editions in one year, the pamphlet today is the rarest of numerous anti-slavery tracts.

The first book by a black American published by a commercial publisher also has the distinction of being the first directory of its kind; so writes Maxwell Whiteman, editor of the *Afro-American History Series*. His statement refers to his Historic Publication number 235, entitled *The House Servant's Directory, or a Monitor for Private Families*. The work, written by Robert Roberts, was published simultaneously in 1827 by a Boston publisher and New York publisher. *The House Servant's Directory*, because it is a sort of Emily Post of the era, is quite valuable as Americana. As black literature, it is valuable to the collector because it was written by a black Philadelphian, one of the city's most successful caterers. As a collectible in general, it is valuable simply because it is rare in being a first edition—or in any other edition.

I enjoy reading the elaborate, if sometimes overly lengthy, subtitles of nineteenth century works. I especially enjoyed a section of *The House Servant's Directory*: " . . . with friendly advice to cooks and heads of families, and complete directions on how to burn Lehigh coal." It seems that many of the cooks of the era heartily refused to replace the tried and tested wood with the new fangled idea of coal.

There are other rare works—so many others, but part of the fun of book collecting is the discovery of what is rare and what is not so rare, and what is not rare at all.

Do not be mislead into thinking that age establishes the rarity of a book. There are books published in 1934 more valuable and even more difficult to find than books published in 1853. A first edition of John Dos Passos' *Three Plays: The Garbage Man, Airways, Inc., and, Fortune Heights*, published in 1934, would be today more valuable than Elizabeth Stuart Phelps' *The Tell-Tale: Or, Home Secrets Told by Old Travelers*, published in 1853. Yet, some booksellers may overprice the older work, hoping to take advantage of an amateur or an antiquarian's love of old books. The first edition of a book is always more desirable, since it will not only retain its present value but increase it as time goes on. Now that the interest in black literature has soared, and the number of collectors searching for this material has increased, first editions are becoming even rarer to find, and when found, the cost is often prohibitive.

I prefer to buy first editions, but I have also bought many reprints, as a reprint is better than no print at all. Regarding dust jackets, I follow a similar philosophy. I prefer a dust jacket, but I will purchase a book without one. Most used books will not have one, and the collector should be wary of a book listed in a catalog as "with d.j." Always remove the dust jacket before purchasing a book. Sometimes a very nice dust jacket will cover not only the book, but an unhealthy coat of mold on the book or a worm hole or two, and perhaps the remains of the worms as well. Perhaps the worms ate through the original dust jacket and the bookseller found another cover. Remember, though, that most reputable book dealers will allow the customer to return books in other than described condition.

The first substantial collections of black literature were undoubtedly amassed in the ancient cultural centers of Alexandria, Songhay, and the University of Sankore. But because those civilizations were destroyed, little is known of any serious effort to collect black literature until the German naturalist and anthropologist, Johann Friedrich Blumenbach, began his studies between 1752 and 1840. Blumenbach was primarily recognized for his work in dividing mankind into five racial classifications, but as a result of this work he accumulated the first known European private collection of black literature, described in his *De Generis Humani Varietati Native*, and including poetry by Phillis Wheatley as an example of distinguished Negro achievement.

While Blumenbach's motives were classically academic in providing tools to improve the understanding of differences within the human species, little did he know that he was preparing a double-edged sword that could be used for or against blacks. Unfortunately, the attention he drew to racial differences offered those with less noble purposes discriminatory information which could then be twisted and adulterated for the malignment of one race by another.

The French Jesuit collector, Abbé Henri Grégoire, credits Blumenbach with compiling the first European library of black literature, but it was the priest himself who wrote the first history of black literature, a research project so complete that his reputation is based primarily on that book. Originally published in 1808, Grégoire's *Enquiry into the Moral and Intellectual Faculties of Negroes* was released in English in 1810 through a publishing house in Brooklyn. Since that time, the treatise has become more than just a prime tool in the research of early black literature and outstanding forerunner of Schomburg's *Bibliographic Checklist of the American Negro*. It is also now a rarity as a collector's item. In 1968, I purchased a copy of the translation for seventy-five dollars, but I have seen it offered more recently for two hundred dollars.

Grégoire compiled his book to strike from France across the ocean at the covert hypocrisy of the President in America. Thomas Jefferson had claimed sympathy for the blacks in slavery, denouncing their abuse in his *Notes on the State of Virginia*. Gregoire admonished, "It's sad to say, Jefferson is not the only American statesman who has spoken high-sounding words in favor of freedom, and then his own children to die slaves." Enraged by Jefferson's condescending position and by the President's failure to release his own slaves from bondage, even the children he sired by those slaves, Grégoire responded to Jefferson's "Notes" by exalting the intellectual capacities of Negroes, further chiding Jefferson for his patronizing treatment of John Melbourn, a self-educated black whom Jefferson invited to parties as a token of his tolerance.

The Jesuit priest's literary effort was amplified by a multitude of other humanistic endeavors, especially as a leader with Lafayette and Robespierre of the Abolitionist society, "Les Amis des Noires." Grégoire instigated the establishment of a French school for blacks, L'Ecole Polytechnique, thereby inspiring a sequence of capable black graduates whose subsequent successes attested to his belief in their intellectual potentials. Among the graduates was Armand Lanusse, who eventually headed an artistic band of poets in New Orleans calling themselves "Les Cenelles." Also during Gregoire's lifetime, Alexandre Dumas reached his peak proficiency as a writer. With the kindly encouragement of Abbé Grégoire, Dumas represented himself proudly to the world as the grandson of a beautiful Haitian woman. All of Paris acknowledged the lineage of the author of *The Three Musketeers* and *The Count of Monte Cristo*, despite the efforts of English and American racists to prove otherwise.

Probably the first known black American book collector was David Ruggles, a well-known black abolitionist of the 1830s. Ruggles as a contemporary of Frederick Douglass, contributed actively to the cause of freedom for the slaves, and was recognized as a man of profound ability and force of character. During most of his active public life, he was a leader of the Underground Railroad in New York City, respected for his editorial abilities and for his intimate knowledge of law in slave cases. Ruggles's *Mirror of Liberty*, published in New York in 1838, was the first black periodical to be produced in America. After that, in 1845, he published *The Genius of Freedom*, the second Afro-American newspaper in this country, following James Russwurm's *Freedom's Journal*. With all this to do, Ruggles still managed to allow time to accumulate a significant body of black writing for posterity.

Professor W. S. Scarborough, a classical Greek scholar, also collected a distinguished library of black literature. He was an academician who earned his degrees at Oberlin College and the Liberia College in West Africa, and then became a professor on the staff at Wilberforce College in Ohio.

One of the finest libraries of black literature compiled during the nineteenth century belonged to Robert M. Adger, a black Philadelphia book merchant. Adger's *Catalogue of Rare Books and Pamphlets* covers "Subjects Relating to the Past Condition of the Colored Race and the Slavery in This Country." This catalog describing rare works is itself considered unique. All I have been able to obtain of Adger's catalog is an incomplete photostatic copy of the 1894 publication, showing the title page, and three or four pages of listings similar to those shown at the 1969 Exhibition of Negro History: 1553-1903, sponsored jointly by the Historical Society of Pennsylvania and the Library Company of Philadelphia.

As the century turned, another black Philadelphian concentrated his attention on building a library of black writings, this time focusing mainly on writers of early periods. William C. Bolivar, also known as "pencil pusher" because for twenty-two years he wrote a column by that name on Philadelphia history for the *Philadelphia Tribune* (a black newspaper), brought many interests to his collecting efforts. He was a member of the American Negro Historical Society, in Philadelphia, and a corresponding member of the Negro Society for Historical Research of Yonkers, New York. Bolivar also served as co-editor of Daniel Murray's *Colored Encyclopedia*.

Leon Gardiner's collection also originated in Philadelphia and is housed at the Pennsylvania Historical Society. In it are examples of his own writings as well as those of many other black luminaries.

The Library of Congress in Washington, D.C., began its compilation of Negro writings in 1900 with an industrious bibliography prepared by one of its staff assistants, Daniel A. P. Murray. Under the direction of the Librarian of Congress, Herbert Putnam, Murray organized a presentation of 500 titles, culled from a list of 1,100, for exhibition in the Negro Authorship section of the Paris Exposition.

According to Thomas J. Calloway, special United States Liaison to the Exposition, the most creditable showing in the exhibit was the Negro Authors collection.

Such contributions were not only the province of black men. Long before black studies became a current popular issue, white collectors Alexander Mott and Lewis Tappan concentrated their efforts on the neglected bodies of black legend. In 1826, Alexander Mott published his *Biographical Sketches and Interesting Anecdotes of Persons of Color*. Little is known about Mott, who may have been related to abolitionist Abigail Mott, but his work served as a storehouse of slave narratives, news items, and other Negro memorabilia. Lewis Tappan's 2,000 piece collection of anti-slavery material was turned over to Howard University in 1873.

Howard University's Africana Library expanded in 1914, when former trustee Jesse Moorland presented his 3,000 books, pamphlets, and pictures portraying a vivid spectrum of the life and legends of the black man. In his name, the Moorland Foundation was established with the expectation that research would be continued in these areas.

The purchase of the Arthur B. Spingarn collection of black literature and music amplified the Moorland Library by more than 7,000 items, and between 1946 and 1972, about 1,000 more pieces annually were acquired by Spingarn for the collection. A lawyer by profession and an early leader of the NAACP, Spingarn was honored to give the 1937 Negro History Week address at Howard. His comments on "Collecting a Library of Negro Literature" were carried in the *Journal of Negro Education* (June 1938) and described his acquisition of the extraordinary collection. At present, the Moorland-Spingarn Library at Howard University ranks first among university holdings in black literature. To facilitate the use of the collection, Mrs. Dorothy Porter, recently retired as curator of the collection, published an extensive bibliography based on its contents: "Library Resources for the Study of Negro Life and History" in the *Journal of Negro Education* (April 1936).

There are some other collectors of black materials who also deserve mention. Henry P. Slaughter, the son of a slave, had a house full of books, and a large part of his collection is at Atlanta University in Georgia. Recently some of his books were auctioned in Washington, D.C. Rev. Charles Martin of New York City had a nice collection back in the 1920s. Dr. R. R. Wright, Sr. and his son both had outstanding works on the A.M.E. Church and on blacks in Pennsylvania history. Glen Carrington, a postal worker of New York City who died not too long ago, had a collection which is now part of the Moorland-Spingarn Collection.

The collection of the great black historian and founder of the Association for the Study of Negro Life and History, Carter G. Woodson, is housed at the Library of Congress. Heritage Hall at Livingstone College is the recipient of the collection which belonged to Bishop W. J. Walls. In Canada, Alvin McCurdy, Sr., collects books primarily on the subjects of anti-slavery movement and blacks in Canada. Another good resource is James Abajian of California, who collects newspaper clippings of importance to or about blacks in California.

Dorothy Porter inspired me. She knew Slaughter, Schomburg, Van Vechten, Spingarn, and several other noted black book collectors, and she helped to set standards for the preservation of black heritage. Her works on early black writers were beneficial to me as a collector and I still use her bibliographies as a guide.

I am a friend of Maxwell Whiteman, who was a book dealer for forty years and is the author of *A Century of Fiction by American Negroes 1853-1952*. Whiteman introduced me to the book by Vernon Loggins, *The Negro Author in America*, and this book helped me to get my collection started. Whiteman also introduced me to *Americana*, a bibliographic catalog written by the noted book dealer Charles F. Heartman. Furthermore, he encouraged me to study the bibliography of the noted educator Monroe N. Work, *A Bibliography of the Negro in Africa and America*, a "must" in black book collecting.

I have enjoyed visiting the home of Clarence Holte in New York City, who has one of the largest private collections on black literature in the United States and who visited and complimented me on my collection for its depth. The strength of his collection lies in his books dealing with Africa.

I have had the fortune of meeting M. A. (Spike) Harris who resides in Brooklyn, New York. He was a prime source for the times in *The Black Book* edited by Tony Morrison, and he has a large collection of anti-slavery coins as well.

Another friend is Robert Welch, now the sports director and reporter at Rutgers University in Newark, New Jersey, who has a great collection of black fiction. Mr. Brook Morris of Philadelphia is a schoolteacher who specializes in the anti-slavery movement and black political conventions. A schoolteacher in Lancaster, Pennsylvania, Ms. Celmast Easton, has a good collection of pro-black and anti-black books and prints. A former schoolteacher from Philadelphia, Mrs. Loretta Cooper collects literature for black children and books related to the black experience with Quakers. Edwin Starr of Boston, Massachusetts, just sold his outstanding collection of black fiction to Boston University. The late William Tasker, a former Philadelphia schoolteacher, had a collection on blacks and slavery which is now disseminated. Harrison Ridely of Philadelphia is a young black collector who specializes on blacks in music and has an excellent record collection.

Pablo Eisenberg of Washington, D.C. has a good collection of black authors. Included in his library is *The Garys' and Their Friends* by Frank Webb, the second novel to be published by a black man in America. Mr. Eisenberg also has a copy of Nancy Cunard's book *Negro*, which is extremely rare.

Book collecting has its agonies and its ecstasies. It is agony when you have just missed getting your hands on a book that you have been searching for for years. It is agony when you have found what you wanted but cannot afford to buy it. And, oh, what agony when you finally possess a rare book like *The Fugitive Blacksmith* by James Pennington and lose it on the train as I did. I have not found another copy yet! But what can compare to the satisfaction of knowing that within your library may lie the knowledge which can eradicate ignorance and inspire a people and yourself to loftier heights of civilization.

32. Black Special Libraries

by   Vivian D. Dewitt, Librarian, Carnegie Endowment for
     International Peace

Special libraries constitute the least familiar form of library for the general public, and they are usually differentiated from other libraries by the following distinguishing characteristics: where they are found, limitations in subject scope, the kinds of people who use them or are served by them, their size, and their emphasis on the information function. Special libraries may be found in private business and industrial organizations such as banks, advertising agencies, television stations, professional and trade associations, newspapers, publishing, engineering firms, and insurance companies. Other are part of the framework of federal, state, county, or municipal governmental bodies. A number of special libraries are in nonprofit institutions such as hospitals, museums and foundations. They may also be subject branches or departments of public or university library complexes, such as the picture collection of a large public library or the international relations library of a university library system.[1] Some concentrate on a particular form of material such as maps, records, and slides. Special libraries are distinguished by having specific, rather than general subject interests, singly or in groups of related subjects, and the special library's collection and services are developed with the needs of the specific organization in mind. This factor is descriptive of special libraries as a type and also distinguishes one special library from another, since uniqueness is largely a matter of subject specialization. The library of a pharmaceutical company bears slight resemblance to one of a petroleum producer, newspaper publisher, or museum.

All kinds of libraries come in all sizes, and some special libraries have dozens of employees and thousands and thousands of volumes in their collections; but surveys and studies of special libraries have led to the conclusion that a majority of them employ only a few persons. The special library is usually small in staff size, small in space occupied, and small in size of collection.

Services of the special library are designed to save the time of employees, which, in turn, saves money for the organization. Many situations and events have led to the establishment of special libraries in organizations; usually this occurs when one or more of the following problems exists, is recognized, and a solution is sought:

> An organization realizes that its funds are being used to buy multiple copies of books and magazines for individuals in the organization, when fewer copies, properly centralized, circulated, and controlled would better serve the needs of all.

---

[1] Edward G. Strable, editor, *Special Libraries: A Guide for Management* (New York: Special Libraries Association, 1975), pp. 1-3.

An organization takes stock and recognizes the extensive and expensive collections of books, magazines, pamphlets, reprints, and other materials scattered among its departments and offices in desk drawers, on the tops of file cabinets, in the back of storerooms.

Employees complain that they have attempted to borrow publications from nonpublic libraries and have been told they must request them on interlibrary loan through their special library—and they do not have one.

Management wonders, and begins to check on, how much time and money are being spent by executives to telephone around the country in search of information.

Junior executives or secretaries are, once again, sent out to the public library to "look something up" and, once again, tardily return without the needed information.

Someone points out, once again, that each day's mail brings quantities of free but valuable information that is being wasted through lack of organization.

Management finds that despite an extensive and valuable accumulation of publications, often including expensive internal research reports, specific ones can never seem to be located to answer specific needs.[2]

The public librarian generally needs a broad educational background and wide range of personal interests, coupled with motivation toward public service. In an academic library, teaching activity provides the strongest influence, with scholarly specialization coming to the fore where advanced degree and research programs are strongly supported. The service programs of the special library, on the other hand, is likely to present some unique staff requirements. Obviously, most skills needed in other libraries are also required in the special library,[3] but the special library often has a special climate and work characteristics. Demands tend to be rapid, frequent, often complex, sometimes overwhelming. It goes without saying that, as in other kinds of libraries, professional education as well as several years of experience in the traditional type of library (BS in LS or MLS degree), plus a specialization in one or more subjects, has equipped the librarian to provide service as quickly and efficiently as possible.

The daily functioning of most libraries requires a large amount of basic clerical work. An organization may assign a clerk or secretary to these chores (typing, filing, clipping, record-keeping; duties too numerous to mention), title the person "librarian," and proclaim itself well served—but these are just custodial functions. Good information service begins at this point with a professional librarian not only

---

[2] *Ibid.*, pp. 7-8.
[3] *Ibid.*, p. 38.

planning and supervising the performance of the clerical work but actually using the results in achieving the library's more extensive goals.

It is essential, however, that the librarian be provided with competent clerical assistance; otherwise, his or her efforts will be vitiated in routine tasks, and the opportunity for active, outgoing contribution to the organization will be lost. Qualifications and local sources for nonprofessional personnel will be much the same as for similar positions elsewhere in an organization. In a large number of special libraries, one clerical employee and the librarian constitute the library staff. In libraries of greater size, the proportion of two nonprofessionals to each professional staff member is often found.[4]

A report titled "Does Your Firm Need Its Own Information Service?" (published in 1963 by the Organization for Economic Cooperation and Development) recommends that any organization, research group, or firm with 30 professional workers can well justify establishing a library.[5]

To recruit a special librarian, an organization may turn to the Special Libraries Association, whose headquarters are at 235 Park Avenue South, New York City. The Association is an international organization of more than 9,500 professional librarians and information experts. It has 45 regional chapters and 26 divisions representing broad subject fields or types of information handling techniques such as advertising and marketing, documentation, social science, public utilities, transportation, and so on.

At various professional meetings and particularly, the Annual Conference of the Association, one can see a gradual swelling of black and other minority librarians, representing all types of libraries. Too, Special Libraries Association's long-standing anti-discrimination policy states:

> It is the policy of Special Libraries Association that membership and participation in the Association and its units is not limited in any respect by race, creed, color, national origin, age, sex or physical disability. In particular, all meetings are conducted so as to assure compliance with this policy. The Association participates in joint meetings only with other organizations having the same policy. The Association is an Equal Opportunity Employer.[6]

Equally important is the honest commitment of the Association to put policy into practice through its Committee on the Positive Action Program for Minority Groups. At present, the Committee is attempting to compile a directory of minority group special librarians, i.e., Native Americans, Asian-Americans, blacks, and native Spanish-speaking persons. The Committee feels that such a directory could be of

---

[4]*Ibid.*, pp. 44-45.

[5]*Ibid.*, p. 61.

[6]Actions of the Board of Directors (June 7/June 8/June 13), "Anti-Discrimination Policy," *Special Libraries* 66 (September, 1975):458.

great value to all special librarians, corporate personnel officers, and others who might need such a source when seeking qualified minority persons for employees, speakers, and the like.[7]

Descriptions of outstanding black special libraries follow:

Johnson Publishing Company Library
820 South Michigan Avenue
Chicago, Illinois 60605   (312) 786-7692
Ms. Pamela J. Cash, Librarian

The Johnson Publishing Company Library holds two distinctions—it is both a showcase in the business world, reserved for use by writers, editors, and other company employees, and a monument to the African-American community, who point to it with pride for having stored information on events that have changed the course of the world. The need for a library at Johnson Publishing Company was felt long before the library was established. Mr. John H. Johnson founded the company in 1942 with the publication of *Negro Digest*, and he also felt the need and selected the first librarian, Mrs. Doris E. Saunders (now director of the Book Division) to establish the library in 1949. Together, they decided to establish the most comprehensive library possible on the contemporary Negro. Historical material such as slavery would be represented, but no attempt would be made to compete with such established collections as the Schomburg in New York, the Moorland Collection at Howard University, or any of the other very famous collections of Negroana. The collection was to be intended for current use.

From the very beginning, the library has been a pivotal point in company operations. The collection includes 8,000 volumes by and about blacks. Many are first editions signed by the authors, others are rare and out of print titles by black writers of the Reconstruction period. The biography section is truly outstanding. The basic reference section consists of tools that serve as indexes to general material, as well as specialized tools to research the massive volumes of Afro-Americana. Of course, all JPC publications are indexed by the library staff, and each magazine is bound and also microfilmed yearly. The microfilm collection also includes many black newspapers, some dating back to 1864. *The New Orleans Tribune* is particularly noteworthy because it was printed in both English and French. The newspapers represent different geographic locations, allowing researchers to investigate contemporary events as they occurred in the lives of blacks across the country a century ago.

During the course of the day, the library staff reads 50 newspapers from across the U.S. and Canada, seeking news stories that may be of interest to its editors to be used either in *Jet*, the weekly magazine, or filed for future use. To supplement the "book" information, the library staff has compiled one of the most extensive newspaper clipping files to be found. The careers of politicians, celebrities, and civic workers can be traced through the years.

The United Press International wire service is monitored daily as well, since it gives current details that help make stories in JPC magazines more accurate. The library subscribes to 150 periodicals, and to 75 newspapers. The library is not open

---

[7]"Directory Information Sought," *Special Libraries* 67 (July, 1976):327.

to the public, and permission from the Executive Office must be granted for use by anyone other than employees. The Johnson Publishing Company has been an institutional member of Special Libraries Association since 1949.[8]

The Martin Luther King, Jr. Center for Social Change, Library-Archives
671 Beckwith Street SW
Atlanta, Georgia 30314   (404) 524-1956
Mrs. Minnie H. Clayton, Librarian-Archivist
Open Monday-Friday, 9:00 A.M.-5:00 P.M.

The Civil Rights Archives of the Martin Luther King, Jr. Center for Social Change developed from the Center's Library-Documentation Project during the establishment of the family-oriented institution and was officially opened for research purposes in January, 1969, through the announcement of Mrs. Martin Luther King, Jr., President of the Center. The primary purpose of the Archives is to preserve the papers of Dr. Martin Luther King, Jr., and make them available for research of the Civil Rights Movement, from the Montgomery Bus Boycott to the assassination of Dr. King in Memphis, Tennessee (1955-1968).

The Archives is presently a repository for the Center's programs and major civil rights organizations and individuals of the 1955-1968 era. The Center continues to encourage persons to donate their correspondence from Dr. King, his speeches and sermons on tapes and recordings, photographs, handbills, posters, buttons from marches, drafts, diaries, scrapbooks, clippings, and other printed materials. The Center exists not only to inform blacks about their heritage, struggle, experiences and accomplishments but also to inform other races so that they may better understand black people's way of life.

The library's first responsibility is to the Center for Social Change and then to its clientele, whether they be scholars, students, instructors, businessmen, institutions, or organizations. The King Library's well-rounded collection consists of a general collection of 4,500 volumes, which places special emphasis on the black experience and the history of the Civil Rights Movement (1955-1968); the Children's Collection basically focuses on contemporary black leadership, the black way of life—rural and urban—and is designed to be symbolic of Dr. King's interaction with children. There are also the Coretta Scott King Award Collection, the Multilingual Collection of books by and about Dr. King, and the Reference Collection. If there are duplicate copies of any books in the collection, they may be secured through interlibrary loans, but other than this courtesy, no books are circulated. The library subscribes to 75 journals and 15 newspapers reflecting the black experience.

The library's archival collection consists of Dr. King's writings, such as the six original manuscripts of his published books, speeches, etc. There are also original records of organizations such as CORE (Congress of Racial Equality founded in 1942); the Montgomery Improvement Association (organized in December, 1955), the forerunner of the Southern Christian Leadership Conference; the Dexter Avenue Baptist Church of Montgomery, Alabama; the Mississippi Freedom Democratic Party;

---

[8]Pamela J. Cash, "Johnson Publishing Company Library: Special Collection of Afro-Americana," *Publishing Division Bulletin, SLA* 27 (Spring, 1975).

SNCC (Student Nonviolent Coordinating Committee); the Delta Ministry, a subsidiary of the National Council of Churches, and other organizations which were affiliated with the Civil Rights Movement.[9]

Minority Business Information Institute, Inc.
295 Madison Avenue
New York, New York 10017   (212) 889-8220
Mr. Earl G. Graves, Publisher and Editor
Ms. Eleanor Hurka, Librarian

The Minority Business Information Institute was founded in June, 1971, by Earl G. Graves, publisher and editor of *Black Enterprise* magazine, in cooperation with the U.S. Department of Commerce, Office of Minority Business Enterprise, to answer the need for a specialized research facility focusing on minority economic development. The Economic Development Administration also contributed to the initial financing of the library, which is open by appointment to qualified members of the general public (business persons, students, teachers, researchers) Monday through Friday, 9:00 A.M. to 5:00 P.M. A librarian is available to answer brief telephone and written inquiries; telephone reference hours are 10:00 A.M.-4:30 P.M., Monday through Friday. Items of interest to minority business persons are published in a bimonthly *MBII Newsletter,* which is distributed throughout the region to all OMBE funded organizations and to others by request.

Although the institute's emphasis is on minority business development information, related areas, such as the history of blacks in the United States, the Caribbean and Africa and relevant novels and biographies, are also in its scope. MBII library contains approximately 1,500 volumes, subscriptions to 110 periodicals, 20 newsletters, and 23 vertical file drawers of clippings, pamphlets, and other nonbook materials. The librarian is a member of the Special Libraries Association.[10]

Western States Black Research Center
3617½ Montclair Street
Los Angeles, California 90018   (213) 737-3292
Mrs. Mayme A. Clayton, Librarian

To many people in the Los Angeles area, Mayme Clayton is known as the proprietor of the Third World Ethnic Bookstore and to others as the founder and Director of the Western States Black Research Center. In both, she controls the largest collection of out-of-print, rare black books, documents, and manuscripts on the West Coast.

When the University of California, Los Angeles, Afro-American Studies Center was organized, its Director asked for a room in the ethnic center for the library. Mrs. Clayton was asked to organize the library. She travelled all over Los Angele County looking for books for the collection and made contact with a rare book dealer who had many books on black history and literature. After looking over his

---

[9]The Martin Luther King, Jr. Center. "Archives," 1975-76, p. 4, mimeo.
[10]*MBII Newsletter* 1 (April, 1974):1.

stock, she decided that some of his holdings should be purchased for the library of the Afro-American Studies Center. She approached the advisory committee on her discovery, but was told to stick to contemporary and current materials. The reason given was that not enough black students were interested in research to warrant the purchase of rare books. She disagreed with the committee.

Mrs. Clayton made a trip to West Africa to research libraries there and to make book purchases to add to her own collection. After returning to Los Angeles, she approached the rare book dealer friend who taught her the mechanics of operating a book business. From these concerted efforts came the beginning of the Western States Black Research Center, a non-profit corporation, organized and founded by Mayme A. Clayton in 1971.[11] WBBRS contains approximately 8,000 books, subscriptions to 15 periodicals, African artifacts, pamphlets, newspapers, clippings and other non-book materials. The Center is for the benefit of the residents of Los Angeles City and County and is centrally located in Los Angeles. The Library is open by appointment only and its services are available for anyone in the world. The mailing address is: P.O. Box 38237, Los Angeles, California 90018.

---

[11] Western States Black Research Center, "First Annual Achievement Awards Presentation," March 21, 1976 (Luncheon Souvenir Programme), p. 4.

33. Library Holdings on Afro-Americans
by   Ernest Kaiser, Associate Editor, *Freedomways*

SURVEYS OF AND CONFERENCES ON UNITED STATES BLACK COLLECTIONS

As early as 1936, Dorothy B. Porter, former longtime curator of the Moorland-Spingarn Research Center [formerly Moorland Foundation Collection] at Howard University, Washington, D.C., published "Library Resources for the Study of Negro Life and History" in the then recently started *Journal of Negro Education* (April 1936). In March 1940, the American Council of Learned Societies held an important conference on the problems of research and scholarship in the field of Black Studies. At this conference L. D. Reddick, in a paper entitled "Bibliographical Problems in Negro Research" (*ACLS Bulletin*, No. 32, September 1941), stated (as he had in his article "Library Facilities for Research in Negro Colleges," *Quarterly Review of Higher Education Among Negroes*, July 1940) that there were then about a half dozen important black collections in the United States, and that they were all suffering from rather indifferent support. Reddick, then curator of the (now) Schomburg Center for Research in Black Culture, emphasized the necessity of building up a few great collections of black literature and history in the United States and called for much greater effort in the area of Black Studies.

He appealed to all sections of the country, including the then largely uninterested states of the Far West. He also pointed to the need for three guides to the sources on blacks: to cover the sources in Europe, in Latin America, and in the United States. Reddick later supplied (and it was probably the first of its kind) a good summary of library holdings on blacks in these three areas in his essay "Library Resources for Negro Studies in the United States and Abroad" in the *Encyclopedia of the Negro: Preparatory Volume* (New York: The Phelps-Stokes Fund, Inc., 1945, 1946), edited by W. E. B. DuBois and Guy B. Johnson.

Since 1945, there have been some things in the way of resource or holdings guides on blacks in the United States. Paul Lewinson compiled in 1947 *A Guide to Documents in the National Archives: For Negro Studies* for the Committee on Negro Studies of the American Council of Learned Societies. Since 1947, some valuable published material on library resources or holdings has been issued in bibliographical essays in books such as the late Gilbert Osofsky's *Harlem: The Making of a Ghetto* (1966; 1968) and August Meier's *Negro Thought in America, 1880-1915* (1963; 1968), and in occasional periodical pieces on individual libraries such as the Schomburg Center or the Moorland-Spingarn Research Center.

The important piece on the extensive holdings of the Library of Congress on American Blacks is John McDonough's "Manuscript Resources for the Study of Negro Life and History" (*Quarterly Journal of the Library of Congress*, Vol. 26, No. 3, July 1969, pp. 126-148). Lorenzo J. Greene started a series titled "Negro Manuscript Collections in Libraries" in the *Negro History Bulletin* in March 1967, and about five articles in the series have appeared. Clifton H. Johnson published "Some Archival Sources on Negro History in Tennessee" (*Tennessee Historical Quarterly*, Winter 1969, pp. 297-316). Dorothy B. Porter wrote "Documentation on the Afro-American: Familiar and Less Familiar Sources" (*African Studies Bulletin*, December 1969). Nancy G. Boles, curator of manuscripts in the Maryland Historical Society Library, has written "Notes on Maryland Historical Society Manuscript Collections: Black History Collections" (*Maryland Historical Magazine*, Spring 1971). Also in the Spring 1971 number of the *Maryland Historical Magazine* is Mary K. Meyer's "Genealogical Notes," giving some useful hints on the search for black genealogy, a subject whose popularity among blacks was given great impetus by Alex Haley's popular book *Roots* (1976). Although no papers on resources for Black Studies have been actually commissioned for meetings of the Association for the Study of African-American Life and History or for the occasional conferences at the Atlanta University School of Library Science, papers were read at the 1973 New York Conference and the 1974 Atlanta Conference.

Collections on blacks are listed in both general and special library directories, but the descriptions of the holdings are brief, inadequate and usually not up to date. The *Guide to the Research Collections of the New York Public Library* (1975), which includes the Schomburg Center, is a considerable improvement over the norm here. However, there are some recently published individual guides to black archives in black university libraries and elsewhere. These are *Guide to Manuscripts and Archives in the Negro Collection of Trevor Arnett Library, Atlanta University* (1971); *Calendar of the Manuscripts in the Schomburg Collection of Negro Literature (1700 to 1941)*, compiled by the Historical Records Survey, Works Projects Administration (Andronicus Publishing Co., 1970); *Black Studies: Select Catalog of National Archives and Records Service Microfilm Publications* (1973); and *Original Resources in Black Studies: A Guide to the Talladega College Historical*

Collections (1972), stemming from the 1969 Conference for the Evaluation of Materials about Black Americans in Huntsville, Alabama, which launched with the Alabama Center for Higher Education, a major archival program on eight campuses.

A Black History Archives Project has been established at The Western Reserve Historical Society, Cleveland, Ohio, to collect letters, manuscripts, speeches, record books, etc., about blacks in Cleveland. *The Ohio Black History Guide* (1975) was published by the Ohio Historical Society, Columbus, and lists personal papers, institutional records, and government (federal, state, county, municipal) records.

The most important publication of manuscript holdings about blacks is the *Directory of Afro-American Resources* (R. R. Bowker, 1970). Compiled by Walter Schatz, former librarian of the Southern Education Reporting Service, Nashville, Tennessee, it is not definitive, but it is an invaluable directory to the holdings of black materials (African and art holdings excluded) in all of the libraries in the United States. Jessie Carney Smith has also written (in 1969) an unpublished, 123-page "Survey of Manuscript and Archival Collections for the Study of Black Culture."

Recently, many catalogs of the black collections in black college libraries and elsewhere have been published such as the *Dictionary Catalog of the Schomburg Collection of Negro Literature and History* plus supplements (G. K. Hall, 1962; 1967); *Dictionary Catalogs of the Jesse E. Moorland Collection of Negro Life and History and the Arthur B. Spingarn Collection of Negro Authors in the Howard University Library* (G. K. Hall, 1971); *Dictionary Catalog of the George Foster Peabody Collection on the Negro in the Collis P. Huntington Memorial Library, Hampton Institute, Hampton, Va.* (Greenwood Press, 1972); *Catalog of the Special Negro and African Collections, Vail Memorial Library*, Lincoln University, Pennsylvania, plus supplement (1970; 1971); *Negro History, 1553-1903*, the joint catalog of the black historical materials in the Library Company of Philadelphia and the adjacent Historical Society of Pennsylvania (Library Company of Philadelphia, 1969); and the *Vivian G. Harsh Collection of Afro-American History and Literature at the George Cleveland Hall Branch of the Chicago Public Library* (G. K. Hall, 1971), which has the Chicago Afro-American Union Analytic Catalog (over 75,000 entries) of the major research libraries of Chicago. Earlier, the *Catalog of the Charles F. Heartman Negro Collection, Texas Southern University Library, Houston*, Texas, was published (1955) with a supplement. Finally there is the *Dictionary Catalog of the Negro Collection at the Fisk University Library* (G. K. Hall, 1974).

Several good, large bibliographies and indexes on blacks have also been published, such as James de T. Abajian's *Blacks and Their Contributions to the American West: A Bibliography and Union List of Library Holdings through 1970* (1974) and Dorothy H. Chapman's *Index to Black Poetry* (1974) (both published by G. K. Hall); Dwight L. Smith's *Afro-American History: A Bibliography* (American Bibliographical Center, Santa Barbara, Calif., 1974), containing almost 3,000 abstracts of articles published in periodicals from 1954 to 1971; *New Jersey and the Negro: A Bibliography, 1715-1966* (New Jersey Library Association, Trenton, 1967); Mary Mace Spradling's *In Black and White: Afro-Americans in Print* (Kalamazoo Public Library, Kalamazoo, Mich., 1976), giving sources of biographical information on 7,392 blacks; and *Black Bibliography* (University of Utah Marriott Library Bibliographic Series, Vol. 2, 1974), listing books, magazine articles, reports, government documents, films, tapes, and recordings covering many subjects.

Dorothy B. Porter's "Bibliography and Research in Afro-American Scholarship" (*The Journal of Academic Librarianship*, Vol. 2, No. 2, May 1976, pp. 78-81) traces the historical development of bibliographies about blacks generally and on specific aspects of black culture. Jessie Carney Smith's two essays, "Developing Collections of Black Literature" (*Black World*, Vol. 20, June 1971) and "Special Collections of Black Literature in the Traditionally Black College" (*College and Research Libraries*, Vol. 35, Sept. 1974), are also quite valuable. Ann Allen Shockley's "Black Book Reviewing: A Case for Library Action" (*College and Research Libraries*, Vol. 34, Jan. 1974) points to the magazine *Freedomways*' extensive, annotated list of recent books in all subject areas, with full bibliographic information and additional titles on similar subjects or themes brought out in the annotations, and the magazine's outstanding feature of special interest to librarians. The National Endowment for the Humanities provided in 1976 a grant of $93,666 to Samuel A. Floyd, Jr., of Southern Illinois University, Carbondale, to prepare a six-volume compilation of musical compositions (sheet music, religious music, etc.) by black American composers from 1750 through 1975.

Eighteen years after Lewinson's *Guide* was published, the Atlanta University School of Library Science and Trevor Arnett Library convened an institute (in October 1965) to discuss the role of United States Afro-American and African collections in libraries. This was, as the call stated, because of the increased and unprecedented interest in blacks in America, in Africa, and throughout the world. It was further pointed out that Arthur A. Schomburg, Henry P. Slaughter, Arthur B. Spingarn, and Carter G. Woodson had labored in relative obscurity to document the blacks' contributions and that their cumulations are the nuclei respectively of the Schomburg Center (New York Public Library) and the Atlanta University, Howard University, and Library of Congress black collections. But now, said the conference call, new black collections are being developed and large sums of money are being spent in this field.

At the October 1970 conference of the Society of American Archivists, there was a panel on Archival Resources for Black Studies, with Dorothy B. Porter, Jessie Carney Smith, Vincent Harding, Willie L. Harriford, Jr., and Stanton F. Biddle participating. Biddle's paper "The Schomburg Center for Research in Black Culture: Documenting the Black Experience," was later published in the *Bulletin of the New York Public Library* (Vol. 76, 1972). Now, a few years after Biddle's article, processed Schomburg Center documents are entered in the *National Union Catalog of Manuscript Collections*, and all books, microfilm, and other materials published after January 1, 1972, and cataloged for the Schomburg Center, are in *The Dictionary Catalog of the Research Libraries of the New York Public Library* and clearly labeled as Schomburg material. This *Dictionary Catalog* is updated continuously by a computer. From June 4-5, 1973, a National Archives Conference on Federal Archives as Sources for Research on Afro-Americans was attended in Washington, D.C., by more than 150 scholars, researchers, and others. Also a Conference to Develop a National Plan for the Acquisition of Materials by and about Blacks was held in Atlanta, Georgia, October 26-28, 1973, sponsored by Urban Resource Systems, Inc. of Haslett, Michigan. As a result of this effort, a proposal was developed and published: *A National Network for the Acquisition, Processing and Dissemination of Materials by and about Blacks* in January 1974.

August Meier described the recent development of great interest in American black history in his article "Black America as a Research Field: Some Comments"

(*American Historical Association Newsletter*, April 1968). He also pointed out what remains to be done in the field of black studies. Perhaps the best example of this is that of the 14,285 biographical sketches in the 22-volume *Dictionary of American Biography* (including the first supplementary volume; the second supplement was not counted), only 89 are about blacks. John A. Garraty, editor of the fourth DAB supplement (which comes up to 1950), was aided by the Schomburg Center in getting blacks for inclusion in that supplement. Wilhelmena S. Robinson's *Historical Negro Biographies* (1967; 1968), Sylvia G. L. Dannett's *Profiles of Negro Womanhood, 1619-1900; Twentieth Century* (2 vols.: 1964; 1966), and Walter Christmas's *Negroes in Public Affairs and Government* (1966) are attempts to make up for the DAB's exclusion of many blacks. The soon-to-be published *Dictionary of American Negro Biography* (Thomas Y. Crowell), edited by Rayford W. Logan and Michael R. Winston, should improve the present deplorable situation although that volume has a cut-off date and will not be current.

Finally, Congressmen James Scheuer (New York City), William D. Hathaway (Maine), and Augustus F. Hawkins (Afro-American—California) of the Select Subcommittee on Labor of the House Committee on Education and Labor, held hearings on March 18, 1968, in New York City, on a bill to establish a national commission on black history and culture. (These hearings and documents were published and are available from the U.S. Government Printing Office, Washington, D.C. They are also in Howard N. Meyer's edited *Integrating America's Heritage* [McGrath Publishing Co., College Park, Md., 1970].) This commission was to: 1) study the steps necessary to unearth, preserve, collect, and catalog historical materials dealing with black history and culture, 2) consider the possibilities of establishing a museum or center of black history and culture, and 3) work out methods of disseminating black history and culture materials so that the information can be best integrated into the mainstream of American education and life. There have been similar Senate hearings on black history and culture (*Integrated Education*, March 1969). In August 1976, Senators Glenn and Taft of Ohio introduced a bill in the Senate directing the Secretary of the Interior to conduct a one-year feasibility/suitability study of a National Museum of Afro-American History and Culture, to be established and operated at or near Wilberforce, Ohio (*Congressional Record*, August 26, 1976).

SURVEYS OF AND CONFERENCES ON AFRICAN COLLECTIONS IN THE UNITED STATES

In the field of African resources in the United States, the record is not too bad even though the period of considerable interest in African materials is much shorter than that for North American black materials. The pioneering and continual lecturing, writing, and publishing on Africa by W. E. B. DuBois, W. Leo Hansberry, and Carter G. Woodson—along with the books of anthropologist Melville J. Herskovits and his building of the African library at Northwestern University—helped to develop African studies over the last four or five decades. The newly independent African countries of the 1960s also stimulated the development of African studies in U.S. universities.

The predominantly white African Studies Association, formed in 1957, has been one of the three organizations largely responsible for the increased interest in this field. It has helped stimulate this interest through its annual conferences and its scholarly quarterly *African Studies Bulletin* (which published its nineteenth volume in 1976), as well as its *Issue* quarterly magazine and *African Studies Newsletter* publications. The *African Studies Bulletin*, over its many years of publication, has carried articles from time to time on the special collections of African materials in the Africana Section of the Library of Congress; in the many university libraries such as those in Northwestern, Boston University and Howard; in the National Archives and in the U.S. Department of State; in the Schomburg Center for Research in Black Culture of the New York Public Library; and in theological seminaries. The *Bulletin* also carried for several years an annual listing and description of all the academic African studies centers and their programs in United States universities. This listing became so extensive that it is now published separately as the *Directory of African Studies in the United States*, with supplement (as the latest, 1973, edition became).

In October 1969, at the then 12-year-old African Studies Association's Montreal, Canada, meeting, the black caucus of students and educators from the 1968 Los Angeles meeting said that the Association perpetuated neo-colonialism and raped the African people culturally and intellectually. They then called on Africans and Afro-Americans to give the proper perspective to African studies. This group of black students and educators, who had proposed a new black organization at a meeting in New York City in December, 1968, broke away from the Association, and they formed the African Heritage Studies Association at their first convention in June 1969. This Association has held annual meetings since that time, and at these meetings, speeches are made and papers are read about many African subjects. The African Heritage Studies Association has become an organization in which all U.S. black Africanists can unite and work out the black perspective on or approach to African studies. This has been helpful to both black and white teachers of African studies in universities.

The third organization which furthered U.S. scholarly interest in Africa was the all-black American Society of African Culture. Organized in 1958 as an affiliate of the older, Paris-based Society of African Culture, it brought out in the same year (with the help of the parent organization, which had been publishing books and the magazine *Présence Africaine* since 1947) the very important book *Africa Seen by American Negro Scholars*, edited by John A. Davis. The scholarly papers read at AMSAC's annual conferences have always been available (mimeographed) to the conferees, and two of its sets of annual conference papers, *Pan-Africanism Reconsidered* (1959) and *Southern Africa in Transition* (1966), as well as Leopold S. Senghor's *On African Socialism* (1965), have been published as books. AMSAC also published the *AMSAC Newsletter* and later the quarterly *African Forum*, as well as the earlier *The American Negro Writer and His Roots* (1960), selected papers from the first conference of black writers, March, 1959, sponsored by AMSAC. In 1968, it was shown that the Central Intelligence Agency had supplied money through foundations to many organizations it favored without their knowing where the money really came from. Two of these were the Paris-based Congress for Cultural Freedom, which had some connections with AMSAC, and AMSAC itself. This stigma made it impossible for AMSAC to continue to operate with any credibility, and it finally closed down early in 1971.

In researching material on African sources, Dorothy B. Porter again pioneered, in 1960, with her "Research Centers and Sources for the Study of African History" (*Journal of Human Relations*, Spring-Summer 1960). Two bibliographical essays of great value to librarians and scholars in developing useful, non-exhaustive collections on Africa are Adelaide C. Hill's "Developing a Collection on Africa South of the Sahara" (*College and Research Libraries*, November 1961) and Robert I. Rotberg's more limited "The Teaching of African History" (*American Historical Review*, Oct. 1963). The Library of Congress has published three editions of *African Newspapers in Selected American Libraries* (1956; 1962; 1965). The first had 16 pages; the third has 135 pages. *The Quarterly Journal of the Library of Congress* (July 1970) was a special issue devoted to the African materials in the Library of Congress. Hans E. Panofsky, head of the Africana Division of the Library of Congress, published *A Bibliography of Africana* in 1975. Also, Moore Crossey compiled "A Survey of Africana in Microform" (*Microform Review*, Vol. 3, No. 2, April 1974, pp. 96-105). *A Catalogue of the African Collection in the Moorland Collection* (at Howard University, Washington, D.C.) was published in 1958. In the early 1960s, G. K. Hall of Boston published dictionary catalogs of the African libraries at Boston University, Northwestern University, the Schomburg Center of the New York Public Library, and others. A review article on the catalogs on Africa published by G. K. Hall was published in *Africana Library Journal* (Autumn 1971, pp. 18-21).

The African Department of Northwestern University libraries continues to publish six times a year a *Joint Acquisitions List of Africana*, which it began in January 1962. The *List* consists of items published in the current year, and in the five preceding years, which have been received after June 1961. Many libraries of Africana contribute to this list. The U.S. Department of State's considerable interest in Africa goes back to the 1950s. It has published two editions of the useful *African Programs of U.S. Organizations: A Select Directory* (1961; 1965).

The Hoover Institution on War, Revolution and Peace (of Stanford University) has published many important, useful bibliographies of and guides to Africa over the past decade—with an occasional deplorable volume on Africa and communism or a defense of European imperialism in Africa. Its *Africana Newsletter* (1962-1964) merged with the *African Studies Bulletin.* In 1963, the Hoover Institution published Robert Collins and Peter Duignan's *Americans in Africa: A Preliminary Guide to American Missionary Archives and Library Manuscript Collections on Africa*, which described 52 Protestant and Catholic missionary archives and 47 private and public library manuscript collections and cited only records and papers of Americans who went to Africa.

The African Studies Association received a grant from the Ford Foundation in 1963 to prepare a descriptive *National African Guide* to Africa-related archival and manuscript sources in the United States, covering the entire continent of Africa and the coastal islands and having no chronological limits. The Association and the Archivist of the United States at the National Archives and Records Services were responsible for this project, which covered materials in American government agencies, commercial concerns, religious and missionary groups, and other non-commercial agencies. Materials of private individuals were to be covered if they were in a depository. Morris Rieger of the National Archives was to prepare the guide, which would also serve as the United States national volume of the projected *Guide to the Sources of African History* (outside of Africa), sponsored by the International Council of Archives. This was published by the Hoover Institution as Peter Duignan's extremely valuable 234-page *Handbook of American Resources for African Studies* (Stanford, Calif.: Hoover Institute on War, Revolution and Peace, 1967), which, though incomplete, attempts to describe all materials relevant to African studies. Descriptions are given of the holdings of 95 library and manuscript collections, mostly in colleges, universities, and historical societies; 108 church and missionary libraries and archives; 95 art and ethnographic collections (mostly in museums and private collections); and four business archives. Presently, the Archives and Libraries Committee of the African Studies Association is preparing, with Duignan's support, a revision of the *Handbook*. The work will update and expand coverage of the materials relevant to Africa and African Studies in the United States.

Warren M. Robbins, founder and director of the Museum of African Art in Washington, D.C., brought out his very useful survey *African Art in American Collections* (1966) with the assistance of Robert H. Simmons. This big book, with text and 347 photographs, covers the African tribal sculpture in American museums and private collections. There is also the 20-volume *Dictionary of African Biography* (Vol. I, Ethiopia-Ghana, 1976) by Reference Publications, Inc. (551 Fifth Avenue, 28th Floor, New York City, N.Y. 10017). This is the first volume of the *Encyclopedia Africana* started by W. E. B. DuBois in Ghana in 1962. Volume II (Nigeria-Zaire) will be published in 1977. Also, there will be three volumes published each year under the direction of L. H. Ofosu-Appiah, the author of *People in Bondage: African Slavery in the Modern Era* (1971).

AMERICAN PUBLIC LIBRARY HOLDINGS ON UNITED STATES BLACKS

There are many black collections in libraries open to the public. The Schomburg Center for Research in Black Culture of the Research Libraries of the New York Public Library consists of over seventy thousand volumes (with some 50 percent about Africa), art objects, musical recordings, photographs, prints, sheet music, manuscripts, scrapbooks, pamphlets, playbills, programs, newspaper clippings, magazine articles, dissertations, black newspaper files (mostly on microfilm), and many black and jazz periodicals (many on microfilm). The basis of the Schomburg Center was the large, important private library on blacks collected by Arthur A. Schomburg (1874-1938), a Puerto Rican of African descent who lived in New York City. In 1926, a Harlem citizens' committee persuaded the Carnegie Corporation to buy Schomburg's library for the New York Public Library and place it in a branch in the heart of Harlem.

The Schomburg Center contains rare books and pamphlets; manuscripts of slavery and abolition; manuscripts on the West Indies; manuscripts of Alexander Crummell, John E. Bruce, and the Citizens' Protective League; the Booker T. Washington correspondence with F. S. Garrison; some Leigh Whipper material; the Hiram R. Revels papers; the John B. Rayner papers; some papers of Christian Abraham Fleetwood, a free black Civil War major and worker in the Freedmen's Bureau and the Freedmen's Savings and Trust Company; some letters of Ira Aldridge, William Stanley Braithwaite, and Richard T. Greener; many Civil War papers; some Paul Laurence Dunbar manuscripts; the William Pickens papers; some Arthur A. Schomburg papers (his main papers are held by his daughter, Mrs. Dolores Schomburg Thomas of Hempstead, N.Y.); files of the International Labor Defense and the Civil Rights Congress; papers of the National Negro Congress; some Paul Robeson papers (restricted—the main Paul Robeson papers are at the Paul Robeson Archives in New York City); the papers of Lawrence Brown, Paul Robeson's long-time accompanist; the papers of Frank R. Crosswaith and the Negro Labor Committee of New York City (1925-1969); the papers of Elmer A. Carter, former chairman of the New York State Division of Human Rights and earlier an editor of the National Urban League's magazine *Opportunity*; former *Ebony* editor Allan Morrison's papers; the papers of Glenn Carrington of New York City and of the black composer Clarence Cameron White; the files of the Community News Service of New York City (1969-1976); some papers of the Central Division, New York City, of Marcus Garvey's Universal Negro Improvement Association (1918-1959) (other Central Division papers, held by the Metropolitan Applied Research Center in New York City until it closed in 1976, have now been returned to Berenice Simms in New York City who had them earlier); the Oakley C. Johnson papers; the Hugh H. Smythe papers; the Kurt A. Fisher collection of documents and manuscripts covering over 200 years of Haitian history; about half of the files of Friendship House, a long-time, now defunct, Catholic settlement house in Harlem; some papers of Bessye J. Bearden, a former Harlem community leader; the papers of the musical Spiller family; the 81 volumes of manuscripts and field notes that Gunnar Myrdal's *An American Dilemma* is based on; the Francis L. Broderick notes on the W. E. B. DuBois papers; the Harry A. Williamson Collection of Negro Masonry; the Lyons family papers (Williamson's family); Pauli Murray's family papers (mostly on microfilm); some letters and unpublished manuscripts of Langston Hughes (second depository); Yale Professor R. W. Winks's research notes and documents on the Negro in Canada; some manuscripts of Claude McKay and others; galley proofs of many books; the National Association of Colored Graduate Nurses material; the Bert Williams scrapbooks; the Rose McClendon scrapbooks; Earl Conrad's Harriet Tubman collection; Stetson Kennedy's Ku Klux Klan material; the Federal Writers' Project's Negroes of New York material; and some Richard Wright papers (the main collection of Richard Wright papers was sold by Mrs. Wright to the James Weldon Johnson Memorial Collection at Yale University in 1976). Mrs. Jean Blackwell Hutson has been curator or chief of the Schomburg Center for over 25 years.

The New York Public Library's Library of the Performing Arts at Lincoln Center has material on blacks in music, theatre, dance, films, and television. It has the main Scott Joplin music collection; impresario Sol Hurok's Marian Anderson materials; some materials on W. C. Handy, etc. The other special collections of the Research Libraries of the New York Public Library contain a huge amount of material on U.S. blacks. Mrs. Aubrey Bowser's T. Thomas Fortune scrapbook (1879-1914) is also held on microfilm by the New York Public Library. Other materials in the Research Libraries are those on slavery and anti-slavery and the Manuscript Division's several thousand letters of Pierre Toussaint (the Santo Domingo free Negro who became famous in New York City), as well as the scrapbooks of the late New York City African model Maurice Hunter.

The Library of Congress has a tremendous amount of United States black material scattered through its special collections. It also has a Folk Archives of black folk songs and tales, the Daniel Murray Collection of black authors, and the Federal Writers' Project's material, which includes thousands of slave narratives and much state and city material. B. A. Botkin's *Lay My Burden Down: A Folk History of Slavery* (1945), George P. Rawick's *From Sundown to Sunup: The Making of the Black Community* (1972), Julius Lester's *To Be a Slave* (1968), and other books are drawn from this slave narrative material. In the Manuscript Division are the papers of Booker T. Washington (see E. Franklin Frazier's "The Booker T. Washington Papers," *Quarterly Journal of the Library of Congress*, Feb. 1945); the NAACP papers; the papers of Carter G. Woodson, the National Urban League, Mary Church Terrell, Robert H. Terrell, James G. Birney, and Matthew C. Perry; Rev. Daniel Coker's *Journal*; the papers of Arthur B. Spingarn and the American Colonization Society; some Christian A. Fleetwood papers; the Robert Todd Lincoln collection of the Abraham Lincoln papers (1790-1916; 194 vols.); the Brotherhood of Sleeping Car Porters papers; the papers of Moorfield Storey, one of the white founders of the NAACP; the Lewis Tappan anti-slavery letters; the Fulham and Lambeth Palace collections; the papers of the Society for the Propagation of the Gospel in Foreign Parts; the papers of Dr. Bray's Associates; and the proceedings of various British anti-slavery societies.

The very important Frederick Douglass papers were originally in the Frederick Douglass Memorial Home in Anacostia, D.C. In the 1960s, they were stored by the National Park Service in Washington, D.C., and in 1972, the papers were transferred to the custody of the Library of Congress (*Quarterly Journal of the Library of Congress*, July 1972). A new microfilm edition of the Douglass papers is now in preparation (*Quarterly Journal*, Oct. 1973). John W. Blassingame, Philip S. Foner, and others are preparing at Yale University Douglass's complete works and papers for publication in book form. The Frederick Douglass and Booker T. Washington papers publication projects are supported by the National Historical Publications and Records Commission, and the Douglass papers project also by two editing awards (totaling $189,992) from the National Endowment for the Humanities Division of Research Grants (both organizations are in Washington, D.C.). Louis R. Harlan has edited and published several volumes of the Booker T. Washington works and papers.

There is important historical material on United States Afro-Americans in the National Archives such as: material on the suppression of the African slave trade; War Records Office material on blacks in the military service of the United States, including Congressional Medal of Honor files; Freedmen's Bureau files; full records of the U.S. Senate; and material on Ku Klux Klan investigations and the black press. (See also Harold T. Pinkett's "Recent Federal Archives as Sources for Negro History," *Negro History Bulletin*, Dec. 1967). The National Historical Publications and Records Commission is supporting the three-volume *Freedmen and Southern Society: A Documentary Record*, edited by Ira Berlin and drawn from the National Archives' large collection of Freedmen's Bureau records. It is also supporting Robert A. Hill's project to publish the *Papers of Marcus Garvey and the U.N.I.A., 1910-1940*. Hill has been searching out and copying the surviving records and papers of Garvey and his movement from archives in England, the West Indies, and the U.S. since 1970. (*Prologue: The Journal of the National Archives*, Vol. 8, No. 3, Fall 1976, pp. 175-176.) See also James M. Gifford's "Black Hope and Despair in Antebellum Georgia: The William Moss Correspondence" (in the National Archives). Moss of Griffin, Georgia, was a young slave who learned about colonization and the American Colonization Society in the 1850s (*Prologue*, Fall 1976, pp. 152-162).

The papers and files of the Harmon Foundation of New York City, an organization that helped and promoted Afro-American and later African artists from the 1920s until the 1960s, when it terminated its activities, went to the Smithsonian Institution in Washington, D.C.

The Detroit Public Library has the E. Azalia Hackley Memorial Collection of Negro Music, Dance and Drama. This collection was presented to the Detroit Public Library by the Detroit Musicians Association in 1943 as a memorial to Mme. E. Azalia Hackley, a pioneer black music educator and concert singer who died in

Detroit in 1923. The Vivian G. Harsh Collection, now housed in the Carter G. Woodson Regional Library of the Chicago Public Library, has a long-established collection by and about blacks. The Paul Cuffe papers some years ago were deteriorating in boxes in the New Bedford (Massachusetts) Free Library, but have now been microfilmed (microfilm copies may be purchased from the Library). The papers of the Congress of Racial Equality are in the library of the State Historical Society of Wisconsin in Madison, as are the papers (1954-1964) of Rev. Milton A. Galamison, the civil rights and education leader of New York City. The Benjamin "Pap" Singleton scrapbooks are in the library of the Kansas State Historical Society in Topeka. John Brown letters and manuscripts are in many libraries and state historical societies' collections.

There is material on black pioneers and explorers and similar subjects in several of the libraries of state historical societies and state archives of the western and far western states—and also at the New York Historical Society. The Paul Laurence Dunbar papers are at the Ohio Historical Society Library in Columbus. There is black material in the Boston Athenaeum, and the William Monroe Trotter papers are at the Congregational Library in Boston. The Boston Public Library has the papers of the abolitionists Parker, Garrison, Child, May, and Phelps and others. The Charles Sumner papers are at the Chicago Historical Society. The minutes of meetings of the Freedmen's Aid and Southern Education Society of the Methodist Church, North, are at the Methodist Board of Education in Nashville, Tennessee. The A. Philip Randolph papers are at the A. Philip Randolph Institute in New York City. A small Carter G. Woodson Memorial Library is in the Queens Borough Public Library central building in Jamaica, New York City. The George Edmund Haynes Memorial Library is in the Mount Vernon Public Library, Mount Vernon, New York.

UNITED STATES UNIVERSITY LIBRARY HOLDINGS ON THE AMERICAN BLACKS

Universities also have many holdings in this field, and the Moorland-Spingarn Research Center at Howard University, Washington, D.C., is the largest. It is basically the extensive Lewis Tappan anti-slavery collection given to Howard University in 1873, plus former Howard trustee Jesse Edward Moorland's gifts in 1914 and 1940 of his large private collection of books, pamphlets, engravings, portraits, manuscripts, curios, pictures, and clippings concerning blacks. Organized as a research library in 1930, this collection has been augmented by purchases and gifts and has been greatly expanded, especially in the field of African materials. The Works Projects Administration brought out in 1939 "A Catalogue of Books in the Moorland Foundation" (mimeographed).

The over 7,000-item Arthur B. Spingarn collection of Negro authors and Negro music was purchased and added to the Moorland Collection in 1946. Spingarn explained how he assembled the collection of Negro authors in a valuable 1937 Negro History Week address, "Collecting a Library of Negro Literature" (*Journal of Negro Education*, Jan. 1938). He also published an annual annotated bibliography of Negro authors all over the world in the NAACP's *Crisis* magazine over 32 years. Spingarn continued to add new and old works (about a thousand annually) to his collection from 1946 nearly to his death in 1971. Howard University published a descriptive brochure of the Spingarn Collection of Negro authors in the 1940s, soon after it was purchased.

The Moorland-Spingarn Research Center also contains the papers of the following: James T. and John Rapier; Kelly Miller; Alain Locke; George L. Ruffin; Blanche K. Bruce; W. J. Whipper; P. B. S. Pinchback; Joel E. Spingarn, an early chairman of the NAACP board of directors; some Arthur B. Spingarn papers; U.S. Works Progress Administration (1934-1941) and NAACP, Washington, D.C., branch papers; the papers of Dr. Louis T. Wright, the Grimké family, Mordecai Johnson, and E. Franklin Frazier; some Marian Anderson papers, mostly on the DAR controversy and the Ralph J. Bunche Oral History Collection. Judge J. Waties Waring's collection of albums on civil rights is in the collection, as are some Leigh Whipper papers and the four volumes of John Mercer Langston clippings. Holdings today are of more than 125,000 catalogued and recorded items including books, pamphlets, periodicals, newspapers, manuscripts, photographs, clippings, musical compositions, phonograph records, and microfilm. Michael R. Winston succeeded Dorothy B. Porter when she retired as director of the Moorland-Spingarn Research Center.

The Black Collection at Fisk University in Nashville, Tennessee, absorbed the collection of the defunct Y.M.C.A. graduate school in Nashville many years ago and became, with additional gifts and purchases, one of the strongest libraries in the South for the study of blacks. Some of its outstanding holdings are the John Mercer Langston papers; the George Gershwin Memorial Collection of Music and Musical Literature, given by Carl Van Vechten; the Charles S. Johnson papers (1893-1956; 478 manuscript boxes and 4 file cabinets); the Charles W. Chesnutt papers; the W. E. B. DuBois papers (over 2,000 volumes) together with some rare manuscripts and files bought in the fall of 1961 by the then librarian of Fisk University, Arna Bontemps, when Dr. DuBois went to Ghana to work on the multivolume *Encyclopedia Africana.* The bulk of the DuBois papers are now at the University of Massachusetts, Amherst, and some DuBois papers are also in Ghana. Herbert Aptheker's "The W. E. B. DuBois Papers" (*Political Affairs,* March 1966) describes the papers as consisting of letters, manuscripts of his writings and speeches, his organizational manuscripts, memoranda on movements and on periodicals he edited, book reviews, newspaper and periodical clippings, diaries, travel notes, memorabilia, photographs, and other items. The University of Massachusetts Press is publishing 10 volumes from the DuBois papers, edited by Herbert Aptheker. *The Education of Black People: Ten Critiques, 1906-1960, The Correspondence of W. E. B. DuBois: Volume I Selections, 1877-1934* and *Volume II Selections, 1934-1944* (with some assistance from Sidney Kaplan and Ernest Kaiser) have been published. Volume III, the last volume of the selected correspondence, will be published soon. Aptheker is also editing the 40-volume published writings of DuBois, being published by Kraus-Thomson, Millwood, N.Y., which began with a mammoth, annotated bibliography of DuBois's writings by Aptheker. Twenty volumes had been published as of 1976.

About 30,000 pieces of the manuscript material of black novelist and poet Jean Toomer have been deposited in the Fisk Black Collection by his widow, following his death in 1967. A part of the Alfred Stieglitz Collection of paintings, sculpture and other works of art is at Fisk. A catalogue of the Stieglitz Collection was published in 1949. Fisk is also the depository for the Southern Education Reporting Service and the Race Relations Information Center. The Aaron Douglas papers, Chicago Congressman William L. Dawson's papers, and some George Edmund Hayes papers are also at Fisk. The Marcus Garvey papers held by his wife,

A. Jacques Garvey, in Jamaica, W.I., at her death in 1973 were deposited at Fisk by her two sons in 1975. Also a small Scott Joplin collection and some Langston Hughes material are at Fisk. Jessie Carney Smith is the director of the library at Fisk, having succeeded Arna Bontemps.

The Black Collection of the Trevor-Arnett Library at Atlanta University, Atlanta, Georgia, has been built up over the last 31 years. After the death of the black New York writer and teacher Countee Cullen in 1946, the late Harold Jackman started the Countee Cullen Memorial Collection at Atlanta University; it consists largely of materials on blacks in writing, drama, painting, and music and includes some Leigh Whipper material which was added later. A committee in New York City has continued to add to this collection since the death of Harold Jackman many years ago. In 1946, Atlanta University purchased the private collection of Henry P. Slaughter of Washington, D.C. This collection, consisting of 15,000 items, contains many pamphlets and prints. It was at this time that the Black Collection was established as a separate department. The Atlanta University Library also has some papers of Thomas Clarkson, a leading British abolitionist. Casper L. Jordan is now university librarian at Atlanta University, following the recent retirement of Gaynelle Barksdale.

Yale University Library has the James Weldon Johnson Memorial Collection of Negro Arts and Letters, donated by Carl Van Vechten in the early 1940s. Opened in 1950, it consists largely of manuscripts, typescripts, letters, photographs, and autographed copies of works by contemporary American black authors. It was the first depository of the letters and manuscripts of the late Langston Hughes, and it contains as well the papers of George Edmund Haynes, James Weldon Johnson, New York businessman John B. Nail, Carl Van Vechten (white), Richard Wright (acquired in 1976 from Wright's wife), and many other black authors. This is one of the country's largest collections relative to twentieth century black arts and letters.

The Amistad Research Center was established in 1966 by the American Missionary Association of the United Church Board for Homeland Ministries when the Association moved its archives of about 300,000 manuscripts (covering the period from 1839 to 1879), plus the AMA Race Relations Department papers and those of the American Home Missionary Society (1817-1902), from Fisk University, to Dillard University, New Orleans, Louisiana. With the Association's archives as a base, the Amistad Research Center's task was to collect, process and make available to research scholars manuscripts, letters, and other primary source materials on the history of American blacks, Indians, Puerto Ricans, Chicanos, Chinese and Caribbean people. The Center was incorporated in 1969 as an independent library and archives for historical research.

Today the Center is a large repository for original ethnic or minority manuscript documentation, with over 8,000,000 primary documents in its collection. The Center's holdings include the records of organizations and the private papers of individuals and families. Here are the basic documents relating to the establishment and early histories of many black educational institutions such as Straight University (Dillard), Fisk University, Tougaloo College (Mississippi), Talladega College (Alabama), Tillotson College (Austin, Texas), Hampton Institute (Virginia), Le Moyne College (Memphis, Tennessee), and Atlanta University (Georgia). The Center also has the papers of the National Association of Intergroup Relations Officials, the Catholic Committee of the South (1939-1955), the Committee on

Civil Rights in Metropolitan New York, the New Orleans Catholic Council on Human Relations, the Anti-Defamation League's race relations records, the National Committee Against Discrimination in Housing's papers, and those of other organizations. Clifton H. Johnson is the executive director. *The Amistad Research Center News* started publishing as a quarterly in 1972.

The Center has the personal papers of Raymond Pace Alexander of Philadelphia, Pennsylvania; Rev. James H. Robinson of New York City, founder of Operation Crossroads Africa; some Mary M. Bethune papers (1923-1936); the papers of Marguerite D. Cartwright; Judge Edward R. Dudley of New York City; Countee Cullen of New York City; George W. Lee of Memphis, Tennessee; Prof. Lillian W. Voorhees; Bishop Robert E. Jones of New Orleans; Rev. Roland T. Heacock of Connecticut; Lillie M. Jackson of Baltimore, Maryland; Alfred Baker Lewis of the NAACP; Prof. Hylan G. Lewis of Brooklyn College, New York City; Bishop Stephen Gill Spottswood of the NAACP; Mabel K. Staupers (1930-1973), leader of black nurses; civil rights attorney Alexander P. Tureaud of New Orleans; actress Fredi Washington (1925-1975); some Judge J. Waties Waring papers; some Richard U. von Dickerson family of Chicago papers; Chicagoan Erwin A. Salk's collection of materials (magnetic tapes, cassettes, brochures, and correspondence) relating to Paul Robeson; the papers of James Egert Allen of New York City; John Hope, II; singer Carol Brice of New York City; the John Wesley Dobbs family of Atlanta, Georgia; Frank S. Horne of New York City; Edward F. Williams; James Sedalia Peters, II, of Connecticut; Kenneth B. M. Crooks of Jamaica, W.I. and the U.S., and others. Also, some copies of W. E. B. DuBois's letters, speeches, and articles, including articles printed in the *Fisk Herald* from 1887 to 1892, are at the Amistad Research Center—from the Michigan Historical Collections.

Morris A. Soper, who was a trustee of Morgan State College, Baltimore, Maryland, left a grant for the purchase of books for a black collection at the college. The result is the large Morris A. Soper Library or Black Collection at Morgan State College which has, among other things, the Emmett J. Scott Collection of papers (about 3,000 pieces on the history of blacks from 1900 to 1951) and the black explorer Matthew Henson Collection, donated by Herbert Frisby of Baltimore. (Some Henson papers are also in the library of the Explorers Club in New York City.) A sizeable body of William Stanley Braithwaite papers is also at Morgan, and Harvard University has sold parts of its Braithwaite papers to dealers.

There is an old, sizeable black collection in the library at Tuskegee Institute in Alabama. Tuskegee also has the material in the department of Records and Research, founded in 1908 by Monroe N. Work, who compiled and published nine editions of the *Negro Year Book* from 1912 to 1938. Work died in 1945 and Jessie P. Guzman brought out two more editions of the *Negro Year Book* in 1947 and in 1952. The George Washington Carver Museum, set up in 1938 and containing Dr. Carver's scientific discoveries and art productions, is also at Tuskegee, but this museum was damaged by fire some years ago. Carver's papers are on microfilm (as of 1975) and for sale at the Carver Research Foundation, Division of Behavioral Science, Tuskegee Institute, Alabama.

The George Foster Peabody Collection on Blacks, in the Collis P. Huntington Memorial Library at Hampton Institute, Hampton, Virginia, is also a large, old library. It contains a magnificent collection of several hundred scrapbooks of clippings on almost every conceivable subject for the years 1898-1920.

Columbia University in New York City has the Alexander Gumby Collection on blacks. This consists of valuable scrapbooks compiled by Mr. Gumby, a New York Afro-American collector, over many decades and sold to Columbia many years ago. Columbia also has the J. G. Phelps Stokes Collection. The papers (speeches, articles, public statements, letters, etc.) of Whitney M. Young, Jr., who died in 1971, are in the Columbia University School of Social Work Library, renamed the Whitney M. Young, Jr. Memorial Library in 1975. The papers of Whitney M. Young, Sr., who died in 1975, were given to Kentucky State University, Frankfort, by one of his two daughters in 1976.

Texas Southern University, Houston, has the Charles F. Heartman Negro Collection. The Mary McLeod Bethune documents and private papers are at Bethune-Cookman College, Daytona Beach, Florida, an institution which Mrs. Bethune founded. Joseph Charles Price, the founder of Livingstone College, Salisbury, North Carolina, has his papers there. Delaware State College, near Dover, has a black collection in its library. Harvard University, the University of Chicago, the University of Michigan and other white universities also have good collections on blacks. There is a collection of William Stanley Braithwaite's letters, etc., at Harvard, parts of which have been sold to the book dealers Ed Starr of Brookline, Massachusetts, and Maxwell Whiteman of Cedar Falls, Pennsylvania. These dealers have also acquired other Braithwaite papers at a sale of his stored materials for storage fees.

The papers of Arna Bontemps and George S. Schuyler are at Syracuse University, Syracuse, New York. Eva Jessye's extensive personal collection of black music memorabilia was given by her to the University of Michigan a few years ago. The May Collection of anti-slavery pamphlets is at Cornell University, Ithaca, New York. The Zora Neale Hurston papers are at the University of Florida Libraries, Gainesville, and some of her letters are in the James Weldon Johnson Memorial Collection at Yale University. Willard Motley's papers (1957-1963) are at the University of Wisconsin, and the rest of his papers are on loan to Northern Illinois University, De Kalb, from the Motley estate. The Talladega College Library, Talladega, Alabama, has papers on African missions (1839-1962), the Buell G. Gallager papers (1930-1962), and the Herman H. Long papers (1962-1970). The records of the Southern Tenant Farmers Union are in the Southern Historical Collection at the University of North Carolina.

Half of the files of Friendship House, a Harlem, New York, settlement house closed many years ago, are at Roosevelt University, Chicago, or the University of Chicago. Bishop Reverdy C. Ransom's papers are at Wilberforce University, Wilberforce, Ohio. The Hallie Q. Brown Black Collection, named for the outstanding black teacher and elocutionist at Wilberforce University, is at Central State University, Wilberforce, Ohio. Some Richard Wright letters are at Kent State University, Kent, Ohio. (See *Richard Wright: Letters to Joe C. Brown*, Occasional Paper No. 1, Kent State University Libraries.) The Martin Luther King, Jr. papers are at Boston University, Boston, Massachusetts, but will be moved to the Martin Luther King, Jr. Memorial Center, to be constructed on the Morehouse College campus in Atlanta, Georgia.

Materials on Afro-Americans in the Far West are found in the Henry E. Huntington Library and Art Gallery, San Marino, California, and in the libraries of the University of California at Berkeley and of Stanford University, as well as in other university libraries in the area.

AMERICAN PRIVATE LIBRARY HOLDINGS
ON UNITED STATES BLACKS

There are many private holdings of the papers of important figures in black history, and there are also good private black collections. The John C. Dancy papers are in the possession of John C. Dancy, Jr., of Detroit and Mrs. Lillian Dancy Reid of Salisbury, North Carolina. Mrs. Mae Miller Sullivan of Washington, D.C., has some papers of her father, Kelly Miller. Dr. Otelia Cromwell of Washington, D.C., who died in 1972, had some papers of John W. Cromwell that very likely went to Howard University. The W. C. Handy papers are in the possession of the Handy family of New Rochelle and Mount Vernon, New York. The Library of Congress, the Music Division of the Research Libraries of the New York Public Library, and the Rutgers University Institute of Jazz Studies all have material on Handy which they used for exhibits on him in 1973, the one hundredth anniversary of his birth. The Institute of Jazz Studies also borrowed from the family papers for its exhibit.

The valuable Hall Johnson manuscripts and papers are held by friends or relatives in New York City (Johnson died in 1970). The late New York African model Maurice Hunter's papers are in the hands of his son, who lives in Queens, New York. The Lewis H. Latimer papers are held by his descendants, the Gerald Norman family of New York City. Fred R. Moore's papers are in the possession of his daughter in New York City. Some papers of Victoria Earle Matthews were held by her relative, Mrs. Carolyne Williams of Queens, New York, until her death in the 1970s. The papers of George T. Downing, a pioneer black fighter for Civil War black troop equality and for school integration, and the papers of black physician John V. De Grasse, who served in the Civil War, are held by Rev. Howard Asbury in Jamaica, New York. Middleton A. Harris of New York City, author of *A Negro History Tour of Manhattan* (1968) and *The Black Book* (1974) with others, had a large collection of documents, manuscripts, photographs and other things about blacks in New York and over the United States, and he recently sold his collection to the Schomburg Center. Franklin D. Brower of New York City, a black former newspaper reporter, has a tremendous collection of basically newspaper clippings (one or two million) and magazine articles on virtually all subjects relating to blacks. Brower, the brother of reporter William Brower of the *Toledo Blade*, has some files of the Brotherhood of Sleeping Car Porters (including many A. Philip Randolph papers) and of the American Negro Theatre in New York City during the 1940s.

There are several large private collections in New York City that have become institutions themselves. The Helen Armstead Johnson Foundation for Theater Research, in the Chelsea Hotel, has a vast collection of material on blacks in the theater. Helen A. Johnson also contributed a long essay on black theater to Mabel M. Smythe's *The Black American Reference Book* (1976) and is writing a two-volume work on black theater. The Hatch/Billops Collection (oral history tapes and slides) of James V. Hatch and Camille Billops is at the Hatch/Billops Studio, New York City, at the Cohen Library of City College, City University of New York, and at the Schomburg Center. James VanDerZee's huge photograph collection of New York City blacks in the twentieth century is now at the Metropolitan Museum of Art in New York City. (The collection was at the James VanDerZee Institute in Harlem until it closed.) *The World of James VanDerZee* (1970) and *James VanDerZee* (1974), edited by Reginald McGhee and Liliane DeCock; Elton C. Fax's

Garvey (1972); and *Harlem on My Mind* (1969), edited by Allon Schoener, all have photographs by the ninety-year-old VanDerZee.

The Hubert T. Delany papers are held by his family in New York City. The Ralph J. Bunche papers are presumably held by Mrs. Bunche in New York City. Anita Bush, founder of the black stage repertory company in Harlem in 1915 (who died in 1974), has papers with relatives or friends in New York City. Lorraine Hansberry's papers are held by Robert Nemiroff, her ex-husband, in Croton-on-Hudson, New York. J. A. Rogers's vast papers are held by Mrs. Rogers in New York City. W. Leo Hansberry's papers are held by his daughter, Gail Hansberry Mattox, in New York City. Eubie Blake's papers are held by him and Mrs. Blake at their home in Brooklyn, New York. Thurgood Marshall's papers will presumably go to the Thurgood Marshall School of Law at Texas Southern University, Houston, named for him in 1976. Horace Mann Bond's papers, held by his family, will probably go to Atlanta University or to Lincoln University, Pennsylvania, where he was president for many years. Adam Clayton Powell, Jr.'s papers are at the Abyssinian Baptist Church in New York City, where both he and his father were pastors.

The location of the papers of many prominent blacks remains unknown, however. Where are the papers of pianist-composer Margaret Bonds, a former resident of New York City who died in Los Angeles, California? Of Charlotta A. Bass, publisher of the *California Eagle* newspaper? Of Josephine Baker in France? Of Robert L. Vann and Mrs. Vann of the *Pittsburgh Courier* newspaper in Pittsburgh, Pennsylvania? Where will the main papers of Duke Ellington, Marian Anderson and William H. Hastie be housed? They are held now by Mercer Ellington's son Mercer, by Marian Anderson herself, and by the Hastie family respectively.

Glenn Carrington, a black social worker and long-time New York City connoisseur and devotee of the fine arts, has a large, invaluable black collection that included rare books, magazines, letters, old record albums and many other things. The *Yale University Library Gazette* (first quarter 1972) called Carrington's extensive Amiri Baraka collection the best in the country. Shortly before his death in 1974, Carrington made a gift of his Amiri Baraka Collection and his Alain Locke materials to Howard University. This material is very valuable since, as Carrington often said, Baraka does not collect his own writings and manuscripts systematically or at all.

Clarence L. Holte, another New Yorker and a former executive in the advertising firm of Batten, Barton, Durstine and Osborn in New York City, has a tremendous, 7,000-volume or more black collection with many rare books. He sells duplicates, and Johnson Reprint Corporation in New York City reprinted a series of old volumes from the Holte collection in the late 1960s. A catalogue of this collection was also published (*Ebony*, April 1970; *New York Times*, March 18, 1972). Charles L. Blockson of Norristown, Pennsylvania, is also one of the great black collectors of black history libraries. *Sepia* magazine carried an article on him, Clarence L. Holte, and a third collector some time ago. Blockson has recently published *Pennsylvania's Black History* (1975), a thorough, in-depth book which his many years of collecting on blacks in Pennsylvania prepared him to write. His collection of Paul Robeson material is one of the best in the country.

Clarence S. Gee of Lockport, New York, and Boyd B. Stutler have good collections of John Brown manuscripts and materials. There are papers and records in the possession of the living descendants of Barzillai Lew, who fought in the

Revolutionary War; of Cyrus Bustill, Paul Robeson's great-great-grandfather, who supplied bread to the Revolutionary Army; of Nat Turner; R. R. Wright, Sr.; R. R. Wright, Jr.; Robert Smalls, and many others. *Ebony* magazine, the *Journal of Negro History* and especially the *Negro History Bulletin* (1937-1950) when Carter G. Woodson was editor, have carried many articles about outstanding black families, based on the family records and photographs held by the descendants. The genealogical and records book of the James M. and Fannie Bolling family of Virginia was published in 1975.

Benjamin Quarles, in "Black History Unbound" (*Daedalus*, Spring 1974), has stated that "by far the most urgent need in black history (and in black studies in general) is for . . . a massive, comprehensive bibliography of black source materials, modeled along the lines of the *National Union Catalog* compiled by the Library of Congress. Such a compilation might take a dual form, providing a catalogue of printed works and another of manuscripts. . . . [P]ublicizing the existing data would be a major step forward in black historiography." Perhaps the time has come, since black materials are now proliferating and are being collected and cataloged in many different places and in many research areas, to make a real effort to bring all black source materials together in a National Black Union Catalog. This essay, expanded and updated from *In Black America, 1968: The Year of Awakening* (1969) edited by Patricia W. Romero in the International Library of Negro Life and History series, is an over-all, beginning survey of black source materials and the writings about them.

34. Major Afro-American Collections

Amistad Research Center
Dillard University
New Orleans, Louisiana 70122   (504) 944-0239

Dr. Clifton Johnson, director; 8 prof, 4 non-prof staff; ILL; lit searches; copying; restrictions.

The Amistad Research Center, located on the campus of Dillard University, was founded in September, 1966. The name for the Center was taken from the Amistad incident of 1839, out of which grew the American Missionary Association, founder of the Center. The subject collections on ethnic history and race relations comprise 7,500 volumes. The center subscribes to 135 periodicals and 20 newspapers. Non-print materials number 1,122 reels of microfilm, 475 microfiche, and ca. 100,000 photographs. The vertical files have 150 major subject headings, and there are guides to the collections.

The 95 manuscript and archival collections include the papers of: Raymond Pace Alexander; American and Foreign Anti-Slavery Society Minutes; American Home Missionary Society Archives; American Missionary Association Archives; Records of the Anti-Defamation League of B'Nai B'Rith; Mary McLeod Bethune; Frederick Leslie Brownlee; Records of the Catholic Committee of the South;

Archives of the Committee on Civil Rights in Metropolitan New York; Congregational Church Extension Board Correspondence; Countee Cullen; John Hope, II; John Wesley Dobbs Family; Ophelia Settle Egypt Collection; Freedmen's Aid Society of the Methodist Episcopal Church Records; George Washington Lee; Archives of the Race Relations Department of the United Church Board for Homeland Ministries; Lewis Tappan Collection; and O. C. W. Taylor-Louisiana Collection.

The Center publishes the *Amistad Research Center News.*

Atlanta University
Trevor Arnett Library
273 Chestnut Street, S.W.
Atlanta, Georgia 30314 (404) 681-0251, ext. 335

Mrs. Lillian Miles Lewis, curator; 1 prof staff; limited ILL; limited lit searches; copying; no restrictions.

The Negro Collection of Atlanta University was founded in 1946. It has as its overall scope of Afro-Americana, with special focus on Atlanta, slavery, Georgia, the United States, Africa, the Caribbean, South America, and other parts of the world. The collection houses 1,500 rolls of microfilm, 100 microfiche, and 1,500 photographs. Twelve vertical files contain ephemeral material.

Of the 25 manuscript and archival collections, particularly outstanding are: The Thomas Clarkson Collection; John Brown; Countee Cullen Memorial Collection; Henry P. Slaughter; C. Eric Lincoln; Henry Ossawa Tanner; Maude Cuney Hare; Chautaqua Circle; Neighbor Union; Project to Study Business and Business Education Among Negroes, 1944-45; Commission on Interracial Cooperation; Association of Southern Women for the Prevention of Lynching; Southern Conference for Human Welfare; and the Atlanta University Archives.

Publications are the *Guide to Manuscript and Archives in the Negro Collection of the Trevor Arnett Library*, Atlanta University, 1971.

Chicago Public Library
Vivian G. Harsh Collection on Afro-American History
   and Literature
Carter G. Woodson Regional Library
9525 South Halstead Street
Chicago, Illinois 60628 (312) 881-6910

Donald F. Joyce, curator; 2 prof, 6 non-prof staff; lit searches; copying; restrictions.

This collection was named in honor of Vivian G. Harsh, first chief librarian of the George Cleveland Hall Branch of the Chicago Public Library and founder of the collection in 1932. The collection covers all phases of Afro-Americana from 1500 to the present, including materials on Africana, with emphasis on West Africa. It has ca. 22,000 volumes, and receives 210 current periodicals and 10 newspapers. Audiovisual items include 2,700 reels of microfilm, 10 films, 13 filmstrips, and 1,300 recordings. The microfilm unit has 291 complete and partial runs. Over 500 photographs are in the graphic collection.

There are 7 manuscript and archival collections, prominent among which are the Langston Hughes Collection (galley proofs and three typewritten drafts of *The Big Sea*); the Richard Wright Collection (original typewritten manuscripts of

Big Boy Leaves Home, Blueprint for Negro Literature, and *The Negro in Chicago*); and the Negro in Illinois Collection (research data on the History of the Afro-American in Illinois from the 1800s through 1940, compiled by the WPA).

Publications include the *New Books in the Vivian G. Harsh Collection,* and *The Chicago Afro-American Union Analytic Catalog,* 1972.

Columbia University Libraries
Rare Book and Manuscript Library
801 Butler Library
New York, New York 10027   (212) 280-2231

Kenneth A. Lohf, librarian; 4 prof, 10 non-prof staff; no services; for graduate students only.

The Columbia University Libraries Rare Book and Manuscript Library covers all fields of the humanities, social sciences, and other areas. Originating in 1930, the collection contains ca. 400,000 volumes and receives 10 current periodicals. Photographs number ca. 10,000 and microfilm 200. Shelflists, catalogs, and indexes are available.

There are 800 manuscript and archival collections. Those containing significant Afro-American resources are: L. S. Alexander Gumby Collection of Negroana, which covers the period 1800-1960 and contains ca. 5,000 items concerned with the various phases of Negro life in America; The Plimpton Manuscripts Collection (1855-1936) of George A. Plimpton, which covers the period ca. 17th century to 1936 and includes the Slavery Collection of 155 letters, documents, broadsides, and pamphlets on slavery (which range in dates from 1650 to 1869)—the majority of the material relates principally to the southern United States in the 19th century, although some items bear on slavery in 17th and 18th century England. The collection of Whitney M. Young, Jr. (1921-1972), executive director of the National Urban League, focuses on civil rights and urban sociology, 1960-1972; the 106,000 items contain press releases and articles of Whitney Moore Young, Jr.

Publications include *Columbia Library Columns.*

Detroit Public Library
5201 Woodward Avenue
Detroit, Michigan 48202   (313) 388-1000

Mrs. Clara Stanton Jones, director; ILL; lit searches; copying; some restrictions.

The Sociology and Economics Departments of the Detroit Public Library has extensive holdings of printed sources on Afro-Americans. The materials range from the history of slavery to all aspects of political, social, and economic life, both past and present.

Outstanding among the manuscript collections are: 1) the Burton Historical Collection, on Negroes in Detroit from 1795 to the present. Extensive source material is contained in out-of-print monographs, indexed clipping files, and in photographs and manuscripts. 2) the E. Azalia Hackley Memorial Collection of research materials documenting the achievements of blacks in music and the performing arts, with emphasis on Afro-America. Materials include: books, pamphlets, manuscripts, musical scores, photographs, phonograph recordings, tape recordings, letters, journals, scrapbooks, programs, playbills, newspaper clippings, and periodicals; 3) the papers of Mary Etta Glenn, first black woman supervisor of the Detroit Post Office in 1951; 4) papers of Rosa L. Gragg of Detroit, prominent in the National Association of Colored Women's Clubs and the National Council of Negro Women; 5) papers of the Housewives League, which originated in Detroit and became a national organization.

Fisk University
Special Collections
Library
Nashville, Tennessee 37203 (615) 329-8646

Ann Allen Shockley, curator; 2 prof staff; lit searches; limited copying; restrictions.

Although it is difficult to date the actual founding of the Special Negro Collection, the presumption is that when Fisk was founded in 1866, there were then some books by and about the Negro in the library. The collection entails all aspects of the Negro in America, Africa, and the Caribbean. Included are 36,565 volumes, 110 serial titles and 76 newspapers currently received. Twelve vertical files comprise innumerable newspaper clippings, photographs, biographical information, and other material. Sheet music totals 400 pieces. Non-print items include 2,000 phonograph records, 3,050 microfilm, and 183 audio-tapes.

Special Collections houses 65 manuscript and archival collections, outstanding among which are those of Arna Bontemps; Charles W. Chesnutt; Aaron Douglas; W. E. B. DuBois; Fisk University Archives; Marcus Garvey; George Gershwin Memorial Collection of Music and Music Literature; George Edmund Haynes; Scott Joplin; Charles S. Johnson; Jubilee Singers; Julius Rosenwald Fund; Jean Toomer; and John W. Work, III.

Publications include *Dictionary Catalog of the Negro Collection*, 6 vols., 1974; *BANC!: Selected Items from the George Gershwin Memorial Collection*, 1947.

Hampton Institute
Collis P. Huntington Memorial Library
Hampton, Virginia 23668 (804) 727-5371

The Collis P. Huntington Memorial Library of Hampton Institute has an outstanding collection of materials by and about blacks. Of particular significance is the George Foster Peabody Collection of 17,000 items of history and literature, in addition to pamphlets on slavery and the slave trade. Other important research materials in the Hampton Collection are art works, phonograph records, scrapbooks, newspapers, journals, clippings, and the Hampton Archives.

Howard University
Moorland-Spingarn Research Center
Founders Library
2400 6th Street, N.W.
Washington, D.C. 20059 (202) 636-7239, ext. 40 or 66

Dr. Michael R. Winston, director; 18 prof, 24.5 non-prof staff; lit searches; copying; restrictions.

The Moorland-Spingarn Research Center, established in 1914, was named for Jesse E. Moorland (an alumnus and trustee of Howard University who donated his private collection) and Arthur B. Spingarn (an attorney and bibliophile whose collection of Negro authors was sold to Howard in 1946). The collection's scope covers Africa, Afro-American, Caribbean, and South America. Volumes total 85,763, with 401 periodicals and 170 newspapers currently received. Vertical files contain 48 boxes and number 3,206, microcards number 103. Thousands of photographs are in the collection, as well as phonograph records, tape recordings, and sheet music.

There are 120 processed manuscript and archival collections, among which are the papers of Marian Anderson; Benjamin Griffith Brawley; Frederick Douglass; Angelina Weld Grimké; Oliver Otis Howard; Howard University Archives; Kelley Miller; Jesse Edward Moorland; National Association for the Advancement of Colored People; Arthur Barnett Spingarn; Joel Ellias Spingarn; Mary Church Terrell; and the Works Progress Administration.

Martin Luther King, Jr. Center Library-Archives
671 Beckwith Street, S.W.
Atlanta, Georgia 30314 (404) 524-1956

Minnie H. Clayton, curator; 1 staff; ILL; copying; restrictions.

The Martin Luther King, Jr. Center Library-Archives was founded in January, 1969. The collection's subject covers the Civil Rights Movement from 1954-1968 in the United States. The book collection has 5,000 volumes; 75 periodicals and 25 newspapers are currently received. Eight file cabinets contain ephemeral material. The center has 25 microfilm reels, 2 films, and 75 filmstrips.

The Civil Rights Archives of the Martin Luther King, Jr. Center for Social Change developed from the Center's Library-Documentation Project during the establishment of the family oriented institution. The primary purpose of the archives is to preserve the papers of Dr. Martin Luther King, Jr. and make them available for research on the Civil Rights Movement, from the Montgomery Bus Boycott to the Assassination of Dr. King in Memphis, Tennessee. It is presently a repository for the Center's programs and major civil rights organizations and individuals of the 1955-1968 era. Major holdings include the papers of the Congress on Racial Equality, Dexter Avenue Baptist Church, Coretta Scott King, Martin Luther King, Jr., Southern Christian Leadership Conference, and the Student Nonviolent Coordinating Committee.

Publications include *Martin Luther King, Jr. Center* brochure (annual), and a *Newsletter*.

New York Public Library
Schomburg Center for Research in Black Culture
103 West 135th Street
New York, New York 10030 (212) 862-4000, ext. 4045

Jean Blackwell Hutson, chief; 6 prof, 4 para-prof, 12 non-prof staff (augmented by NEH staff of 3 prof, 7 para-prof, 4 non-prof; ILL; lit searches; copying; restrictions.

The Schomburg Center for Research in Black Culture originated in 1925 and was named after Arthur A. Schomburg, whose collection was added to the former Negro Division in 1926. The name of the Collection was changed to Center in 1972, when it was transferred administratively to the Research Libraries of the New York

Public Library. The overall subject is black culture and encompasses the history, literature, and art of all peoples of African descent. The collection houses 66,000 volumes, and receives 332 periodicals and 105 newspapers. Vertical files number 32. Non-print materials comprise 15,592 microfilm, 2,004 microfiche, 60,000 photographs, 117 films, 29 filmstrips, 6,481 slides, thousands of phonograph records, tape recordings, art work and artifacts.

The Schomburg Center for Research in Black Culture has 90 manuscript and archival collections. These include the papers of Paul Laurence Dunbar; the Federal Writers' Project; Claude McKay; field notes and manuscripts of Gunnar Myrdal's *An American Dilemma*; National Negro Congress Record Groups; National Association of Colored Graduate Nurses; Negro Labor Committee; Arthur A. Schomburg; Universal Negro Movement Division; and Paul Robeson.

Publications include *Dictionary Catalog of the Schomburg Collection*, 9 vols. (1962), 2 supplements (1967) and (1972) 4 vols.; *The Negro in New York* (1907); *Harlem, 1900-1929*, an exhibit portfolio (1974); and *From These Roots* (1975), a film.

Tuskegee Institute
Hollis Burke Frissell Library
Tuskegee, Alabama 36088   (205) 727-8477

Daniel T. Williams, archivist; 1 prof, 2 non-prof staff; lit searches; copying; restrictions.

The Tuskegee Collection is comprised of the Booker T. Washington Collection and Tuskegee Institute Archives. The collection, founded in 1895, covers Afro-American history and Civil Rights. The Washington Collection, named after Tuskegee's founder, contains 25,000 volumes, and receives 35 current periodicals and 7 black newspapers. Ephemeral material is housed in 98 five-drawer vertical files. Audio-visual materials include 10,500 photographs, 7 films, 44 filmstrips, 319 slides, 700 phonograph records, and 75 pieces of sheet music. The microfilm collection has 210 reels.

Collections number 37. Significant papers include those of George Washington Carver; Sadie Peterson Delaney; Jessie Parkhurst Guyman; Robert Russo Morton; Monroe Nathan Work; the Tuskegee Lynching Reports; and Booker T. Washington.

Publications include *Tuskegee Institute: A Guide to the Special Collections and Archives*, 1974.

U.S. General Services Administration
National Archives and Records Service
Washington National Records Center
Washington, D.C. 20409   (202) 440-7729

James B. Rhodes, Archivist of the United States; lit searches.

The National Archives and Records Service is charged with selecting, preserving, and making available to the government and public the permanently valuable noncurrent records of the federal government. Additional duties include publishing the laws, constitutional amendments, and administrative regulations having general applicability and legal effects; and promoting improved current records management and disposal practices in federal agencies.

Materials are classified according to record group. Record groups having Afro-American related information include the U.S. District Courts for the District of Columbia, 1789-1929; Naval Records Collection; Office of National Records and Library, 1775-1931; Office of Indian Affairs, 1795-1933; Select Committee on Slavery and the Treatment of Freedmen; Bureau for Colored Troops; Slave Claims Commissions; and the 25th Army Corps.

Publications include *A Guide to Documents in the National Archives: For Negro Studies*, 1947; *Selected List of Documents and Photographs Relating to Negro History*, n.d.; and *The Publications of the National Archives and Records Service*.

U.S. Library of Congress
10 First Street, S.E.
Washington, D.C. 20540   (202) 426-5000

Daniel Boorstin, Librarian of Congress; ILL; lit searches; copying; restricted to inquiries that cannot be answered by state libraries; refuses requests for information on academic exercises, debates, and contests.

The U.S. Library of Congress serves as the reference library and research center of the U.S. Congress and other government agencies, libraries, and the adult public. The Library of Congress in its general and special collections houses books, newspapers, monographs, unbound serials, photographs, films, music, and sound recordings related to Afro-Americans. The Slave Narrative Collection of the Federal Writer's Project is a distinctive part of the collection.

Among the more than 5,000 collections, prominent among those with Afro-American materials are the American Colonization Society, Henry Ward Beecher, James Gillespie Birney, John Brown, Harmon Foundation, Julia Ward Howe, Abraham Lincoln, Myrtilla Miner, National Association for the Advancement of Colored People, and the National Urban League.

Publications include *Library of Congress Quarterly Journal*; *National Union Catalog of Manuscript Collections*; *Negro Newspapers on Microfilm*; *The Negro in the United States*.

University of Massachusetts
University of Massachusetts Archives
W. E. B. DuBois Collection
University Library
Amherst, Massachusetts 01003   (413) 545-2780

Katherine Emerson, curator; 8 prof, 2 non-prof staff; lit searches; copying; the collection is being organized for research, and prospective users should contact the library for information on availability.

The W. E. B. DuBois papers were acquired by the University of Massachusetts from his widow, Mrs. Shirley Graham DuBois, in 1973. The collection of 150 linear feet includes correspondence files of about 125 linear feet, covering his life's activities with special emphasis on the period after 1934. Manuscript versions of DuBois's published and unpublished writings are included in the collection, along with photographs, sound recordings, motion picture films, and artifacts collected during his life. Major correspondents include: Countee Cullen; James Weldon Johnson; Alain Locke; Walter White; Marcus Garvey; Carter G. Woodson; Mary White Ovington and other individuals.

Publications include occasional articles in the *University of Massachusetts Library Newsletter.*

Western States Black Research Center
3617 Mont Clair Street
Los Angeles, California 90018   (213) 737-3292

Mayme A. Clayton, director; 3 prof, 3 non-prof staff; lit searches; copying; restrictions.

The Western States Black Research Center was founded in 1972 by Mayme A. Clayton and is dedicated to the preservation of black culture and heritage through its special collection of books, communication material, and other black historical memorabilia. The collection contains 8,000 volumes of books, documents, pamphlets, ephemera, artifacts, posters, and memorabilia. Audiovisual items include 500 photographs, 30 films, and 25 slides. Over 30 periodicals and 25 newspapers are currently received. The collection is named the Mayme A. Clayton Collection after its owner and collector. The collection of primary source documents total 150.

Yale University
The James Weldon Johnson Memorial Collection of
  Negro Arts and Letters
The Beinecke Rare Book and Manuscript Library
New Haven, Connecticut 06520

Donald C. Gallup, curator; 2 prof, 1 non-prof staff; lit searches; limited copying; restrictions.

The James Weldon Johnson Memorial Collection of Negro Arts and Letters was founded by Carl Van Vechten in 1941, and is a part of the Yale Collection of American Literature. The collection emphasis is on the fine arts of this century. There are approximately 10,000 volumes, 700 titles of magazines and newspapers, 26 microfilm, 48 file drawers of printed material, 55 drawers of correspondence, 62 file boxes of Langston Hughes printed material, and 20,000 photographs.

The James Weldon Johnson Memorial Collection contains 35 important manuscripts and correspondence of Langston Hughes, Walter White, Claude McKay, Countee Cullen, James Weldon Johnson, Richard Wright, and others. Additional Afro-American archival and manuscript collections are also a part of the Sterling Memorial Library of Yale University.

Publications include *Exercises Marking the Opening of the James Weldon Johnson Memorial Collection of Negro Arts and Letters Founded by Carl Van Vechten.* Sprague Hall, January 7, 1950. New Haven, 1950.

35. Major Black Oral History Programs

Columbia University
Oral History Collection
Butler Library
Columbia University
New York, New York 10027

Louis M. Starr, director; Elizabeth B. Mason, associate director; 5 staff; organized 1948; sponsored by the University; budget is $100,000 to $150,000 (30% private; 30% federal; 40% university); ongoing; limited photocopying of transcripts; no ILL; 40 hours weekly; restrictions.

The collection is designed to provide source materials on 20th century history, with the focus largely on leaders in the fields of public affairs, literature, law, medicine, journalsim, music, architecture, painting, sculpture, business, labor, pure science. The collection is about equally divided between oral autobiographies, transcribed memoirs of book length or longer, and special projects containing clusters of interviews centered on specific topics. There is a biographical index, and reports are made to the *National Union Catalog of Manuscript Collections* and *Oral History Collections.*

The program participates in the *New York Times Oral History Program*, which offers about one third of the total collection on microform. Micropublication is limited to material for which special permission was obtained from the interviewees or heirs.

It is difficult to estimate the number of tapes because most were re-used after transcription during 1948-62. Those relating to black interests that have been saved since that time number 200. There are 450 hours of tape and all are transcribed, with 12,500 pages. Some major oral autobiographies conducted with blacks include: Sam Battle; William Stanley Braithwaite; W. E. B. DuBois; A. Philip Randolph; John Warren Davis (continuing); Kenneth Clark (continuing); John Lewis; Lester Granger; Dorothy Height (continuing); Ernest R. McKinney (continuing); George Schuyler; Roy Wilkins; and Mrs. Whitney Young (continuing).

Special projects have focused on the Black Press in America, which contains 92 memoirs; Civil Rights in Alabama in 1964, with 6 memoirs; the Little Rock School Crisis; Eisenhower Administration, with 15 memoirs; and the U.S. Air Force and integration, having 10 memoirs.

Publications include annual report; catalog.

Fisk University
Library and Media Center
Special Collections—Black Oral History Program
Nashville, Tennessee 37203

Ann Allen Shockley, director; organized 1970; sponsored by Library and Media Center; budget from library; ongoing; no photocopying; no ILL; open on request; restrictions.

The Black Oral History Program was strengthened and supported by a $86,377 grant from the National Endowment for the Humanities from 1971-73. The program was designed to tape persons from all walks of life who have been eyewitnesses, participants, or contributors to black history and culture. The program also supplements the Library's Archival and Manuscript resources by interviews with significant figures represented in the collection. The tapes are preserved, indexed, and cataloged. Reports are made to the *National Union Catalog of Manuscript Collections* and to the *Oral History Collections*.

Over 500 tapes are in the collection, representing ca. 240 hours of tape, along with 657 pages of transcripts. In addition, the collection contains approximately 150 donated taped interviews by persons doing personal research. A few of the major interviews have been conducted with such people as: Mrs. Jean Toomer; Mrs. Shirley Graham DuBois; Hank Aaron; Mrs. Countee Cullen; Aaron Douglas; Mrs. John W. Work, III; Dr. Dorothy L. Brown; John Hope Franklin; Benjamin A. Quarles; Alex Haley; J. Saunders Redding; Dudley Randall; Florynce Kennedy; Aileen Hernandez; Arna W. Bontemps; Clara Stanton Jones; William Grant Still; Nikki Giovanni; Hoyt W. Fuller; Margaret Walker Alexander; Nathan Hare; Joyce Ladner; and Lt./Col. Ellen R. Willis.

Special projects have included black women in all fields of endeavor; Viet Nam veterans; history of Fisk University (ongoing); librarians; the Harlem Renaissance; black mayors; the Catholic Church; and all-black towns.

Publications include *A Manual for the Fisk University Library's Black Oral History Program*, and *An Annotated Bibliography of the Fisk University Library's Black Oral History Collection*.

Hatch-Billops Collection, Inc.
Archives of Black American Cultural History
491 Broadway
New York, New York 10012

Camille Billops and James Hatch, directors; 2 staff; organized 1975; budget from National Endowment and New York State Council; ongoing; no photocopying; no ILL; open only by appointment; restricted to graduate level.

The collection consists of taped interviews with black artists in film, dance, theatre, visual arts, music, literature, and related subjects. The tapes are reproduced for educational purposes only, and commercial rights are retained by the individuals interviewed. The tapes are housed at the Cohen Library of the City College, the Schomburg Research Center in Black Culture, and the Hatch/Billops Studio.

Over 350 Hatch/Billops interviews have been conducted with approximately 5,250 hours of tape. One third of the collection has been abstracted. The tapes are preserved. Interviews have been conducted with Regina Andrews; William Branch; Ed Bullins; Dick Campbell; Alice Clutchens; Lonne Elder, III; Elton Fax; Samella Lewis; John Steptoe; Raoul Abdul; Eubie Blake; William Grant Still; Maxine Sullivan; William Warfield; Carmen de Lavallade; Katherine Dunham; Larry Neal; Sonia Sanchez; Askia M. Toure; and John Williams. A complete list is available upon request.

Howard University
Moorland-Spingarn Research Center
Ralph J. Bunche Oral History Collections
(Manuscript Division)
Washington, D.C. 20059

Michael R. Winston, director; Thomas C. Battle, curator of manuscripts; 55 full and part-time staff; organized 1974; sponsored by Oral History Department, Manuscripts Division, Moorland-Spingarn Research Center; budget from University; ongoing; photocopying of transcripts; no ILL; 35 hours weekly; some restrictions.

The Ralph J. Bunche Oral History Collection was originally the Civil Rights Documentation Project. The department has a continuing program to interview donors of personal and organizational records to the Research Center for securing as complete a record as possible of the activities of black people.

The collection contains over 700 tapes with 1,500 hours. The bulk of the tapes have been transcribed. Interviews were conducted with practically all persons of significance involved in the Civil Rights activities during the sixties. An index is available to the collection.

The Interdenominational Theological Center
Religious Heritage of the Black World
671 Beckwith Street, S.W.
Atlanta, Georgia 30314

George B. Thomas, director; 6 staff; organized 1960; sponsored by the Center; budget of $90,000 (private foundation); ongoing; no ILL; no photocopying; no hours of service; restrictions.

The Religious Heritage of the Black World's documentation program has many significant research functions. The personal interviews concern religion, family, politics, economics, and education. To coincide with this, there are recordings of sermons, lectures and dialogues and book reviews. It is a member of the consortium of the International Theological Center and Institute of the Black World.

The collection has 5,000 one-hour tapes. Twenty-five transcripts of 750 pages are in the collection. Interviews have been conducted with Alen Boesak, pastor, Dutch Reform Church, South Africa; Clinton Marsh, moderator, United Presbyterian Church, U.S.A.; Osmundo Alfonso Mirando, professor of religion and philosophy, Stillman College; the Rev. Chrisperi Renner, Assistant to the Secretary of the President of Sierre Leone, West Africa; Victor Vokeroit of South Africa; Martin Luther King, Sr.; and Benjamin Mays.

Mary Holmes College
Oral History Program
Box 2217
West Point, Mississippi 39773

Richard D. Tucker, director; 2 staff; organized 1969; sponsored by General Studies; budget of $48,000 (federal for three years); not ongoing—program terminated August 15, 1972; photocopying of transcripts; no ILL; 45 hours weekly; restrictions.

The program has taped interviews of the reminiscences of rural black Mississippians seventy years of age and above. The information pertained to education, sex life, economic status, religion, environment as related to the sharecropping system, and civil rights experiences to determine the extent of their participation and comprehension of historical developments during their lifetimes. The tapes have been preserved, indexed, and reports made to the *Oral History Collections*.

The collection has a repository of 600 tapes of 900 hours. All 600 tapes have been transcribed, with transcripts ranging between 15 and 65 pages. Interviews of particular note have been conducted with Alvin Thomas, Midland Green, and Mr. Calvin.

Memphis State University
Oral History Research Office
Memphis, Tennessee 38152

Charles W. Crawford, director; staff of one secretary and volunteer interviewers; organized 1967; sponsored by History Department; budget of $18,950 (university); ongoing; photocopying of transcripts; ILL; 49 hours weekly; only the Church Family Project is restricted for use at this time.

The program aims to preserve the memoirs of men and women who have made significant contributions to society in recent times, and it encourages faculty research and publication by aiding researchers in locating and collecting source material. It is temporarily oriented toward people and events in the lower Mississippi Valley region. The office may take advantage of unusual opportunities to conduct interviews with distinguished people of any discipline who are visiting the area. The tapes are preserved, indexed, and reports made to the *Oral History Collections*.

Approximately 360 tapes relate to the Memphis Events of 1968 and 260 are transcribed; five tapes of nine interviews concern the Robert Church Family; and 17 tapes of approximately 15-20 interviews are on Memphis jazz and blues. Transcribing is ongoing. Interviews have been with a number of musicians and other persons.

Talladega College Historical Collections
Talladega College
Talladega, Alabama 35160

Leon P. Spencer, director; staff of student assistants and history majors; organized 1970; sponsored by History Department; budget is from the general archival budget (with approximately $500 federal funding) and salary support is through the Alabama Center for Higher Education Consortium; ongoing; photocopied transcripts must be returned; no ILL; 35 hours weekly; ordinary controls.

This project originated as part of the Statewide Oral History Program of the Alabama Center for Higher Education Consortium. It followed a broadly interpreted Civil Rights theme. The program is responsible to particular issues in the community and special research interests of students. The collection seeks also to complement the manuscript collections by interviews with persons covered in the papers. The tapes are preserved and reports are made to the *National Union Catalog of Manuscript Collections*.

The collection houses 58 tapes totaling approximately 80 hours. Approximately 12 tapes have been transcribed, comprising 300 pages of transcript. Interviews of significance have been with Teddy Wilson; Henry C. McDowell; Aaron M. McMillan; Laura R. Daly; Alfred B. Lewis; and Everett McNair. Special subject projects have been based on the Sharecroppers Union of Alabama (1930s); jazz in Chicago (1930s); the black Congregational Church in the South; black Americans in Angola; mill strikes in Talladega; civil rights demonstrations (1960s); African Missionaries; and school integration.

Publishes *Original Resources in Black Studies.*

INITIAL ORAL HISTORY PROGRAMS

Oral history programs focusing on blacks that have been recently organized are the following:

1. Afro-American Historical Association of the Niagra Frontier
   The Buffalo Afro-American Historical Collection
   332 East Utica
   Buffalo, New York 14208

   The program is aimed at preserving Buffalo's black experience through interviews with residents of the black community.

2. Radcliffe College
   The Schlesinger Library
   3 James Street
   Cambridge, Massachusetts 02138

   A two-year grant of $98,700 from the Rockefeller Foundation was awarded to Radcliffe College to support a biographical oral history project on the lives of black women. Interviews will be conducted with women educators, businesswomen, entertainers, writers, artists, social workers, community organizers, religious leaders, and women in politics, government, and the health professions. Interviews will be with older women who began their involvement in civic and professional activities prior to the 1930s. The grant will be administered by the Schlesinger Library.

3. Bishop College
   Zale Library
   Black Oral History Program
   Southwest Research Center
   3837 Simpson-Stuart Road
   Dallas, Texas 75241

   Program in formulation stage.

36. Afro-American Museums

ALABAMA
Tuskegee

George Washington Carver Museum
Tuskegee Institute
Tuskegee, Alabama 36088   (205) 727-8479

Elaine F. Thomas, curator; 9 staff; founded 1938; subsidized by Tuskegee Institute; 39 hours weekly; member The American Association of Museums.

The Museum was authorized by the Trustees of Tuskegee Institute, at the request of President F. D. Patterson in 1938, as a memorial to the eminent scientist who became director of agricultural research at Tuskegee in 1896. George Washington Carver received world-wide recognition for his research program in developing numerous products from sweet potatoes and peanuts. Formally dedicated in 1941 by the late Henry and Mrs. Ford, the building is a brick structure of two levels, air conditioned, neon lighted, and can accommodate three hundred guests. The collection includes dioramas, African art, paintings, sculpture, and exhibits of Carver's products, as well as his plant, mineral, and bird collections.

Publishes museum brochures and bulletins by George Washington Carver.

CALIFORNIA
Oakland

The Oakland Museum
1000 Oak Street
Oakland, California 94607   (916) 273-3819

Ben Hazard, curator; Dorothy Delahoussaye, assistant curator; 4 staff; subsidized by City Museum; 35 hours weekly; member The American Association of Museums.

Publishes *Mine Okubo; Three Generations of Chinese; Black Filmmakers Hall of Fame, 1974-76.*

DISTRICT OF COLUMBIA

Howard University
Howard University Museum
Moorland-Spingarn Research Center
500 Howard Place, N.W.
Washington, D.C. 20059   (202) 636-7239

Thomas C. Battle, acting curator; 5 staff; founded 1973; subsidized by University; 40 hours weekly; member The American Association of Museums.

The physical quarters occupy 1,700 square feet divided into four gallerys. The collection includes African, Afro-American and Caribbean artifacts, documents, photographs, textiles, art, rare volumes, and other items.

Publishes catalogs, facsimiles, reproductions.

FLORIDA

Jacksonville

Joseph E. Lee Memorial Library and Museum
1424 East 17th Street
Jacksonville, Florida 32206   (904) 358-2096

Isiah J. Williams, III, curator; 7 staff; groundbreaking ceremonies, September 5, 1975; dedication, January 28, 1976; budget of $35,000; subsidized by grants and contributions; 50 hours weekly.

The Joseph E. Lee Memorial Library and Museum was named in honor of the first black lawyer to be admitted to the Florida bar. He had a significant role in developing an important black community in Jacksonville, served in the state legislature for several terms, and was a federal official until his death in 1913. The library and museum consist of a reading room of 660 square feet and 2,000 square feet of decks, with approximately 800 square feet of the deck under the roof for exhibitions. The Joseph E. Lee papers consist of 1,000 letters from 350 persons who were active in the political, educational, and religious community between 1876 and 1884. Records of the Human Relations Council of Northwest Florida and Jacksonville are there as well.

Publishes materials on Joseph E. Lee Library and Museum.

ILLINOIS

Chicago

DuSable Museum of African American History
740 East 56th Place
Chicago, Illinois 60637   (312) 947-0600

Charles G. Burroughs, curator; 16 full-time, 14 part-time staff; founded October 29, 1961; budget of $128,450; subsidized by memberships, sales, foundations; 39.5 hours weekly; member The American Association of Museums and Midwest Association of Museums.

The museum occupies a one-story building with a full basement, having approximately 20,000 square feet for exhibits, offices, library, and workshops. The collection includes African, Haitian, and Jamaican sculpture and paintings; a research library; clipping file; periodicals; and a photo file.

Publishes an annual calendar and historical material.

MASSACHUSETTS

Boston

Museum of the National Center of Afro-American Artists
300 Walnut Street
Boston, Massachusetts 02122

Edmund Barry Gaither, curator; Debra Spencer, assistant curator; 4 staff; founded October, 1969; budget of $100,000; subsidized by the National Center of Afro-American Artists and the Museum of Fine Arts, Boston; 28 hours weekly, closed Mondays; member The American Association of Museums.

Formerly housed in the auditorium of the Elma Lewis School of Fine Arts, the museum is now located in a renovated private mansion, built in the late 1850s, which affords 1,500 square feet of space. It was founded by the National Center of Afro-American Artists with assistance from the Boston Museum of Fine Arts. The museum was initiated by Elma Lewis, and Edmund Barry Gaither has been the chief designer of programs. The collection includes prints, sculptures, photographs and slides of works by Afro-Americans, Africans, and West Indians.

Publications include *Lampblack*; *Our Elders*; *Crite and Dames*; *Ah Haiti*; *Glimpses of Voudou*; *Roxbury Yesteryears*; *Affairs of Black Artists: Flashback, Ancestral Vibrations*; *African Art for Children: Reflective Moments*; and *Lois Mailou Jones*.

MICHIGAN
Detroit

Afro-American Museum of Detroit
1553 West Grand Boulevard
Detroit, Michigan 78208   (313) 899-2500

Masha Harris and Charles Lewis, curators; 4 staff; founded March 10, 1965; budget of $35,000; subsidized by membership donations, state and federal funds; 40 hours weekly.

The Afro-American Museum of Detroit was officially opened in January 1966. It is housed in an early twentieth century three-family complex. The collection includes the original gas mask and traffic signal of Jarrett Morgan, Jr., and paintings by Leroy Foster.

Publications include newsletters, brochures, bi-annual catalog.

MINNESOTA
Minneapolis

African American Cultural Center
258 Hennepin Avenue
Minneapolis, Minnesota 55401   (612) 332-3506

Gloria D. Ali, curator; 3 staff; founded December 10, 1969; budget of $146,000; subsidized by City of Minneapolis (Community Development Block Grant Fund); 59 hours weekly.

The museum was founded as a project of the Sabathani Community Center under the auspices of the Model Cities Program. It is presently located on the west side of the second floor of the center. Plans are projected for the museum to be housed in a multi-million dollar center in the heart of the city within three to five years. The collection specializes in African and Afro-American sources from the general to the specific, including all subject areas.

NEW JERSEY

New Egypt

Merabash Museum (Galleries)
40 Main Street
New Egypt, New Jersey 08533   (609) 758-7113

P.O. Box 752
Willingboro, New Jersey 08046

Mark Henderson, Jr., president; 4 full-time, volunteer staff; founded September 2, 1971; budget of $50,000-$60,000; subsidized by membership, contributions, CETA funding; 35 hours weekly and by appointment; member The American Association of Museums.

A non-profit organization, the Merabash Museum was founded to educate society about the contributions made by Afro-Americans. It has a goal to build a multipurpose research, education, and exhibition complex. The museum is a brick and shingle contemporary building with two upper galleries, library, conference room, lower gallery, workshops, and administrative offices, containing approximately 5,000 square feet. The collection includes African artifacts, panel exhibits, art treasures, and items from estates, collectors, and transfers from other institutions. The library has 3,000 reference books. The museum assembles exhibition packages for display at shipping malls, large auditoriums, and places of business with high pedestrian density. Trained staff members install the displays and execute on-site presentations.

Publishes *MERABASH: A Sense of Dignity.*

NEW YORK

Jamaica

Store Front Museum/Paul Robeson Theatre
162-02 Liberty Avenue
Jamaica, New York 11433   (212) 523-5199

Tom Lloyd, executive director; 3 full-time, 8 part-time staff; founded February 2, 1971; subsidized by National Endowment for the Arts, New York State Council on the Arts, Parks Department (New York City), private contributions; 30.5 hours weekly (includes Saturdays); member The American Association of Museums.

The Store Front Museum, a non-profit museum, was established to alleviate some of the major cultural disadvantages encountered by residents of Southeast Queens. It aims to cultivate and promote participation by the community in the arts, and to emphasize the contributions that black people have made to the United States and mankind. The museum established the first art museum and cultural center in the Borough of Queens, and founded the second public theatre in Queens, the Paul Robeson Theatre. The Store Front Museum is the only museum in greater New York with a complete studio and mobile video communications training program. The building housing the museum was a former automobile warehouse of 20,000 square feet, with three workshop areas, exhibit gallery, a 330 seat modern theatre (Paul Robeson Theatre), and an outdoor amphitheatre with a seating capacity for 3,000 people. There is a permanent collection of works of art, relics, memorabilia, photographs, souvenirs, artifacts, and documents relating to black history, both past and present. Of note is an exhibit of Romare Bearden's pen and ink drawings, and African poetry. A library of black literature is a part of the museum's holdings.

OHIO
Cleveland

Afro-American Cultural and Historical Society
1839 East 81st Street
Cleveland, Ohio 44103

Icabod Flewellen, curator; 4 staff; founded April 15, 1953; budget of $2,500; subsidized by membership contributions; 2 hours, Saturdays and Sundays.

The Society is a civic, cultural, non-political, educational, and non-profit organization whose purpose is to promote the study of the black man's contribution through clubs, schools, churches and periodicals. The collection covers the history of Afro-Americans in Ohio, blacks in the Army Air Corps, and black theology.

RHODE ISLAND
Providence

Rhode Island Black Heritage Society
110 Benevolent Street
Providence, Rhode Island 02906   (401) 861-2917

Mrs. Rowena Street, curator; 5 full-time, 3 summer staff; incorporated December 1975; budget of $39,782; subsidized by RICH grant, VISTA grant, Providence Library, Urban League tours, charter membership, donations; 40 hours weekly.

The Rhode Island Black Heritage Society occupies the Aldrich house, which is a restored mansion. Artifacts, books, photographs, newspapers and manuscripts are collected for the purpose of preserving all periods of black life in Rhode Island. There are over 1,000 books, and the total collection is valued at $25,000. The information collected and researched is periodically exhibited during the year.

Publishes *Blacks in Rhode Island.*

TENNESSEE
Knoxville

Beck Cultural Exchange, Inc.
1927 Dandridge Avenue
Knoxville, Tennessee 37915   (615) 524-8461

4 staff; founded September 21, 1975; budget of $55,000; subsidized by Community Development Funds; 39 hours weekly (including Saturday and Sunday); member The American Association of Museums.

The Beck Cultural Exchange, Inc. was eatablished by the Project Area Committee of Morningside Urban Renewal Project R-111. The idea was created and put into action by residents in the urban renewal project area who remained to live in the area. The museum is the eighty-year-old former home of James and

Ethel Beck, which was renovated for the cultural center. It is of brick American and Dutch architecture with nine rooms. The first floor is designed for exhibits, and the second floor has an art gallery, meeting rooms and offices, which include one for Oral History. The collection includes art work and paintings of Buford Delaney, Joseph Delaney, Ruth Brice and other local artists; photography and historical materials on outstanding Knoxvillians, such as Squire William Yardly who ran for Governor in 1876, and William H. Hastie, first black U.S. Federal Judge.

Publishes a brochure.

TEXAS

Dallas

Bishop College
Southwest Research Center and Museum
3837 Simpson-Stuart Road
Dallas, Texas 75241   (214) 376-4311, ext. 270

Harry Robinson, Jr., director; Mildred Honore, associate director; 1.5 staff; founded January 15, 1975; subsidized by grants and contributions; 28 hours weekly including Saturday; member Texas Association of Museums.

The Southwest Research Center and Museum for the Study of African-American Life and Culture is concerned with the systematic study of the African-American people, their culture and development, both historically and contemporary. The museum's exhibition area is on the main floor of the Zale Library. The collection includes African art, brass collection, and works of Southwest black artists.

Publishes a newsletter and brochure.

37. Afro-American Historical Societies

Afro-American Historical Association of the Niagara Frontier
332 East Utica
Buffalo, New York 14208   (716) 883-4418

Monroe Fordham, president; founded 1974; membership—25, open to organizations, students and individuals.

The Afro-American Historical Association of the Niagara Frontier was founded in 1974 for the purpose of locating and preserving papers, records, and other historical materials pertaining to the life and history of Afro-Americans on the Niagara Frontier. Programs are sponsored to encourage research and produce written articles aimed at promoting a greater understanding and appreciation of the life and history of Afro-Americans of the area. It is a non-profit community organization without a paid staff.

Various services include: 1) working with organizations and individuals in helping them to organize and preserve their records; and 2) indexing and microfilming of such records free of charge to place the microfilm in the Buffalo Afro-American Historical Collection and Research Center and the Buffalo State College Archives.

Publishes *Afro-Americans in New York Life and History: An Interdisciplinary Journal.*

Black American Cinema Society
3617 Montclair Street
Los Angeles, California 90018   (213) 737-3292

Edgar Goff, president; Mayme A. Clayton, founder/director; founded May 1976; membership—125, open to interested persons.

The non-profit Black American Cinema Society was established under the auspices of the Western States Black Research Center. The Society seeks to broaden historical awareness of the black American's contribution to the motion picture industry by identifying, acquiring and preserving their history, folklore, and historical characters on film. The society's objective is to initiate a film society for film buffs, in relationship to black Americans. The collection presently houses early black American films, posters, books, pamphlets, and billboard posters.

Rhode Island Heritage Society
110 Benevolent Street
Providence, Rhode Island   (401) 861-2917

Albert Klyberg, director; Mrs. Rowena Stewart, project director; founded December 1975; membership—first year limited to charter membership primarily as a fund raising mechanism.

The Society was organized to research, document, purchase, collect, and preserve all periods of black life in Rhode Island. The information collected and researched is periodically exhibited during the year with emphasis on showing this generation how other generations of blacks in Rhode Island lived. A non-profit community-based organization, it is sponsored by the Rhode Island Historical Society and funded by the Rhode Island Committee for the Humanities. Among the Society's many services are: 1) exhibits, 2) tours throughout the state to inform the general public about the contribution of blacks, 3) community-based projects that teach local black history and stimulate research, and 4) a resource bank for locating information relating to the black heritage in libraries, private collections, and historical societies.

Publications include a brochure and *Blacks in Rhode Island—A Heritage Discovered.*

Western Pennsylvania Research and Historical Society, Inc.
1810 Funston Street
Pittsburgh, Pennsylvania 15235   (412) 682-0491

Albert Goldsmith, president; Bernard Morris, executive director; founded November 1955; membership—25.

The society grew out of discussions between its co-founders, S. Carter Robinson and Walter Worthington. Prior to this, Mr. Worthington had unsuccessfully tried twice since 1927 to organize such an organization. The society was incorporated and a charter was issued in 1960. After the death of Mr. Robinson, Samuel Golden served as president until his death. The society's membership is integrated. The majority of the society's collection material is being held by individuals until a permanent building is acquired.

UNDERGRADUATE LIBRARY SCHOOL DEPARTMENTS IN PREDOMINANTLY BLACK COLLEGES AND UNIVERSITIES

ALABAMA
Montgomery

Alabama State University
950 South Jackson Street
Montgomery, Alabama 36101   (205) 262-3581

Katie R. Bell, acting coordinator; under College of Education; 2 full-time, 3 part-time faculty; undergraduate library science, graduate library educational media training; degrees—undergraduate 27 (quarterly), graduate 45 (quarterly) hrs; degrees—undergraduate B.S. (minor), graduate M.Ed.

ARKANSAS
Pine Bluff

University of Arkansas at Pine Bluff
Pine Bluff, Arkansas 71601   (501) 535-6700, ext. 304

Helen Mei-ju Chen, head; under Educational Media and Services; 1 full-time faculty; school librarian training; 12 hrs; degree; summer session.

DISTRICT OF COLUMBIA

University of the District of Columbia
724 9th Street, N.W.
Room 309
Washington, D.C. 20001   (202) 727-2756

Edith M. Griffin, acting chairperson; under School of Education; 8 full-time, 2 part-time faculty; Media Science training; degrees—B.S., M.S, A.A.; summer session.

FLORIDA
Tallahassee

Florida Agricultural and Mechanical University
Tallahassee, Florida 32307   (904) 222-8031, ext. 369

Mrs. Margaret B. Jones, acting head; under College of Education; 2 full-time, 1 part-time faculty; school media services, AV technical training; 42 qtr hrs specialized, 180 qtr hrs; degree—B.S. in Education; summer session.

GEORGIA
Atlanta

Atlanta University
School of Library Service
223 Chestnut Street, S.W.
Atlanta, Georgia 30314 (404) 681-0251, ext. 312

Virginia Lacy Jones, director; under School of Library Service; 11 full-time, 2 part-time faculty; degree–B.S.; 27 hrs; summer session.

Fort Valley

Fort Valley State College
State College Drive
Fort Valley, Georgia 31030 (912) 825-6251

George Jowers, Jr., head; under Division of Education; 1 full-time, 1 part-time faculty; minor in library science; 20 hrs; no summer session.

Savannah

Savannah State College
Savannah, Georgia 31404 (912) 356-2183, -2184, or -2185

A. J. McLemore, head; under library; 3 part-time faculty; four courses required for certification of teacher-librarian; 20 total hrs; no degrees; summer session.

LOUISIANA
Grambling

Grambling State University
Grambling, Louisiana 71245 (318) 247-6941

Mrs. Hazel Johnson Jones, head; under Education Department; 5 part-time faculty; certification for school librarianship–elementary, secondary; 21 hrs; library education minor; summer session.

MISSISSIPPI
Itta Bena

Mississippi Valley State University
Itta Bena, Mississippi 38941 (601) 254-9041, ext. 274, 275, or 276

Mary Ruth Prince, head; under library; 1 full-time faculty; major in library science by majoring in elementary ed with additional hours in library science to have a double major; 24 hrs; no degrees; summer session.

Jackson

Jackson State University
1325 Lynch Street
Jackson, Mississippi 39217 (601) 968-2391

Cozetta W. Buckley, head; under Education Department; 2 full-time, 2 part-time faculty; certificate program for school librarians and a minor program in which any student may enroll; 24 semester hrs; no degrees; two five week summer sessions.

NORTH CAROLINA
Durham

North Carolina Central University
School of Library Science
1805 Fayetteville Street
Durham, North Carolina 27707 (919) 683-6485

Annette L. Phinazee, director; under School of Library Science; 9 full-time faculty; undergraduate minor, school associate media coordinator training; 27 hrs; degrees—B.S., B.A.; summer session.

Greensboro

North Carolina Agricultural and Technical State University
Greensboro, North Carolina   (919) 379-7782, ext. 7783

Tommie M. Young, head; under library; 1 full-time faculty; teacher-librarian curriculum; 18 hrs; no degrees; summer session.

SOUTH CAROLINA

Orangeburg

South Carolina State College
College Avenue, N.E.
Orangeburg, South Carolina 29117   (803) 534-7103

Mrs. Bernice B. Middleton, head; under School of Education; 2 full-time faculty; undergraduate geared toward school media programs; 131 hrs, 31 hrs in library service; degree—B.S. in education; summer session.

TENNESSEE

Nashville

Fisk University
17th and Jackson Street
Nashville, Tennessee 37203   (615) 329-9111, ext. 207, 208

Jessie Carney Smith, head; under Department of Education; 3 part-time faculty; certification as a teacher-librarian—elementary, secondary; 15 hrs; no degrees; no summer session.

Tennessee State University
3500 Centennial Boulevard
Nashville, Tennessee 37203

Evelyn Fancher, head; under Curriculum and Instruction; 1 full-time, part-time faculty varies; minor in librarianship (18 sem hrs), certification as librarian (27 sem hrs); minor in library science; no summer session.

TEXAS

Prairie View

Prairie View Agricultural and Mechanical University
Prairie View, Texas 77445   (713) 857-3311

Frank Francis, Jr., Administrative Librarian, head; under library; 7 full-time, 2 part-time faculty; college, public, school training; 24 hrs; degree—B.S. in education, major in library science; summer session.

VIRGINIA

Petersburg

Virginia State College
Petersburg, Virginia 23803   (804) 526-5111, ext. 208

Ruth Moore Jackson, coordinator; under Library Science-Educational Media; school librarianship training; 33-36 hrs; degree—B.S.; summer session.

PREDOMINANTLY BLACK
GRADUATE LIBRARY SCHOOLS

Alabama Agricultural and Mechanical University
School of Library Media
Normal, Alabama 35762				(205) 859-7216

Dorothy M. Haith, dean; 5 full-time, 1 part-time faculty; 66 full-time, 7 part-time students; M.S.L.S., M.A.; scholarships or financial aid; summer program; 114 degrees conferred.

The Department of Media Instruction was initiated during the spring semester of 1969. Dr. Carl H. Marbury headed a faculty of three part-time teachers; approximately 25 students enrolled in the school. By an act of the University's Executive Council on February 1, 1971, the name was changed from Department to School of Library Media. The school was accredited as a single-specialization program by the American Library Association.

Atlanta University
School of Library Service
223 Chestnut Street, S.W.
Atlanta, Georgia 30314				(404) 681-0251, ext. 312

Virginia Lacy Jones, dean; 11 full-time, 2 part-time faculty; 56 full-time, 20 part-time students; degrees—M.S.L.S., M.A., post-masters, S.L.S. (Specialist in Library Service); scholarships or financial aid; summer program; 1,463 degrees conferred.

The Atlanta University School of Library Service was founded in September, 1941, for the purpose of training professional black librarians. The school was designed to replace the Hampton Institute Library School which closed in 1939. The establishment of the school was supported by the Carnegie Corporation of New York, the General Education Board, and Atlanta University. Eliza Atkins Gleason served as the first director of the school, with Wallace Van Jackson and Virginia Lacy Jones as two full-time faculty members, and Lillie K. Daly, secretary-librarian. Twenty-five selected students were enrolled. In July, 1943, the school was fully accredited by the ALA Board of Education for Librarianship as a standard type II school offering the B.S. in L.S. The graduate program leading to the master's degree was initiated in 1949.

North Carolina Central University
School of Library Science
1805 Fayetteville Street
Durham, North Carolina 27707			(919) 683-6485

Annette L. Phinazee, dean; 9 full-time faculty; 25 full-time, 20 part-time students; degrees— M.L.S.; scholarships or financial aid; summer program; 455 degrees conferred.

North Carolina Central University was authorized by the legislature in 1939 when it restructured the then North Carolina College for Negroes and thereby reaffirmed its position in regard to graduate and professional instruction for North Carolina College at Durham in 1957. The College library science program began in the fall of 1939. The School of Library Science, as a professional school, was organized in 1941. The School is accredited by the American Library Association and the Southern Association of Colleges and Schools. During the first two years of its operation, the School of Library Science offered three programs: the program for the B.L.S. degree for persons holding a baccalaureate degree at the time of entrance, a major in the College of Arts and Sciences, and a minor also in the undergraduate program. The undergraduate major was discontinued. The last B.L.S. degree was awarded in 1953. The masters program began in 1950. The degree of Master of Library Science was first awarded in 1951.

LIBRARIES OF PUBLIC LIBRARY SYSTEMS
SERVING PREDOMINANTLY BLACK COMMUNITIES

Directory entries include the following information: name of library (branch); address, telephone number; name of (branch) librarian; number of staff (professional, para-professional, non-professional); annual library materials budget; annual operating budget; number of volumes in library; number of periodicals received; description and number of audiovisual materials; availability of interlibrary loan (ILL), copying facilities, and teletype (with number, if available); hours of service; names of former librarians; subject specialization, if any. (Libraries are assumed to have general collections, but some do report subject specializations.) If no report was made for a category, then those services are unavailable or the information was not provided to the compilers. A brief history of the library completes the entry; if the name of the library has been starred (*), this indicates that it was named for a black individual, and the significance of that name is explained at the end of the entry.

ALABAMA

Birmingham

East Ensley Branch Library
900 - 14th Street, Ensley
Birmingham, Alabama 35218   (205) 787-1928

Mrs. Earline Girgsby, branch librarian; 1 prof, 2.5 non-prof staff; $5,356 materials budget; part of system budget; 17,370 volumes; records and films available through AV Department at Central Library; ILL through Main Library; copying; 46.5 hours weekly; Mrs. Geneva Blackburn, former head librarian; emphasis is placed on black history and science.

East Ensley Branch, built in 1965, serves a high school and several elementary schools. The building is 4,000 square feet and serves both adult and juvenile patrons.

Ensley Branch Library
1201 - 25th Street, Ensley
Birmingham, Alabama 35218   (205) 785-2625

Mrs. Virginia Guthrie, branch librarian; 1 prof, 3.5 non-prof staff; $11,611 materials budget; part of system budget; 31,483 volumes; 34 periodicals; extensive collection available citywide through AV Department at Central Library; phono records; ILL, copying at the Main Library; 47 hours weekly; Miss Ione McKnight, Mrs. Eunice Collins, former head librarians; general collection.

The library was established in 1955. One of the busier branches, it is noted for its "Outreach" programs. Ensley Branch is between a community predominantly black and one predominantly white. A continuing trend forecasts that the entire area will be a black community within the foreseeable future.

Georgia Road Branch Library
501 - 43rd Street, North
Birmingham, Alabama 35222　　　　　　　(205) 595-2080

Mrs. Ada Blount, branch librarian; 1 prof, 1.5 non-prof staff; $6,304 materials budget; part of system budget; 35,338 volumes; 30 periodicals; extensive AV Department at Central Library available throughout the entire system; ILL, copying through Main Library; 24 hours weekly; black history.

George Road Branch Library was built in 1961. It contains 4,250 square feet with meeting room seating approximately 50 persons.

North Birmingham Branch Library
3200 North 27th Street
Birmingham, Alabama 35207　　　　　　　(205) 254-2658

Mrs. Edith Harwell, branch librarian; 1 prof, 3 non-prof staff; $5,821 materials budget; part of system budget; 24,308 volumes; 28 periodicals; AV Department at Central Library available; ILL; copying through Main Library; 49 hours weekly; Mrs. Carolyn Macready, Miss Margaret Harrell former head librarians; this branch also handles the Books-by-Mail program of this library, a service for persons over 65 who cannot get to the library, or who are physically handicapped.

This branch replaced an old Carnegie Library in 1967; it contains 6,000 square feet.

Pratt City Branch Library
820 - 2nd Street, Pratt City
Birmingham, Alabama 35214　　　　　　　(205) 798-5071

Mrs. Louise Stack, branch librarian; 1 prof, 2 non-prof staff; $5,941 materials budget; part of system budget; 24,246 volumes; 27 periodicals; extensive AV collection available at Central Library; ILL, copying through Central Library; 26 hours weekly; present librarian has been head since 1946; general collection.

The Pratt City branch was built in 1963. Located in a once thriving community but not a desirable location at present, the Library was formerly housed in a community building.

Slossfield Branch Library
1916 - 25th Court North
Birmingham, Alabama 35234　　　　　　　(205) 254-2656

Mr. Jimmie Hayes, branch librarian; 1 prof, 1.5 non-prof staff; $3,385 materials budget; part of system budget; 12,234 volumes; 24 periodicals; AV available through Central Library; ILL, copying; Mrs. Geneva Blackburn, Mrs. Tywanna Burton, Mrs. Gwendolyn Hooks, Mrs. Dianne Humphries, former head librarians; general collection.

This is a small branch in a disadvantaged area and a freeway made access to library difficult. Interest in the facility is apparently on the downgrade. Staff works with retarded in adjacent school.

Smithfield Branch Library
One 8th Avenue West
Birmingham, Alabama 35204　　　　　　　(205) 254-2654

Mrs. Wilma Cottrell, branch librarian; 1 prof, 2.5 non-prof staff; $7,480 materials budget; part of system budget; 34,162 volumes; 43 periodicals; AV available through the Central Library; ILL, copying at Central Library; 44 hours weekly; Miss Vivian Bell, Mr. Oscar Smith, Mrs. Earline Barron, former head librarians; information on all phases of black history, literature, culture, etc.

The Library was constructed in 1956 near a housing development, and has meeting room with seating for 98 persons. It was moved from a room in the Masonic Building in central Birmingham.

Southside Branch Library
No. 2 - 5th Avenue, S.W.
Birmingham, Alabama 35211   (205) 254-2652

Mrs. Mary Pugh, branch librarian; 1 prof, 1.5 non-prof staff; $5,721 materials budget; part of system budget; 24,248 volumes; 30 periodicals; records only available at the branch, extensive AV materials available through the Central Library; ILL, copying through Central Library; 29 hours weekly; Mrs. Geneva Blackburn, Mrs. Hollie Brown, Mrs. Maxine Matthews, and Mrs. Geneva Brandon, former head librarians; emphasis on material by and about blacks.

The Southside branch was constructed in 1957 and contains 4,250 square feet. It has a meeting room with seating for 75 persons. It is near a housing project and a residential area is within walking distance.

Mobile

Toulminville Branch Library
2318 St. Stephens Road
Mobile, Alabama 36617   (205) 457-1396 or 457-1397

Mrs. Virginia Dillard Smith, branch librarian; 2 prof, 7 non-prof staff; $341,745 system materials budget; $858,726.67 system operating budget; 29,720 volumes; 142 periodicals; there are recordings, cassettes, 8mm films, filmstrips, and a pamphlet collection, and all audiovisual materials circulate; ILL, copying; 66 hours weekly; Ailene Cooper, Juanita Simmons, Eran Corsby, former head librarians; social science, young adult services.

The original Toulminville branch was dedicated May 12, 1956; it was located on Gorgas Park under the same roof with the War Memorial Auditorium. The population outgrew this building and the present site was opened November 24, 1974. The branch has 12,600 square feet of floor space, which includes two meeting rooms, an adult reference section, reading and study areas, and a children's department. There is shelving capacity for 100,000 volumes.

ARIZONA

Phoenix

Harmon Branch Library
411 Yavapai Street
Phoenix, Arizona 85003   (602) 262-6371

Mrs. Sylvia Williams, branch librarian; 1 prof, 4 non-prof, 2 para-prof staff; $13,765 materials budget; part of system budget; 32,480 volumes; 75 periodicals; phonodiscs, cassettes, filmstrips, film; ILL; copying; 52 hours weekly; Donna Stephenson, Sr. Claire Hughes, Harry Houle, former head librarians; emphasizes material for Black-Americans and Mexican-Americans.

The Harmon branch was constructed in 1949 to serve people in South Phoenix. It was the first branch library to be constructed in Phoenix.

ARKANSAS

Little Rock

Study Center, East Little Rock Community Complex
2500 East 6th
Little Rock, Arkansas   (501) 376-9011

Lillian Dawson, branch librarian; 1 prof staff; part of system budget; 25 hours during school year, daily during summer; general collection.

The Study Center is located in the East Little Rock Community Complex in a predominantly black community.

CALIFORNIA

Berkeley

South Berkeley Branch Library
1901 Russell Street
Berkeley, California 94703   (415) 644-6860

Mr. James Jacobs, branch librarian; 2 prof, 2.6 non-prof staff; $12,625 materials budget; $67,710 operating budget; 21,007 volumes; 55 periodicals; ILL; copying; teletype no. 910-366-7020; 60 hours weekly; Mrs. Dorothy Daffield, Mr. Bruce Manly, Ms. Mary Jane Rowe, former head librarians; black history, Civil Service books.

The branch has been in existence since 1927. The present building was dedicated in 1961. In 1966, it received an ALA architectural award of merit. The community multipurpose room was added in 1974, made possible by passage of Library Bond issue in 1971.

West Berkeley Branch Library
1125 University Avenue
Berkeley, California 94702   (415) 644-6870

Mrs. Carol Mullane, branch librarian; 2 prof, 3 non-prof staff; $12,690 materials budget; $70,930 operating budget; 22,742 volumes; 95 periodicals; ILL; copying; teletype no. 910-366-7020; Mrs. Macway, Mrs. Florence Catone, Mrs. Helen Roop, former head librarians; black history, minorities in the U.S., Civil Service test books.

The branch was constructed in 1923 and extensively remodeled and enlarged in 1974, which was made possible by passage of a Library Bond issue in 1971.

Fresno

Fresno County Free Library
2420 Mariposa
Fresno, California 93721   (209) 488-3191

Mrs. Tommie Foote, branch librarian; 1 prof, 3 non-prof staff; part of system budget; 12,900 volumes; 27 periodicals; one record listening table, record collection of 450, film projector and access to collection of 636 films; ILL; copying from headquarters; teletype no. 910-362-1181; 47 hours weekly; William T. Cash, Mrs. Mildred Madsen, Mrs. Cynthia King, Daniel Smith, former head librarians; black history and literature.

Ivy Center Branch Library was formerly the West Fresno Branch, which was two small school-housed libraries serving West Fresno. The library was moved to Ivy Community Center in November 1973, when that complex was built.

Long Beach

Burnett Branch Library
560 East Hill Street
Long Beach, California 90806   (213) 591-8604

Mrs. Eleanor Newhard, branch librarian; 2.5 prof, 2.5 non-prof staff; $9,155 materials budget; $58,755 operating budget; 41,484 volumes; 89 periodicals; 16mm projector, 8mm projector, record/cassette player, slide/recorder projector, slide projector, video monitor and receiver, record players and tape recorders; ILL; copying; teletype no. 910-341-7287; 44 hours weekly; Despoina Navari, Jean Eustice, Jean Taggart, Claribel J. Atwood, former head librarians; general collection.

This branch was established as a school-based library in 1910. It was located in rented quarters from 1917 to 1924, and then was housed in its own building until 1968, when that building was demolished. In 1969, it was moved to new quarters, an 8,120 square foot building with a 1,200 square foot auditorium.

Mark Twain Branch Library
1325 East Anaheim Street
Long Beach, California 90318   (213) 591-7412

Mrs. Eleanor Newhard, branch librarian; .8 prof, 2.4 non-prof staff; $3,797 materials budget;

$24,981 operating budget; 17,189 volumes; 46 periodicals; 16mm projector, 8mm projector, record player; ILL; no copying; teletype no. 910-341-7287; 35 hours weekly; Chizuru Boyea, Robert Bellinger, Luan Gordon, Elaine Winkey, former head librarians; general collection.

The branch was established in February 1930, as an enrichment to the central city neighborhood. It is a satellite operation under the Burnett Branch.

Los Angeles

Angeles Mesa Branch Library
2700 West 52nd Street
Los Angeles, California 90043   (213) 292-4328

Elizabeth Hoage, branch librarian; 2.5 prof, 2.75 non-prof staff; $17,500 materials budget; part of system budget; 24,386 volumes; 106 periodicals; 421 disc, 6 cassette, 26 filmstrips, 39 study prints; ILL; 44 hours weekly; Mary R. Grier, Charles Wulach, Margaretha Winchester, Gertrude Goetz, former head librarians; general collection.

A library here was first opened by a local church group in 1914 to provide books to children. In 1917, this area became part of the city of Los Angeles, and the library system. Since 1923, it has been housed in a city-designated building.

Ascot Branch Library
256 West 70th Street
Los Angeles, California 90003   (213) 759-4817

Tracy Mochizuki, branch librarian; 2.5 prof, 4.25 non-prof staff; $16,300 materials budget; part of system budget; 22,844 volumes; 104 periodicals; 854 discs, cassettes, and filmstrips; ILL; 47 hours weekly; Ruth Olson, Donald Read, Gwendolyn Timmons, Margaret D. Jansen, former head librarians; general collection.

The branch was opened in 1921 and has been in its present location since 1939.

Baldwin Hills Branch Library
2906 South La Brea Avenue
Los Angeles, California 90016   (213) 733-1196

Eleanor Nishita, branch librarian; 4 prof, 4.5 non-prof staff; $23,500 materials budget; part of system budget; 32,935 volumes; 124 periodicals; 122 cassettes, 95 discs, 401 study prints, 56 filmstrips; ILL; 47.5 hours weekly; Mary Grier, Gloria Elliott, Joel Martinez, Florence Purdy, former head librarians; general collection.

This branch was formerly called the La Cienega Branch; it opened on January 2, 1923, and moved to larger rented quarters in 1932. It then moved to its present location on April 19, 1961.

Exposition Park–Dr. Mary McLeod Bethune Branch*
3665 South Vermont Avenue
Los Angeles, California 90007   (213) 732-0169

Helen Schwarz, branch librarian; 2.5 prof, 4 non-prof staff; $29,000 materials budget; part of system budget; 28,254 volumes; 101 periodicals; 80 cassettes, 848 discs, 130 filmstrips; ILL; 47 hours weekly; Hazel Merry, Helen Spotts, Mildred Sowers, former head librarians; black studies.

This is the former University Branch. It opened on July 1, 1905, in a room; in 1923, it moved to a permanent building opposite the University of Southern California. In 1965, it moved to a temporary building when the University bought the library property as part of its master plan. The present building opened on May 15, 1974, under the new name of Dr. Mary McLeod Bethune Branch, after community groups and citizens submitted petitions.

*Mary McLeod Bethune, a distinguished educator founded Bethune-Cookman College, was an advisor to Presidents Herbert Hoover and Franklin D. Roosevelt, and was the only woman to serve in President Roosevelt's unofficial "Black Cabinet."

Hyde Park Branch Library
6527 Crenshaw Boulevard
Los Angeles, California 90043   (213) 750-7241

Wilma M. Dean, branch librarian; 2.5 prof, 2.75 non-prof staff; $19,000 materials budget; part of system budget; 16,527 volumes; 112 periodicals; 91 cassettes, 258 discs, 1 16mm film, 73 filmstrips; ILL; 43.5 hours weekly; Mathilde Rehse, Frances Hays, Mildred Adams, Marjorie Kearney, former head librarians; general collection.

    County library service was taken over by the city by annexation in 1923. The first building was built in 1925 and was replaced by the present structure in August 1960.

Jefferson Branch Library
2211 West Jefferson Boulevard
Los Angeles, California 90018   (213) 734-8573

Dorothy Askenazy, branch librarian; 2.5 prof, 3.75 non-prof staff; $16,200 materials budget; part of system budget; 26,544 volumes; 81 periodicals; 34 cassettes, 95 discs, 23 filmstrips; ILL; 47.5 hours weekly; Bernice Barth, Lily Schoop, former head librarians; general collection.

    The library began as a deposit station in 1912, became a sub-branch in 1915 in rented quarters, and moved into the present permanent building in November 1923.

John Muir Branch Library
1005 West 64th Street
Los Angeles, California 90044   (213) 759-4184

Inez Brown, branch librarian; 2.5 prof, 2.75 non-prof staff; $16,300 materials budget; part of system budget; 23,263 volumes; 88 periodicals; 67 discs, 24 cassettes, 17 filmstrips; ILL; 47 hours weekly; Susan Ikeda, Beatrice Yasui, Mary Grier, Elizabeth Higbie, former head librarians; general collection.

    The branch opened in 1923 with a donation from a private citizen. In 1930, the branch moved to its permanent location and at that time was one of the largest and busiest branches in the system.

Junipero Serra Branch Library
4255 South Olive Street
Los Angeles, California 90037   (213) 234-1685

James Page, branch librarian; 2.5 prof, 3.75 non-prof staff; $13,500 materials budget; part of system budget; 18,505 volumes; 87 periodicals; 20 cassettes, 389 discs, 11 filmstrips, 13 study prints; ILL; 46.5 hours weekly; Stirling Yeargain, Ida Davis, Aurilda Jones, Mary Brooks, former head librarians; general collection.

    The library was originally established as a delivery station in 1908. The library moved to the present building in August 1923.

Mark Twain Branch Library
9621 South Figueroa Street
Los Angeles, California 90003   (213) 755-4088

Wanda Johnson, branch librarian; 2.5 prof, 3.75 non-prof staff; $17,500 materials budget; part of system budget; 28,412 volumes; 91 periodicals; 5 cassettes, 793 discs, 20 filmstrips, 22 picture sets; ILL; 47 hours weekly; John Phillips, Frances Hayes, Genevieve Thompson, former head librarians; general collection.

    The library opened in 1928 as a station; it later became a branch. It moved to the present permanent location from a rented store building on December 19, 1960.

Vermont Square Regional Branch Library
1201 West 48th Street
Los Angeles, California 90037

Judith Tetove, branch librarian; 4 prof, 7.5 non-prof staff; $27,550 materials budget; part of system budget; 47,431 volumes; 187 periodicals; 780 discs, 362 cassettes, 21 filmstrips; ILL; 62.5 hours weekly; James A. Page, Eleanor Nishita, Mary S. Hestwood, Charlotte Jackson, former head librarians; black studies and Civil Service test tutors.

Opened in 1913 in the first library building to be built by the city of Los Angeles, this branch was funded by the Carnegie Foundation.

Vernon Branch–Leon H. Washington Memorial Library*
4504 South Central Avenue
Los Angeles, California 90011   (213) 234-9106

Hortense Woods, branch librarian; 2.5 prof, 4.75 non-prof staff; $34,000 materials budget; part of system budget; 22,710 volumes; 138 periodicals; 375 cassettes, discs, and filmstrips; ILL; 44 hours weekly; Barbara G. Placide, Eleanor Nishita, Johanna G. Sutton, Lois M. Green, former head librarians; black history, complete file of *Los Angeles Sentinel* (local black paper) on microfilm.

This branch was an outgrowth of a delivery station opened in 1901. In 1912, it was moved to a Carnegie Branch Building and was at that time one of the most popular branches. This building was closed due to earthquake damage; it was replaced by the present building in 1975.
*Leon H. Washington was the founder and publisher of the *Los Angeles Sentinel*, the leading Afro-American newspaper in Los Angeles.

Washington Irving Branch Library
1803 South Arlington Avenue
Los Angeles, California 90019   (213) 734-6303

Mary Brooks, branch librarian; 2.5 prof, 3.75 non-prof staff; $18,000 materials budget; part of system budget; 33,472 volumes; 95 periodicals; 7 cassettes, 409 discs, 71 filmstrips; ILL; 47 hours weekly; Anell Knutson, Florence Purdy, Evelyn Greenwald, Johanna Sutton, former head librarians; general collection.

The initiative for the establishment of the library was taken by the West Washington Improvement Association in 1922 and it resulted in the opening of this branch at its present location on January 10, 1927.

Watts Branch Library
1501 East 103rd Street
Los Angeles, California 90002   (213) 567-2297

Ida Davis, branch librarian; 2.5 prof, 4.25 non-prof staff; $16,300 materials budget; part of system budget; 19,925 volumes; 85 periodicals; 1,028 discs, 66 cassettes, 93 filmstrips; ILL; 47 hours weekly; Barbara H. Clark, Helen J. Collins, Myrtle L. Yand, Giovanna V. Castelfranco, former head librarians; general collection.

First opened by the city of Watts in 1914 through a Carnegie Grant, the branch, when Watts was annexed to Los Angeles in 1926, became a part of the Los Angeles system and has remained in the same location.

Los Angeles County

A. C. Bilbrew Library*
150 East El Segundo Boulevard
Los Angeles, California 90061   (213) 538-3350

Miss Louise Moses, branch librarian; 4 prof, 12 non-prof staff; $2,106,100 system materials budget; $20,457,683 system operating budget; 31,707 volumes; 195 periodicals; 800 phonograph records, projector and 2 screens for in-house use, 2 television sets, and 6 reading machines;

ILL; copying; teletype no. 910-321-2877, 910-321-2878; 66 hours weekly; Mrs. Virginia Bruce, Miss Lois Edwards, Mrs. Carolyn Robinson, former head librarians; black history, social studies, music, literature.

The library was established as North Enterprise Library, January 11, 1967. Now the A. C. Bilbrew Library, it was dedicated November 2, 1974. The building contains 21,000 square feet. *Mrs. A. C. Bilbrew was a pioneer civil rights leader in Los Angeles, a poet, musician, and the first black to host a radio show in the Los Angeles area.

Compton Library
240 West Compton Boulevard
Compton, California 90220   (213) 637-0202

Mrs. Margaret McKnight, branch librarian; 5 prof, 10 non-prof staff; $2,106,100 system materials budget; $20,457,683 system operating budget; 56,380 volumes; 220 periodicals; 800 phonograph records, 60 cassettes, 40 films, listening facilities, projector and screen for in-house use; ILL; copying; teletype no. 910-321-2877, 910-321-2878; 59 hours weekly; Corinne Wicks, Bess McCook, Joe Schwartz, former head librarians; bilingual-bicultural collection (Spanish) with two bilingual aids, black history and periodical collection in book and microform, government publications.

The library was established in July 1913, has 20,000 square feet, and was dedicated August 12, 1974.

East Compton Library
4205 East Compton Boulevard
Compton, California 90221   (213) 632-6193

Mrs. Elaine Hughes, branch librarian; 1 prof, 5 non-prof staff; $2,106,100 system materials budget; $20,457,683 system operating budget; 23,709 volumes; 98 periodicals; 75 phonograph records, projector and screen for in-house use; ILL; teletype no. 910-321-2877, 910-321-2878; 48 hours weekly; Suzanne Hess, Mrs. Beryl Sherman, Anne Myhre, Geneva Chase, former head librarians; general collection.

The library was established on March 17, 1952. The present building contains 5,000 square feet and was opened on October 3, 1956.

Enterprise Library
2411 West Compton Boulevard
Compton, California 90220   (213) 631-9223

Mr. Lloyd Mayfield, branch librarian; 1 prof, 5 non-prof staff; $2,106,100 system materials budget; $20,457,683 system operating budget; 16,921 volumes; 101 periodicals; 200 phonograph records, projector and screen for in-house use; ILL; teletype no. 910-321-2877, 910-321-2878; 41 hours weekly; Rose Reynolds, Mrs. Margaret McKnight, Louise Moses, Gladys Lindsey, former head librarians; Mexican-American and black literature, and materials on Samoans.

The library was established in November 1916. The present building of 3,000 square feet was opened August 29, 1956.

Florence Library
1610 East Florence Avenue
Los Angeles, California 90001   (213) 581-8028

Mrs. Corrinne Bateman, branch librarian; 1 prof, 5 non-prof staff; $2,106,100 system materials budget; $20,457,683 system operating budget; 19,168 volumes; 95 periodicals; 400 phonograph records, projector and screen for in-house use, television set; ILL; teletype no. 910-321-2877, 910-321-2878; 48 hours weekly; Mrs. Bessie Zink, William Dohman, Mrs. Dorothy Nukes, Mrs. Bernese Rodgers, former head librarians; black history and Spanish language collection.

The library was established in May, 1914. The present building of 5,000 square feet was dedicated on February 2, 1970.

Graham Library
1900 E. Firestone
Los Angeles, California 90001   (213) 582-3809

Mrs. Jean Bolton, branch librarian; 1 prof, 7 non-prof staff; $2,106,100 system materials budget; $20,457,683 system operating budget; 19,678 volumes; 98 periodicals; 500 phonograph records, projector and screen for in-house use; ILL; teletype no. 910-321-2877, 910-321-2878; 51 hours weekly; Mrs. Evelyn Vollnogle, Mr. Anthony Wilson, Dolores Christopher, Mrs. Mary McWeeney, former head librarians; Spanish language and black history.

The library was established in April, 1915. The present building of 5,000 square feet was dedicated on November 14, 1969.

Holly Park Library
2150 West 120th Street
Hawthorne, California 90250   (213) 757-1735

Mr. Dennis Martin, branch librarian; 1 prof, 6 non-prof staff; $2,106,100 system materials budget; $20,457,683 system operating budget; 33,582 volumes; 82 periodicals; 300 phonograph records, cassette listening center with 30 cassettes, record player for in-house use; ILL; teletype no. 910-321-2877, 910-321-2878; 43 hours weekly; James Gear, Hermina Melcon, Jack Burke, former head librarians; black history.

The library of 7,760 square feet was opened on November 14, 1964.

View Park Library
5400 Harcourt Avenue
Los Angeles, California 90043   (213) 294-0390

Mrs. Dorothy Nukes, branch librarian; 1 prof, 7 non-prof staff; $2,106,100 system materials budget; $20,457,683 system operating budget; 19,875 volumes; 62 periodicals; 200 to 300 phonograph records, projector and screen for in-house use; ILL; teletype no. 910-321-2877, 910-321-2878; 43 hours weekly; Richard Little, Mrs. Vivian Dutton, Minerva Freudenberger, former head librarians; general collection.

The library of 2,350 square feet was established in July, 1940.

Willowbrook Library
2326 East El Segundo Boulevard
Compton, California 90222   (213) 631-4311

Mrs. Gene Hopkins, branch librarian; 1 prof, 5 non-prof staff; $2,106,100 system materials budget; $20,457,683 system operating budget; 14,964 volumes; 70 periodicals; 400 phonograph records, projector and screen for in-house use; ILL; teletype no. 910-321-2877, 910-321-2878; 36 hours weekly; Raphael Gonzales, Josue Aranda, Mrs. Annette Walker, Mrs. Joyce Sumbi, former head librarians; Spanish language collection.

The library was established in April, 1913 (first library in the Los Angeles County system). The building today contains 4,500 square feet.

Woodcrest Library
1340 West 106th Street
Los Angeles, California 90044   (213) 757-9373

Mrs. Carolyn Robinson, branch librarian; 1 prof, 5 non-prof staff; $2,106,100 system materials budget; $20,457,683 system operating budget; 26,282 volumes; 79 periodicals; projector and screen for in-house use; ILL; teletype no. 910-321-2877, 910-321-2878; 45 hours weekly; Monica Burdex, Ruth Williams, Camille Kazadi, Margaret Thatcher, former head librarians; general collection.

The library was established in October, 1913. The present building of 7,500 square feet was opened September 21, 1967.

Oakland

Golden Gate Branch Library
5606 San Pablo Avenue
Oakland, California 94608 (415) 652-3584

Mrs. Rosa L. Wooten, branch librarian; 1 prof, 4 non-prof staff; $2,301 materials budget; part of system budget; 8,366 volumes; 66 periodicals; records and cassettes; ILL; copying; 30 hours weekly; Miss Linda L. Minor, Miss Emily P. Otis, Miss Mary Dunn, Mr. Robert L. Highberg, former head librarians; general collection.

The Golden Gate Library was opened in October 1899, in what City Librarian Charles S. Greene described as "a little box of a store at 5893 San Pablo Avenue." It outgrew this place, and in June 1908, it was moved to more spacious quarters in the Golden Gate Building at 5706 San Pablo Avenue.

Melrose Branch Library
4805 Foothill Boulevard
Oakland, California 94601 (415) 532-6800

Patrick Haggarty, branch librarian; 1.5 prof, 4 non-prof staff; $7,000 materials budget; part of system budget; 20,000 volumes; 100 periodicals; records only; ILL; copying; teletype no. 910-366-7016; 45 hours weekly; Sumika Yamshita, Barbara Humes, Syria Baptiste, former head librarians; California history, limited black studies collection.

The library was organized in 1911, the Carnegie-donated building was dedicated in 1915, and it has been active since that year.

North Oakland Branch Library
3134 San Pablo Avenue
Oakland, California 94608 (415) 654-0307

Barbara W. Edwards, branch librarian; 1 prof, 1 non-prof staff; $2,467 materials budget; part of system budget; 18,113 volumes; 52 periodicals; ILL; copying; teletype no. 910-366-7016; 30 hours weekly; Genevieve Wilson, Yvonne Cam, Ed Nyland, Asline S. Jones, former head librarians; books about, written by, and for black Americans.

North Oakland Branch was opened in 1887 on 35th and San Pablo Avenue. It moved to 3134 San Pablo Avenue on July 18, 1966.

West Oakland Branch Library
712 Peralta Street
Oakland, California 94607 (415) 832-3519

Ms. Yvonne M. Cam, branch librarian; 1 prof, 1 non-prof staff; $2,301 materials budget; part of system budget; 10,770 volumes; 50 periodicals; records only; ILL; copying; 50 hours weekly; Mrs. Elinora Young, Mrs. Thelma Keith, Mrs. Mary Wrinkle, Mrs. Peggy Foster, former head librarians; black history, job materials, newspaper clipping file.

The West Oakland Reading Room was the first library in Oakland, founded in 1878.

Sacramento

Del Paso Heights Library
920 Grand Avenue
Sacramento, California 94838 (916) 927,1133; 449-6561

Ms. Mary Mijares, branch librarian; 1 prof, 4 non-prof staff; approximately $9,000 materials budget; part of system budget; approximately 15,000 volumes; 85 periodicals; 16mm projector, automatic sound filmstrip viewer, 4 silent filmstrip viewers, 2 cassette tape players, circulating records LPs, and system-wide circulation of 16mm films; ILL; copying; teletype no. 910-367-0289; 47.5 hours weekly; black studies (adult and juvenile).

The branch was established on July 15, 1913. For several years, the library was located in the home of the "Library Custodian," Mrs. C. P. Van Alstine, and in a post office, and in other private homes in the area. On June 28, 1963, after Del Paso Heights was annexed to the

City of Sacramento, the library moved to a storefront location at 815 Grand Avenue. Ground breaking ceremonies for the present structure were held on May 3, 1972. This branch library has a number of unique features which set it apart from other branch libraries in Sacramento: 1) first public building to have a requirement that a minority person be in joint ventured with the general contractor and have a share in the profits, 2) first public building to have minorities of all races participating in its total development, 3) first public library to have community participation through the decoration of its sidewalks by residents.

Oak Park Branch Library
3301 5th Avenue
Sacramento, California 95817   (916) 455-8522

Rose Marks, supervisor; 1 prof, 4 non-prof staff; $8,750 materials budget; part of system budget; approximately 14,000 volumes; 98 periodicals; sound filmstrip projector, silent filmstrip projectors, disc recrodings cassette recordings and AM-FM cassette tape player; ILL; copying; 46 hours weekly; Mrs. Fiscus, Mrs. Tanner, former head librarians; Civil Service and black studies.

Oak Park Branch Library was the first city branch established in Sacramento and has been at its present location since April 22, 1930.

San Bernardino

Mary Belle Kellogg Branch
1322 Muscott Street
San Bernardino, California 92411   (714) 885-6254

Bill Greeley, extension services librarian and supervisor; 0 prof, 2 non-prof staff; part of system budget; 9,747 volumes; 22 periodicals; 167 phonograph records, film showings administered out of headquarters; ILL; copying through headquarters; teletype no. 910-390-1145; 20 hours weekly; Katherine Goodman, former head librarian; black culture.

Mary Belle Kellogg Branch opened in 1964, named for a retired city librarian. Because of excessive vandalism, and other negative influences, the branch will soon be moved to a new security-protected building being erected by Operation Second Chance, where the premises will be guarded at all times.

San Francisco

Anna E. Waden Branch Library
5075 3rd Street
San Francisco, California 94124   (415) 468-1323

Mrs. Akilimali Funua, acting librarian; 3 prof, 7 non-prof staff; $6,155 materials budget; part of system budget; 25,922 volumes; 115 periodicals; George Alfred, Blanche Maulef, Annie M. Young, Esther Scott, former head librarians; Anna E. Waden has a community and black information section of the card catalog consisting of references to articles, books, magazines not indexed anywhere else (this includes the indexing of most of the 38 black periodicals and newspapers they receive), this on topics of general community and black interest, including definitions of terms related to the black experience in America and the world. The extensive vertical file of clippings, pamphlets on Bayview-Hunters Point, Africans and African-Americans (including North, Central, South America and the Islands) is waiting for a 4-drawer cabinet of its own. The library has a collection of college catalogs from black schools in the United States, containing now more than 50, with requests in for all 103 black colleges and universities. The black book collection has been separated from the general collection and offers coverage of blacks throughout the world. The library is in the process of developing a black picture file that will circulate.

After a history of temporary stations and storefront branches since 1922, the Bayview-Hunters Point area of San Francisco received a permanent facility made possible through a bequest from a former city clerical worker, Anna E. Waden, after whom the library is named. The development of the new branch from the start was a cooperative community project spearheaded by black branch librarian, George Alfred, and was opened in 1969. Although the library is not named after a black, the name has become synonymous with a superior black book collection and black information and reference services.

Western Addition Branch
1550 Scott Street
San Francisco, California 94115   (415) 346-9531

Blanch Maulet, branch librarian; 3 prof, 3 non-prof staff; $10,249 materials budget; part of system budget; 30,991 volumes; 108 periodicals; phonograph records; 51 hours weekly; Glenda T. Hooper, Hiroshi Kashiwagi, Margaret J. Wyatt, Joe Sugg, former head librarians; black history, black interest books and periodicals, Japanese language books—mainly fiction, but various topics, Japanese periodicals and records.

The library was completed in 1966, built from funds voted on in bond election. The library is located in the midst of one of the city's most ambitious urban renewal areas. The collection was started from scratch at this time.

Stockton

Fair Oaks Branch Library
2125 East Main Street
Stockton, California 95202   (209) 464-2171

Ms. Virginia Struhsaker, branch librarian; 1 prof, 3 non-prof staff; $5,100 materials budget; part of system budget; 17,711 volumes, paperbacks not included; 63 periodicals; 2 16mm projectors and screen, 1 tape recorder, 1 3-speed phonograph, 1 filmstrip projector; ILL; copying; teletype no. 510-765-6668; 51 hours weekly; Kearney Leeper, Ms. Gertrude K. Plotkin, Jasper Wright, and James Koping, former head librarians; black history and literature, Chicago history and literature.

From 1913-1949, the library was housed in various odd places. During the early years, it was housed in Fair Oaks School. Since 1949, it has been housed in its own building constructed from two war surplus buildings containing 3,000 square feet. It has the highest circulation (67,000) in the system.

Southeast Neighborhood Branch Library
2326 South Airport Way
Stockton, California 95206   (209) 463-8025

Branch librarian position vacant; 1 prof, 2 non-prof staff; $5,400 materials budget; part of system budget; 9,962 volumes, paperbacks not included; 44 periodicals; 1 projector and screen, 1 viewer with 45 cassettes, 1 slide projector, 1 tape recorder with 15 cassette programs, and 1 solid state record player; ILL; copying; teletype no. 510-765-6668; Ms. Mary Federman, Ms. Christine Poole, former head librarians; black history and literature, Chicago history and literature.

The library was opened September 30, 1971, as a federal "outreach" project in a 2,400 square foot storefront rented building. It became a branch in the city/county system on July 1, 1973.

COLORADO

Denver

Dahlia Library
3304 Dahlia Street
Denver, Colorado 80220   (303) 333-5932

Jo Coker, branch librarian; 1 prof, 2.5 non-prof staff; $10,068 materials budget; part of system budget; approximately 2,440 volumes; 35 periodicals; 1 8mm film loop machine, 6 8mm loops, 148 music cassettes, 13 framed prints; ILL; copying; 20 hours weekly; Margaret E. Hedgecock, Doris Gray, Verna Johnson, Leo Gerstner, former head librarians; black history and culture; job training.

The library was opened in 1968 in the Dahlia Shopping Center as the Dahlia Neighborhood Library in rented quarters. It is a satellite of Park Hill Library.

Ford-Warren Library and Five Points Library*
2825 High Street
Denver, Colorado 80205   (303) 892-1735

Mrs. Maureen K. Crocker, branch librarian; 2 prof, 6 non-prof staff; approximately $25,000 materials budget; part of system budget; approximately 21,000 volumes; 74 periodicals; approximately 500 items of audiovisual materials with formats including videotapes, 8mm film loops, sound filmstrips and silent ones, 8mm films, music and spoken cassettes, framed pictures, sculptures, and AudioCardReader tapes; ILL; copying; Ford-Warren, 51½ hours weekly; Five Points, 20 hours weekly; Mrs. Jean Edgeworth, Mrs. Eleanor Swanson, Mrs. Pauline Robinson, Ms. Marjorie B. Wilson, former head librarians; black, Chicano, and Native American ethnic materials.

The original Henry White Warren Library was the first branch of the Denver Public Library system, built in 1912, through a grant of the Andrew Carnegie Corporation and named after a nationally prominent churchman in the Methodist Episcopal Church. In 1972, a library bond issue was passed to provide a new library for the community to stimulate library use. This new facility opened on July 6, 1975, with the addition of the name Ford. Previous to the opening of the new library, a satellite storefront library was opened in November, 1974, in a nearby city community services center, called the Five Points Library.

*The Ford part of the library's name honors Dr. Justina L. Ford, the first black woman doctor in Colorado with a general practice in Denver.

Park Hill Library
Montview & Dexter
Denver, Colorado 80207   (303) 322-3631

Dennis Kane, branch librarian; 3 prof, 5.5 non-prof staff; approximately $34,338 materials budget; part of system budget; approximately 52,982 volumes; 55 periodicals; 200 adult and juvenile cassettes, 2 cassette players, 1 record player, 500 adult and juvenile records, 1 8mm projector, 79 8mm films, 1 16mm projector, 1 8mm loop machine, 20 8mm loops, 1 slide projector and filmstrip projector combination, 10 filmstrips; ILL; copying; 51½ hours weekly; Harry J. Mooney, Jr., John Ward, Pearl Hallett, Georgiana Tiff, former head librarians; black history and culture, handicrafts, independent learning material, African history and culture.

Park Hill Library was built in 1920 with an addition in 1964. It was originally surrounded by an all-white community, and it is now 55% black.

CONNECTICUT

Hartford

Albany Branch Library
1250 Albany Avenue
Hartford, Connecticut 06112   (203) 525-9121

Floyd E. Wyche, branch librarian; 2 prof, 3 non-prof staff; $8,350 materials budget; $69,110 operating budget; 23,553 volumes; 39 periodicals; phonorecords and cassettes available at branch, but not part of branch's collection, up to 150 records at branch; ILL; copying; teletype through Central Library; 43 hours weekly; Florence N. Adams, former head librarian; general collection.

Albany Branch was established in 1926 in a public school. It moved to rented quarters in 1927 and has occupied its own building since 1950.

Barbour Branch Library
205 Barbour Street
Hartford, Connecticut 06120   (203) 525-9121

Carol DeLoach, branch head; 3 non-prof staff; $2,465 materials budget; $33,840 operating budget; 13,305 volumes; 27 periodicals; phonograph records and cassettes available at branch but not part of branch's permanent collection, and sculpture and realia are rotation collections; ILL; copying; teletype through Central Library; 43 hours weekly; Jeannette Simpson, former head librarian; general collection.

Barbour Branch was established in 1927, and moved to new rented quarters in 1939, occupying its own building. In 1974, it moved to Unity Plaza.

Blue Hills Branch Library
655 Blue Hills Avenue
Hartford, Connecticut 06112

Helen Spector, acting branch head; 3 non-prof staff; $2,835 materials budget; $34,605 operating budget; 9,092 volumes; phonograph records and cassettes available at branch but not part of branch's permanent collection, up to 150 records at branch, cassettes borrowed on demand, sculpture and relia are rotating collections; ILL; copying; teletype through Central Library; 43 hours weekly; Patricia Berberich, Dorothy Busby, Anna Addison, former head librarians; general collection.

Blue Hills Branch, a small but active storefront branch, started in 1931 but was discontinued because of the Depression. It reopened in 1949.

Stamford

South End Branch Library
96 Broad Street
Stamford, Connecticut 06901   (203) 325-4354

Geraldine Sydney Ewart, branch librarian; 1 prof, 1 non-prof staff; $4,500 materials budget; part of system budget; approximately 6,000 volumes; 13 periodicals; film projector, filmstrip viewer; 37.5 hours weekly; Marie V. Hurley, Mary L. Alexander, Alice M. Colt, Elizabeth Van Hoevenberg, former head librarians; approximately 3,500 of the titles are by and about blacks.

The South End Branch came into being in 1968, when the community took over a former school building for use as a multi-service facility. As the residents are predominantly minority Americans (60% black, 25% Puerto Rican, 15% Polish) and non-library users, it was reduced to open a sub-branch (one large room) providing print materials relating to history, culture and reading interests of the community.

DISTRICT OF COLUMBIA

District of Columbia Public Library/
Martin Luther King Memorial Library*
901 G Street, N.W.
Washington, D.C. 20001   (202) 727-1101

Hardy R. Franklin, director; 175 prof, 475 non-prof staff; $668,000 materials budget; $8,051,000 operating budget; 1,280,000 volumes; 5,200 periodicals; microfilm reels–23,500, microcards–29,300, newspapers–20, films and filmstrips–5,300, recordings–83,000, framed prints and posters–6,800; ILL; copying; teletype; 64 hours weekly; George Bowerman, Clara Herbert, Harry N. Peterson, Joe Y. Lee (acting), Milton S. Byam, former head librarians; arranged by subject divisions–Black Studies and Washingtoniana Divs. have local history collections, Special Services has Braille and talking books.

The District of Columbia Public Library system was established in 1896, and now is comprised of one central library (Martin Luther King Memorial Library), 20 major branches, three community libraries, 4 bookmobiles, service to blind, physically handicapped, homebound.

*This library is the central library of the District of Columbia Public Library System. Martin Luther King, Jr., considered the foremost civil rights leader of the twentieth century, utilized a policy of non-violent protest that captured the imagination of the world. He was the youngest person to receive the Nobel Peace Prize. A theologian and a scholar, he was a Boston University Ph.D. and author of several books.

Anacostia Branch Library
Good Hope Road & 18th Street, S.E.
Washington, D.C. 20020   (202) 727-1329

Margaret W. Kemp, branch librarian; 4 prof, 4 non-prof staff; $16,100 materials budget; part of system budget; 68,940 volumes; 145 periodicals; phonograph records–1,144, pictures–140, filmstrips—125, cassettes—74; copying; winter—56 hours weekly, summer—40 hours weekly; general collection.

The library was opened on April 12, 1956.

Benning Branch Library
Benning Road near Minnesota Avenue, N.E.
Washington, D.C. 20027 (202) 727-1333

Althea V. Howard, branch librarian; 3 prof, 5 non-prof staff; $14,000 materials budget; part of system budget; 73,889 volumes; 125 periodicals; phonograph records—1,778, pictures—320, filmstrips—168, cassettes—83; copying; winter—56 hours weekly, summer—40 hours weekly; general collection.

The library was opened May 17, 1962.

Capitol View Branch Library
Central Avenue & 50th Street, S.E.
Washington, D.C. 20019 (202) 727-1337

Charles Brown, branch librarian; 4 prof, 4 non-prof staff; $15,600 materials budget; part of system budget; 57,938 volumes; 123 periodicals; phonograph records—1,478, pictures—365, cassettes—103, filmstrips—111; copying; winter—56 hours weekly, summer—40 hours weekly; general collection.

The library was opened January 12, 1965.

Ft. Davis Branch Library
Alabama Avenue and 37th Street, S.E.
Washington, D.C. 20020 (202) 727-1349

Sharon Suggs, branch librarian; 4 prof, 4 non-prof staff; $16,300 materials budget; part of system budget; 62,502 volumes; 98 periodicals; phonograph records—1,557, pictures—172, filmstrips—41, cassettes—91; copying; winter—56 hours weekly, summer—40 hours weekly; general collection.

The library was opened January 27, 1961.

Langston Branch Library
701 24th Street, N.E.
Washington, D.C. 20002 (202) 727-1357

James Quinn, branch librarian; 1 prof, 1 non-prof staff; $5,000 materials budget; part of system budget; 27,415 volumes; 25 periodicals; phonograph records—273, pictures—45, cassettes—105, filmstrips—96; copying; 40 hours weekly; general collection.

The library was opened September 24, 1943.

Mt. Pleasant Branch Library
16th and Lamont Streets, N.W.
Washington, D.C. 20010 (202) 727-1361

Dr. Ralph Csoke, branch librarian; 4 prof, 4 non-prof staff; $16,500 materials budget; part of system budget; 83,383 volumes; 129 periodicals; phonograph records—1,286, pictures—149, cassettes—87, filmstrips—74; copying; winter—56 hours weekly, summer—40 hours weekly; general collection.

The library was opened May 15, 1925.

Northeast Branch Library
Maryland Avenue and 7th Street, N.E.
Washington, D.C. 20002 (202) 727-1365

June D. Sweeny, branch librarian; 4 prof, 5 non-prof staff; $16,100 materials budget; part of system budget; 50,278 volumes; 125 periodicals; phonograph records—1,124, pictures—215, filmstrips—75, cassettes—96; copying; winter—56 hours weekly, summer—40 hours weekly; general collection.

    The library was opened March 11, 1932.

Petworth Branch Library
Georgia Avenue and Upshur Street, N.W.
Washington, D.C. 20011   (202) 727-1373

Deborah R. Lockhart, branch librarian; 4 prof, 4 non-prof staff; $15,600 materials budget; part of system budget; 72,362 volumes; 125 periodicals; phonograph records—1,500, pictures—200, filmstrips—50, cassettes—50; copying; winter—56 hours weekly, summer—40 hours weekly; general collection.

    The library was opened January 27, 1939.

R. L. Christian Branch Library*
1007 H Street, N.E.
Washington, D.C. 20002   (202) 727-1347

Roderick Meyers, branch librarian; 1 prof, 1 non-prof staff; $6,000 materials budget; part of system budget; approximately 5,000 volumes; 10 periodicals; phonograph records—50, filmstrips—50; 40 hours weekly; general collection.

    The library was opened in August, 1972. *R. L. Christian was an active community supporter of the District of Columbia Public Library. He was highly regarded by his neighbors for his unselfish contribution to civic improvement.

Southeast Branch Library
7th and D Streets, S.E.
Washington, D.C. 20003   (202) 727-1377

John R. Belcher, branch librarian; 4 prof, 4 non-prof staff; $15,600 materials budget; part of system budget; 46,048 volumes; 125 periodicals; phonograph records—875, pictures—242, filmstrips—91, cassettes—53; copying; winter—56 hours weekly, summer—40 hours weekly; general collection.

    The library was opened December 8, 1922.

Southwest Branch Library
Wesley Place and K Streets, S.W.
Washington, D.C. 20024   (202) 727-1381

Margaret Pitsenberger, branch librarian; 4 prof, 3 non-prof staff; $15,800 materials budget; part of system budget; 56,794 volumes; 149 periodicals; phonograph records—1,743, pictures—229, filmstrips—73, cassettes—95; copying; winter—56 hours weekly, summer—40 hours weekly; general collection.

    The library was opened October 22, 1965.

Sursum Corda Branch Library
1112 First Terrace, N.W.
Washington, D.C. 20001   (202) 727-1348

Korea Strowder, branch librarian; 1 prof, 2 non-prof staff; $6,000 materials budget; part of system budget; approximately 7,000 volumes; 11 periodicals; phonograph records—89, filmstrips—58; 40 hours weekly; general collection.

    The library was opened March 15, 1971.

Takoma Park Branch Library
5th and Cedar Streets, N.W.
Washington, D.C. 20012   (202) 727-1385

Lessie V. Owens, branch librarian; 4 prof, 3 non-prof staff; $16,200 materials budget; part of system budget; 57,575 volumes; 130 periodicals; phonograph records—1,008, pictures—186, cassettes—85, filmstrips—58; copying; winter—56 hours weekly, summer—40 hours weekly; general collection.

The library was opened November 16, 1911.

Trinidad Branch Library
1603 Montello Avenue, N.E.
Washington, D.C. 20002

Gloria M. Rice, branch librarian; 1 prof, 2 non-prof staff; $6,000 materials budget; part of system budget; approximately 5,000 volumes; 10 periodicals; phonograph records—50, filmstrips—50; 40 hours weekly; general collection.

The library was opened March 15, 1971.

Washington Highlands Branch Library
Atlantic Street and South Capitol Terrace, S.W.
Washington, D.C. 20032 · (202) 727-1393

Sigrid M. Washington, branch librarian; 4 prof, 4 non-prof staff; $16,300 materials budget; part of system budget; 56,273 volumes; 110 periodicals; phonograph records—1,298, pictures—293, cassettes—87, filmstrips—73; copying; winter—56 hours weekly, summer—40 hours weekly; general collection.

The library was opened October 14, 1959.

Watha T. Daniel Branch Library*
8th and Rhode Island Avenue, N.W.
Washington, D.C. 20001 (202) 727-1228

Brenda J. Cox, branch librarian; 6 prof, 6 non-prof staff; $20,000 materials budget; part of system budget; 21,616 volumes; 164 periodicals; phonograph records—350, cassettes—143, filmstrips—396, films—109, pictures—51; copying; winter—56 hours weekly, summer—40 hours weekly; general collection.

The library was opened September 28, 1975. *Watha T. Daniel was Chairman of the District of Columbia Model Cities Commission and was instrumental in helping to plan and acquire land to build the library. Active in many areas, Mr. Daniel served also on the Board of Education Examiners for Trade Instructors and as chairman of the City Housing Advisory Council. He was the first and only black person to have been appointed to the D. C. Plumbers Board at the time of his death in 1973.

Woodridge Branch Library
Rhode Island Avenue and 18th Street, N.E.
Washington, D.C. 20018 (202) 727-1401

Kathleen A. Woods, branch librarian; 5 prof, 6 non-prof staff; $16,300 materials budget; part of system budget; 67,648 volumes; 149 periodicals; phonograph records—1,146, pictures—292, filmstrips—59, cassettes—109; copying; winter—56 hours weekly, summer—40 hours weekly; general collection.

The library was opened on November 16, 1958.

FLORIDA

Jacksonville

Eastside Branch Library
1390 Harrison Street
Jacksonville, Florida 32206 (904) 633-5609

No branch librarian; branch is run by library-operated Outreach Program staff; part of system budget; 4,613 volumes; 40 periodicals; branch is operating as Outreach center and it stocks only children's books and easy-to-read materials for adults; 40 hours weekly; Mrs. Willye Dennis, Mrs. Elaine Kitchings, Mrs. Millicent Norman, former head librarians.

The Eastside Branch was opened in 1961.

Myrtle Avenue Branch Library
2304 North Myrtle Avenue
Jacksonville, Florida 32209   (904) 633-5605

Mrs. Etta Brooks, branch librarian; 2 prof, 1 non-prof staff; $1,700 books budget; part of system budget; 26,765 volumes; 52 periodicals; 37 hours weekly; Afro-American materials including biography file and information on black history.

The Myrtle Avenue Branch opened June 22, 1965, in present location to replace Wilder Park.

St. Petersburg

James Weldon Johnson Branch Library*
1035 3rd Avenue, South
St. Petersburg, Florida 33705   (813) 822-4905

Mrs. Helen Edwards, branch librarian; 1.5 non-prof staff; $6,500 materials budget; $17,000 operating budget; 14,407 volumes; 35 periodicals; record player, recordings used in children's programs; 40 hours weekly; Mrs. Lessie Burke, former head librarian; black history and literature collection.

James Weldon Johnson Branch was eatablished in rented quarters at 1035 3rd Avenue, South, April 1, 1947. *James Weldon Johnson, a black intellectual of many talents, was a high school principal, a lawyer, a diplomat, and the first Executive Secretary of the NAACP. His books include *Fifty Years and Other Poems, The Book of American Negro Poetry, God's Trombones, St. Peter Relates an Incident of the Resurrection,* and *Along This Way.* He is most widely remembered for his lyrics to the song "Lift Every Voice and Sing," which is considered to be the Negro National Anthem.

GEORGIA

Atlanta

Collier Heights Branch Library
3571 Gordon Road, S.W.
Atlanta, Georgia 30331   (404) 691-1988

Mrs. Bertha Campbell, branch librarian; 2 prof, 3 non-prof staff; $11,880 materials budget; $57,976.80 operating budget; 18,200 volumes; 78 periodicals; 1 projector, 1 set of earphones, 836 recordings, 1 record player, 51 cassettes, 2 tape players; copying; 60 hours weekly; general collection.

The library was opened March 1971, in a small shopping center. The community indicated the desire for service to replace a bookmobile stop.

Dixie Hills Branch Library
2189 Verbena Street, N.W.
Atlanta, Georgia 30314   (404) 799-3266

Ms. Cora Flynt, branch librarian; 3 non-prof staff; $5,400 materials budget; $12,129 operating budget; 4,500 volumes; 281 recordings, 119 cassettes, 1 record player, 1 film projector, 1 cassette player; copying; 45 hours weekly; general collection.

The library was opened February 27, 1973.

Dogwood Branch Library
1953 Bankhead Highway, N.W.
Atlanta, Georgia 30318   (404) 794-8261

Mrs. Melzetta P. Laws, branch librarian; 1 prof, 2 non-prof staff; $10,800 materials budget; $36,759 operating budget; 13,523 volumes; 1 record player, 168 recordings, 1 cassette player, 178 cassettes, 1 projector; copying; 42 hours weekly; general collection.

The library was opened June, 1965.

Dunbar Branch Library
447 Windsor Street, S.W.
Atlanta, Georgia 30312 (404) 523-2873

Mrs. Renelda Thomas, branch librarian; 2 non-prof staff; $4,320 materials budget; part of system budget; 3,182 volumes; 85 periodicals; 1 projector, 1 television, 1 cassette player, 63 recordings, 50 cassettes; 40 hours weekly; general collection.

The library was opened January 16, 1974. Dunbar is a result of Model Cities 4 Storefront Libraries closing.

Georgia Hill Branch Library
250 Georgia Avenue, S.W.
Atlanta, Georgia 30312 (404) 658-6738

Ms. Carolyn L. Garnes, branch librarian; 1.5 prof, 2.5 non-prof staff; $12,960 materials budget; $26,255 operating budget; 10,552 volumes; 68 periodicals; 1 projector, 1 record player, 1 video cassette player, 142 recordings, 73 cassettes; copying; 60 hours weekly; general collection.

The library was opened November 24, 1975.

Kirkwood Branch Library
106 Kirkwood Road, N.E.
Atlanta, Georgia 30317 (404) 377-6471

Mr. Isaac Washington, branch librarian; 1 prof, 3 non-prof staff; $9,720 materials budget; $25,578 operating budget; 11,218 volumes; 41 periodicals; 1 16mm film projector, 1 record player, 2 cassette players, 400 recordings, 150 cassettes; copying; 45 hours weekly; Bobby Henderson, Charlie M. Ford, former head librarians; general collection.

The library was opened in 1942.

West Hunter Branch Library
1116 Hunter Street, S.W.
Atlanta, Georgia 30314 (404) 758-0811

Mrs. Marva G. Ivey, branch librarian; 1 prof, 2.5 non-prof staff; $9,720 materials budget; $30,045 operating budget; 14,989 volumes; 80 periodicals; 1 projector, 2 headphones, 419 recordings, 1 record player, 154 cassettes, 2 cassette players; copying; general collection.

The library was opened in 1949.

Columbus

Fourth Avenue Library
640 Fourth Avenue
Columbus, Georgia 31901 (404) 327-8278

Mrs. Mildred L. Terry, branch librarian; 2 prof, 6 non-prof staff; part of system budget; 30,000 volumes; 161 periodicals; projectors, microfilm readers, opaque projector, controlled reader projector, tape recorders, radio, television, record players, public address system, microphones, piano; ILL; copyings; 51 hours weekly; black culture collection developing marketing and advertising.

The library opened January 5, 1963. It is an ultra-modern building that was built under the administration of the Muscogee County Board of Education.

Savannah

Carnegie Branch Library
537 East Henry Street
Savannah, Georgia 31401 (912) 232-1420

Mrs. Betty Bynes, branch librarian; 1 prof, 4 non-prof staff; part of system budget; 43,690 volumes; 45 periodicals; 1 16mm film projector, 1 filmstrip projector, 1 record player, 1 screen; 53 hours weekly; C. A. R. McDowell, Miss C. G. Hatcher, former head librarians; general collection.

The library was erected in 1913 with funds from the Carnegie Corporation.

Robert M. Hitch Branch Library
840 Hitch Drive
Savannah, Georgia 31401

Mrs. Demetra Williams, branch librarian; 1.5 non-prof staff; part of system budget; 6,869 volumes; 13 periodicals; 1 filmstrip projector, 1 record player, 1 screen; 21 hours weekly; Mrs. Florance Branch, Mrs. Fay Hall, Mrs. Janette Scott, Mrs. Betty Bynes, former head librarians; general collection.

Located in a housing development, the library was opened to the public in 1958.

Hubert W. Kayton Branch Library
Administration Building
624 West Gwinnette Street
Savannah, Georgia 31401

Mrs. Demetra Williams, branch librarian; 3 non-prof staff; part of system budget; 8,756 volumes; 10 periodicals; 1 record player, 1 filmstrip projector, 1 screen; 17 hours weekly; Mrs. Janette Scott, Miss Theolia Kirkland, Mrs. LaBlanche Bonds, former head librarians; general collection.

Located in a housing development, the library was opened to the public in 1963.

Ogeechee Branch Library
1820 Ogeechee Road
Savannah, Georgia 31401   (912) 322-1339

Mrs. Ruth Pope, branch librarian; 1 prof staff; part of system budget; 10,220 volumes—combined holdings of Ogeechee and W. W. Law Branches; 20 periodicals; 1 filmstrip projector, 1 record player, 1 16mm film projector (shared with W. W. Law Branch), 1 screen; 30 hours weekly; general collection.

The library was opened as a Model Cities branch in 1971.

W. W. Law Center Branch
905 East Bolton Street
Savannah, Georgia 31401   (912) 236-8040

Mrs. Idella O'Neal, branch librarian; 1 prof, 3 non-prof staff; part of system budget; 10,220 volumes—combined holdings of W. W. Law and Ogeechee Branches; 17 periodicals; 1 filmstrip projector, 1 record player, 1 screen; 34.5 hours weekly; general collection.

The library is located in the W. W. Law Center and was opened in 1971 as a Model Cities branch.

Yamacraw Branch Library
349 West Bryan Street
Savannah, Georgia 31401

Mrs. Theolia Kirkland, branch librarian; 2 non-prof staff; part of system budget; 7,975 volumes; 11 periodicals; 1 record player, 1 filmstrip projector, 1 screen; 31 hours weekly; Mrs. Ellen Alston, Miss Carolyn Boles, Miss Betty Bynes, former head librarians; general collection.

The library opened in 1946 in the Yamacraw housing development.

ILLINOIS

Chicago

Altgeld Branch Library
841 East 132nd Street
Chicago, Illinois 60627   (312) 264-5952

Catherine Sanders, branch librarian; 4 non-prof staff; $4,300 materials budget; part of system budget; 17,890 volumes; 59 periodicals; 1 movie projector, 1 slide projector; ILL; teletype no. 910-221-1401; 40 hours weekly; Ms. Inez Walton, former head librarian; general collection.

The branch was opened in 1949. The community is lower income and patrons have varied interests.

Auburn Branch Library
1364 West 79th Street
Chicago, Illinois 60620 (312) 783-5927

Melnee Simmons, branch librarian; 2 prof, 1 para-prof, 7.5 non-prof staff; $7,075 materials budget; part of system budget; 33,692 volumes; 129 periodicals; 1,077 phonodiscs, 60 filmstrips, 10 multimedia sets, 21 pictures/posters, 4 16mm films, 16 toys/games, 17 maps; ILL; copying; teletype no. 910-221-1401; 65 hours weekly; Q. Esther Smith, Adele Beaton, Jule Conroy, Esther Wilcox, former head librarians; black culture and heritage, social sciences.

The branch opened for service June 7, 1963, after moving from a location a few blocks east of the present location utilized since 1938.

Austin Branch Library
5615 West Race
Chicago, Illinois 60644 (312) 287-0667

Randall Menakes, branch librarian; 3 prof, 9 non-prof staff; $8,375 materials budget; part of system budget; 50,731 volumes; 102 periodicals; 1,690 phonodiscs, 50 cassettes, 10 16mm films, 125 filmstrips, 178 multimedia sets; ILL; copying; teletype no. 910-221-1401; 68 hours weekly; Paula Hamilton, Ann Beckerdite, former head librarians; general collection.

Austin Branch Library is located in Austin Town Hall Park and was first opened in 1910. Only ten years ago, the community rapidly changed to a black population.

Avalon Library
8828 South Stony Island
Chicago, Illinois 60617 (312) 768-5234

Janet Taylor, branch librarian; 1 prof, 6 non-prof staff; $6,200 materials budget; part of system budget; 28,000 volumes; 108 periodicals; 5 16mm films, 942 recordings, 25 filmstrip sets; ILL; copying; teletype no. 910-221-1401; 65 hours weekly; Adele Beaton, Dorothy Gilliard, Charlotte Kohn, A. Sullivan, former head librarian; general collection.

The library was established in 1927 as a sub-branch and was located in a church. It became a full service agency in 1963, and moved to its present location in 1976. The library serves a community of single family homes of predominantly black families.

T. B. Blackstone Branch Library
4904 South Lake Park
Chicago, Illinois 60615 (312) 624-0511

Alfred L. Woods, branch librarian; 3 prof, 13 non-prof staff; $13,300 materials budget; part of system budget; 47,457 volumes; 70 periodicals; 9 16mm films, 68 filmstrips, 2,049 phonodiscs, 83 multimedia sets; ILL; copying; teletype no. 910-221-1401; 65 hours weekly; Suzanne Whelden, Dorothy Gilliard, Bernice Towles, Arlene Chamberlain, former head librarian; general collection.

This branch is the oldest of the Chicago Public Library branches. It was opened for service on January 8, 1904, as a memorial for T. B. Blackstone, a former president of the Alpon Railroad.

Brainerd Branch Library
8945 South Loomis
Chicago, Illinois 60620

Anne Echols, branch librarian; 1 prof, 1 para-prof, 7.5 non-prof staff; $5,100 materials budget; part of system budget; 42,480 volumes; 111 periodicals; 373 phonodiscs, 61 filmstrips, 5 multimedia sets, 26 pictures/posters, 9 toys/games, 8 16mm films; ILL; copying; teletype no. 910-221-1401; 65 hours weekly; Jule Conroy, former head librarian; black culture and heritage, juvenile picture books.

The branch was opened August 27, 1971, in a rented storefront facility in a small business section.

Carter G. Woodson Regional Library*
9525 South Halsted Street
Chicago, Illinois 60628   (312) 881-6905

Mrs. Alice H. Scott, director; 15 prof, 10 para-prof staff; $90,000 materials budget; $750,000 operating budget; 142,000 volumes; 948 periodicals; 489 films, 392 filmstrips, 92 slides, 11,000 microfilm reels, 451 microfiche, 1,766 cassettes, 307 transparencies, 31 multimedia sets, 105 study prints; ILL; copying; teletype no. 910-221-1401; 75 hours weekly.

The library opened December 19, 1976. It is located on Chicago's south side and serves primarily as a reference and research library for the intermediate college level. *Carter G. Woodson, distinguished historian, organized the Association for the Study of Negro Life and History in 1915, as well as writing many books. Dr. Woodson, a Harvard Ph.D., served as Dean of the School of Liberal Arts, Howard University. He also founded the Associated Publishers.

Garter G. Woodson Regional Library—Community Library
9525 South Halsted Street
Chicago, Illinois 60628   (312) 881-6918

Dorothy S. Gilliard, branch librarian; 4 prof, 3 para-prof, 6 non-prof staff; $27,690 materials budget; part of system budget; 40,000 volumes; 200 periodicals; children's services only—120 filmloops, 94 cassettes, 1,261 recordings, 392 filmstrips, 478 study prints, 112 games, 44 16mm films; ILL; copying; teletype no. 910-221-1401; general collection.

The Community Library is located in the Woodson Regional Library, a new concept in library service. It was opened December 19, 1975, on the 100th birthday of Carter G. Woodson.

Douglass Branch Library*
3353 West 13th Street
Chicago, Illinois 60623   (312) 762-3725

Wallace Williams, branch librarian; 5 prof, 16 non-prof staff; $3,375 materials budget; part of system budget; 81,904 volumes; 108 periodicals; 615 phonodiscs, 69 filmstrips, 9 16mm films; ILL; copying; teletype no. 910-221-1401; 68 hours weekly; Eileen Lawrence, former head librarian; general collection.

The Douglass Branch was opened at its present site in 1930. It had been located in two previous sites. *Frederick Douglass, a former slave, became one of the most articulate voices of the abolitionist movement. His autobiography, *My Bondage and My Freedom*, is an American classic. He held many posts, including police commissioner of the District of Columbia, Federal Marshal, Recorder of Deeds, and diplomat.

George C. Hall Branch Library*
4801 South Michigan Avenue
Chicago, Illinois 60615   (312) 536-2275

Eileen B. Lawrence, branch librarian; 1 prof, 2 para-prof, 12 non-prof staff; $11,975 materials budget; part of system budget; 48,584 volumes; 98 periodicals; 1 movie projector, 1 filmstrip projector, 1 tape recorder, 1 phonograph, 1 tape cassette, 12 films, 56 filmstrips, 72 multimedia sets, 992 recordings; ILL; copying; teletype no. 910-221-1401; 65 hours weekly; Vivian Harsh, Alice Scott, Ollie Coffin, Donald Joyce, former head librarians; Afro-American books and magazines.

The library opened in 1932. It housed a large Black Heritage Collection until 1975.
*Dr. George C. Hall was chief of staff, Providence Hospital in Chicago, as well as the co-founder of the Chicago Chapter of the Association for the Study of Negro Life and History. A member of the board of directors of the Chicago Public Library, he was instrumental in procuring funds from Julius Rosenwald to purchase the land on which the library that honors him is located.

George M. Pullman Branch Library
11001 South Indiana
Chicago, Illinois 60643   (312) 881-6943

Charlene Snelling, branch librarian; 1 prof, 11 non-prof staff; $13,250 materials budget; part of system budget; 54,125 volumes; 156 periodicals; 13 films, 1,279 records, 101 filmstrips;

ILL; copying; teletype no. 910-221-1401; 65 hours weekly; Dorothy Latiak, Elizabeth Woods, Mary Carroll, Sara Shaw, former head librarians; historic files of Pullman Community and environs.

The library was established in old Pullman town for the Pullman Car workers. It moved to its present site in 1926; the building was donated by Mrs. George M. Pullman.

Hamilton Park Library
7200 South Normal Boulevard
Chicago, Illinois 60621   (312) 846-7491

Idell Collins, branch librarian; 1 para-prof, 4 non-prof staff; $4,600 materials budget; part of system budget; 20,041 volumes; 40 periodicals; 60 filmstrips, 29 recordings; ILL; teletype no. 910-221-1401; 48 hours weekly; Alice Mays, Jean Scott, Barbara Thomas, Annie Allen, former head librarians; black history collection.

The library has been serving the community of the Hamilton Park Fieldhouse facility for the last 71 years.

Hiram Kelly Branch Library
6151 South Normal Boulevard
Chicago, Illinois 60621   (312) 487-1545

Naomi S. Williams, branch librarian; 2 prof, 4 para-prof, 9 non-prof staff; $23,400 materials budget; part of system budget; 85,656 volumes; 82 periodicals; 12 tape cassettes, 1,162 records, 34 films, 197 filmstrips, all keyed to the needs of all community segments; ILL; copying; teletype no. 910-221-1401; 65 hours weekly; Ellyn A. Hill, Esther Belous, Marcella McGee, Mary Farrell, former head librarians; general collection.

The library was erected in 1910 and named for its benefactor, Hiram Kelly, a leading Chicago merchant who left a legacy of $200,000 to the Chicago Public Library system.

Jeffery Manor Branch Library
2435 East 100th Street
Chicago, Illinois 60617   (312) 374-6479

Dolores Smith, branch librarian; 4 non-prof staff; $8,200 materials budget; part of system budget; 18,143 volumes; 57 periodicals; 1 filmstrip projector, 1 movie screen, 6 multimedia sets, 310 recordings; ILL; teletype no. 910-221-1401; 48 hours weekly; Jean Buchanan, Artis Pilgrim, former head librarians; emphasis on black materials.

The Jeffery Manor Branch was originally opened as a sub-branch in 1969. The neighborhood has undergone a racial change and is now predominantly black.

Legler Regional Branch Library
115 South Pulaski Road
Chicago, Illinois 60624   (312) 638-7730

Reginald Adams, branch librarian; 3 prof, 19 non-prof staff; $39,000 materials budget; part of system budget; 136,331 volumes; 339 periodicals; 1,614 phonodiscs, 82 filmstrips, 269 multimedia sets; ILL; copying; teletype no. 910-221-1401; 68 hours weekly; J. Ingrid Lesley, Alonzo Jackson, Ruth Fambro, former head librarians; black heritage collection.

Legler Regional Branch Library was the first of three regional libraries in Chicago. It was opened in 1920 serving a totally white community which is now a predominantly black one.

Lorraine B. Hansberry Branch Library*
4314 South Cottage Grove
Chicago, Illinois 60619

Raymon Hightower, branch librarian; 1 prof staff; funds for organizing this agency are being obtained from a building fund used for organizing new agencies; being organized to include 20,000+ volumes; 115 periodicals; ILL; copying; teletype no. 910-221-1401; general collection.

The Hansberry Branch Library is located on the near south side of Chicago and is housed within the Dr. Martin L. King, Jr. Community Service Center. The center, which also houses several social service agencies (such as Illinois State Unemployment, Mental Health, the Mayor's Office for Senior Citizens, and the Abraham Lincoln Day Care Center), is a new concept in which the library has become involved. *Lorraine B. Hansberry won the New York Drama Critics Award for her first play, "A Raisin in the Sun." In addition to her plays, she wrote two books. A native of Chicago, she is the only woman with a branch library of the Chicago Public Library named in her honor.

Martin Luther King, Jr. Branch Library*
3436 South King Drive
Chicago, Illinois 60616   (312) 225-7543

Jessie Fountain, branch librarian; 1 prof, 11 non-prof staff; $11,850 materials budget; part of system budget; 47,812 volumes; 88 periodicals; 708 recordings, 12 16mm films, 88 multimedia sets, 16 filmstrips; ILL; copying; teletype no. 910-221-1401; 65 hours weekly; Arlene Chamberlain, Naomi Williams, former head librarians; general collection.

The library was opened in March, 1967. It is located near several schools and large housing developments and is one of the sites of the Model Cities Library Program. *For significance of name, see DISTRICT OF COLUMBIA.

Near North Branch Library
451 West North Avenue
Chicago, Illinois 60610   (312) 664-6575

Ms. Blonnie Lee, branch librarian; 1 para-prof, 7 non-prof staff; $3,989 materials budget; part of system budget; 23,000 volumes; 40 periodicals; 40 filmstrips, 110 recordings; ILL; copying; teletype no. 910-221-1401; 48 hours weekly; Jeanne Armstrong, Ola Mae Jarrell, former head librarians; black history, children's collection.

The library has been in its present location since June, 1965. It was previously known as Olivet Institute Sub-Branch.

Roosevelt Branch Library
1329 South Racine
Chicago, Illinois 60608   (312) 666-5656

Calvin Robinson, branch librarian; 1 prof, 6 non-prof staff; $3,933 materials budget; part of system budget; 23,000 volumes; 42 periodicals; 20 filmstrips, 100 recordings; ILL; copying; teletype no. 910-221-1401; 48 hours weekly; Inalee Berry, Frances Langford, former head librarians; black history, children's collection.

The library opened in its present location in 1967. It was previously located at Taylor and Halsted Streets.

Sherman Park Branch Library
5440 South Racine
Chicago, Illinois 60617   (312) 268-1753

Annie Miller, acting branch librarian; 1 prof, 3 para-prof, 9.5 non-prof staff; $6,800 materials budget; part of system budget; 27,066 volumes; 101 periodicals; 1,427 phonodiscs, 84 filmstrips, 17 multimedia sets, 9 posters/pictures, 26 toys/games, 19 16mm films; ILL; copying; teletype no. 910-221-1401; 65 hours weekly; Janet Russell, Grace Thatcher, Viola Neeson, former head librarians; black culture and heritage.

The neighborhood around Sherman Park Branch has had library services since 1904: a reading room, 1904; a branch, 1910; and the present facility, October 18, 1973.

South Shore Branch Library
2505 East 73rd Street
Chicago, Illinois 60649   (312) 734-4780

Ms. Bernice C. Smith, branch librarian; 2 prof, 8.5 non-prof staff; $7,325 materials budget; part of system budget; 58,994 volumes; 88 periodicals; 884 phonodiscs (adult), 10 tapes and cassettes (juvenile), 342 phonodiscs (juvenile), 27 films, 186 filmstrips: ILL; copying;

teletype no. 910-221-1401; 65 hours weekly; Jane Finder, Suzanne K. Harhen, Hilda Lukas, Mildred Waters, former head librarians; general collection.

The library opened in May, 1929. The community has been in a state of transition for about ten years.

Southeast Branch Library
1934 East 79th Street
Chicago, Illinois 60649

Evelyn Stewart, branch librarian; 2 prof, 9 non-prof staff; $7,500 materials budget; part of system budget; 34,060 volumes; 93 periodicals; 886 phonodiscs, 16mm films, filmstrips, multimedia sets, toys, and games; ILL; copying; teletype no. 910-221-1401; 65 hours weekly; Adele Beaton, Raymon Hightower, former head librarians; general collection.

The library is located in a middle class business area, with predominantly privately owned homes and few apartments.

Tuley Park Sub-Branch Library
90th Street and St. Lawrence Avenue
Chicago, Illinois 60619 (312) 846-7608

Naomi Washington, branch librarian; 4 non-prof staff; $4,200 materials budget; part of system budget; 18,011 volumes; 58 periodicals; 1 filmstrip machine with record player, 134 records, 27 filmstrips; teletype no. 910-221-1401; 48 hours weekly; Ruth A. Cahill, Julia Buggs, former head librarians; Negro history, sports, music, woodcraft and sewing.

In February, 1928, a sub-branch was opened in the fieldhouse of Tuley Park.

Walker Branch Library
11071 South Hoyne
Chicago, Illinois 60643 (312) 881-6942

Sandra Weir, branch librarian; 3 prof, 1 para-prof, 8 non-prof staff; $9,600 materials budget; part of system budget; 39,587 volumes; 121 periodicals; 1,178 phonodiscs, 154 multimedia sets, 6 pictures/posters, 81 toys/games, 11 16mm films; ILL; copying; teletype no. 910-221-1401; 65 hours weekly; Suzanne Harhen, Elizabeth Woods, Marguerite Gallagher, Mildred Waters, former head librarians.

The present branch (a large building in a residential area) was Morgan Park Village Library from 1890 until April 15, 1914, when the village became part of Chicago and the library part of the Chicago Public Library branch system. The area served now is approximately 50% black residents.

Washington Park Branch Library
448 East 61st Street
Chicago, Illinois 60637 (312) 363-1168

Mrs. Nannie W. Pinkney, principal clerk; 4 non-prof staff; $4,200 materials budget; part of system budget; 14,664 volumes; 65 periodicals; 1 record player, 1 filmstrip projector, 229 recordings, 19 filmstrips, 71 multimedia sets; ILL; teletype no. 910-221-1401; 48 hours weekly; Miss Bennie Brown, Miss Irene A. Watkins, Mrs. Phyllis Stadeker, Mrs. Inez Walton, former head librarians; general collection.

Washington Park Branch Library was opened July 21, 1942, by the Chicago Public Library in a double storefront.

Wendell Smith Branch Library*
722 East 103rd Street
Chicago, Illinois 60628 (312) 995-1700

Florine E. Pratt, branch librarian; 2 prof, 2 para-prof, 9 non-prof staff; $10,500 materials budget; part of system budget; 31,000 volumes; 90 periodicals; 1 filmstrip projector, other equipment can be borrowed from the schools' collection (see below); teletype no. 910-221-1401; 65 hours weekly; general collection.

Wendell Smith Branch was opened to the public on September 11, 1974. It is a joint school-public facility serving both school and public during the day and night hours. *Wendell Smith was a prominent sportswriter and sportscaster with radio station WGN in Chicago. Very active in the promotion of black athletes, he assisted Jackie Robinson during his early years in professional baseball and wrote *The Jackie Robinson Story*.

Whitney M. Young, Jr. Branch Library*
7901 South Dr. Martin Luther King, Jr. Drive
Chicago, Illinois 60619   (312) 723-2133 or 723-4029

Hattie L. Power, branch librarian; 3 prof, 13 non-prof staff; $13,000 materials budget; part of system budget; 60,000 volumes; 100 periodicals; 1,500 records; ILL; copying; teletype no. 910-221-1401; 65 hours weekly; Ms. Evelyn Morgan, Mrs. Naomi S. Williams, Mrs. Bernice Tolles, former head librarians; black heritage collection.

The Chatham Branch Library was officially opened in 1927. The building of the new branch was commenced in 1970, and on September 13, 1973, the Chatham Branch became the Whitney M. Young, Jr. Branch Library. *Whitney M. Young, Jr., served as Executive Director of the National Urban League from 1961 to 1971. A prominent advocate of social justice for Afro-Americans, he received the nation's highest civilian award, the Medal of Freedom from President Johnson in 1969.

Woodlawn Regional Branch Library
6247-49 South Kimbark Avenue
Chicago, Illinois 60637   (312) 752-3761

Mae Gregory, branch librarian; 2 prof, 17 non-prof staff; $35,600 materials budget; part of system budget; 118,575 volumes; 284 periodicals; 49 films, 290 filmstrips, 1,830 phonodiscs; ILL; copying; teletype no. 910-221-1401; 65 hours weekly; Calvin Robinson, Elizabeth Taylor, Alice Scott, Jane Finder, former head librarians; general collection.

Woodlawn Regional Branch Library was established in 1917. The present building was erected in 1938-1939.

Rockford

Montague Library Center
1238 South Winnebago Street
Rockford, Illinois 61102   (815) 965-1912

Estelle M. Black, branch librarian; 1 prof, 3 non-prof staff; $2,728 (1975) materials budget; $41,218 (1975) operating budget; 18,373 volumes; 107 periodicals; 381 phonograph records, 39 kits, 27 sound filmstrips, 50 games, 15 filmstrips, 1 16mm film, 18 tape cassettes; ILL; copying; teletype no. 910-631-3428; 32 hours weekly; Polly Hays, Jan Sarver, Mary Gene Winne, Dorothy Church, former head librarians; black literature, Spanish literature.

From 1913 to 1918, the library was a deposit collection in a community center; in 1918, a branch was established in a room of a neighborhood school; in 1922, a voter referendum passed for a new building; and May 1923, the building was dedicated. In 1971, one half of the building was converted to a Community Information Center as part of a special effort to reach the unserved; in 1972 a licensed pre-school program was initiated.

West End Branch Library
1618 West State Street
Rockford, Illinois 61102   (815) 963-8532

Marilyn Rehnberg, branch librarian; 1 prof, 2 non-prof staff; $2,354 (1975) materials budget; $30,067 (1975) operating budget; 14,013 volumes; 30 periodicals; 192 phonograph records, 11 kits, 38 sound filmstrips, 21 games; ILL; copying; teletype no. 910-631-3428; 30 hours weekly; Arthur Means, Gail Reeves, Marian Brown, Elaine McHone, former head librarians; general collection.

The library was established in 1917 in a rented storefront on a main traffic artery. This is in a low income, transition neighborhood. Most users are very young or very old. Successful art/crafts programming.

INDIANA

Evansville

East Branch
840 E. Chandler Avenue
Evansville, Indiana   (812) 425-2621

Mrs. Carolyn Outlaw, branch librarian; 4.5 non-prof staff; $4,000 materials budget; $33,146 operating budget; 18,000 volumes; 95 periodicals; phonograph records; ILL; copying; teletype no. 810-353-0580; 56 hours weekly; Zella Lockhart (1920-1947), Bettye E. Miller (1947-1969), Frances Klinger (1969-1971), Huge E. Hunt (1971-1974), former head librarians; Afro-American history, biography, studies.

East Branch was one of two gifts from the Carnegie Corporation in 1912. It served the carriage trade until the mid-sixties when the neighborhood began to change and use of the agency began to decline.

Fort Wayne

Pontiac Branch Library
3304 Warsaw Street
Fort Wayne, Indiana 46806   (219) 444-0403

Mary Jane Wood, branch librarian; 1 prof, 1 non-prof staff; $9,000 materials budget; part of system budget; 32,963 volumes; 56 periodicals; AV in central library collection; ILL; copying; teletype no. 810-332-1409; 69 hours weekly; Mavis Dean, Robert Vegeler, Virginia Williams, former head librarians; general collection.

The library is located in a mixed neighborhood. It has its own building with community room for meetings and viewing pictures.

Hammond

Brooks House Branch Library
1047 Conkey Street
Hammond, Indiana 46320   (219) 931-5100, ext. 64

Willie Mae Durr, branch librarian; 1 para-prof, 2 non-prof staff; $3,000 materials budget; $15,000 operating budget; 9,620 volumes; 28 periodicals; record player and vocational materials; ILL; 28 hours weekly; Georgia Barnett, Norma Bethea, Sue Erickson, former head librarians; general collection.

The library was established in 1919. It is located in a neighborhood community center.

Indianapolis

Brightwood Branch Library
2435 North Sherman Drive
Indianapolis, Indiana 46218   (317) 546-1910

Mr. Charles Ransom, branch librarian; 2 prof, 1 non-prof staff; $9,364 materials budget; $40,000 operating budget; 18,967 volumes; 43 periodicals; projector and screen, with other AV equipment available through films division; ILL; 44 hours weekly; Mrs. Inez Babb, Mrs. Mary Ann Parks, James Leachman, Ms. Gilda Bothwell, former head librarians; concentration on Afro-American materials, but not any exclusive subject specialization.

The library opened in rented building in 1901. It has moved four times and has been in its present quarters since 1971.

IOWA

Des Moines

Mid City Library Information Center
1305 University Avenue
Des Moines, Iowa 50314   (515) 283-4070

Daniel M. Bakke, branch librarian; 1 prof, 4.5 non-prof staff; approximately $20,000 materials budget; approximately $50,000 operating budget; 13,000 volumes; 30 periodicals; 300 records, 120 cassettes and filmstrips, 3 recorders, and various equipment for loan; ILL; copying; teletype no. 910-520-2665; 59 hours weekly; Donald Dimmitt, former head librarian; black studies.

The library began in one room in 1972, moved to old community center later that year, and moved to its new building in January, 1976.

KANSAS
Wichita

Wichita Public Library
223 South Main
Wichita, Kansas 67202   (316) 265-5281

Ola Mae Sanders, branch librarian; 3 non-prof staff; part of system budget; 18,500 volumes; ILL; copying; teletype no. 910-741-5989; 62.5 hours weekly; Ruth Hammond (1923-1948), Ford Rockwell (1948-1976), former head librarians; books on blacks.

The library has enjoyed branch status for 10 years. Originally, it was located in a recreation room of a park. It will soon become part of a new neighborhood center.

KENTUCKY
Louisville

Harris Memorial Branch*
1719 South 34th Street
Louisville, Kentucky 40211   (502) 778-7067

Mrs. Martha McCoy, area head; 1 prof, 1 non-prof staff; $2,574 materials budget; $10,706.96 operating budget; 8,500 volumes; 7 periodicals; ILL; 20 hours weekly; Mrs. Madge Bulware, Mrs. Benjamin Jordon, former head librarians; general collection.

The Harris Branch opened in 1954 in the Cotter Homes housing project. * Mrs. Rachel Harris was formerly head of the Western Branch Library Negro Division.

Parkland Branch Library
2743 Virginia Avenue
Louisville, Kentucky 40211   (502) 772-1212

Mrs. Martha McCoy, area head; 2 prof, 2 non-prof staff; $6,000 materials budget; $23,596.84 operating budget; 22,535 volumes; 54 periodicals; ILL; 44 hours weekly; Mrs. Ruth Harn, Mrs. May Alyce Stinger, Miss Laura Jefferies, Miss Jessie M. Taylor, former head librarians; general collection.

A $20,000 building was erected in 1908 with funds from the Andrew Carnegie Foundation. It was formerly an all white branch in a blue collar neighborhood.

Shawnee Branch Library
3912 West Broadway
Louisville, Kentucky 40211   (502) 774-5122

Mrs. Martha McCoy, area head; 2 prof, 1 non-prof staff; $6,000 materials budget; $38,708.08 operating budget; 23,157 volumes; 63 periodicals; ILL; 35 hours weekly; Mrs. May McClure Curray, Miss Alma St. Clair, former head librarians; general collection.

The first Shawnee Branch was opened in 1922 and was destroyed by a flood in 1937. The new building was built with $30,000 of WPA funds in 1938. The branch was formerly in an all white, middle class neighborhood; now it is in a middle to upper class black neighborhood.

Western Branch Library
604 South Tenth Street
Louisville, Kentucky   (502) 584-5526

Mrs. Ruth Harry, branch librarian; 1 prof, 2 non-prof staff; $7,722 materials budget; $31,776.75 operating budget; 49,297 volumes; 71 periodicals; ILL; 44 hours weekly; Mrs. Naomi Lattimore, Mrs. Rachel Harris, Mr. Thomas F. Blue, former head librarians; black literature.

Western Branch was built from a Carnegie grant at the cost of $30,935 in 1908. In 1975, Western Branch received national landmark designation as the first Negro branch library in the United States.

LOUISIANA
Baton Rouge

Carver Branch Library*
1214 East Boulevard
Baton Rouge, Louisiana 70802   (504) 389-3360

Mrs. Robbie Mack, branch librarian; 1 non-prof staff; $11,214.64 operating budget; 14,191 volumes; 18 periodicals; ILL; 39.5 hours weekly; Mrs. Laverne Baker, Mrs. Mary Blakes, Mrs. Mattie Bennett, former head librarians; black history.

The Carver Branch opened in April, 1943, at 1263 Government Street; it later moved to a Louise Street location. It has been at its present location since 1959. *George Washington Carver, the famous Afro-American agricultural scientist, was born a slave in Missouri. Dr. Carver made many scientific discoveries and dedicated his life to teaching and research at Tuskegee Institute.

Scotlandville Branch Library
1492 Harding Boulevard
Baton Rouge, Louisiana 70807   (504) 389-3360

Mrs. Marsha Harrison, branch librarian; 2 non-prof staff; $25,983.91 operating budget; 11,086 volumes; 31 periodicals; movies, projector and screen provided through Main Library; ILL; 49.5 hours weekly; black history.

The Scotlandville Branch opened in July, 1974.

New Orleans

Nora Navra Memorial Branch Library
1902 St. Bernard Avenue
New Orleans, Louisiana 70116   (504) 947-6822

Bruce Horton, branch librarian; 0.5 prof staff, 2 non-prof staff; approximately $5,000 materials budget; part of system budget; 20,000 volumes; 39 periodicals; all audio visual materials of the library system are available to branch from central location and branch owns projector, screen, and other hardware; ILL; copying; 40 hours weekly; Barbara Belisle, Mary Mayo, Mike Wiltenmuth, former head librarians; general collection.

Dedicated on May 2, 1954, and designed by Jules de la Vergne to house 15,000 volumes at a cost of $60,000.00, this branch is a small neighborhood library serving a compact community.

MICHIGAN
Detroit

Abraham Lincoln Branch Library
1221 East Seven Mile Road
Detroit, Michigan 48203   (313) 833-9813

Patricia E. Smee, branch librarian; 4 prof staff, 2.25 non-prof staff; $19,550.00 materials budget; part of system budget; 28,500 volumes; 122 periodicals; 15mm sound film projector for use in the building, 50 record albums, 100 cassette tapes, 125 records and 300 tapes; ILL; copying; 40 hours weekly; Marsha Allen, Aleda Cady, Olga Pobutsky, Kathleen J. Schwab, former head librarians; general collection.

The library was established in 1926 as the North Woodward Branch, and it moved to its present location October 29, 1951. The building has 6,078 square feet with a capacity of 24,000 volumes. In 1956, a special weekly program for Senior Citizens was begun. Pre-School Story Hour and Consumer Programs are offered, and free meeting space is available to civic groups, block clubs, and scouting organizations.

Duffield Branch
2507 West Grand Boulevard
Detroit, Michigan 48208   (313) 833-9808

James Evenhuis, branch librarian; 4 prof, 3 non-prof staff; approximately $15,000 materials budget; part of system budget; 19,000 volumes; 72 periodicals; 1 16mm movie projector and screen, 1 stereo phonograph, 2 filmstrip projectors, 20 LP records (popular in nature, circulating), 12 filmstrips dealing with black materials; ILL; copying; 40 hours weekly; Ellen Sibley, Doris McLeod, Alice Downs, Virginia Dickerson, former head librarians; only specialization books are on black America.

Duffield opened just prior to World War I and has continuously served a community of approximately 50,000 persons in the near-west side area of Detroit.

Frederick Douglass Branch Library*
3666 Grand River
Detroit, Michigan 48208   (313) 833-9714

Mrs. Sue Hoag, branch librarian; 3 prof, 2.5 non-prof staff; $20,400 materials budget; part of system budget; 25,000 volumes; 72 periodicals; 681 phonograph records, films available from main library for viewing at branch, unknown number of Model Neighborhood films available for loan from Main Library; ILL; copying; 40 hours weekly; Mrs. Jane Morgan, former head librarian; general collection.

Frederick Douglass Branch opened in 1971 with Mrs. Jane Morgan, now deputy director, as head librarian. *Renowned American abolitionist. See entry under CHICAGO, ILLINOIS.

Gabriel Richard Branch Library
9876 West Grand River
Detroit, Michigan 48204   (313) 833-9763

Carol Bignell, branch librarian; 3 prof, 4.5 non-prof staff; $15,900 materials budget; part of system budget; 20,922 volumes; 83 periodicals; approximately 250 records, circulating; ILL; copying; 40 hours weekly; Patricia Smee, Freddie Mae Brown, Jane Wickham, Virginia Kelte, former head librarians; black culture.

The library was opened in 1923 and dedicated to the memory of Fr. Gabriel Richard, a French Catholic priest.

George V. Lothrop Branch Library
1529 West Grand Boulevard
Detroit, Michigan 48208   (313) 833-9710

Mamie Might, branch librarian; 4 prof, 3.5 non-prof staff; $15,870 materials budget; part of system budget; 15,277 volumes; 71 periodicals; records, juvenile picture file; ILL; copying; 40 hours weekly; Helen Bennett, Virginia Dickerson, Helen Wilkinson, Olga Pobutsky, former head librarians; black history.

The library was opened in December, 1912. It is named for George Van Ness Lothrop, for many years a Minister to Russia and then Attorney General of Michigan. It was built with aid of a grant of $40,000 from the Carnegie Foundation.

Gray Branch in Butzel Family Center
7737 Kercheval
Detroit, Michigan 48214   (313) 833-9154

Dorothy S. Baker, branch librarian; 4 prof, 4 non-prof staff; $14,000 materials budget; part of system budget; 13,100 volumes; 79 periodicals; one movie projector; ILL; copying; 48 hours weekly; Mrs. Mary Masterton, Mr. Kenneth Nielson, Miss Jeanne Norris, Mrs. Alice James, former head librarians; general collection.

On June 1, 1976, Gray Branch Library had been giving service to Detroit's public for seventy years. The branch, located on the east side of the city, was at its original location, 1117 Field Street, for sixty-eight years. With a shifting of population, services declined considerably. In April 1975, the branch was relocated and is now housed in the Butzel Family Center, six blocks away from the old location. The Center, a multi-center, houses many other agencies. Putting the library in the midst of these services has increased its use.

Mark Twain Branch Library
8500 Gratiot Avenue
Detroit, Michigan 48213   (313) 833-9150

Mrs. Alice E. James, branch librarian; 3 prof, 8 non-prof staff; $16,700 materials budget; part of system budget; 40,000 volumes; 35 periodicals; ILL; copying; Miss Elsie Gordon, Miss Helen Ransom, Miss Dorothy Hagberg, Mrs. Emmy Lou Wilson, former head librarians; general collection.

Mark Twain Branch opened formally in 1939. It was originally named George Osivs Branch in 1913, and was renamed Mark Twain in 1939.

Parkman Branch Library
1766 Oakman Boulevard
Detroit, Michigan 48238   (313) 833-9770

Alice Downs, branch librarian; 4 prof, 5 non-prof staff; $20,400 materials budget; part of system budget; 50,000 volumes; 94 periodicals; 36 cassettes, 500 recordings; ILL; copying; 40 hours weekly; Doris McLeod, Virginia Dickerson, Kenneth Hartline, Thekla Hodgson, former head librarians; black America.

The library was opened in 1931 as a regional branch library in a largely Jewish community.

Flint

North Flint Branch Library
North Flint Shopping Plaza
West Pearson and Detroit Street
Flint, Michigan 48505   (313) 785-9879

Catherine Alexander, branch librarian; 3.25 prof, 2.5 non-prof staff; $13,080 materials budget; $55,000 operating budget; 20,266 volumes; 73 periodicals; 640 recordings; ILL; copying; 43 hours weekly; adult collection arranged by Detroit Reader Interest, black life and literature, Spanish and American Indian literature.

The branch is located in a shopping center facility located at the north end of the city. It opened October 16, 1973, in a renovated retail store.

MINNESOTA

Minneapolis

Hosmer Community Library
347 East 36th Street
Minneapolis, Minnesota 55408   (612) 824-4848

Ruth Johnson, head of community libraries; 1 prof, 0.5 para-prof, 2 non-prof staff; $811,887 system materials budget; $5,560,272 system operating budget; 18,085 volumes; 6,564 periodicals (entire system); phonodiscs and cassettes; ILL; copying; 50 hours weekly; emphasis on black history and black culture.

Hosmer Community Library is located on the south side of the city, serving a population of middle income citizens. Blacks have always resided in the area. The branch was erected in 1916 with bond money for land and a Carnegie grant for the building.

Sumner Community Library
611 Emerson Avenue North
Minneapolis, Minnesota 55411   (612) 374-5642

Ruth Johnson, head of community libraries; 1 prof, 0.5 para-prof, 2 non-prof staff; $811,887 system materials budget; $5,560,272 system operating budget; 14,278 volumes; 6,564 periodicals (entire system); phonodiscs and cassettes; ILL; copying; 50 hours weekly; emphasis on black history and black culture.

MISSOURI
St. Louis

Cabanne Branch Library
1106 Union Boulevard
St. Louis, Missouri 63113   (314) 367-0717

Mrs. Lois Stovall, branch librarian; 1 prof, 3.5 non-prof staff; $8,050 materials budget; $59,597 operating budget; 21,171 volumes; 73 periodicals; educational videotape cassettes, phonodiscs; ILL; copying; teletype no. 910-761-1120; 47 hours weekly; Miss Jane McFarlane, Miss Marcella Ahrens, Mrs. Ida H. Shaw, Mrs. Vera B. Heim, former head librarians; general collection.

Cabanne Branch opened on July 29, 1907, at 1106 Union Boulevard in the St. Louis suburb of Cabanne. This building was built with Carnegie funds and the structure was extensively remodeled in 1967.

Crunden Branch Library
2008 Cass Avenue
St. Louis, Missouri 63106   (314) 241-6639

Miss Barbara Stewart, branch librarian; 1 prof, 2.5 non-prof staff; $6,100 materials budget; $46,041 operating budget; 23,875 volumes; 44 periodicals; phonodiscs; ILL; copying; teletype no. 910-761-1120; 35 hours weekly; Michael E. Powell, Mrs. Thelma Price, Mrs. Ellen Q. Clauss, former head librarians; general collection.

The present Crunden Branch was opened December 21, 1959, in the Pruitt-Igoe Housing area. It replaced the Carnegie-funded Crunden building located at 14th Street and Cass Avenue, which opened on September 11, 1909, in honor of Frederick M. Crunden, Librarian of St. Louis Public Library from 1877 to 1909.

Des Peres Branch Library
5960 Kingsbury Boulevard
St. Louis, Missouri 63112   (314) 726-2653

Mrs. Jean Roberts, branch librarian; 1 prof, 3.5 non-prof staff; $6,700 materials budget; $54,376 operating budget; 21,736 volumes; 64 periodicals; phonodiscs; ILL; copying; teletype no. 910-761-1120; 48 hours weekly; Mrs. Judith Schneider, Mr. Dale Poertner, Mrs. Patricia Smith, Miss Jane McFarlane, former head librarians; general collection.

Des Peres Branch opened in rented quarters March 26, 1963, at 6003 Kingsbury Boulevard. It was moved to larger rented facilities at 5960 Kingsbury Boulevard in 1970.

Divoll Branch Library
4234 North Grand Boulevard
St. Louis, Missouri 63107   (314) 534-0313

Michael E. Powell, branch librarian; 2 prof, 3.5 non-prof staff; $8,970 materials budget; $71,203 operating budget; 22,947 volumes; 76 periodicals; 8-track cassettes, phonodiscs, ILL; copying; teletype no. 910-716-1120; 51 hours weekly; Miss Ruth Brennan, Miss Margaret G. Curran, former head librarians; general collection.

The new branch of Divoll was dedicated on April 16, 1967. Divoll Branch was originally opened on December 5, 1910, and named for Ira Divoll, Superintendent of Schools in St. Louis from 1857 to 1868.

John Berry Meachum Branch Library*
3701 Grandel Square
St. Louis, Missouri 63108   (314) 652-3319

Mrs. Jeanette Smith, branch librarian; 1 prof, 2.5 non-prof staff; $6,960 materials budget; $47,034 operating budget; 8,539 volumes; 33 periodicals; 8-track cassettes, phonodiscs; ILL; copying; teletype no. 910-761-1120; 46½ hours weekly; Mr. Robert Robinson, Mr. Fred Rogers, Jr., former head librarians; black literature.

The Meachum Branch was formerly the Mid-City Branch, which opened January 17, 1971, at 3974 Delmar Boulevard after three years of effort between the library and the Mid-City Community Congress, Inc., under a federal grant. It was moved to Vandeventer and Washington and, in 1974, was re-named the John Berry Meachum Branch and moved to 3701 Grandel Square in the St. Louis Urban League Building. *John Berry Meachum was born a slave in Virginia, May 3, 1789. He bought his freedom and gained an education. In 1825, he founded the First African Baptist Church in St. Louis and became a widely respected abolitionist and educator.

Julia Davis Branch Library*
4666 Natural Bridge Road
St. Louis, Missouri 63115   (314) 383-3021

Dudley Colbert, branch librarian; 1 prof, 2.5 non-prof staff; $8,270 materials budget; $50,906 operating budget; 20,952 volumes; 85 periodicals; filmstrips, phonodiscs; ILL; copying; teletype no. 910-761-1120; 46 hours weekly; Miss Karen McAdoo, Miss Robbie Porter, Mrs. Penny Peterson, Mr. Benjamin Zabel, former head librarians; black literature.

This branch, originally named the Sherman Park Branch, moved several times after its initial opening on April 17, 1925, in the Sherman Park Community House. In 1974, it was moved to its present location and re-named. *Julia Davis is a beloved and respected retired Afro-American public school teacher. She is also a researcher in Afro-American history and a contributor to the St. Louis Public Library.

Wellston Branch Library
5886 Dr. Martin Luther King Drive
St. Louis, Missouri 63112   (314) 385-4042

Mrs. Esther Cline, branch librarian; 1 prof, 2.5 non-prof staff; $6,925 materials budget; $51,756 operating budget; 22,582 volumes; 59 periodicals; phonodiscs; ILL; copying; teletype no. 910-761-1120; 42½ hours weekly; Miss Carolyn Herbert, Miss Karen McAdoo, Mrs. Lois Stovall, Mrs. Agnes McBride, former head librarians; general collection.

The Wellston Branch was opened March 3, 1925, as a sub-branch in a store room that was provided rent free for three years through the efforts of the Wellston Chamber of Commerce. The present Wellston Branch opened March 26, 1964, at 5886 Easton Avenue, now Dr. Martin Luther King Drive.

NEBRASKA

Omaha

North Branch Library
29th and Ames
Omaha, Nebraska 68111   (402) 451-4388

Mrs. Carolyn Green, branch librarian; 2 prof, 2 non-prof staff; $10,400 materials budget; part of system budget; 26,665 volumes; 74 periodicals; 1 16mm projector (sound), 1 filmstrip projector, 1 tape recorder-player, 1 record player, 1 sound-filmstrip projector; ILL; copying; teletype no. 910-622-0755; 70 hours weekly; Julanne Brown, Saundra Harry, Doris Mayfield, Inga Anderson, former head librarians; some emphasis on black heritage.

An earlier building was constructed in 1938 and replaced by a new one in October, 1972. It received a First Honor award from the American Institute of Architects in 1974.

Kellom Branch Library
2211 Paul Street
Omaha, Nebraska 68102   (402) 345-0334

Mrs. Wanda Fagan, branch librarian; 1 prof, 0.5 non-prof staff; $4,800 materials budget; part of system budget; 9,552 volumes; 34 periocials; 1 tape recorder, 1 filmstrip projector, 2 record players, 1 sound filmstrip projector, access to 16mm projector on request; ILL; teletype no. 910-622-0755; 39.5 hours weekly; some emphasis on black heritage.

A community club library became a small branch of the Omaha Public Library in the Logan Fontenelle Multi-Service Center when it was built in February 1971.

NEVADA
Las Vegas

West Las Vegas Library
1402 North "D" Street
Las Vegas, Nevada 89106 (702) 648-9421

G. William Ludwig, branch librarian; 3 prof, 1 non-prof staff; $7,000 plus special grant funds materials budget; approximately $60,000 operating budget; 15,000 volumes; 90 periodicals; resources of entire system plus 25 black films, 300 cassettes, 500 records, 25 filmstrip/slide sets, 5,000 picture file, 100 posters/art reproductions, 6 cassette players, all of which are circulating; ILL; copying; teletype no. 910-397-6890; 58 hours weekly; black resource materials, community information, strong community involvement and programming.

The library was established because of community pressure and opened in December 1973.

NEW JERSEY
Jersey City

Claremont Branch Library
291 Martin Luther King Drive
Jersey City. New Jersey 07305 (201) 435-6262

Branch librarian position vacant as of March 25, 1976; 1 prof, 2 non-prof staff; approximately $1,000 materials budget; part of system budget; approximately 4,000 volumes; 54 periodicals; 1 record player, 1 16mm film projector, 1 filmstrip projector, 1 screen, phonograph records and filmstrips; ILL; copying; 30 hours weekly; Spencer Brown, Florence Gibbs, Valentine Allen, former head librarians; black history and culture, consumer information.

The library was opened in 1954 in a white residential/commercial area. As the area changed to a largely black populace, the branch was relocated in a prominent location on the main business street, easily accessible to all parts of the community.

Newark

Clinton Branch Library
739 Bergen Street
Newark, New Jersey 07108 (201) 733-7757

Wilhelmina Person, branch librarian; 3 prof, 3 non-prof staff; $4,950 materials budget; $62,300 operating budget; 25,000 volumes; 111 periodicals; films, filmstrips and recordings provided from Main Library for programs; ILL; copying; 46.5 hours weekly; Walter Pezda, Della Elsenberg, former head librarians; black history and culture, occupational training and careers.

The library opened in 1925. It originally served a large Jewish and German population and the neighborhood is now predominantly black.

Springfield Branch Library
50 Hayes Street
Newark, New Jersey 07103 (201) 733-7736

Lewis Graves, branch librarian; 3 prof, 2 non-prof staff; $4,700 materials budget; $59,000 operating budget; 25,200 volumes; 111 periodicals; recordings, films, and filmstrips provided from Main Library for programs; ILL; 44 hours weekly; J. Bernard Schein, Eleln Weitz, Ruth Stevenson, Mary Pannon, former head librarians; black history and culture, vocational training and career information.

The library opened in 1923. The neighborhood was largely Slavic, Jewish, and Greek; it is now a black community.

Weeguchic Branch Library
355 Osborne Terrace
Newark, New Jersey 07108   (201) 733-7751

Dolores Whitehead, branch librarian; 3 prof, 3 non-prof staff; $4,850 materials budget; $62,000 operating budget; 42,800 volumes; 111 periodicals; films, filmstrips, and recordings provided from Main Library for programs; ILL; 42.5 hours weekly; James Brown, Edward Small, Harriet Spottiswoode, Lillias Nichols, former head librarians; black history and culture, vocational training and career materials.

The library opened in 1929 and originally served a mostly Jewish population; the community is now predominantly black.

Paterson

First Ward Branch Library
56 North Main Street
Paterson, New Jersey 07522   (201) 742-0992

Bertha Hinton, branch librarian; 3 non-prof staff; $5,300 materials budget; $23,000 operating budget; 17,500 volumes; 60 periodicals; System 80 teaching machine, record player; ILL; copying; 40 hours weekly; Lilliam Worman, Cesarina Augusto, Anne Soskin, Mrs. De Vries, former head librarians; general collection.

The library opened in October 1907, at 98 North Main Street. It moved to its present location on February 16, 1942.

Trenton

East Trenton Branch Library
North Clinton and Girard Avenue
Trenton, New Jersey 08618   (609) 392-7188

Howard Crossland, branch librarian; 1 prof, 3 non-prof staff; 18,000 volumes; film projector and screen, and all other equipment is borrowed from the Main Library; ILL; copying; 45 hours weekly; Mrs. Mildred Norris, Lus Aletha, Ramsdell Ditmars, former head librarians; general collection.

The library opened in the old Dickenson Building on November 10, 1926. For a period of 7 months the library was located in temporary quarters while the building was being renovated; it was reopened on November 1, 1934.

NEW YORK

Albany

Arbor Hill Branch Library
50 North Lark Street
Albany, New York 12208   (518) 463-7803

Hemwatie Jaipershad, branch librarian; 2 prof, 1 non-prof staff; $2,800 materials budget; $28,000 operating budget; 12,000 volumes; 41 periodicals; films are available at main library; ILL; copying; teletype no. 518-474-5269; 39 hours weekly; some emphasis on black history, politics, literature and the arts.

The library was established in March 1973, in response to community requests for library services in the Arbor Hill area.

John A. Howe Branch Library
Schuyler, Broad & Clinton Streets
Albany, New York 12202   (518) 472-9485

George W. Vealey, branch librarian; 2 prof, 2 non-prof staff; $10,830 materials budget; $91,386 operating budget; 10,000 volumes; 66 periodicals; 16mm sound movie projector, 1 cassette filmstrip projector, 3 headsets, 1 cassette recorder/player, and all 16mm films, filmstrips, and records that are held by the Albany Public Library are used as well; ILL; teletype no. 518-474-5269; 42.5 hours weekly; John A. Howe, Lillian Callaham, Mary Collins, Hertensia Stoyan, Barbara Smith, former head librarians; black history books by and about black people, high interest-low reading level materials.

The library was established in 1891, and the present building was built in 1929. Service to the foreign-born was first emphasized, then in 1932, black programs and collection began. The majority of patrons are now black.

Brooklyn

Bedford Branch Library
496 Franklin Avenue
Brooklyn, New York 11238   (212) 638-9544

Clara Mayer, branch librarian; 3 prof, 9 non-prof staff; $17,350 materials budget; part of system budget; 17,400 volumes; 100 periodicals; 440 records and cassettes; ILL; copying; teletype no. 212-488-3529; black history and literature.

The library is located in a 1904 Carnegie Building; Bedford was the first branch of the Brooklyn Public Library built in the middle of a wealthy white residential neighborhood. The 1920s and 30s brought a population shift, so that the neighborhood is now black. The building was rehabilitated in 1966. It houses the office and collection of the Bookmobiles. In addition, Bed-Stuy Youth Council uses the premises, as does the Library's Bed-Stuy Community Coordinator.

Brower Park Library
725 St. Marks Avenue
Brooklyn, New York 11216   (212) 778-6262

Doris P. Graham, branch librarian; 2 prof, 4 non-prof staff; $15,200 materials budget; part of system budget; 13,508 volumes; 122 periodicals; browsing collection of 764 records for adults and juveniles; ILL; copying; teletype no. 212-488-3529; 35 hours weekly; general collection.

Brower Park was named in honor of George V. Brower (Commissioner of Parks in Brooklyn for 13 years) and was opened to the public for service on July 30, 1963.

Brownsville Community Library
61 Glenmore Avenue
Brooklyn, New York 11212   (212) 345-1212

Mrs. Anna Fluker, center manager; served by New Lots District Adult and Children's Specialists; 5 non-prof staff; $11,900 materials budget; part of system budget; 14,505 volumes; 60 periodicals; ILL; copying; teletype no. 212-488-3529; 26 hours weekly; public library service to adults, children and young people, with popular black and Hispanic collections highlighted.

The Brownsville Community Library marked its 70th year of service in 1975. During the early years, immigrant groups (predominantly Russian and Polish Jews) used the library, and in 1909, Brownsville led the library system in circulation. The children's department shifted to a new branch in 1914—the Brownsville Children's Branch at Stone and Dumont Avenues. Many Negroes and Italians used the Brownsville Branch during the lean 1930s. 1950 saw an "upsurge in activity" with the restoration of children's services. The Brownsville Branch became the Brownsville Community Library, a satellite of the New Lots District Library in the 1960s. Today, 95% of the users of the Brownsville Community Library are of black or Hispanic descent.

Clinton Hill Branch Library
380 Washington Avenue
Brooklyn, New York 11238   (212) 857-8038

Doris J. Lyda, branch librarian; 4 prof, 5 non-prof staff; $13,000 materials budget; part of system budget; 23,500 volumes; 114 periodicals; 16mm projector, phonograph, color TV, 2 cassette players, 944 records and cassettes (adult and juvenile); ILL; copying; teletype no. 212-488-3529; 38 hours weekly; special black studies collection.

Clinton is a new branch library that opened on November 19, 1974, and provides a full range of materials and services. Community support is active and vocal.

Crown Heights Branch
560 New York Avenue
Brooklyn, New York 11225   (212) 773-1223

Mrs. Beverly Vance, branch librarian; 3.5 prof, 5 non-prof staff; $18,000 materials budget; part of system budget; 20,280 volumes; 120 periodicals; 1 16mm sound projector, 1 record player, 1 cassette tape recorder; ILL; copying; teletype no. 212-488-3529; 31 hours weekly; general collection.

Crown Heights Branch, originally established in a storefront location in 1931, moved to its current location in 1957. It is an 8,000 square foot, one-floor building that serves a fairly stable community of Hasidic Jews and West Indians.

East Flatbush Branch Library
9612 Church Avenue
Brooklyn, New York 11212   (212) 498-0033

Sara Trolinger, branch librarian; 3 prof, 3 non-prof staff; $15,000 materials budget; part of system budget; 11,559 volumes; 95 periodicals; 385 records and cassettes; ILL; copying; teletype no. 212-488-3529; 29 hours weekly; general collection.

East Flatbush was established in 1952 to serve a predominantly Jewish neighborhood, which has been changing over the years.

Eastern Parkway Branch Library
1044 Eastern Parkway
Brooklyn, New York 11213   (212) 756-5150

Frances H. Ricks, branch librarian; 5 prof, 8 non-prof staff; $22,156 materials budget; part of system budget; 26,875 volumes; 310 periodicals; 1 16mm projector, 1 AM-FM multiplex stereo; ILL; copying; teletype no. 212-488-3529; 29 hours weekly; general collection.

The branch opened in 1914 in a predominantly Jewish community. It was closed for renovation on January 14, 1970, and after extensive work, it reopened on March 13, 1972.

Macon Community Library
374 Lewis Avenue
Brooklyn, New York 11233   (212) 453-3333

Vivian Henderson, community library manager; 3 non-prof staff; $11,500 materials budget; part of system budget; 13,900 volumes; 90 periodicals; as part of the Bedford Stuyvesant Media Center, the library has access to 16mm projector, 8mm projectors, 8mm movie film cameras, 35mm slide projector, 35mm camera, filmstrip projectors, 8mm film editing equipment, record players, cassette players, rear projector screen, head set units, public announcement system, laminating machine, transparency making projector, opaque projector, TV monitors, filmstrips, 8mm films, and 35mm films; ILL; teletype no. 212-488-3529; 30 hours weekly; general collection.

Macon Branch Library opened in 1907, as one of 20 libraries in Brooklyn provided for by a grant from Andrew Carnegie. In 1963, it was converted to a community library and became part of the DeKalb District Library structure.

New Lots District Library
665 New Lots Avenue
Brooklyn, New York 11207   (212) 649-3700

Doris L. Gustafson, branch librarian; 4 prof, 7.5 non-prof staff; $22,700 materials budget; part of system budget; 20,733 volumes; 296 periodicals; filmstrip projector, film sound projector, 2 screens, record player; ILL; copying; teletype no. 212-488-3529; 35 hours weekly; adult, children's, and young people's services, black and Spanish culture sections, and a "Learn Your Way" center.

The New Lots District Library has served eastern Brooklyn for over a quarter of a century and was established and maintained by the Womens Club of the East New York "Y" from 1941 to 1949. Heavy use was made by a predominantly Jewish (of Russian and Polish descent) community during the early years. Today, black and Spanish residents make up the majority of the users. The present building is located on the site of the "Old New Lots Burying Ground."

Red Hook Community Library
7 Wolcott Street
Brooklyn, New York 11231   (212) 875-4412

Ms. Shirley S. Townes, manager; 1 prof, 5 non-prof staff; approximately $10,000 materials budget; part of system budget; approximately 15,000 volumes; 82 periodicals; 16mm movie projector, record player with headphones, movie screen, cassette tape recorder, 300 records, 75 cassettes; ILL; copying; teletype no. 212-488-3529; 31 hours weekly; general collection.

The first Red Hook Branch opened on April 22, 1915, in a Carnegie building, but eventually closed due to a fire in 1947. The following year, the branch moved into the Red Hook Housing Project but again shifted quarters to rented facilities in March 1957. In the early 1960s, the branch became a "Family Reading Center" as a satellite unit of the Prospect District. In 1975, a much larger building was erected in the heart of the Red Hook community, opening on March 17. The one-story brick structure has 7,500 square feet of space, is air-conditioned, and has a capacity for 100 in the Reference/Reading Room and 50 in its mini-auditorium.

Saratoga Community Library
8 Hopkinson Avenue
Brooklyn, New York 11233   (212) 455-3078

Douglas L. James, community library manager; 1 prof, 5 non-prof staff; $18,850 materials budget; part of system budget; 11,300 volumes; 95 periodicals; 200 records and 200 cassettes, and as part of the Bedford Stuyvesant Media Center, it has access to 16mm projectors, 8mm projectors, 8mm movie film cameras, 35mm slide projector, 35mm camera, filmstrip projectors, 8mm film editing equipment, record players, cassette players, rear projector screen, head set units, public announcement system, laminating machine, transparency making projector, opaque projector, TV monitors, filmstrips, 8mm films and 16mm films; ILL; copying; teletype no. 212-488-3529; 31 hours weekly; black history and other materials related to black culture and strong in biographies of Afro-Americans.

Saratoga Branch Library opened on Putnam Street in 1902 with less than 1,500 books. In 1908, it moved to Hopkinson Avenue into a new Carnegie building. The neighborhood remained largely German and Jewish until the 1950s, when it became a black residential area. In the 1960s, the branch was converted to a Community Library as part of the DeKalb District Library.

Stone Avenue Community Library
581 Stone Avenue
Brooklyn, New York 11212   (212) 385-3737

Mrs. Lola Eigen, library manager; 1 prof, 5 non-prof staff; $15,250 materials budget; part of system budget; 10,247 volumes; 68 periodicals; 365 discs, 9 cassettes, 16mm film projector; ILL; copying; teletype no. 212-488-3529; 29.5 hours weekly; general collection.

Stone Avenue Branch Library opened in 1914 with the first complete Children's Room in the Brooklyn Public Library System. It became a Reading Center as part of New Lots District on April 19, 1965.

Walt Whitman Community Library
93 St. Edwards Street
Brooklyn, New York 11205   (212) 855-1508

Mrs. Martha Bettis, manager; 0.4 prof, 5 non-prof staff; $15,350 materials budget (not including periodicals); part of system budget; 16,718 volumes; 68 periodicals; browsing collection of 280 phonodiscs and 31 audio tape cassettes; ILL; copying; teletype no. 212-488-3529; 30 hours weekly; black literature and Hispanic culture.

The library was first opened July 22, 1901, at 186 Bridge Street. It became the City Park Branch in 1907, and moved into the Carnegie building at the present site in September, 1908. On May 31, 1944, it was renamed Walt Whitman Branch, became Walt Whitman Reading Center in 1967, then the Walt Whitman Community Library in 1969.

Buffalo

Martin Luther King Branch Library*
451 William Street
Towne Gardens Plaza
Buffalo, New York 14204   (716) 854-2070

Mrs. Joanne Bliss, branch librarian; 2 prof, 5 non-prof staff; $4,300 materials budget ($1,600 of which is for special Black History Collection); $13,244 operating budget (includes rental but not supplies and salaries); 7,779 volumes; 71 periodicals; 16mm film projector, 2 cassette recorder-players, 1 record player, 100 viewmasters, 1 filmstrip projector, 1 video tape receiver; ILL; copying; teletype no. 716-842-4501; 48 hours weekly; Wendy Colquhoun, Linda Carroll, Denis Kay, Virginia Nestor, former head librarians; black history circulating and non-circulating collections.

This branch was known as the William Street Branch when it was opened on September 8, 1913, at 356 William Street, the center of a section in which people of many nationalities lived. In addition to the Yiddish, Hebrew, and Russian books asked for, there were requests for others in German, French, Italian, Polish, Hungarian, and Swedish. In 1918, the branch was moved to 326 William Street, to larger quarters. In 1921, it was stated that the branch was located in the most cosmopolitan district of the city. In April, 1927, the branch was moved to 433 William Street, near the largest group of black people in the city. In May, 1941, the branch moved to a newly decorated store on the corner of William and Sherman Streets (664 William Street). In 1954, the former William Street Branch was relocated in more spacious quarters in the Willert Park Community House at 406 Jefferson Avenue, and renamed Willert Park Branch. In 1972, the Willert Park Branch moved to a modern new library in the Towne Gardens Plaza at 451 William Street and was renamed the Martin Luther King Branch. *For significance of name, see DISTRICT OF COLUMBIA.

North Jefferson Branch
332 East Utica Street
Buffalo, New York 14208   (716) 883-4418

Melvin Watkins, branch librarian; 2 prof, 7 non-prof staff; $6,640 materials budget ($2,000 of which is for the Black History Collection); $4,459.04 operating budget (city-owned building, does not include salaries or supplies); 17,152 volumes; 69 periodicals; 1 16mm film projector, 1 TV, 1 record player, 50 viewmasters; ILL; copying; teletype no. 716-842-4501; 48 hours weekly; Sharon Jordan, Benjamin Williams, Linda Carroll, Peter Brand, former head librarians; black history and black culture, Buffalo Afro-American History Collection.

The Utica Street Branch was established at 306 East Utica Street on January 6, 1911. In 1928, the residents of the neighborhood gained a new building, being led by the officers of the North Jefferson Business Men's Association. The Utica Street Branch was renamed the North Jefferson Branch and opened on November 19, 1929, at 332 East Utica Street. In the 1960s, the neighborhood began to change from a predominantly Jewish community to a black community, and at present, the population served by the branch is almost entirely black. In July, 1965, the resources and services of the North Jefferson Branch were expanded as a result of funds received under the Library Services and Construction Act—Title I.

Corona

Langston Hughes Library and Cultural Center*
102-09 Northern Boulevard
Corona, New York 11368   (212) 651-1100, 651-1101

Ms. Charlyne Gadsden, Ms. Angela Vricella, branch librarians; 2 prof, 15 non-prof staff; approximately $12,000 materials budget; $180,000 operating budget; approximately 29,250 volumes (mainly paperbacks); 97 periodicals; video portapak, cassette tape recorders with sync., electronic programmer, stereo AM-FM receiver with record player, reel-to-reel tape recorder, ekta graphic visual maker, slide projector, filmstrip projector, opaque projector, color TV set, head sets, 35mm camera, public address system, color tran kit, 16mm projector; ILL; copying; 58 hours weekly; Yvonne Bennett, Gwendolyn Weaver, Martha Andujar, Judy James, former head librarians; materials to improve self image, high interest simple vocabulary, popular fiction, how-to-do-it, children's collection, children's picture books, careers, employment, Arco test books.

The library was funded in 1968 as a Neighborhood Information and Cultural Center to be operated jointly by the Queens Borough Public Library and a Board of Corona-East Elmhurst Community Residents. This center was established to experiment with non-traditional approaches in library services through community participation. The entire staff including the supervisors of the center are community residents. The professional librarians serve as advisers to the staff and community. *Langston Hughes, one of the most important American writers of the twentieth century, was the editor of several anthologies as well as a poet and lyricist. Hughes worked also in prose; *Not Without Laughter, The Big Sea, The Weary Blues, Shakespeare in Harlem*, and many other books were written by him.

New York (branches of the New York Public Library)

Countee Cullen Regional Branch Library*
104 West 136th Street
New York, New York 10030   (212) 281-0700

Jomarjo Bowen, branch librarian; 3 prof, 5 non-prof staff; $48,975 materials budget; $216,330 operating budget (estimated New York City expense); 43,052 volumes; 118 periodicals; records, cassettes, an art gallery with murals by Aaron Douglas and art work by Ellis Wilson, Jacob Lawrence, and others; ILL; copying; the James Weldon Johnson Memorial Collection contains book for children on the black experience.

The Countee Cullen Regional Branch Library is the largest library in Harlem. It was opened in 1905 at 103 West 135th Street (present home of the Schomburg Center for Research in Black Culture). In 1941, the branch was moved to its present location on 136th Street, and in 1951 it was renamed. *Countee Cullen was one of the leaders of the "Harlem Renaissance." In his 43 years of life, he published 6 volumes of poetry and one novel, *One Way to Heaven*. Following his death in 1946, a selection of his works were collected and published in a volume entitled *On These I Stand*.

George Bruce Branch Library
518 West 125th Street
New York, New York 10027   (212) 662-9727

Miriam Fleischer, branch librarian; 2 prof, 3.5 non-prof staff; $22,805 materials budget; $138,240 operating budget (estimated New York City cost); 27,365 volumes; 76 periodicals; records, cassettes, film programs, and games; ILL; copying; teletype (number not provided); 30 hours weekly; general collection.

In 1877, the daughter of a typefounder, George Bruce, gave the New York Public Library a gift of $50,000 for a library and books to be dedicated to the memory of her father. The original structure was built at 226 West 46th Street. In 1915, it was moved to its present location. It has an auditorium that is used by community groups.

Hamilton Grange Branch Library
503 West 145th Street
New York, New York 10031   (212) 926-2147

Robert Calere, branch librarian; 2 prof, 4 non-prof staff; $12,005 materials budget; $125,430 operating budget; 12,940 volumes; films; teletype no. 212-889-1238; general collection.

The branch opened in 1907, built from funds provided by the Carnegie Corporation. In 1970, it was declared a landmark building.

Harlem Branch Library
9 West 124th Street
New York, New York 10035   (212) 348-5620

Mrs. Pauline Singletary, branch librarian; 1 prof, 3 non-prof staff; $18,885 materials budget; $100,880 operating budget (estimated New York City expense); 24,000 volumes; has film programs; ILL; copying; teletype (no number provided); 29 hours weekly; general collection.

The Harlem Branch Library has served the east Harlem area since 1826, one of the first libraries to become incorporated into the branch system of the New York Public Library. The library had three homes before moving to its present site, a Carnegie building, in 1909.

Macomb's Bridge Branch Library
2650 Seventh Avenue
New York, New York 10039   (212) 281-4900

Mrs. Lillie Prioleau, branch librarian; 0.5 prof staff; $6,940 materials budget; $22,395 operating budget (estimated New York City expense); 5,563 volumes; ILL; teletype (no number provided); 17 hours weekly; black studies and the Clinton Henry Memorial Collection.

Macomb's Bridge Branch Library is in the Harlem River Houses Project. The library's unique name comes from the Macomb's Dam Bridge, which crosses the Harlem River from Manhattan to the Bronx. The library opened on July 11, 1955.

Morrisania Branch Library
610 East 169th Street
Bronx, New York 10456   (212) 589-9268

Dorothy Fludd, branch librarian; 2 prof, 3.5 non-prof staff; $24,420 materials budget; $132,760 operating budget (estimated New York City expense); 24,867 volumes; 46 periodicals; records, cassettes, film programs; ILL; copying; teletype (no number provided); 36 hours weekly; general collection.

The Morrisania Branch was opened in 1908, constructed from funds given by Andrew Carnegie. There is an auditorium used for library and community programs.

115th Street Branch Library
203 West 115th Street
New York, New York 10026   (212) 666-9393

Bonnie Sterling, branch librarian; 2 prof, 3 non-prof staff; $20,945 materials budget; $122,920 operating budget (estimated New York City expense); 19,000 volumes; 47 periodicals; records, cassettes, and film programs; ILL; copying; teletype (no number provided); 27 hours per week; general collection.

The library building was constructed from Carnegie funds and completed in 1908. Because of its "handsome facade" it was designated as a New York City Landmark Building. Community organizations make use of its auditorium for programs and meetings.

125th Street Branch Library
224 East 125th Street
New York, New York 10035   (212) 534-5050

Mrs. Rose Jackson, branch librarian; 2 prof, 2.5 non-prof staff; $20,800 materials budget; $113,150 operating budget; 20,000 volumes; 60 periodicals; records, cassettes, and film programs; ILL; teletype (no number provided); 24 hours weekly; black culture, pamphlets on Africa, American Indians, Puerto Ricans in America, and books in Spanish.

The library has served the East Harlem community since 1904. The building is a neo-Gothic structure and a gift from Carnegie. There is an activities room used for programming for library affairs and events sponsored by community groups.

Tremont Branch Library
1866 Washington Avenue
Bronx, New York 10457   (212) 299-5177

Mrs. Phyllis Mack, branch librarian; 3 prof staff; $22,825 materials budget; $104,705 operating budget (estimated New York City cost); 21,000 volumes; 45 periodicals; records and films; ILL; teletype (no number provided); 34 hours weekly; black culture, Spanish books.

The Tremont Branch has served the Bronx since 1905 from a Carnegie building. A meeting room for library programs and community groups is a feature of the building.

Washington Heights Branch Library
1000 St. Nicholas Avenue
New York, New York 10032

Constance Van Tilburg, branch librarian; 2 prof, 4 non-prof staff; $20,375 materials budget; $136,890 operating budget (estimated New York City expense); 36,237 volumes; 50 periodicals; records, cassettes, film programs, and local history collection on Washington Heights; ILL; copying; teletype (no number provided); 25 hours weekly; black history, Spanish-American history and culture.

A subscription library, opened in 1868, was the forerunner of the Washington Heights Branch. It became a free library with a $100 monthly gift from J. Hood Wright in 1883, and was named the Washington Heights Free Library. In 1901, it became a part of the New York Public Library branch system.

West Farms Branch Library
2085 Honeywell Avenue
Bronx, New York 10460   (212) 367-5376

Raymond Markey, branch librarian; 3 prof, 3 non-prof staff; $27,200 materials budget; $181,105 operating budget (estimated New York City cost); 28,432 volumes; records, cassettes; ILL; teletype (no number provided); 36 hours weekly; Spanish literature, German, French, Italian and Yiddish literature.

The library was established in 1929 and has been at its present location since 1954. The library program is varied to serve the many nationalities that make up its clientele.

Woodstock Branch Library
761 East 16th Street
Bronx, New York 10456   (212) 635-9068

Mrs. Theresa Lott, branch librarian; 3 prof, 3 non-prof staff; $22,970 materials budget; $146,280 operating budget (estimated cost borne by New York City); 30,000 volumes; 42 periodicals; records, cassettes, and film programs; ILL; copying; teletype (no number provided); 32 hours weekly; general collection.

The library was established in its present location in 1917 in a building given by Andrew Carnegie. A very active branch, it is used by many community groups.

Rochester

Lincoln Branch Library
585 Clifford Avenue
Rochester, New York 14621   (716) 232-4554

Audrey Wright, branch librarian; 3 prof, 5.5 non-prof staff; $15,400 materials budget; $80,000 operating budget; 21,000 volumes; 70 periodicals; 725 recordings, 150 16mm films, 325 8mm films, 200 filmstrips, 25 slide sets; ILL; teletype no. 716-546-5330; 43 hours weekly; David Thompson, Linda Bretz, Berenice Milner, former head librarians; general collection.

The library opened in 1915 in rented quarters and moved in 1925 to a city-purchased building. The building was remodeled and refurbished in 1969-70.

Phillis Wheatley Community Library*
13 Bronson Avenue
Rochester, New York 14608   (716) 235-3682

James Wright, branch librarian; 3 prof, 5.5 non-prof staff; $14,125 materials budget; $95,500 operating budget; 32,000 volumes; 103 periodicals; 2,300 recordings, 175 16mm films, 250 8mm films, 180 filmstrips, 36 slide sets; ILL; teletype no. 716-546-5330; 43 hours weekly; Afro-American literature and studies, high interest, low reading level materials.

The library opened in 1971, a new building constructed with city and LSCA funds, in an urban renewal area. *A poet of the eighteenth century, Phillis Wheatley was the first Afro-American woman to publish a book. Ms. Wheatley published her first poem, "A Poem by Phillis, A Negro Girl, on the Death of Reverend George Whitefield," in 1770.

Yonkers

Broadway Branch Library
70 South Broadway
Yonkers, New York 10701   (914) 337-1500

Roslyn G. Drucker, branch librarian; 11.5 prof, 18 non-prof staff; $36,200 materials budget; $441,150 operating budget; 25,418 volumes; 573 periodicals; 2,445 record discs, 25 filmstrips, 17 videocassettes; ILL; copying; 48 hours weekly; Jacqueline E. Miller, Virginia E. Wolven, Grinton I. Will, former head librarians; business and technical materials, young adult books by and about Afro-Americans, books in 15 foreign languages.

The library was established from 1850-54 as the Young Men's Library Association; from 1854-66 it was operated as the Yonkers Circulation Library Association. In 1884, it became the Yonkers Public Library under the aegis of the Board of Education. In 1904, the present library building opened to the public.

NORTH CAROLINA

Charlotte

Belmont Center Branch Library
700 Parkwood Avenue
Charlotte, North Carolina 28205   (704) 374-2470

Kutricia Spann, head; 3 non-prof staff; $1,900 materials budget; approximately $26,287.82 operating budget (1974-75), part of system budget; 3,553 volumes; 47 periodicals; 16mm projector, 8mm projector, technicolor loop projector, tape recorders, slide projectors, phonograph records, slides, tapes, framed prints, etc.; 66 hours weekly; James Blue, Mrs. Dorothy Waiters Ware, former head librarians; general collection.

The Belmont Center Branch Library was established as a LSCA (Library Service and Construct Act) project in July 1972, as the Alexander Street Branch. In May 1973, it was combined with the Piedmont Courts Branch, and in May 1975, the library was relocated in the Belmont Center.

North Branch Library
2324 LaSalle Street
Charlotte, North Carolina 28216   (704) 374-2882

Branch librarian position vacant; 1 prof, 2.5 non-prof staff; $6,900 materials budget; approximately $62,113.29 operating budget; part of system budget; 25,129 volumes; 44 periodicals; 16mm projector; copying; 69 hours weekly; Dorothy Holt Person, Robbie Grant Dolphus, Pearlee Coefield, Victoria Tsai, former head librarians; early Afro-American materials.

The library opened June, 1957, as one of 9 new branches. It incorporated the basic collection from the Brevard Street facility.

Greensboro

Southeast Branch Library
900 South Benbow Road
Greensboro, North Carolina 27401 (919) 373-2392

Helen B. Walden, branch librarian; 1 prof, 3.5 non-prof staff; $15,000 materials budget (estimated); $60,570 operating budget (July 1, 1975-June 30, 1976); 20,000 volumes; 72 periodicals; 1 opaque projector, 2 16mm film projectors, Audio-Study Mage cassette player, 2 Borg-Warner System 80 reading machines; 1 sound filmstrip viewer; ILL; copying; 66 hours weekly; Martha Sebastian, Willie M. Grimes, former head librarians; black history and race relations.

Southeast Branch is an extension of the old Carnegie Negro Library which was organized in 1924 as an independent separate library. Library services under the Greensboro Public Library central administration began July 1, 1963, as an integrated service.

Raleigh

Richard B. Harrison Branch Library*
1313 New Bern Avenue
Raleigh, North Carolina 27610 (919) 832-2942

Ms. Joanne Canady, branch librarian; 4.5 non-prof staff; part of system budget; 45,000 volumes; 99 periodicals; phono-records, access to county and state film and filmstrip collections, circulating art prints, projection equipment available to circulate, listening stations, and projection booth facilities; ILL; copying; 65 hours weekly; Mollie H. Lee, only former librarian; Mollie H. Lee Collection of Black Literature, which is devoted to a wide range of subjects of interest to, by, and about blacks.

The library was founded in 1935. The initial appropriation was $3,250; it became the sole black branch in Raleigh. During the tenure of Mrs. Mollie H. Lee as librarian, the library developed into a cultural center in the black community. The library was incorporated into the Wake County Library System in 1965. A new modern building was completed in 1968.
*Richard B. Harrison was a distinguished actor who became internationally known for his characterization of "De Lawd" in *Green Pastures* and for giving one-man performances of *Macbeth, Julius Caesar,* and *Damon and Pythias.*

South Raleigh Branch Library
1965 Rock Quarry Road
Raleigh, North Carolina 27610 (919) 834-1533

Mr. Wes Alston, branch librarian; 2.5 non-prof staff; part of system budget; 5,000 volumes; 47 periodicals; 150 phonorecords, access to county and state film collections, circulating art prints, listening station, projection equipment available for circulation; ILL; copying; 53 hours weekly; general collection.

The library was opened in 1972 to serve southeast Raleigh. It is located in Southgate Shopping Center.

Winston-Salem

East Winston Branch Library
1110 East 7th Street
Winston-Salem, North Carolina 27101 (919) 727-2202

Judie DeJonge, branch librarian (professional), Ann Gray (para-professional); 0.05 prof, 2 non-prof staff; $4,000 materials budget; $30,000 operating budget; 28,000 volumes; 75 periodicals; 400 phonorecords, access to 16mm films in the system-wide collection; ILL; 51 hours weekly; Emmalene Goodwin, Mary Bruce, Martha Young, former head librarians; general collection.

The East Winston Branch was constructed in 1954 to serve the entire black population of Winston-Salem. Blacks were barred from use of the Main Library until 1965. Located less than a mile from the main library, the branch has suffered a decline in use since integration of the library system took place in 1965. Also affecting the usage factor is the fact that much of the residential housing once located close to the branch has since been relocated. There are presently plans to close the branch and build another in a more suitable location. The library system now conducts an extensive Children's Outreach program in the East Winston area through deposit collections in four community centers and 25 day care centers, plus providing two fully equipped media mobiles. This program includes 8 full-time and 4 part-time staff, two of which are professionals, and is based in the main library.

OHIO

Cincinnati

Avondale Branch Library
3566 Reading Road
Cincinnati, Ohio 45229   (513) 369-6900

Mrs. Louise Dixon, branch librarian; 1 prof, 2 non-prof staff; $8,385 materials budget; $62,308 operating budget; 12,992 volumes; 93 periodicals; recordings; ILL; copying; teletype no. 810-461-2300; 46.5 hours weekly; Mrs. Vivian Baldwin, Mrs. Carol Daniel, Mrs. Elizabeth Hammond, Mr. Donald Spencer, former head librarians; business reference library, black history, humanities (art, music, literature, drama) geared to the black experience.

A deposit station library opened in 1899. On March 1, 1913, a new Carnegie building was opened. In 1970, a Business Reference Library was dedicated.

Lincoln Park Branch Library
805 Lincoln Park Drive
Cincinnati, Ohio 45203   (513) 369-6900

Mary Jo Holcomb, branch librarian (extension office); 0.5 prof, 2.5 non-prof staff; $7,800 materials budget; $37,821 operating budget; 10,926 volumes; 81 periodicals; ILL; copying; teletype no. 810-461-2300; 38 hours weekly; Mrs. Hattie Walker, Mrs. Mary Finley, Miss Judith Dickens, Mr. Mike Suedkamp, former head librarians; black materials, job information.

The Lincoln Park Branch opened in 1923 as Stowe Branch in a public school building. The name changed to Lincoln Park Branch when it moved into a new building in 1961.

Madisonville Branch Library
4830 Whetsel Avenue
Cincinnati, Ohio 45227   (513) 369-6900

Mrs. Phyllis Moore, branch librarian; 2 prof, 1 non-prof staff; $9,282 materials budget; $55,141 operating budget; 18,935 volumes; 97 periodicals; recordings; ILL; copying; teletype no. 810-461-2300; 46.5 hours weekly; Mr. George Soete, Ms. Virginia Kerr, Mrs. Elizabeth Cotton, Mrs. Anita Connelly, former head librarians; black history and literature collection, job information and gardening collection.

The Madisonville Branch Library was organized as a village library in 1892; a deposit station opened in 1899. It was absorbed by the public library in 1902, and in 1925, a new branch library was opened to the public.

Walnut Hills Branch Library
2533 Kemper Lane
Cincinnati, Ohio 45206   (513) 369-6900

Mr. Stan Schmidt, branch librarian; 2 prof, 2 non-prof staff; $12,880 materials budget; $58,683 operating budget; 21,092 volumes; 99 periodicals; recordings; ILL; copying; teletype no. 810-461-2300; 56 hours weekly; Eulalie Spilman, Alice Isphording, Anita Gorius Meyer, Helen Knecht, former head librarians; black history and literature, business reference, excellent general reference collection.

The Walnut Hills Branch Library was established in 1899, when a deposit collection was placed in the Walnut Hills area. In April 1906, the present branch was opened in a newly built Carnegie facility.

Cleveland

Arlington Branch Library
12332 Arlington Avenue
Cleveland, Ohio 44108 (216) 451-0306

Mrs. Eunice Peters, branch librarian; 1 prof, 3 non-prof staff; $10,000 materials budget; $36,926 operating budget (1975); 17,530 volumes; 49 periodicals; movie projector and films on request from the Main Library; ILL; copying; 42.5 hours weekly; Shirley Lee, Loraine U. Gooding, Fritz Stein, Loraine A. Slater, former head librarians; black history collection.

The library opened as a station on April 6, 1942. On October 31, 1949, it was converted into a branch. In June 1954, additional store space on the corner of Arlington and Eddy Road was remodeled to enlarge the branch.

Collinwood Branch Library
856 East 152nd Street
Cleveland, Ohio 44110 (216) 541-4220

Mrs. Sandra A. Emery, branch librarian; 3 prof, 2.5 non-prof staff; $16,100 materials budget; $69,436.62 operating budget (1975); 29,695 volumes; 73 periodicals; 387 phonodiscs, films available from the Main Library; ILL; copying; 49.5 hours weekly; Helen M. Reed, M. Irene Adair, Mable H. Houser, Mary E. Hoover, former head librarians; black collection and railroad collection.

The Collinwood Branch opened as a school library in 1892 before Collinwood was annexed to the city. In 1910, it was annexed to the Cleveland Public Library. On August 14, 1912, it opened as a smaller branch.

East 131st Street Branch Library
3830 East 131st Street
Cleveland, Ohio 44120 (216) 561-6133

Jo Ann Petrello, branch librarian; 2 prof, 3 non-prof staff; $17,000 materials budget; $49,554.29 operating budget (1975); 26,742 volumes; 16mm projector, phonodisc collection of approximately 600 records; ILL; copying; 49.5 hours weekly; black history and literature.

The library began as a station in Kominsky Hall on September 19, 1923. It closed temporarily and moved to a store on East 131st Street at Benwood Avenue in October 1925. On September 4, 1928, it was made a branch and opened in a new building in 1929.

East 79th Street Branch Library
1215 East 79th Street
Cleveland, Ohio 44103 (216) 881-7266

Mrs. Phyllis J. Martin, branch librarian; 2 prof, 3 non-prof staff; $14,700 materials budget; $54,782.32 operating budget (1975); 21,119 volumes; 60 periodicals; records and 16mm projector; ILL; copying; 42.5 hours weekly; Iris B. Boyd, Frances M. Rodstein, Mathilda Kelsey, Gertrude M. Kahne, former head librarians; black history and literature.

The library opened as a station in 1909 and later became a school branch. In 1914, it moved to a rented store room, and in July 1915, it was made a smaller branch. In April 1916, a new building was opened.

55th East Branch Library
5510 Superior Avenue
Cleveland, Ohio 44103 (216) 361-6232

Mr. Ivan Miletic, branch librarian; 1 prof, 1 non-prof staff; $10,000 materials budget; $35,895.92 operating budget (1975); 22,514 volumes; 16mm projector; ILL; copying; 42.5 hours weekly; Mrs. Swanson, Miss Justine Gehring, Bonnie Landgrabe, former head librarians; general collection.

The library was opened August 7, 1967, in three rented store spaces.

Garden Valley Branch Library
7100 Kinsman Road
Cleveland, Ohio 44104 (216) 883-9096

Mrs. Eleanor Robinson, branch librarian; 2 non-prof staff; $6,000 materials budget; $21,707.02 operating budget (1975); 6,910 volumes; 16mm projector; ILL; copying; general collection.

The library opened in the Garden Valley Housing Project on April 7, 1969, and it was moved to 7100 Kinsman Road on January 15, 1973.

Glenville Branch Library
660 Parkwood Drive
Cleveland, Ohio 44108 (216) 681-2040

Lena L. Nance, branch librarian; 3 prof, 2 non-prof staff; $15,590 materials budget; $63,683.43 operating budget (1975); 32,327 volumes; 105 periodicals; phonodiscs; ILL; copying; teletype (no number provided); 41 hours weekly; Laura L. Haupt, Alice K. Hatch, Catherine Graves, Marcella Hecthman, former head librarians; general collection.

In March, 1909, the library opened as a sub-branch. The village of Glenville became a part of Cleveland and the old Town Hall was used as a branch library. In January 1911, it was made into a branch. A new building was opened in March 1927.

Harvard-Lee Branch Library
4125 Lee Road
Cleveland, Ohio 44128 (216) 751-9955

Mrs. Ann A. Marks, branch librarian; 3 prof, 3.25 non-prof staff; $16,900 materials budget; $79,388.78 operating budget (1975); 28,919 volumes; 88 periodicals; 510 phonodiscs, 100 cassettes, 12 hand projectors, 8 filmstrips with records, 1 portable record player, 1 built-in listening center with earphones, 1 16mm movie projector with sound; ILL; copying; 41 hours weekly; Mrs. Jane Piwonka, Mr. Arnold McClain, Mrs. Edrice Ivory, Miss Karen Jamison, former head librarians; black history, biography, literature and fiction.

The library opened as a station on May 11, 1953, in leased quarters. It moved to a new site in 1962. The library is now housed in a shopping center, and one of its unique programs is the story hour for children.

Langston Hughes Branch Library*
2390 East 79th Street
Cleveland, Ohio 44104 (216) 431-6118

Mrs. Ruth B. Walker, branch librarian; 2 non-prof staff; $4,000 materials budget; $13,833.91 operating budget; 15,804 volumes; 42 periodicals; 16mm projector, films available from Main Library; ILL; copying; black literature.

The library was called the Quincy Branch when, in 1914, it was built with Carnegie funds. The name was changed to Langston Hughes Branch Library on July 15, 1973. *For significance of name, see CORONA, NEW YORK.

Martin Luther King, Jr. Regional Branch Library*
1962 East 107th Street
Cleveland, Ohio 44106 (216) 795-4117

Mr. Robert W. H. Vokes, branch librarian; 4 prof, 2 non-prof staff; $15,800 materials budget; $108,083.30 operating budget (1975); 53,278 volumes; 107 periodicals; phonodiscs and 8mm films; ILL; copying; 41 hours weekly; Mrs. Louis F. Bolden, former head librarian; black collection, general reference, literature, fairy tales.

The Martin Luther King, Jr. Regional Branch Library opened in a new building on June 14, 1970. The building has 18,600 square feet of floor space with an exterior arcade of 3,700 square feet and book capacity for 125,000 volumes. *For significance of name, see DISTRICT OF COLUMBIA.

Miles Park Branch Library
Miles Park and East 93rd Street
Cleveland, Ohio 44105   (216) 641-4990

Mr. Joseph E. Mock, branch librarian; 2 prof, 3 non-prof staff; $14,000 materials budget; $58,301.39 operating budget (1975); 24,548 volumes; 69 periodicals; phonodisc record player and 400 records; ILL; copying; 41 hours weekly; Robert W. Vokes, Olive A. Osmun, Ellie B. Hunt, Marion Ewing, former head librarians; history, psychology, black literature, American and English literature.

The library was opened September 10, 1894, the second branch library of the system. On March 23, 1906, a new building, built with Carnegie funds, was opened.

Mt. Pleasant Branch Library
14000 Kinsman Road
Cleveland, Ohio 44120   (216) 561-4790

Mrs. Shirley T. Lee, branch librarian; 3 prof, 3 non-prof staff; $16,100 materials budget; $60,837.54 operating budget (1975); 31,775 volumes; 76 periodicals; 761 phonodiscs (music) and 63 spoken language phonodiscs (plays, speeches, poetry readings, storytelling); ILL; copying; 41 hours weekly; Mrs. Mildred H. Smith, Mrs. Evelyn Mickens, Miss Elizabeth Lindsey, Mr. George Scherma, former head librarians; black history and culture.

The library opened as a station in 1923, then as a branch in February 1928. In August 1930, it moved into a remodeled frame house. In 1937, it moved into a remodeled bank building.

Rice Branch Library
2820 East 116th Street
Cleveland, Ohio 44120   (216) 231-5062

Mrs. Olive A. Osmun, branch librarian; 3 prof, 2.5 non-prof staff; $9,800 materials budget (1975); $73,709 operating budget (1975); 34,845 volumes; 91 periodicals; 16mm projector, screen, listening center, stereo, phonodiscs; ILL; copying; Martha Kling, Lorine Kolbeck, Rosalie Booker, Charlotte Fairchild, former head librarians; Hungarian language materials, art history and drama sections.

The library opened as a school library at Harvey Rice School in 1916, and in March 1924, was made a branch. A new building opened on February 28, 1927.

Sterling Branch Library
2200 East 30th Street
Cleveland, Ohio 44115   (216) 621-5766

Mrs. Agnes K. Linhart, branch librarian; 1 prof, 2 non-prof staff; $10,000 materials budget; $41,819.36 operating budget; 18,780 volumes; 43 periodicals; projector, screen, stereo, listening table, monaural head phones, 429 phonodiscs; ILL; copying; 42.5 hours weekly; Mrs. Patricia Saunders, Miss Melanie E. Maczkov, Miss Ruth C. Epstein, Mrs. Louise Bolden, former head librarians; early childhood education, black history, biography, literature.

The library opened August 1, 1913, built with Carnegie funds.

Superior Branch Library
1347 East 105th Street
Cleveland, Ohio 44106   (216) 795-4249

Mrs. Janet J. Powell, branch librarian; 1 prof, 2 non-prof staff; $6,000 materials budget; 17,267 volumes, 39 periodicals; ILL; copying; 42.5 hours weekly; Mrs. Lillie B. Joyce, Mr. Joseph E. Mock, Mrs. Louise F. Bolden, Miss Catharine Graves, former head librarians; black collection.

The library opened as Oakland Station at Oakland School in 1899 and was made into a smaller branch in April 1912. The library received full branch status when it moved into a new building built with Carnegie funds in September 1920.

Treasure House Branch Library
Crawford Road and East 86th Street
Cleveland, Ohio 44106   (216) 795-4383

Miss Willelma M. Aldana, branch librarian; 1 prof, 2 non-prof staff; $10,000 material budget; 16,271 volumes; 37 periodicals; movie projector, filmstrip viewer, record player; ILL; copying; 42.5 hours weekly; Roger Mae Johnson, Elaine Dockens, Arnold McClain, Lena Nance, former head librarians; Afro-American books and magazines.

The library is the former Hough Branch, which opened as a sub-branch in two rented rooms on the second floor of a business building in 1904. In January 1907, it opened in a new building and was made a branch. In January 1966, the name was changed to the Treasure House Branch Library.

Union Branch Library
9319 Union Avenue
Cleveland, Ohio 44105   (216) 641-4961

Mrs. Nellie Rucker, branch librarian; 2 prof, 1 non-prof staff; $14,200 materials budget; 17,778 volumes; 52 periodicals; projector and screen; ILL; copying; 41 hours weekly; Agnes H. Harnett, Agnes B. Tarjon, Lillian Hricko, Myrtle Graves, former head librarians; Afro-American collection.

The library opened as a station in a store room in November 1930. In January 1938, it was made a branch. The library moved to a new building (a remodeled store) in December 1939.

Woodhill Branch Library
2973 Woodhill Road
Cleveland, Ohio 44104   (216) 721-7970

Mrs. Lucille T. Conde, branch librarian; 2 non-prof staff; $9,000 materials budget; $17,797.59 operating budget (1975); 10,358 volumes; 16mm projector, films are supplied from the main library; ILL; copying; 25 hours weekly; general collection.

In 1925, the library opened as a station in the East End Neighborhood House. In April 1950, it moved to rented quarters, and it was classified an "A" branch in November 1955.

Woodland Branch Library
5806 Woodland Avenue
Cleveland, Ohio 44104   (216) 361-7255

Miss Germaine Gibian, branch librarian; 2 prof, 3 non-prof staff; $14,000 materials budget; $78,383.67 operating budget (1975); 17,770 volumes; 65 periodicals; 16mm projector and picture file; ILL; copying; 42.5 hours weekly; Jewel Harris, Alice Smith, Nellie Rucker, Agnes Harnett, former head librarians; black culture.

The library opened as a branch in a small Methodist chapel on January 31, 1896. In July 1904, it moved to a new and larger building that was built with Carnegie funds. The Russian Collection was in this library, but later was moved to the main library.

Columbus

Driving Park Branch Library
1566 East Livingston Avenue
Columbus, Ohio 43205   (614) 461-5612

Sue E. Henderson, branch librarian; 4 non-prof staff; part of system budget; 22,210 volumes; 70 periodicals; video cassettes, access to 16mm and 8mm projectors and films; ILL; copying; teletype no. 810-482-1161; 61 hours weekly; black history.

The library is a five-year-old branch in a predominantly black neighborhood serving seven elementary schools and two junior high schools.

Martin Luther King Memorial Branch Library*
1600 East Long Street
Columbus, Ohio 43203 (614) 461-6522

Verdi Fitz, branch librarian; 1 prof, 3 non-prof staff; part of system budget; 35,233 volumes; 80 periodicals; 16mm film projector, color TV cassette set, video cassette; ILL; copying; teletype no. 810-482-1161; 40 hours weekly; Mrs. Bertha Campbell, former head librarian; black history collection.

The new library opened in 1969 to replace the old East Side Branch Library. *For significance of name, see DISTRICT OF COLUMBIA.

Shepard Branch Library
2185 East 5th Avenue
Columbus, Ohio 43219 (614) 461-6535

Mrs. Rubye R. Kyles, branch librarian; 5 non-prof staff; part of system budget; 17,869 volumes; 75 periodicals; 8mm silent projector, 100 8mm silent films, 1,000 audio-cassette tapes; ILL; copying; teletype no. 810-482-1161; 48 hours weekly; Phyllis Baker, Jean Grant, Sue Henderson, Nancy Katz, former head librarians; general collection.

The library opened in February 1939, in its present location.

Dayton

Madden Hills Branch Library
2542 Germantown Street
Dayton, Ohio 45429 (513) 224-1651

Mrs. Nancy Tanner, branch librarian; 1 prof, 3 non-prof staff; part of system budget; 32,013 volumes; 64 periodicals; phonograph records; ILL; copying; teletype no. 810-459-1609; 51 hours weekly; Mrs. Margarett Cooper, Miss Estella Grayson, former head librarians; black history, Afro-American authors, and small business collection.

The library originally opened in 1914 as the West Carnegie Branch Library in a racially mixed neighborhood. It was replaced by a new building at a different location in 1970 and is now called the Madden Hills Branch Library.

Westwood Branch Library
3207 Hoover Avenue
Dayton, Ohio 45407 (513) 224-1651

Mrs. Nancy Tanner, branch librarian; 1 prof, 2 non-prof staff; part of system budget; 28,600 volumes; 43 periodicals; phonograph records; ILL; copying; teletype no. 810-459-1609; 51 hours weekly; black history, Afro-American authors.

The Westwood Branch was opened in 1938 in an all-white neighborhood. Changes started in the late 1950s, and by 1965 it became a predominantly black community.

Toledo

Kent Branch Library
3101 Collingwood Boulevard
Toledo, Ohio 43610 (419) 242-7361

James Marshall, branch librarian; 2 prof, 6 non-prof staff; $26,440 materials budget; part of system budget; 14,347 volumes; 85 periodicals; records; ILL; copying; teletype no. 810-442-1649; 27 hours weekly; Lillian Francois, Margaret Longworth, Elizabeth Mayberry, Lillian Baumgardner, former head librarians; black history and culture, child development and infant care.

The Kent Branch Library opened December 12, 1917, one of five branches built with Carnegie funds. The building was destroyed by fire on December 1, 1974, and the library moved to its present location November 17, 1975.

Mott Branch Library
1085 Don Street
Toledo, Ohio 43607   (419) 242-7361

Cynthia Stilley, branch librarian; 1.5 prof, 4 non-prof staff; $10,660 materials budget; part of system budget; 23,786 volumes; 69 periodicals; records; ILL; copying; teletype no. 810-442-1649; 32.5 hours weekly; Henry Doder, Florence Moodey, Marian Wadsworth, Luella Gilson, former head librarians; black history and culture, and career materials.

The Mott Branch Library opened January 3, 1918, as a result of a Carnegie gift. In 1975, the library expanded its services with a new addition to the building.

Youngstown

South Side Library
1771 Market Street
Youngstown, Ohio 44507   (216) 747-6424

Betty W. Armstrong, branch librarian; 1 prof, 5 non-prof staff; $15,000 materials budget; part of system budget; 39,548 volumes; 90 periodicals; films and other AV programs provided by another agency; ILL; copying; 40.5 hours weekly; Lucile Fitch, Catharine Stuart, former head librarians African history, African literature, Shakespeare.

The library opened in a nearby high school in 1919; it moved to permanent quarters in 1929. It was extensively remodeled and enlarged in 1971-72.

OKLAHOMA

Oklahoma City

Ralph Ellison Branch Library*
2000 Northeast 23rd Street
Oklahoma City, Oklahoma   (405) 424-1437

Mrs. Gertrude Richard, branch librarian; 2 prof, 3 non-prof staff; $11,870 materials budget; part of system budget; 34,014 volumes; 81 periodicals; art prints, framed posters, audio-cassettes and disc recordings, listening stations, 16mm sound film projector, and system collection of 16mm films available; ILL; copying; teletype no. 405-232-9312; 48 hours weekly; Rosalie Starks, Joan Bierman, former head librarians; history of black community in greater Oklahoma city; and Black Heritage Chronicles, a special collection that deals with civil and human rights in the United States.

The library opened in June, 1975, replacing a smaller storefront branch that had operated since 1967. The branch is located in the same community but in a different location. *Ralph Ellison is one of America's foremost novelists. A native of Oklahoma City, he was the National Book Award winner for his greatly acclaimed book, *Invisible Man* (1952).

OREGON

Portland

Albina Branch Library
3630 North Vancouver Avenue
Portland, Oregon 97227   (503) 287-7147

Miss Betty Hodges, branch librarian; 2.62 non-prof staff; $3,600 materials budget; $41,332 operating budget; 10,000 volumes; 48 periodicals; recordings; 30.5 hours weekly; black history and literature.

The proposal for the Albina Branch Library Demonstration Project, to create a branch library service in a culturally deprived area, was submitted to the Albina Citizens War-On-Poverty Committee and was approved by the Metropolitan Steering Committee in April 1966. Funding was requested from the Community Action Program, Office of Economic Opportunity, and funding for start-up costs was provided through the State of Oregon with Library Service Construction Act funds. The branch opened in June 1967.

North Portland Branch Library
512 North Killingsworth Avenue
Portland, Oregon 97217   (503) 284-5622

Miss Mary Griffin, branch librarian; 2 prof, 2.87 non-prof staff; $9,450 materials budget; $74,700 operating budget; 15,000 volumes; 76 periodicals; 75 framed art prints; copying; 48 hours weekly; black history.

Library service was established in North Portland in 1909. The building was erected in 1913 with Carnegie funds and remodeled in 1961. The gift of the land came from W. B. Ayer and local residents.

PENNSYLVANIA

Philadelphia

Columbia Avenue Branch Library
2320 West Columbia Avenue
Philadelphia, Pennsylvania 19121   (215) 236-9736

Mary Miller, branch librarian; 1.5 prof, 4 non-prof staff; $11,430 materials budget; part of system budget; 25,986 volumes; 40 periodicals; ILL; copying; teletype no. 710-670-9719; 37 hours weekly; Stuart McDougall, Victoria Fan, Elliot Shelkrot, Ellen M. Whitney, former head librarians; general collection.

The Columbia Avenue Branch was opened on April 11, 1962, the successor to a branch library opened in 1892. This agency was the first extension of the library system.

Cobbs Creek Branch Library
59th Street and Baltimore Avenue
Philadelphia, Pennsylvania 19143   (215) 476-0760

Sandra Farrell, branch librarian; 2 prof, 4 non-prof staff; $12,140 materials budget; part of system budget; 23,238 volumes; 46 periodicals; ILL; copying; teletype no. 710-670-9719; 37 hours weekly; Bernard Berman, Norman Long, Judith Segel, Irma Dillon; general collection.

This agency was opened for service on December 30, 1925. The building was completely renovated and refurbished in 1957.

George Institute Library
52nd Street below Lancaster Avenue
Philadelphia, Pennsylvania 19131   (215) 477-9977

Hedra L. Peterman, branch librarian; 1 prof, 4 non-prof staff; $9,445 materials budget; part of system budget; 16,558 volumes; 42 periodicals; ILL; copying; teletype no. 710-670-9719; 37 hours weekly; Joseph Costello, Ida C. Benders, Helen M. Mullen, Esther R. Sexton; general collection.

The George Institute Library opened in 1872 under private auspices. Its original charter was dissolved in 1926, and since 1927, the agency has been operated by the Free Library of Philadelphia. The present building was erected in 1919.

Germantown Branch Library
Vernon Park, Germantown
Philadelphia, Pennsylvania 19144   (215) 844-0120

Martin T. Kasker, branch librarian; 2 prof, 4 non-prof staff; $10,000 materials budget; part of system budget; 30,539 volumes; 53 periodicals; ILL; copying; teletype no. 710-670-9719; 37 hours weekly; Dorothy Harris, Susanna B. Quinn, Martha Lamb, Kathryn E. Hayes, former head librarians; general collection.

The Germantown Branch opened in 1895 and became an operation of the library system in 1896. It has occupied two buildings, the current one being erected in 1907 with Carnegie funds. Partial rehabilitation was carried out in 1963.

Kingsessing Branch Library
51st Street below Chester Avenue
Philadelphia, Pennsylvania 19143   (215) 766-5022

Michele Gendron, branch librarian; 1 prof, 4 non-prof staff; $11,445 materials budget; part of system budget; 26,957 volumes; 44 periodicals; 129 filmstrips, 52 cassettes, 57 phonodiscs; ILL; copying; teletype no. 710-670-9719; 37 hours weekly; Richard Dissinger, Doris Kessler, Warren King, Marianne Promos, former head librarians; general collection.

The Kingsessing building opened in 1919 as the 22nd library constructed in Philadelphia with Andrew Carnegie funds. Rehabilitation of the building was made in 1959.

Lehigh Avenue Branch Library
6th Street and Lehigh Avenue
Philadelphia, Pennsylvania 19133   (215) 228-6760

Marie Guertin, branch librarian; 2 prof, 4 non-prof staff; $12,230 materials budget; part of system budget; 23,880 volumes; 42 periodicals; ILL; copying; teletype no. 710-670-9719; 37 hours weekly; Helen Miller, Charles Peguese, Beatrice Gottlieb, Guntina S. Lielkjas, former head librarians; general collection.

Lehigh Avenue Branch was built with Andrew Carnegie funds in 1906. Extensive renovation and rehabilitation was completed in 1966.

Nicetown-Tioga Branch Library
3720 North Broad Street
Philadelphia, Pennsylvania 19140   (215) 225-8733

Jessie Birtha, branch librarian; 2 prof, 7.5 non-prof staff; $12,730 materials budget; part of system budget; 27,218 volumes; 49 periodicals; 119 filmstrips, 64 cassettes, 68 phonodiscs; ILL; copying; teletype no. 710-670-9719; 37 hours weekly; Dorothy Harris, Michael Coyle, Ruth Ann Robinson, Alice E. Moore, former head librarians; general collection.

The Nicetown-Tioga Branch, established in 1897, was the twelfth branch established in the Free Library of Philadelphia. The current building is its third and was opened in 1961.

Queen Memorial Library
1315 Point Breeze Avenue
Philadelphia, Pennsylvania 19146   (215) 467-4025

Richard Dissinger, branch librarian; 1 prof, 3 non-prof staff; $9,426 materials budget; part of system budget; 16,605 volumes; 46 periodicals; ILL; copying; teletype no. 710-670-9719; 37 hours weekly; Patricia Hoberg, Lewis Buckingham, Omema Howerton, Clarence Eaton, former head librarians; 37 hours weekly; general collection.

Queen Memorial Library opened in 1913 and was housed in a church building until 1957. It was re-opened in a new storefront building and has increased service to the public.

Wadsworth Avenue Branch Library
Wadsworth and Michener Avenues
Philadelphia, Pennsylvania 19150   (215) 247-2954

Dorothy E. Harris, branch librarian; 2 prof, 6 non-prof staff; $12,481 materials budget; part of system budget; 35,436 volumes; 65 periodicals; ILL; copying; teletype no. 710-670-9719; 37 hours weekly; Stephanie West, Gail Stefanski, Evelyn Diehm, Faith McDowell, former head librarians; general collection.

The Wadsworth Avenue agency was opened in a new building in mid-1959 to broaden service in the northwest area of the city.

West Oak Lane Branch Library
74th Avenue and Washington Lane
Philadelphia, Pennsylvania 19138   (215) 424-4587

Ruth Ann Robinson, branch librarian; 3 prof, 6 non-prof staff; $13,581 materials budget; part of system budget; 53,918 volumes; 66 periodicals; ILL; copying; teletype no. 710-670-9719; 44 hours weekly; Daphne Labega, Henry Kapenstein, Frances Peters, Harold West, former head librarians; general collection.

The West Oak Lane Branch opened in 1957. For many years this was one of the busiest branches in the library system, but a changing community has altered the usage and service patterns of the agency.

Widener Branch Library
2531 West Lehigh Avenue
Philadelphia, Pennsylvania 19132   (215) 229-3541

Branch librarian position vacant; 1 prof, 4 non-prof staff; $9,930 materials budget; part of system budget; 30,979 volumes; 46 periodicals; ILL; copying; teletype no. 710-670-9719; closed due to renovation; Florinda Roma, Kathleen M. Eagleson, Loretta J. McElvaine, Steve Adams, former head librarians; general collection.

The Widener Branch was first established in 1908 in a large mansion donated by its owners. A renovated building was acquired in 1946, and the branch was merged with another area branch library. The branch is undergoing renovation (1976).

Wynnefield Branch Library
54th Street and Overbrook Avenue
Philadelphia, Pennsylvania 19131   (215) 473-4686

Vickie Lange, branch librarian; 3 prof, 6.5 non-prof staff; $13,143 materials budget; part of system budget; 50,338 volumes; 65 periodicals; ILL; copying; teletype no. 710-670-9719; 44 hours weekly; Alice C. Moore, Frank Bradley, Edmond Doherty, former head librarians; general collection.

The Wynnefield Branch, built in 1964, is a joint building project in cooperation with the City Recreation Department. Dual services are offered from one facility.

Pittsburgh

Homewood Branch Library
7101 Hamilton Avenue
Pittsburgh, Pennsylvania 15208   (412) 731-3080, 731-7205

Marjorie T. Franklin, branch librarian; 2 prof, 3 non-prof staff; $14,085 materials budget; part of system budget; 44,578 volumes; 125 periodicals; 12 sets of filmstrips on black history or culture, 15 sets of filmstrips for the improvement of reading and mathematics, 1,000 records (all music), 40 cassettes (black), 25 transparencies (black); ILL; copying; teletype no. AS11-9807-L; 36 hours weekly; Ruth Rhen, Alice Breiner, Elizabeth Brunot, Laura Selkregg, former head librarians; black culture collection of more than 5,000 items.

This branch opened in 1910 in a wealthy white neighborhood. The population started to shift in 1925, and by 1970 approximately 90 percent of the residents were black. It is a spacious, well-preserved Carnegie building.

Martin Luther King, Jr. Reading Center*
Herron Avenue and Milwaukee Street
Pittsburgh, Pennsylvania 15219   (412) 621-6185

Supervised by clerical assistant; Inner-City Services provides two professional consultants (one adult and one juvenile), 5 non-prof staff; approximately $2,000 materials budget; approximately $15,000 operating budget; 5,000 volumes; 57 periodicals; 200 records (popular, religious, etc., which are black oriented), 16mm motion picture projector; ILL; teletype no. AS11-9807-L; 32 hours weekly; Mrs. Ethel Hampton, Clerical Assistant, former head; black materials.

This is a remodeled storefront which opened in 1970 as an informal community cultural center. There are a reading room and a multi-purpose room which serve the materials resources and programming activities needs for this 98 percent black community. This branch is a division of Inner-City Services of the Outreach department of the Carnegie Library of Pittsburgh. *For significance of name, see DISTRICT OF COLUMBIA.

Wylie Avenue Branch Library
1909 Wylie Avenue
Pittsburgh, Pennsylvania 15219 (412) 281-3753

Mrs. Helen M. McClain, branch librarian; 1 prof, 4 non-prof staff; $3,100 materials budget (books only); part of system budget; 27,000 volumes; 92 periodicals; 16mm film projector; ILL; teletype no. AS11-9807-L; 40 hours weekly; Elizabeth McCombs, Sue H. Weir, Eugenia Brunot, Enid Boli, former head librarians; black oriented collection; Civil Service examination collection.

The library opened to the public on June 1, 1899 (the third branch built in the Carnegie Library of Pittsburgh system) in a section called the "Hill District." The population during the early years was predominantly Russian-Jewish, but it is now 99 percent black. In the very near future, the library will be relocated in a mini-shopping mall in the same area.

TENNESSEE

Chattanooga

South Chattanooga Branch Library
2500 South Market Street
Chattanooga, Tennessee 37408 (615) 757-5312

Mrs. Ola Boatner, branch librarian; 1 prof, 1.5 non-prof staff; $6,000 materials budget; $20,000 operating budget; 14,827 volumes; 60 periodicals; phonograph records, with films supplied from the Main Library; ILL; teletype no. 810-573-5289; 27 hours weekly (September-May), 43 hours weekly (June-August); Kate Brown Hunter, Helen Millsaps, former head librarians; black history.

On March 4, 1913, a branch library for Negroes was established in the Howard High School, and it became the Howard Branch Library of the Chattanooga Public Library in 1921. The library moved to new quarters when the new Howard High School was built in 1954, and the library has since been renamed the South Chattanooga Branch Library.

Knoxville

Burlington Branch Library
3615 McCalla Avenue
Knoxville, Tennessee 37914 (615) 525-5431

Trenie Cooper, branch librarian; 1 prof, 5 non-prof staff; $9,000 materials budget; part of system budget; 20,000 volumes; 82 periodicals; record collection, projector, films; ILL; copying; 40 hours weekly; Margaret Dickson, Billie Barnett, former head librarians; black studies.

The library opened in 1945 and serves the East Knoxville area.

East Knoxville Branch Library
2301 McCalla Avenue
Knoxville, Tennessee 37915 (615) 522-8052

Loyce Stracener, branch librarian; 1 non-prof staff; $1,900 materials budget; part of system budget; 2,300 volumes; 53 periodicals; phonographs and head sets, 16mm projector and films; ILL; 20 hours weekly; Andrena Coleman, former head librarian; black studies, adult education.

The library started in 1972 with federal money. It was incorporated as a branch in 1974 by Knoxville-Knox County Library system.

Memphis

Cherokee Branch Library
3300 Sharpe Avenue
Memphis, Tennessee 38111 (901) 743-3655

Miss Harriet Fuller, branch librarian; 2 prof, 3.5 non-prof staff; $10,923 materials budget; part of system budget; 23,887 volumes; 115 periodicals; 350 recordings, 93 cassettes; ILL; copying; teletype no. 810-591-1347; 50 hours weekly; black history, black achievement.

The library building was constructed in 1974 and opened in 1975.

Levi Branch Library
3676 Highway 61 South
Memphis, Tennessee 38109   (901) 789-3140

Mrs. LaRosa Greene, branch librarian; 4.5 non-prof staff; $4,300 materials budget; part of system budget; 22,657 volumes; 53 periodicals; 303 recordings, 54 cassettes; ILL; copying; teletype no. 810-591-1347; 60 hours weekly; Miss Dianne Cofer, Miss Elizabeth Johnston, former head librarians; black history.

    The library was built in 1967.

North Branch Library
1192 Vollintine
Memphis, Tennessee 38107   (901) 276-6631

Mrs. Thelma McKissic, branch librarian; 3.25 non-prof staff; $4,300 materials budget; part of system budget; 27,327 volumes; 56 periodicals; 301 recordings, 49 cassettes; ILL; teletype no. 810-591-1347; 60 hours weekly; black history.

    North Branch Library was constructed in 1961.

Shelby State Community College Library
737 Union Avenue
Memphis, Tennessee 38103   (901) 528-6743

Mr. Joe Lindenfeld, branch librarian; 3 prof, 8 non-prof staff; $115,000 materials budget; $234,650 operating budget; 32,000 volumes; 320 periodicals; 42 recordings, 349 cassettes; ILL; copying; teletype no. 810-591-1347; 75 hours weekly; black studies.

    The Shelby State Community College Library is one of the most unique branch libraries in a public library system in the country. In three locations and operating primarily as the community college's library, it also serves as a public library branch. It opened in 1972.

South Branch Library
185 East Norwood Avenue
Memphis, Tennessee 38109   (901) 946-8518

Mrs. Katherine Kuehn, branch librarian; 2 prof, 5.25 non-prof staff; $7,000 materials budget; part of system budget; 36,039 volumes; 67 periodicals; 716 recordings, 78 cassettes; ILL; copying; teletype no. 810-591-1347; 66 hours weekly; Mrs. Margaret Barr, former head librarian; black history.

    The South Branch was constructed in 1968.

Vance Branch Library
531 Vance Avenue
Memphis, Tennessee 38126   (901) 528-2980

Mrs. Geneva Cooper, branch librarian; 3.25 non-prof staff; $4,300 materials budget; part of system budget; 20,265 volumes; 66 periodicals; 245 recordings, 43 cassettes; ILL; teletype no. 810-591-1347; 54 hours weekly; Mrs. Pearl Oates, Miss Lillian Campbell, Miss Rachel Lymon, former head librarians; black history.

    The building was constructed in 1935 and was purchased in 1938 for renovation as a library.

Nashville

Edgehill Branch Library
1409 12th Avenue South
Nashville, Tennessee 37203   (615) 298-3173

Runcie Prince, branch librarian; 1 prof, 4 non-prof staff; part of system budget; 17,214 volumes; 37 periodicals; 16mm projector, 8mm projector, filmstrip projector, record player, and records; ILL; 52 hours weekly; Mrs. Celestine Turner, Ms. Gloria L. Coleman, former head librarians; general collection.

    The Edgehill Branch was opened to the public in 1967.

Hadley Park Library
1039 28th Avenue North
Nashville, Tennessee 37208   (615) 329-4774

Mrs. Edith Brooks, branch librarian; 2 prof, 3 non-prof staff; part of system budget; 18,608 volumes; 32 periodicals; 16mm projector, filmstrip projector, cassette player, and records; 53 hours weekly; Mrs. Ophelia Lockhart, former head librarian; general collection.

Hadley Park Branch was opened to the public in 1952.

Z. Alexander Looby Branch Library*
2301 Metro Center Boulevard
Nashville, Tennessee 37228   (615) 255-9503

Ms. Gloria L. Coleman, branch librarian; 2 prof, 4 non-prof staff; part of system budget; 8,000 volumes; 48 periodicals; 1 16mm projector, 1 8mm projector, 1 record player, 1 screen and 1 projection stand; ILL; 52 hours weekly; general collection.

The branch opened on November 1, 1976, a $900,000 modern structure located in the MetroCenter Complex. *The late Z. Alexander Looby was an outstanding black N.A.A.C.P. attorney and civil rights leader in Nashville. Active in politics, he was for many years a Councilman in the Metropolitan Nashville and Davidson County local government.

TEXAS

Austin

George Washington Carver Branch Library*
1165 Angelina
Austin, Texas 78702   (512) 472-5433

Mr. Clifton Griffin, branch librarian; 1 prof, 1.5 non-prof staff; part of system budget; 13,500 volumes; 49 periodicals; films, posters, storytime and puppet show presentations to children; ILL; 52 hours weekly; Mrs. Carolyn Watkins, Mrs. Jo Cappleman, Mrs. Elva Pearson, Mrs. Vinella Orr, former head librarians; black literature and black studies.

The George Washington Carver Branch building was originally the Austin Public Library's central library and was constructed in 1927; the library moved to its present site in 1933. *For significance of name, see BATON ROUGE, LOUISIANA.

Oak Springs Branch Library
2135 West Anderson Lane
Austin, Texas 78757   (512) 472-5433

Mr. Walter Davis, branch librarian; 1 prof, 3 non-prof staff; part of system budget; 29,000 volumes; 60 periodicals; films, storytime and puppet show presentations to children; ILL; copying; 57 hours weekly; Mrs. Joanna Chambers, Mrs. Carolyn Watkins, former head librarians; black literature, adult basic education.

The Oak Springs Branch Library was constructed in 1967. It is the largest branch library in the Austin Public Library system serving a predominantly black community.

Dallas

Dallas West Branch Library
2332 Singleton Boulevard
Dallas, Texas 75212   (214) 748-9071

Jo Iris Smith, branch librarian; 3 prof, 1 para-prof, 3 non-prof staff; $27,910 materials budget; $238,109 operating budget; 40,696 volumes; 116 periodicals; 220 toys, 7 8mm films, 117 filmstrips, 50 games, 559 posters, 75 video cassettes; ILL; copying; 44 hours weekly; Bill Ludwig, JoBelle Burk, Clarence Tyler, former head librarians; black and Mexican-American culture, social sciences, useful arts.

The Dunbar Branch opened in 1931. It was renamed Dallas West Branch and was moved to a leased storefront location in 1958. In August 1975, the Dallas West Branch moved into a new library building with 14,896 square feet.

Lancaster-Kiest Branch Library
3039 South Lancaster
Dallas, Texas 75216　　　　　　　　　(214) 748-9071

Branch librarian position vacant (1976); 3 prof, 5.5 non-prof staff; $31,750 materials budget; $248,623 operating budget; 67,853 volumes; 110 periodicals; 54 framed prints, 586 posters; ILL; copying; 43 hours weekly; Dick Miller, Geoff Gilson, Linda Allmand, Marcel Carroll, former head librarians; black history, literature and culture, picture books for deposit collection program.

　　　The library was built in 1964 to serve a white community. However, an abrupt neighborhood change one year after its opening created a continuing effort to change materials and services to meet the needs of the community.

Martin Luther King, Jr. Library/Learning Center*
2922 Forest Avenue
Dallas, Texas 75201　　　　　　　　　(214) 421-4171

Donna Johnson, branch librarian; 3 prof, 1 para-prof, 3 non-prof staff; $27,445 materials budget; $237,644 operating budget; 61,484 periodicals; 1,274 cassettes, 425 toys, 175 films, 56 8mm films, 328 filmstrips, 120 games, 64 kits, 98 framed pictures, 107 puzzles, 100 slides, 95 video cassettes; ILL; copying; 48 hours weekly; Cordie Hines, Charles Allen, Myrtle Berry, former head librarians; special collection on Martin Luther King, black culture, and non-book materials.

　　　The Sanger Branch opened in 1932 in a Carnegie library building. In 1968 it moved to a new location and was renamed the Forest Avenue Branch. It was renamed the Martin Luther King, Jr. Library/Learning Center and in 1974 became located in a new social service campus complex containing approximately 13,000 square feet. This branch interacts with other agencies to meet all the social needs of the community. *For significance of name, see DISTRICT OF COLUMBIA.

Houston

Alice Young Branch Library
6003 Beekman Road
Houston, Texas 77021　　　　　　　　(713) 643-8556

Anita Scott, branch librarian; 3 prof, 4.5 non-prof staff; $20,000 materials budget; $78,417 operating budget; 56,876 volumes; 108 periodicals; wide variety of records, cassettes and kits for juvenile readers; ILL; copying; 51 hours weekly; Betty Privette, Claudia Pettigrew, former head librarians; general collection.

　　　The branch library opened in 1957 and was very enthusiastically received by residents of south central Houston.

Dixon Branch Library
8002 Hirsch Road
Houston, Texas 77016　　　　　　　　(713) 633-2147

Ursula Tant, branch librarian; 2 prof, 3 non-prof staff; $17,000 materials budget; $35,000 operating budget; 15,638 volumes; 106 periodicals; AV kits and records for juvenile readers; ILL; copying; 49 hours weekly; Grace Brown, Evelin Fowler, former head librarians; black studies collection.

　　　The library opened in 1972. The Trinity Gardens community had previously rented two rooms in 1967 which were later vacated for a rented building at 7200 Hirsch Road.

Johnson Branch Library*
3511 Reed Road
Houston, Texas 77051　　　　　　　　(713) 733-1983

Pollye Brown, branch librarian; 1.5 prof, 3.5 non-prof staff; $13,000 materials budget; $55,162 operating budget; 30,746 volumes; 90 periodicals; record and cassette kits for juvenile readers; ILL; copying; Anita Scott, former head librarian; general collection.

The library opened in June, 1964. *The library was named for W. L. D. Johnson, Sr., who for 31 years was principal of Blackshear School in the Houston Public School system.

Kashmere Gardens Branch
5411 Pardee
Houston, Texas 77026   (713) 674-8461

Evelin Fowler, branch librarian; 4 prof, 6.5 non-prof staff; $20,000 materials budget; $113,132 operating budget; 34,219 volumes; 164 periodicals; juvenile audiovisual materials including records, cassettes, and kits, as well as learning kits for adult readers; ILL; copying; 53 hours weekly; Ella Epivey, Gail Carstens, former head librarians; adult learning center, black studies collection.

The library opened in 1971. A 1969 survey authorized by the Library Board and the City Planning Commission indicated the need for a library in Kashmere Gardens.

Lonnie E. Smith Branch Library*
3624 Scott Street
Houston, Texas 77004   (713) 741-6220

Grace Brown, branch librarian; 4.5 prof, 7 non-prof staff; $20,000 materials budget; $136,396 operating budget; 26,546 volumes; 197 periodicals; variety of records and cassettes for adults, as well as records, cassettes, and kits for juvenile readers; ILL; copying; 53 hours weekly; Grace Brown, former head librarian; black studies materials.

The branch opened in February 1974. It has 10,500 square feet and a collection emphasizing black materials. *Lonnie E. Smith was a black dentist active in the civil rights movement.

Pleasantville Branch Library
1520 Gellhorn
Houston, Texas 77029   (713) 676-0693

Sandra Stuart, branch librarian; 2 prof, 3 non-prof staff; $13,000 materials budget; $32,657 operating budget; 9,761 volumes; 108 periodicals; record and cassette kits for juvenile readers; ILL; copying; 49 hours weekly; Raymona Jones, former head librarian; general collection.

The library opened in 1974.

VIRGINIA

Portsmouth

Portsmouth Public Library
601 Court Street
Portsmouth, Virginia 23704   (804) 393-8501

Dean Burgess, chief librarian; 3 prof, 11 non-prof staff; $15,000 materials budget; part of system budget; 100,000 volumes; 650 periodicals; 6,000 records, 2 16mm films, record listening areas, films, filmstrips, and viewers; ILL; copying; 68 hours weekly; Helen Kirkpatrick, former head librarian; local history, black history.

The main library of the Portsmouth Public Library serves the largest number of black citizens. The library was founded in 1914.

Norfolk

Berkley Branch Library
229 East Berkley Avenue
Norfolk, Virginia 23523   (804) 441-2853

Olivia Venable, branch librarian; 1 prof, 2.5 non-prof staff; $7,500 materials budget; $39,000 operating budget; 14,305 volumes; 36 periodicals; ILL; 56.5 hours weekly; Mrs. Simmons, Mrs. Nix, Mr. Brockington, Mr. Dixon, former head librarians; black collection.

The Berkley Branch Library was established in 1921 in rented quarters. A new building was constructed in 1957, and present plans call for a move to another new building in 1977.

Blyden Branch Library*
879 East Princess Anne Road
Norfolk, Virginia 23504   (804) 441-2852

Mrs. Shirley Johnson, branch librarian; 3 non-prof staff; $7,500 materials budget; $45,000 operating budget; 19,297 volumes; 54 periodicals; ILL; 57 hours weekly; Mrs. Moon, Mrs. Johnson, Mrs. Curtis, former head librarians; black collection.

The Blyden Branch Library was established in 1921, and it was moved into a new building in 1957. *Edward W. Blyden was a distinguished black editor.

Brambleton Branch Library
1520 East Brambleton Avenue
Norfolk, Virginia 23504   (804) 441-2843

Mrs. Armitta King, branch librarian; 2.5 non-prof staff; $6,000 materials budget; $32,000 operating budget; 10,116 volumes; 51 periodicals; ILL; 49 hours weekly; Mrs. Abbitt, Miss Drewry, Mrs. Slate, former head librarians; black collection.

The Brambleton Branch Library was established in 1922 and relocated in 1947. It has always occupied rental quarters.

Van Wyck Branch Library
345 West 15th Street
Norfolk, Virginia 23517   (804) 441-2844

Mr. William Baker, branch librarian; 1 prof, 2.5 non-prof staff; $6,500 materials budget; $34,000 operating budget; 61 periodicals; ILL; 52 hours weekly; Mrs. King, Mrs. Tucker, Mrs. Washington, Mrs. Freeman, former head librarians; black collection.

The Van Wyck Branch Library was established in 1916 with a $20,000 Carnegie grant. It still occupies the same building.

WASHINGTON

Seattle

Douglass-Truth Branch Library*
23rd and East Yesler Way
Seattle, Washington 98122   (206) 625-4904

Cheryl Watson, branch librarian; 2.1 prof, 2.6 non-prof staff; $11,312 materials budget; $62,451 operating budget; 22,943 volumes; 51 periodicals; 111 cassettes, 250 records, 20 16mm films (rotating collection among 3 service units), 8mm projector, record player; ILL; copying; 40 hours weekly; Audrey Wright, James Welsh, Donna Edwards, Jean Glafke, former head librarians; Afro-American collection.

The library was established in 1914 as the Yesler Branch, named after a noted Seattle citizen. The name changed in 1975. *Concerning Frederick Douglass, the abolitionist, see CHICAGO, ILLINOIS. Sojourner Truth was an ardent abolitionist and orator. After her freedom from slavery as a result of the New York State Emancipation Act of 1827, she travelled across the country lecturing in behalf of her people.

WISCONSIN

Milwaukee

Atkinson Neighborhood Library
1960 West Atkinson Avenue
Milwaukee, Wisconsin 53206   (414) 278-3068

Mary Pickett, branch librarian; 4 prof, 5 non-prof staff; $22,672 materials budget; $118,577 operating budget; 55,536 volumes; 70 periodicals; member of the Milwaukee County Federated Library System which supplies videotapes, 16mm films, audio cassettes, filmstrips, and equipment to play videotapes and filmstrips, and each neighborhood library has its own film projector;

ILL; copying; teletype no. 910-262-1120; Mr. Nolan Neds, Ms. Alice Krahn, former head librarians; black experience in the U.S., world, literature, handicrafts.

The Atkinson branch was built in 1961 as a library facility, and it sponsors a community council.

Center Street Neighborhood Library
2620 West Center Street
Milwaukee, Wisconsin 53206   (414) 278-3090

Ms. Lynn Fell, branch librarian; 3 prof, 4 non-prof staff; $16,250 materials budget; $89,101 operating budget; 25,162 volumes; 70 periodicals; member of the Milwaukee County Federated Library System which supplies videotapes, 16mm films, audio cassettes, filmstrips, and equipment to play videotapes and filmstrips, and each neighborhood library has its own film projector; ILL; copying; teletype no. 910-262-1120; Ms. Mary Carian, Ms. Jo Reitman, Ms. Helen Nagle, Ms. Dorothy Arnold, former head librarians; black collection and Bible subjects.

The library opened in 1920 in a building previously a firehouse. For many years it served a white community, but the community has changed to a black community.

Martin Luther King Neighborhood Library*
310 East Locust Street
Milwaukee, Wisconsin 53202   (414) 278-3098

William J. K. Beaudot, branch librarian; 4 prof, 6 non-prof staff; $24,000 materials budget; $134,847 operating budget; 60,221 volumes; 65 periodicals; member of the Milwaukee County Federated Library System which supplies videotapes, 16mm films, audio cassettes, filmstrips, and equipment to play videotapes and filmstrips, and each neighborhood library has its own film projector; ILL; copying; teletype no. 910-262-1120; 50 hours weekly; black subjects, urban studies, early education, psychology.

The library opened in 1971 and was designated the Locust Library. The name was changed to Martin Luther King Neighborhood Library in a new facility designed for library purposes. *For significance of name, see DISTRICT OF COLUMBIA.

BLACK ACADEMIC LIBRARIES

Directory entries include the following information: name of library and school; address; telephone number; chief librarian's name; number of staff (professional, para-professional, non-professional); annual library materials budget; annual operating budget; number of volumes in library; number of periodicals received; description and number of audiovisual materials; availability of interlibrary loan (ILL), copying facilities, and teletype (with number, if available); any publications by the library; hours of service; names of former librarians; subject specializations if any. If information is not provided in each of these categories, this is because it was not reported to the compilers. (Library collections are assumed to be general in nature, but some do report subject specializations.) A brief history of each institution and its library was requested, but not always provided. Libraries named for black individuals are starred (*), and a note concerning that person will be found at the end of the entry.

ALABAMA

Birmingham

Daniel Payne College Library*
Daniel Payne College
2101 West Sayreton Road
Birmingham, Alabama 35214   (205) 798-8240, ext. 29

Emsie D. Colvin, chief librarian; 2.5 prof, 2 non-prof staff; $117,690 materials budget; $1,187,210 operating budget; 25,000 volumes; 185 periodicals; 200 records, 53 filmstrips; 32 slides and transparencies; 10 microforms, 9 maps and charts; ILL; copying; 70 hours weekly; Lula Driver, Jeanette Long, Alyce Ligeon, former chief librarians; general collection.

No date has been established for the founding of the library of Daniel Payne College, which was founded in 1889. In 1928, the College was reorganized and moved to Birmingham. Since the library was housed in the administration building, this could be the year the library was organized. Daniel Payne was a Bishop of the A. M. E. Church.

William A. Bell Library
Miles College
5500 Avenue G, Vinesville, Box 3800
Birmingham, Alabama 35208   (205) 780-6490, ext. 260

Mrs. H. R. Patterson, head librarian; 70,000 volumes; enquire concerning services; Afro-American Materials Center.

The college was founded in 1905, and the library was named after the ninth president of the college, William E. Bell, who served from 1912-1913.

Huntsville

Eva B. Dykes Library*
Oakwood College
Huntsville, Alabama 35806   (205) 837-1630, ext. 275 and 276

Jannith Louise Lewis, chief librarian; 5 prof, 3 non-prof staff; $25,000 materials budget; $135,000 operating budget; 70,000 volumes; 400 periodicals; 50 films, 450 records and cassettes, 150 filmstrips, 450 slides and transparencies, 100 other items; ILL; copying; 65 hours weekly; James Towery, former chief librarian; black studies, Seventh-Day Adventist black history.

     Oakwood College was founded in 1896, but the exact date of the founding of the library is not known. *Dr. Eva B. Dykes was the first black woman to meet the requirements for the Ph.D. degree in the United States. She was awarded the degree in 1921 by Radcliffe College, and has served as an English professor at Howard University, Oakwood College, and other academic institutions for over fifty years. The author of several books and many periodical articles, Dr. Dykes is also a member of the Seventh-Day Adventist Church, which founded Oakwood College.

Montgomery

G. W. Trenholm Memorial Library*
Alabama State University
Montgomery, Alabama 36101   (205) 262-3581, ext. 251 and 252

Dr. John Chen, chief librarian; 10 prof, 11 non-prof staff; $324,900 materials budget; $327,866 operating budget; 139,507 volumes; 771 periodicals; 898 audio recordings and tapes, 194 filmstrips, 802 slides and overhead transparencies, 1,119 pictures, games and other realia, 2,396 microforms (book titles), 78 microforms (periodical titles); ILL; copying; publications— newsletter, *Afro-American Resources Bibliography*; 78 hours weekly; Dr. Harry Robinson, Mr. Eligah Singley, John L. Buskey, Dr. Frances Pollard, Ollie L. Brown, former chief librarians; education, music, and Afro-American resources.

     The George W. Trenholm Library, founded in 1948, is the main university library, with special laboratories for classes in library education. The university library has seating capacity for 332 readers. Duplicating services are available on two floors. A $125,000 addition to the stack area was completed in 1963, and the building was air-conditioned in 1964. Plans for an ultramodern university library and learning resources complex are well underway, and the facility is scheduled to be completed in July 1977. *George W. Trenholm was the fourth president of the university.

Normal

J. F. Drake Memorial Learning Resources Center*
Alabama A&M University
Normal, Alabama 35762   (205) 859-7309, ext. 309

Mrs. Birdie O. Weir, chief librarian; 13 prof, 19 non-prof staff; part of university budget; 238,634 volumes; 1,114 periodicals; 2,963 tapes-cassettes, video, records, sound films, projectors, record players, study prints, art prints, games, kits, models, slides; ILL; copying; 80 hours weekly; Lucille A. Love, James Miller, Binford Conley, Dorothy Briscoe, former chief librarians; general collection.

     The first library building was constructed in 1906 with funds donated by Andrew Carnegie. It contained approximately 4,092 square feet of floor space and also housed many offices. In 1931, Miss Lucille A. Love, a graduate of Hampton Institute Library School, became the first librarian of the College. A new building was constructed and occupied in January 1968. The three-story structure contains 60,000 square feet of floor space, has a 300,000 volume capacity, and will seat 1,000 patrons. *Dr. Joseph F. Drake was president of the university from 1927-1962.

Talladega

Savery Library*
Talladega College
Talladega, Alabama 35160   (205) 362-2882

Mrs. Juliette S. Smith, chief librarian; 2 prof, 2 non-prof staff; $30,000 materials budget; $59,000 operating budget; 64,000 volumes; 412 periodicals; 1,102 records, 170 phonotape cassettes and reels, 12 films, 290 filmstrips, 4,690 slides, 2,001 microfilm, 27 microfiche; ILL; copying; publications—library handbook for faculty and staff, a handbook for freshmen and new students; 65 hours weekly; Miss Margaret H. Scott, Miss Mabel Carter, Mrs. Mary Cleveland, Miss Elizabeth C. Williams, former chief librarians; art, black studies.

    Through the generosity of the General Education Board, the American Missionary Association, Mr. Edward S. Harkness of New York City, eight hundred other donors, and the sale of some of its own land, the College was able, in 1939, to build a spacious and modestly beautiful library.

    The Savery Library, in New England colonial style, was completed during the one-hundredth year anniversary of the Amistad incident. Embedded in the terrazzo floor of the central library, in soft colors of blue, green, and white with strips of brass, is the picture of the ship, the Amistad. The students themselves decreed that it should not be stepped upon, for it symbolizes the circumstances that gave birth to the American Missionary Association. On the walls above this floor-piece are murals painted by Hale Woodruff that give the story of the Amistad slave mutiny and depict a station along the "underground railroad," registration on the first day of school at Talladega, and the building of the library. *William Savery was an enslaved carpenter who led the Freedmen's Bureau and the American Missionary Association to purchase Swayne Hall, which he helped to build, for a campus site. He became an original trustee and incorporator of the College.

Tuscaloosa

William H. Sheppard Library*
Stillman College
3600 15th Street
Tuscaloosa, Alabama 35401   (205) 752-2548, ext. 52

Martha L. O'Rourke, chief librarian; 6 prof, 4 non-prof staff; $26,300 materials budget (funds for media equipment, materials not included); $91,109 operating budget (funds for media staff not included); 72,000 volumes; 326 periodicals; 2,481 microforms, 440 audio recordings, 422 filmstrips, silent-sound, 455 slides and transparencies; ILL; copying; publications—student library handbook, faculty library handbook; 72.5 hours weekly; Martha E. Riddick, Mary L. Hill, Charlotte Dean, James R. O'Rourke, Sr., Grace Tooson, former chief librarians; black studies, business and economics.

    The library had its beginning as a small collection of books located in the Old Chapel. Early in 1930, when the library was moved to a room above the dining hall, a part-time librarian who also taught classes in English was employed. In 1936, when the enrollment reached 168 students, a full-time librarian was hired.

    When Stillman became a four-year liberal arts college in 1948, the library was moved to the first floor of Snedecor Building, which had sufficient stack space to house the book collection of 9,000 volumes and 122 periodicals and to seat 100 persons. The present library was built in 1956. In 1971, the media program was organized and incorporated into the service patterns of the library under a single administration with a staff of specialists and support personnel. The library became a learning center with programmed materials, electronic and photographic equipment in addition to print materials. *The Reverend William H. Sheppard was an alumnus of the college and a missionary who, in 1890, helped Samuel Lapsley to establish the Congo mission of the Presbyterian Church. For this work, he was made a Fellow of the Royal Geographic Society of London.

Tuskegee

Hollis Burke Frissel Library
Tuskegee Institute
Tuskegee Institute, Alabama 36088 (205) 727-8237

Annie G. King, chief librarian; 9 prof, 9 non-prof staff; $97,600 materials budget; $249,900 operating budget; 225,176 volumes; 1,103 periodicals; 44,459 microfilm, microfiche, cassettes, film loops, filmstrips, transparencies; ILL; copying; publications—*Guide to Archives and Special Collections at Tuskegee Institute* (publication pending), selected list of current acquisitions (monthly with local distribution), *Guide to Hollis Burke Frissell Library*; 85 hours weekly; M. D. Sprague, Lucile E. Wheelock, LePearl Howard, Walter B. Williams, former chief librarians; black experience, veterinary medicine, government document depository, nursing, architecture, engineering.

The library dates back to the founding of the Institute, when a small collection of materials was gathered under the supervision of Alice E. Jones, who served as librarian from 1881-1894.

ARKANSAS

Little Rock

M. L. Harris Library*
Philander Smith College
Little Rock, Arkansas (501) 375-9845, ext. 46

Alice M. Martin, chief librarian; 3 prof, 1 non-prof staff; part of university budget; 55,000 volumes; 125 periodicals; 2,000 microforms, 2,000 audio-recordings, 300 filmstrips, 8,500 slides and transparencies, 40 miscellaneous; ILL; copying; 78 hours weekly; Mrs. Atlene Vincent, Mrs. Hazel Kenicutt, Mrs. Shirley Tolefree, Mrs. June Fleming, former chief librarians; black studies.

Accession records were begun in 1925. The present library was constructed as part of the Fine Arts Center in 1959. *Bishop Marquis LaFayette Harris was president of the College from 1936-1961.

Pine Bluff

John Brown Watson Memorial Library*
The University of Arkansas at Pine Bluff
Pine Bluff, Arkansas 71601 (501) 535-6700, ext. 232, 318, and 319

Edward Fontennette, librarin; 3 prof, 11 non-prof staff; $40,000 materials budget; $152,477 operating budget (1975-76); 71,002 volumes; 800 periodicals; 333 filmstrips, 4 films, 700 phonodiscs, 150 slides, 18 overhead transparencies, 50 tapes; ILL; copying; 81 hours weekly; Mrs. J. Palmer Howard, former chief librarian; general collection.

The collection in 1928 consisted of 600 books that were housed in one small reading room of the main building of the old Branch Normal School. In 1929 the library was moved into half the space of the second floor of the present administration building, where the reading room seated 144 patrons. Between January, 1930, and the end of the fiscal year, June 30, 1931, the book stock increased by 3,556 volumes, which brought the total accessions to 4,156. The unusual growth was due in large measure to the Rosenwald Fund donation of $2,500 and a special state appropriation of $5,000. During the Depression years of the thirties, a donation of nearly 1,000 volumes was made from Howard University of Washington, D.C., and contributions from friends. In 1939, the library moved into a modern two-story structure located near the center of the quadrangle. The main reading room accommodated 240 patrons and the periodical room, an additional 30 people. The present site was occupied in 1968. *John Brown Watson was president of the College during the years 1928-1942.

DELAWARE

Dover

William C. Jason Library-Learning Center*
Delaware State College
Dover, Delaware 19901   (302) 678-5111 or 678-5112

Dr. Daniel E. Coones, chief librarian; 6 prof, 11 non-prof staff; $137,500 materials budget; $183,000 operating budget; 117,000 volumes (22,000 of which are microtexts); 516 periodicals; 500 audio and video tapes, films, filmstrips, and recordings; ILL; copying; publications—monthly newsletter and acquisitions list; 90 hours weekly; E. J. Josey, Arthur Gunn, Juanita R. Williams, Gertrude W. Jackson, Justina Henderson, former chief librarians; black studies, Delaware history.

The library was founded with the establishment of the College in 1891. It moved into what was the chapel in the 1940s, additions were made during the 1950s, and the present William C. Jason Library-Learning Center was constructed in 1975. *Dr. William C. Jason was the second president and first black to hold this office, serving with distinction from 1895 to 1923.

DISTRICT OF COLUMBIA

Library and Media Services Division
University of the District of Columbia
425 2nd Street, N.W.
Washington, D.C. 20001   (202) 727-2174

Mrs. Lottie Mae Wright, director; 28 prof, 37 non-prof staff; $352,359 materials budget; $567,449 operating budget; 286,000 volumes; 1,560 periodicals; films, filmstrips, slides, tapes (vodeo, cassettes, reel-to-reel), phonodiscs; ILL; publications—media news, new acquisitions, *Media Center* (brochure), *Media Power, Guide to Media Services, Media Services to Faculty, Capital Media Guide* (I and II), *Understanding Media* (newsletter); Robert T. Jordon, Matthew Woods, former chief librarians; general collection.

The Library of Federal City College was established in 1968 to coincide with the beginning of the College. Located in the basement of FCC's Main Campus at 425 2nd Street, N.W., Washington, D.C., it was called the Media Center and was organized with a multi-media approach to library development and to education itself.

Howard University Libraries
Howard University
500 Howard Place N.W.
Washington, D.C. 20059   (202) 636-7234

Binford H. Conley, director of university libraries; 62 prof, 69 non-prof staff; $611,406 materials budget; $2,596,678 operating budget; 837,055 volumes; 7,606 periodicals; 7,121 microfilm reels, 429,366 microfiche, 449 reel-to-reel tapes, 525 audio cassettes, 5,295 records, 185 filmstrips, 402 motion picture films, 19,147 slides, 197 video tapes; ILL; copying; teletype no. TWX 710-822-9798; publications—Howard University libraries' staff newsletter (bi-weekly), school of business and public administration library (monthly); accessions—*Moorland-Spingarn Research Center* (bi-monthly except July/August); 97 hours weekly during academic year; Dr. Walter G. Daniel (1935-46), Dr. Joseph H. Reason (1946-71), William D. Cunningham (1971-73), Kenneth S. Wilson, acting director (1973-75), former chief librarians; Afro-American, curriculum materials.

Library services at Howard can be traced back nearly to the founding of the University. In April, 1867, the Board of Trustees appointed a committee to select books for the library of the newly founded institution. Danforth B. Nichols, the first librarian and one of the 17 incorporators of the University, moved his private library to the campus and began to collect and organize the material. Since then, the library system has grown to include the main library, Founders Library, which was opened in 1939, and eleven branches serving the various departments, schools, and colleges of the University. Howard also has the Moorland-Spingarn Research Center, a law library, and an Afro-American Studies Resource Center, all of which also provide library services to the university community but which are independent of the central University Libraries system. All figures include both the Howard University Libraries and the independent libraries (Moorland-Spingarn Research Center, Law Library, and the Afro-American Studies Resource Center) and are accurate for the year ending June 30, 1975.

FLORIDA
Jacksonville

H. Y. Tookes Library*
Edward Waters College
1658 Kings Road
Jacksonville, Florida 32209   (904) 353-5053

Mrs. Jean S. Jones, chief librarian; 3 prof, 4 non-prof staff; $6,000 materials budget; $53,200 operating budget; 37,000 volumes; 153 periodicals; 249 phonorecords, 75 cassette tapes, 296 filmstrips, 17 maps, 680 slides, the entire collection of ERIC Microfiche consisting of some 133,000 separate pieces of microfiche—years 1968-76; copying; publications—staff manuals and library guide; 52 hours weekly; Mrs. Willye F. Dennis, James Lockett, Mrs. Elizabeth Reddin, Mrs. Olga L. Bradham, former chief librarians; Afro-American, curriculum materials.

The present library facility, a carpeted, air-conditioned, one-story building, was built in 1945, when the college was operating as a junior college. In 1955, an annex was added. Before this time, there was a library located in one room of the B. F. Lee Theological Seminary, which is now the administration building. *Henry Young Tookes was a bishop of the African Methodist Episcopal Church.

Tallahassee

Samuel H. Coleman Memorial Library*
Florida Agricultural & Mechanical University
P.O. Box 78-A, Florida A&M University
Tallahassee, Florida 32307   (904) 222-2030, ext. 338 and 354

Dr. Nicholas E. Gaymon, chief librarian; 15 prof, 23 non-prof staff; $262,182 materials budget; $778,894 operating budget; 260,000 volumes; 2,250 periodicals; 9,026 reels of microfilm, 4,602 phonodiscs, 805 filmstrips, 16,391 slides, 7,781 microfiche, 1,130 pictures, 2,088 microfilm, 79 films, 8 tapes, and maps, charts, and graphs; ILL; copying; teletype (no number provided); publications—student library handbook, *A Classified Catalogue of the Negro Collection in the Samuel H. Coleman Library*, Florida Agricultural & Mechanical University, December, 1969 (photocopied); 81 hours weekly; J. Luther Thomas, Maude Watkins, Joseph Reason, E. C. Ware, Jeannie Baker, former chief librarians; general collection.

In 1902, Florida A&M University began its library development with a collection of 1,023 volumes which had been donated by friends and purchased through a special fund set aside for that purpose. The first building, Carnegie Library, was completed in 1914. In 1948, the present building was completed at a cost of $580,000, and there were 20,000 volumes. To date, the collection numbers over 260,000 volumes housed in the main library and six branch/reading libraries (Pharmacy, Sociology, Business, Technology, Nursing Reading Room, and Media Specialization). In 1972, this building was completely renovated with an addition, at a cost of over $800,000. *Samuel H. Coleman was the earliest graduate of the University.

GEORGIA
Albany

Margaret Rood Hazard Library
Albany State College
Albany, Georgia 31705   (912) 439-4065

Guy C. Craft, chief librarian; 6 prof, 4 non-prof staff; $62,789.38 materials budget; $221,507 operating budget; 96,000 volumes; 591 periodicals; audiovisual materials are located in the Education Department; ILL; copying; 71 hours weekly; Mrs. Mary L. McCoy, Miss Gloria Williams, Mrs. Minnie M. Finch, former chief librarians; general collection.

338 / Black Academic Libraries

The original library of Albany State College was completed in 1934, a gift of the late Miss Caroline Hazard, former president of Wellesley College. The building was named in memory of her mother, Mrs. Margaret Rood Hazard. The new building was constructed with funds provided by the Georgia Board of Regents, when it became apparent that the original building was inadequate for the needs of a constantly growing student body. This building was completed and available to readers on May 25, 1959. A three-story wing has been added to this building, completed in 1970.

Atlanta

Trevor Arnett Library
Atlanta University
273 Chestnut Street, S.W.
Atlanta, Georgia 30314   (404) 681-0251, ext. 225

Casper LeRoy Jordan, chief librarian; 15 prof, 6 non-prof staff; $116,000 materials budget (1974-75); $377,510 operating budget (1974-75); 309,565 volumes; 1,084 periodicals; 1,029 filmstrips; ILL; copying; publications—book notes, library handbook, *Guide to Special Collections*; 85 hours weekly; Charlotte Templeton (1931-42), Wallace Van Jackson (1942-48), L. D. Reddick (1948-57), William Bennett (1959-65), Miles Jackson (1965-68), Gaynelle Barksdale (1968-74), former chief librarians; blacks in Georgia, U.S. and Africa.

The library of Atlanta University began its existence in the second year of the institution's life in South Hall of the old Atlanta University campus (now Morris Brown College). The catalog of 1872-73 gives first mention of it as a library. Gifts and donations were solicited, and the generosity of R. R. Graves of Brooklyn, New York, caused the first name of the library to be in his honor. In 1883, the library was moved to Stone Hall, now Fountain Hall, on the Morris Brown campus. With funds donated by Andrew Carnegie for a site and building, the Carnegie Library was opened in 1905 to serve the Atlanta University academic community and the black public until the municipal library provided service to blacks. The success of the Atlanta University Center idea, begun in 1929 with the affiliation of Atlanta University and Morehouse and Spelman Colleges, was largely dependent upon the establishment of a central library. In June 1930, the General Education Board gave a gift of $450,000 for this purpose, and the present Trevor Arnett Library was dedicated in April, 1932.

Marquis L. Harris Library*
Clark College
240 Chestnut Street, S.W.
Atlanta, Georgia 30314   (404) 681-3080, ext. 232

Mrs. Fannie Burrell Hogan, chief librarian; 4 prof, 3 non-prof staff; $21,000 materials budget; $120,450 operating budget; 60,000 volumes; 415 periodicals; 3,889 items including cassettes, filmstrips, films, film loops, microfiche, records, slides, tapes, microfilms and manuals, guides, texts and notes; ILL; copying; publications—student handbook, faculty handbook, bibliographies; 90 hours weekly; Mrs. C. Riley, Mrs. Dovie T. Patrick, Mrs. Margaret Hunton, and Mr. Henry James, former chief librarians; physics, education, chemistry and mathematics.

The library, then known as Georgia Smith Keeney Library (after the wife of the resident Bishop Keeney of the Methodist Episcopal Church), had its beginning in Leete Hall in South Atlanta, on the site of Gammon Theological Seminary. In 1941, under the administration of Mrs. C. L. Riley, the library was located on the second floor of the present Haven-Warren Administration Building. In 1970, the Marquis L. Harris Library became a part of the McPheeter-Dennis Building, its present location. *Bishop Marquis LaFayette Harris was a former resident bishop of Atlanta, president of Philander Smith College, and an alumnus of Clark College.

Jordan-Thomas Library*
Morris Brown College
643 Hunter Street, S.W.
Atlanta, Georgia 30314   (404) 525-7831, ext. 37

Mrs. Victoria W. Jenkins, chief librarian; 3 prof, 2 non-prof staff; $63,802 materials budget; $118,802 operating budget; 49,000 volumes; 385 periodicals; AV materials are housed in two locations and the basic equipment includes projectors (16mm, 8/super, filmstrips, overhead, opaque), recorders, record players, video tape, TV receiver, previewers, and listening stations; ILL; copying; 80 hours weekly; H. Eugene Craig, G. T. Johnson, Alta McKnight Anderson, Mary McAfee, former chief librarians; business administration and chemistry.

A small reading room was set up in 1885, shortly after the college was founded, and the library was moved to its present site in August, 1968. *The joint names are derived from the Right Reverend Frederick Douglas Jordan, clergyman, bishop, and chief ecumenical officer of the African Methodist Episcopal Church, and his mother's maiden name, Carrie Thomas Jordan.

Fort Valley

Henry Alexander Hunt Memorial Library*
Fort Valley State College
Ft. Valley, Georgia 31030   (912) 825-6342

Homie Regulus, chief librarian; 8 prof, 11 non-prof staff; $148,000 materials budget; $193,504 operating budget; 130,664 volumes; 1,352 periodicals; about 138,000 volumes of microtext, including fiche, film, filmstrip, records, cassette tapes, and reel-to-reel; ILL; copying; publications—semi-quarterly book list, departmental newsnotes; 83 hours weekly; Sarah H. Rogers, Beulah E. Cooper, Edith Thomas, Lillie Adkins, former chief librarians; home economics, agriculture, education, ethnic heritage.

Since its founding in 1895, the College has offered library service. Its first library was a division of the high school program. The first formal library program began in 1925 with a gift of a building from the Carnegie Foundation. *Henry Alexander Hunt was the second principal of the Fort Valley High and Industrial School. Under his administration, the school became a normal school, and just before his death (1938), he completed all arrangements for the school to be transferred to the state. At that time, the school became a four-year degree granting institution.

Augusta

Warren A. Candler Library
Paine College
Augusta, Georgia 30901   (404) 722-4471, ext. 253

Miss Helen Gilbert, chief librarian; 3 prof, 3 non-prof staff; $23,000 materials budget; $68,701 operating budget; 59,000 volumes; 422 periodicals; 954 recordings, 192 slides, 16 motion picture films, 3,101 microfilms, 348 filmstrips, 277 cassettes, 31 kits; ILL; copying; publications—student handbook, student assistant handbook, faculty handbook; 66 hours weekly; Mrs. Lenna Hall, Dr. Ruth Bartholomew, former chief librarians; liberal arts.

The Warren A. Candler Library was completed in 1947, a two-story, brick veneer building. Funds for constructing the building were given by the General Education Board of the Methodist Churches in Georgia, alumni, friends, and the Christian Methodist Episcopal Church.

Savannah

Asa H. Gordon Library*
Savannah State College
Savannah, Georgia 31404   (912) 356-2183, 356-2184, and 356-2185

A. J. McLemore, chief librarian; 14 prof, 5 non-prof staff; approximately $120,000 materials budget; approximately $250,000 operating budget; 107,385 volumes; 917 periodicals; 9,921 microfilms, 1,891 microcards, 128,578 microfiche, 122 audio-cassettes, 88 films, 302 filmstrips with cassettes, 478 records and hardware; ILL; copying; publications—various bibliographies on current issues; 75 hours weekly; Mrs. Ben Ingersoll, Mrs. Luella Hawkins, E. J. Josey, former chief librarians; Negro collection.

The library was established in 1891, when the institution began operating as the Georgia State Industrial College, a branch of the University of Georgia. By 1900-1901, the collection numbered 600 books. The first mention of a librarian in available records appeared in the 1930-31 catalog with the name of Miss Ursuline Belcher (later Mrs. Ben Ingersoll). In 1959, a new

Savannah State College Library was opened. *Asa H. Gordon was a faculty member, author, and civil rights activist whose employment at Savannah State College was terminated because of a series of articles attempting to equalize black teachers' salaries with whites. His most notable publication was *Sketches of Negro Life and History in South Carolina*.

KENTUCKY
Frankfort

Blazer Library
Kentucky State University
Frankfort, Kentucky 40601   (502) 564-5852

Donald W. Lyons, Director of Libraries; 6 prof, 14 non-prof staff; $140,000 materials budget; $288,218 operating budget; 155,000 volumes; 931 periodicals; 350 films, 80 film loops, 50,000 microfilm and microfiche; ILL; copying; teletype (no number provided); publications—*The Blazer Bugle, K.S.U. Libraries Newsletter, African and African-American History and Culture: A Bibliography*; 78 hours weekly; Olie Atkins Carpenter (1929-30), Emma B. Lewis (1930-34), Ann Rucker Anderson (1934-43), Catherine O. Vaughn (1943-49), James R. O'Rourke (1949-75), former chief librarians; African and Afro-American history and culture.

A room or area has been designated as a library since the founding of the school in 1886; however, in the fall of 1929, Kentucky State's first professionally trained librarian assumed the head librarianship. From 369 books in 1929, the collection has grown to a total in excess of 155,000. The present Blazer Library was constructed in 1958 with an addition in 1967 that more than doubled the floor space.

LOUISIANA
Baton Rouge

Southern University Library
Southern University
Southern Branch Post
Baton Route, Louisiana 70813   (504) 771-4990, ext. 0

Mrs. Georgia Brown, acting director; 17 prof, 13 non-prof staff; $116,621 materials budget; $411,748 operating budget; 257,000 volumes; 1,558 periodicals; 2 microfilm reader-printers, 2 microfilm readers, 2 microfiche readers, 10,350 microforms; ILL; copying; publications—library handbook, bibliographies for departments; 92 hours weekly; Mrs. Camille Shade (1929-70), Mr. Edward Fontenette (1970-74), Mrs. Adele Jackson, acting director (1974-75), former chief librarians; general collection.

In 1928, the library began with a small collection of books supplied by the teaching staff, and Mrs. Camille Shade began as the first professional librarian in 1929. The present building was constructed in 1941 with expansions in 1958. The staff has grown to thirty, serving 9,000 students.

Grambling

A. C. Lewis Memorial Library
Grambling State University
Grambling, Louisiana 71245   (318) 247-6941, ext. 220

Mrs. Hazel S. Johnson Jones, chief librarian; 9 prof, 8 non-prof staff; $115,000 materials budget; $376,000 operating budget; 122,000 volumes; 1,032 periodicals; 5,612 microfilm reels, 156 cassettes, 373 filmstrips, 76,652 microfiche (ERIC, LAC, ELE and Update/Newsbank); ILL; 76 hours weekly; Dr. Mary Watson Hymon (1947-74), Mrs. Virginia Hill, Mrs. Carrie Robinson, former chief librarians; general collection.

New Orleans

Will W. Alexander
Dillard University
2601 Gentilly Boulevard
New Orleans, Louisiana 70122   (504) 944-8751, ext. 240

Carole R. Taylor, chief librarian; 6 prof, 3 non-prof staff; $51,505 materials budget; $170,270 operating budget (fiscal year ending June 30, 1975); 111,033 volumes; 658 periodicals; 1,977 newspapers and magazines on microfilm, 2,146 microcards, 135 phonograph records, 200 cassettes, Schomburg Collection of 64 titles and 305 microfilm; ILL; copying; 78 hours weekly; Dr. Nicholas Gaymon, Mr. Ernest Wagner, Mr. Paul Smith, Ms. Rita W. McCoy, former chief librarians; general collection.

Prior to 1961, the Dillard Library was housed in the administration building. A separate building was erected October 22, 1961, and dedicated in honor of Will W. Alexander, the first Administrative Officer of Dillard University. Under his leadership, the original building of the campus was constructed, the first educational program designed, and the first faculty selected.

Southern University in New Orleans Library
6400 Press Drive
New Orleans, Louisiana 70126   (504) 282-4401, ext. 224

Mrs. Eddie Mae Young, chief librarian; 10 prof, 2 non-prof staff; $55,784 materials budget; $119,051 operating budget; 119,042 volumes; 692 periodicals; ILL; copying; publications— library manual; 75 hours weekly; Mr. Leonard S. Washington, former chief librarian; general collection.

The library was established in September 1956, when the university was created by Act 28 of the extraordinary session of the Louisiana Legislature. The institution is a branch unit of Southern University, Baton Rouge.

Xavier University Library
7325 Palmetto and Pine Street
New Orleans, Louisiana 70124   (504) 486-7411, ext. 317

Leslie R. Morris, chief librarian; 8.5 prof, 11 non-prof staff; $75,000 materials budget; $250,000 operating budget; 99,112 volumes; 445 periodicals; 820 tapes, 5,600 records, 500 slide sets, 90 films, 1,023 filmstrips, 300 transparencies; ILL; copying; publications—library handbook; 82 hours weekly; Sr. Marie Christine, S.B.S., Sr. M. Redempta, S.B.S., Sr. Mary Stanislaus, S.B.S., former chief librarians; general collection.

Xavier University of Louisiana was founded by the Sisters of the Blessed Sacrament in 1925, and it is the only black Catholic university in the western hemisphere. The library was built in 1937.

MARYLAND

Baltimore

Parlett Moore Library*
Coppin State College
2500 West North Avenue
Baltimore, Maryland   (301) 383-7371

Joseph A. Boyce, acting director; 9 prof, 9 non-prof staff; $206,000 materials budget; $405,300 operating budget; 93,226 volumes; 40,000 microfiche, 2,524 phonograph records, 112 films, 18 loop films, 1,402 filmstrips, 2,106 slides, 1,247 pictures, 56 reel tapes, 154 cassette tapes, 73 transparencies, and curriculum kits, photographs, art prints, and study prints; ILL; copying; publications—bibliography of recent additions, library fact sheet; 65 hours weekly; Mrs. Leone Thompson, Mrs. Hilda B. Clark, former chief librarians; education, special education.

Prior to 1952, when Coppin State College became a state-funded institution, it was called Coppin Demonstration School and was located on Mount Street and Riggs Avenue in Baltimore City. Here the school maintained just a scattered collection of books without a professional librarian. Coppin moved to its present location in 1952 and became Coppin State Teachers College.

The library occupied a portion of the second floor of the original building of the college, presently known as Connor Hall. *Dr. Parlett Moore was a past president of the College.

Morgan State University Library
Cold Spring Lane and Hillen Road
Baltimore, Maryland 21239 (301) 893-3489

George C. Grant, chief librarian; 17 prof, 4 para-prof, 17 non-prof staff; $86,000 materials budget; $612,387 operating budget; 154,032 volumes; 1,378 periodicals; 69,580 microforms, 1,934 recordings, 3,355 slides, 1,103 tapes, 634 card-set tapes, 366 art prints, 106 small sculpture, 33 kits, 2 filmstrips; ILL; copying; 90 hours weekly; Beulah M. Davis (1926-1965), Helen Florine Williams, acting librarian (1965-66), Walter Fisher (1966-75), Helen Florine Williams, acting director (1975-76), former chief librarians; Afro-American/black studies.

Morgan's library evolved from the personal libraries of ministers and teachers associated with the Centenary Biblical Institute (1867-1890). This institute's subsequent growth into Morgan College (1890-1939) saw the continuation and development of a "quasi-ministerial" library into one supportive of this liberal arts college. Prior to the school's take-over by the State of Maryland in 1939, the library was moved into a new facility, where it continued to expand. In 1973, the library was moved into a larger, newly constructed building.

Bowie

Thurgood Marshall Library*
Bowie State College
Bowie, Maryland 20715 (301) 262-3350, ext. 237 or 289

Mrs. Courtney H. Funn, chief librarian; 11 prof, 12 non-prof staff; $83,508 materials budget; $396,071 operating budget; 118,908 volumes; 1,206 periodicals; 57 motion pictures, 285 audio recordings, 857 filmstrips, 92 slides and overhead transparencies, 58 maps and charts, 875 items of other materials (mixed media, kits, etc.); ILL; copying; 80 hours weekly; Ms. Angela Smith, Ms. Lillian M. Gary, former chief librarians; Maryland Collection, Thomas G. Pullen, Jr. Collection, Ford Foundation Black Collection (paperbacks), Negro Collection, Graves Collection of Rare Materials, Bowie State College Archives.

The old Thomas G. Pullen, Jr. Library was completed in 1959, and was designed to house 60,000 volumes. The new Thurgood Marshall Library is a three-story structure that houses 600,000 volumes and provides 137,400 square feet of space for bookstacks and readers. *Thurgood Marshall, distinguished civil rights attorney, is the first black to be appointed to the Supreme Court.

Princess Anne

Frederick Douglass Library*
University of Maryland, Eastern Shore
Princess Anne, Maryland 21853 (301) 651-2200, ext. 229

Mrs. Jessie Cottman Smith, chief librarian; 8 prof, 7 non-prof staff; $136,000 materials budget; 93,000 volumes; 920 periodicals; 113,548 items consisting of cassettes, filmstrips, microbook, microfiche, microfilm, recordings, slides, study prints, and transparencies; ILL; copying; publications—new acquisitions print-out, *Your Library Guide*, staff procedural manual, library book mark, student assistants' manual; 72 hours weekly; Mr. Baine R. Maddox, Mrs. Ann R. Anderson, Jason Grant III, Mrs. Olie Carpenter, former chief librarians, general collection.

Under the control of the Centenary Biblical Institute, the branch known as the Delaware Conference Academy was founded on September 13, 1886, with an enrollment of nine students. Subsequently, it became Industrial Branch of Morgan State College, still under the control of the Delaware Conference, and as operated by Morgan State College under the control of the Methodist Church, the institution was known as Princess Anne Academy. The State of Maryland, in its land-grant program at the Maryland Agricultural College at College Park (to which Afro-Americans were not admitted as students), sought to provide a land-grant program for Afro-Americans and assumed control of the Princess Anne Academy, renaming it the Eastern Shore Branch of the Maryland Agricultural College. The arrangement was effected in 1919. In

1926, the College passed into complete control by the state, and the University of Maryland was designated as the administrative agency. In 1948, the Eastern Shore Branch of the University of Maryland (Princess Anne College) became officially Maryland State College. On July 1, 1970, Maryland State College became the University of Maryland, Eastern Shore. *Frederick Douglass was a well-known black orator and abolitionist in the nineteenth century.

MISSISSIPPI

Holly Springs

Leontyne Price Library*
Rust College
Holly Springs, Mississippi 38635   (601) 252-4661, ext. 250

Johnny W. Jackson, chief librarian; 4 prof, 1 non-prof staff; $53,693 materials budget; $89,118 operating budget; 73,998 volumes; 306 periodicals; 30 16mm films, 829 audio recordings (including disc, audio tapes and cassettes), 214 filmstrips and filmstrip record sets, 2,274 reels of microfilm, 914 slides and overhead transparencies; ILL; copying; 79 hours weekly; Mr. Wilfred T. Mayfield, Mr. James D. Lockett, Mr. Frank Moorer, Mrs. Earnest A. Smith, former chief librarians; general collection.

*Leontyne Price, an internationally famed lyric soprano, was born in Laurel, Mississippi.

Itta Bena

James Herbert White Library*
Mississippi Valley State University
Itta Bena, Mississippi 38941   (601) 254-9811, ext. 275

Robbye R. Henderson, chief librarian; 7 prof, 18 non-prof staff; $71,387 materials budget (1975-76); $287,434 operating budget (1975-76); 88,259 volumes; 251 periodicals; 195 filmloops, 293 films, 1,346 filmstrips, 36 maps, 1,132 microfilms, 696 records, 922 slides, 221 cassette tapes, 61 open reel tapes, 586 transparencies; ILL; 72 hours weekly; Mrs. Mary E. Kidd, Mr. Joseph Perches, Mrs. Birdie Weir, Mrs. Clara L. Bendenfield, former chief librarians; general collection.

The library at Mississippi Valley State University began in 1952 (one year after the founding of the institution) in a classroom building with teachers serving as librarians. In 1957, a two-story wing of the old Science-Library building became the library's quarters. A stable and qualified staff, sizeable budgets, and services of qualified consultants contributed greatly to the growth of the library program from 1958-1972. In April 1973, the new James Herbert White Library was dedicated, with construction and equipment costing over one million dollars. It has a book capacity of 160,000 volumes and seating for 750. *Dr. James Herbert White was the first president of the institution.

Jackson

Henry T. Sampson Library*
Jackson State University
1325 J. R. Lynch Street
Jackson, Mississippi 39217   (601) 968-2123

Dr. Lelia G. Rhodes, chief librarian; 13 prof, 21 non-prof staff; $154,966.14 materials budget; $483,842 operating budget; 350,000 volumes (including 70,000 titles on microfilm); 2,002 periodicals; 2,114 recordings, 314 tapes, 6,074 slides, 676 films, 635 filmstrips, 100 8mm film loops, 118,656 microfiche; ILL; copying; publications—*A Classified Bibliography of the Afro-American Collection and Selected Works on Africa, New Acquisitions—Henry T. Sampson Library, A Selected Bibliography of Works by Participants of the Phillis Wheatley Poetry Festival . . . in the Henry T. Sampson Library*; 83 hours weekly; Rubye E. Stutts Lyells, Jane Watts, Ernestine A. Lipscomb, former chief librarians; education, black studies.

The earliest reference to "library" service appeared in the Natchez Seminary Catalog, 1882-83, after the institution was founded by the American Baptist Home Mission Society in 1877. The college moved to its present site in 1903, and by 1909, the library was housed in

Chivers Hall, a new building. When the college changed to a state institution in 1946, the one-room library was enlarged. In 1944, the library was moved from Chivers Hall to the basement of the newly constructed Johnson Hall, and this was expanded in 1952. Construction of the new library was completed by the end of 1958, at a cost of $450,000, with one-third of that sum coming from the General Education Board. The library was moved to its new building and present site in January 1959. *Henry T. Sampson was dean of Jackson College from 1933-38, and he returned to Jackson State in 1942 (after service at Savannah State College) to serve as executive dean until his death in 1967.

Lorman

Alcorn State University Library
Alcorn State University
Lorman, Mississippi 39096   (601) 877-3711, ext. 221

Mrs. Epsy Hendricks, chief librarian (on leave); 6 prof, 10 non-prof staff; $127,258 materials budget (1975-76); $63,234 operating budget (1975-76); 100,000 volumes; 863 periodicals; 5,000 microfilms, 300 microfiche, 2,188 records, 300 cassettes, 12 film loops, 10 reel-to-reel tapes, 820 filmstrips, 182 transparencies; ILL; copying; 68 hours weekly; Ms. Lillian A. Ward, Mrs. Ruby Stutts Lyles, Ms. Julia Batey, Ms. Thelma Richardson, former chief librarians; general collection.

Tougaloo

L. Zenobia Coleman Library
Tougaloo College
Tougaloo, Mississippi 39174   (601) 956-4941, ext. 29

Jeannetta C. Roach, chief librarian; 3 prof, 6 non-prof staff; $37,750 materials budget; $94,070 operating budget; 81,679 volumes; 424 periodicals; 2,247 phonograph records, 122 cassettes, 417 filmstrips, 1,721 microfilms, 936 microfiche; ILL; copying; publications—library handbook, *Bibliography of the Black Collection*; 68 hours weekly; Miss L. Zenobia Coleman, Mrs. Ellen Upson Woodworth, Mrs. Helen Holmes, former chief librarians; civil rights and black studies.

The L. Zenobia Coleman Library was completed in November, 1972, and named for the former head librarian, Mrs. L. Zenobia Coleman. It is located just behind the Mansion (the oldest building on campus) in the center of the campus.

MISSOURI

Jefferson City

Inman E. Page Library*
Lincoln University
Jefferson City, Missouri 65101   (314) 751-2325, ext. 326

Mrs. Freddye G. Ashford, chief librarian; 6 prof, 6 non-prof staff; $53,418 materials budget; $197,462 operating budget; 114,678 volumes; 985 periodicals; 79,099 AV items, which include microfiche, microfilms, films, slides, tapes, microcrads, maps, charts, phonodiscs, filmstrips, cassettes, and microprint; restricted ILL; copying; publications—selected bibliographies, student handbook, staff manual, newsletter; 80 hours weekly; Lovey Anthony, D. Eric Moore, Mrs. Mary Turner, A. P. Marshall, former chief librarians; black studies and other minority ethnic groups.

Plans for Inman E. Page Library were begun in 1940 and finally after many altered blueprints, in 1948, the architect Louis Edwin Fry was commissioned to supervise the construction of the building. It was dedicated May 20, 1950. *Inman E. Page was born a slave in Virginia, became the assistant principal of Lincoln Institute in 1878, and two years later was installed as the first president. After twenty years of dedication, he left, in 1898, to become president of Langston University.

NORTH CAROLINA

Charlotte

James B. Duke Memorial Library
Johnson C. Smith University
100 Beatties Ford Road
Charlotte, North Carolina 28216   (704) 372-2370, ext. 211, 212, or 213

Mrs. Mary C. Flows, chief librarian; 5 prof, 6 non-prof staff; $28,000 materials budget; $127,155 operating budget; 84,743 volumes; 795 periodicals; 1,642 microfilm, 2,495 microfiche, 230 filmstrips, 157 films, 77 film loops, 246 cassettes, 521 records, 1,822 slides, 214 transparencies; ILL; copying; publications—library newsletter (quarterly); 74 hours weekly; Mr. T. L. Gunn, Mrs. Mattie Grigsby, former chief librarians; general collection.

In 1911, a library was built from funds contributed primarily by Andrew Carnegie. In 1967, a new library was built, mainly from gifts donated by the Duke Endowment.

Concord

Sage Memorial Library
Barber Scotia College
145 Cabarrus Avenue
Concord, North Carolina 28025   (704) 786-5171, ext. 438

Pearlee A. Coefield, chief librarian; 3 prof, 2 non-prof staff; $9,700 materials budget; $90,000 operating budget; 60,000 volumes; 240 periodicals; 25 cassette tapes, 35 films, 64 reel-to-reel tapes, 1 study print, 23 film loops, 30 slide sets, 250 phonodiscs, 135 filmstrips, 45 sound filmstrips; ILL; copying; 67 hours weekly; Carrie M. Shute, Jean Davis, Elizabeth Mosby, Jean Williams, former chief librarians; general collection.

Durham

James E. Shepard Memorial Library*
North Carolina Central University
Durham, North Carolina 27707   (919) 683-6475

Pennie E. Perry, chief librarian; 21 prof, 17 non-prof staff; $216,770 materials budget; $756,803 operating budget; 311,031 volumes; 2,140 periodicals; 856 video tapes, 320 slides, 9,939 filmstrips, 5,301 audio recordings, 1 16mm film; ILL; copying; publications—*J. E. S. Echoes* (varying regularity from Librarian's Office), *SIN* (quarterly library staff), *Annual Report* (Librarian); 92 hours weekly; Miss Marjorie Shepard (until 1937), Miss Parepa Watson (1937-1951), Dr. Benjamin E. Smith (1951-1965), former chief librarians; music, law, library science, and black literature.

From 1922, the university's library, composed mostly of gift items, was housed in the basement of a wooden structure that also served as the school's administration building. By 1929, a new administration building was constructed and a room was designated as the library. In 1937, a library building was constructed with capacity for 67,000 volumes. The James E. Shepard Memorial Library, named for the school's founder, was dedicated in 1951, with capacity for 200,000 volumes. A new annex to the library opened January 12, 1976. The old building is undergoing complete renovation and, with the new annex, will have the capacity for 500,000 volumes and more than a thousand users. *Dr. James Edward Shepard, a pharmacist and native of Raleigh, North Carolina, was instrumental in establishing the National Religious Training School and Chautauqua for the education of black youth. (In 1923, it became known as the North Carolina College for Negroes, the first state-supported liberal arts college for blacks in America. Subsequent name changes made the institution the North Carolina College at Durham, then, in 1967, the North Carolina Central University.)

Elizabeth City

G. R. Little Library
Elizabeth City State University
1001 Parkview Drive
Elizabeth City, North Carolina 27909   (919) 335-0551, ext. 332

Claude Green, chief librarian; 5 prof, 7 non-prof staff; $103,000 materials budget; $204,000 operating budget; 89,000 volumes; 774 periodicals; 96,403 items, which include microfilm, records, filmstrips, films, and 72,000 microfiche (ERIC Collection); ILL; copying; 74 hours weekly; E. Pose, C. P. Bell, G. J. Midgette, H. Thompson, Jr., former chief librarians; general collection.

For more than two decades after it was established in 1891, the Elizabeth City State Normal School had no formal library—instructors supplemented textbooks with their personal books and other materials. A library room was provided in the new administration building, Lane Hall, in 1914. Apparently no one on the staff was "librarian" until 1924, when the library moved into the present administration building, Moore Hall. By 1935, the books numbered 3,450. In 1938, the first trained librarian (a B.S. in Library Science) was appointed. There was still very little budgetary support for the library and the librarian was constrained to solicit materials from graduates and former students. The collection numbered some 6,900 books in 1939, when the library was finally housed in a building constructed for that purpose, now known as the Administration Annex (Old Library). The present building, the G. R. Little Library, named for the longtime chairman of the Board of Trustees, was occupied in the fall of 1966.

Fayetteville

Charles W. Chesnutt Library*
Fayetteville State University
Fayetteville, North Carolina 28301   (918) 483-6144, ext. 369

Mrs. Nathalene R. Smith, chief librarian; 6 prof, 8 non-prof staff; $113,555 materials budget; $309,668 operating budget; 100,000 volumes; 1,000 periodicals; 322 tapes, 7,344 microfilm, 1,267 recordings, 640 flat pictures, 1,121 slides, 45,639 microfiche; ILL; copying; teletype (no number provided); publications—*Favorite Study Habits and Locations of Students at Fayetteville State College* (by Nathalene Smith), *A Classified Bibliography of Works By and About Blacks Held by the Charles Waddell Chesnutt Library Fayetteville State University* (by Nettie Thigpen), *Periodicals and Newspaper Holdings* (by Mary Hightower); 87 hours weekly; Ms. Hazel C. Edwards, Mr. M. L. James, Miss Alice Jackson, Miss Mamie Wilkerson, former chief librarians; general collection.

*Charles Waddell Chesnutt was a renowned novelist, short story writer, and lawyer. He attended the public schools of Fayetteville, and later became an English teacher and principal of the Fayetteville State Normal School for nine years.

Greensboro

F. D. Bluford Library*
North Carolina A & T State University
Greensboro, North Carolina 27411   (919) 379-7782, ext. 83

Tommie M. Young, director; 13 prof, 27 non-prof staff; $170,101 materials budget; $660,999 operating budget; 167,150 volumes; 1,643 periodicals; over 200,000 microfiche, 45,020 other microforms and AV holdings; ILL; copying; publications—quarterly newsletter; 95 hours weekly; F. D. Bluford, Alma Morrow, Paul Smith, C. C. Dean, B. C. Crews, former chief librarians; engineering, agriculture, literature on developing nations (black), black studies.

The library began in the office of president John O. Crosby in 1894, when $600.00 was allocated for books. Gifts and donations were added to the purchase to form the collection. President Dudley, the second chief executive, designated two rooms on the fourth floor of the administration building (Dudley Hall) for the library. Elizabeth Hill, the first professional librarian, came to the College in 1924. Alma Morrow became Head Librarian in 1937, and held this position when the present structure was occupied in 1955. The present structure is named for F. D. Bluford, a teacher of English and later president of the college.

Thomas F. Holgate Library
Bennett College
Greensboro, North Carolina 27420   (919) 273-4431, ext. 139

Mrs. Edna J. Williams, chief librarian; 4 prof, 5 non-prof staff; $12,000 materials budget; $107,431 operating budget; 76,000+ volumes; 261+ periodicals; filmstrips, film loops, microfilm, recordings, flat pictures, charts, miscellaneous teaching aids which total approximately 1,712 in number; ILL; copying; publications—*African and Afro-American Materials* (a bibliography); 61 hours weekly; Miss Beulah Cooper, Mrs. Artis, Mrs. Constance Marteena, Mrs. Barbara H. Bryan, former chief librarians; art, black studies, humanities, human and behavioral sciences.

The Thomas F. Holgate Library was completed in the spring of 1939, the generous gift of Mr. and Mrs. Henry Pfeiffer of New York City and the General Education Board of the Methodist Church. The library is named in honor of Thomas F. Holgate, treasurer of the Bennett College Board of Trustees, educator, and a leader in the cause of higher education for Negroes.

Raleigh

Saint Augustine College Library
Saint Augustine College
Oakwood Avenue
Raleigh, North Carolina 27611   (919) 828-4451, ext. 236

Everett A. Days, chief librarian; 5 prof, 4 non-prof staff; $45,000 materials budget; $140,000 operating budget; 88,000 volumes; 540 periodicals; 300 films, filmstrips, and other media materials housed in the curriculum materials collection; ILL; copying; publications— guide to the new college library, monthly acquisition lists, and newsletters; 78 hours weekly; Billie Hooker, Ophelia M. Irving, Muriel Walker, Pearl Snodgrass, former chief librarians; black studies, management, and education.

The private collections and books of the first principals of the school served as the school's first library. In 1896-97, the Benson Library was completed, made possible by a gift of $1,600 from Miss Mary Benson of Brooklyn, New York. The Benson Library facility was occupied until the summer of 1974, when the new college library was completed.

Learning Resources Center
Shaw University
118 East South Street
Raleigh, North Carolina 27602   (919) 755-4930

Miss Mildred H. Mallette, chief librarian; 2 prof, 4 non-prof staff; $51,661 materials budget; $125,000 operating budget; 66,500 volumes; 416 periodicals; media kits, cassettes, filmstrips, films, maps, film loops, phonograph records, microfilm, slides, microfiche; ILL; copying; publications—library handbook (student, faculty and staff), student assistants' handbook, area manuals, staff handbook, bibliographies (new additions to the collection), and information on specific library services as needed; 76 hours weekly; Mrs. Carolyn Johnson, Mr. Eddie LeFrancois, Miss Mernell Martin, Mrs. Zeta Dawes, former chief librarians; general collection.

The historical records of the University indicate the existence of library resources. The present library setting is the Learning Resources Center.

Salisbury

Andrew Carnegie Library
Livingstone College
Salisbury, North Carolina 28144   (704) 633-7960, ext. 62

Louise M. Rountree, chief librarian; 4 prof, 3 non-prof staff; $15,000 materials budget; $59,646 operating budget; 60,001 volumes; 495 periodicals; 5,990 volumes micro text, 66 film loops, 266 filmstrips, 78 kits, 63 tapes, 13 cassettes, 498 recordings, 306 transparencies and slides; ILL; copying; publications—occasional bibliographies; 65.5 hours weekly; Professor Frank Nolde (1886-87), Miss Mary A. Lyncy (1903), Miss Victoria Richardson (1926-28),

Mrs. Josephine Price Sherrill (1928-1969), former chief librarians; Afro-American history and African history.

Andrew Carnegie was persuaded in 1905 by Bishop G. W. Clinton, Booker T. Washington, and President Goler to donate $12,000 for the construction of the building (1908) because Livingstone was nonsectarian. Expansion and renovation of the library with fireproof stacks occurred at a cost of $28,500 in 1947. To alleviate crowded conditions, a new wing was added by 1958, and a second wing ten years later, at a cost of $180,000.

Winston-Salem

C. G. O'Kelly Library*
Winston-Salem State University
Winston-Salem, North Carolina 27102   (919) 761-2128

Mrs. Lucy Hyman Bradshaw, chief librarian; 6 prof, 10 non-prof staff; $109,502 materials budget (1976-77); $316,754 operating budget (1976-77); 122,421 volumes; 991 periodicals; 6,936 pictures, charts, maps, photographs and other items, and 1,743 phonograph records, 660 filmstrips, 977 slides, 140 tapes, 115 transparencies, and other learning resource media (units, workbooks, charts, etc.); ILL; copying; publications–library handbooks (students and faculty) and manuals of library departments; 74 hours weekly; Mrs. Leola M. Ross, Mr. A. P. Marshall, Miss Evelyn Dorsey, Miss Elliott, Miss Mollie Dunlap, former chief librarian; general collection.

In 1924, the library holdings were approximately 3,200 volumes. The library was moved into new quarters, the Blair Library and Administration Building, on March 10, 1940. The present C. G. O'Kelly Library is a completely air-conditioned, three-story plant containing 32,990 square feet of floor space. The library building was completed on March 28, 1967, with an addition plus renovations to the existing building completed on March 18, 1971.
*Cadd Grant O'Kelly was a former president of the university (1904-1910).

OHIO

Wilberforce

Hallie Q. Brown Memorial Library*
Central State University
Wilberforce, Ohio 45384   (513) 376-6522

Mr. George T. Johnson, chief librarian; 5 prof, 9 non-prof staff; $125,000 materials budget; $320,000 operating budget; 130,000 volumes; 825 periodicals; 240,000 microforms, but other AV materials not part of library services; ILL; copying; publications–*Index to Periodical Articles By and About Negroes* (annual publication); 75 hours weekly; Miss Mollie E. Dunlap, Mr. George Gardiner, Mrs. Thelma Harper, former chief librarians; Afro-American materials.

The library grew out of the parent institution, Wilberforce University, which was founded in 1856. A separate library was established in 1947 and was expanded again in 1959, when a multi-storied structure was erected. This building was virtually destroyed by a tornado on April 3, 1974, so the present library occupies quarters in a separate, temporary building until a new one is constructed. *Hallie Q. Brown was a distinguished educator and lecturer. A graduate of Wilberforce College in 1873, she returned to the institution to teach and serve on the Board of Trustees. Miss Brown was the author of several books, including *Homespun Heroines and Other Women of Distinction*.

Carnegie Library
Wilberforce University
Wilberforce, Ohio 45384   (513) 376-9310 or 376-2911, ext. 311

Frank Edward Moorer, chief librarian; 3 prof, 3 non-prof staff; $18,000 materials budget; $101,000 operating budget; 55,000 volumes; 350 periodicals; AV materials are housed in the Department of Education; ILL; copying; 80 hours weekly; Mr. Casper L. Jordan, Mrs. Rachael Tanner, Mr. Richard Z. Smith, Mr. Lee E. Sellers, former chief librarians; A.M.E. church history.

As early as 1890, students petitioned Bishop Payne requesting that a room be set aside for the library. The present building was completed in 1904 and enlarged in 1938.

OKLAHOMA

Langston

G. Lamar Harrison Library*
Langston University
Langston, Oklahoma 73050   (405) 466-2281, ext. 231

Ella P. Morgan, acting librarian; 3 prof, 4 non-prof staff; part of university budget; 118,849 volumes; 480 periodicals; microfilms, filmstrips, audiotapes, transparencies, films, cassettes; ILL; publications—library handbook, student library assistant handbook; 71 hours weekly; Dr. Elmira R. Davis, Dr. William B. Scott, Mr. Laron Clark, Mrs. Virginia M. Crowell, former chief librarians; M. B. Tolson Black Heritage Center.

*Dr. General Lamar Harrison was president of Langston University for twenty years, during which time the library was built and named in his honor.

PENNSYLVANIA

Cheyney

Leslie Pinckney Hill Library*
Cheyney State College
Cheyney, Pennsylvania   (215) 399-6880, ext. 208

Mrs. V. R. Smith, director of library services; 8 prof, 16 non-prof staff; $200,000 materials budget; approximately $500,000 operating budget; 145,000 volumes; 1,647 periodicals; films, filmstrips, cassettes, records, loops, transparencies, slides, records, video tapes; ILL; copying; 82.5 hours weekly; Mrs. Margaret Prioleau, Miss Manley, former chief librarians; ethnic studies.

*Leslie Pinckney Hill, an educator and author, was president of the institution from 1913-1951, when it was named the Cheyney Training School for Teachers.

Lincoln

Langston Hughes Memorial Library*
Lincoln University
Lincoln University, Pennsylvania 19352   (215) 932-8300, ext. 359

Emery Wimbish, Jr., chief librarian; 8 prof, 7 non-prof staff; $44,000 materials budget (1974-75); $208,148 operating budget; 125,000 volumes; 698 periodicals; 78 cassettes, 58 filmstrips, 26 multi-media kits, 38 phonotapes, 1,143 microcards, 3 motion pictures, 1,057 slides, 124 transparencies, 806 phonograph records, 11,481 microfiche, 4,188 reels of microfilm; ILL; copying; teletype (no number provided); publications—*Self Guided Tour, Langston Hughes Memorial Library* (Lincoln University, Pa., 1973, Vail Memorial Library), *Catalog of the Special Negro and African Collections* (2 vols. and supplement, 1970, Vail Memorial Library), *Reference Handbook* (1972, Vail Memorial Library), *Reference Handbook of Special Collections* (1972, Vail Memorial Library), *Selected Bibliography on Malcolm X* (Yelton, Donald C.), *A Survey of the Special Negro Collections in Vail Memorial Library* (Lincoln University, Pa.); 99.5 hours weekly; Dr. Donald C. Yelton, Dr. Armstead O. Grubb, Charles Katz, Mrs. Carrie Williams, former chief librarians; minority studies, Afro-American studies, African studies.

Ashmun Hall, the first building of Ashmun Institute (later Lincoln University), contained a "library" room. The 1865-66 catalog published by Lincoln University in 1866 mentions that "a library has already been founded, which though small, is of great value to the students." In 1898, the Vail Memorial Library was constructed with a book capacity of 30,000 volumes, and in addition to the building in 1954 more than doubled the book capacity. The Langston Hughes Memorial Library was completed in 1972, a modern four-story building with shelf space for more than 250,000 volumes. *Langston Hughes, black poet and novelist, was a key figure in the Harlem Renaissance in the 1920s and 1930s, and a 1928 graduate of the university.

SOUTH CAROLINA

Columbia

J. S. Flipper Library
Allen University
Columbia, South Carolina 29204   (803) 779-6430

Mrs. Charlotte Alston Ferebee, chief librarian; 4 prof, 2 non-prof staff; $69,600 materials budget; $90,466 operating budget; 50,000 volumes; 378 periodicals; 35 motion picture films, 315 audio recordings, 440 filmstrips, 1,047 slide and overhead transparencies, 94 maps and charts; 65 hours weekly; Mrs. Edith R. Holmes, Mr. James Black, Mrs. Louisa Robinson, Mrs. Georgie E. Cooke, former chief librarians; general collection.

Allen University has been in operation since 1870, but little, if anything, is known of its library during its early days. The first library was completed in 1941. Extensive renovations were made in 1965, giving the library an entirely new look.

Benjamin F. Payton Learning Resource Center*
Benedict College
Taylor and Harden Streets
Columbia, South Carolina 29204   (803) 779-4930

Mae S. Johnson, chief librarian; 7 prof, 11 non-prof staff; $25,000 materials budget; $392,804 operating budget (1975-76); 111,854 volumes; 1,050 periodicals; 225 motion pictures, 150 slides, 350 records, 12 print sets, 200 filmstrips, 50 overhead transparencies; ILL; copying; publications—newsletter, library rules and regulations; 73 hours weekly; Ms. Jane Watts, former chief librarian; Afro-American, juvenile.

*Dr. Benjamin F. Payton was president of the college at the time the building was planned. (The old structure was named the Starks Memorial Library in honor of Dr. J. J. Starks, first black president of the college, and his wife.)

Denmark

Voorhees College Library
Voorhees College
Denmark, South Carolina 29042   (803) 793-3346, ext. 261

Jaynie M. Shelton, acting administrative librarian; 4 prof, 5 non-prof staff; $60,000 materials budget; $133,129 operating budget; 80,566 volumes; 573 periodicals; 34 motion pictures, 221 records, 39 cassettes, 13 tapes, 83 filmstrips, 793 slides, 35 maps and charts, 24 mixed media kits; ILL; copying; publications—library handbook; 71 hours weekly; Maisie V. Curtis, Esther M. Crenshaw, Jaynie M. Shelton, Claude Green, former chief librarians; social sciences and humanities.

The Vorhees College Library began as a small classroom collection at the beginning of the school's history in 1897. The first regular library was located on the second floor of the Administration Building and served the Junior College Department and also grades one through twelve.

Orangeburg

H. V. Manning Library*
Claflin College
Orangeburg, South Carolina 29115   (803) 534-2710, ext. 56

Mrs. Louisa S. Robinson, chief librarian; 4 prof, 4.5 non-prof staff; $106,000 materials budget; $214,334 operating budget; 72,749 volumes; 585 periodicals; 5 cassette tape players and recorders, 3 carousel projectors and players, 1 listening center, 1 record player, 1 filmstrip previewer, 2 35mm filmstrip projectors (sound), 1 rear screen previewer, 1 screen and 1 overhead projector; ILL; copying; 78.5 hours weekly; Dr. Paul Smith, Mrs. Fannie B. Hogan, Miss Harvey L. Ward, Mrs. Gracia Dawson, former chief librarians; general collection.

Information concerning the very first library is scarce. However, the second library, Lee Library, was built in 1898. In 1948, the library was moved into a larger building and named

Bowen Library. In 1967, a new library was constructed and named the H. V. Manning Library.
*Dr. H. V. Manning became president of the College in 1956 and still occupies that office.

Miller F. Whittaker Library*
South Carolina State College
P.O. Box 1991
Orangeburg, South Carolina 29117   (803) 536-7045 or 536-7046

Barbara J. Williams, chief librarian; 8 prof, 18 non-prof staff; $211,046 materials budget; $400,608 operating budget; 273,431 volumes; 635 periodicals; AV acquisitions are limited to library oriented materials, maps, and charts; ILL; copying; publications—*The Katalog* (list of new publications, monthly), *The Martin Luther King, Jr. Memorial Booklist* (annual), *Library News and Notes* (quarterly newsletter to faculty and staff); *Across the Librarian's Desk* (monthly statistical report to faculty and staff); *Miller F. Whittaker Library Faculty Handbook, Miller F. Whittaker Library Student Handbook, A Guide to the Miller F. Whittaker Library, About ERIC, Basic Reference Sources, How to Locate and Use the Government Documents, How to Locate and Use Library of American Civilization, Serial Holdings of the Miller F. Whittaker Library* (annual), *Afro-American Subject Headings in the Miller F. Whittaker Library*; 81.5 hours weekly; Miss H. B. Lawson, Mrs. Athelma R. Nix, Mrs. Jestina Henderson, Mr. Binford H. Conley, former chief librarians; black collection.

The library began in 1913, with a very small collection of books contributed by faculty and friends of the college. The Rev. P. P. Watson, head of the history department, was in charge of the library, which was housed in the Morrill Hall Academic Building, which, in 1916, was completely destroyed by fire. Another effort to establish a library was made by members of the faculty and friends who donated books to the college. In 1921, the library was located in a small room on the second floor of White Hall, and Judge C. P. Brunson willed his personal books to the school. The first trained librarian, Miss Celeste Hatcher, was employed in 1925, and the library received a grant of $4,000 from the Julius Rosenwald Fund and moved to the first floor of White Hall. Later, a grant from the General Education Board provided a reading room. The collection then included 8,000 volumes. In 1938, the library was moved to Wilkinson Hall, erected with funds from the General Education Board and the state. In 1967, the school received funds from the state and the Higher Education Facilities Act to build a new library, and on April 20, 1969, the Miller F. Whittaker Library was dedicated. *Dr. Miller Fulton Whittaker, a native of Sumter, South Carolina, was professor of physics and head of the Division of Mechanic Arts, 1913-1932. He served as college president from 1932-1949. A registered architect in South Carolina and Georgia, he designed many buildings on the campus, as well as schools, churches, residences, and businesses in South Carolina and Georgia.

Sumter

I. D. Pinson Memorial Library*
Morris College
North Main Street
Sumter, South Carolina 29150   (803) 775-9371, ext. 216

Clara B. Gordon, chief librarian; 3 prof, 2 non-prof staff; $16,900 materials budget (1974-75); $46,456 operating budget (1974-75); 25,400 volumes; 190 periodicals; 1 chart, 3 films, 266 filmstrips, 38 games, 11 kits, 197 phonograph records, 1 slide set, 4 slides with cassette tape sets, 10 sound filmstrips with cassette tapes, 46 sound filmstrips with phonorecords, 40 tape cassettes, 57 reel-to-reel tapes, 14 transparency sets, 55 booklets; ILL; copying; 75 hours weekly; Mrs. Fannie M. Davis, Mr. Days, Miss McAlister, Mr. Thompson, former chief librarians; general collection.

The I. D. Pinson Memorial Library building was built in 1946. *Dr. I. D. Pinson was college president from 1930-1939.

TENNESSEE

Jackson

J. K. Daniels Library*
Lane College
545 Lane Avenue
Jackson, Tennessee 38301   (901) 424-4600, ext. 274

Mrs. Anna L. Cooke, chief librarian; 4 prof, 3 non-prof staff; $28,000 materials budget; $96,000 operating budget; 76,733 volumes; 449 periodicals; 319 recordings, 422 filmstrips, 498 slides, 68 films and film loops; ILL; copying; publications–presently indexing *Lane College Reporter*, alumni quarterly; 65 hours weekly; Louise H. Graves, Muriel Osborne, Ruth Smith, Annie M. Brown, James W. Sloan, Clara Hewitt, former chief librarians; general collection.

Lane College was founded in 1882 as a Christian Methodist Episcopal High School. The name was changed to Lane College in 1896, a year after college courses were added. The library was located in a room in the main building. In 1928, the library was moved to the first floor of the science building. In 1954, the building was remodeled with UNCF funds and the entire structure has since been used as a library. *In November, 1878, the Rev. J. K. Daniels presented a resolution to build a school for black youths to the Tennessee Annual Conference of the C.M.E. Church. Rev. Daniels was a member of the committee that brought the college into existence, and because of his untiring efforts, the present renovated structure was named in his honor in 1954.

Knoxville

Alumni Library
Knoxville College
Knoxville, Tennessee 37921   (615) 546-0751, ext. 285

Mrs. Lois N. Clark, chief librarian; 3.5 prof, 6 non-prof staff; $23,500 materials budget; $101,772 operating budget; 65,824 volumes; 452 periodicals; 1,137 reels of microfilm and college has separate AV center; ILL; copying; publications–student library handbook, faculty library handbook, *Other Americans: A Selected Bibliography of Multi-Ethnic Materials, Part I and Part II for Junior and Senior High Schools*; 88 hours weekly; Reverend H. J. Bell (1909-11), Miss Harriet Ann Kerr (1911-25), Miss Mabel Grace Robb (1927-47), Miss J. Rea Whetstone (1947-61), former chief librarians; general collection.

The Knoxville College Library began in 1876 (one year after the founding of the College) in room 209 on the second floor of the Administration Building. In 1909, the old Carnegie building was completed, using student labor and bricks made in the college kiln. In September, 1965, the Carnegie Building was razed so that construction of the new one could begin on the old site (the ground floor of the College Center served as temporary quarters). The new library opened for use on February 6, 1967, and was rechristened the Alumni Library because of the Alumni Association's significant financial support of the library.

Memphis

Hollis F. Price Library*
LeMoyne-Owen College
807 Walker Avenue
Memphis, Tennessee 38126   (901) 948-6626, ext. 50

Mae Isom Fitzgerald, chief librarian; 3 prof, 3 non-prof staff; $49,100 materials budget; $105,335 operating budget; 71,733 volumes; 215 periodicals; approximately 650 items of AV materials (microfilms, recordings), but most non-book materials are housed in the Learning Resources Center; ILL; copying; publications–acquisitions lists, bibliographies; 65 hours weekly; Mr. Francis Allen, Miss Bessie K. Meacham, former chief librarians; black studies.

In the fall of 1968, LeMoyne College and Owen College merged to form LeMoyne-Owen College. LeMoyne College had its beginning in 1862, when the American Missionary Association sent Miss Lucinda Humphrey to open an elementary school for "contraband" Negroes and "freedmen" at Camp Shiloh, just below Memphis, Tennessee. In 1863, the school was moved to Memphis and in 1866 was known as Lincoln Chapel School. In the race riots that followed withdrawal of federal troops in 1866, Lincoln Chapel was destroyed by fire. It was immediately rebuilt and reopened in 1867 with 150 pupils and 6 teachers. The school acquired its present site in 1914. It became a junior college in 1924 and was chartered by the State of Tennessee as a four-year, degree granting institution, in 1934, when the name was changed to LeMoyne College. The library provides over 70,000 volumes. *Hollis F. Price was president of the college from 1943 to 1970, fund raising director for the United Negro College fund in New York (1954), and director of the Rapid Social Change Study in Liberia for the World Council of Churches and the Phelps-Stokes Fund (1954). He was the recipient of the 1975 Brotherhood Award given annually by the Memphis Roundtable, National Conference of Christians and Jews.

Morristown

Miriam Parlin Library
Morristown College
Morristown, Tennessee 37814   (615) 586-5262, ext. 34

Samuel E. Richardson, chief librarian; 1 prof, 1 non-prof staff; $5,000 materials budget; $25,000 operating budget; 24,000+ volumes; 125 periodicals; audio-text cassettes, disc and filmstrip programmed modules; copying; publications–library handbook, *Bibliography of Books By and About Blacks, Annotated Bibliography of Biographical and Autobiographical Materials About Blacks*; 67 hours weekly; Miss Laura E. Jones, Miss Laura Decker, Miss Jessie L. Matthews, Miss Lillian Wood, former chief librarians; sociology, black literature, black studies, black religion.

Since the founding of Morristown College in 1881, library facilities have fluctuated because of the lack of funding, poor planning, and an ever-changing curriculum. In the early years, the library was housed in a small classroom. The library was the Carnegie Library until the name was changed to Miriam Parlin Library in 1975.

Nashville

Fisk University Library and Media Center
Fisk University
17th and Jackson Street
Nashville, Tennessee 37203   (615) 329-9111, ext. 207 or 208

Dr. Jessie Carney Smith, chief librarian; 7 prof, 7 non-prof staff; $72,133 materials budget; $288,560 operating budget; 177,627 volumes; 608 periodicals; 4,085 reels microfilm, 24 16mm films, 15 filmstrips, 8 video recordings, 10 reel tapes, 1,000 microfiche, 56 tape cassette recordings, 400 phonograph records, 8mm cartridge film; ILL; copying; publications– *Fisk University Library Guide, A Handbook for the Organization of Black Materials, A Bibliography of Charles S. Johnson's Published Writings* (1960), *Selected Items from the George Gershwin Memorial Collection of Music and Music Literature*, department manuals, *A Handbook for the Administration of Special Negro Collections*; Louis Shores (1928-33), Frances Yocum (acting, 1933-34), Carl White (1934), Arna Bontemps (1943-65), former chief librarians; materials by and about blacks.

Mr. George C. White began the first library at Fisk in 1867 with a bookcase in his office, and the 1871-72 catalog mentions a reading room. When Jubilee Hall was occupied in 1875, the library was housed in a "pleasant and cozy apartment" on the second floor. Later, Fisk appealed to Andrew Carnegie, who, in 1905, offered $20,000 for a building when Fisk raised a matching sum for the maintenance of the library. Work on the new building was begun May 4, 1908, the cornerstone laid on May 22, 1908, and on February 25, 1909, the building was occupied. By 1927, extensive renovations were made on the Carnegie building. In 1928, the General Education Board offered Fisk University $400,000 for the construction, equipment and endowment of a new library building to be used jointly by Fisk University and Meharry Medical College. Fisk moved into the Erasmus Milo Cravath Library in November 1930. The striking new Fisk University Library and Media Center of contemporary design was occupied in December 1969, a three-floor building constructed at a cost of $1,408,000.

S. S. Kresge Learning Resources Center
Meharry Medical College
Nashville, Tennessee 37208   (615) 327-6319

Blondell M. Strong, chief librarian; 5 prof, 12 non-prof staff; $67,479 materials budget; $228,001 operating budget; 40,000 volumes; 975 periodicals; ILL; copying; publications—library printout acquisitions list, library brochure and guide; 99 hours weekly; Mrs. Jean Cazort, former chief librarian; health sciences, access to MEDLARS.

Martha M. Brown Memorial Library*
Tennessee State University
Centennial Boulevard
Nashville, Tennessee 37203   (615) 320-3682

Dr. Evelyn P. Fancher, chief librarian; 11 prof, 10.5 non-prof staff; $106,730 materials budget; operating budget under revision; 229,301 volumes in TSU collection, 7,500 volumes in UT-School of Social Work collection; 1,415 periodicals; 8,597 physical units of microform, 3,853 microfiche; ILL; copying; 82 hours weekly; Mrs. Martha M. Brown (1912-51), Miss Lois Daniel (1945-76), former chief librarians; general collection.

The library began with a small collection of books donated by the faculty and others in 1912 and housed in a classroom, which later burned. Through the efforts of Mrs. Brown, in 1927, the first building was erected. Then, in the fall of 1945, Miss Lois H. Daniel was appointed Director, and plans were made for increasing the staff and upgrading the collection. By 1949, an annex was completed for the building. A new library is nearing completion and should be opened early in 1977. *Mrs. Martha M. Brown was a member of the school's first faculty of 1912. As librarian, she directed the library's development until the fall of 1945, when she relinquished administrative duties to serve as Library Consultant until her retirement in August, 1951.

TEXAS

Austin

Downs-Jones Library*
Huston-Tillotson College
1820 East 8th Street
Austin, Texas 78702   (512) 476-7421, ext. 300

Mrs. Vivian L. Dorn, chief librarian; 2 prof, 3 non-prof staff; $26,000 materials budget; $91,726 operating budget; 60,678 volumes, 295 periodicals; 60 motion pictures, 1,420 recordings, 1,575 audio recordings, 525 microfilm reels, 219 filmstrips, 241,137 microfiche sheets, 1,400 slides and transparencies, 2 maps and charts; ILL; copying; publications—student library handbook, recent additions list; 63 hours weekly; Samuel Huston College—Leonella Hutton (1945-47), Fannie Foster (1947-49), Essie Tatum (1949-50), Adye Bel Sampson (1950-52), and Tillotson College—Fannie H. Ussery (1932-35), Carrie L. Robinson (1937-41), Beatrice Inez Schuck (1941-43), Olive D. Brown (1943-75), former chief librarians; teacher education, business administration.

The Downs-Jones Library had its beginning a century ago in two institutions, Samuel Huston College and Tillotson College. Each library of the antecedent institutions was housed in the respective administration building. Subsequent to the merger of the colleges in 1952, library services were continued on both campuses for three years. In 1955, the libraries were combined on the Tillotson campus, and the first permanent structure for library use was opened in 1960. *The Downs-Jones Library was named in 1969 for two former presidents of the antecedent institutions. The Reverend Karl E. Downs, an alumnus of Samuel Huston College, was a pioneer in the National Council of Methodist Youth. He assumed the presidency of Samuel Huston College in 1943 and remained there until his death in 1948. Dr. William H. Jones, a professor of sociology, was dean of Tillotson College for fifteen years and president, 1945-52. At the merger of the two institutions, Dr. Jones became vice-president in charge of curriculum development, in which position he remained until his retirement.

Dallas

The Zale Library
Bishop College
3837 Simpson-Stuart Road
Dallas, Texas 75241 (214) 376-4311, ext. 270

Harry Robinson, Jr., chief librarian; 6 prof, 8 non-prof staff; $65,000 materials budget; $247,000 operating budget; 135,000 volumes; 750 periodicals; ILL; copying; teletype (no number provided); publications—newsletter, occasional paper; 74 hours weekly; G. T. Johnson, R. A. Hudson, Mary Bledsoe, Everett Coby, former chief librarians; Afro-American materials.

Bishop College was founded in 1881 in Marshall, Texas, by a band of illiterate ex-slaves and a group of missionaries from the Home Mission Society of the Northern Baptist Convention. Its name derived from its chief benefactor of those early days, Colonel Nathan Bishop.

Hawkins

Olin Library and Communication Center
Jarvis Christian College
Drawer G
Hawkins, Texas 75765 (214) 769-2223, ext. 154

Mrs. Doris P. Rutherford, chief librarian; 3 prof, 4 non-prof staff; $26,707 materials budget; $75,447 operating budget; 50,000+ volumes; 480 periodicals; 44 projectors with specialized attachments for 16mm, 8mm, filmstrips, sound filmstrips, slides, and transparencies, as well as 3 cameras, 3 microfilm readers, 6 record players, and 2 combination record player/tape recorders; ILL; 66 hours weekly; Agnes Cobbins, Spaesio Mothershed, Alvis Price, Abbas Mozaher, former chief librarians; teacher education.

The library has withstood some lean years, including its destruction by fire in 1928. The first organized library at Jarvis was the W. J. Fuller Library, named for the late W. J. Fuller of Greenville, Texas, who gave $500.00 for its establishment. As the school grew, the library expanded and was moved to the Emma B. Smith Building. At the 1964 Commencement Exercises, the Olin Foundation presented the school a grant of $585,000 for constructing and equipping a library and communication center. On September 17, 1965, the magnificent Olin Library and Communication Center, consisting of two and one-half floors, was dedicated. The conference room of the new library, which will also house the Jarvis Archival and History Collection, is now named for Mr. Fuller.

Houston

Texas Southern University Library
Texas Southern University
3201 Wheeler
Houston, Texas 77004 (713) 527-7147

Spaesio W. Mothershed, chief librarian; 11 prof (excluding law), 36 non-prof staff (excluding law); $264,000 materials budget; $571,218 operating budget (including materials budget); 265,214 volumes; 2,093 periodicals; 131,120 microforms including audio cassettes, video cassettes, filmstrips, film loops, slides; ILL; copying; teletype no. 910-881-3745; publication—*Heartman Catalog*; 91 hours weekly; Howard Bell, H. E. Davis, Richard Griffin, Wallace Van Jackson, former chief librarians; black history, teacher education, urban programming.

The Texas Southern University library came into being in 1947, when the Texas Legislature voted to create the Texas State University for Negroes. To house the new university, the State purchased the municipally-operated Houston College, including its library. The Texas State University for Negroes changed its name to Texas Southern University in 1951. The library existed in small collections housed in several buildings on campus until the completion of its present modern building in 1956. In 1967, a new wing was added to this building to increase book capacity to over 350,000 volumes and its seating capacity to over 1,100 patrons.

Marshall

Thomas Winston Cole, Sr. Library*
Wiley College
Marshall, Texas 75670   (214) 938-8341, ext. 70

Mrs. Mary Louise Cleveland, chief librarian; 4 prof, 2 non-prof staff; $48,450 materials budget; $48,950 operating budget; 75,351 volumes; 429 periodicals; 2,000 pieces including slides, filmstrips, records, models, transparencies; ILL; 69 hours weekly; Mrs. R. C. Hunt, Dr. Herman Totten, Mrs. Gertrude Mason, Mr. Robert Todd, former chief librarians; general collection.

      The library was first housed in a Carnegie library building, 1907-1967. *Dr. Thomas Winston Cole, Sr., was the tenth president of the college (1958 to 1971).

Prairie View

W. R. Banks Library*
Prairie View A&M University
Prairie View, Texas 77445   (713) 857-3311, ext. 2012

Frank Francis, Jr., chief librarian; 8 prof, 12 non-prof staff; $353,924 materials budget; $521,152 operating budget; 165,000 volumes; 1,200 periodicals; 717 16mm films, 912 audio tapes, 1,803 filmstrips, 65 sound filmstrips, 318 LP records, 870 slides, 76 video cartridges, 12 video tapes, 620 transparencies; ILL; copying; teletype (no number provided); publication– *W. R. Banks Library Focus*; 87 hours weekly; Gertrude Williams (1923-31), O. J. Baker (1931-66), William Scott (1966-68), former chief librarians; black studies, chemistry and biology.

      The building housing the library had two stages of physical growth. The first section was completed in 1945 at a cost of $171,867.91. The half million dollar addition was completed in 1968. The building has three floors, a book stack section with five levels, book capacity of 301,000 volumes, and study space for 800 students simultaneously. *Willette Rutherford Banks was an outstanding educator, former president of the institution, and a pioneer in higher education for blacks.

San Antonio

St. Philip's College Library
St. Philip's College
2111 Nevada Street
San Antonio, Texas 78203   (512) 534-4211, ext. 200

Mrs. Georgene I. Bias, chief librarian; 7 prof, 2 non-prof staff; materials budget is part of college budget; $43,300 general budget; 42,834 volumes; 69 periodicals; 951 AV items, which include slides, films, filmstrips, video tapes, audio tapes, records, and cassettes; ILL; copying; teletype (no number provided); Maude Rebecca Hill, Adye Bell Sampson, Dolly Davis Smith, Julia H. Taylor, former chief librarians; black studies.

      St. Philip's Normal and Industrial School was founded in 1898 as a parochial day school, gradually developed into a normal and industrial school, then became a first class junior college. All of this growth was under the direction of Miss Artemisia Bowden, who became Principal in 1902. Miss Katherine Greene was the first librarian in 1927.

Terrell

Hogan-Steward Learning Resources Center*
Southwestern Christian College
Box 10
Terrell, Texas 75160   (214) 563-3341, ext. 41

Doris Johnson, chief librarian; 2 prof, 12 student staff; $10,000 materials budget; $41,462 operating budget; 16,596 volumes; 196 periodicals; 1,628 AV items, which includes audio recordings, filmstrips, slides, transparencies, tapes, and mixed media kits; ILL; copying; 60 hours weekly; Mrs. Mary Carpenter, Mrs. Myrtle Fraizer, former chief librarians; general collection.

The library is located in the new Hogan-Steward Learning Center, constructed in 1974.
*R. N. Hogan and G. E. Steward are gospel preachers and board members of the college.

Tyler

The D. R. Glass Library
Texas College
2404 North Grand Avenue
Tyler, Texas 75701

Mrs. Vivian F. Jeffries, chief librarian; 3 prof, 4 non-prof staff; $30,000 book budget; $95,000 operating budget; 90,000 volumes; 539 periodicals; 18 microfiche (424 titles), 974 microfilm reels, 681 cassettes, 1,334 disc recordings, 1,302 filmstrips, 18 kits, 85 motion pictures, 475 slides, 82 transparencies; ILL; copying; 73 hours weekly; Mrs. W. R. Banks, Mr. Wilk Peters, Mr. Leroy Thompson, Mrs. Emma Patterson Clark, former chief librarians; general collection.

The first library on the Texas College campus was housed in the Administration Hall. On April 19, 1910, the Administration Hall burned as a result of lightning, and all the school fixtures and the library were lost. During the administration of Bishop Martin, the present administration building, Martin Hall, was erected in 1924. The library, temporarily housed on the first floor of Phillips Hall, was moved to the third floor of this building. In 1929, Bishop McKinney moved the library to the new McKinney Hall. The D. R. Glass Library, a modern brick building constructed in 1951 at a cost of $500,000 is a two and one-quarter level brick structure. *Dr. Dominion R. Glass was president of the college from 1931 to 1961, during which time it became an accredited institution.

VIRGINIA

Petersburg

Johnston Memorial Library*
Virginia State College
Petersburg, Virginia 23803   (804) 520-6181

Catherine V. Bland, chief librarian; 12 prof, 16 non-prof staff; $173,890 materials budget (1974-75); $481,013 operating budget (1974-75); 1,357 periodicals; 23,000 AV items consisting of filmstrips, filmloops, 16mm films, games, modules transparencies, records, tapes, study prints, video cassettes; ILL; copying; teletype no. 710-957-2334; 78 hours weekly; Alpha Rogers, Thelma Nelson Jenkins, Mamie White Campbell, Wallace Van Jackson, former chief librarians; education, black studies.

The college was founded on March 6, 1882. From the earliest records available, a library of more than 2,000 volumes was organized and located in Virginia Hall, the main campus building. The library was relocated in a new structure in 1937, where it remained until the present building was occupied in 1960. *James Hugo Johnston was the second president of the college (1888-1914).

Richmond

William J. Clark Library
Virginia Union University
Richmond, Virginia 23220   (804) 359-9331, ext. 256 or 257

Verdelle V. Bradley, chief librarian; 4 prof, 4 non-prof staff; $48,597 materials budget; $153,691 operating budget; 122,477 volumes; 639 periodicals; 2,380 recordings, 203 films, 292 tapes, 612 filmstrips, 3,471 slides, 695 microcards, 8,499 microfilm, 54 cassettes, 76 transparencies; restricted ILL; copying; 74 hours weekly; Mr. Wallace Van Jackson, Mr. William A. Griffev, Mrs. Bertha W. Gibbs, former chief librarians; black studies.

The library at Virginia Union University was established in 1900 on the first floor of Cobburn Hall. It grew from 8,000 volumes to 13,000 during the administration of Dr. George Rice Hovey (1904-1918). In 1919, Dr. William J. Clark became president and also acted as librarian. During this administration, Mr. Wallace Van Jackson was hired as the first trained librarian, and by 1933, the volumes increased to 22,000. Under the administration of Dr. John M. Ellison (the first black president, 1941-1955), the library moved from Cobburn Hall to its present location, the Belgian Building. The library was named and dedicated as the William J. Clark Library, June, 1949.

WEST VIRGINIA

West Virginia

Drain-Jordan Library*
West Virginia State College
Institute, West Virginia 25112   (304) 766-3116

John E. Scott, chief librarian; 6 prof, 8 non-prof staff; $70,000 materials budget; $211,000 operating budget; 155,000 volumes; 1,006 periodicals; 844 filmstrips, 2,606 microfilm, 4,931 microfiche, 2,645 phonodiscs, 717 slides; ILL; copying; teletype no. 710-938-1683; publications—library handbook, recent accessions list; 82 hours weekly; Mrs. Leaonead P. Bailey, Mr. Miles Jefferson, former chief librarians; education.

*Mrs. Leonard P. Drain Baily, an alumna of the school, became head librarian in 1927, after receiving her B.A. degree that year. (From the University of Illinois, she received her degree in Library Science in 1929.) She left on November 15, 1956. Mr. L. V. Jordan came to West Virginia State College in 1934, and he was principal of the Laboratory High School, professor of education, and chairman of the Department of Education (1963-67). He retired in 1968. Both people contributed greatly to the development of the library's collection.

ADDITIONAL LIBRARIES NAMED FOR AFRO-AMERICANS

NEW YORK
Brooklyn

Medgar Evers College Library
1150 Carroll Street
Brooklyn, New York 11225

Medgar Evers is considered to be one of the great heroes of the Civil Rights movement of the 1960s, having fought the injustices and the inhumane treatment suffered by black Americans in Mississippi. Because of his leadership in a voter registration campaign, he was assassinated on June 13, 1963, in Jackson, Mississippi.

New Paltz

Sojourner Truth Library
State University of New York at New Paltz
New Paltz, New York 12561

Born in slavery at Hurley, New York, in 1797, Sojourner Truth was freed after twenty-eight years of bondage. She spent the remainder of her life working diligently for the abolition of slavery and for women's rights.

New York

Whitney M. Young, Jr. Memorial Library of Social Work
Columbia University
301 Butler Library
New York, New York 10027

Whitney M. Young, Jr. was a distinguished social worker, educator and civil rights leader. During his tenure as Executive Director of the National Urban League, he developed programs of national and international importance. In 1969, he received the nation's highest civilian award, the Medal of Freedom.

Schomburg Center for Research in Black Culture
103 West 135th Street
New York, New York 10030

The Schomburg Center is a part of the New York Public Library Research Libraries but is included here because of its significance. (See MAJOR AFRO-AMERICAN COLLECTIONS.) Arthur A. Schomburg was a pioneer collector of materials by and about blacks, and his collection formed the nucleus of this research center.

SELECTIVE LIST OF BLACK-OWNED BOOKSTORES

CALIFORNIA

Berkeley

Marcus Bookstores
2977 Sacramento Street
Berkeley, California 94702   (415) 845-5600

Julian and Raye G. Richardson, owners; founded in 1960; books, posters, maps, art magazines, and newspapers by and about blacks all over the world.

Long Beach

Afro-American Bookstore
1708 Atlantic Avenue
Long Beach, California 90813   (213) 591-5911

Dave Kelley, owner; Afro-American literature and history, and everything on black people.

Los Angeles

Aquarian Bookshop
1302 West Santa Barbara Avenue
Los Angeles, California 90037   (213) 296-1633

Alfred and Bernice Ligon, owners; founded in 1940; books concerning Africans and Afro-Americans, occult literature.

Third World Ethnic Books
3617 Mont Clair Street
Los Angeles, California 90018   (213) 737-3292

Mayme A. Clayton, owner; founded in June 1972; black literature and history, documents, ephemera, memorabilia; out-of-print, rare and current materials.

San Francisco

Marcus Bookstores
540 McAllister Street
San Francisco, California 94102   (415) 863-2248

Julian and Raye G. Richardson, owners; founded in 1960; books, posters, maps, art magazines, and newspapers by and about black people all over the world.

New Day Bookstore
613 Davisadeno Street
San Francisco, California 94117   (415) 346-8537

Joseph Goncalves, owner; founded in 1973; black books.

ILLINOIS
Chicago

A-S Stationery & Books
751 East 80th Street
Chicago, Illinois 60019   (312) 994-5700

Alma S. Graham, owner; founded in 1967; black literature, school books from kindergarten through college, career books—Civil Service, high school preparatory and college, general literature, black greeting cards, general greeting cards, stationery—business forms, school supplies, and African gifts and costume jewelry.

Book & Magazine Distributing Company
6809 South Ashland
Chicago, Illinois 60636   (312) 737-3600

Richard and Warren Brown, owners; founded in 1963; distribution of paperbacks and magazines.

Ellis Bookstores
6447 Cottage
Chicago, Illinois 60637   (312) 493-1177

C. N. Ellis, Sr., owner; founded in September 1959; African-American literature and college textbooks.

Third World Press/Institute of Positive Education
7524 South Cottage Grove
Chicago, Illinois 60619   (312) 651-0700

Third World Press/Institute of Positive Education, owner; founded in 1968; Third World Press and Institute of Positive Education titles.

Zion Bookstore
606 East 50th Street
Chicago, Illinois 60653   (312) 624-9769

Holy Mt. Zion Pentecostal Church, owner; founded in 1961; church supplies and Christian literature.

MICHIGAN
Detroit

Shrine of the Black Madonna Cultural Center
 & Bookstore No. 1
13535 Livernois
Detroit, Michigan 48238   (313) 491-0777

Shrine of the Black Madonna Church, owner; founded in 1970; black history, religion, and literature.

Vaughn's Bookstore
12135 Dexter
Detroit, Michigan 48206   (313) 933-1380

Edward Vaughn, owner; founded in 1964; African and Afro-American history, culture, and literature.

NEW YORK

Brooklyn

East Distribution and Publications
10 Claver Place
Brooklyn, New York 11238   (212) 636-9400

The East, owner; founded in 1972; publication of books on or about black people.

Freedom Book Store
526 Nostrand Avenue
Brooklyn, New York

James Jones, owner; history, literature, children's books (primarily black materials).

Jamaica, Queens

The Written Word, Inc. Bookstore
89-61 165th Street
Jamaica, Queens, New York 11432   (212) 658-4487

N. Walden, owner; founded in 1965; black history, culture, poetry, contemporary magazines, and African history and religion.

New York

Afro-American Book Center
532 West 145th Street
New York, New York 10031   (212) 234-3369

Mr. Earl Hadley, owner; founded in 1973; children's books, wide selection of books for adults in Afro-American and African history, literature and sociology, metaphysics and the occult.

Liberation Bookstore
421 Lenox Avenue at 131st Street
New York, New York 10037   (212) 281-4615

Una G. Mulzac, owner; founded in 1967; books, magazines and pamphlets on black studies in Africa, Asia, the Caribbean, North and South America.

Tree of Life Book Store
101 West 125th Street
New York, New York 10027

Kanya KeKumbha, owner; Africa, black books in all subjects and including Marxist materials.

TEXAS

Houston

Afro-American Book Distributors
2537 Prospect
Houston, Texas 77004   (713) 522-9707

Dr. J. B. Jones, owner; Gary Jones, manager; founded in 1968; black authors and titles on black subjects, and black children's books.

ENGLAND

London

New Beacon Bookshop
76 Stroud Green Road
London N4 3EN England   01-272-4889

John LaRose, Sarah White, Andrew Salkey, directors; founded in 1966; Africa, Caribbean, Afro-America, Brazil to U.S.A. International booksellers with an international bookservice for libraries and individuals all over the world.

BLACK BOOK PUBLISHERS

(This section is alphabetical by name of publisher.)

Africana Publishing Company
Division of Holmes & Meier Publishers, Inc.
101 Fifth Avenue
New York, New York 10013   (212) 691-5252

M. J. Holmes, owner; founded in 1969; Kathleen McCarthy, Abe Goldman, senior editors; publishes scholarly books on African studies. Published 15 books in 1975-76.

Afro-Am Publishing Company, Inc.
1727 South Indiana Avenue
Chicago, Illinois 60616   (312) 921-1147

David P. Ross, president; Eugene Winslow, secretary-treasurer, senior editor; incorporated in Illinois, 1963; publishes Elhi supplementary social studies, language arts and science, child development teaching aids, and black studies reference text and display prints. Published 1 book in 1975-76.

Alkebu-Lan Books Assoc.
209 West 125th Street
Suite 218
New York, New York 10027   (212) 866-9220

Alkebu-Lan Foundation, Inc., owner; founded in 1971; George E. Simmonds, senior editor; publishes African history, black philosophy, and religion as it affects black people; Published 1 book in 1975-76.

Associated Publishers, Inc.
1401 14th Street, N.W.
Washington, D.C. 20005   (202) 667-2822

Association for the Study of Afro-American Life and History, Inc. (ASALH), owner; founded in 1915; Mrs. Thelma Perry, senior editor; publishes historical books. Published 7 books in 1975-76.

Black River Writers
Box 1591
East St. Louis, Illinois 62205   (916) 482-0799

        and

Black River Writers: West
P.O. Box 15853
Sacramento, California 94813

Eugene Redmond, owner; founded in 1967; Eugene Redmond, senior editor; publishes poetry and short stories. Published 5 books in 1975-76.

Bogle-l'Ouverture Publications Limited
5a Chignell Place
Ealing, London W13 OTJ, England   01-579-4920

Jessica E. Huntley, Eric L. Huntley, owners; founded in 1968; Br. Andrew-Salkey, senior editor; publishes books suitable for children, poetry, and political science. Published 6 books in 1975-76.

Broadside Press
12652 Livernois
Detroit, Michigan 48228

Dudley Randall, owner; founded in 1965; Dudley Randall, senior editor; publishes poetry and literary criticism. Published 9 books in 1975-76.

E. A. Publishing House Limited
P.O. Box 30571
Nairobi, Kenya, East Africa   557417

East African Cultural Trust, owner; founded in 1965; Richard C. Ntiru, senior editor; publishes novels, academic books, and biographies. Published 50 books in 1975-76.

East African Literature Bureau
Ngong Road
P.O. Box 30022
Nairobi, Kenya   28713

East African Community, owner; founded in 1948; N. G. Ngulukulu, director; publishes scholarly books, reference books, journals, fiction, adult education primers, and follow-up readers in English, Swahili, and local languages. Published 60 books in 1975-76.

Edward W. Blyden Press
P.O. Box 621 Manhattanville P.O.
New York, New York 10027   (212) 226-6000

A. Faulkner Watts, owner; founded in 1968; Rupert Garfia, senior editor; publishes educational materials dealing with all facets of the black experience in the United States, Africa, Latin America, and the Caribbean, and materials include teachers' resource guides, and books for children of elementary grades as well as high school students. Published 4 books in 1975-76.

Heritage of Hope Press
P.O. Box 125
Tillery, North Carolina 27887   (919) 693-1211

Evan-Redd Productions, Inc., owner; founded in 1976; Ferne Thorpe Dixon, senior editor; publishes fiction, non-fiction, poetry, children's materials, art, history, politics, economics, education and sociology. Published 1 book in 1975-76.

Howard University Press
2935 Upton Street, N.W.
Washington, D.C. 20059   (202) 686-6696

Howard University, owner; founded in 1972; Fay Acker, managing editor; publishes scholarly works, poetry, fiction, and biography. Published 26 books in 1974-76.

Institute of Positive Education
7524 South Cottage Grove Avenue
Chicago, Illinois 60619   (312) 651-0701

Institute of Positive Education, owner; founded in 1969; Haki R. Madhubuti, Jabari Mahiri, senior editors; publishes *Black Books Bulletin* (quarterly magazine), *Black Pages* (regular pamphlet series), educational posters, and other materials related to the development of educational models. Published 8 books in 1975-76.

Johnson Publishing Company, Inc.
820 South Michigan Avenue
Chicago, Illinois 60605   (312) 786-7600

Johnson Publishing Co., Inc., John H. Johnson, president; founded in 1961; Ms. Doris E. Saunders, director; publishes non-fiction, juvenile, and scholarly works primarily by and about black people. Published 5 books in 1975-76.

Lotus Press
P.O. Box 601
College Park Station
Detroit, Michigan 48221   (313) 862-5695

Leonard and Naomi Andrews, owners; founded in 1972; Naomi Andrews, senior editor; publishes poetry, usually by black authors, and no special ideology but simply of high literary merit. (We are particularly interested in presenting authors who are perhaps not sensational enough to attract large audiences merely because of content without regard for form. We find our authors among young persons previously unpublished and older authors with experience and some degree of prestige. We are particularly interested in providing black poetry for the classroom.) Published 6 books in 1975-76.

New Beacon Books
76 Stroud Green Road
London N43EN, England   01-272-4889

John LaRose, Sarah White, Andres Salkey, Matthew Butler, directors; founded in 1966; John LaRose, senior editor; publishes fiction, literary criticism, history, politics, education, linguistics, poetry. Published 4 books in 1975-76.

New Day Press, Inc.
2355 East 89th Street
Cleveland, Ohio 44106   (216) 795-7070

New Day Press, owner; founded in 1972; John McCluskey, senior editor; publishes educational books. Published 6 books in 1975-76.

People's War Publishing (formerly Jihad Productions)
P.O. Box 663
Newark, New Jersey 07101   (201) 621-2300

Congress of Afrikan People, owner; founded in 1967; Amiri Baraka, Katibu, senior editor; publishes books on black liberation (i.e., by Pres. A. Sekou Toure, Amilcar Cabral, Amiri Baraka), poetry, and ideological papers. Published 1 book in 1975-76.

Third World Press
7524 South Cottage Grove Avenue
Chicago, Illinois 60619   (312) 651-0700

Haki R. Madhubuti, Jabari Mahari, Jawanza Kunjufu, Safisha Madhubuti, Soyini Olamina, and others, owners; founded in 1967; Haki R. Madhubuti, senior editor; publishes non-fiction, fiction, poetry, children's books. Published 12 books in 1975-76.

Sapphire Publishing Company
P.O. Box 15072
San Francisco, California 94115

Patsy G. Fulcher, Aileen C. Hernandez, Jean Kresy, Jessica Minor, Eleanor R. Spikes, Maxine Ussery, E. Anne Warren, owners; founded in 1973; publishes works which reflect life and history relevant to black women, fiction, non-fiction, biography, autobiography, poetry, technical "know how," art, humor, and essays. Specialized area of children's books, preschool and beyond, and related educational materials. Published 1 book in 1975-76.

Yardbird Publishing Company, Inc.
Box 2370, Station A
Berkeley, California 94702

B. Wayne Daniels, Ishmael Reed, Al Young, William Lawson, Doyle Foreman, Carl Thompson, Lois Cunningham, Glenn Myles, owners; founded in 1971; Ishmael Reed, senior editor; publishes *Yardbird Readers* (collections of short stories), excerpts from novels (usually in progress), poetry, interviews, and articles (*Yardbird, Wing Editions*, editor Al Young, is publishing Youth Law Handbook, "Changing All Those Changes," by J. P. Girard, and "Zeppelin Coming Down," by William Lawson). Published three *Yardbird Readers* plus the above mentioned *Wing Editions* in 1975-76.

INDEX

Compiled by Sanford Berman
Head Cataloger
Hennepin County Library
Edina, Minnesota

Current and former branch library heads whose names appear in the directory have not been indexed unless also mentioned earlier in the text itself.

AAMP. *see* African-American Materials Project
AASL. *see* Alabama Association of School Librarians
ABIP. *see African Books in Print*
ABRP. *see African Book Publishing Record*
ACLO. *see* Association of Cooperative Library Organizations
ACRL. *see* Association of College and Research Libraries
AFSCME. *see* American Federation of State, County, and Municipal Employees
AHSA. *see* African Heritage Studies Association
A. L. A. *see* American Library Association
A. L. A. Notable Book List, 156-60
A. N. C. (South Africa). *see* African National Congress of South Africa
A. S. A. *see* African Studies Association
ASALH. *see* Association for the Study of Afro-American Life and History
ASTA. *see* Alabama State Teachers Association
Aaron, Hank, 254
Abajian, James De T., 184, 220, 230
Abdul, Raoul, 254
abolitionist literature, 212, 217, 220, 235, 237-38, 240, 242, 245-46, 251
Abrahams, Peter, 157
academic librarians, 30-31, 40-41, 43-46, 88-89
academic libraries, 127-33, 332-58
Access to Public Libraries, 20
Accessions List: Eastern Africa, 171, 178
accredited library schools, 103, 269-70
acquisition of Africana, 167-79
acquisition of Afro-Americana, 184-88

Action Library Program (Philadelphia), 104
actors. *see* theater
Adams, Charles M., 54
Adams, Elaine Parker, 89
Adams, Russell L., 134
Adelbert College Library, 11, 15, 30
Adger, Robert M., 219
Africa: an international business, economic, and political monthly, 143
Africa: Journal of the International African Institute, 143
Africa Quarterly, 144
Africa Report, 144
Africa Seen by American Negro Scholars, 233
African Adult Education, 170
African Affairs, 144
African American Cultural Center (Minneapolis), 260
African-American Institute, 144
African-American Materials Project, 22
African-American Scholars Council, 44, 74
African and Afro-American Materials (Bennett College Library), 347
African Art for Children, 260
African Art in American Collections, 235
African Arts, 144
African Book Publishing Record, 172, 186
African Books in Print, 169, 171-72
African exchange program (A. L. A. Black Caucus), 73-76
African Forum, 233
African Heritage Studies Association, 233
African Journey (Robeson), 159
African libraries, 44-45, 73-75
African Music and Oral Data: A Catalog of Recordings, 1902-1972, 180
African National Congress of South Africa, 181

African Newspapers in Selected American Libraries: A Union List (1965), 173, 234
African Research and Documentation, 172
African Review, 170
African Revolutionary Movements Collection (Hoover Institution), 181
African Scientist, 170
African Studies Association, 144, 232-34
African Studies Review, 144
Africana collections, 179-81, 246-47
Africana i nordiska vetenskapliga bibliotek, 173
Africana Journal, 145, 172-73, 175, 186
Africana Publishing Corporation, 169, 363
Africana resources, 105-06, 143-45, 167-81, 186
Africanus, Leo, 215-16
Afro-Am Publishing Co., 363
Afro-American academic libraries, 127-33, 332-58
Afro-American Book Distributors (Houston), 362
Afro-American colleges and universities, 127-29, 203-08, 240, 332-58
Afro-American Cultural and Historical Society (Cleveland), 262
Afro-American Encyclopedia (1895), 137
Afro-American Encyclopedia (1974), 135
Afro-American Historical Association of the Niagara Frontier, 257, 263
Afro-American Museum of Detroit, 260
Afro-American Resources Bibliography (G. W. Trenholm Memorial Library), 333
Afro-American Subject Headings in the Miller F. Whittaker Library, 351
Afro-Americana collections, 182-208, 222-65, 333-58
Afro-Americana resources, 82, 98, 105-06, 134-42, 145-52, 157-60, 182-265, 360-67
Afro-Americans in New York Life and History: An Interdisciplinary Journal, 264
Afro-Canadians, 236
After the Killing, 163
Alabama A. & M. College Library, 16
Alabama A. & M. University School of Library Media, 41, 103, 269
Alabama academic libraries, 332-35
Alabama Association of School Librarians, 47-51
Alabama Dept. of Education, 41-42
Alabama Education Association, 50
Alabama Instructional Media Association, 51
Alabama Library Association, 48-49
Alabama public library branches, 271-73
Alabama School Library Association, 49, 51
Alabama State College Dept. of Library Education, 41, 47

Alabama State Teachers Association, 47-48, 50
Alabama State University Library School, 266
Alain, Alex P., 71
Aldridge, Ira, 210, 235
Alexander Gumby Collection, 242, 247
Alexander, Margaret Walker. *see* Walker, Margaret A.
Alexander, Raymond Pace, 241, 245
Alford, Thomas, 67, 69
Ali, Gloria D., 260
Alkebu-Lan Books, 363
Alston, Clarice Jones, 52-53
Aman, Mohammed M., 74, 89, 178
American Association of Law Librarians. Southwestern Chapter, 21
American Bar Association, 66
American Black Women in the Arts and Social Sciences, 142
American Colonization Society, 237, 251
American Dilemma, 236, 250
American Federation of State, County, and Municipal Employees. Federal Council, 23
American Home Missionary Society, 245
American Library Association, 18, 19, 20, 35, 42, 67
American Library Association. Ad Hoc Committee on Opportunities for Negro Students in the Library Profession, 20
American Library Association Annual Conference, 1922, 32
American Library Association Annual Conference, 1926, 32
American Library Association Annual Conference, 1936, 44
American Library Association Annual Conference, 1956, 19
American Library Association Annual Conference, 1961, 20
American Library Association Annual Conference, 1964, 20
American Library Association Annual Conference, 1971, 71-72
American Library Association Annual Conference, 1972, 76, 81-82
American Library Association Annual Conference, 1973, 43, 75
American Library Association Annual Conference, 1974, 75, 87
American Library Association Annual Conference, 1976, 23, 76
American Library Association. Black Caucus, 21, 23, 42-43, 66-77, 81
American Library Association. Black Caucus. Task Force on Librarians for Africa, 44-45, 73-75

Index / 369

American Library Association Centennial Awards, 24, 45
American Library Association chapters, 19, 55
American Library Association. Children's Services Division, 19
American Library Association. Committee on Accreditation, 42
American Library Association. Committee on Racial Discrimination, 44
American Library Association Council, 22, 44, 55, 67-71
American Library Association. Executive Board, 20, 69
American Library Association Executive Director, 22, 72
American Library Association honorary members, 22, 23, 24, 43
American Library Association. Intellectual Freedom Committee, 70-71
American Library Association Midwinter Meeting, 1970, 68-69, 81
American Library Association Midwinter Meeting, 1971, 69-71
American Library Association Midwinter Meeting, 1972, 73
American Library Association Midwinter Meeting, 1974, 82
American Library Association. Nominating Committee, 20, 67
American Library Association. Office for Library Services to the Disadvantaged, 82
American Library Association. Public Library Association. *see* Public Library Association
American Library Association. Reference and Adult Services Division, 156
American Library Association. Social Responsibilities Round Table, 68
American Library Association. Social Responsibilities Round Table. Task Force on Recruitment of Minorities, 69
American Library Association. Work with Negroes Round Table, 17, 32
American Missionary Association, 240, 245
American Negro Academy, 16
American Negro: His History and Literature, 187
American Negro Reference Book, 141
American Negro Theatre, 243
American Negro Writer and His Roots, 233
American Society of African Culture, 233
Amistad Research Center, 240-41, 245-46
Amistad Research Center News, 241, 246

Amos and Andy (Radio Program), 94
AMSAC. *see* American Society of African Culture
Amsterdam News (New York), 189
Anderson, Jewett Langford, 47
Anderson, Marian, 157, 236, 239, 244, 249
Andrews, Naomi, 365
Andrews, Regina, 254
Angelou, Maya, 154-55, 157
Angola, 257
Anowuo Educational Publications, 170
Anthology of the American Negro in the Theatre, 138
Anti-Defamation League, 241, 245
antiquarian book collectors. *see* book collectors
anti-Semitism, 153
anti-slavery literature. *see* abolitionist literature
Apartheid, 157, 158, 159
Aptheker, Herbert, 239
Aquarian Bookshop (Los Angeles), 360
Arata, Ester Spring, 140
archives, 191, 197, 202-08, 226, 229-30, 235-37, 239-42
Arizona public library branches, 273
Arkansas public library branches, 273
Arkansas University. *see* University of Arkansas
art galleries, 258-61, 263, 310
Arthur Spingarn Collection of Black Authors. *see* Moorland-Spingarn Collection
artists, 135, 139, 142, 254, 259, 263
Askov, Eunice, 118
Associated Publishers (Washington, D.C.), 363
Association for the Study of Afro-American Life and History, 82, 151-52, 363
Association for the Study of Negro Life and History, 17
Association of American Library Schools, 21
Association of College and Research Libraries, 22, 23, 75, 129
Association of Cooperative Library Organizations, 22
Association of Research Libraries, 88
Association of Southern Women for the Prevention of Lynching, 246
ASTA. *see* Alabama State Teachers Association
athletes, 137, 147
Atkins, Hannah D., 20, 21
Atkinson, Hugh, 68
Atlanta Daily World, 189
Atlanta Public Library, 23, 288-89

Atlanta University Data Bank on
    Black Librarians, 76, 103
Atlanta University Library, 16, 17, 338
Atlanta University Library Conference,
    1941, 18
Atlanta University Library. Countee
    Cullen-Harold Jackman Collection.
    see Countee Cullen-Harold Jackman
    Collection
Atlanta University Library. Negro
    Collection, 19, 26, 194, 196, 240,
    246
Atlanta University Press, 16
Atlanta University School of Library
    Service, 18, 19, 24, 42-43, 103,
    105, 130, 267, 269
Atlanta University. Trevor-Arnett
    Library. see Atlanta University
    Library
audio-visual materials, 102, 118-26,
    131, 190
Austriad, 216
authors, 135, 140-42, 153-55, 157-66,
    185, 233, 236, 238, 240, 244,
    246, 250, 252, 254
Autobiography of Miss Jane Pittman,
    158
autograph parties, 78-79
Ayer, Thomas Parker, 64
Azalia Hackley Memorial Collection.
    see E. Azalia Hackley Memorial
    Collection

BLS University. see University of
    Botswana, Lesotho, and Swaziland
Bailey, Leaonead Pack, 135
Baily, Mrs. Leonard P. Drain, 358
Baird, Syvil, 49
Baker, Augusta, 19, 23, 52, 60, 87,
    96, 140
Baker, Josephine, 244
Baker, Michael, 83
Baldwin, James, 154-55, 157, 213
Ballard, Allen B., 128
Ballard, Robert, 89
Ballard, Ruby, 78
Bambara, Toni Cade, 149
Banks, Willette Rutherford, 356
Banneker, Benjamin, 135, 212
Baraka, Amiri, 244, 365
Barker, Tommie Dora, 62
Bass, Charlotta A., 244
Battle, Sam, 253
Battle, Thomas C., 74, 255, 258
Bayview-Hunters Point Area (San
    Francisco), 281
Beal, Marjorie, 54-55
Bearden, Bessye J., 236

Bearden, Romare, 262
Beasley, Nancy, 52-53
Beasley, William D., 52-53
Beck Cultural Exchange (Knoxville),
    262-63
Beecher, Henry Ward, 251
Bell, Geraldine W., 51
Benedict College Library, 16, 350
Benjamin, Lillie, 53
Bennett College Library (Greensboro),
    347
Berninghausen, David K., 70-71
best sellers, 153-55
Beta Phi Mu, 23
Bethune, Mary McLeod, 241-42, 245,
    275
Between Ourselves, 165
*Bibliographical Checklist of American
    Negro Poetry*, 17, 186
*Bibliographie nationale courante des
    pays d'Afrique d'expression française*,
    171
bibliographies, 105-06, 115-18, 134-52,
    171-74, 178-79, 184-86, 213, 228-32
Bibliography of Africa (1970), 171
*Bibliography of European Colonization
    and the Resulting Contacts of People,
    Races, and Culture*, 27
*Bibliography of the Negro in Africa and
    America*, 18, 26-27, 142, 213, 221
bibliophiles, 25-26, 194-95, 209-21
bibliotherapy, 17, 34-35
Biblo, Mary, 83
Biddle, Stanton F., 231
Bilalian News, 190
Bilbrew, Mrs. A. C., 278
bilingual public library collections,
    278-79, 282, 301, 306, 308, 311-12
Billops, Camille, 243, 254
Bingham, Rebecca T., 22
*Bio-Bibliography of Countee P. Cullen,
    1903-1946*, 164
Biographical Directory of Negro Ministers,
    142
biographical sources, 134-42
Birney, James Gillespie, 237, 251
Bishop College (Dallas). Southwest
    Research Center and Museum, 263
Bishop College Library (Dallas), 355
Bishop College Library (Dallas). Black
    Oral History Program, 257
Bishop, Minnie Slade, 45
Black Almanac, 137
Black American Cinema Society, 264
Black American in Books for Children, 106
Black American Reference Book, 141,
    243
Black American Writers Past and Present,
    140

Black Americana collections. *see* Afro-Americana collections
Black Athlete, 137
Black Bibliography, 230
Black Book, 221, 243
"Black Book Reviewing: A Case for Library Action" (Shockley), 231
Black Books Bulletin, 145, 364
Black Boy, 153-54, 160
Black Caucus (American Library Association). *see* American Library Association. Black Caucus
Black Caucus (California Library Association). *see* California Librarians Black Caucus
Black Caucus (Chicago). *see* Chicago Area Black Librarians
Black Caucus (New York). *see* New York Black Librarians Caucus
Black Caucus Newsletter, 23, 76, 164
Black Caucus (U. S. Congress). *see* Congressional Black Caucus
"Black College Library" (Josey), 127-33
Black colleges and universities. *see* Afro-American colleges and universities
Black Collegian, 146
Black Economic Research Center, 152
Black Employees Association (Library of Congress), 75
Black Enterprise, 146, 227
Black Experience in Children's Books, 105, 140
Black Experience in the United States: A Bibliography Based on Collections of the San Fernando Valley State College Library, 135
Black History Archives Project, Western Reserve Historical Society, 230
Black Law Journal, 146
Black Liberation, 66, 365
Black Librarian in America, 21, 67-68
"Black Librarians: A Statement of Concern" (1970), 69
Black Librarians Caucus of Queens, 84, 87
Black Librarians Data Bank (Atlanta University), 76, 103
Black Muslims, 190, 212
Black Oral History Conference, 1972, 22
Black Oral History Program (Fisk University Library), 253
Black Pages, 364
Black Panther, 190, 212
Black Perspective in Music, 146, 189
Black Poets, 163
Black Rage, 127, 132, 155, 158

Black Representation on Library Governing Boards Resolution (A. L. A. Council), 69, 73
Black River Writers (East St. Louis/Sacramento), 363
Black Scholar, 147
Black Sports, 147
Black Studies Librarianship Institute. *see* Fisk University Institute on Black Studies Librarianship
Black Studies resources, 82, 105-06, 134-52, 157-60, 167-265, 360-66
Black Thunder, 161
Black Times, 189
Black/White information transfer, 132-33
Black Woman Speaks, 79
Black World, 78, 149
Blacks in American Films, 22
Blacks in Rhode Island, 262
Blake, Eubie, 244, 254
blind persons, 34
Blockson, Charles L., 244
Blue, Thomas Fountain, 16, 17, 18, 31-32, 36, 37, 299
Bluford, F. D., 346
Blumenbach, Johann Friedrich, 218
Blyden, Edward W., 330
Blyden Press, 364
Blyden, Wilmont, 211
Boesak, Alen, 255
Bogle-l'Ouverture Publications, 364
Bolden, Ethel, 61
Boles, Nancy G., 229
Bolivar, William C., 219
Bolling Family, 245
Bomar, Cora P., 60
Bond, Horace Mann, 244
Bond, Julian, 75
Bonds, Margaret, 244
Bontemps, Arna, 18, 52, 161-62, 183, 190, 194, 196, 239, 242, 248, 254, 353
book collectors, 25-26, 196, 209-21, 243-45
Book Development in Africa (1969), 168
book selection. *see* collection development
bookmobiles, 98
books-by-mail services, 272
bookstores, 210, 360-62
Boston Guardian, 29
Boston Public Library. West End Branch, 15, 29
Botswana, Lesotho, and Swaziland University. *see* University of Botswana, Lesotho, and Swaziland
Bowie State College Library, 342
Braithwaite, William Stanley, 235, 241-42, 253
branch public libraries. *see* public library branches

Branch, William, 254
Brawley, Benjamin Griffith, 135, 249
Brice, Carol, 241
Brice, Ruth, 263
Broadside Authors and Artists, 135
Broadside Press, 20, 86, 135, 162-63, 165, 212, 364
Broderick, Francis L., 236
Brooklyn Story, 166
Brooks, Gwendolyn, 19, 23, 102, 157, 162
Brooks, Hallie Beacham, 18
Brotherhood of Sleeping Car Porters, 237, 243
Brower, Franklin D., 243
Brown, Claude, 155, 157
Brown, Dorothy L., 254
Brown, Hallie Q., 135, 242, 348
Brown, John, 244, 246, 251
Brown, Lawrence, 235
Brown, Lorene Byron, 89
Brown, Martha M., 354
Brown, Olive Durden, 40
Brown, Ollie L., 45, 47, 49
Brown, Richard, 80
Brown University Library, 22
Brown v. Board of Education, 15, 19
Brown v. Louisiana, 20
Brown, William Wells, 211
Brownlee, Frederick Leslie, 245
Brownridge, Ina C., 23
Bruce, Blanche K., 239
Bruce, John E., 28, 135, 235
Bruner, Jerome S., 114
Buffalo, New York, 257, 263, 309
buildings, 131-32
Bullock, Penelope L., 89
Bullins, Ed, 254
Bunche, Ralph J., 244
Burkel, Nicholas C., 191
Burnett, Lenel L., 53
Burns, Ben, 152
Burroughs, Charles G., 259
Burroughs, Sadie, 58
Burton Historical Collection (Detroit Public Library), 247
Busara, 170
Bush, Anita, 244
business, 146, 148, 227
Bustill, Cyrus, 245
Butler, Charles, 52
Butler, Susan Dart, 32-33, 58, 61
Byam, Milton S., 21, 22, 70, 87

CCLC. *see* Cooperative College Library Center
C.E.M.B.A. *see* Conference for the Evaluation of Materials about Black Americans, 1969
CIBC. *see* Council on Interracial Books for Children
CLA. *see* California Library Association
CLA Journal (College Language Association), 147, 189
CLBC. *see* California Librarians Black Caucus
C.U.N.Y. *see* City University of New York
Cables to Rage, 165
Cabral, Amilcar, 365
California bookstores, 360
California Librarians Black Caucus, 77-81
California Library Association, 77
California Library Association. Black Caucus. *see* California Librarians Black Caucus
California public library branches, 274-82
CAMP, 178-79
Campbell, Dick, 254
Capitein, Jacobus Elijah, 212, 216
CARDAN, 173
career guidance. *see* vocational guidance
Career Guide: Opportunities and Resources, 137
Carmichael, Stokely, 182
Carmichael, T. A., 52
Carnegie Corporation, 17, 18, 25, 27, 33, 35-36, 62, 198, 269
Carnegie libraries, 16, 91
Carr, Kathryn P., 77-79
Carrington, Glen, 220, 236, 244
Carter, Elmer A., 236
Cartwright, Marguerite D., 241
Carver, George Washington, 241, 250, 258, 299, 327
Cash, Pamela J., 225
cataloging of audio-visual materials, 122
Catalogue of the African Collection in the Moorland Foundation, 19
Catholic Committee of the South, 245
CEMBA. *see* Conference for the Evaluation of Materials about Black Americans, 1969
Center for Research Libraries, 179
Central State University Library, 348
Central State University Library. Hallie Q. Brown Collection. *see* Hallie Q. Brown Collection
Chandler, Sue P., 22, 141
Chapman, Dorothy, 136, 230
Chariot in the Sky, 161
Charles F. Heartman Negro Collection. *see* Heartman Negro Collection
Charleston County (South Carolina) Free Public Library, 33, 58
Charlotte (North Carolina) Public Library, 16, 313
Chatham Bookseller, 184
Chesnutt, Charles W., 197, 239, 248, 346
Cheyney State College Library, 16, 349
Chicago Afro-American Union Analytic Catalog, 184, 230, 247

Chicago Area Black Librarians, 81-83
Chicago Black Caucus. *see* Chicago Area Black Librarians
Chicago Defender, 189
Chicago Public Library, 82, 290-96
Chicago Public Library. Vivian Harsh Collection. *see* Vivian Harsh Collection.
Chicago University. *see* University of Chicago
Chicano librarians, 76
Chicano resources, 273, 278-79, 283, 327
children's librarians, 95-96
children's literature, 95, 101-02, 105-06, 140, 146, 165-66, 185, 226, 362, 364-65
children's services, 86-87, 93-118
Children's Television Workshop, 126
Childs, Leroy C., 53
Choice of Weapons, 159
Christian, R. L., 286
Christmas, Walter, 232
Christopher, R. A., 175-76
chronology of Afro-American librarianship, 15-24
Church Family, 256
Churchwell, Charles D., 22, 89
circulation policies, 110
Cities Burning, 163
Citizens' Protective League, 235
City University of New York. Cohen Library, 243, 254
City University of New York Council of Chief Librarians, 23
Civil Rights Congress, 235
Civil Rights Movement, 226, 249, 253, 255-56
Clack, Doris, 89
Clarence Day Award, 23
Clark, Kenneth B., 123, 131, 150, 157, 253
Clarke, John Henrik, 88, 150
Clarkson, Thomas, 240, 246
Clayton, Mayme A., 227, 252, 264, 360
Clayton, Minnie H., 249
Cleaver, Eldridge, 155, 158, 182
Clift, David, 72
Clifton, Lucille, 102
clipping files, 225, 227, 228, 235, 238-39, 241, 243, 247-48, 259, 280-81
Cloud, Annie, 61
Clutchens, Alice, 254
Cobbs, Price M., 127, 132-33, 155, 158
Cohen Library (City University of New York), 243, 254
Coker, Daniel, 237
Cole, Ernest, 158
Cole, Thomas Winston, Sr., 356
Coleman, Barbara, 77-78

Coleman, James S., 111
Coleman, Jean E., 82
Coleman, Samuel H., 337
Coley, Hattie, 56
collection development, 86-87, 92, 101-02, 111-13, 122, 131, 184-92
College Language Association, 147
college librarians. *see* academic librarians
college libraries. *see* academic libraries
Collings, Dorothy, 89
Collins, Leslie Morgan, 89, 163
Collis P. Huntington Library. *see* Hampton Institute Library
colonialism, 158
Color and Democracy, 158
Colorado public library branches, 282-83
"Colored People" (South Africa), 157
Columbia University Library. Alexander Gumby Collection. *see* Alexander Gumby Collection
Columbia University Library. Oral History Collection, 253
Columbia University Library. Rare Book and Manuscript Library, 247
Commission on Interracial Cooperation, 246
Committee on Scientific and Technical Information. Subcommittee on Negro Research Libraries, 21
computer-assisted instruction, 125
computer data banks. *see* data banks
Conference for the Evaluation of Materials about Black Americans, 1969, 21
Congregational Church Extension Board, 246
Congress of Afrikan People, 365
Congress of Racial Equality. *see* CORE
Congressional Black Caucus, 66, 72, 149
Conley, Binford H., 336
Connecticut public library branches, 283-84
Conover, Helen F., 174, 178
Constance Lindsay Skinner Award, 21
consumer education, 113
Coombs, Orde, 149
Cooper, Loretta, 221
Cooperative Africana Microfilm Project, 178-79
Cooperative College Library Center, 21
Copeland, Emily, 61, 189
CORE, 226, 238, 249
Coretta Scott King Award, 101, 166
Coretta Scott King Award Collection, 226
COSATI. *see* Committee on Scientific and Technical Information
Cosby, Bill, 94
Cossitt Library (Memphis, Tennessee), 16

Council on Interracial Books for Children, 75
Council on Interracial Books for Children Award, 101, 106, 166
counseling, 130
Countee Cullen-Harold Jackman Collection, 196, 240, 246
Cousins, R. L., 52
Crawford, Agnes, 58
Crawford, Charles W., 256
Crayton, James E., 77-78
Crisis, 147, 161
Cromwell, John W., 28, 243
Crooks, Kenneth B. M., 241
Cross, James, 89
Crossey, Moore, 176, 234
Crosswaith, Frank R., 235
Crummell, Alexander, 16, 210, 235
Cruzat, Gwendolyn, 89
Cuffe, Paul, 135, 214, 238
Cullen, Countee, 34, 196, 240-41, 246, 251-52, 310
Cullen, Mrs. Countee, 254
cultural identity, 92-93, 98-99, 102, 123, 126
Cunard, Nancy, 221
Cunningham, William D., 72, 336
CUNY. *see* City University of New York
curators, 192-202
Curley, Arthur, 69
Current Bibliography on African Affairs, 172
Curtis, Florence Rising, 17, 36-40, 64
Cuthbert, Evelyn, 61

D. C. P. L. *see* District of Columbia Public Library
Daddy Was a Number Runner, 159
Daly, Laura R., 257
Dancy, John C., Sr., 243
Daniel, Lois H., 45
Daniel, Robert P., 56
Daniel, Watha T., 287
Daniels, J. K., 352
Danner, Margaret, 163
Dannett, Sylvia G. L., 232
Dark Ghetto, 157
Data Bank on Black Librarians (Atlanta University), 76, 103
data banks, 92
Davenport, Vivien, 89
Davies, Nolan, 79
Davis, Angela Y., 66
Davis, Hillis, 21
Davis, John A., 233
Davis, John Warren, 253
Davis, Julia, 303

Davis, Sara Bond, 60
Dawson, William L., 197, 239
Day, Nancy Jane, 60
Daystar Press, 170
DeGrasse, John V., 243
DeJohn, William, 69
Delaney, Buford, 263
Delaney, Joseph, 263
Delaney, Sadie Peterson, 17, 34-35, 49, 250
Delany, Hubert T., 244
Delany, Martin, 211
De Lavallade, Carmen, 254
Delaware academic libraries, 336
Delta Ministry, 227
desegregated library associations. *see* integrated library associations
desegregated library conferences. *see* integrated library conferences
Detroit Afro-American Museum, 260
Detroit Public Library, 21, 247, 299-301
Detroit Public Library. E. Azalia Hackley Memorial Collection. *see* E. Azalia Hackley Memorial Collection.
"Developing Collections of Black Literature" (Smith), 189, 231
Dewey, Melville, 119
Dickinson, Charles W., Jr., 62-63
Dictionary of African Biography, 235
Dictionary of American Biography, 232
Dictionary of American Negro Biography, 232
Dillard University. Amistad Research Center. *see* Amistad Research Center
Dillard University Library, 341
Dimensions Dance Theatre, 80
Di Nigro Press, 170
Diop, Alioune, 145
Directory of African Studies in the United States, 233
Directory of Afro-American Resources, 140, 230
Directory of Black Literary Magazines, 136
discrimination in library service. *see* racism in library service
displays, 111, 113
District of Columbia academic libraries, 336-37
District of Columbia Public Library, 22, 74, 284-87
District of Columbia public library branches, 284-87
District of Columbia University. *see* University of the District of Columbia
Dix, William, 68
Dixon, Rosebud, 53
Dobbs Family, 246

Doctorates in librarianship, 18, 19, 89
doctors, 138, 243, 283, 292
Doherty, Amy S., 191
Doms, Keith, 72
Douglas, Aaron, 197, 239, 248, 254, 310
Douglas, Mary Peacock, 55
Douglass, Frederick, 212, 237, 249, 292, 300, 330, 342
Downing, George T., 243
Downs, Karl E., 354
Drake, Joseph F., 333
dramatists. see authors
Drew, Charles, 114
Drums at Dusk, 161
DuBois, Shirley Graham, 209, 251, 254
DuBois, W. E. B., 16, 29, 152, 158 161, 196-97, 210, 229, 232, 235-36, 239, 241, 248, 251, 253
Dudley, Edward R., 241
Duignan, Peter, 136, 181, 234
Dumas, Alexandre, 219
Dunbar, Paul Laurence, 210, 235, 238, 250
Duncan, S. E., 56
Dunham, Katherine, 254
Durant, Hattie I., 45
DuSable Museum of African American History, 259
Dykes, Eva B., 333

EAPH. see East African Publishing House
E. Azalia Hackley Memorial Collection, 19, 237, 247-48
Early Negro Writing: 1760-1837, 138, 185
East African Journal of Rural Development, 170
East African Literature Bureau, 170, 364
East African Publishing House, 169-70, 364
East African Research Information Center, 172
East Distribution and Publications (Brooklyn), 362
Easton, Celmast, 221
Ebony, 148, 245
Ebony Handbook, 136
Ebony Success Library, 136
education, 151
Education and Race Relations Conference, 1933, 18
education, higher. see higher education
Education of Black Folk (1973), 128
education, urban. see urban education
Educational Media Association, 49
educational television, 125-26

Edward W. Blyden Press, 364
Ehrhardt, Margaret, 60
Eisenberg, Pablo, 221
Elder, Lonne, 254
Elder, Lucius W., 195
Electric Company (Television Program), 126
Ellington, Duke, 244
Ellis, Elinor, 89
Ellison, Ralph, 158, 321
Emerson, Katherine, 251
Eminent Negro Men and Women, 135
Emory University Library School, 35
Encore, 148
Encyclopedia Africana, 235
Encyclopedia of the Negro: Preparatory Volume (1945), 229
English, Jeanne, 76, 81
ephemeral materials, 202-08
Equal Opportunity: The Minority Student Magazine, 148
Essence, 149
Estes, Rice, 20
Ethiope Publishing Corporation, 170
ethnic library caucuses, 76
ethnic pride. see cultural identity
Evans, Mari, 149
Evers, Medgar, 359
exchange librarians, 74, 76

Fair Employment Practice Laws Resolution (A. L. A. Council), 69
Famous Blacks Give Secrets of Success, 137
Fancher, Evelyn, 89, 268, 354
Fanon, Frantz, 160
Fauset, Jessie Redmond, 153
Fax, Elton, 87, 243-44, 254
Fayetteville State University Library, 346
federal aid, 132, 198
Federal City College (Washington, D. C.). see University of the District of Columbia
films, 22, 180, 264, 304
Films on Africa, 180
Fire Next Time, 155, 157
first Afro-American
    A. L. A. Children's Services Division President, 19
    A. L. A. Executive Board member, 20
    A. L. A. Executive Director, 22
    A. L. A. honorary member, 22
    A. L. A. Nominating Committee Chairperson, 20
    A. L. A. program speaker, 17
    A. L. A. President, 23, 75
    Association of American Library Schools President, 21

376 / Index

first Afro-American (cont'd)
    Association of College and Research Libraries President, 22
    Atlanta Public Library Director, 23
    best seller, 153
    Beta Phi Mu President, 23
    Clarence Day Award winner, 23
    Constance Lindsay Skinner Award winner, 21
    Dean of White library school, 23
    Detroit Public Library Director, 21
    District of Columbia Public Library Director, 21
    Doctorate in librarianship, 18
    Fisk University Librarian, 18
    Georgia Library Association member, 20
    Grolier Foundation Award winner, 19
    Harvard University graduate, 15
    independent library, 16
    Joseph Wharton Lippincott Award winner, 24
    Journal of Library History Award winner, 21
    Kentucky Library Association President, 22
    library training in South, 17
    Melville Dewey Medal winner, 23
    Missouri Library Association President, 20
    New York Library Association President, 24
    New York Library Club President, 23
    New York Public Library administrator, 19
    New York State Regents Advisory Council on Libraries member, 22
    Newbery Medal winner, 101
    Oklahoma Chapter, Special Libraries Association President, 20
    Pacific Northwest Library Association President, 19
    periodical, 219
    professionally trained librarian, 16
    Public Library Association President, 22
    public library branch, 16, 299
    public library branch head, 16, 99
    Pulitzer Prize winner, 19
    Queens Borough Public Library Director, 22
    school library consultant, 41
    Southwest Chapter, American Association of Law Librarians, President, 21
    SUNY library director, 23
    Supreme Court Justice, 342
    Tennessee Library Association President, 22

first Afro-American (cont'd)
    Virginia Library Association members, 44
    West Virginia Library Association President, 20
    woman doctor in Colorado, 283
    woman Ph.D., 333
First Cities, 165
First World, 149
Fisher, Mary L., 138
Fisk University Institute on Black Studies Librarianship, 1970, 21
Fisk University Library, 16, 18, 22, 134, 161, 197, 353
Fisk University Library. Black Oral History Program, 253-54
Fisk University Library. Julius Rosenwald Archives. *see* Julius Rosenwald Archives
Fisk University Library. Negro Collection, 25, 185, 193-94, 201, 230, 239-40, 248
Fisk University Library School, 268
Flaherty, Thomas, 158
Fleetwood, Christian Abraham, 235, 237
Flewellen, Icabod, 262
Florida A. & M. University Library, 337
Florida A. & M. University Library School, 266
Florida academic libraries, 337
Florida public library branches, 287-88
Floyd, Samuel A., Jr., 231
Forbes, George Washington, 15, 28-29
Ford, Anne, 79
Ford Foundation, 130, 168
Ford, Justina L., 283
Fordham, Monroe, 263
Fort Valley State College Library, 339
Fort Valley State College Library School, 267
Fortune, Thomas, 236
Foss, Sam Walter, 95
Foster, Leroy, 260
Foxes of Harrow, 153-54
Francis, Frank, Jr., 268
Franklin Book Programs, 168-69
Franklin, Hardy, 22, 89, 284
Franklin, John Hope, 141, 254
Frazier, Edward Franklin, 158, 239
Freedmen's Bureau, 237
Freedom's Journal, 219
Freedomways, 150, 213, 231
Frissell Library. *see* Tuskegee Institute Library
From a Land Where Other People Live, 165
From Man to Superman, 211
From These Roots, 250
Frost, Carolyn, 89
Fugitive Blacksmith, 221

fugitive materials, 202-08, 360
Fuller, Hoyt W., 149, 254
fund raising, 198
Funua, Akilimali, 78, 281
Future Shock, 121

GTEA. *see* Georgia Teachers and Education Association
Gaines, Ernest, 80, 158
Gainsboro Branch, Roanoke Public Library, 39-41
Gaither, Edmund Barry, 259
Galamison, Milton A., 238
Gallager, Buell G., 242
Gallup, Donald C., 252
Galveston, Texas. Rosenberg Library. *see* Rosenberg Library (Galveston, Texas)
Gardiner, Leon, 219
Garraty, John A., 232
Garrison, F. S., 235
Garvey, Marcus, 197, 214, 236-37, 239-40, 248, 251
Garys' and Their Friends, 221
Gaymon, Nicolas E., 89, 337, 341
Gee, Clarence S., 244
genealogy, 229
General Education Board, 16, 18, 35-36, 38, 269, 338-39, 344, 351, 353
Genius of Freedom, 219
Gentleman's Agreement, 153
George Foster Peabody Collection on the Negro, 16, 241, 248
George Gershwin Memorial Collection of Music and Music Literature (Fisk University Library), 248, 353
George Washington Carver Museum, 258
Georgia academic libraries, 337-40
Georgia Library Association, 20
Georgia library schools, 267, 269
Georgia public library branches, 288-90
Georgia State Teachers and Educational Association, 51
Georgia Teacher and Education Association. Librarians' Section, 51-53
Gershwin Memorial Collection of Music and Music Literature. *see* George Gershwin Memorial Collection of Music and Music Literature
Ghana Publishing Corporation, 170
ghetto libraries. *see* inner city libraries
Giles, Louise, 23, 75
Gillespie, Marcia, 149
Giovanni, Nikki, 102, 196, 254
Giovanni's Room, 213
Glass, Dominion R., 357
Gleason, Eliza Atkins, 18, 30, 89, 269
Glenn, Mary Etta, 248
Gloster, Hugh M., 56

God Sends Sunday, 161
Goff, Edgar, 264
Golden, Samuel, 265
Goldsmith, Albert, 264
Goodloe, Robbie, 46
Gordon, Asa H., 340
Gordon, Voree, 82
Gosebrink, Jean E. Meeh, 180
government publications, 174-76
graduate programs in librarianship, 19, 37, 103, 269-70
Gragg, Rosa L., 248
Graham, Alma S., 361
Graham, Clarence R., 19
Grambling State University Library, 340
Grambling State University Library School, 267
Granger, Lester, 253
Graves, Earl G., 227
Gray, Beverly, 175
Great Men of Color (Rogers), 210
Great Negroes Past and Present, 134
Green, Lucille, 47
Green, Midland, 256
Greene, Lorenzo J., 229
Greener, Richard T., 11, 15, 235
Greenfield, Eloise, 102
Gregoire, Henri, 15, 212, 218-19
Gregory, James H., 17
Grier, William H., 127, 132-33, 155, 158
Griffin, Mary, 61
Grimke Family, 239, 249
Grolier Foundation Award, 19
Gross, Robert E., 114
Guide to Negro Periodical Literature, 55, 137
Gumbs, Laurette, 64
Gumby Collection. *see* Alexander Gumby Collection
Guyman, Jessie Parkhurst, 250
Guzman, Jessie P., 241

Hackley Memorial Collection. *see* E. Azalia Hackley Memorial Collection
Hadley, Earl, 362
Hairston, Mary H., 55
Haith, Dorothy M., 89, 269
Haiti, 236
Haley, Alex, 24, 154-55, 158, 229, 254
Haley, James T., 137
Hall, George C., 292
Hallie Q. Brown Collection, 242
Hamilton, Virginia, 101
Hammon, Jupiter, 212
Hampton Institute Library, 16, 230, 248

Hampton Institute Library Conference, 1927, 18
Hampton Institute Library. George Foster Peabody Collection. see George Foster Peabody Collection on the Negro
Hampton Institute Library School, 17, 18, 24, 35-46, 54, 62
Handbook for the Organization of Black Materials, 353
Handbook of American Resources for African Studies, 136, 234
Handy, W. C., 236, 243
Hansberry, Lorraine, 244, 293
Hansberry, W. Leo, 232, 244
Harders, Walter, 168
Harding, Vincent, 231
Hare, Julia, 81
Hare, Maude Cuney, 246
Hare, Nathan, 146, 254
Harlan, Louis R., 237
Harlem Gallery, 159
Harlem Renaissance, 25, 34, 153, 161, 212, 254
Harmon Award, 25, 27
Harmon Foundation, 251
Harper, Charles Lincoln, 52
Harriford, Willie L., Jr., 231
Harris, Marquis LaFayette, 335, 338
Harris, Masha, 260
Harris, Middleton A. "Spike," 221, 243
Harris, Rache D., 37, 298-99
Harrison, General Lamar, 349
Harrison, Hubert H., 194
Harrison, Richard B., 314
Harsh Collection. see Vivian Harsh Collection
Hart, James D., 195-96
Harvard University, 15
Hastie, William H., 244, 263
Hatch/Billops Collection, 243, 254
Hawkins, Louella, 133
Hayden, Robert E., 24, 162
Hayes, Carol W., 48, 50
Hayes, George Edmund, 238-40 248
Haynes, Lemuel, 212
Haytian Papers, 211, 214
Hazard, Ben, 258
Heacock, Roland T., 241
Head, Bessie, 149
Heartman Negro Collection (Texas Southern University), 230, 242, 355
Hedgeman, Anna Arnold, 87
Height, Dorothy, 253
Helen Armstead Johnson Foundation for Theater Research, 243

Henderson, Edwin B., 137
Henderson, Mark, Jr., 261
Hendricks, Espy, 89, 344
Henne, Frances, 48
Henry Proctor Slaughter Collection. see Atlanta University Library. Negro Collection
Henson, Matthew, 241
heritage, cultural. see cultural identity
Heritage of Hope Press, 364
Hernandez, Aileen, 254, 365
Herring, Joan, 43
Hershaw, L. M., 28
Herskovits Library of African Studies. see Melville J. Herskovits Library of African Studies
Herskovits, Melville Jean, 232
Hewitt, Vivian, 74
Heyward, DuBose, 153
Hicks, Jeannette, 55
High John The Conqueror Program (Baltimore), 104
higher education, 127-30
Hightower, Mary, 346
Hill, Adelaide E., 186, 234
Hill, Harriet Dorothy Miles, 41
Hill, Leslie Pinckney, 349
Hill, Robert A., 237
His Eye is on the Sparrow, 159
Historical Negro Biographies, 140, 232
historical societies, 263-65
Historical Society of Pennsylvania, 230
History of the Black Men in the Life of the Republic, 29
History of the Negro in Medicine, 138
Hobson, Laura Z., 153
Hogan, Lloyd L., 152
Hollis Burke Frissell Library. see Tuskegee Institute Library
Holte, Clarence L., 221, 224
Homespun Heroines and Other Women of Distinction, 135
honorary A. L. A. members, 22, 23, 24, 43
honorary Doctorates, 89
Hoole, W. S., 49
Hoover Institution on War, Revolution, and Peace, 181, 234
Hope, John II, 241, 246
Horne, Frank S., 241
Hornsby, Alton, 137
hospital librarians, 34-35
House of Bondage, 158
House, Robert B., 55
House Servant's Directory, 217
Housewives League, 248
How Far the Promised Land, 159
Howard, Oliver Otis, 249
Howard University Library, 16, 31, 74, 129, 336

Howard University Library Conference on Black Bibliography, 1969, 21
Howard University Library. Moorland Foundation Collection. *see* Moorland-Spingarn Collection
Howard University Library. Moorland-Spingarn Collection. *see* Moorland-Spingarn Collection
Howard University Museum, 258
Howard University Press, 364
Howe, Julia Ward, 251
Hughes, Langston, 34, 102, 153, 160, 161, 212, 236, 240, 246, 252, 310, 317, 349
Hulbert, James A., 64
Humphrey, Moss, 79
Hundred Penny Box, 166
Hunt, Henry Alexander, 339
Hunter, Maurice, 236, 243
Huntington Library (Hampton Institute). *see* Hampton Institute Library
Huntington Library (San Marino, California), 242
Hurka, Eleanor, 227
Hurston, Zora Neale, 153, 242
Huston-Tillotson College Library, 40, 354
Hutson, Jean Blackwell, 194, 236, 249

IAI Notes and News, 143
I Know Why the Caged Bird Sings, 154-55, 157
I Too Am America: Documents from 1619 to the Present, 140
Ibadan University Press, 169
identity, cultural. *see* cultural identity
Illinois bookstores, 361
Illinois Manpower Advisory Committee, 82
Illinois public library branches, 290-96
Image of the Black in Children's Fiction, 106
In a Mecca: Poems, 157
In Freedom's Footsteps, 141
In the Castle of My Skin, 158
Index Africanus, 181
Index to Black Poetry, 136, 230
Index to Periodical Articles by and about Negroes, 137, 348
Indian Centre for Africa, 144
Indiana public library branches, 297
Indiana University Library, 180
inner city libraries, 80, 90-93, 97-101
inner city schools, 123-26
Inquiry Concerning the Intellectual and Moral Faculties and Literature of Negroes, 15

Institute of Positive Education, 145, 361, 364
Institute on Black Studies Librarianship. *see* Fisk University Institute on Black Studies Librarianship
Integrated Education, 150
integrated library associations, 19, 20, 49, 51-52, 56, 61, 65, 224
integrated library conferences, 19, 44
integrated schools, 150, 257
Integrating America's Heritage (1970), 232
intellectual freedom, 64
Intellectual Freedom Committee (A. L. A.). *see* American Library Association. Intellectual Freedom Committee
intelligence tests, 124
Interdenominational Theological Center, 255
Intergroup Education in Kindergarten-Primary Grades, 108
International African Bibliography, 143, 172, 186
International African Institute, 143, 173, 185
International Book Year, 73-75
International Labor Defense, 235
Interracial Books for Children Bulletin, 106
Introduction to Black Literature in America: From 1746 to the Present, 138
Invisible Man, 158, 321
Iowa public library branches, 297-98

Jackman, Harold, 196, 240
Jackson, Alice A., 40
Jackson, George, 158
Jackson, J. Arthur, 17, 27
Jackson, Lillie M., 241
Jackson, Maynard, 143, 148
Jackson, Miles M., 89, 105
Jackson, Parepa Watson, 46
Jackson, Ruth Moore, 89, 268
Jackson State University Library, 343
Jackson State University Library School, 267
Jackson, W. Carl, 72
Jackson, Wallace Van. *see* Van Jackson, Wallace
Jacksonville, Florida, 259, 287-88
Jacobs, Alma, 19, 20, 89
James, Jerry, 170, 177
James Weldon Johnson Collection, 18, 161, 192, 240, 242, 252
Jane Adams Book Award, 161
Japanese-American resources, 282
Jason, William C., 336
Jeanes Teachers, 54, 62

Jefferson, Thomas, 218
Jeffersons (Television Program), 92
Jenkins, Cynthia, 84
Jenkins, Harriet, 61
Jessye, Eva, 242
Jet, 92, 150, 225
Jewish Daily Forward, 29
Jews, 29, 76, 153, 194, 241, 245, 307
Jihad Productions. see People's War Publishing
John West Publications, 170
Johnson, Ann M., 56
Johnson, C. Elizabeth, 47
Johnson C. Smith University Library, 16, 345
Johnson, Charles S., 239, 248, 353
Johnson, Clifton H., 229, 241, 245
Johnson, Georgia Douglas, 161
Johnson, Guy B., 229
Johnson, Hall, 243
Johnson, Harry A., 105, 123-25, 190
Johnson, Helen Armstead, 243
Johnson, J. Albert, 28
Johnson, James Weldon, 153, 161, 194, 240, 251-52, 288
Johnson, John H., 148, 150, 365
Johnson Memorial Collection (Yale University Library). see James Weldon Johnson Collection
Johnson, Mordecai, 239
Johnson, Oakley C., 236
Johnson Publishing Co., 20, 136, 148, 150, 365
Johnson Publishing Co. Library, 225-26
Johnson, W. L. D., Sr., 329
Johnston, James Hugo, 357
Joint Acquisitions List of Africana, 173, 181, 234
Jones, Carolyn L., 64
Jones, Clara Stanton, 21, 23, 69, 75, 80, 87, 89, 247, 254
Jones, Clarice. see Alston, Clarice Jones
Jones, LeRoi. see Baraka, Amiri
Jones, Robert E., 241
Jones, Thomas J., 17
Jones, Virginia Lacy, 19, 20, 21, 23, 24, 42-43, 52, 53, 60, 87, 267, 269
Jones, William H., 354
Joplin, Scott, 236, 240, 248
Jordan, Casper Leroy, 76, 240, 328, 348
Jordan, Frederick Douglas, 339
Jordan, Gwendolyn, 64
Jordan, L. V., 358
Jordan, Patricia, 89
Jordan, Vernon E., 75, 141, 148

Joseph E. Lee Memorial Library and Museum, 259
Joseph Wharton Lippincott Award, 24
Josey, E. J., 20, 21, 22, 42, 53, 66-71, 74-75, 87-88, 89, 336, 339
Journal of African History, 145
Journal of Black Studies, 151
Journal of Library History Award, 21
Journal of Modern African Studies, 145
Journal of Negro Education, 151, 189
Journal of Negro History, 151, 189, 245
Joyce, Donald F., 76, 81, 246
Jubilee Singers, 248
Julius Rosenwald Archives (Fisk University), 197, 248
Julius Rosenwald Fund, 18, 33, 35-36, 54, 62, 351
Jussin, Estelle, 121-22
Justice, Hermia, 77-78

Kaiser, Ernest, 150
Kamara, Harry, 74
Kansas public library branches, 298
Kantrowitz, Adrian, 114
Kaser, David, 72
Katz, William Loren, 105
KeKumbha, Kanya, 362
Kelley, Emma, 215
Kelsey, Anne, 89
Kennedy, Florynce, 254
Kent State University Library, 242
Kentucky academic libraries, 340
Kentucky Library Association, 22
Kentucky public library branches, 298-99
Kerner Report, 109, 128
Killens, John, 160
King, Coretta Scott, 249
King, Martin Luther, Jr., 140, 158, 182, 226, 242, 249, 284, 294, 309, 317, 320, 324, 328, 331
King, Martin Luther, Sr., 255
Kingsblood Royal, 153
Kirkpatrick, Oliver Austin, 162
Klein, Arthur J., 18
Klyberg, Albert, 264
Knoke, Susan, 176-77
Knollenberg, Bernhard, 192
Knoxville College Library, 16, 352
Konadu, Asare, 170
Kotei, S. I. A., 179
Ku Klux Klan, 210, 236-37
Kuumba Liberation Award, 163

Ladner, Joyce A., 254
Lamkin, Burton E., 21
Lamming, George, 158

Langford, Mattie Lee, 47
Langston, John Mercer, 239
Langston University Library, 349
Lanusse, Armand, 219
LaRose, John, 365
Larsen, Nela, 153
Latimer, Lewis H., 243
Latino, Juan, 216
Latino librarians, 80
Latino resources, 273, 278-79, 283, 301, 306, 308-09, 311-12, 327
law, 146
Lawrence, Jacob, 310
Layman's Guide to Negro History, 140
learning resource centers. *see* school libraries
Lee, Don. *see* Madhubuti, Haki R.
Lee, George Washington, 241, 246
Lee, Joseph E., 259
Lee, Mollie Huston, 54-55, 60, 314
Lee, Virginia Young, 39-40
Lemoyne Institute, 16
Let My People Go, 159
Lew, Barzillai, 244-45
Lewinson, Paul, 229
Lewis, Alfred B., 257
Lewis, Charles, 260
Lewis, Elma, 260
Lewis, Ida, 148
Lewis, Alfred Baker, 241
Lewis, Hylan G., 241
Lewis, John, 253
Lewis, Laura S., 53
Lewis, Lillian Miles, 246
Lewis, Samella, 254
Lewis, Sinclair, 153
Liberation, Black. *see* Black Liberation
Liberation Bookstore (New York City), 362
Liberia, 181
librarian authors, 160-66
Librarian-for-a-Day programs, 86
Librarians for Africa Task Force. *see* American Library Association. Black Caucus. Task Force on Librarians for Africa
Library of Congress, 15, 21, 23, 28, 197, 219, 229, 236-37, 251
Library of Congress Affirmative Action Programs Coordinator, 22
Library of Congress. African Section, 173-74, 233
Library of Congress Consultant in American Cultural History, 161
Library of Congress Consultant in Poetry, 24
Library of Congress. Loan Division, 23
Library of Congress. National Program for Acquisitions and Cataloging. Nairobi Office, 171, 177-78

Library Company of Philadelphia, 15, 230
library educators, 30-31, 36, 38-39, 41-43, 46
Library Institute for Negro Librarians, 1930, 18
Library Materials on Africa, 173
libraries named for Afro-Americans, 275, 277, 283-84, 286-88, 292-96, 300, 302, 310, 313-14, 317, 320-21, 324, 327-46, 348-52, 354, 356-59
Libraries of the South (1936), 62
Library of Congress personnel policies, 22, 72, 75
Library of Congress Specialist in Afro-American History and Culture, 22
library schools, 103, 266-70
Library Service Review, 56
Library Service to Segregated Schools Report (A. L. A. Black Caucus), 70-71, 75
Lincoln, Abraham, 237, 251
Lincoln, C. Eric, 246
Lincoln Center Performing Arts Library, 236
Lincoln University Library, 344, 349
Lincoln University Library. Negro and African Collection, 186, 230, 349
Lippincott Award. *see* Joseph Wharton Lippincott Award
Listen for the Fig Tree, 166
literacy, 102
Little Black Sambo, 94
Little, Doris P., 53
Little Rock School Crisis, 253
Living Black American Authors: A Biographical Directory, 22, 141, 164
Livingstone College Library, 16, 242, 347
Lloyd, Tom, 261
local history collections, 133, 263-65, 309, 321, 336, 342
Locke, Alain, 209, 239, 244, 251
Logan, Rayford W., 232
Logan, Spencer, 159
Loggins, Vernon, 213, 220
Lohf, Kenneth A., 247
Lomen, Sylvia Green, 89
Lonesome Road, 159
Long, Herman H., 242
Looby, Z. Alexander, 327
Lord, Audre, 149, 165
Los Angeles County Public library personnel policies, 76-77, 80
Los Angeles Sentinel, 266
Lotus Press, 365
Louisiana academic libraries, 340-41
Louisiana libray schools, 267
Louisiana public library branches, 299

382 / Index

Louisville (Kentucky) Free Public Library, 16, 17, 19, 31-32, 37, 99, 298-99
Love, Eleanor Young, 89
Love, Lucille A., 333
Love, Nate, 212
Love You, 163
Lovell, Marguerite, 60
Loving Her, 164
Lubin, Maurice A., 202
Luthuli, Albert, 159
lynching, 246, 250

MBII Newsletter, 227
M. C. Higgins, the Great, 101
McBlain Books, 184
McCain, Ella, 48
McClaron, Georgia, 22
McClendon, Joyce, 60
McClendon, Rose, 236
McCord, Inez Boddy, 89
McCurdy, Alvin, 220
McDonald, Jack, 23
McDonough, John, 229
McDowell, Henry C., 257
McKay, Claude, 34, 236, 250, 252
McKinney, Ernest R., 253
McKissick, Mabel, 61
McLuhan, Marshall, 119, 121
McMillan, Aaron M., 257
McNair, Everett, 257
Madgett, Naomi, 81, 199
Madhubuti, Haki R., 145, 364-65
Mahiri, Jabari, 364-65
Malcolm X, 349
Mamba's Daughters, 153
Man Called White, 159
Manchild in the Promised Land, 155, 157
Manley, Dorothy Shepard, 46
Manning, H. V., 351
manuscript collections. see archives
"Manuscript Resources for the Study of Negro Life and History" (1969), 229
Mapp, Edward C., 22, 23, 89
Marblehead Libraries, 17
Marbury, Carl H., 269
Marcus Bookstores (Berkeley/San Francisco), 360
Marsh, Clinton, 255
Marshall, Albert P., 20, 55-56, 67, 137, 344
Marshall, Thurgood, 244, 342
Marshall, William, 79
Marteena, Constance, 56
Martin, Allie Beth, 121
Martin, Charles, 220

Martin Luther King, Jr., Center for Social Change Library/Archives, 226, 249
Martin, William E., 108
Marxism, 147, 362
Mary Holmes College. Oral History Program, 255-56
Maryland academic libraries, 341-43
Maryland University. see University of Maryland
mass media treatment of Afro-Americans, 92
Master's programs in librarianship. see graduate programs in librarianship
Materials by and about American Negroes Conference, 1965, 20
materials selection. see collection development
Mathis, Sharon Bell, 102, 165-66
Matthews, Helen, 89
Matthews, Victoria Earle, 243
Mays, Benjamin, 255
Meachum, John Berry, 303
media centers. see school libraries
media specialists. see school librarians
Megda, 215
Meier, August, 229, 231-32
Melville Dewey Medal, 23, 43
Melville J. Herskovits Library of African Studies, 180-81, 185, 232
Memphis State University. Oral History Research Office, 256
Men of Mark, 141
Merabash Museum (New Egypt, N. J.), 261
Meriwether, Louise, 159
Metropolitan Museum of Art (New York City), 243
Meyer, Mary K., 229
Micheaux, Lewis, 87, 210
Michigan bookstores, 361
Michigan public library branches, 299-301
Middleton, Bernice B., 61, 268
Midgette, Gwendolyn Jordan, 41
Miller, Elizabeth W., 137-38
Miller, Kelly, 243, 249
Miller, Marian, 58
Mills, Joyce, W., 105
Miner, Myrtilla, 251
ministers, 142, 227, 241, 255
Minnesota public library branches, 301-02
Minority Business Information Institute, 227
Mirando, Alfonso, 255
Mirror of Liberty, 219
Mississippi, 256
Mississippi academic libraries, 343-44

Mississippi Freedom Democratic Party, 226
Mississippi library schools, 267
Mississippi Valley Region, 256
Mississippi Valley State University Library, 343
Mississippi Valley State University Library School, 267
Missouri academic libraries, 344
Missouri Library Association, 20
Missouri public library branches, 302-03
Modern African Studies, 145
Monro, John U., 128-29
Montana Library Association, 19
Montana State Librarians, 21
Montgomery Improvement Association, 226
Moon, Eric, 42, 71
Moore, Fred R., 243
Moore, Mrs. Ray N., 56
Moore, Parlett, 342
Moorland Foundation Collection. see Moorland-Spingarn Collection
Moorland, Jesse Edward, 17, 238, 248-49
Moorland-Spingarn Collection, 17, 19, 185, 195, 220, 230, 238-39, 248-49, 255, 258, 336
Moorland-Spingarn Research Center, 336
Morais, Herbert M., 138
More to Remember, 163
Morgan, Jarrett, Jr., 260
Morgan State University Library, 342
Morgan State University Library. Black Collection, 241
Morris A. Soper Collection. see Morgan State College Library. Black Collection
Morris, Bernard, 264
Morris, Brook, 221
Morris, Effie Lee, 19, 20, 22, 67-68, 77
Morrison, Allan, 236
Morristown College Library, 353
Morton, Robert Russo, 250
Moses, Kathleen, 61
Moses, Louise, 78
Moss, William, 237
Motley, Willard, 242
Mott, Alexander, 220
Muhammad Ali, 92
multicultural education, 108-09, 150, 352
multicultural public library collections, 278-79, 282-83, 301, 306, 308-09, 311-12, 327
multi-media materials. see audio-visual materials

Murray, Daniel Alexander Payne, 15, 16, 17, 24, 27-28, 219
Murray, Pauli, 236
Murray's Historical and Biographical Encyclopedia of the Colored Race throughout the World, 28, 219
Museum of the National Center of Afro-American Artists, 259-60
museums, 258-63
music, 146, 180, 231, 236-38, 240, 242, 247-48, 250, 256-57, 353
musicians, 139, 142, 146, 157, 236-37, 240-41, 244, 248, 254
Myers, Carol Fairbanks, 140
Myrdal, Gunnar, 236

NAACP. see National Association for the Advancement of Colored People
NCLIS. see National Commission on Libraries and Information Science
NCNLA. see North Carolina Negro Library Association
NPAC. see Library of Congress. National Program for Acquisitions and Cataloging
N. Y. L. A. see New York Library Association
N. Y. P. L. see New York Public Library
Nail, John, 194, 240
Nairobi Office (Library of Congress), 171, 177-78
Naja the Snake and Mangus the Mongoose, 162
National Archives (U.S.), 237, 250-51
National Association for the Advancement of Colored People, 70, 73, 76, 147, 197, 236-37, 239, 241, 249, 251
National Association of Black Social Workers, 66
National Association of Colored Graduate Nurses, 250
National Association of Colored Women's Clubs, 248
National Black Union Catalog (Proposed), 245
National Book Award, 24
National Center of Afro-American Artists Museum, 259-60
National Commission on Black History and Culture (Proposed), 232
National Commission on Libraries and Information Science, 80
National Conference of Black Lawyers, 66
National Conference of Black Political Scientists, 66
National Council of Negro Women, 248
National Cyclopedia of the Colored Race, 138
National Historical Publications and Records Commission, 237

national liberation movements, 181
National Library Board (Sierra Leone), 74
National Memorial Bookstore (Harlem), 210
National Museum of Afro-American History and Culture (Proposed), 232
National Negro Congress, 235
National Program for Acquisitions and Cataloging (LC). *see* Library of Congress. National Program for Acquisitions and Cataloging
National Urban League, 17, 25, 75, 237, 247, 251
National Urban League Woman of the Year Award, 35
Native American resources, 283, 301
Neal, Larry, 254
Nebraska public library branches, 303-04
NECZAM, 170
Negro a Beast, 212
Negro Almanac, 20, 139
Negro Americans in the Civil War, 141
Negro Bibliographic and Research Center, 136
Negro Builders and Heroes, 135
Negro Collection, Atlanta University Library. *see* Atlanta University Library. Negro Collection
Negro Collection, Fisk University Library. *see* Fisk University Library. Negro Collection
"Negro College Libraries and ACRL Standards" (1963), 129
Negro (Cunard), 221
"Negro Digs up His Past" (Schomburg), 25
Negro Education (1917), 17
Negro Educational Review, 151
Negro Handbook, 20, 138
Negro History Bulletin, 152, 245
Negro History Tour of Manhattan, 243
Negro History Week, 17
Negro in America: A Bibliography, 137-38, 185
Negro in Illinois Collection, 247
Negro in Music and Art, 139
Negro in the United States (Frazier), 158
Negro in the United States: A Selected Bibliography, 21, 139, 184, 186
Negro Labor Committee, 235-36, 250
Negro Library Conference, 1930, 18, 32
Negro Library Conference, 1931, 18

"Negro Manuscript Collections in Libraries" (Greene), 229
Negro Society for Historical Research, 17, 25
Negro Yearbook, 17, 26-27, 138, 241
Negroana collections. *see* Afro-Americana collections
Negroes in Public Affairs and Government (1966), 232
Negro's Faith in America, 159
Nelson, Thelma, 56
Nevada public library branches, 304
New Beacon Books, 365
New Beacon Bookshop (London), 362
New Day Bookstore (San Francisco), 360
New Day Press (Cleveland), 365
New Jersey and the Negro: A Bibliography, 1715-1966, 230
New Jersey public library branches, 304-05
New Negro (Locke), 209
New Orleans Tribune, 225
New York Amsterdam News, 189
New York Black Librarians Caucus, 84-88
New York bookstores, 362
New York Head Shop and Museum, 165
New York Library Association, 24
New York Library Club, 23
New York Public Library, 19, 34, 310-12
New York public library branches, 305-13
New York Public Library. Division of Negro Literature, History and Prints, 17, 194
New York Public Library. Lincoln Center Performing Arts Library, 236
New York Public Library. Research Collections, 229
New York Public Library. Schomburg Collection. *see* Schomburg Collection
New York State Education Dept. Bureau of Academic and Research Libraries, 21
New York State Library School, 16, 30, 36
New York State Regents Advisory Council on Libraries, 22
newspapers. *see* periodicals
Nigeria, 181
Nix, Athelma, 61
Nixon, Richard Milhous, 66
Nobody Knows My Name, 157
non-print materials. *see* audio-visual materials
Norfolk State College Library, 45
North American Negro Poets: A Bibliographical Checklist, 19

North Carolina A. & T. State University Library, 346
North Carolina A. & T. State University Library School, 268
North Carolina academic libraries, 345-48
North Carolina Central University Library, 46, 345
North Carolina Central University School of Library Science, 18, 23, 46, 56, 103, 267-69
North Carolina College School of Library Science. *see* North Carolina Central University School of Library Science
North Carolina Index, 56
North Carolina Library Association, 54, 56
North Carolina Negro Library Association, 19, 54-57
North Carolina public library branches, 313-15
Northern Nigerian Publishing Co., 169
Northwestern University Library. Melville J. Herskovits Library of African Studies. *see* Melville J. Herskovits Library of African Studies
Notable Books List (A. L. A.), 156-60
Ntiru, Richard C., 364
Nwamife Publishers, 170

OLSD. *see* American Library Association. Office for Library Service to the Disadvantaged
Oakland Museum, 258
Obi, Dorothy, 89
Office of Education (U. S.), 22
Ofosu-Appiah, L. H., 235
Ohio, 262
Ohio academic libraries, 348
Ohio Black History Guide, 230
Ohio Historical Society Library, 238
Ohio Library Association, 30
Ohio public library branches, 315-21
O'Kelly, Cadd Grant, 348
Oklahoma academic libraries, 349
Oklahoma Chapter, Special Libraries Association. *see* Special Libraries Association. Oklahoma Chapter
Oklahoma public library branches, 321
Old South (Bontemps), 162
Omoerha, Thompson, 174-75
One by One, 78
O'Neill, David, 215
Onibonoje, Gabriel, 168
open houses, 100

Operation Headstart, 85
Opposition to Support of Racist Institutions Resolution (A. L. A. Council), 68-69, 75
oral history, 22, 190, 206, 239, 243, 253-57
Oregon public library branches, 321-22
Oregon University. *see* University of Oregon
orientations, 130
Orne, Jerrold, 131-32
Osahon, Naiwo, 170
Other Americans: A Selected Bibliography of Multi-Ethnic Materials, 352
Otto, Wayne, 118
out-of-print works, 184, 360
outreach services, 86, 98-100, 271-72, 284, 315
Ovington, Mary White, 251
Owens, Major, 87

PEA. *see* Palmetto Education Association
PSTA. *see* Palmetto State Teachers' Association
Page, Inman E., 344
Palmer, Warren, 89
Palmetto Education Association, 57, 59
Palmetto Library Association. *see* South Carolina State Library Group
Palmetto State Teachers' Association, 57-58, 60
Panofsky, Hans E., 179-80, 234
paraprofessionals, 85, 110
Paris Exposition, 1900, 16, 28, 219
Parker, Eunice, 80
Parks, Gordon, 159
Patterson, Lillie, 102
Patterson, Lindsay, 138-39
Paul Robeson Theatre (Jamaica, N. Y.), 261
Payne, Daniel, 332
Payne, Foster, 55
Payton, Benjamin F., 350
Peabody Collection on the Negro. *see* George Foster Peabody Collection on the Negro
Pendergrass, Margaret, 61
Pennington, James 221
Pennsylvania academic libraries, 349
Pennsylvania Historical Society, 230
Pennsylvania public library branches, 322-25
Peoples, Marie, 49
People's War Publishing, 365
Performing Arts Library (Lincoln Center, New York), 236
periodical directories, 136
periodical indexes, 55, 137

periodicals, 86, 143-52, 170, 173-74, 189-90, 346
Periodicals Published in Africa, 179
Perry, Margaret, 164
Perry, Matthew C., 237
Perry, Penny, 56, 345
Perry, Thelma, 363
Peterkin, Julia, 153
Peters, James Sedalia, II, 241
Petry, Ann, 160, 213
Ph.D.s in librarianship. *see* Doctorates in librarianship
Philadelphia Library Company, 15, 230
Phinazee, Annette Hoage, 20, 89, 268-69
Phylon, 44, 152, 189
Pickens, William, 210, 235
Pickett, Leo, 89
Picot, J. Rupert, 152
Pinchback, P. B. S., 239
Pinson, I. D., 351
Pitiful and the Proud, 159
Pittsburgh Courier, 189
playwrights. *see* authors
Plessy v. Ferguson, 15
Plimpton, George A., 247
Ploski, Harry A., 139
Poem Counterpoem, 163
poetry, 86, 102, 149, 160-63, 165, 185, 212, 217, 343, 363-66
poetry indexes, 136
poets. *see* authors
Pollard, Francie, 89
Pope, Evelyn B., 46
Porter, Dorothy B., 19, 21, 89, 136, 139, 184-86, 194-95, 197, 202, 213, 220, 228-29, 231, 233
Potts, Muriel, 59
Povey, John, 144
Powell, Adam Clayton, Jr., 244
Prairie View A. & M. University, 42
Prairie View A. & M. University Library, 356
Prairie View A. & M. University Library School, 268
Preliminary List of Books and Pamphlets by Negro Authors, 16, 28
Presence Africaine, 145, 233
presses. *see* publishers
Price, Hollis F., 352
Price, Joseph Charles, 242
Price, Leontyne, 343
Prince le Boos, 214
printism, 120-21
prisoners' writings, 158
private book collectors. *see* book collectors
private libraries, 243-45

programmed learning, 125, 130
programming, 92-93, 100-01, 103-04, 109
public librarians, 19, 28-29, 31-33, 37, 39-40, 84-88
public libraries, 64, 73, 84-88, 90-93
Public Library Association, 22
public library branches, 16, 17, 31-34, 37, 39-40, 104, 271-331
public library main facilities, 19
"Public Library Service to Negroes" (Shores), 18
publishers, 20, 76, 104, 162-63, 167-70, 225-26, 363-66
Publishing in Africa Conference, 1973, 167-68
Pulitzer Prize, 24
Purcell, Mae H., 58
Putnam, Herbert, 28, 219

Quarles, Benjamin, 146, 245, 254
Queens Borough Public Library, 22, 84-87, 238
Quest for Equality, 141

race relations, 245
Race Relations Information Center, 140, 239
Racial and Sexual Parity in Library Staffing Resolution (A. L. A. Council), 69
racism, 158, 182
Racism and Sexism Awareness Resolution (A. L. A. 1976 Conference), 75
racism in bookselling, 213
racism in children's literature, 106
racism in library associations, 48-49, 66, 68
racism in library employment, 42, 69, 72, 75, 82, 84-86
racism in library service, 20, 67-71, 84-87
racism in medicine, 138
racism in publishing, 153-54
Radcliffe College Library, 257
Ralph J. Bunche Oral History Collection (Howard University Library), 255
Randall, Ann Knight, 89
Randall, Dudley, 20, 149, 162-63, 254, 364
Randolph A., Philip, 238, 243, 253
Ransom, Reverdy C., 242
Rapier, James T., 239
Rapier, John, 239
rare book collectors. *see* book collectors
Ray Charles, 166
Rayner, John B., 235
reading lists. *see* bibliographies

reading skills. *see* literacy
Reason, Joseph H., 22, 56, 89, 336-37
recruitment programs, 69, 86
Reddick, Lawrence, 194, 228-29, 338
Redding, Joy Saunders, 159, 254
Redmond, Eugene, 363
Reed, Ishmael, 366
reference works, 134-42
REFORMA, 80
Reid, Helen Cephas, 64
Reid, John D., 152
Religious Heritage of the Black World Program, 255
Render, Sylvia Lyons, 22
Rene Lemarchand Collection (Hoover Institution), 181
Renner, Chrisperi, 255
reprints, 184, 187, 212, 217
research libraries, 21
Resolution on Action Now to Achieve Racial and Sexual Parity in Library Staffing (A. L. A. Council), 69
Resolution on Application of Fair Employment Practice Laws (A. L. A. Council), 69
Resolution on Ensuring Black Representation on Library Governing Boards (A. L. A. Council), 69, 73
Resolution on Opposition to Support of Racist Institutions (A. L. A. Council), 68-69, 75
Resolution on Racism and Sexism Awareness (A. L. A. 1976 Conference), 75
Revels, Hiram R., 235
"reverse discrimination" suits, 128
Review of Black Political Economy, 152
Rhode Island Black Heritage Society, 262, 264
Rhodes, James B., 250
Rhodes, Lelia, 89
Rhodesia, 181
Richards, Beah, 79
Richardson, Raye, 81
Ridely, Harrison, 221
Ringer, Barbara, 75
Rising in the Sun: A History of Georgia Teachers and Education Association, 53
Roanoke Public Library, 39-41
Robbins, Warren M., 235
Roberts, Robert, 217
Robertson, Alpha A., 51
Robeson, Eslanda Cardoza, 159
Robeson, Paul, 209, 212-13, 235, 241, 244, 250
Robinson, Carrie Coleman, 41-42
Robinson, Harry, 75, 89
Robinson, Harry, Jr., 263, 355
Robinson, James H., 241

Robinson, S. Carter, 265
Robinson, Wilhelmena S., 140, 232
Rogers, Alpha S., 44, 62-63, 357
Rogers, Joel A., 210-11, 244
Rollins, Charlemae, 19, 21, 22, 49, 52, 96, 106
Rollock, Barbara, 105, 140
Romero, Patricia E., 140
Roosevelt, Eleanor, 34
Roots, 24, 154-55, 158, 229
Rose, Ernestine, 194
Rosenberg Library, Galveston, Texas, 16
Rosenwald Fund, 18, 33, 35-36, 54, 62, 351
Rose, Claudine, 61
Rowan, Carl T., 159
Royal African Society, 144
Ruffin, George L., 239
Ruggles, David, 219
Rush, Theressa Gunnels, 140
Russwurm, James, 214, 219
Rywell, Martin, 135

SNCC, 227, 249
S. R. R. T. *see* American Library Association. Social Responsibilities Round Table
S. U. N. Y. *see* State University of New York
St. John's University Dept. of Library Science, 21
Salk, Erwin A., 140, 241
Salkey, Andrew, 362, 364
Samoa, 278
Sampson, Henry T., 343-44
Sampson, Robert, 63
San Francisco Negro Historical and Cultural Society, 78
San Francisco Public Library, 20, 281-82
Sanchez, Sonia, 254
Sanford Bishop College Library (Mobile), 45
Sapphire Publishing Co., 365
Saunders, Doris E., 136, 225, 365
Savannah, Georgia, 133, 289-90
Savannah State College Library, 131, 339
Savannah State College Library School, 267
Savery, William, 334
Scarborough, William S., 28, 219
Scarlet Sister Mary, 153
Schatz, Walter, 140, 230
Schenk, Gretchen, 49
Schomburg, Arthur Alphonso, 17, 18, 24-25, 28, 34, 186, 194, 196, 198, 209-11, 218, 235, 250, 359
Schomburg Collection, 17, 18, 25, 40, 183, 185, 194, 196, 209-10, 230-31, 235, 243, 249-50, 254

school histories, 203-08, 240
school integration. *see* integrated schools
school librarians, 47-53, 62-65, 114
school libraries, 106-18
school libraries in the South, 62-65
schools, inner city. *see* inner city schools
Schuyler, George S., 242, 253
SCOLMA, 172-74, 179
Scott, John E., 20
Scott, Lavinnia, 181
segregated libraires, 15, 20, 32
segregated library associations, 48-49, 54, 57, 61, 63
segregated library conferences, 18, 20
segregated schools, 19, 67-71, 75
Select Bibliography of the Negro American, 16
Senghor, Leopold S., 233
Senior Citizens' services, 300
"Separate But Equal" doctrine, 15
Sepia, 152
serials. *see* periodicals
Sesame Street (Television Program), 94, 126
Seventh Day Adventist Church, 333
sexism in publishing, 154
Shagaloff, June, 70-71
Sharecroppers Union of Alabama, 257
Shaw, Spencer, 96
Shaw University Library, 54, 347
Sheffield, Charliese P., 58
Shepard, James E., 345
Shepard, Marjorie, 55
Sheppard, William H., 334
Sherrard, Mrs. Ollie, 61
Sherrill, Josephine P., 55
Shockley, Ann Allen, 22, 23, 76, 141, 163-64, 231, 248, 253
Shores, Louis S., 18, 36, 56, 119, 353
Shrine of the Black Madonna Cultural Center and Bookstore No. 1, 361
Sidewalk Story, 166
Sierra Leone, 74, 214
Simmons, William J., 141
singers. *see* musicians
Singletary, Lola Johnson, 69, 73
Singleton, Benjamin "Pap," 238
Sinnette, Elinor, 89
Skinner Award. *see* Constance Lindsay Skinner Award
SLAGS. *see* Student Library Assistants of Georgia
Slater Fund, 36
Slaughter Collection. *see* Atlanta University Library. Negro Collection
Slaughter, Henry Proctor, 24-26, 196, 220, 240, 246
slave narratives, 236, 251

Slavery Collection (Columbia University Library), 247
Smalls, Robert, 245
Smith, Benjamin, 56, 89
Smith, Dwight L., 230
Smith, Elizabeth M., 77
Smith, Henrietta M., 89
Smith, Jessie Carney, 21, 23, 89, 189, 230-31, 240, 268, 353
Smith, Lillian, 153
Smith, Lonnie E., 329
Smith, Paul, 89
Smith, Wendell, 296
Smythe, Hugh H., 236
Smythe, Mabel M., 141, 243
Snodgrass, Pearl, 55
Social Responsibilities Round Table (A. L. A.). *see* American Library Association. Social Responsibilities Round Table
Soledad Brother: Prison Letters, 158
Solomon, Walker E., 57
Soper Collection. *see* Morgan State College Library. Black Collection
Sorkin, Alan L., 129
Soul on Ice, 155, 158
Souls of Black Folk, 210
South Africa, 157, 158, 159, 181
South Carolina academic libraries, 350-51
South Carolina Education Association, 57
South Carolina Library Association, 61
South Carolina State College. Dept. of Library Service, 60, 268
South Carolina State College Library, 351
South Carolina State Library Group, 57-61
South Carolina University. *see* University of South Carolina
South of Freedom, 159
Southeastern Black Librarians Colloquium, 1976, 23
Southeastern Library Association, 36
Southern African Collection (Hoover Institution), 181
Southern Christian Leadership Conference, 249
Southern Conference for Human Welfare, 246
Southern Tenant Farmers Union, 242
Southwest Research Center and Museum (Dallas), 263
"Special Collections of Black Literature in the Traditionally Black College" (Smith), 231
"Special Collections of Negroana" (Bontemps), 183

special libraries, 222-28
Special Libraries Association, 224
Special Libraries Association. Oklahoma Chapter, 20
Speller, Benjamin F., Jr., 89
Spencer, Anne, 160
Spencer, Leon P., 256
Spingarn, Arthur B., 237, 239, 249
Spingarn Collection of Black Authors. see Moorland-Spingarn Collection
Spingarn, Joel Ellias, 239, 249
Spofford, Ainsworth Rand, 15
sports, 137, 147
Spottswood, Stephen Gill, 241
Spradling, Mary Mace, 230
SRRT. see American Library Association. Social Responsibilities Round Table
Standing Conference on Library Materials in Africa, 172-74, 179
Stanford University. Hoover Institution on War, Revolution, and Peace, 181
Stanford University Library, 242
Staples, Robert, 146
Starks, S. W., 16, 27
Starr, Edwin, 221, 242
Starr, Louis M., 253
state library agencies, 88
State University of New York at Binghamton Libraries, 23
statistics, 88-89
Staupers, Mabel K., 241
Stendler, Celia Burns, 108
Steptoe, John, 102, 254
Stewart, Rowena, 264
Still, William Grant, 254
Store Front Museum/Paul Robeson Theatre (Jamaica, N. Y.), 261
Storey, Moorfield, 237
story hours, 102, 317
Story of the Negro (Bontemps), 161
Strange Fruit, 153
Strategy for Public Library Change, 121
Street (Petry), 213
Street, Rowena, 262
Strength to Love, 158
Stride toward Freedom, 158
student achievement, 124
student counseling, 130
student library assistants, 50, 53, 60, 110, 201
Student Library Assistants of Georgia, 53
Student Nonviolent Coordinating Committee, 227, 249
students' rights, 110
Stutler, Boyd B., 244
Sub-Saharan Africa: A Guide to Serials (1970), 173

Successful Blacks, 136
Sullivan, Maxine, 254
Sullivan, Peggy, 60
Sumbi, Joyce, 78, 279
Sumner, Charles, 212, 238
SUNY. see State University of New York
Survey of Negro Colleges and Universities, 18
survival information, 92, 111-13

Talladega College Historical Collections, 256
Talladega College Library, 16, 229-30, 242, 334
Talley, Julia W., 58, 61
Tanner, Henry Ossawa, 246
Tanzania, 181
Tanzania Publishing House, 169
Tappan, Lewis, 220, 237-38, 246
Task Force on Librarians for Africa. see American Library Association. Black Caucus. Task Force on Librarians for Africa
Tasker, William, 221
Tate, Binnie, 67, 70-71
Tate, Horace E., 52
teacher-librarian training, 38, 62
Teacup Full of Roses, 166
teen-agers' services, 99, 113, 118-26
television, educational. see educational television
Tell Me How Long the Train's Been Gone, 155
Tennessee academic libraries, 352-54
Tennessee Library Association, 22
Tennessee library schools, 268
Tennessee public library branches, 325-27
Tennessee State University Library, 354
Tennessee State University Library School, 268
Terrell, Mary Church, 237, 249
Terrell, Robert H., 237
Terry, Lucy, 138, 217
Texas academic libraries, 354-57
Texas bookstores, 362
Texas library schools, 268
Texas public library branches, 327-29
Texas Southern University Library, 355
Texas Southern University Library. Charles F. Heartman Negro Collection. see Heartman Negro Collection
textbook treatment of Afro-Americans, 18
theater, 138, 185, 236-37, 243, 247-48, 254, 261
Theus, Theodosia M., 52-53
Thigpen, Nettie, 346
Third World, 346
Third World Ethnic Bookstore (Los Angeles), 227, 360

390 / Index

Third World Press, 361, 365
Thomas, Alvin, 256
Thomas, Charles, 80
Thomas, Dolores Schomburg, 235
Thomas, Elaine F., 258
Thomas, George B., 255
Thomas, Lucille C., 22, 23, 24, 87
Thompson, Elizabeth Jett, 47
Toffler, Alvin, 121
Tolson, Melvin B., 159, 349
Tookes, Henry Young, 337
Toomer, Jean, 197, 239, 248
Toomer, Mrs. Jean, 254
Totten, Herman L., 23, 89, 356
Tougaloo College Library, 344
Toure, Askia Muhammad, 254
Toure, Sekou, 365
Toussaint, Pierre, 236
Townley, Charles, 76
Transafrican Journal of History, 170
traveling library extension service, 17
Travis, William H., 53
Tree of Life Book Store (New York City), 362
Trenholm, George W., 333
Trevor-Arnett Library. *see* Atlanta University Library
Trotter, William Monroe, 29, 238
trustees, 69-70, 73, 76, 80
Truth, Sojourner, 135, 330, 359
Tubman, Harriet, 135, 236
Tucker, Harold W., 84
Tucker, Richard D., 255
Tucker, T. Vivian, 63
Tureaud, Alexander P., 241
Turner, Nat, 212, 245
Tuskegee Institute Dept. of Records and Research, 17, 26, 138, 241
Tuskegee Institute Library, 16, 241, 250, 335
Tuskegee Veterans Hospital Library, 17, 34

U. S. Library of Congress. *see* Library of Congress
U. S. National Archives. *see* National Archives (U. S.)
U. S. Office of Education. *see* Office of Education (U. S.)
undergraduate programs in librarianship, 266-69
Understanding Media, 119
unit teaching, 115-18
Universal Books, 184
Universal Negro Improvement Association, 236-37, 250
university librarians. *see* academic librarians

university libraries. *see* academic libraries
University Microfilms, 184
University of Arkansas at Pine Bluff Library School, 266
University of Botswana, Lesotho, and Swaziland, 44, 74
University of California at Berkeley Library, 242
University of Chicago Library School, 18, 19
University of Ife Press, 169
University of Maryland School of Library and Information Services, 75
University of North Carolina Library. Southern Historical Collection, 242
University of Oregon School of Librarianship, 23
University of South Carolina, 11, 15
University of the District of Columbia. Library and Media Services Division, 336
University of the District of Columbia Library School, 266
urban education, 106-26, 150
Urban League. *see* National Urban League
Uwechue, Ralph, 143

Vail Memorial Library. *see* Lincoln University Library
Van Der Zee, James, 243
Van Jackson, Wallace, 24, 38, 43-45, 63, 74, 194, 269, 338, 355, 357
Van Vechten, Carl, 18, 192, 195, 239, 252
Vann Family, 244
Vassa, Gustavus, 210, 216-17
Vaughn's Bookstore (Detroit), 361
Virginia academic libraries, 357-58
Virginia Dept. of School Libraries and Textbooks, 62-63
Virginia Education Association, 65
Virginia Library Association, 44, 63
Virginia public library branches, 329-30
Virginia State College Library, 40, 44, 357
Virginia State College Library School, 268
Virginia State Teachers Association. Division of Librarians, 62-65
Virginia Union University, 63
Virginia Union University Library, 357-58
Vivian Harsh Collection, 183, 230, 238, 246-47
vocational guidance, 113, 137, 146, 148
Vokeroit, Victor, 255
Voorhees, Lillian W., 241

W. E. B. DuBois Collection (University of Massachusetts), 196, 251

Walker, David, 217
Walker, Estellene, 60
Walker, Margaret A., 162, 254
Walker, Margaret L., 52, 60
Walls, W. J., 220
Walton, Emma, 50
Walton, Eugene, 22
Warfield, William, 254
Waring, J. Waties, 239, 241
Washington, Booker T., 29, 91, 235-37, 250
Washington, D. C. *see* District of Columbia
Washington, Ernestine, 84
Washington, Etta, 61
Washington, Fredi, 241
Washington, Leon H., 277
Washington (State) public library branches, 330
Waters, Ethel, 150
Watson, John Brown, 335
Watts, California, 90, 277
Webb, Frank, 221
Webster, Bill, 78
Wedgeworth, Robert, 22, 89
Welch, Robert, 221
Wells, Ida B., 135
Wesley, Charles H., 141
West End Branch, Boston Public Library. *see* Boston Public Library. West End Branch
West Indies, 211, 235, 246, 248, 364
West Virginia Library Association, 20
West Virginia State College Library, 358
West Virginia State Librarians, 16, 17, 27
Western Pennsylvania Research and Historical Society, 264
Western Reserve Historical Society. Black History Archives Project, 230
Western Reserve University. Adelbert College. *see* Adelbert College
Western Reserve University Library School, 16, 30
Western States Black Research Center, 227-28, 252, 264
What Black Librarians Are Saying, 22
"What of the Black and Yellow Races?" (Yust), 17
Wheatley, Phillis, 135, 210, 212, 218, 313
Wheeler, Katherine, 61
Whipper, Leigh, 210, 235, 239-40
Whipper, W. J., 239
White/Black information transfer, 132-33
White, Carl W., 18, 193-94
White, Clarence Cameron, 236
White, James Herbert, 343

White racism. *see* racism
White, Walter F., 159, 251-52
Whiteman, Maxwell, 186, 213, 217, 220-21, 242
Whitenack, Carolyn L., 50-51
Whitlow, Roger, 187-88
Whittaker, Miller F., 351
Who's Who Among Black Americans, 141-42
Who's Who in Colored America, 142
Why We Can't Wait, 182
Wilberforce University Library, 16, 242, 348
Wiley College Library, 16, 356
Wilkins, Roy, 253
Williams, Avery, 75, 83
Williams, Bert, 236
Williams, Bertha Pleasant, 47
Williams, Daniel Hale, 114
Williams, Daniel T., 250
Williams, Edward Christopher, 11, 15, 16, 24, 30-31, 37
Williams, Edward F., 241
Williams, Ethel L., 142
Williams, Eva Glass, 46
Williams, Isiah, J., III, 259
Williams, John, 254
Williams, Joslyn, 23, 72
Williams, Ora, 79, 142
Williams, W. Hazaiah, 81
Willis, Ellen R., 254
Wilmington, Delaware, 15
Wilson, Agnes Hildebrand, 60-61
Wilson, Ellis, 310
Wilson, Flip, 92
Wilson, Louis R., 54
Wilson, Lucy, 80
Wilson, Teddy, 257
Wink, R. W., 236
Winston, Eric, 89
Winston, Michael R., 239, 248, 255
Winston-Salem State University Library, 348
Winston-Salem Teachers College Library, 55-56
Wisconsin Design for Reading Skill Development: Rationale and Guidelines, 118
Wisconsin public library branches, 330-31
Witherell, Julian, 174, 177
women, 79, 135, 142, 149, 157, 158, 201, 232, 248, 250, 254, 257, 365
women artists, 142
women authors, 142, 154, 160-61, 163-66, 215, 217, 244, 254
women musicians, 159
Wood, Johanna Smith, 89
Woods, Alfred L., 83
Woodson, Carter G., 17, 220, 232, 237-38, 245, 251, 292
Work, John W., III, 248

Work, Mrs. John W., III, 254
Work, Monroe Nathan, 17, 18, 24, 26-27, 138, 142, 213, 221, 241, 250
Work with Negroes Round Table. *see* American Library Association. Work with Negroes Round Table
Working Bibliography on the Negro in the United States, 139, 186
Worthington, Walter, 265
Wright, James R., 75, 89
Wright, Louis T., 239
Wright, R. R., Jr., 28, 220, 245
Wright, R. R., Sr., 220, 245
Wright, Richard, 153-54, 160, 236, 240, 242, 246, 252
writers. *see* authors
Written Word, Inc. Bookstore (Jamaica, N. Y.), 362

Yale University Library. James Weldon Johnson Collection. *see* James Weldon Johnson Collection
Yardbird Publishing Co., 366
Yardly, William, 263
Yates, Ella Gaines, 23
Yerby, Frank, 153-55, 212-13
Young, A. S. "Doc," 79
Young, Mrs. Whitney M., Jr., 253
Young, Tommie M. A., 89, 268, 346
Young, Whitney M., Jr., 242, 247, 296, 359
Young, Whitney M., Sr., 242
youth services, 99, 113-26
Yust, William F., 17

Zell, Hans, 167-68, 169, 172
Zimmerman, Geraldine P., 58

Z
711.9
H35

AUG 30 1978